# EUROPEAN CONSTITUTIONAL LANGUAGE

If the task of constitutional theory is to set out a language in which the discourse of constitutional law may be grounded, a question of the utmost importance is how this terminology is created, defined and interpreted. In this ground-breaking new work, András Jakab maps out and analyses the grammar and vocabulary on which the core European traditions of constitutional theory are based. He suggests understanding key constitutional concepts as responses to historical and present-day challenges experienced by European societies. Drawing together a great and diverse range of literature, much of which has never before been touched upon by scholarship in the English language, Jakab reconceptualises and argues for a new understanding of European constitutional law discourse. In so doing, he shines new light on what constitutes its distinctively European nature. This remarkable book is essential reading for all scholars and students of constitutional theory in Europe and beyond.

ANDRÁS JAKAB is the director of the Institute for Legal Studies at the Centre for Social Sciences at the Hungarian Academy of Sciences in Budapest, where he holds a tenured research chair. He is also a Schumpeter Fellow at the Max Planck Institute for Comparative Public Law and International Law in Heidelberg.

# EUROPEAN CONSTITUTIONAL LANGUAGE

ANDRÁS JAKAB

*Hungarian Academy of Sciences (Budapest)*
*Max Planck Institute for Comparative Public Law and International Law (Heidelberg)*

CAMBRIDGE
UNIVERSITY PRESS

**CAMBRIDGE**
**UNIVERSITY PRESS**

University Printing House, Cambridge CB2 8BS, United Kingdom

Cambridge University Press is part of the University of Cambridge.

It furthers the University's mission by disseminating knowledge in the pursuit of education, learning and research at the highest international levels of excellence.

www.cambridge.org
Information on this title: www.cambridge.org/9781107130784



First published 2016

*A catalogue record for this publication is available from the British Library*

*Library of Congress Cataloguing in Publication data*
Jakab, András, author.
European constitutional language / Andras Jakab.
pages cm
ISBN 978-1-107-13078-4 (hardback)
1. Language policy – European Union countries. 2. Language and languages – Political aspects. I. Title.
P119.32.E85J35 2016
342.4001'4–dc23
2015032255

ISBN 978-1-107-13078-4 Hardback

*Lisának, Emilynek és szüleimnek*

# CONTENTS

# TABLES

# PREFACE

This book has taken more than ten years to write. Many other scholarly challenges, of course, interrupted the work, and some of the chapters have been thoroughly rewritten, partly because new literature or legal developments arose, and partly because I had reconsidered my original position. I taught most of this book at different European universities and was often inspired by my students, especially by their original perspectives and outspoken questions about constitutional law, which made me rethink many fundamental issues. I also greatly benefitted from discussions with colleagues in Budapest, Nottingham, Liverpool, Madrid and Heidelberg, where I have been working over the last decade; I thank them by name at the beginning of each chapter to which their thoughts (and doubts or objections) contributed. I would especially like to thank Giuseppe Martinico, Giulio Itzcovich, Lando Kirchmair, Dimitry Kochenov, Zoltán Szente, Emese Szilágyi, Péter Takács, Allan Francis Tatham and Attila Vincze who endeavoured to read the whole manuscript. At Cambridge University Press, Elizabeth Spicer and Rebecca J Roberts provided an attentive service during the different phases of the publication process. The comments of the Press's anonymous reviewers were greatly appreciated. I am grateful for research assistance to Barbara Agatha Baldauf, for library help to Adrienn Aczél-Partos, Judit Elek, Stefan Hampele, Sara von Skerst and Ali Zakouri, for linguistic help to Miklós Könczöl, Lisa Giles and Allan Francis Tatham, for institutional and financial support during the final stage of writing to the Max Planck Institute for Comparative Public Law and International Law in Heidelberg, to the VolkswagenStiftung (in the form of a generous Schumpeter Fellowship) and to the Hungarian Academy of Sciences.

*Budapest/Heidelberg*
*7 April 2015*

# 1

# Introduction

> The ideas of economists and political philosophers, both when they are right and when they are wrong, are more powerful than is commonly understood. Indeed the world is ruled by little else. Practical men, who believe themselves to be quite exempt from any intellectual influence, are usually the slaves of some defunct economist.[1]

This book provides a theory for constitutional lawyers about *fundamental questions of European constitutional law.*[2] My intention was: (1) to present a map (or a structured and concise overview) of the immense literature on these questions; (2) to show in an intelligible methodological manner my own answers to these questions; and (3) to demonstrate the practical relevance of constitutional theory by presenting concrete examples of its application and by showing how different theoretical answers (presuppositions) lead to different legal solutions.

Before beginning the actual enquiry, it is necessary to clarify the methodological presuppositions of the work, which I believe distinguish this book sharply from similar ones in the field. To a certain extent, a major part of this book itself is about the method of (how to pursue a discourse on) constitutional law,[3] but to go one abstraction level higher and to analyse the 'method of the method' would necessarily lead to very

[1] John Maynard Keynes, *The General Theory of Employment, Interest and Money*, London, Palgrave Macmillan 1936, 383.

[2] I am grateful to Paul Behrens, Paul Blokker, Armin von Bogdandy, Péter Cserne, Arthur Dyevre, Tamás Győrfi, Marek Hrubec, Zoltán Novák, Howard Schweber, Jiří Přibáň, Pál Sonnevend, Esther Vogel and Hans Vorländer, in addition to the participants of the MPI Heidelberg weekly workshop on 26 February 2013, to the participants of the PPKE BTK Constitutional Culture conference in Budapest on 14 November 2013 and to my colleagues at the Institute for Legal Studies at the Centre for Social Sciences of the Hungarian Academy of Sciences for critical remarks.

[3] On constitutional theory as the analysis of the methods of constitutional law enquiries, see Helmuth Schulze-Fielitz, Staatsrechtslehre als Wissenschaft, in: *id.* (ed.), *Staatsrechtslehre als Wissenschaft*, Berlin, Duncker & Humblot 2007, 11–48, especially 14. I strongly disagree with Gustav Radbruch, *Einführung in die Rechtswissenschaft*, Stuttgart, KF Köhler Verlag [12]1969, 253, according to whom it is a sign of the sickness of an academic

general philosophical issues, which we need to minimise here. This is not a book about legal epistemology. The following pages should, therefore, be understood rather as revealing presuppositions than as proving their truth. Their ambition is just to provide a theoretical context to the following chapters.

## 1.1 Constitutional theory as a language suggestion for a constitutional discourse

If we do not want to pretend that legal expressions have some kind of ontological 'essence', then we have two ('anti-essentialist') options: either (1) we should view their meanings as their role played in the constitutional discourse (*description* of the meanings of legal terms),[4] or (2) we should recognise that the definition and re-definition of constitutional concepts are never just descriptions, but they are rather *suggestions* about their meanings which are consistent with our political preferences. The latter option, which I believe is nearer to the reality of constitutional discourses than the first one, means that there is an ongoing political struggle over who defines concepts and how,[5] and concepts are viewed something like squares on a chessboard which can be occupied (by our own, strategically designed definitions) in order to have a better position than our (potential) opponents. Thus, when we 'describe' the constitutional concepts, we actually do not just *de*scribe them but rather implicitly *pre*scribe a use which favours our political preferences (be it emotional-ideological preferences or interest preferences).[6] This constitutional discourse has three types of participants in my simplified model: politicians, scholars and judges. These all have different types of interactions or interwovenness, and they all have different ranks of importance in different countries, but from time to time they are all inspired or even forced by the people (as an extraordinary, fourth participant) to alter

discipline if it is concerned with its own method. A certain level of concern is quite healthy, the question is rather that of proportions.

4 Cf. more general Ludwig Wittgenstein, *Philosophical Investigations*, Oxford, Blackwell 1953, 43. For an application of this idea to general legal concepts see HLA Hart, Definition and Theory in Jurisprudence, *Law Quarterly Review* 70 (1954), 37–60.

5 Pierre Bourdieu, La force du droit. Éléments pour une sociologie du champs juridique, *Actes de la recherche en sciences sociales* 64/9 (1986) 3–19, especially 4.

6 At the end of the day, most of these interpretation struggles *(Deutungskämpfe)* will be decided by the constitutional court (or supreme court) of the given legal order, see Hans Vorländer (ed.), *Die Deutungsmacht der Verfassungsgerichtsbarkeit*, Wiesbaden, VS-Verlag 2006, with further references. See also below the introductory text to Part B.

their own discoursive behaviour, for instance, through elections or through constitutional complaints.

I will refer to some of the most important legal expressions as '(legal/constitutional) key concepts', deliberately ignoring the possible difference between 'expression' and 'concept' because of the already mentioned anti-essentialist methodological presupposition.[7] The key concepts are chosen according not only to their frequency of use, but also to their centrality in either explaining other concepts or in justifying constitutional norms (if we see concepts as a network, then they would be the major nodes). They are not necessarily often mentioned (as a matter of fact, most of them are very often mentioned, but that is not the point), but they would be or could be mentioned if you asked enough questions in order to find the key concepts of the discourse.

The task of *constitutional theory* is to suggest a *language* for the discourse on constitutional law. Language, in the sense used here, comprises a list of key concepts,[8] the meaning of these key concepts[9] and the grammar of the discourse (i.e., what constitutional reasoning looks like).[10] None of these elements is entirely objective; they all imply a certain political vision (see below *1.2 The political nature of constitutional theory*). The language therefore is necessarily (at least partly) normative, but it also has to fit the current discourse (as it does not intend to be the language of a fictitious constitutional discourse, but wants to shape the current one).[11] Constitutional theory is thus an advice (and the

[7] For a similar view see Michael Stolleis, *Rechtsgeschichte schreiben. Rekonstruktion, Erzählung, Fiktion?*, Basel, Schwabe 2008, 25; *id.*, *Rechtsgeschichte als Kunstprodukt. Zur Entbehrlichkeit von 'Begriff' und 'Tatsache'*, Baden-Baden, Nomos 1997, 12.

[8] Participating in the constitutional discourse and even creating a constitutional regime itself mean the acceptance of a very specific language with its key words and conceptualisations, see Howard Schweber, *The Language of Liberal Constitutionalism*, Cambridge, Cambridge University Press 2007.

[9] As to this second element of the language, I was highly inspired by the work of Christoph Möllers, *Staat als Argument*, München, CH Beck 2000. I am indebted to Armin von Bogdandy who placed this book into my hands ten years ago (when I was just about to begin writing an essentialist *Staatslehre* which, as I realised through Möllers' book, was an absolutely futile idea) and to Christoph Möllers with whom since then I have had the opportunity to personally discuss methodological issues of constitutional law.

[10] The latter could be decoded for German ears approximately as 'Metatheorie der Verfassungsdogmatik', see Martin Morlok, *Was heißt und zu welchem Ende studiert man Verfassungstheorie?*, Berlin, Duncker & Humblot 1988, 52–55.

[11] Even though I see in many aspects law as a discourse, this work shares hardly any of the theoretical presuppositions of Habermas's discourse theory. My theory is much more fragmented and sceptical, it does not contain any master plan (see below *1.3 The role of historical and sociological knowledge*), and its implied anthropology is much less

constitutional theorist is the advisor) as to the terminology of constitutional law, that is, how to conceptualise constitutional issues.

The structure of the book is, partly following from the above definition of *language*, going to be tripartite. In the first major part (Part A), I am going to analyse the general rules (or the grammar) of the constitutional discourse, that is, the rules of constitutional reasoning.[12] In the largest and most important part (Part B), an analysis of the different conceptualised responses ('key concepts') will be given. And finally, I will collect some conceptual dead-ends in Part C.

## 1.2 The political nature of constitutional theory

Constitutional lawyers are often accused of being politically biased[13] and, to be fair, for good reason. Constitutional lawyers are, and ought to be, politically biased (or to put it nicely: they should not be politically neutral). However, they should only be political in a very specific narrow sense: they ought to have a political vision.[14] Without a political vision, key concepts of constitutional law (democracy, the rule of law, etc.)

optimistic as to the rationality and morality of humans, than that of Habermas. My theory is normative only in the sense that it hopes to influence the European constitutional discourse and indirectly also European politics, but it is not meant to be a moral philosophy (even though it does imply certain moral assertions). My anthropological views are near to those of Anthony Quinton as exposed in his *The Politics of Imperfection*, London, Faber & Faber 1978.

12 For a similar grammar metaphor see Martti Koskenniemi, *From Apology to Utopia. The Structure of International Legal Argument*, Cambridge, Cambridge University Press 2005, esp. 562–617. I differ from Koskenniemi's view, however, on several points: (1) He uses a wider concept of grammar, which also includes the 'grammar of concepts', and he considers the description of the whole argumentative practice as 'grammar': according to his terminology, the present book should have been entitled the 'Grammar of European Constitutional Law'. (2) I do not share his critical-emancipatory normative ambition, I rather consider this work as an intellectual contribution to European institution-building. (3) Consequently, I provide a more constructive approach, as I am always suggesting a certain interpretation instead of just rejecting others. For a narrower understanding of the concept of 'grammar' including only rules of reasoning, like the concept of the present author, see Jack M Balkin – Sanford Levinson, Constitutional Grammar, *Texas Law Review* 72 (1994) 1771–1803.

13 On the tendency of political insinuations, see Hans Peter Ipsen, Die deutsche Staatsrechtswissenschaft im Spiegel der Lehrbücher, *Archiv des öffentlichen Rechts* 106 (1981) 161–204, especially 198.

14 Cf. Rudolf von Laun, Der Staatsrechtslehrer und die Politik, *Archiv des öffentlichen Rechts* NF 2 (1922) 145–199, 174 stating that a constitutional lawyer without a political vision is 'ridiculous' *(lächerlich)*. For a similar conclusion, with different terminology, see David Robertson, *The Judge as Political Theorist*, Princeton, Princeton University Press 2010.

cannot be meaningfully interpreted, and borderline cases (or cases that have never come up before) cannot be decided in a predictable manner. Without a political vision, you either obtain absurd results through legal formalism, or you end up making arbitrary decisions. Political visions are often unconscious or fragmentary, very vague and even sometimes purposely hidden, but they are normally there, and rightly so. Sometimes you hint at them, but even more often your discoursive opponents try to debunk them in order to discredit you.[15] But you do not speak about them openly in detail *as a lawyer*, because that would undermine your social role. If the matter of the debate is the political vision, then political theorists (political philosophers, political scientists) are better qualified and politicians have more legitimacy to speak than lawyers. But I believe that lawyers do have an important role: they tame ideological and political conflicts by transforming them into technical-legal issues (and this transformation is ideally enforced by the institution of judicial review of statutes). When lawyers talk about the solution of a case, they do not mention who is morally good or bad, smart or stupid, fascist (communist) or democrat, nice or ugly, corrupt or clean (unfortunately, all too often, these are debatable and instrumentalisable categories), but they refer to legal texts, and in our case, to constitutions. They refer to constitutions because these are, normally, fixed points. Of course, their interpretations can differ hugely, but again we have (unwritten) rules about how to deal with this. Constitutional discourse by scholars and judges is therefore functionally superior (as it tames politicians by providing a behavioural framework for them, which will then be institutionally enforced by constitutional courts or supreme courts),[16] but also more formalised (as it has more discourse rules) than the usual everyday discourse of politicians. Constitutional lawyers (even though their job is political) have to distance themselves from everyday politics, primarily by the way they speak about political issues (i.e., via references to constitutional law), but also through remaining outside of everyday

15 In order to ease the job of my critics, I would hint at the following political vision behind many of my writings (including most chapters of this book): 'a federal Europe (meaning the European Union) which is a strong contestant on the political and economic world stage and which is based on its common constitutional traditions'. On how the rule of law, constitutionalism and democracy make economic development more likely (and step-by-step even change the mentality of peoples), see Daron Acemoglu – James Robinson, *Why Nations Fail: The Origins of Power, Prosperity and Poverty*, New York, Random House 2012, especially 302–334.

16 This means both influence and responsibility, see Andreas Voßkuhle, Die politischen Dimensionen der Staatsrechtslehre, in: Schulze-Fielitz (n. 3) 135–158, especially 138.

party politics.[17] If they participate in everyday party politics, they should do it openly, and they should make it clear that they do not do it as constitutional lawyers, as otherwise they are abusing their standing and endangering the fulfilment of the social function of their fellow constitutional lawyers.[18] Thus constitutional lawyers have to be political, but they should not interfere with everyday politics, and they should follow certain discourse rules when speaking up.

Constitutional theorists might even be one degree more political than constitutional lawyers,[19] because constitutional theorists have the ambition to form the thoughts of constitutional lawyers and to advise them about how to argue in the constitutional (scholarly or judicial) discourse.[20] The nature of the job of a constitutional theorist is thus somewhere between that of (a) a constitutional lawyer and (b) a political philosopher, but his or her task is different from any of the other two.

Ad (a). A constitutional theorist's job is different from that of a constitutional lawyer, because: (a/1) s/he also has to work on a theoretically more abstract level than constitutional lawyers; *and* (a/2) s/he has to be able to sell his/her ideas to the constitutional lawyers by showing their concrete relevance for the solution of cases.[21] A constitutional theorist advises constitutional lawyers about the language which they should use in their discourse. The discourse itself is carried on by constitutional lawyers (judges or scholars), but the communication advisors are constitutional theorists (even if sometimes constitutional theorists cannot resist the temptation to take part in the actual constitutional discourse too). Constitutional theory itself is also a discourse: a discourse about a discourse (or to put it nicely: a meta-discourse), a reflection about what the constitutional law discourse should look like, what constitutional language it should use.

Ad (b). A constitutional theorist's job is also different from that of a political philosopher as well, because: (b/1) s/he also has to connect the

[17] Voßkuhle (n. 16) 153–157.

[18] Michael Stolleis, *Staatsrechtslehre und Politik*, Heidelberg, CF Müller 1996, 26–27.

[19] On the political nature of constitutional theory see Morlok (n. 10) 178 and (with a different terminology) Nicholas William Barber, *The Constitutional State*, Oxford, Oxford University Press 2010, 1–16 and TRS Allan, *The Sovereignty of Law. Freedom, Constitution, and Common Law*, Oxford, Oxford University Press 2013, 1–16, 333–349.

[20] Thus indirectly, constitutional theorists form constitutional law itself, see Morlok (n. 10) 81.

[21] I strongly disagree with Helmuth Schulze-Fielitz, *Der informale Verfassungsstaat*, Berlin, Duncker & Humblot 1984, 151 and with Morlok (n. 10) 52 according to whom, constitutional theory is not developed in order to solve cases. It should be developed in order to solve cases, but in a more indirect way than concrete doctrinal analysis. Without this (at least indirect) ambition, the outcome of the analysis remains unclear.

abstract political ideas to the legal discourse by translating them into the more rigid (because being legally fixed) constitutional language, and consequently, his/her choice of terminology is rather limited; and (b/2) finally, bearing in mind the non-philosopher audience, philosophical issues have to be slightly simplified, especially if they are not directly essential to the actual thesis.

Now, after we have clarified the nature of the job of constitutional scholars (be they constitutional lawyers or constitutional theorists), an additional question arises: whether we should speak about it. Sometimes the truth should remain unspoken. We do not tell our neighbour that he is fat (even if he is), and we do not tell a scholar friend that his book which has just been published is useless (even if it is). Some might think that the ideology of perfect neutrality (even if everybody knows it is not really true) might contribute to the healthy running of the constitutional machinery: rhetorically confirming neutrality (e.g., stating that 'constitutional scholars are just the mouthpiece of the constitution') might be a lie, but a sweet, little and, most importantly, necessary lie. I think this would be a mistaken position to take. If constitutional scholars pretend to be fully neutral, then they are vulnerable to bold debunking exercises by destructive critical scholars, who then justify their own abuse of constitutional law for everyday party politics with reference to the general political nature of constitutional scholarship. Nevertheless, we should differentiate between the general political nature of the job and the melding with everyday politics. It is better to admit openly a certain general type of political attachment (i.e., attachment towards the values of constitutionalism), in order to be able to detach from the everyday business of politics. Without this detachment, constitutional lawyers cannot plausibly determine the framework of everyday politics, cannot tame it; and without this detachment, constitutional theorists cannot plausibly advise constitutional lawyers about the language which should be used to fulfil this task.

## 1.3 The role of historical and sociological knowledge

We can perceive constitutional key concepts in two distinct ways. One is to trace them back to (or justify them with) certain general moral principles, like human dignity or equal freedom (i.e., to see a unified teleological masterplan behind all the key concepts of constitutional law). The other is to view them as historical responses to social challenges.

I believe in the latter path and think that even moral ideas can be explained as long-term default responses to social challenges.[22]

Following Toynbee, I view societies (including European societies) as facing – from time to time – new historical challenges, to which they try to find the right responses.[23] A challenge in this context means a new situation or problem[24] (even a bold response to a former challenge), which cannot be solved by the methods known to that society, but which makes creativity necessary. This creativity can mean technical innovation or the introduction of new ideas on how to organise society (my emphasis here lies with this latter issue).[25] If the technical innovation or the new idea was not the right one to tackle the problem (wrong response), then the society (culture or nation) in question stagnates or even declines until the right response is found (or loses its distinctive identity and is dissolved in another).

The language of constitutional law itself is a type of answer to different historical challenges.[26] If we want to use this language consciously (and if we want to be able to reject certain parts of it), then we have to know the original historical and sociological context in which a constitutional-conceptual innovation arose. We are going to return to this methodological problem in more detail in the introduction to Part B, and I also hope that when we consider our *concrete* topics, that is, constitutional key concepts in Part B, these *abstract* methodological issues will become clearer as well.

[22] Richard A Posner, *The Problematics of Moral and Legal Theory*, Cambridge, Mass., London, Belknap Press of Harvard University Press 1999, 17–38.

[23] Arnold J Toynbee, *A Study of History*, vol. I, London, Oxford University Press 1933, 271. While different aspects of Toynbee's work have been subject to justified criticism (especially the role of religion, the relationship between civilisations, certain concrete historical details), his basic scheme of challenge-and-response does seem to fit the historical facts. For an account of recent literature on Toynbee see Marvin Perry, *Arnold Toynbee and the Western Tradition*, New York, Peter Lang 1996, especially 103–128; for a good introduction to his work see CT McIntire – Marvin Perry, Toynbee's Achievement, in: CT McIntire – Marvin Perry (eds.), *Toynbee. Reappraisals*, Toronto, University of Toronto Press 1989, 3–31; for classic literature on him (and some of his own methodological essays) see MF Ashley Montagu (ed.), *Toynbee and History. Critical Essays and Reviews*, Boston, Porter Sargent 1956.

[24] On wars as challenges to the constitutional systems and on modern constitutional solutions as responses to wars (or to the threats thereof) see Philip Bobbitt, *The Shield of Achilles. War, Peace, and the Course of History*, New York, Anchor 2002, 69–209.

[25] See András Sajó, *Limiting Government. An Introduction to Constitutionalism*, Budapest, New York, Central European University Press 1999, 1–7 on constitutional ideas as expressions of what kind of past experiences the constitution-giver wanted to avoid.

[26] On the role of historical knowledge in understanding contemporary constitutional key concepts see Gustavo Zagrebelsky, *Historia y constitución*, Madrid, Trotta $^{2}$2011.

## 1.4 Why 'European'?

This is not a general (or universal) constitutional theory in a geographic sense. On the one hand, it is debatable whether it is possible to write a general constitutional theory at all.[27] There is a universal constitutional discourse (both judicial and scholarly), but it is definitely not as dense as the European one.

On the other hand, however, it is also not the constitutional theory of just one single state.[28] Its geographic ambition is much broader, and it attempts to develop a constitutional theory for Europe. For different reasons, it seemed possible to have a common constitutional theory for Europe: (1) The role of law in the political system (especially the 'rule of law') connects these legal systems together (as compared to China or Africa). (2) The social challenges are similar (e.g., multi-ethnic democracies in post-industrial societies). (3) European integration (including the law of the European Convention on Human Rights [ECHR]) gives a common, but very new type of legal framework to these responses. We could even say that Europe is the laboratory of constitutional theory because European integration required many of the traditional constitutional key concepts to be partly redefined.[29] (4) The European constitutional discourse, consisting of the constitutional discourses of the Member States and the constitutional discourse of the EU, is strongly interwoven, both in its judicial and its scholarly components, and is becoming more so each year. Comparative law became a standard part of domestic constitutional work, and mostly through the use of European materials (and only rarely non-European materials).

[27] Hermann Heller, *Staatslehre*, Leiden, Sijthoff 1934, 3–4. As a less ambitious rejection, simply stating that his own theory is not universal, see Ronald Dworkin, *Law's Empire*, London, Fontana 1986, 102–103.

[28] Cf. Otto Depenheuer – Christoph Grabenwarter (eds.), *Verfassungstheorie*, Tübingen, Mohr Siebeck 2010, which is (despite of its general title: 'Constitutional Theory') a theory of the German constitutional doctrine (with some passages on other countries); a thorough and interesting one, no doubt, but destined to advise only the German discourse. The same applies to a former British analysis, see Geoffrey Marshall, *Constitutional Theory*, Oxford, Clarendon Press 1971.

[29] Cf. the flourishing literature on the topic Anne Peters, *Elemente einer Theorie der Verfassung Europas*, Berlin, Duncker & Humblot 2001; Amaryllis Verhoeven, *The European Union in Search of a Democratic and Constitutional* Theory, The Hague, Kluwer Law International 2002; Peter Häberle, *Europäische Verfassungslehre*, Baden-Baden, Nomos [7]2011; John Erik Fossum – Agustín José Menéndez, *The Constitution's Gift. A Constitutional Theory for a Democratic European Union*, Lanham, Rowman & Littlefield 2011.

And finally, the geographic scope, is of course also influenced by the specific political vision behind the present theory (see above *1.2 The political nature of constitutional theory*). The purpose of the following chapters is also to provide tools or argumentative strategies for those constitutional lawyers who share this vision of a strong and unified Europe.

# PART I

# The grammar: the rules of constitutional reasoning

We are not final because we are infallible, but we are infallible because we are final.[1]

The grammar of a constitutional language is made up of the rules of constitutional reasoning. In this Part we are going to analyse how constitutional lawyers are able to extract the most meaning from a (relatively) short text,[2] such as a constitution, with the use of sophisticated tricks (or methods) of interpretation. Partly with the help of these methods, and partly on the basis of text-independent speculations, constitutional courts and legal scholars are able to develop a system of concepts (a *Rechtsdogmatik*[3] or its specific constitutional part, the *Verfassungsdogmatik*) which is considerably more sophisticated than the one of the actual text of the Constitution in order to serve as a helping toolkit for the solution of future cases.[4] After having analysed some

[1] Robert L Jackson in *Brown v. Allen*, 344 US 443 (1953), 540.

[2] The short and abstract nature of the constitutions is not to be explained by a cynical attempt to make it more difficult to control state power (but for such a view see Napoleon Bonaparte: '[i]l faut qu'une constitution soit courte et obscure' [a constitution has to be short and obscure]). The actual reason for this is rather that, on the one hand, the constitution maker could not decide everything beforehand, and on the other hand, that too many detailed rules would inflate the text of the constitution (and this would also make it necessary to modify it often, which would ruin its prestige). See Meinhard Hilf, Die sprachliche Struktur der Verfassung, in: Josef Isensee – Paul Kirchhof (eds.), *Handbuch des Staatsrechts der Bundesrepublik Deutschland VII.: Normativität und Schutz der Verfassung – internationale Beziehungen*, Heidelberg, CF Müller 1992, 79–102, especially 90.

[3] The German term *Rechtsdogmatik* is normally translated into English either as 'doctrine' or as 'dogmatic'. I would, however, stick to the German original, as 'doctrine' is too general and does not express the systematic conceptual nature of the genre, and 'dogmatic' has a rather pejorative connotation in English which I would like to avoid. One of the reasons for translation problems is that in common law countries the conceptual system as developed by legal scholarship is relatively simplistic (it is rather done by judgments on a case-by-case basis).

[4] A sophisticated conceptual system also helps (a) to decide future cases (if their relevant facts are the same) in the *same* way, and (b) to give *reasons* for this, i.e., not to decide

preliminary issues in Chapter 2, in its largest part we are going to deal with the different methods of constitutional interpretation (Chapter 3). The nature of this conceptual system will then be analysed (Chapter 4), before we turn to the question of styles of constitutional reasoning in different European countries (Chapter 5). The analysis concentrates on the European constitutional discourse, though for purposes of classification and comparison, non-European discourses will also be mentioned.

arbitrarily (and also not to appear to decide arbitrarily). See Eike von Savigny, Methodologie der Dogmatik: Wissenschaftstheoretische Fragen, in: Ulfrid Neumann – Joachim Rahlf – Eike von Savigny, *Juristische Dogmatik und Wissenschaftstheorie*, München, CH Beck 1976, 7–13, 8.

2

# Constitutional reasoning in general

> 'In the beginning was the Word.' This quote from the Holy Bible stands also on the ceiling of our discipline's temple. The job of legal scholarship is interpreting, and the base of every interpretation is the word.[1]

Constitutional reasoning in this chapter refers to a special type of legal reasoning, namely, a type of reasoning that is using arguments based on constitutional law in order to solve a case.[2] The concept of 'constitutional law' is, unfortunately, not as simple as it looks at first sight. (a) If we define it as a legal document (or a group of documents) which is more difficult to amend than (other, ordinary) statutes, then organic laws may also fall into this category, expanding it too far. (b) If we look for the norms of the highest rank in a legal order on which the validity of all new norms is measured, then it could mean only the *Ewigkeitsklausel* (those provisions of the constitution that cannot be modified) of constitutions, thus we would narrow the concept too much. (c) If we call a constitution the norm(s) which regulate(s) the creation of statutes (following Kelsen), then the Standing Orders of parliaments would be part of the constitution, which also does not conform to our usual understanding.[3] (d) If we consider the constitution as a norm or as a bundle of norms which regulate the most important questions (state organisation, fundamental rights) of a legal order, then the definition would be very vague, as 'most

[1] '"Kezdetben vala az ige." A szentírás e szava tudományunk csarnoka felett is áll. A jogtudomány minden munkája értelmezés és minden értelmezés alapja a szó.' Gusztáv Szászy-Schwarz, *Parerga*, Budapest, Athenaeum 1912, 420 (present author's translation).

[2] For comments on earlier versions of Chapters 2–5, I am grateful to Armin von Bogdandy, Damiano Canale, Lourens du Plessis, Arthur Dyevre, Jeffrey Goldsworthy, Christoph Grabenwarter, Giulio Itzcovich, Katalin Kelemen, Mitchel Lasser, Oliver Lepsius, Otto Pfersmann, Oreste Pollicino, Alec Stone Sweet, Zoltán Szente and Giovanni Tuzet, in addition to the participants of the Ius Publicum Europaeum workshop of 18 February 2011 in Heidelberg, of the judicial reasoning workshop of 13 December 2011 in Milan, and of the Berger Lecture of 10 April 2012 at Cornell Law School.

[3] Theo Öhlinger, *Der Stufenbau der Rechtsordnung. Rechtstheoretische und ideologische Aspekte*, Wien, Manz 1975, 17.

important' can be defined in very different manners. (e) And finally, if we consider constitutions those documents which bear the name constitution, then the *Grundgesetz* would fall outside of this category. Thus we need a more sophisticated definition.[4]

I am actually going to use the expression 'constitution' in the sense of (f) 'a norm or a group of norms which are of the highest rank in a legal order in the sense that the validity of all other norms is measured on them'. This definition is different from the (b) above, because here we measure the validity of all other norms on the constitution, whereas in (b) we measured only the validity of *new* norms on the constitution. The difference is important, as we cannot measure the validity of the original (ordinary) constitutional text on the *Ewigkeitsklausel* (which are formally part of this document), thus our new (f) definition does not merge the concept of *Ewigkeitsklausel* with that of the constitution, but it simply conceives the *Ewigkeitsklausel* as part of the constitution. This also conforms to our usual use of the word 'constitution'.

In situations leading to legal decisions, there are three fundamental requirements: (A) the issue has to be decided, (B) the decision has to be sound (i.e., acceptable also from non-legal, e.g., political, social, moral or economic, points of view); and (C) it also has to be acceptable from a legal point of view, that is, traceable back to the constitution. Requirement (A) is not within the scope of the present chapter,[5] but (B) and (C) sometimes require considerable lawyerly efforts if they are to be met at the same time, and this is exactly what we shall discuss here. If taken separately, (B) and (C) can be fulfilled quite easily, but their simultaneous accomplishment may raise difficulties. In later parts of this chapter and in Chapter 3 we are therefore going to focus on how one can have a set of legal arguments which allows for the delivery of a sound decision [i.e., (B)] without being accused of departing from the constitution, as this would result in arbitrariness [i.e., (C) would not be fulfilled]. The problem here is that making a good decision in a non-legal (non-lawyerly) sense does *not always* qualify as a legal argument.[6] One of the presuppositions of the present chapter is

[4] For substantive (material, content-based, evolutionary, historical) definitions of the word 'constitution', and for their rejection, see below 8.1.1.

[5] For such a problem see the Spanish Constitutional Court being unable to decide about the Statute of Catalonia for several years: BGG, Cuatro años de encarnizada batallas política, *El País* 16.04.2010.

[6] Cf. András Jakab, What makes a good lawyer?, *Zeitschrift für öffentliches Recht* 62 (2007) 275–287 on purposive (teleological) reasoning as a bridge or a method facilitating the translation of non-legal considerations into legal ones. Teleological arguments ensure that we are able to respond to new social challenges without modifying the text of the constitution. See below 3.3.1 and 3.6.

that from a lawyerly point of view, there is quite often no single good decision (though sometimes there is), but that some of the possible (i.e., legally not absurd) decisions are socially, morally etc. more acceptable, while others are less so. The problem can be conceptualised in two different ways: either we can say that finding the *legally* most acceptable decision sometimes involves subjective factors; or (if we work with a more positivistic concept of law, i.e., if we strictly differentiate between description and prescription as to the content of the law, then) we can admit that sometimes we choose the legally second best solution because of non-legal factors.[7]

One of the theses of the present chapter, which will be developed later, is that this is not a perversion of constitutional interpretation, but rather that the presence of subjective factors is a necessary and unavoidable feature. Thus, legal methodology is somewhere between complete (objective) certainty and complete (subjective) arbitrariness, as to the outcome of legal interpretation. The existence of debates in constitutional law may suggest that there is general disagreement amongst constitutional lawyers on the most important issues and that the subjective factor plays a major role in constitutional interpretation. This, however, is a false impression: we do agree on most problems, but we do not discuss these, as it would be terribly boring to keep repeating each other. Moreover, the general (implicit and tacit) opinion of the professional community serves as an objective control mechanism *on most questions,* thus preventing arbitrariness. This chapter reflects the conviction that one may indeed aim for more objectivity (which is required by the rule of law, and its conceptual component legal certainty), but complete objectivity[8] (like the axis of a hyperbola) can, and should, never be achieved.

[7] For a traditional positivist conceptualisation, separating sharply between the interpretation of the text, on the one hand, and then the actual legal decision as a choice from the different options offered by the interpretation, on the other hand (and criticising Robert Alexy, Michel Troper and Ronald Dworkin for not doing this separation), see Otto Pfersmann, Le sophisme onomastique: changer au lieu de connaître. L'interprétation da la Constitution, in: Ferdinand Mélin-Soucramanien (ed.), *L'interprétation constitutionnelle*, Paris, Dalloz 2005, 33–60. If we follow this positivistic path, then our legal theoretical task becomes quite complicated: for the first (interpretative) step we also have to clarify precisely what we interpret, i.e., what the law is. See Otto Pfersmann, Ontologie des normes juridiques et argumentation, in: Otto Pfersmann – Gérard Timsit (eds.), *Raisonnement juridique et interpretation,* Paris, Sorbonne 2001, 11–34. Non-positivists (or non-traditional positivists) have it easier at this point, as they can avoid this hopelessly complicated ontological question.

[8] By objectivity we mean here the lack of arbitrariness, i.e., 'it can be supported by arguments thought to be relevant which are independent from the person of the speaker/author of those arguments'.

Legal norms in general, and the constitution (due to the abstract nature of its text) in particular, mostly allow for different interpretations.[9] To use the words of Neil MacCormick:[10]

> In short, rules can be ambiguous in given contexts, and can be applied in one way or the other only after the ambiguity is resolved. But resolving the ambiguity in effect involves choosing between rival versions of the rule ... once that choice is made, a simple deductive justification of a particular decision follows. But a complete justification of that decision must hinge then on how the choice between the competing versions of the rule is justified.

According to European legal traditions, any choice between these options has to be justified: one ought to argue for his or her decision.[11] Such a reasoning has to provide a (rational) *justification* for the solution chosen, on the one hand, and – partly overlapping this – *convince* (both rationally and emotionally) the audience, on the other.[12] In the case of constitutional reasoning, the audience comprises the whole of the political community, yet in practice it is limited (because of the expert knowledge needed to understand such reasoning) to the citizens who have at least some education in constitutional law. Reasoning is essentially addressed to the latter group: the decision-maker (a constitutional court) wants to show its audience (especially politicians and constitutional lawyers) that its decision was not an arbitrary one (or *horribile dictu,* motivated by party politics).

[9] Different outcomes of different interpretations are called 'norm hypotheses' *(Normhypothesen)*; see, e.g., Karl Korinek, Zur Interpretation von Verfassungsrecht, in: Heinz Mayer (ed.), *Staatsrecht in Theorie und Praxis. Festschrift für Robert Walter*, Wien, Manz 1991, 363–385, 367 or 'interpretative alernatives' *(Auslegungsalternativen),* see Aulis Aarnio, *Denkweisen der Rechtswissenschaft*, Wien, Springer 1979, 95.

[10] Neil MacCormick, *Legal Reasoning and Legal Theory*, Oxford, Clarendon Press 1978, 67–68.

[11] It was not always the case; the practice of the Middle Ages is very diverse from this point of view, see Tony Sauvel, Histoire du jugement motivé, *Revue du droit public et de la science politique* 1955, 5–53. On the obligation to give reasons for legal decisions (with historical, theoretical and German constitutional perspectives), see Uwe Kischel, *Die Begründung*, Tübingen, Mohr Siebeck 2003. For the French minimalistic justificatory tradition, see below 5.2.

[12] On the difference between convincing and justifying, see Eugenio Bulygin, Normative Positivism vs. The Theory of Legal Argumentation, in: Tomasz Gizbert-Studnicki – Jerzy Stelmach (eds.), *Law and Legal Cultures in the 21st Century. Diversity and Unity*, Warszawa, Oficyna 2007, 221–228, 224. On convincing as the purpose of legal reasoning, see Chaïm Perelman, *Logique juridique – nouvelle rhétorique,* Paris, Dalloz 1976. For a critical discussion of this approach (especially that of Perelman), see Manuel Atienza, *Las razones del Derecho. Teorías de la argumentación jurídica,* Madrid, Centro de Estudios Constitucionales 1991, 65–101.

One may argue before the actual decision, searching open-mindedly for the best interpretation; but also after the decision is made, trying to persuade others about one's decision (i.e., providing arguments supporting the decision already made). Thus constitutional reasoning can be both an honest endeavour to find the solution for the case, or it can be just an ideological mask to find support for a choice which we already made well before we actually began the reasoning. Different schools in legal theory place a stronger emphasis on one or the other of these phases, but we do not intend to take sides here on this issue, and accept both argumentative situations as possible.

## 2.1 Constitutional reasoning and constitutional interpretation

We have to say something briefly about the relationship between the concepts of 'interpretation' and 'argumentation' (the latter is used as synonymous throughout this book with 'reasoning'). 'Interpretation' (in the sense used here) means determining the content of a normative text. This determination of content can be argued for (or against) with the help of arguments. Consequently, what is traditionally called 'a method of interpretation', is in fact a type of argument used to interpret a text.

Most arguments in constitutional reasoning aim to interpret the constitution, even if sometimes they just presuppose its existence and the debate will be about some logically secondary question (like the interpretation of a precedent). There are three main exceptions where the arguments are not interpretative in their nature: (a) analogies, (b) establishing the text of the constitution, and (c) arguments about why the text of the constitution should or should not be applied.

Ad (a). Analogies are used if there is a legal gap or lacuna and one wants to solve a problem not covered by the text of the constitution.[13] There are two kinds of gaps: (a) real, ideological or axiological and (b) technical or institutional.[14] Technical or institutional gaps exist where the constitution itself raises a question, but fails to answer it (e.g., a provision makes a reference to another, which does not exist; or the

13 E.g., in the judgment by the Spanish Constitutional Court No. 36/82.

14 Hans Kelsen, *Reine Rechtslehre*, Leipzig, Wien, Franz Deuticke 1934, 100–104. Likewise Pavel Holländer, *Verfassungsrechtliche Argumentation – zwischen dem Optimismus und der Skepsis*, Berlin, Duncker & Humblot 2007, 107–108; Riccardo Guastini, *L'interpretazione dei documenti normativi*, Milano, Guiffrè 2004, 224–227; Norberto Bobbio, *Teoria generale del diritto*, Torino, Giappichelli 1993, 257–259.

rules of succession of a state organ are simply missing).[15] Real (axiological or substantive) gaps, in turn, are found where a rule does not regulate a question, and from this would follow an obviously unacceptable legal solution (*planwidrige Rechtslücke*).[16] The difficulty here is that this (i.e., what 'obviously unacceptable' means) is a question of evaluation. Therefore, if one claims that there is a substantive legal gap, this argument has to be supported by a reference to the objective *ratio legis* (3.3.1) or the subjective intention of the constitution-maker (3.3.2), or to substantive (e.g., moral) arguments (3.3.3). This is the reason why the use of analogy (without a particularly firm reasoning) in the case of a substantive constitutional gap may run the risk of being accused of arbitrariness.[17] Fear of that may explain why in some legal cultures it is not accepted at all,[18] and mostly general principles are referred to instead.

The basic idea of analogy is to look for a rule containing provisions not exactly for our case but for cases similar to it (i.e., the accusation of arbitrariness can be rebutted by showing this 'similarity' together with the 'gap in law'). The more similar the case is, the more convincing the analogy. The typical problems here, too, are (1) when a case can be regarded as 'similar' to another and (2) which of two 'similar' cases (being similar to ours in different aspects) is *more* similar. To answer these, teleological arguments may be of some help.

A distinction well known in literature is the one between *analogia legis* and *analogia iuris*.[19] The former means applying a particular (but not immediately relevant to the case) norm of positive law (possibly not even of constitutional rank), while in the case of the latter the norm to be applied is inferred from general principles not explicitly codified (which may be collected from several enactments).

[15] Katja Hemke, *Methodik der Analogiebildung im öffentlichen Recht*, Berlin, Duncker & Humblot 2006, 43 calls these 'Existenzlücke' ('existence gap').

[16] Hemke (n. 15) 44 calls these 'Relationslücke' ('relation gap'), as they exist *in relation* to the legal system or its values as a whole.

[17] One way of escaping the charge or arbitrariness is trying to trace the substantive gap back to provisions of the normative text (e.g., to principles of the constitution, perhaps combined with particular provisions). A thorough argument (i.e., answering the possible counter-arguments – especially of the types 'Why this very provision?' and 'Is there no other, more important principle that would suggest the use of analogy from another particular provision?') is not used normally, however.

[18] One of the usual rejections of the use of analogy by the Austrian Constitutional Court: VfSlg 11.663/1988.

[19] Miklós Szabó, *Ars juris. A jogdogmatika alapjai*, Miskolc, Bíbor 2005, 182–183.

Analogy is not a method of interpretation, but rather the application of a rule (which of course has to be interpreted too, in order to be applied) which actually does not cover the case. If one uses the 'analogous' rule only for interpreting the rule one has to apply, then it is rather either a contextual/harmonising argument (*in pari materia,* see below 3.2.1) or 'interpretation in the light of doctrinal concepts and principles' (see below 3.2.3).

The inverse of analogy is teleological reduction (*teleologische Reduktion*): a norm which covers the case is not applied, as it would contradict a general principle, the objective *ratio legis* or the subjective intention of the constitution-maker.[20]

Making use of analogy may raise serious doubts in terms of its legality (as the case is admittedly not covered by the norm applied; or in the case of teleological reduction one fails to apply the relevant norm),[21] and is also likely to make the resulting interpretation unforeseeable (thus contradicting legal certainty), therefore such arguments are usually avoided.[22] The most acceptable situation for using analogies is that of technical legal gaps – provided that one's argument is founded on positive law (e.g., reference to several – concordant – provisions of positive law made for similar cases) to the greatest extent possible.

Ad (b). The second type of non-interpretative constitutional arguments is about establishing the valid text of the constitution, which is a preliminary question of interpretation. It can be problematic in times of revolutionary regime changes (when it is unclear whether the new constitution or the old one is valid), or also when constitutional amendments take place (where either the application of the unwritten *lex posterior derogat legi priori* rule might be the issue, or there are some promulgation problems).

Ad (c). The third type of non-interpretative constitutional arguments is about whether the valid constitution can be applied or not. This is again a preliminary question of interpretation. To this category belong arguments stating that some questions cannot be judged from a legal point of

20 Cf. Karl Larenz, *Methodenlehre der Rechtswissenschaft*, Berlin, Springer [6]1991, 391–395. Against teleological reduction for fundamental rights, see BVerfGE 51, 97 (110).

21 Teleological reduction, if used contrary to the statutes, may conceal a decentralised constitutional review. Its disadvantages are even worse, as it is not even based on positive law (viz. the constitution). For arguments against decentralised constitutional review, see Attila Vincze, Die unmittelbare Anwendbarkeit der ungarischen Verfassung, *Jahrbuch für Ostrecht* 2009, 83–94.

22 This is the reason why most criminal law regimes forbid the use of analogy in disfavour of the defendant, see, e.g., BVerfGE 92, 1. Similarly problematic is analogy if used by the state for any limitation of individual rights (e.g., in tax law or in administrative law), see, e.g., BVerfGE 71, 108.

view, as they are *too* political (thus the constitution cannot be applied)[23] or about the extra-legal nature of state of emergency.[24] In this conceptualisation, the normativity of constitutional regulation of the state of emergency always depends on uncodifiable pre-legal rules governing emergencies. We are going to discuss these arguments in Chapter 11 in more detail (see below 11.3).

Beyond these rare exceptions, the vast majority of arguments are interpretative in their nature. They have to be 'rooted into the constitution', if the judge wants to avoid the risk of being accused of arbitrariness and unfounded argumentation. In the UK, in the absence of such a document, constitutional reasoning is either simply missing in courts (especially in the former House of Lords, today's Supreme Court) as with matters of the relationship between the highest state organs (and the norms are conceptualised as non-legal constitutional conventions), or limited to human rights issues as found in the ECHR (Human Rights Act 1998).

## 2.2 Constitutional interpretation and statutory interpretation

Constitutional interpretation should be understood as just a specific case of statutory interpretation. There is no need to draw a sharp distinction between these two types of interpretation.[25] In general, there are two kinds of arguments for a sharp distinction between the two: (a) the constitution is 'political law' (*Verfassungsrecht als politisches Recht*), thus it is substantially different from other norms of non-constitutional rank; or (b) the norms of the constitution are much more abstract and/or value-laden than the rather concrete

[23] For similar Jellinekian arguments, see Georg Jellinek, *Allgemeine Staatslehre*, Berlin, Häring $^{3}$1914, 16–17 (*Vorbehalt des 'politisch Möglichen'*) and 18 (*Vermutung für die Rechtmäßgkeit der Handlungen der obersten Staatsorgane*). For a convincing critique of the latter see Hans Kelsen, *Vom Wesen und Wert der Demokratie*, Tübingen, Mohr $^{2}$1929, 80. As soon as you try to find a base for such doctrines in the text of the constitution, these doctrines become issues of constitutional interpretation. Without this they are rather just bold attempts to limit constitutionalism.

[24] For an overview of extra- (or pre-)textual constitutional arguments, see below Chapter 11.

[25] On constitutional interpretation using basically the general methods of statutory interpretation (with certain differences in degree), see Guastini (n. 14) 277–278; Ernst Forsthoff, Die Umbildung des Verfassungsgesetzes, in: Hans Barion – Ernst Forsthoff – Werner Weber (eds.), *Festschrift für Carl Schmitt zum 70. Geburtstag*, Berlin, Duncker & Humblot 1959, 35–62, especially 36; and Zoltán Szente, *Érvelés és értelmezés az alkotmányjogban*, Budapest, Pécs, Dialóg Campus 2013, 113–115.

statutory norms.[26] Ad (a) The first argument is dangerous from the perspective of the rule of law on the one hand (as it places some questions outside the scope of judicial review), and fails to recognise that also statutes below constitutional rank may also have a 'political' content, on the other hand. Referring to the 'political' nature of constitutions in order to depart from the usual country-specific methods of statutory interpretation is mostly just a way of removing some kind of political activity from constitutional or judicial control or supporting an interpretation of the constitution which cannot be justified by any of the methods of interpretation (as it rests on the arbitrary, possibly party political, preferences). Thus such arguments are hard to reconcile with the rule of law; they should rather be avoided.[27] Ad (b) Referring to the different nature of norms is likewise mistaken, as it does not take into account the fact that general clauses in civil codes are at least as abstract and/or value-laden as the provisions of the constitutions concerning fundamental rights, and that constitutions also contain a number of rather concrete (e.g., procedural) rules. True, constitutions contain abstract and general provisions in a greater proportion, but this only means that one has to use certain methods more frequently (see below 3.6).

The vast literature on constitutional interpretation (greater than on any other particular norm in the legal order, such as civil or criminal codes) is due to the higher stakes that are at issue, and not to the entirely different legal nature. The stakes are higher because the interpretation often concerns the institutional structure of society as well as political power; and also because the law-maker cannot as easily correct judicial interpretation in the same way as it can with ordinary statutes.

A sharp difference in terms of nature is thus rather a myth and, moreover, a harmful one, as it would place constitutional review beyond the traditional limits of *Verfassungsdogmatik*, thus making it more difficult to control. Over-emphasising the difference can serve two purposes: 1. a rhetorical tool used to make constitutional interpretation look mystical and complex, thus making the author or the court look very smart; or 2. escaping from the control of usual methods, thus being able

[26] See the description and convincing refutation of these arguments by María Luisa Balaguer Callejón, *Interpretación de la Constitución y ordenamiento jurídico*, Madrid, Tecnos 1997, 39–40.

[27] Convincingly, Werner Kägi, *Die Verfassung als rechtliche Grundordnung des Staates*, Zürich, Polygraph 1945, 65–66, 120.

to smuggle one's own moral preferences masked as the result of some special kind of interpretation. The methods of constitutional interpretation are thus not different from the methods of statutory interpretation, only the emphasis placed on the specific methods and the frequency of their use are different.

Such gradual differences can be explained by the fact that constitutions are more difficult to amend, thus judges have to interpret constitutions often in a more creative way to adjust them to new challenges. Further the degree of generality of constitutional provisions is *on average* higher than that of statutory provisions, which again indicates a higher probability for creative (i.e., non-literal) interpretation. But this difference is, again, just gradual.

In some legal orders, though, there does exist a rather pronounced difference between the style of argumentation in ordinary courts, on the one hand, and that in the constitutional court, on the other. This can mostly be explained by different positive legal rules on how judgments should be delivered in the different courts, such as whether dissenting opinions are possible or not. It is also usual that the ratio of university professors or former politicians is higher amongst constitutional court judges, which influences their typical arguments (e.g., whether they rely on arguments of public morality or of legal scholarship). In some constitutional courts, the *locus standi* rules (e.g., the requirement of claiming the violation of a fundamental right) make it more likely that the ratio of fundamental rights cases will be higher; thus usual arguments about fundamental rights (e.g., proportionality tests) will also be more likely to appear. Different *locus standi* rules (e.g., *actio popularis* in which no fundamental rights' violations have to be claimed, but instead constitutional grievances can be conceptualised with the help of general principles like the rule of law or democracy),[28] however, can reduce such differences.

The differences between the style of argumentation in ordinary courts and that in constitutional courts thus do *not* follow from the 'nature' of constitutional interpretation as such; they are usually accidental features, which do exist in some countries, not in others.

[28] In Europe, there are currently four constitutional courts where *actio popularis* exists: Bavaria, Serbia, Montenegro and Macedonia. In Croatia, there is a similar type of popular claim, but the constitutional court is not obliged to begin the procedure. See Bernd Wieser, *Vergleichendes Verfassungsrecht*, Wien, Springer 2005, 140. In Hungary, the *actio popularis* was abolished by the end of 2011, and the new constitution introduced a German-type constitutional complaint in which the violation of a fundamental right has to be claimed.

## 2.3 The structure of arguments

There are three general types of legal argumentative structures: (a) deploying one conclusive argument (or a chain of arguments following from one another); (b) cumulative-parallel arguments or a reasoning like 'the legs of a chair'[29] (several arguments support a certain legal interpretation independently; every argument would suffice on its own, but there are more of them);[30] and (c) mentioning only relevant factors, any of which is not conclusive, but if taken together, they provide a certain solution (discursive or dialogic style; making use of *topoi*).[31] The most transparent is (a), the least is (c); depending on the legal culture, different structures are preferred.[32]

Legal argumentation is usually enthymematic in structure: that is, not all the steps are explained, but some of them are only implied, or based on implied premises.[33] What we find in judicial decisions is therefore necessarily only a sketch or abbreviation of all the arguments: only those steps will be analysed which are susceptible to debate.

[29] William Twining - David Miers, *How to Do Things with Rules: A Primer of Interpretation*, London, Weidenfeld and Nicolson $^{2}$1982, 268 [following John Wisdom, Gods, *Proceedings of the Aristotelian Society* 1944, 185–194]. In the original text of Wisdom, the phrase 'legs of a chair' also implied that single arguments are not conclusive, but if we used the expression in this sense here, we could not distinguish between this type and that of topical reasoning. We therefore use the phrase in a sense slightly different from the original (i.e., for a reasoning in which every argument is conclusive in itself).

[30] See, e.g., László Kiss (dissenting) in Dec. Hung. CC 41/2005. (X. 27.) AB, ABH 2005, 459, 502.

[31] Following Theodor Viehweg, *Topik und Jurisprudenz*, München, Beck 1953. On the jurisprudence of the German Federal Constitutional Court sometimes accepting this argument, see (the criticism by) Ernst-Wolfgang Böckenförde, Die Methoden der Verfassungsinterpretation, *Neue Juristische Wochenschrift* 1976, 2089–2099, especially 2092–2094.

[32] The third (topical) pattern of argumentation is more frequent in German constitutional review, but e.g. hardly ever used in Hungary, see András Jakab, Az Alkotmány kommentárjának feladata, in: András Jakab (ed.), *Az Alkotmány kommentárja*, Budapest, Századvég $^{2}$2009, para 5. A convincing set of arguments against it (namely: it is unclear, uncontrollable and leads to arbitrary and unpredictable decisions) is given by Ulrich Karpen, *Auslegung und Anwendung des Grundgesetzes*, Berlin, Duncker & Humblot 1987, 54–55, with further references.

[33] Franz Horak, Zur rechtstheoretischen Problematik der Begründung, in: Rainer Sprung (ed.), *Die Entscheidungsbegründung in europäischen Verfahrensrechten und im Verfahren vor internationalen Gerichten*, Wien, New York, Springer 1974, 1–26, especially 9, 14–15.

## 2.4 The need for clarifying the methods of interpretation

The methods of interpretation are norms themselves: norms about how norms ought to be interpreted.[34] Normally these methods are uncodified; they follow only from the specific legal culture in which they are used and in which they are considered as obvious truths (at least amongst those who did not do comparative law).[35] Codification of the methods of interpretation arises normally only if the legislator (more specifically: the constitution-maker) wants to change the traditionally cultivated (and sometimes even unspoken) presuppositions about the methods of interpretation. For example, after the downfall of internationally isolated nationalist dictatorships, a typical answer of the new democratic constitution-maker can be to rely explicitly on international law as an aid in constitutional interpretation (especially concerning human rights); this happened in Spain and Portugal.[36]

Another example where the constitution-maker has regulated the interpretation of the constitution is Art. R of the Hungarian Basic Law of 2011:

> (3) The provisions of the Basic Law shall be interpreted in accordance with their purposes, with the Avowal of National Faith contained therein, and with the achievements of our historical constitution.

It lists – somewhat randomly, without any hint why other methods are missing – three methods: the objective teleological method ('in accordance with their purpose'), interpretation in light of the preamble (called 'National Avowal') and interpretation in light of the 'achievements of our historical constitution'. It defines then in Art. 28 what the expression 'purpose' means:

> When interpreting the Basic Law or legal rules, it shall be presumed that they serve moral and economic purposes which are in accordance with common sense and the public good.

[34] Jerzy Wróblewski, Legal Reasoning in Legal Interpretation, *Logique et Analyse* 1969, 3–31, especially 7.

[35] See esp. Anna Gamper, *Regeln der Verfassungsinterpretation*, Wien, New York, Springer 2012 on codified and uncodified rules of constitutional interpretation.

[36] See Art. 16(2) Constitution of Portugal: 'The provisions of the Constitution and laws relating to fundamental rights are to be read and interpreted in harmony with the Universal Declaration of Human Rights.' and Art. 10(2) Constitution of Spain: 'The norms relative to basic rights and liberties which are recognised by the Constitution shall be interpreted in conformity with the Universal Declaration of Human Rights and the international treaties and agreements on those matters ratified by Spain.'

None of these provisions, however, contains all the methods (they do not contain the word 'only' when listing the methods; some obvious ones, like the literal one, are missing), and they do not give any ranking of the listed methods. The second method ('National Avowal') is considered as being named superfluously, as preambles are used anyway to help the interpretation of constitutions.[37] The third method ('historical constitution') is considered either as legally inoperable and serving only purposes of historicising political rhetoric, or as referring to the past case-law of the Constitutional Court, which was used anyway as an aid of interpretation.[38] The explicit reference to the objective teleological method was necessary because of the socialist legacy of interpretation (mainly in ordinary courts), which had to be broken (see below pp. 44, 80); the two others were mentioned only for political reasons.

This example shows that also in the rare cases where we find explicit provisions about the interpretation of the constitution, it will most likely be incomplete: a constitution, by its nature, cannot contain a handbook of its own interpretation. A detailed guide can only be delivered by legal scholarship. But why should we have a detailed guide at all?

Because it means a standard on which we can measure the judges and their decisions. Having such a standard is a way of controlling their power through a soft manner, which at the same time conforms to the idea of judicial independence. Such scholarly critique can be especially effective on those judges who are themselves legal scholars. Beyond scholarly critique, another way to control judges' power is to use judges of the same court: to allow them to write minority opinions and to criticise the majority opinions as equals 'from inside' the judicial branch.

Interpretation inevitably involves subjective factors (or, to put it more mildly, factors which lawyers cannot determine objectively with their traditional legal doctrinal methods): if this were not the case, legal interpretation could be worked out similarly to a mathematical or logical problem, and there would only be one correct interpretation in every case.[39] Very often

[37] On the Hungarian traditions of interpretive preambles, see Márton Sulyok – László Trócsányi, Preambulum, in: Jakab (n. 32), 83–105, especially 91. On the topic in general see Liav Orgad, The preamble in constitutional interpretation, *International Journal of Constitutional Law* 8 (2010) 714–738 with further references.

[38] András Jakab – Pál Sonnevend, Kontinuität mit Mängeln: Das neue ungarische Grundgesetz, *Zeitschrift für ausländisches öffentliches Recht und Völkerrecht* 2012, 79–102, 85.

[39] On the (failed) attempt of Leibniz, aiming at this, see Fritjof Haft, Recht und Sprache, in: Arthur Kaufmann – Winfried Hassemer (eds.), *Einführung in die Rechtsphilosophie und Rechtstheorie der Gegenwart*, Heidelberg, Müller [6]2006, 269–291, 278; Benoît Frydman,

there is no 'single right solution', just better or worse ones.[40] Interpretation is, however, not mathematics, and this is the reason why minority opinions are allowed by several courts (including constitutional courts) in the world. A minority opinion does not (necessarily) mean that the respective judge made a mistake, or that (s)he was not properly trained, or 'misinterpreted' the law (even though this can also happen). A majority decision mostly means only that another interpretation was considered by the greater part of the judges to be more convincing.

The introduction of the institution of concurring and dissenting opinions in constitutional courts reveals the dilemmas: it shows that the law is not straightforward,[41] and that the (constitutional court) judge is not simply 'the mouth-piece of the law [or of the constitution]' (as Montesquieu put it).[42] Moreover, this institution raises the quality of reasoning, since those delivering a concurring reasoning or dissenting opinion have to explain why they do not agree with the majority – and, in turn, those drawing up the majority opinion have to deal with the embarrassing situation in front of a professional audience that a fellow judge is picking to pieces their argument in his dissenting opinion (as it *de facto* happens at times). Certainly one could cite counter-examples, when the majority opinion was not troubled at all, but on the whole its positive influence on the quality of constitutional reasoning is incontestable.

The inevitable subjective factors are to be minimised as far as possible (but a full elimination is both impossible and undesirable).[43]

*Le sens des lois. Histoire de l'interprétation et de la raison juridique*, Paris, Bruxelles, Librairie Générale de Droit et de Jurisprudence – Bruylant 2005, 274–277.

40 This is also the self-understanding of the German Federal Constitutional Court; see BVerfGE 82, 30 (38f).

41 For a recent normative theory underpinning this fact, see Conrado Hübner Mendes, *Constitutional Courts and Deliberative Democracy*, Oxford, Oxford University Press 2013.

42 This makes the style of European continental constitutional court judgments normally more discursive than that of ordinary courts, where normally there is no dissenting opinion; see, e.g., Lech Morawski – Marek Zirk-Sadowski, Precedent in Poland, in: Neil MacCormick – Robert S Summers (eds.), *Interpreting Precedents. A Comparative Study*, Aldershot: Ashgate 1997, 219–258, 225. On the institution of dissenting opinions in constitutional courts, see Katalin Kelemen, The Road from Common Law to East-Central Europe, in: Péter Cserne – Miklós Könczöl (eds.), *Legal and Political Theory in the Post-National Age*, Frankfurt aM, Peter Lang 2011, 118–134.

43 Even within the subjective factors, one can distinguish legitimate (e.g., a different conception of democracy) and illegitimate (e.g., party allegiance) ones. The former may be referred to in an argument, while the latter may not. See Ralf Dreier, Zur Problematik und Situation der Verfassungsinterpretation, in: *id.*, *Recht – Moral – Ideologie. Studien zur Rechtstheorie*, Frankfurt aM, Suhrkamp 1981, 106–145, especially 126.

Accordingly, the text has to be massaged (with methods of interpretation) until it provides a solution in a given case. The choice between these methods cannot eliminate subjective factors,[44] but (a) the decision has to be traced back to the text; and (b) supported with arguments.

The reason for this is that the text has stronger legitimacy than the judge (in cultures respecting the rule of law). For the text is shaped through usually more transparent steps of procedure and in closer relation to the bearer of popular sovereignty (i.e., the people themselves, or organs representing the people), than judicial decision-making (which, according to its mandate, should be based on the text anyway).[45]

One of the means of minimising the subjective factor is to review the methods (or canons) of legal (statutory, constitutional) interpretations.[46] In the following, we are going to give such a review, with the disclaimer that the acceptance of any specific method differs strongly between legal systems.[47] We are going to return to the problem of country-specificity many times in later parts of this book.

[44] This is reflected in an exaggerated form by the lawyerly adage cited by Schneider: 'Tell me who is interpreting the norm, and I tell you what it means.' Hans-Peter Schneider, Verfassungsinterpretation aus theoretischer Sicht, in: Hans-Peter Schneider – Rudolf Steinberg (eds.), *Verfassungsrecht zwischen Wissenschaft und Richterkunst. Konrad Hesse zum 70. Geburtstag*, Heidelberg, CF Müller 1990, 39–52, especially 39.

[45] Judicial procedures themselves are transparent, but how they shape the interpretation of statutes or constitutions is very far from transparent: only in the rarest cases do we find an *explicit* change of former case-law.

[46] The idea of narrowing down the circle of acceptable arguments to a canon stems from ancient Rome, and is alien to Asian or African legal cultures, see AM Honoré, Legal Reasoning in Rome and Today, *South African Law Journal* 1974, 84–94, especially 92.

[47] The discussion of the methods follows Robert S Summers – Michele Taruffo, Interpretation and Comparative Analysis, in: Neil MacCormick – Robert S Summers (eds.), *Interpreting Statutes*, Aldershot, Dartmouth 1991, 461–510, especially 464–465.

# 3

# A scheme of the specific methods of interpretation

> It must be observed that in addition to the usual reasons which make ancient writings more or less difficult to understand, there are some which are peculiar to the Bible. For the language of the Bible is employed to express, under the inspiration of the Holy Ghost, many things which are beyond the power and scope of the reason of man – that is to say, divine mysteries and all that is related to them. There is sometimes in such passages a fullness and a hidden depth of meaning which the letter hardly expresses and which the laws of grammatical interpretation hardly warrant. Moreover, the literal sense itself frequently admits other senses, adapted to illustrate dogma or to confirm morality. Wherefore, it must be recognized that the Sacred Writings are wrapt in a certain religious obscurity, and that no one can enter into their interior without a guide.[1]

In the following, a scheme of specific methods of interpretation will be given.[2] This is meant to be a general conceptual framework which on the one hand helps us to understand issues of constitutional interpretation through examples while showing general theoretical features, but which on the other hand can also be used when describing the different style of constitutional reasoning in later parts of this chapter.

The following scheme of specific methods of interpretation is not entirely exhaustive, but it does contain the vast majority of arguments, and it does contain all binding arguments which are methodologically acceptable. Many other, methodologically unacceptable and unusual arguments can be imagined ('the Court was bribed yesterday to decide so', 'my spouse told me to quash the statute', 'it is usual *factual* political practice, thus it is allowed by constitutional *law*') which we do not list in a separate category. Amongst non-binding arguments, some more types of arguments are possible, like referring to legal history in the same manner as referring to comparative law (e.g., as an inventory of ideas or in order to show that

[1] Providentissimus Deus. Encyclical of Pope Leo XIII on the Study of Holy Scripture (1893), para 14.

[2] An early version of this chapter was published as Judicial Reasoning in Constitutional Courts. A European Perspective, *German Law Journal* 14 (2013) 1215–1278.

the question was well considered, but not as a decisive argument, see below 3.4.2), but they seemed to be rather rare so they are not listed either.

The argumentation on the choice of interpretation is carried out on two levels: (A) on the one hand, it is about the interpretation according to the various methods discussed below; (B) on the other, it is about which of those arguments one should use, or which of the different interpretations obtained (by different methods) one ought to adopt in a particular case ('meta-argumentation'). As for the latter, there is no exact and general rule ('a ranking of methods of interpretation'), only an approximate one as outlined above;[3] the subjective factor (i.e., personal conviction of the person interpreting the text) cannot be eliminated. Yet a certain limit is imposed by the interpretational views of the professional community of constitutional lawyers of the respective country.[4] These limits can always be stretched carefully, yet they cannot be completely neglected (without running the risk of being accused of an arbitrary decision threatening legal certainty).[5] The popularity of specific methods differs by legal cultures.

A technique of simplification, rather than a method of interpretation, is that of reasoning from hypotheticals; thus it will not be included in the scheme of methods.[6] Reasoning from hypotheticals means that one argues for a certain interpretation in a given case by (1) constructing a simpler case instead of the complicated one that has to be decided; (2) which, in turn, cannot be distinguished from our case in terms of the actual legal issue. Then the solution thereby obtained can be applied to the complicated original (real) case.

[3] See, with a focus on German and American preferences in methodology, David M Beatty, The Forms and Limits of Constitutional Interpretation, *American Journal of Comparative Law* 49 (2001) 79–120. The American ranking of methods [viz. (a) precedents, (b) textualist and originalist arguments, (c) others] is discussed by Richard H Fallon, A Constructivist Coherence Theory of Constitutional Interpretation, *Harvard Law Review* 100 (1987) 1189–1286.

[4] Fish calls these supplementary norms of the interpretive community, into which the new members (in our case young lawyers at the beginning of their careers) are 'socialised'. Stanley Fish, Doing What Comes Naturally: Change, Rhetoric and the Practice of Theory in Literary and Legal Studies, Durham, Duke University Press & Clarendon Press 1989, 133.

[5] This kind of limit works only if the 'web of beliefs in the legal community' clearly shows the solution to the given (easy) case; if, however, views on the problem diverge or there are no views yet (it being a new problem), then it is a hard case. See Steven J Burton, *An Introduction to Law and Legal Reasoning*, Boston, Toronto, Little, Brown and Company 1985, 125–143.

[6] Melvin Aron Eisenberg, *The Nature of the Common Law*, Cambridge, Mass., Harvard University Press 1988, 99–103.

### 3.1 The ordinary or technical meaning of the words

This method essentially focuses on the dictionary meaning or ordinary meaning (*sens courant*),[7] relying on grammatical (or orthographic) rules.[8] The approach that prefers this method is usually called the textualist approach.[9] It is also referred to as 'grammatical interpretation', and is often used if a constitutional court wants to decide the question without examining other methods.[10] In the UK, the rule providing for reference to this method is called the *literal rule*, in the United States, it is the *plain meaning rule*. A special form of this method is used when arguments are made not from the (current) ordinary meaning, but from the ordinary meaning at the time when the respective words were included in the Constitution.[11] In American constitutional law, the latter is termed the *original meaning*. Antonin Scalia, the foremost advocate of historical-grammatical arguments in contemporary American jurisprudence, describes this method as follows, distinguishing it from another historical originalist method of interpretation (namely, the subjective teleological one, see below at pp. 48–49):[12]

[7] E.g. BVerfGE 92, 130 (134); 102, 26 (39).

[8] The technical meaning is that used by some particular community (e.g., lawyers) as opposed to the whole of the society. See Susan J Brison – Walter Sinnott-Armstrong, A Philosophical Introduction to Constitutional Interpretation, in: Susan J Brison – Walter Sinnott-Armstrong (eds.), *Contemporary Perspectives on Constitutional Interpretation*, Boulder, Westview 1993, 1–25, especially 5. An idiosyncratic terminology makes the text more difficult to understand, but it improves its clarity (and thus contributes to legal certainty).

[9] One of the most influential formulations of the textualist theory is John F Manning, Textualism as a Nondelegation Doctrine, *Columbia Law Review* 97 (1997) 673–739, supporting his theory by arguments of legitimacy. Richard Posner's contrary theory of 'pragmatic judgement' (i.e., it is only the best solution of the actual case and the filling of legal gaps that one has to aim for) is critically discussed in Cass R Sunstein – Adrian Vermeule, Interpretation and Institutions, *Michigan Law Review* 101 (2003) 885–951, especially 910–913, with detailed references.

[10] E.g. Dec. Hung CC 1/1999. (II. 24.) AB, ABH 1999, 25, 37.

[11] See Mark Tushnet, The United States: Eclecticism in the Service of Pragmatism, in: Jeffrey Goldsworthy (ed.), *Interpreting Constitutions. A Comparative Study*, Oxford, Oxford University Press 2006, 7–55, 28.

[12] Antonin Scalia, Judicial Adherence to the Text of Our Basic Law: A Theory of Constitution Interpretation, *The Progressive Conservative* 5/225 (2003), www.proconservative.net/PCVol5Is225ScaliaTheoryConstlInterpretation.shtml. For a recent explanation of his views in a similar vein see Antonin Scalia, *Reading Law: The Interpretation of Legal Texts*, St. Paul, Thomson/West 2012. A convincing collection of anti-originalist arguments [in essence: (a) the constitution has to develop, (b) yet it is difficult to amend, (c) therefore it has to be adapted to the changing circumstances through interpretation] is given (under the heading *open ended modernism*) by Erwin Chemerinsky, *Interpreting the Constitution*, New York, Praeger 1987.

> The theory of originalism treats a constitution like a statute, and gives it the meaning that its words were understood to bear at the time they were promulgated. You will sometimes hear it described as the theory of original intent. You will never hear me refer to original intent, because as I say I am first of all a textualist, and secondly an originalist. If you are a textualist, you don't care about the intent, and I don't care if the Framers of the U.S. Constitution had some secret meaning in mind when they adopted its words. I take the words as they were promulgated to the people of the United States, and what is the fairly understood meaning of those words.

Arguments referring to the grammatical interpretation presume that the norms (in our case, the constitutional provisions) have been drafted without errors (i.e., they expressed everything and exactly in the way they were meant to), being aware of all grammatical rules and the meaning of words.[13] Yet even if these conditions are met (which is not always the case), such a grammatical interpretation does not always offer an unambiguous result.[14] The reason for this is partly the vagueness of natural languages, partly that certain questions may be kept open deliberately,[15] or the emergence of new problems, which the constitution-maker could by no means foresee, even in the course of an otherwise perfect codification (technical development).

A special problem arises, if the text of the constitution has several official language versions. The obvious solution for such situations is to give precedence to one specific language version, as Art. 25(4)(6) does: in case of conflict between the English and the Irish version of a law, including laws amending the Constitution, the Irish version shall prevail. The other solution is chosen by the EU where all language versions of the founding treaties are supposed to have equal relevance – even if it is practically quite difficult to comply with this.[16]

[13] Pierre-André Côté, *Interprétation des lois*, Montréal, Yvon Blanc [2]1990, 240.

[14] See the convincing examples in Glanville Williams, Language and the Law, *Law Quarterly Review* 61 (1945) 71–86, 179–195, 293–303, 384–406; 62 (1946) 387–406.

[15] Carl Schmitt, *Verfassungslehre*, München, Leipzig, Duncker & Humblot 1928, 31–32 calls this *dilatorischer Formelkompromiß*, i.e., when the solution of a question is delayed (and placed to courts) by formulating the norm very vaguely. For a different terminology ('incompletely theorized agreements') on this issue, see Cass R Sunstein, *Legal Reasoning and Political Conflict*, Oxford, Oxford University Press 1996, 35.

[16] 283/81 *CILFIT* [1982] ECR 3415 para 23–27; Joxerramon Bengoetxea, Multilingual and Multicultural Legal Reasoning: The European Court of Justice, in: Anne Lise Kjær – Silvia Adamo (eds.), *Linguistic Diversity and European Democracy*, Farnham, Ashgate 2011, 97–122; Mattias Derlén, *Multilingual Interpretation of European Union Law*, Alphen aan den Rijn, Kluwer Law International 2009.

## 3.2 Systemic arguments: arguments from the *legal* context

These arguments do not concentrate on the text of a legal provision on its own (unlike the previously mentioned group), but refer to other legal provisions, legal acts (including judicial decisions), legal principles and general legal concepts in order to determine its meaning. If there is no relevant provision, one may argue for a legal solution from the very absence of a legal provision (arguments from silence). These arguments are united by their focus on the *legal* context. These arguments presuppose that law is a coherent and complete system (for more detail on these presuppositions see below in 4.1).

### *3.2.1 Contextual harmonising arguments*

Contextual harmonising arguments support a certain interpretation by referring to other legal norms.[17] The latter may be a rule from within the same legal act (i.e., from the constitutional document: perhaps a definition amongst the interpretative provisions, a heading of the constitution),[18] or a provision from another document of equal constitutional rank (see the American principle of *in pari materia*).[19] Constitutional interpretation may conform to a norm higher in rank of the same legal order (e.g., interpreting constitutional provisions in the light of an *Ewigkeitsklausel* or of a basic principle of the constitution which is more difficult to amend than ordinary constitutional law)[20] or to rules

[17] E.g. BVerfGE 62, 1 (35, 38ff, 44); 69, 1, 57 (61). Documents containing informal interpretations (e.g., explanatory notes by the ministries) are not like this, as they are not legal acts. Their use is forbidden in Hungary for reasons of legal certainty; see the decision Dec. Hung. CC 37/2001 (X. 11.) AB, ABH 2001, 302, 305, with further references.

[18] This is called *intrinsic aid* in English scholarship. *Extrinsic aid*, in turn, refers to other legal acts or scholarly works, or even parliamentary materials. See, e.g., Alisdair A Gillespie, *The English Legal System*, Oxford, Oxford University Press 2007, 43–50.

[19] With reference to constitutional law, see Chester James Antieau, *Constitutional Construction*, London, Oceana 1982, 21–22.

[20] E.g. in Austria (*baugesetzkonforme Interpretation*) VfSlg 11.829/1988, 11.927/1988, 16.327/2001. When interpreting statutes below the rank of the constitution, the usual form of this type of argument is the interpretation in the light of the constitution. See Harald Bogs, *Die verfassungskonforme Auslegung von Gesetzen*, Stuttgart, Kohlhammer 1966; Joachim Burmeister, *Die Verfassungsorientierung der Gesetzesauslegung*, Berlin, Frankfurt aM, Franz Vahlen 1966; Peter Raisch, *Juristische Methoden. Vom antiken Rom bis zur Gegenwart*, Heidelberg, CF Müller 1995, 179–180, with further references. A statutory interpretation in the light of the constitution is essentially a presumption of the validity (constitutionality) of the statute, see Tobias van Reenen, Tendances actuelles

of another legal order imposing duties on the legal order concerned (e.g., interpreting national constitutional law in accordance with EU-law [indirect effect of EU law]; or with international law[21]). In the case of enumerations, English-speaking countries use the principles of *noscitur a sociis* ('the unknown may be known from its companions')[22] and *ejusdem generis* ('of the same kind').[23] Here also belongs the well-known principle of *exceptio est strictissimae interpretationis*,[24] that is, the strict interpretation of exceptions.

Special contextual arguments of German constitutional law are the *Prinzip der Einheit der Verfassung* ('principle of the unity of the constitution', i.e., particular constitutional provisions have to be interpreted in accordance with the other constitutional provisions)[25] and *praktische Konkordanz* (conflicts of general provisions [principles] have to be decided by 'practical reconciliation', that is, finding some compromise, rather than on an all-or-nothing approach).[26] In American jurisprudence, advocates of

dans l'interprétation de la Constitution de l'Afrique du Sud, *Revue française de droit constitutionnel* 2002, 355–375, especially 360–361.

21 On the principle of *völkerrechtskonforme Auslegung* as part of the interpretation according to the general hierarchy, see Ernst Zeller, *Auslegung von Gesetz und Vertrag*, Zürich, Schulthess 1989, 372. In the United States, this general principle is known as the '*Charming Betsy*' *canon*, after the first case where it was deployed: The Schooner Charming Betsy, 6 U.S. (2 Cranch) 604 (1804) (Marshall, CJ). An excellent analysis of the topic is Curtis A Bradley, The Charming Betsy Canon and the Separation of Powers: Rethinking the Interpretive Role of International Law, *Georgetown Law Journal* 86 (1998) 479–537. On international-law arguments used in constitutional interpretation (in American constitutional law), see Gerald L Newman, The Uses of International Law in Constitutional Interpretation, *American Journal of International Law* 98 (2004) 82–90. On the fact that the influence of Strasbourg jurisprudence on national constitutional law is similar to that of the *Supreme Court* on the practice of the states, see Gerda Kleijkamp, Comparing the Application and Interpretation of the United States Constitution and The European Convention on Human Rights, *Transnational Law and Contemporary Problems* 12 (2002) 307–334.

22 The meaning of a word, particularly in enumerations, can be determined with the help of the words adjacent to it. See Antieau (n. 19) 22–23.

23 If words of specific meaning are followed by a more general expression in a list, then the latter has to be understood as a broader expression having a meaning similar to those of the preceding specific words. In an enumeration like 'cars, vans and other vehicles', the word 'vehicle' cannot mean ship or bicycle, only land motor vehicles. See Peter Goodrich, *Reading the Law: A Critical Introduction to Legal Method and Techniques*, New York, London, Basil Blackwell 1986, 110.

24 In another formulation: *exceptiones non extendendae*, see Aleksander Peczenik, *On Law and Reason*, Dordrecht, Kluwer 1989, 399.

25 E.g. BVerfGE 19, 206 (220); 55, 274 (300) with further references. An example from Hungarian practice is the Dec. Hung. CC 48/1991. (IX. 26.) AB, ABH 1991, 217, 242.

26 Konrad Hesse, *Grundzüge des Verfassungsrechts der Bundesrepublik Deutschland*, Heidelberg, Müller [20]1999, 28.

*holistic interpretation* use a modified version of this argument by claiming that, in the interpretation of legal texts, later amendments have greater weight than earlier ones, as older parts have to be interpreted in the light of more recent ones, and not *vice versa.*[27]

A historical version of contextual harmonising arguments is the *Versteinerungstheorie* ('petrification theory') of Austrian constitutional law. This means that (as a general rule) the words describing the division of competences between the federal and the state level have to be interpreted according to the meaning they had (in the statutes then in force) at the time they were incorporated into the text of the constitution.[28] Later changes of definitions in statutes (or at an even lower level) are not relevant to the interpretation.[29]

A special case of contextual harmonising arguments is inferring the meaning of the constitutional provision from its place within the constitution.[30] For example, we can argue that a constitutional provision looking like a fundamental right is not a fundamental right, as it is not in the chapter of the constitution on fundamental rights.

### *3.2.2 Referring to precedents which interpret the constitution*

In order to establish what the text of the constitution says, one may also refer to past decisions of the constitutional court interpreting the constitution.[31] The question is, then, whether single decisions can be taken as conclusive arguments or whether it is only an established

[27] Vicki C Jackson, Holistic Interpretation: Fitzpatrick v. Bitzer and Our Bifurcated Constitution, *Stanford Law Review* 53 (2001) 1259–1310. This doctrine, however, is not yet accepted by the courts, only a scholarly opinion.

[28] Classical formulations: VfSlg 4349/1963, 4680/1964, 11.503/1987. It differs from references to the American *original meaning* (see above at p. 30) to the extent that here the meaning is inferred from other legal rules, while there is no such limit in the case of the *original meaning.*

[29] See e.g. Felix Ermacora, *Österreichische Verfassungslehre*, Wien, Verlag Österreich 1998, 96. This kind of argument is not unknown to the BVerfG either; see BVerfGE 7, 29 (44); BVerfGE 33, 125 (152–153); BVerfGE 42, 20 (29); BVerfGE 61, 149 (175); BVerfGE 68, 319 (328), but it is used as a less strict and conclusive argument.

[30] On the problem in general, with reference to statutes, see Rolf Wank, *Die Auslegung von Gesetzen*, München, Vahlen [5]2011, 65–68.

[31] The school of American constitutional interpretation focusing on such arguments is called 'doctrinalist'; see Walter F Murphy – James E Fleming – Sotirios A Barber – Stephen Macedo, *American Constitutional Interpretation*, New York, Foundation Press [3]2003, 405–410.

practice (a series of past decisions, a *jurisprudence constante*) that qualifies as such.[32] Another question is whether in the case of contradictory case-law the more recent or rather the older decisions should prevail.[33] In some countries precedents have a formal binding force (common law),[34] in others only a (sometimes very strong) persuasive value.

The principle justifying the following of precedents is that similar cases ought to be decided in a similar way. The question here is what 'similar' means. Ordinary (not constitutional) courts usually define 'similar' as having the same *material facts*. In the case of constitutional review, this means that the norm to be interpreted has the *same* content *from the relevant* (constitutional) *perspective*.[35] If it does not, then the previous decision does not have to be followed, so the current case can be *distinguished* from the earlier case. In certain cases, however, the court, while acknowledging the identity of the relevant aspects of the cases, does not follow the previous decision for reasons of social changes which have taken place in the meantime or by simply stating that it was mistaken, and thus creating a new precedent (*overruling*).[36]

[32] Cf. Edgar Reiners, *Die Normenhierarchie in den Mitgliedstaaten der europäischen Gemeinschaften*, vol. i, Hamburg, Fundament-Verlag 1971, 275–276. Most constitutional courts consider 'established practice' stronger, since if it was otherwise, they would quote the most recent decision only, but they usually quote several decisions if they can.

[33] In the UK, in case of contradictory precedents, the judge is free to choose amongst them. See *Young* v. *Bristol Aeroplane* Co Ltd [1944] KB 718 CA.

[34] Also common law countries differ in whether a court binds itself for the future by a decision, or whether it only binds courts lower in the hierarchy. The latter is the case in the United States, the former (with the exception of the House of Lords, today Supreme Court) in the UK. Patrick S Atiyah – Robert S Summers, *Form and Substance in Anglo-American Law: A Comparative Study of Legal Reasoning, Legal Theory and Legal Institutions*, Oxford, Clarendon Press 1987, 118–127.

[35] See the Dec. Hung. CC 75/2008. (V. 29.) AB, ABH 2008, 651, 656. on the issue that there is *res iudicata* in the Court, only if a certain statute has already been examined from the *same* constitutional aspect. The same statute can thus be examined again, if it is challenged on the basis of another constitutional provision.

[36] Explicit overruling, e.g., BVerfGE 85, 264 (285f). Mostly, overruling happens in silence; see, e.g., the Spanish Constitutional Court: Alfonso Ruiz-Miguel – Francisco J Laporta, Precedent in Spain, in: Neil MacCormick – Robert S Summers (eds.), *Interpreting Precedents: A Comparative Study*, Aldershot, Ashgate 1997, 259–292, 285. A special technique of *overruling* allowing for legal certainty is the so-called *prospective overruling*, see Eisenberg (n. 6) 127–132. This means that although the new rule is applied for the actual case (or not even for it), the former one will be applied for all other cases that happened before the decision. Thus, the newly declared rule is going to be valid for cases emerging after the decision. Implicit suppression without an explicit modification is called *transformation*, whereas the narrowing of the scope of the previous case is *overriding*. *Ibid.* 132–136. 'Anticipatory overruling' in the United States is when a lower court

A limit to the latter is set by legal certainty – which in our case means that citizens should be able to have trust in the stability of the legal system and that the constitutional court is going to overrule its previous decisions only if there are very strong reasons for doing so.[37] Moreover, as the constitutional court is the main organ protecting the constitution or, expressed in another way, the primary guardian of the constitution, it has to use higher standards than other courts when judging itself. A possibility of overruling can be reasonably considered where the social circumstances have undergone rather serious changes (i.e., new facts have emerged, which the court could not possibly have taken into account),[38] or if the previous decision was passed *per incuriam*. The latter means (in the context of constitutional review) that a relevant precedent or constitutional rule was not even considered by the constitutional court.[39] It is not enough if that norm were simply misinterpreted: the legal authority has to have been completely ignored.

Yet even if one adheres to precedents (previous choices of interpretation), there is still some room for innovative decisions: precedents (like the texts of the norms) only define a framework, quite often without providing an unambiguous outcome for the new case. Precedents themselves have to be interpreted. This situation was described by Dworkin as writing a 'chain novel', each chapter of which is composed by a different author.[40] One always has to keep an eye on how the story has developed so far, and this is what has to be continued (i.e., one does not have unlimited freedom), but how the story is going to proceed is not completely bound by past decisions.

There may be different reasons for following previous decisions:[41] (a) Rejecting the possibility of an arbitrary innovative decision. If one keeps to his or her previous decision, (s)he also thereby shows that in that

does not follow the precedent by a higher court, because it expects the higher court to overturn its decision anyway.

37 Cf. '[t]he whole function of [stare decisis] is to make us say that what is false under proper analysis must nevertheless be held to be true.' Antonin Scalia, Response in: Amy Gutmann (ed.), *A Matter of Interpretation*, Princeton, Princeton University Press 1997, 129–150, 139.

38 Cf. *House of Lords* for the proper development of the law: *Practice Statement* [1966] 3 All ER 77.

39 On the notion of decisions *per incuriam*, see *Morelle Ltd v. Wakeling* [1955] 1 All ER 708, [1955] 2 QB 379.

40 Ronald Dworkin, *Law's Empire*, London, Fontana 1986, 228–232.

41 Following Grant Lamont, Precedent and Analogy in Legal Reasoning, in: Edward N Zalta (ed.), Stanford Encyclopedia of Philosophy (plato.stanford.edu/ 2006) section 3.

case the decision was made not arbitrarily but on the basis of some (legal) rule (*rule of law*). This is not a very convincing argument, however, as following a decision does not say anything about the followed decisions. If the original decision was a bad one, the reasons to repeat it are rather weak. (b) Satisfying expectations to follow precedents. This reason is flawed as it rests on circularity: one ought to follow precedents precisely because there is a doctrine of following them. Thus the doctrine itself cannot be justified in this way. (c) Efficiency in time or intellectual efforts. It is less difficult to repeat, as one does not have to consider all the potential choices again.[42] Normally this provides a good explanation for the nature of precedents, but, alas, this is not always the case. In some cases, precedents are not time saving, but rather make the decision more cumbersome. For example, judges can sometimes clearly and quickly see how they should decide a new case, but the relevant old precedent they are supposed to follow is a mistaken one; thus they make a huge effort to explain why they are not following the old precedent. Therefore, the problem with this kind of justification is that it cannot explain the huge efforts one sometimes puts into *distinguishing*. (d) The need for (interstitial) legislation or constitution-making.[43] According to this reasoning, one considers past decisions as binding because this allows for constitutional rules of behaviour, the contents of which are (on the basis of their text only) uncertain, to become easier to predict in the future, and also because the respective constitution-maker may not have the time or may not be in the position to go through the cumbersome procedure for making a constitutional amendment.[44] If we want to conceptualise this point not as a justification, but rather as an incentive mechanism, then we can say that judges by following precedents empower themselves to make laws; thus they enhance their own power as a social group.[45] (e) Formal justice: similar cases have to be decided in a similar way for reasons of justice.[46] This argument tacitly

[42] Frederick Schauer, Precedent, *Stanford Law Review* 39 (1987) 571–605, 597–598.

[43] Cf. Joseph Raz, *The Authority of Law*, Oxford, Oxford University Press $^{2}$2009, 194–201, arguing that courts ought to have law-making competence because there are unforeseen situations. For a similar approach to the ECJ, see Marc Jacob, *Precedents and Case-Based Reasoning in the European Court of Justice*, Cambridge, Cambridge University Press 2014.

[44] A similar view is held by John Bell, *Policy Arguments in Judicial Decisions*, Oxford, Oxford University Press 1983, 17–20, claiming that the judge is in fact an *interstitial legislator*.

[45] Eric B Rasmusen, Judicial Legitimacy as a Repeated Game, *Journal of Law, Economics & Organization* 1994/1, 63–83.

[46] Martin P Golding, *Legal Reasoning*, New York, Knopf 1984, 98, following Aristotle (*Nicomachean Ethics* V. 3, 1131a10–b15).

presupposes that the right decision was made last time (i.e., it is not a mistake that is going to be reiterated), which may (regrettably) not be the case.[47] It cannot be 'just' to condemn someone by mistake just because it was done to someone else already. (f) Self-confirmation: if a court considers itself to be bound by its own precedents, it also expresses the court's belief in its own legitimacy.[48]

This phenomenon (i.e., following earlier decisions) is also reflected by a notion used by the Hungarian Constitutional Court when presided over by László Sólyom, that of the invisible constitution.[49] The invisible constitution comprises (a) a coherent (non-contradictory) conceptual system derived from decisions of the Constitutional Court, (b) the norms inferred (by such decisions) from the text of the Constitution and (c) those norms added to the Constitution (in such decisions) (e.g., the proportionality test), which are beyond the text of the Constitution. What these have in common is that their content can be understood from the decisions of the Constitutional Court and that they make, after all, a possible (and, as it is shared by the Hungarian Constitutional Court, a binding) interpretation of the Constitution. The invisible constitution is essentially the system of the court's decisions: every new decision is another brick in the building of the invisible constitution.[50]

Some constitutional courts do *not* recognise the difference between the binding force of the *ratio decidendi* (the reason underlying the decision: i.e., the part of the reasoning that contains the arguments necessary for the given decision; without these the decision would not have been made or at least not in that way)[51]

[47] Brison – Sinnott-Armstrong (n. 8) 1–25, especially 13.

[48] Steven Schäller, Präjudizien als selbstreferentielle Geltungsressource des Bundesverfassungsgerichts, in: Hans Vorländer (ed.), *Die Deutungsmacht der Verfassungsgerichtsbarkeit*, Wiesbaden, VS-Verlag 2006, 205–234.

[49] See the Dec. Hung CC 23/1990. (X. 31.) AB, ABH 1990, 88, 97–98. For the general phenomenon of having an operative constitution which differs very much from the constitutional text exemplified by US constitutional law, see Laurence H Tribe, *The Invisible Constitution*, Oxford, Oxford University Press 2008.

[50] On the dangers (narrowing the room for politics [without democratic legitimacy]) and advantages of this phenomenon (solving situations where politics came to a standstill), see Christian Starck, Verfassung und Gesetz, in: Christian Starck (ed.), *Rangordnung der Gesetze*, Göttingen, Vandenhoeck & Ruprecht 1995, 29–38, especially 32–33.

[51] The definition stems from Arthur L Goodhart, Determining the Ratio Decidendi of a Case, *Yale Law Journal* 40 (1930) 161–183; Arthur L Goodhart, The Ratio Decidendi of a Case, *Modern Law Review* 22 (1959) 117–124. A more subtle discussion is that of Peczenik (n. 24) 334, who means by 'construed *ratio decidendi*' also the arguments which may not be mentioned in the reasoning, but were (implicitly) essential for passing a decision. A special difficulty arises in cases where (because of concurring reasoning and dissenting

and the *obiter dicta* (other considerations).[52] The consequence of the absence of this difference is that they never reject an argument of one of their past decisions with the reason that it was merely *obiter dictum*.

The binding force of precedents is different in every country. In some, there is an expectation that an explanation will be provided as to why a former precedent has not been followed; in others there is no such requirement. Even if the court's own precedents do not seem to bind strictly the court itself (i.e., the precedent is only of persuasive force, only to be considered as a possible solution),[53] it is still possible to differentiate between the weight of different precedent arguments. If it is a judgment from a previous constitutional regime or if it is the case-law of other countries' courts, then the weight is smaller. The latter, as there are special problems related to it, will be dealt with separately later (comparative law arguments, see below 4.2.1).

A special case of referring to precedents is when one does not refer to the interpretation that had been adopted in previous decision(s), but claims that the interpretation changed gradually and therefore (continuing this trend) a decision would have to be made that had not been made before. Here, then, one opts for a certain interpretation because it follows from past tendencies of interpretation: for instance, 'the Court has gradually interpreted this provision more and more broadly, so (albeit never interpreted it as broadly as I now suggest) one ought to interpret it even more broadly than ever before'. This kind of argument would need the courts to admit that their own jurisprudence is subject to changes, which constitutional courts are rather unwilling to do. On the difference between precedents interpreting norms and mere practice without formal decisions, see below at p. 68.

opinions) there is no reasoning accepted by the majority, thus the *ratio* cannot be established with certainty either.

52 In Germany the situation is not entirely clear: we find statements that only the *ratio decidendi* is binding, see BVerfGE 1, 14 (37); 19, 377 (392); 20, 56 (87); 40, 88 (93); but we also find judgments which say that the Federal Constitutional Court can disregard its own precedents, if the circumstances require it to do so, see BVerfGE 4, 31 (38); 20, 56 (87); 77, 84 (104). Yet another judgment states that a precedent should be followed not because it is a precedent, but because it contains sound reasoning, see BVerfGE 84, 212 (227). This unclear situation is of course favourable to the court, as it can pick the doctrine favouring its own moral preferences.

53 Further on this concept see Richard Bronaugh, Persuasive Precedent, in: Laurence Goldstein (ed.), *Precedent in Law*, Oxford, Clarendon Press 1987, 217–247.

### 3.2.3 *Interpreting the constitution in the light of doctrinal concepts and principles*

There is another possible argument to the effect that a certain concept found in the text means *x*, because this follows from a doctrinal legal concept (e.g., that of an 'organ' or its being described as such)[54] or a legal principle (e.g., the principle of non-arbitrary use of rights or the principle of *nemo plus iuris*). If this doctrinal concept or principle is defined by referring to another legal rule, then it is a contextual harmonising argument; if by referring to, for instance, a precedent, then it is a reference to an interpretive precedent. 'Interpreting the constitution in the light of doctrinal concepts and principles' in the strict sense means that neither of the above is used for supporting the content of the given general concept, but this content is just defined as obvious.

Given that a conceptual definition is not usually regarded as binding in itself (without a background in a legal rule or a decision),[55] such interpretative references to legal concepts are methodologically questionable. A characteristic example of such arguments in Hungary is the reference to the separation of powers without linking it to any particular provision of the Constitution.[56] In Spanish case-law, the principle of interpreting all statutes in conformity with the Constitution is said to be a general (constitutional) principle.[57]

### 3.2.4 *Arguments from silence*

Real lawyerly reasoning makes use not only of the text, but also of its absence in order to interpret the constitution. Characteristic forms of this include principles like *expressio unius exclusio alterius* ('expressing the one means excluding the other'), *qui de uno dicit, de altero negat* ('stating the one means rejecting the other'),[58] *argumentum a contrario* (stating

[54] We call arguments from a name or designation *argumentum a notatione.*

[55] In the case of an argument, the lack of binding force means that it may be countered by asking 'So what?'. Arguments with no binding force show the mere possibility of a solution, the acceptance of which has to be supported with arguments having binding force.

[56] See, e.g., Dec. Hung. CC 42/2005. (XI. 14.) AB, ABH 2005, 504, 526, with further references.

[57] Decision of the Spanish Constitutional Court No. 2/81 and 77/83.

[58] François Ost – Michel van de Kerchove, *Entre la lettre et l'esprit. Les directives d'interprétation en droit*, Bruxelles, Bruylant 1989, 54.

something about *A* may be denying the same about *non-A*)[59] or *enumeratio ergo limitatio* (i.e., 'an enumeration is presumed to be exhaustive').

A similar way of reasoning is used by the two forms of *argumentum a fortiori: argumentum a maiori ad minus* and its inverse (*argumentum a minori ad maius*). The former argument holds, for instance, that if the constitution-maker has explicitly allowed something, some other action is also allowed (although it is not mentioned explicitly), while the latter holds that, for instance, the constitution-maker has explicitly forbidden something, and therefore another, more grave, action – although not mentioned explicitly – is also forbidden. Which of the two has to be applied can often be decided by way of teleological considerations only.[60]

## 3.3 Evaluating arguments: arguments from beyond the legal context

These arguments are grouped together because they do not refer to the legal provision itself or its legal context, but to its (subjective or objective) intention/purpose, or even to admittedly non-legal (moral, sociological or economic) considerations. These arguments contain more (or at least more apparent) evaluative elements than the two previous groups.

### *3.3.1 Relying on the objective purpose of the norm*

This kind of reasoning justifies choosing a certain interpretation by claiming that it corresponds to the objective purpose of the norm in question.[61] The objective purpose can be inferred directly from the text (e.g., its title or preamble) or indirectly on the basis of it (like the presumable intention of an assumed abstract author).[62] The purpose itself is generally defined as a social purpose (*le but social*) or *ratio legis*.[63] The name of this method is

[59] See e.g. László Kiss (dissenting) Dec. Hung. CC 18/1999. (VI. 11.) AB, ABH 1999, 137, 143. Sometimes the *a contrario* argument is referred to as *e contrario*, meaning the same though.

[60] Cf. Miklós Szabó, *Ars juris, A jogdogmatika alapjai*, Miskolc, Bíbor 2005, 208.

[61] BVerfGE 57, 43 (62ff), 69, 1, 57 (72). For the thoroughest explanation of this method see Stephen Breyer, *Active Liberty: Interpreting our Democratic Constitution*, New York, Alfred Knopf 2005.

[62] 'Intent of any reasonable author'. Aharon Barak, *Purposive Interpretation in Law*, Princeton, Princeton University Press 2005, xi.

[63] An interesting way of dealing with this problem is the Québec Interpretation Act, providing that 'Every provision of an Act is deemed to be enacted for the recognition of rights, the imposition of obligations or the furtherance of the exercise of rights, or for

*objektiv-teleologische Auslegung* in German,[64] *purposive interpretation* in Anglo-American scholarship,[65] while French-speaking authors call it *méthode téléologique*.[66] The idea is not a new one, it was also known to the Romans: *Scire leges non hoc est verba earum tenere, sed vim ac potestatem*. [Knowing the laws does not mean knowing their words, but their intent and purpose.] (Celsus, Dig. 1,3,17).

We call this argument the 'objective teleological' argument or reference to the 'objective purpose' of the norm. This denomination does *not* mean, however, that the objective purpose can be established in an entirely objective way; the word 'objective' simply refers to the origin of the purpose: we establish it on the basis of an object, that is, the norm (and not on the basis of a subject, i.e., the law-maker). What actually this purpose (in Greek: *telos* or *τέλος*) is, is very much open to the partly subjective interpretations of scholars and judges.

In German works, such arguments are sometimes to be found under the heading *Natur der Sache* (i.e., 'it follows from the nature of the thing').[67] Also the principle *Antwortcharakter der Verfassung* (the response character of the constitution), widespread in Austrian jurisprudence, should be mentioned here.[68] Two particular cases of the argument are the EU-law principle *effet utile* and the *implied powers doctrine* of

the remedying of some injustice or the securing of some benefit. Such statute shall receive such fair, large and liberal construction as will ensure the attainment of its object and the carrying out of its provisions, according to their true intent, meaning and spirit.' Interpretation Act (Québec) sect. 41.

64 Franz Bydlinski, *Juristische Methodenlehre und Rechtsbegriff*, Wien, New York, Springer $^2$1991, 453.

65 A special case of this is where the establishment of representative democracy is considered to be the purpose of the constitution, and its text is interpreted in this light. This idea leads to *judicial self-restraint*, since *judicial review* (by a constitutional court) is a limit to representative democracy. If, however, the purpose is understood to be the protection of fundamental rights, then it may justify activism. See Murphy (n. 31) 419–426.

66 Côté (n. 13) 353 n. 1. 67 Raisch (n. 20) 176–178.

68 This is an historical argument, where one refers not to what a norm says but what it *does not* ('eloquent silence'). This is to mean that the norm is actually silent on an issue, which seems doubtful to us, because it was beyond any question at the time of enacting. E.g., the B-VG does not prescribe whether the cabinet decides unanimously or by majority vote, but since this (viz. unanimous decision) was evident at the time Art. 69 B-VG was enacted, one has to assume that this is implied by the B-VG even today (or else the constitution-makers would have amended it explicitly). Silence means that the purpose of the norm is to stick to the old (then obvious) solution. See Bernhard Raschauer, Art. 69, in: Karl Korinek – Michael Holoubek (eds.), *Österreichisches Bundesverfassungsrecht*, Wien, Springer [loose-leaf edn., December 2003], para 28.

international law, which rest on the assumption that the supposed constitution-maker (would certainly have preferred a special interpretation, even if she did not mention this explicitly, for she) wants her own norms to be effective (and therefore, e.g., competences for implementation have to be interpreted broadly etc.). Also the common law principle *magis est ut res valeat quam pereat* ('That the thing may rather have effect than be destroyed.', i.e., legal provisions have to be given a meaning which enables them to be effective) follows this line of reasoning.[69]

There are principles of interpretation which at first sight do not seem to have an objective teleological character, but they still rest on such assumptions. Such as the Austrian idea of *intrasystematische Fortentwicklung* ('development within the limits of the system'), according to which rules of competence can be understood in a broader sense than those according to the original *Versteinerungstheorie* (see above at p. 34), and particularly in the case of new technologies: for instance, 'telegraph' also means 'video phone', as the latter did not exist at that time)[70] and the Canadian doctrine of the *living tree* (i.e., the interpretation of the text has to be adapted to changes rather than limited to a static 'original meaning', since the constitution is like a living tree, accommodating itself to the circumstances dynamically and gradually).[71] For the application of these principles, we have to presuppose that there is some inherent purpose of the text beyond what is written in it, and that this purpose can be followed even against the text.

In some countries, objective teleological interpretation is strongly favoured (Germany); in others, such as Austria or especially in Hungary, it is traditionally much weaker, and it is becoming stronger exactly due to German (and ECHR) influence. The weakness in Hungary can be traced back to socialism, which tried to minimise judicial creativity (as creativity seemed dangerous in the dictatorship because of its

[69] Lord Diplock in *Attorney-General of The Gambia v. Momodou Jobe* [1984] A.C. 689, 702.

[70] VfSlg 2720/1954.

[71] Peter W Hogg, Canada: From Privy Council to Supreme Court, in: Goldsworthy (n. 11) 85–87; Wil Waluchow, Constitutions as Living Trees: An Idiot Defends, *Canadian Journal of Law and Jurisprudence* 18 (2005) 207–247. The same idea has made a career in the United States under the name *living constitution*; see David A Strauss, *The Living Constitution*, Oxford, Oxford University Press 2010. For an originalist criticism, see William H Rehnquist, The Notion of a Living Constitution, *Texas Law Review* 1976, 693–706 with further references. For a supporting view assuming that the original framers themselves would have wanted this approach, see Jack M Balkin, Framework Originalism and the Living Constitution, *Northwestern University Law Review* 103 (2009) 549–614.

uncontrolled nature).[72] The Austrian anti-teleological feature is partly due to traditional (nineteenth-century) Austrian positivism, partly as a legacy of Hans Kelsen.[73]

#### 3.3.1.1 Excursus on a special type of objective teleological interpretation: Dworkin

A special kind of teleological interpretation internationally popular amongst constitutional lawyers is put forward by Ronald Dworkin. According to his view, every case has only one right solution (*one right answer thesis*), which has to be found by the judge applying the law by way of constructive (creative) interpretation.[74] This means that the right answer gives the best possible interpretation of the legal rule in question; the best interpretation, in turn, should be understood as the interpretation most compatible with the political morality of the given community (the result of the interpretation obtained in this way may be very remote from the result of a plain grammatical interpretation). Performing interpretation this way is a particularly difficult task, which demands almost superhuman skills. Dworkin calls the ideal person having these superhuman skills of a judge Hercules.[75] This view implies that every legal provision has the objective purpose (i.e., the actual intention of the constitution-maker may not be relevant) of supporting the moral principles of the given political community and contributing to their effectiveness. The judge has to presume that there is one single coherent moral view behind the legal system as a whole (the constitution-maker of which is the personified political community itself), which fits to the social practices based on law (including the legal rules) while at the same time also justifies them (*law as integrity*).[76] From the possible moral views behind the legal order (which 'fit' to the legal order), the one that should be selected is the one which has the strongest moral 'appeal'.

The most important problem with this kind of theory is that it substitutes the legal debate, at least partially, with a debate on the political morality of the community, for which there are fewer rules of discussion

[72] For more detail and further references, see András Jakab, Surviving Socialist Legal Concepts and Methods, in: András Jakab – Péter Takács – Allan F Tatham (eds.), *The Transformation of the Hungarian Legal Order 1985–2005*, The Hague, Kluwer Law International 2007, 606–619.

[73] András Jakab, Two Opposing Paradigms of Continental European Constitutional Thinking: Austria and Germany, *International and Comparative Law Quarterly* 58 (2009) 933–955 with further references.

[74] Dworkin (n. 40) viii–ix. [75] Dworkin (n. 40) 239.

[76] Dworkin (n. 40) 225–228, 254–258.

(i.e., constitutional lawyers are trained to follow rules of legal methodology, but none of us are trained to follow the 'rules of political philosophy debates' as there are just no such rules), and on which it is much more difficult to make compromises.[77] The less technical we become, the more emotional the debate will be. Therefore, if possible, one should argue with reference to the specific purposes of specific rules rather than to the overall purpose of the legal system as a whole. Unfortunately, this purpose-narrowing is not always possible, as our ideas about the specific purposes of specific provisions may depend on our general views of political philosophy.[78] But at least, *direct* reference to such considerations should be minimised in constitutional interpretation as far as possible. Otherwise, we lose one of the main reasons for having constitutional reasoning: taming ideological and political conflicts by transforming them into technical-legal issues.[79] Referring to general purposes (or general moral reasons underlying the legal system) is further made difficult by the fact that if one does not want to give a long list of truisms but something that may be relevant in deciding an actual legal case, then a range of competing narratives can be offered as the moral sense behind the legal system.[80] Sometimes this may be true for finding the *telos* behind the particular legal rules as well, but there one has at least slightly

[77] Dworkin as 'the Taliban of Western legal thought': Richard A Posner, The Problematics of Moral and Legal Theory, *Harvard Law Review* 111 (1997–1998) 1637–1715, especially 1695.

[78] Burton (n. 5) 101–123.

[79] On this function see Gustavo Zagrebelsky – Valeria Marcenò, *Giustizia costituzionale*, Bologna, Il Mulino 2012, 100.

[80] It is for this reason that the theory stemming from Rudolf Smend, according to which the constitution as a whole aims for 'integration', has to be rejected. Integration in the Smendian sense in pluralist societies is verging on the impossible. Smend (and the reception of Schmitt) are heavily criticised as the projection of a conservative state-centred (etatist) morality by Robert Chr van Ooyen, *Der Begriff des Politischen des Bundesverfassungsgerichts*, Berlin, Duncker & Humblot 2005. For fitting argument possibly scaring away liberals in some European countries from Dworkin, see also the opinion of an Irish judge: 'the political philosophy of our constitution owes infinitely more to Thomas Aquinas than Thomas Paine' in *Director of Public Prosecutions v. Best*, 2 IR 17, 65 (2000). Dworkin would probably answer to this that his theory is geographically not universal (i.e., it has been developed solely for the United States or at the most for democracies of a similar liberal approach, cf. Dworkin (n. 40) 102–103), but if he does so, then it would be simpler, more open and more honest just to leave aside the 'fit' part of his argument as what he does is interpreting constitutional law in the light of his own (liberal) moral preferences. With the anti-universal approach, he basically filters out those cases where there could be a contradiction between 'fit' and 'appeal', and he seems to filter the possible legal orders (thus the 'fit'-side) based on his own political philosophy (i.e., based on his 'appeal' preferences).

more chance of not delving into fundamental questions, and therefore the debate will be less vehement, the minority accepting the outcome more easily.[81] In a pluralist democratic system (such as we have in Europe), different narratives on the political and moral nature of the legal system ought to be considered as normal, and therefore a general 'moral base' of the legal system (except for a minimal notion of pragmatic common self-interest) does not exist. To rely on the general 'moral base' of the legal system usually just masks our own moral preferences as legal necessities. True, one's moral preferences cannot be completely eliminated from legal reasoning; yet their role ought to be limited to the minimum for reasons of legitimacy in a pluralist society. Dworkin's theory of interpretation does not replace legal reasoning with a moral one, but it does strengthen considerably the role of moral arguments, encouraging the interpreter to use them more overtly. In light of the above considerations, his view is thus open to serious objections.[82]

We all have, of course, a more or less coherent (sometimes just unconscious) political philosophy which can help us to make choices of constitutional interpretation; however, it is quite a different thing to have such a general theory in the back of our mind and to refer to it in debates on constitutional reasoning. The latter is alien from the genre and due to its emotional nature is likely to damage the taming nature of constitutional reasoning. Constitutional reasoning can fulfil its function of justifying decisions in its specific way exactly because certain touchy issues remain unspoken.

#### 3.3.1.2 Objections to objective teleological arguments and how to respond to them

The most frequent objections are (a) that the same text can have several purposes, which may lead to interpretations contradicting each other (and the choice amongst them being unclear); and (b) that even a clear *ratio legis* sometimes fails to show which interpretation could support it best as to its consequences (e.g., because this would need an empirical survey, which the

[81] A similar criticism on Dworkin: Nigel E Simmonds, *Central Issues in Jurisprudence: Justice, Law and Rights*, London, Sweet & Maxwell $^{2}$2002, 217, with further references.

[82] Similarly problematic is John Hart Ely, *Democracy and Distrust*, Cambridge, Mass., Harvard University Press 1981, who suggests that the (US) constitution should always be interpreted in a way which reinforces the nation's system of democratic representation. The supposition of such overarching purposes behind the constitution leads to never-ending political philosophical debates.

interpreter cannot carry out).[83] These objections are relevant, but they do not mean that in general we cannot successfully use teleological arguments, only that these do not always bring a suitable result.

It may also be argued that the text has no intention: only persons have intentions. Indeed, texts do not have intentions, but, just as one can say that the function/purpose of a hammer is to drive in nails (rather than to sweep), the provisions of the constitution may also have functions/purposes attributed to them.

An argument against a particular form of objective teleological arguments (i.e., referring to the intention of an assumed abstract constitution-maker rather than the purpose of the text) may be that there are no 'abstract authors', only actual ones. This is true, and therefore it is preferable to refer to the purpose of the text than to the intention of an abstract author.

### *3.3.2 Relying on the intention of the constitution-maker (subjective teleological arguments)*

Unlike in the previous section, here we deal with arguments referring not to the (more or less concrete) objective purpose of a particular provision of the constitution or the legal system as a whole, but rather to the actual purpose (intention) of the constitution-maker.[84] Some even call it a 'psychological argument'.[85] One refers to this not because one thinks that the constitution-maker 'knows better than anyone else how to interpret the provision [b]ut simply because this is *her* interpretation'.[86] The reason for this is that normally the constitution-maker has stronger legitimacy (being closer to the source of sovereignty) than those interpreting or applying it. A means of investigating the constitution-maker's

[83] Peczenik (n. 24) 412, 414–415.

[84] This may be difficult to prove (particularly in the case of a group decision where some may not be aware of what they vote for; or different persons may have different purposes); therefore some consider this concept as fiction. See Côté (n. 3) 13–14, with further references. The same problems arise to an even greater extent if one refers to the will of the 'people' in the case of a statute; see, e.g., Ekkehart Stein – Götz Frank, *Staatsrecht*, Tübingen, Mohr Siebeck [21]2010, 36. One may refer to the intent of the drafter(s) instead; see, e.g., Robert Bork, Neutral Principles and Some First Amendment Problems, *Indiana Law Journal* 47 (1971) 1–35, especially 17. This, however, raises problems in terms of legitimacy, since it is not the drafters but the constitution-maker that makes the constitution. On the conceptual problems of original intent, see José Juan Moreso, *Legal Indeterminacy and Constitutional Interpretation*, Dordrecht, Kluwer 1998, 162–165.

[85] Giovanni Tarello, *L'interpretazione della legge*, Milano, Giuffrè 1980, 364–367.

[86] János Kis, *Alkotmányos demokrácia*, Budapest, Indok 2000, 134.

intention may be consulting the *travaux préparatoires* of the constitution-making process.[87]

References to the subjective purpose can be divided in two groups, according to their content. (a) The first type raises the question of what the constitution-maker intended at the particular historical moment.[88] In contemporary American literature on constitutional law, this is called *original intent*. In French literature, such arguments were traditionally put forth by adherents of the so-called exegetic school (*école de l'exégèse*),[89] but since Blackstone it is also a well-known method in England.[90] (b) The other group of references to the subjective purpose concentrate on the question of what the constitution-maker would say today (amongst the altered historical circumstances). French authors call this the *méthode évolutive*.[91]

The most plausible objection (in addition to the objection of fiction mentioned above) as to the arguments of group (a) was formulated by Thomas Jefferson:[92]

> Some men look at constitutions with sanctimonious reverence, and deem them like the ark of the covenant, too sacred to be touched. They ascribe to the men of the preceding age a wisdom more than human. . . . I knew that age well. . . . It was very like the present, but without the experience of the present. . . . Let us follow no such examples, nor weakly believe that one generation is not as capable as another of taking care of itself, and of ordering its own affairs.

Moreover, the constitution-maker's intention may be manifold, and in particular cases these may lead to interpretations contradicting one another.[93] The constitution-maker may even have intended to leave a question open.[94] The most important problem concerning arguments of type (b) is that they are rather hypothetical and unverifiable (i.e., 'in such a case the constitution-maker would say that'). A reference to the point of

[87] A Hungarian example is Dec. Hung. CC 4/1997. (I. 22.) AB, ABH 1997, 41, 45–46.

[88] E.g. BVerfGE 88, 40 (56f.); 102, 176 (185).

[89] Pierre Pescatore, *Introduction à la science du droit*, Luxembourg, Centre Universitaire de l'État 1960, 333–335.

[90] 'The fairest and most rational method to interpret the will of the legislator, is by exploring his intentions at the time when the law was made.' William Blackstone, *Commentaries on the Laws of England*, Oxford, Clarendon Press $^{8}$1765, 59.

[91] Cf. Pescatore (n. 89) 331 on statutory interpretation in general.

[92] Letter of Thomas Jefferson to Samuel Kercheval (12 July 1816) in: Merrill D Peterson (ed.), *The Portable Jefferson*, New York, Penguin 1975, 558–559.

[93] Brison – Sinnott-Armstrong (n. 8) 1–25, especially 11.

[94] See above n. 15.

view of those to whom the norm is addressed is a serious argument against both types:[95]

> it is simply incompatible with democratic government – or indeed, even with fair government – to have the meaning of a law determined by what the lawgiver meant, rather than by what the lawgiver promulgated. It was said of the tyrant Nero that he used to have his edicts posted high up on the pillars, so that they would be more difficult to read, thus entrapping some into inadvertent violation. A legal system that determines the meaning of laws on the basis of what was meant rather than what was said is similarly tyrannical.

In the case-law of the Hungarian Constitutional Court, the most relevant objections to subjective teleological arguments were formulated by László Kiss:[96]

> Moreover, the concept of 'the legislator's intent' – which the majority decision too makes use of – is a rather contradictory one both in terms of the Constitution and the interpretation of law. Possible objections are of two kinds. First, one has to answer the question of whether the 'uniform' intent of a collective body (the assembly comprising 386 representatives) can be traced back at all? (A possible message of accepting the reference to the intent is that in cases allowing for deliberation those applying the law may identify the assumed intent of the legislator with their own intent, which may not be free from all arbitrariness.)
>
> ... In defining the intent, can one construct a ranking to the effect that what was said by the person introducing the bill – who, being a minister, is not even necessarily one of the representatives – is more important than the votes of the representatives saying 'yes' or 'no'? Even if one cannot exclude the theoretical possibility of several hundreds of people having the same intent in a given moment: are the Official Protocols of the National Assembly a sufficient evidence of this? [On the problem of the legislator's intent, see, e.g., Max Radin, Statutory Interpretation, *Harvard Law Review* 43 (1930) 863–885, 870–871; Oliver Wendell Holmes, The Theory of Legal Interpretation, ('We do not enquire what the legislature meant; we ask only what the statute means.') *Harvard Law Review* 12 (1899) 417–420, 417–419.]
>
> Another, even stronger objections may be found on the second level of objections, which I call 'normative'. If there exists empirically 'the legislator's intent', can one argue that it has any power? The legislator speaks through the written text, not her assumed intention. In a constitutional state under the rule of law it is the rule of law that has to be effective, not the intentions of the actual legislators ('government of laws, not men'). The Constitutional Court, in turn, is bound by the text of the Constitution

95 Antonin Scalia, Common Law Courts in a Civil-Law System: The Role of United States Federal Courts in Interpreting the Constitution and Laws, in: Gutmann (n. 37) 3–48, 17.

96 In one of his dissenting opinions, Dec. Hung. CC 675/B/2001, ABH 2002, 1320, 1344–1345.

> only, it cannot consider the assumed intent of those drafting the Constitution (in the case of constitutional interpretation), or that of the legislature (when declaring the norm in question contrary to the constitution) when seeking to find firm ground for the legitimacy of a decision. This argument resembles the concurring reasoning of László Sólyom to the decision 23/1990. (X. 31.) AB, where he opposed the freedom of the legislature, by virtue of which the National Assembly can decide following any reason, scientific, political or practical, to that of the Constitutional Court, which can pass decisions founded upon arguments of constitutional law only, and is therefore not even bound by the legislator's intent. (ABH 1990, 88, 97.) In a constitutional state under the rule of law, one cannot expect those bound by law to use a concept, which is obscure and has no binding force, as the compass of their lawful/unlawful behaviour.

In order to eliminate the above problems, it may be helpful (a) to reformulate (if possible) the subjective teleological arguments into objective teleological arguments (i.e., one should speak of the *ratio* of the constitutional provision rather than some purpose of the constitution-maker); and (b) to trace this back to the text itself rather than to *travaux préparatoires* or other documents of a non-legal kind.

Alongside the positive type of subjective teleological arguments (i.e., what the constitution-maker intended), these arguments also appear in negative forms (i.e., what the constitution-maker could not have intended). Typical examples of these are cases where a certain interpretation is accepted with the rationale that the constitution-maker 'might not want to contradict herself', 'might not want to infringe international law', 'might not want to codify meaningless or irrational rules', 'might not want to proceed in an unfair way'. These arguments too (just as the positive subjective teleological arguments mentioned above) all rest on the assumption of rationality from the part of the constitution-maker,[97] and may justify, for instance, the interpretation of misspelled texts (without any official correction) so that they become meaningful. Also the English *golden rule*, or as it is called in the United States, the *soft plain meaning rule* (i.e., the grammatical interpretation is basically accepted, yet one may depart from it if it leads to an absurd result, since this cannot be what the constitution-maker wanted)[98] is based on this logic (in continental European terminology we would say: the

[97] For a more detailed discussion of these arguments, see François Ost, L'interprétation logique et systématique et le postulat de rationalité du législateur, in: Michel van de Kerchove (ed.), *L'interprétation en droit. Approche pluridisciplinaire*, Bruxelles, Facultés universitaires Saint Louis 1978, 97–184, especially 159–177.

[98] Cf. James Holland – Julian Webb, *Learning Legal Rules*, Oxford, Oxford University Press [6]2006, 234–236 on statutory interpretation in general.

grammatical interpretation has been corrected by an *argumentum ad absurdum*).[99] There are no general methodological objections to these negative subjective teleological arguments. Still, negative subjective teleological arguments are sometimes so abstract (i.e., not linked to the actual constitution-maker), that they seem to be in fact rather objective teleological arguments.

### 3.3.3 *Substantive (non-legal: moral, sociological, economic) arguments*

Arguments of a substantive (or prudential) character are seldom used in most European constitutional courts. Examples of them can be found in cases where no other arguments can help, or they lead to interpretations contradicting one another and one has to choose.[100] Such arguments may especially appear in cases involving rather abstract general clauses or abstract and value-laden legal provisions.

In an Anglo-Saxon context, such arguments are linked to the *Law and Economics* movement[101] (the so-called *Brandeis Briefs*[102] may also be considered as a manifestation of them), in French-speaking cultures (following François Gény) to the slogan *Libre Recherche Scientifique*, while in German-speaking jurisprudence (following Eugen Ehrlich) to the *Freirechtsschule.*[103] Adherents of substantive arguments are split on

99 On the *argumentum ad absurdum* see Szabó (n. 60) 210.

100 For a famous explicit rule from outside of Europe, see s. 1 Israeli Foundations of Law Act 1980: 'Where the court, faced with a legal question requiring decision, finds no answer to it in statute law or case-law or by analogy, it shall decide it in the light of the principles of freedom, justice, equity and peace of Israel's heritage.'

101 On its impact on legal interpretation see William N Eskridge, Politics without Romance: Implications of Public Choice Theory for Statutory Interpretation, *Virginia Law Review* 74 (1988) 275–338, with examples. For a consequence-based theory of interpretation under the heading 'pragmatism', see Richard A Posner, Interpretation Revisited, in: Brison–Sinnott-Armstrong (n. 8) 102–117.

102 Louis Brandeis (justice of the Supreme Court between 1916 and1939) argued as an attorney in the case *Muller v. Oregon* 208 U.S. 412 (1908) by delivering a detailed sociological presentation of the social effects of long working hours on women.

103 On these German and French schools see Jean-Louis Bergel, *Méthodologie juridique*, Paris, Presses Universitaires de France 2001, 249–253; Jean-Cassien Billier – Aglaé Maryioli, *Histoire de la philosophie du droit*, Paris, Armand Collin 2001, 189–194, with further references.

whether you can use both sociological-economic[104] and moral arguments[105] or just one of them.[106]

Sociological-economic arguments are often just implied in constitutional reasoning, but sometimes they are explicitly used. In many of these cases, however, the arguments are mistaken, as lawyers are not trained to deal with sociological or economic data, and they easily misinterpret them.[107]

Using moral arguments has to be distinguished from the Dworkinian theory of interpretation discussed above (p. 44), which does not refer to moral arguments as such, but to moral arguments which can be found *within* the legal order in force and which serve to justify that very legal order. Thus, the Dworkinian reason for a particular interpretation cannot be that the meaning of a constitutional provision is a 'moral' one, but that the given interpretation fits best to the best reading of the principles morally justifying the legal order. Here, however, one finds a reference less subtle and more direct than that of Dworkin.

In Germany, this direct form of the moral argument normally arises under the heading of natural law[108] or, in a somewhat similar form to

[104] On the 'right' interpretation of fundamental rights based on a cost-benefit analysis, with examples from US constitutional interpretation, see Richard A Posner, The Costs of Enforcing Legal Rights, *East European Constitutional Review* 1995/Summer 71–83. He is criticised on moral grounds by János Kis, From Costs and Benefits to Fairness: Comments on Richard Posner, *East European Constitutional Review* 1995/Summer 84–87.

[105] E.g., BVerfGE 84, 212 (221). Within moral arguments one may further distinguish between references to critical morality ('the' right approach of morality) and references to the moral views of the majority of the society (social morality); see, e.g., Rainer Arnold, Réflexions sur l'argumentation juridique en droit constitutionnel allemande, in: Otto Pfersmann – Gérard Timsit (eds.), *Raisonnement juridique et interprétation*, Paris, Sorbonne 2001, 49–63, especially 61. The latter emerges very rarely in Hungarian constitutional case-law: 154/2008. (XII. 17.) AB, ABH 2008, 1203, 1235.

[106] For a combined example see Dec. Hung. CC 23/1990. (X. 31.) AB, ABH 1990, 88, 93, with references to values on the one hand, and the lack of effectiveness, on the other.

[107] See Niels Petersen, Avoiding the Common-Wisdom Fallacy: The Role of Social Sciences in Constitutional Adjudication, *International Journal of Constitutional Law* 2013, 294–318 with examples and further literature.

[108] See the commentary to the decision BVerfGE 95, 96, in: Jörg Menzel (ed.), *Verfassungsrechtsprechung*, Tübingen, Mohr Siebeck 2000, 605–611, with further references. On German references to natural law, see BVerfGE 3, 88; 6, 132; 23, 98. On the arguments for and against the references to values in the jurisprudence of the German Constitutional Court, see Ernst-Wolfgang Böckenförde, Zur Kritik der Wertbegründung des Rechts, in: Ralf Dreier (ed.), *Rechtspositivismus und Wertbezug des Rechts*, Stuttgart, Steiner 1990, 33–46, especially 45; Christian Starck, Zur Notwendigkeit der Wertbegründung des Rechts, in: *ibid.* 47–61, especially 59–61, with further references to German constitutional case-law.

Dworkin's theory, as the 'value system' *(Werteordnung)* of the Constitution.[109] In Hungary, however, such approaches were explicitly rejected by the Constitutional Court with reference to legal certainty.[110] The then President of the Court termed this approach as constitutional positivism (*Verfassungspositivismus*).[111]

Constitutional positivism is indeed a plausible approach, as almost any argument can be 'translated' into objective teleological arguments, thus giving them a legal form. Once we talk about legal arguments, they are exposed to criticism through other *legal* arguments, which opens the way for a rational legal discourse again.[112]

## 3.4 Further arguments

The last group of methods is unified just by the fact that these can merely serve as sources of inspiration or a toolkit of ideas; that is, they can only show the theoretical possibility of a certain interpretation or give a persuasive authority, without being a binding reason for choosing that very interpretation.

### *3.4.1 Referring to scholarly works*

A certain interpretation can be supported by the fact that it appears in scholarly literature (preferably in the works of a jurist of high reputation [*argumentum ab auctoritate*], or as the commonly accepted view [*herrschende Meinung*]). In some legal cultures, it has a heavy persuasive weight (e.g., Germany where as a consequence of the prestige of legal scholarship, constitutional law professors will often be appointed as judges to the Federal Constitutional Court), in others the situation is rather the opposite (UK, except for a *very* few references to some dead

[109] Joachim Detjen, *Die Werteordnung des Grundgesetzes*, Wiesbaden, VS 2009.

[110] Dec. Hung. CC 11/1992. (III. 5.) AB, ABH 1992, 77, 82, 84–85. Unlike, e.g., the United States, where such arguments do play a major role, see Mark Tushnet (n. 11) 38–40.

[111] László Sólyom, Aufbau und dogmatische Fundierung der ungarischen Verfassungsgerichtsbarkeit, *Osteuropa-Recht* 2000, 230–241, especially 235.

[112] Further objections to moral arguments: (a) Giving them a legal form (i.e., forbidding direct references to morality) serves the taming and easing of ideological oppositions; see Ernst Forsthoff, *Zur Problematik der Verfassungsauslegung*, Stuttgart, Kohlhammer 1961, especially 22–25. (b) References to morality are not representative of the whole of society, as they reflect the morality of (upper middle-class) lawyers and are therefore anti-democratic, see Ely (n. 82) 59.

classics like Dicey).[113] In the United States, reference to academic writing mostly serves only to point to factual information, or to decorate the conclusion already defended by other interpretive techniques.[114]

### 3.4.2 *Arguments from comparative law*

Last but not least, arguments from comparative law have to be mentioned.[115] It is interesting to note that Sect. 35.1 of the South African Interim Constitution,[116] as well as Sect. 39.1 of the now valid Constitution of the Republic of South Africa,[117] explicitly encourages the study of foreign cases in constitutional review.[118] Like scholarly works, such arguments have no binding force,[119] yet they may help to give the impression that a decision was arrived at after careful consideration.

[113] On the historical reasons of the differences see András Jakab, Seven Role Models of Legal Scholars, *German Law Journal* 12 (2011) 757–784. An example of deference of the German Federal Constitutional Court to academic critique see BVerfGE 84, 212 (227).

[114] Tushnet (n. 11) 44 n. 109.

[115] E.g., BVerfGE 84, 239 (269); 89, 155 (189); 95, 408 (423f.). Peter Häberle, Grundrechtsgeltung und Grundrechtsinterpretation im Verfassungsstaat – Zugleich zur Rechtsvergleichung als 'fünfter' Auslegungsmethode, *Juristen-Zeitung* 1989, 913–919, mentions comparative law arguments as the fifth method of interpretation in addition to the traditional four (grammatical, logical, systematic and historical) of Savigny.

[116] 'In interpreting the provisions of this Chapter a court of law shall promote the values which underlie an open and democratic society based on freedom and equality and shall, where applicable, have regard to public international law applicable to the protection of the rights entrenched in this Chapter, and may have regard to comparable foreign case law.'

[117] 'When interpreting the Bill of Rights, a court, tribunal or forum (a) must promote the values that underlie an open and democratic society based on human dignity, equality and freedom; (b) must consider international law; and (c) may consider foreign law.' For a detailed commentary of this Section (with general considerations on the topic), see Lourens du Plessis, Interpretation, in: Stu Woolman – Michael Bishop (eds.), *Constitutional Law of South Africa*, Cape Town, Juta $^{2}$2008, Chapter 32, 1–193.

[118] On this topic see DM Davis, Constitutional borrowing: The influence of legal culture and local history in the reconstruction of comparative influence: The South African experience, *International Journal of Constitutional Law* 1 (2003) 181–195, especially 189–191.

[119] This is called 'soft use' by Taavi Annus, Comparative Constitutional Reasoning: The Law and Strategy of Selecting the Right Argument, *Duke Journal of Comparative & International Law* 14 (2004) 301–350. According to an even more radical description, such references have a merely 'ornamental function', see Ulrich Drobnig, The Use of Comparative Law by Courts, in: Ulrich Drobnig – Sjef van Erp (eds.), *The Use of Comparative Law by Courts*, The Hague, Kluwer Law International 1999, 3–21, especially 18.

Reasoning with arguments of comparative law in constitutional interpretation is a global phenomenon or trend.[120] One may or may not like this trend,[121] but its existence is beyond doubt.[122] The main causes of it are the general trend of globalisation (and, as a consequence, the overall weakening of national isolation), the emergence of inter- or supranational courts[123] (as meeting points of different legal cultures, where the practice of legal comparison spreads the culture of comparative law even beyond its own institutional limits)[124] and the similar role-perception of judges (i.e., that of guarding the basic values of constitutionalism, which are considered as being some kind of modern or postmodern natural law or as a modern *ius gentium*)[125] in liberal democracies (this common identity then serves as the ground for a feeling of global community, which in turn leads to a dialogue,[126] that manifests itself in references made in decisions to each other's works).[127] Beyond these reasons for the use of comparative law

120 Christopher McCrudden, A Common Law of Human Rights? Transnational Judicial Conversation on Constitutional Rights, *Oxford Journal of Legal Studies* 20 (2000) 499–532, especially 506.

121 Bruce Ackerman, The Rise of World Constitutionalism, *Virginia Law Review* 83 (1997) 771–794; Donald P Kommers, Comparative Constitutional Law: Its Increasing Relevance, in: Vicki C Jackson – Mark Tushnet (eds.), *Defining the Field of Comparative Constitutional Law*, Westport, Praeger 2002, 61–70; Lorraine E Weinrib, Constitutional Conceptions and Constitutional Comparativism, in: *ibid.* 3–34.

122 This is characteristic not only of 'small' countries, but may also be observed, e.g., in the United States; see, e.g., Cheryl Saunders, The Use and Misuse of Comparative Constitutional Law, *Indiana Journal of Global Legal Studies* 13 (2006) 37–76, especially 39. An interesting figure is that 60% of the cases referred to by Québécois courts are of foreign law (e.g., French or common law). See H Patrick Glenn, Persuasive Authority, *McGill Law Journal* 32 (1987) 261–299, especially 294.

123 In the context of the ECJ, see T. Koopmans, Comparative Law and the Courts, *International and Comparative Law Quarterly* 45 (1996) 545–556, especially 546.

124 On the clarification of vague principles through comparison in international law, see Sigrid Jacoby, *Allgemeine Rechtsgrundsätze. Begriffsentwicklung und Funktion in der europäischen Rechtsgeschichte*, Berlin, Duncker & Humblot 1997, 184–190. From EU law, she discusses the example of Art. 288. 2 [ex Art. 215.2] of the EC Treaty, *ibid.* 210–215.

125 See Gábor Halmai, The Use of Foreign Law in Constitutional Interpretation, in: Michel Rosenfeld – András Sajó (eds.), *The Oxford Handbook of Comparative Constitutional Law*, Oxford, Oxford University Press 2012, 1328–1348, especially 1331–1332 with further references.

126 On the dialogue model of this phenomenon, see Sujit Choudhry, Globalization in Search of Justification: Toward a Theory of Comparative Constitutional Interpretation, *Indiana Law Journal* 74 (1998–1999) 819–892, especially 855–865; Filippo Fontanelli – Giuseppe Martinico – Paolo Carrozza (eds.), *Shaping Rule of Law through Dialogue. International and Supranational Experiences*, Groningen, Europa Law Publishing 2010.

127 On this phenomenon as part of the international communication between courts, see Anne-Marie Slaughter, A Typology of Transjudicial Communication, *University of Richmond Law Review* 29 (1994) 99–137, especially 129–132.

arguments, the explicit reference to foreign case-law might be especially relevant for new constitutional courts of transitional countries, which try to show themselves in a prestigious society of well-established foreign constitutional (or supreme) courts in order to collect some more credibility in their respective domestic discourses. And finally, considering a foreign interpretation might be helpful even if, for some reason, we eventually reject that specific interpretation: it can still be used for purposes of contrast, by showing what we do *not* want to adopt. In this negative way, it can help to understand and to crystallise the reasons behind our own interpretation better (for others as well as for ourselves).

Arguments against this approach form three groups: objections (a) based on legitimacy,[128] (b) on methodology[129] or (c) criticising the mindless borrowing of foreign ideas.[130] The first objection can be dealt with by making it clear that the argument is not a conclusive one (i.e., only an idea for further consideration). As for the second objection, the comparison has to be as broad as possible, and the arguments considered as sources of inspiration (and not necessarily as solutions), given the difference in contexts. The usual trick of choosing only those countries which apply the same solutions that we prefer should thus be avoided. These two answers also give

[128] The defence of authentic national identity against the 'new imperialism': Carlos F Rosenkrantz, Against Borrowings and Other Nonauthoritative Uses of Foreign Law, *International Journal of Constitutional Law* 1 (2003) 269–295. General concerns of legitimacy: Justice Antonin Scalia, Foreign Legal Authority in the Federal Courts, *American Society of International Law Proceedings* 2004, 305–310. For a more detailed and critical analysis of these arguments see Vicki C Jackson, *Constitutional Engagement in a Transnational Era*, Oxford, Oxford University Press 2010, 18–38.

[129] The choice of foreign material is not only arbitrary (or, more properly, one looks for support for an already given conclusion) and uncontrollable; it is also dangerous for stability, delivering arguments for departing from the already established case-law: Günter Frankenberg, Critical Comparisons: Re-Thinking Comparative Law, *Harvard International Law Journal* 26 (1985) 411–455; George P Fletcher, Comparative Law as a Subversive Discipline, *American Journal of Comparative Law* 46 (1998) 683–700. Borrowing is always problematic because of the different contexts: Wiktor Osiatynski, Paradoxes of Constitutional Borrowing, *International Journal of Constitutional Law* 1 (2003) 244–268; Richard A Posner, No Thanks, We Already Have Our Own Laws, *Legal Affairs* Aug. 2004, 40–42, especially 41–42. Every country has a different argumentative culture, so legal reasoning cannot be borrowed: Pierre Legrand, *Le droit comparé*, Paris, Presses Universitaires de France 1999, 81–99. The tacit presupposition that constitutional laws converge, is not true: Ruti Teitel, Comparative Constitutionalism in a Global Age, *Harvard Law Review* 117 (2004) 2570–2596, especially 2584.

[130] Christian Walter, Dezentrale Konstitutionalisierung durch nationale und internationale Gerichte: Überlegungen zur Rechtsvergleichung als Methode im öffentlichen Recht, in: Janbernd Oebbecke (ed.), *Nicht-normative Steuerung in dezentralen Systemen*, Stuttgart, Franz Steiner 2005, 205–230, especially 224.

a response to the third objection, since by considering comparative law only as an idea and by bearing in mind the contextuality of constitutional solutions, we make it clear that we have to think through the particular foreign solutions and find out whether they can be applied to us or not.

The most important argument for the comparative method is the common-sense principle of 'two heads are better than one' or 'wise men learn by other men's mistakes'.[131] Such theoretical arguments, however, are usually only of secondary importance for undertaking or not undertaking legal comparison: whether one goes for an international overview or not basically depends on whether one has sufficient time and knowledge of the relevant languages.

In recent years, a decline of the number of references to foreign court judgments can be seen at various constitutional courts. The reason for this phenomenon is that the growing number of references to the judgments of international courts (ECtHR and IACHR) make comparative law arguments less needed (a reference to the judgments of international courts is not a comparative law argument in the terminology of the present volume, if there is an international obligation to follow their decisions, see above 3.2.1).[132]

### 3.5 The relationship between the methods

In our survey, we discussed four major types of arguments: (a) linguistic (or grammatical or textualist) methods, (b) systemic arguments, (c) evaluative arguments and (d) arguments from scholarship and comparative law, which only have persuasive force. When inquiring about the relationship between them, we have to make general theoretical statements knowing that constitutional courts in practice sometimes do not follow any theoretical pattern in weighing the arguments (or sometimes they pay lip service to old and outdated theories of interpretation, e.g. that of Montesquieu's famous saying that judges are simply 'mouthpieces of the law').[133] Thus any

[131] Mark Tushnet, The Possibilities of Comparative Constitutional Law, *Yale Law Journal* 108 (1999) 1225–1309, 1307.

[132] Tania Groppi – Marie-Claire Ponthoreau, Conclusion. The Use of Foreign Precedents by Constitutional Judges: A Limited Practice, An Uncertain Future, in: *id.* (eds.), *The Use of Foreign Precedents by Constitutional Judges*, Oxford, Hart 2013, 430.

[133] Such Montesquieu-like statements are pronounced not only on the European continent, but also in the United States: 'Judges are like umpires. Umpires don't make rules, they apply them' (John G Roberts, Jr); see Confirmation Hearing on the Nomination of John G Roberts, Jr to be Chief Justice of the United States Before the S. Comm. on the Judiciary, 109th Cong. 55 (2005).

*description* about the weighing of methods of interpretation necessarily becomes also a *prescription.* The following passages are to be read in the light of this disclaimer.

When interpreting constitutions, the first step is usually the examination of the arguments of type (a) (even without explicitly mentioning them, just as an implied starting point). This is followed by the use of (more or less subtle, according to the country-specific sophistication of *Verfassungsdogmatik*) systemic arguments. Arguments of types (a) and (b) are basically accepted everywhere as general lawyerly methods (though with different weight). Evaluative arguments of type (c) (or rather their explicit use) are, however, deliberately rejected or limited by some constitutional cultures (mostly due to their arbitrariness).[134] Arguments of type (d), which lack binding power in European constitutional cultures, are used occasionally, and, as their inventory is almost infinite, they are deployed primarily depending on the time and/or the languages one knows.

Choices between different arguments or types of arguments are often determined by the concerns of legitimacy mentioned above (p. 27).[135] Arguments of type (a) pose the least problem from this aspect, those of type (c) being the most problematic (those of type (d) do not count in this regard, as they admittedly serve only as sources of inspiration with no binding force). This situation has led to the formulation of principles like *interpretatio cessat in claris,*[136] *quand la loi est claire, il faut la suivre* (if the statute is clear, it has to be observed) or *l'esprit l'emporte sur la lettre* (the spirit [of a statute] is expressed by its letter).[137] It is hard, however, to keep to these less legitimacy-demanding methods, if the interpretation thus obtained would remain too obscure (or too vague) or even absurd (cf. the British *golden rule*, see above at p. 50). In such cases, one cannot

[134] The attitude towards the creative arguments of type (c) also depends on which institutions one trusts. if one thinks that the legislature is short-sighted, populist and incompetent, then constitutional courts are likely to prefer creative interpretative techniques, while if the prestige of judges is low (because they are considered to be anti-democratic, elitist or even corrupt, maybe adherents of the *ancien régime*), then one opts for a text-based interpretation. See Sunstein (n. 15) 169.

[135] There are also (tacit) political philosophies (conceptions of democracy) underlying the preferences in terms of methods of legal interpretation, but we shall not discuss these here. For a detailed analysis, see Martin Kriele, *Theorie der Rechtsgewinnung entwickelt am Problem der Verfassungsinterpretation,* Berlin, Duncker & Humblot [2]1976, 27–31.

[136] It is described as an argument used in Belgian jurisprudence by François Ost – Michel van de Kerchove, Les directives d'interprétation en théorie du droit et en droit positif belge. La lettre et l'esprit, in: Jean-François Perrin (ed.), *Les règles d'interprétation,* Fribourg, Éditions Universitaires Fribourg Suisse 1989, 7–39, 25–27.

[137] It is formulated (also) somewhat differently: Côté (n. 3) 265–285.

help but move on towards more legitimacy-demanding grounds: *Quand elle est obscure, il faut en approfondir les dispositions* (if [the statute] is obscure, its provisions have to be examined more closely).[138]

Methods of type (a) provide, firstly, a field which is certainly within the scope of the expression interpreted ('black core'); secondly, one which is definitely outside of it ('white environment'); and thirdly, a blurred 'grey penumbra'.[139] Through methods (b), (c) and (d), the cases in the grey penumbra will then be classified as either white or black. Sometimes even clear cases of black will be classified as white, or the other way around, but in such cases very strong arguments from (b), (c) or (d) are needed to make this result acceptable. Alongside the legitimacy concerns mentioned above, one may also refer to legal certainty in order to support type (a) [or perhaps type (b)] interpretation. Focusing on the constitution, Goldsworthy puts this as follows:[140]

> A constitution laid down by a founding generation empowers as well as restricts subsequent generations, by providing them with the incalculable benefits of an established and accepted set of procedures for making collective decisions binding on all their members. . . . If some attempt is made to evade the restrictions, others may be tempted to follow suit, leading eventually to the collapse of the constitution and the loss of the empowerment it provided.

In the case of constitutional interpretation, however, there are strong arguments for attributing evaluative arguments of type (c) a greater weight than usual. The reason for this is that constitutions are generally rather abstract,[141] difficult to amend (i.e., one cannot always adapt to a new social situation simply by amending the text)[142] and sometimes ancient as well.[143] Therefore, sometimes the constitution can be made

[138] On debates concerning this problem in Austrian scholarship, see Jakab (n. 73) 943–945, with further references.

[139] HLA Hart, *The Concept of Law*, Oxford, Clarendon Press $^{2}$1994, 124–135 uses the metaphor of 'the open texture of law'. For Hart's thesis being applied to constitutional interpretation, see Moreso (n. 84) especially 131–171.

[140] Jeffrey Goldsworthy, Originalism in Constitutional Interpretation, *Federal Law Review* 25 (1997) 1–50.

[141] Moreover, constitutional ideas (and therefore the abstract provisions implementing them) partly contradict one another, see Edward H Levi, *An Introduction to Legal Reasoning*, Chicago, London, The University of Chicago Press 1949, 58–60.

[142] Benjamin L Cardozo, *The Nature of the Judicial Process*, New Haven, Yale University Press 1921, 83.

[143] Jeffrey Goldsworthy, Introduction, in: *id.* (n. 11) 1–6, 5. This argument does not apply, though, to most European countries where constitutions are usually younger than civil or criminal codes.

to fit the altered circumstances by modifying the interpretation.[144] The concerns of legitimacy and legal certainty can be answered, in turn, by always tracing the arguments back to the text of the constitution and referring to (c) moderately (as opposed to complete abstinence). Moreover, most (but not all) of type (c) arguments can be substituted by a skilful use of the systemic arguments of type (b). There is no general standard as to the proportions; one cannot but rely on the country-specific expectations of the professional community of constitutional lawyers (see above at p. 29).

### 3.6 Conclusion on the suggested method of constitutional interpretation

If we had to formulate the most essential thesis of the present chapter as regards to methods of constitutional interpretation, it might be the following. The constitution has to be interpreted (a) always according to its text, (b) yet adapting to the changing circumstances. Amongst the several methods of interpretation discussed above, which all aim to solve the apparent tension between these, the most important one is the objective teleological method, even though some European legal cultures do not really use its potential. This method can reduce (if the objective *telos* is determined on the basis of actual passages of the constitution) the danger of arbitrariness (legal uncertainty) while allowing for flexibility. In determining the *telos* of the text, one has to be as exact as possible, not speaking of general purposes of the legal order or of the constitution, as these may well lead to quasi-religious debates of political philosophy, which are (in practice) regrettably difficult to carry out in a reasonable way.

The objective teleological method can be used not only as a particular method of interpretation, but also as a meta-argument for choosing between the different possible interpretations obtained by the other methods. If, however, the interpretation obtained by an objective teleological argument can also be constructed by systemic arguments (i.e., those of type (b)), then arguments of type (b) have to be preferred, as they

[144] A change in the constitution without a formal amendment to the text (i.e., modification through interpretation) is called *Verfassungswandlung* by Jellinek [*Verfassungswandlung* or *Verfassungswandel*]. Georg Jellinek, *Verfassungsänderung und Verfassungswandlung*, Berlin, Häring 1906, especially 9, 21, 26–27. On the interplay between formal amendment and informal re-interpretation see Xenophon Contiades (ed.), *Engineering Constitutional Change*, London, Routledge 2013.

may raise fewer legitimacy concerns. The objective teleological line of thought serves in such cases as an unspoken control (i.e., we do it quietly, internally, but it is unnecessary to mention it in the reasoning, and it does not need to be referred to explicitly, as one has the desirable outcome anyway). One has to see, however, that in the case of fundamental rights one almost always comes to the teleological arguments, as the systemic arguments cannot in themselves help here.

4

# The conceptual system of constitutional law

> [S]ystème n'est autre chose que la disposition des différentes parties d'un art ou d'une science dans un état où elles soutiennent toutes mutuellement, et où les dernières s'expliquent par les premières[1]

The aim of constitutional reasoning is to find the solution for a case in the constitution. Yet with the help of the above techniques and based on the text of the constitution, an abstract (i.e., separate from actual cases, generally valid) conceptual system (*Rechtsdogmatik*, or constitutional conceptual system: *Verfassungsdogmatik*) can be constructed,[2] which may help to decide future cases, by eliminating contingencies and apparent contradictions in the text.[3] This conceptual system is, however, not always based on the text of the constitution; it goes beyond that and stems from beyond that: it can partly be the result of a text-independent abstract speculation. *Verfassungsdogmatik* is a usual and probably also necessary phenomenon in constitutional courts and in constitutional

1 'System is nothing else but putting the different parts of an art or a science into a state in which they mutually support each other and in which the latter ones are explained by the former ones' [s.n.] Système, in: Denis Diderot – Jean D'Alembert (eds.), *Encyclopédie ou Dictionnaire raisonné des sciences, des arts et des métiers*, vol. 15, Neufchatel, Samuel Faulche 1765, 777.

2 A broader conception of *Rechtdogmatik* (i.e., including not only the conceptual system, but the job building it up) is used, e.g., by Ulfrid Neumann, Wissenschaftstheorie der Rechtswissenschaft, in: Arthur Kaufmann – Winfried Hassemer – Ulfrid Neumann (eds.), *Einführung in die Rechtsphilosophie der Gegenwart*, Heidelberg, Müller [8]2011, 385–400, with further references. We use the concept here in a more narrow sense, which likewise allows for a thorough explanation of methodological problems, while making the explanation clearer and easier to understand.

3 Contradictions have to be eliminated by way of interpretation; otherwise one cannot contribute to the solution of future problems. If contradictions are merely highlighted, those applying the law will stare puzzled at the two passages, then decide by tossing a coin, as it were. Our task is to help to avoid this, thus making a calculable functioning of the system possible. See Eike von Savigny, Die Rolle der Dogmatik – wissenschaftstheoretisch gesehen, in: Ulfrid Neumann – Joachim Rahlf – Eike von Savigny, *Juristische Dogmatik und Wissenschaftstheorie*, München, CH Beck 1976, 100–109, 104.

scholarship in every area of constitutional law, but its most obvious area is that of fundamental rights (in the form of building tests for fundamental rights restrictions), as their usually short and vague formulation alone would not be sufficient for solving cases.[4]

*Verfassungsdogmatik* is built partly by the (constitutional) courts, partly by legal scholars. A conceptual system is, then, like a semi-prepared product, which one may finish (i.e., have a solution for the case) any time. Like the good host, who – thinking of the future – fills her fridge with semi-prepared meals (frozen pizzas) which can easily and quickly be used when needed, the good jurist builds a conceptual system in preparation for future situations where law has to be applied.[5]

## 4.1 Coherence

The building of such a conceptual system is largely neglected in dictatorships, as debates of constitutional law are not decided by constitutional courts, but on the basis of *ad hoc* political reasons:[6] there is normally no formalised procedure for settling debates amongst state organs.[7] Similar problems can be seen in the UK and France, where the judicial review of legislation (*Verfassungsgerichtsbarkeit*) is or was until recently very limited. In dictatorships, a further obstacle facing the construction of a *Verfassungsdogmatik* is that it necessarily also means judicial or scholarly rule-making, thus a certain self-empowerment by judges and scholars which is not welcomed in any centralised system.

The requirement of building a coherent conceptual system consists of several elements. The first and most obvious one is non-contradiction. Yet one used to expect more than that. On the one hand, the system

[4] See, e.g., in Austria: Karl Spielbüchler, Grundrecht und Grundrechtsformel, in: Oswin Martinek e.a (eds.), *Arbeitsrecht und soziale Grundrechte. Festschrift für Hans Floretta*, Wien, Manzsche 1983, 289–307.

[5] If one introduces a legal concept only for understanding and describing ('heuristics'), but does not intend to argue with it when deciding legal cases, then one has no doctrinal ambitions with it.

[6] It is similar to the conceptual system of administrative law: it becomes sophisticated only if there is judicial review of administrative acts; see András Jakab, Wissenschaft vom Verwaltungsrecht: Ungarn, in: Armin von Bogdandy – Sabino Cassese – Peter M Huber (eds.), *Ius Publicum Europaeum IV.*, Heidelberg, CF Müller 2011, 365–396, para 5 and 16. Constitutional courts are a necessary, but on their own, not a sufficient precondition of a sophisticated *Verfassungsdogmatik*.

[7] As explained below (pp. 75–78), in the absence of judicial review of statutes, the elaboration of a detailed constitutional *Rechtsdogmatik* would really be rather just a 'useless lawyerly pursuit'.

(which cannot be built up in a value-neutral way) should be compatible with the fundamental values of the political community.[8] On the other hand, some internal structural criteria have to be met, like the presence of conceptual cross-references, or the pyramidal and logical nature of the system of used concepts.[9] The latter requirement can be fulfilled only to a certain extent (unlike, e.g., the idea of non-contradiction).

## 4.2 In defence of *Begriffsjurisprudenz*

Elaboration of legal concepts as a goal of jurisprudence may be easily – and pejoratively – tagged as *Begriffsjurisprudenz*,[10] which used to imply that this approach cannot live up to the challenges of the present, being some sort of an outdated (and 'out of touch with reality') project. In order to dispel any misunderstanding, this problem has to be briefly addressed here.

1. Let us take the problem of unrealism first. In legal arguments (i.e., those of legal practice) one cannot use arguments commonly accepted in everyday life like 'effective', 'immoral' or 'unprofitable'. Such arguments have to be translated somehow into legal arguments ('unlawful').[11] Arguments of effectiveness and so forth are not necessarily irrelevant to law, but they cannot be deployed directly ('naked'): it has to be explained why they are relevant and through which gate they were introduced to legal reasoning (e.g., constitutional principles).[12] Legal scholarship in a traditional narrow sense (which does not cover topics of policy, sociology, history, political philosophy or legal philosophy) also stays within these limits.

[8] Neil MacCormick, Coherence in Legal Justification, in: Aleksander Peczenik – Lars Lindahl –Bert van Roermund (eds.): *Theory of Legal Science*, Dordrecht, Reidel Publishing 1984, 235–251.

[9] Following Robert Alexy – Aleksander Peczenik, The Concept of Coherence and Its Significance for Discursive Rationality, *Ratio Juris* 3 (1990) 130–147, with some simplification and modification.

[10] The concept comes from Rudolph von Jhering, *Scherz und Ernst in der Jurisprudenz*, Leipzig, Breitkopf & Härtel 1884, 337, who used it primarily for Puchta. An excellent overview of Puchta's scholarship is Hans-Peter Haferkamp, *Georg Friedrich Puchta und die 'Begriffsjurisprudenz'*, Frankfurt aM, Klostermann 2004.

[11] Interests and benefits have to be formulated as rights and duties. See Philippe A Mastronardi, *Juristisches Denken*, Bern, Haupt 2001, 264–276. Moral arguments have to be translated likewise. As it is formulated in a decision by the ICJ: 'It is a court of law, and can take account of moral principles only in so far as these are given a sufficient expression in legal form. Law exists, it is said, to serve a social need; but precisely for that reason it can do so only through and within the limits of its own discipline. Otherwise, it is not a legal service that would be rendered.' (South West Africa Case. I. C.J. Reports 1966, 6, para. 49.)

[12] It is for this reason that journalists and (proper) constitutional lawyers argue in an apparently different way on the same problem. Cf. above pp. 24–27 on the canon of acceptable arguments.

The basic problem of the original nineteenth-century form of *Begriffsjurisprudenz* was something else. It was out of touch with everyday life, not (only) in this sense (since this is true essentially for all traditional kinds of legal conceptual analysis), but also in that in many cases it did not even try to translate the extra-legal arguments into legal ones but neglected these *tout court.*[13] It is also worth noting that the *Interessenjurisprudenz*, frequently referred to as the opposite of *Begriffsjurisprudenz*, was not in fact its counterpart but rather complementary to it.[14] Criticism of *Begriffsjurisprudenz*[15] can therefore be justified only to the extent that it addresses actual logical mistakes;[16] but we cannot criticise *Begriffsjurisprudenz* in general as a conceptual game which is out of touch with everyday life, since lawyers necessarily work with concepts.[17]

2. As for the elaboration of the conceptual system, one may state the following. It is not some kind of self-indulgent worship of the systematic nature as such, but a requirement of legal certainty, since a detailed and thoroughly constructed system of legal concepts makes the application of law more predictable. Moreover, one may add that legal certainty itself is far from being a goal in itself, but it does serve the effective functioning of society (or the economy) through predictability. This elaboration of concepts, however, is not to be made in a vacuum, but always with an eye on legal practice. *Rechtsdogmatik* and its specific constitutional form, *Verfassungsdogmatik*, are therefore aids to practice, having the task of building up an accurate conceptual system for the sake of legal certainty (i.e., the predictability of future practice).[18]

[13] Eugen Bucher, Was ist 'Begriffsjurisprudenz'?, in: Werner Krawietz (ed.), *Theorie und Technik der Begriffsjurisprudenz*, Darmstadt, Wissenschaftliche Buchgesellschaft 1976, 358–389 especially 372.

[14] This is well shown by the fact that the four traditional methods of Savigny (grammatical, logical, systemic and historical) are not replaced by the teleological interpretation (of which Jhering is thought to be the inventor): it is added to them as a fifth method, cf. Géza Kiss, *A jogalkalmazás módszeréről*, Budapest, Athaeneum 1909, 53–58. The opposite of *Begriffsjurisprudenz* is rather the 'School of Free Law' (*Freirechtsschule*), see Bucher (n. 13) 372–373.

[15] See especially Philipp Heck, Was ist die Begriffsjurisprudenz, die wir bekämpfen?, *Deutsche Juristenzeitung* 1909, 1457–1461.

[16] Bucher (n. 13) 388; Horst-Eberhard Henke, Wie tot ist die Begriffsjurisprudenz?, in: Krawietz (n. 13) 390–415, 415.

[17] Bucher (n. 13) 389.

[18] Some of the concepts of legal theory do not directly contribute to legal certainty, but only as a building block of the system. This means that they are mostly not directly used in the application of law, yet they are necessary for building a consequent system, and in this way they help the predictable introduction of new elements (of positive law and *Rechtsdogmatik*) into the system, thereby improving the predictability of the application of law indirectly.

A complete separation from legal practice would result in the inability of those applying the law to make use of the insights delivered by legal scholarship (due to the absence of links); that is, scholarly works could by no means contribute to the increase of legal certainty. Therefore, our starting point has to be the content of concepts (even if this may not always be very elegant) as perceived by the relevant legal actors (in the case of a constitution: the constitutional court).[19] If all the relevant actors 'falsely' think 'x' to be the content of a given concept (while it is in fact 'y'), then the content of that concept becomes 'x' (*communis error facit ius*). This, however, does not mean that the common opinion (*herrschende Meinung*) could not be questioned. If an implicit – and hitherto undiscovered – consequence of a commonly held opinion '*A*' contradicts the likewise commonly accepted opinion '*B*', one of these views may be challenged (the one that is more important according to commonly held opinion '*C*'). What the relevant actors exactly think the content of a given legal text (and its concepts) is, becomes manifest through their interpretational practice.[20]

A mere collection of the commonly held views on individual legal issues does not suffice, however, as these do not cover all the possible problems[21] without gaps[22] or contradictions.[23] Such completeness can

[19] Cf. the constitutional-law proverb: 'The Constitution is what the judges say it is.' Charles Evans Hughes, *Speech at Elmira*, 3 May 1907, cited by Bernard Schwartz, *Constitutional Law*, New York, The Macmillan Company 1972, vii. For a similar view by Rudolf Smend, Festvortrag zur Feier des zehnjährigen Bestehens des Bundesverfassungsgerichts am 26. Januar 1962, in: *Das Bundesverfassungsgericht*, Karlsruhe, Müller 1963, 23–37, 24: 'The Basic Law is now virtually identical with its interpretation by the Federal Constitutional Court.'

[20] Cf. the dictum of Dec. Hung. CC 57/1991. (XI. 8.) AB (ABH 1991, 236, 239.): 'the content and meaning of a legal rule is what is attributed to it by the permanent and uniform practice of courts.' A detailed discussion of this concept of Italian origin (*diritto vivente* or living law) is, e.g., Antonio Ruggeri – Antonino Spadaro, *Lineamenti de giustizia costituzionale*, Torino, Giapichelli 2004, 134.

[21] Building a conceptual system instead of mere reproductivity is advocated also by Henke (n. 16) 414.

[22] The ideal of gaplessness is characteristic not only of *Begriffsjurisprudenz*, but also of the rationalist natural-law tradition; see Gustav Boehmer, *Grundlagen der bürgerlichen Rechtsordnung. 2.1. Dogmengeschichtliche Grundlagen des bürgerlichen Rechtes*, Tübingen, Mohr 1951, 63; with reference to Christian Wolff, see Werner Krawietz, Begriffsjurisprudenz, in: Krawietz (n. 13) 432–437, especially 436. The beginnings of conceptual system-building in law are traced back to scholastics (or its reflections in the works of the glossators and commentators) by Harold J Berman, The Origins of Western Legal Science, in: JC Smith – David N Weisstub (eds.), *The Western Idea of Law*, London, Butterworths 1983, 399–413, especially 401, 405.

[23] Even authors outside of the *Begriffsjurisprudenz* tradition often assume non-contradiction in the case of a legal *system*, see, e.g., JW Harris, *Law and Legal Science: An Inquiry into the Concepts* Legal Rule *and Legal System*, Oxford, Clarendon Press 1979, 11, 81–83.

only be achieved by building up a system, and being aware that this goal (i.e., covering all the possible future legal problems without any gaps) can never be achieved, but also that one may come closer to this goal by building a *Rechtsdogmatik* rather than by merely reproducing all the past views.

You can build concepts of *Rechtsdogmatik* from two directions (and both are acceptable): either you construct more general concepts from concrete existing ones, or you deduce concrete ones from more general ones (by splitting them into sub-concepts or by constructing more concrete concepts to more concrete situations). The former is called constructivism, the latter (if the deduction is from a formerly constructed concept) inversion procedure.[24] This part of the legacy of the *Begriffsjurisprudenz* can also be accepted today,[25] but only if we always take into account and refer to objective teleological considerations. Without objective teleological considerations it could easily seem like an arbitrary ploy, word-magic, a scholastic essentialist exercise or, even worse, cheating and abusing the position of a legal scholar for reasons which are not transparent to the public.

### 4.3 Typical mistakes when building a conceptual system of constitutional law

One common mistake is to believe that the meaning of a constitutional provision is defined by implementing or detailing statutes. To accept this would lead to the absurdity that the ordinary legislator would have the power to modify the meaning of the constitution.[26] In a constitutional democracy, however, it is actually the constitution that has to be used as a

24 Bucher (n. 13) 358–389, especially 361–363. The latter expression stems from Philipp Heck (he used it in a pejorative sense), see Heck (n. 15) 1456–1461, especially 1456.

25 Views of the end of *Begriffsjurisprudenz* are clearly refuted by, e.g., Robert Alexy, *Theorie der Grundrechte,* Frankfurt aM, Suhrkamp 2001, 38. While rejecting mere logical inference, he still thinks that the elaboration of the conceptual system is the primary goal of legal scholarship, and on this point he explicitly sides with the tradition of *Begriffsjurisprudenz.*

26 See Francis Delpérée, La Constitution et son interprétation, in: Michel van de Kerchove (ed.), *L'interprétation en droit. Approche pluridisciplinaire,* Bruxelles, Facultés universitaires Saint Louis 1978, 187–210, especially 193. A radical declaration of this methodological tenet was given by the Spanish Constitutional Court, according to which it is unconstitutional to give a statutory definition to any concept of the Constitution. See quoting (STC 76/83) María Luisa Balaguer Callejón, *Interpretación de la Constitución y ordenamiento jurídico,* Madrid, Tecnos 1997, 119.

tool for interpreting the statutes (*verfassungskonforme Auslegung*), rather than the statutes for interpreting the constitution. Norms of lower rank can be used to interpret the constitution only within an historical interpretation (see above *Versteinerungstheorie* at p. 34).

Another error is mistaking the constitution (*Sollen*) for the political practice based upon it (*Sein*). There is a view according to which a given interpretation of a constitutional provision can be argued for on the basis of how its addressees (e.g., the government or the parliament) interpret it.[27] This view has to be rejected, since the constitution is a norm on which political practice has to be measured. Any factual practice (custom) of the addressees is only a sign of how they understand the respective provision (and this can be of interest, particularly if we think that it contradicts the constitution), but has nothing to say about the right interpretation of the constitution. Amongst the state organs, it is only the constitutional court that can give an interpretation of the constitution that is final and binding for all.[28] Political practice may be mentioned in an analysis of *Verfassungsdogmatik*, if this contributes to the exploration of the meaning of the constitution (as the document providing the framework rules of politics), but essentially such issues (i.e., which particular solution the practice opts for between the limits imposed by the constitution) are remote from the genre of traditional legal scholarship – they belong rather to the field of political science.

A thorough legal argument also has to answer possible counterarguments and it has to be able to be generalised to future cases. This is

27 E.g., Chester James Antieau, *Constitutional Construction*, London, Oceana 1982, 44–45. In French works, such arguments are referred to as *coutume constituante* or *coutume constitutionelle* ('constitutional custom'), see, e.g., Marcel Prélot – Jean Boulouis, *Institutions politiques et droit constitutionnel*, Paris, Dalloz 1990, 207–216. On the German debate, see Christian Tomuschat, *Verfassungsgewohnheitsrecht*, Heidelberg, Winter 1972.

28 The same claim is made (focusing on the US Supreme Court) in a more detailed form by Larry Alexander – Frederick Schauer, On Extrajudicial Constitutional Interpretation, *Harvard Law Review* 110 (1997) 1359–1387. Contrary to this (and to our view) is the pluralist (viz. involving the whole of society: *die offene Gesellschaft der Verfassungsinterpreten*) approach of constitutional interpretation put forth by Peter Häberle; see Peter Häberle, *Verfassung als öffentlicher Prozess*, Berlin, Duncker & Humblot $^{2}$1996, 150–152, which ignores the place of constitutional courts within constitutional law. For criticism on Häberle in the same vein (and emphasising the obscurity of his theory) see Christian Starck, Die Verfassungsauslegung, in: Josef Isensee – Paul Kirchhof (eds.), *Handbuch des Staatsrechts der Bundesrepublik Deutschland VII.: Normativität und Schutz der Verfassung – internationale Beziehungen*, Heidelberg, CF Müller 1992, 189–229, especially 205–206.

to say, we not only want to give a systematic description of constitutional provisions and cases that have occurred so far, but we also want to help and provide direction for future interpretations.[29] The fact that a problem has not yet occurred does not mean that one cannot tell, on the basis of (similar) past cases and indirectly applicable general rules (e.g. principles),[30] which solution would be more 'constitutional' than the other.

[29] On this task of the commentaries see Helmuth Schulze-Fielitz, Was macht die Qualität öffentlich-rechtlicher Forschung aus?, *Jahrbuch des öffentlichen Rechts der Gegenwart. Band 50*, Tübingen, Mohr Siebeck 2002, 1–68, especially 20.

[30] On the nature of principles, especially their role as aids of interpretation, see below 13.3.2.

# 5

# Dialects or local grammars: the style of constitutional reasoning in different European countries

> But the Lord came down to see the city and the tower the people were building. The Lord said, 'If as one people speaking the same language they have begun to do this, then nothing they plan to do will be impossible for them. Come, let us go down and confuse their language so they will not understand each other.'[1]

The style of constitutional reasoning differs from country to country.[2] Style can be characterised by (a) whether creativity or dilemmas are admitted; (b) how technical the language is; (c) how elaborate the reasoning is (e.g., whether possible counter-arguments are answered in advance); (d) the degree of generalisation; (e) whether the style is discursive or rather magisterial (hierarchical); (f) the degree of rhetoric (i.e., how grandiose the reasoning is); (g) the specific methods usually preferred in the respective constitutional cultures; and (h) the typical length, layout and internal structure of judgments (including the possibility of dissenting opinions). Features (b), (c) and (d) are defined by the *Verfassungsdogmatik* (constitutional conceptual system)of the country: the more sophisticated it is, the more technical, the more elaborate and the more generalised the reasoning becomes.

We might be tempted to assume that the features of argumentative style could be divided into two main groups: external (form, layout, rhetorical and linguistic style etc.) and internal (actual legal content).

[1] Genesis 11:5–7 (New International Version), describing the Tower of Babel.

[2] The (organic) statutes often contain the requirement that constitutional/supreme court decisions have to be somehow justified (e.g., in Austria, § 26(2) VfGG: 'mit den wesentlichen Entscheidungsgründen ... zu verkünden'), but on how exactly it should be done, explicit legal rules (except for the question whether there are dissenting or parallel opinions) usually do not say anything. Internal standing orders often refer to certain necessary parts of the judgment (e.g., statement of facts, submissions, applied law, whether to separate these under different headings; decision on costs), but they also do not say much about the style of the reasoning.

But this assumption would be wrong. External and internal features are interconnected; form and content in legal reasoning are difficult to separate from each other; or if we do separate them, then our results will be painfully incomplete. It would be unsatisfactory to say that we only analyse the number of references to case-law, but do not know whether they are actually followed as to their content or rather just mentioned for the sake of ornamenting the text; or the other way around, it would be unfulfilling to say that the actual number of references to precedents is unimportant and we are interested only in the 'real' influence of precedents as to the outcome of new disputes. One is normally indicative of the other, and if not, then exactly this lack of connection would be an important result of the analysis. Until now, there has been no overarching in-depth comparative analysis of *European* styles of constitutional reasoning, so we can only present a tentative sketch on the issue with the hope of further development in the future.[3]

## 5.1 Austria and Germany: focusing on the conceptual system

Both Germany and Austria have a very sophisticated *Verfassungsdogmatik*, the elaboration of which is considered to be the main task of constitutional scholarship, and the constitutional courts of these countries do make use of

[3] Cf. Jeffrey Goldsworthy (ed.), *Interpreting Constitutions. A Comparative Study*, Oxford, Oxford University Press 2006, which includes from Europe only Germany (from outside Europe the United States, India, Canada, South Africa and Australia); Mitchel de S.-O.-l'E. Lasser, *Judicial Deliberations. A Comparative Analysis of Judicial Transparency and Legitimacy*, Oxford, Oxford University Press 2004 which compares the US Supreme Court, the ECJ and the French *Cour de cassation*, thus not treating any national constitutional court in Europe. For some European reports (with serious contributions only from Germany, Austria and France, though), but without an actual comparison, see Georg Lienbacher (ed.), *Verfassungsinterpretation in Europa*, Wien, Jan Sramek 2011. For general studies in judicial style see Basil Markesinis, Conceptualism, Pragmatism and Courage, *American Journal of Comparative Law* 34 (1986) 349–367; Basil Markesinis, A Matter of Style, *Law Quarterly Review* 110 (1994) 607–628; Jean Louis Goutal, Characteristics of Judicial Style in France, Britain, and the USA, *The American Journal of Comparative Law* 24 (1976) 43–72; Bernard Rudden, Courts and Codes in England, France and Soviet Russia, *Tulane Law Review* 48 (1974) 1010–1028; Neil MacCormick – Robert S Summers (eds.), *Interpreting Statutes*, Aldershot, Dartmouth 1991; Neil MacCormick – Robert S Summers (eds.), *Interpreting Precedents. A Comparative Study*, Aldershot: Ashgate 1997. In September 2011, a research group began to work at the Max Planck Institute for Comparative Public Law and International Law in Heidelberg in the framework of a five-year project on 'Comparative Constitutional Reasoning' to fill in this research gap; see András Jakab – Arthur Dyevre – Giulio Itzcovich (eds.), *Comparative Constitutional Reasoning*, Cambridge: Cambridge University Press, forthcoming.

this scholarship (in Germany, the Federal Constitutional Court (FCC) explicitly refers to it in judgments; in Austria, the Constitutional Court uses it mostly without reference).[4] Consequently, constitutional reasoning in these countries is technical, elaborate and open for generalisation. Solutions for constitutional problems are mostly depicted as necessary consequences of the conceptual system, and not as dilemmas to be decided by judges. There are, however, important differences between these two countries.

In Austrian *Verfassungsdogmatik*, legal issues are more often conceptualised in the language of theory of norms. For example, competence conflicts between the federal government and the governments of the *Länder* are conceptualised as conflicts between the federal constitution, federal statutes and *Länder* constitutions, without any reference to the concept of sovereignty.[5] Argumentation tends to be simpler and more readily comprehensible than in Germany. Austrians consider their own argumentative style to be more elegant and more modest (applying less rhetoric, also trying to be shorter)[6] than the German style. Austrian argumentation seldom includes the reinforcing, secondary or 'backup' arguments typical in Germany. Kelsen's theoretical legacy is used frequently (the *Stufenbaulehre*, further the three-circle theory of the federal state). All in all, in Austria, his influence is enormous, as arguments based on natural law and sociology are generally not highly regarded.

German *Verfassungsdogmatik* still employs many basic terms from the period of constitutional monarchy.[7] Instead of Hans Kelsen, the key figures are Rudolf Smend (and Konrad Hesse) and Carl Schmitt, whose

[4] The relevance of scholarship for constitutional reasoning may be the consequence of the fact that, most of the time, the majority of these constitutional courts consists of law professors or former university assistants.

[5] András Jakab, Two Opposing Paradigms of Continental European Constitutional Thinking: Austria and Germany, *International and Comparative Law Quarterly* 58 (2009) 933–955, especially 935–940.

[6] The short style has the advantage of being able to hand down faster decisions, thus contributing to a faster enforcement of constitutional claims. Peter Pernthaler – Peter Pallwein-Prettner, Die Entscheidungsbegründung des österreichischen Verfassungsgerichtshofs, in: Rainer Sprung (ed.), *Die Entscheidungsbegründung in europäischen Verfahrensrechten und im Verfahren vor internationalen Gerichten*, Wien, New York, Springer 1974, 199–227, 210.

[7] Cf. Klaus Stern, *Das Staatsrecht der Bundesrepublik Deutschland*, vol. 2, München, Beck 1980, 584–586. Reference is frequently made to such traditional platitudes as, for example, the equating of executive power with the application of the law without any mention of government decrees/regulations. See, e.g., Konrad Hesse, *Grundzüge des Verfassungsrechts der Bundesrepublik Deutschland*, Heidelberg, CF Müller [20]1999, 88.

lines of argumentation often appear in the Federal Constitutional Court's jurisprudence.[8] These arguments often make use of terms that do admittedly have an intuitive, descriptive value but cannot be strictly legally defined (for example, 'community', 'integration' or '*Gesamtheiten*'[9]). This tendency brings with it an inclination towards compound nouns and somewhat mysterious (or, one could say, pretentious) rhetorical figures: 'the law as an ordering factor'[10] or 'the federal order is a form of federative structure.'[11] One often comes across reasoning based on political science and also occasionally on natural law.[12] This style of thinking has the advantage of facilitating argumentation ('fruitful lack of clarity'); in exchange, the disadvantage lies in the unpredictability of the results of such argumentation. In general, one argues from a greater number of premises and attempts to find more (alternative) arguments for the desired result. Thus, argumentation follows more than one line, and these lines are more complicated and less pointed. Germans argue more often from broad, general principles (democracy, human dignity, etc.) to concrete problems; in Austria, such activist tendencies are less common (albeit not unheard of). Opinions of the FCC are often lengthy, written almost in scholarly monographic style,[13] while their Austrian counterparts are usually much shorter.

Also the political context has influence on the style of reasoning: In Austria, the almost permanent constitution-making majority of the government since the Second World War ('grand coalition') made the Constitutional Court less likely to venture into creative interpretation against the legislature.[14] In Germany, however, the FCC considered itself right from the beginning as the missionary of liberal and democratic values after the downfall of Nazism, and on those rare occasions when a

[8] Robert Chr. van Ooyen, *Der Begriff des Politischen des Bundesverfassungsgerichts*, Berlin, Duncker & Humblot 2005.

[9] Hesse (n. 7) 97. [10] *Id.* at 86 (in German, *Recht als Ordnungsfaktor*).

[11] *Id.* at 97 (in German, *Bundesstaatliche Ordnung ist Form föderativer Gestaltung*). One can only guess as to its meaning.

[12] Or etatistic (state-centred) combinations of both, such as the figure of a state's recognition of a right. See Stern (n. 7) 588.

[13] Matthias Jestaedt, Phänomen Bundesverfassungsgericht, in: Matthias Jestaedt – Oliver Lepsius – Christoph Möllers – Christoph Schönberger, *Das entgrenzte Gericht*, Berlin, Suhrkamp 2011, 77–158, 125.

[14] For a different explanation referring to the dismissal of the judges of the Constitutional Court in 1929, see Ewald Wiederin, Verfassungsinterpretation in Österreich, in: Lienbacher (n. 3) 81–114, 105.

grand coalition existed with constitution-making majority, a conflict with the FCC would have been taboo in German political culture.

In Austria, dissenting opinions are not allowed at all in the Constitutional Court, as the authority of law is perceived to be better protected by a unified voice. In Germany, they are used rather rarely for the very same reason. This also results in hiding contentious general (non-legal) issues, and concentrating on strictly legal approaches. The German references to supra-positive norms or to an *objective value order* are unknown. Dissenting opinions or references to scholarly opinions are also avoided in Austria.[15] Otherwise, the structure of the constitutional court judgments is very similar. As Professor Kommers has described:[16]

> Doctrinal elaboration dominates the approach to constitutional argument and legal writing generally. The FCC's full senate opinions tend to be heavily oriented toward normative theorizing and definitional refinement. In contrast to the breathtaking brevity of and incisiveness of French Constitutional Council decisions, the typical German opinion is an exercise in encyclopaedic scholarship. The typical case reads like a sophisticated – and often turgid – American law student research note.... It seems rather clear that these opinions, which reflect a thorough survey of the literature pertaining to a particular set of constitutional issues, are written less for the general public than for the academic legal profession. Opinion writing on the FCC is designed largely to persuade the academic legal community – and other informed readers – of the rightness, neutrality, and integrity of decisional outcomes. The typical case begins with *Leitzsätze* (leading sentences) or 'headnotes' summarizing its essential holding. The opinion then proceeds systematically (1) to describe the case's factual, legal, and procedural background, (2) to recapitulate – usually in great detail – arguments advanced by petitioners and respondents, (3) to rule on the admissibility of the complaint or the legitimacy of the issue referred to the Court, and (4) to pass upon the merits of the case in an extended judgment that seeks to resolve all relevant constitutional issues.

[15] See Pernthaler – Pallwein-Prettner (n. 6) 207–208 referring to VfSlg 2455/1952 where the Austrian Constitutional Court explicitly refused to discuss scholarly opinions. But, in fact, scholarly opinions (often contained in the submissions) hugely influence the decisions.

[16] Donald P Kommers, Germany: Balancing Rights and Duties, in: Goldsworthy (n. 3) 161–214, 210. On the distinctively scholarly style of BVerfG decisions see Peter Lerche, Stil und Methode verfassungsgerichtlicher Entscheidungspraxis, in: Peter Badura – Horst Dreier (eds.), *Festschrift 50 Jahre Bundesverfassungsgericht*, vol. 1, Tübingen, Mohr Siebeck 2001, 333–361. The abstract style serves also as a means of self-empowerment, as the FCC creates in this way long-term detailed (and seemingly objective) standards for politics, see Oliver Lepsius, Die maßstabsetzende Gewalt, in: Schönberger (n. 13) 159–279, 171–181.

As a final remark, one can say that both German and Austrian legal scholars depict each other as proponents of an outdated methodology. From a traditional Austrian vantage point, German constitutional scholarship appears to be a scholarship stuck at a (pre-)Jellinekian methodological level (that is, the mixing of legal and sociological arguments and the presentation of personal views on legal policy as theoretically compulsory legal conclusions). From the other side of the border, in contrast, the Kelsenian style in Austria is viewed as an absurd and unproductive caricature of an outmoded formalistic nineteenth-century *Begriffsjurisprudenz*.[17] But from a French or British perspective, these two Germanic styles can look very similar indeed.

## 5.2 France and the UK: limited judicial review resulting in limited conceptual sophistication

In both France and the UK, we find significantly fewer references to scholarly works in judgments. In the UK, this is because of the generally low prestige of legal scholarship; in France references to scholarly works are rare because of legitimacy concerns (legal scholars have not been elected democratically). The German-Austrian style of *Verfassungsdogmatik* is considered as being rather quixotic, which can be explained partly by the lack or at least the late birth of an overarching constitutional review of statutes in these countries.

In France, until very recently there was only *a priori* constitutional review,[18] and consequently only a very few cases came to the Constitutional Council.[19] Most constitutional conflicts were consequently not enforceable in courts; thus, building any sophisticated conceptual system of constitutional law would have been futile, as the

[17] See, e.g., Norbert Achterberg, Hans Kelsens Bedeutung in der gegenwärtigen deutschen Staatslehre, *Die öffentliche Verwaltung* 1974, 445–454 citing, inter alia, Hermann Klenner, *Rechtsleere: Die Verurteilung der Reinen Rechtslehre*, Berlin, Verlag Marxistische Blätter 1972. See also Horst Dreier, *Rezeption und Rolle der Reinen Rechtslehre*, Wien, Manz 2001, 25, 29 with numerous references to further German literature on this issue; Horst Dreier, *Rechtslehre, Staatssoziologie und Demokratietheorie bei Hans Kelsen*, Baden-Baden, Nomos 1986, 19–25.

[18] Federico Fabbrini, Kelsen in Paris: France's Constitutional Reform and the Introduction of a Posteriori Constitutional Review of Legislation, *German Law Journal* 9 (2008) 1297–1312.

[19] The original 1958 French Constitutional Council was classified as an example of the 'political [i.e., non-judicial] control of constitutionality' by Mauro Cappelletti, *Judicial Review in the Contemporary World*, New York, Bobbs-Merrill Inc. 1971, 2–6.

conflicts were decided by politicians anyway (according to the rules of politics). Also, the commentary literature (explaining the meaning of each constitutional provision in the form of individual scholarly contributions containing references to academic literature and case-law), so popular in Germany and Austria, is rather a rarity in France.[20] We can predict that with the recent introduction of *a posteriori* constitutional review, the situation is likely to change. The need for a more sophisticated *Verfassungsdogmatik* will be more obvious; the literature of constitutional commentary will become stronger; even references to scholarly works in judgments may become more usual.

The language and the form of the decisions of the Constitutional Council are extremely technical (being one very long sentence), the elaboration of the reasoning is sometimes questionable (decisions are mostly a few lines long, rarely longer than two printed pages, thus much shorter than German or Austrian decisions, even if lately they have been slightly increasing in length), and dilemmas are practically never shown (this is aggravated by the fact that there are no dissenting or concurring opinions). Solutions are presented as stemming from the text of the Constitution (or from the 1789 Declaration) without any trick of interpretation.[21] This can be explained by a certain traditional timidity on the part of the French judges, who do not consider themselves as possessing the legitimacy to decide cases and thus simply point at the Constitution as if they were just its mouthpiece.[22] Academic *doctrine* does have a high

[20] For two of the very few exceptions, noticeably shorter and less sophisticated versions of their German counterparts, see Michel de Villiers – Thierry Renoux (eds.), *Code constitutionnel*, Paris, LexisNexis $^{4}$2011; François Luchaire – Gérard Conac – Xavier Prétot (eds.), *La Constitution de la République française*, Paris, Economica $^{3}$2009.

[21] On French constitutional reasoning see Luc Heuschling, Verfassungsinterpretation in Frankreich, in: Lienbacher (n. 3) 37–68.

[22] This still lasting judicial timidity can be depicted as the legacy of the French Revolution of 1789. At that time, judges were considered as corrupt and (as far as it was possible within the limits of corruption) as royalist, both for good reasons. Thus the revolutionaries and their imperial successors under Napoleon did everything to limit their power ranging from the explicit prohibition in the *Code civil* of the binding power of judgments on future cases to placing the judicial review of administrative actions into the hands of the State Council (a traditional advisory institution, filled with high-profile bureaucrats and reliable politicians) instead of ordinary courts. See Goutal (n. 3) and Rudden (n. 3). They even introduced the institution of *référé legislatif*, which basically meant that judges had to ask the legislature if they were uncertain about the correct interpretation of a statute (see *loi du 27 novembre 1790* and *loi de 1er décembre 1790*), that resulted in slowing down trials and in the legislature's constantly rewriting of the statutes which it was asked about. The institution is now only legal history which, however, was widely used also in German

standing in France (as opposed to the UK),[23] but it is not quoted in judgments; it exerts influence on future decisions, and it is widely read by judges (again, as opposed to the UK). Moral or policy perspectives are not mentioned explicitly in the judgments themselves (which does not mean of course that they are not considered behind the scenes).[24]

The structure of the decisions of the Constitutional Council is always strictly the same.[25] 1. At the beginning of the decision, there is an introductory head note about the constitutional empowerment of the Constitutional Council and a short history of the procedure (initiators, submission date). 2. Then, under the heading 'Le Conseil constitutionnel', we find a list of the titles of the relevant statutes and submissions. Each entry is a new paragraph which finishes with a semicolon, resulting in one huge sentence, consisting of paragraphs beginning with 'Vu' ('Having seen'); the list ends with the entry 'Le rapporteur ayant été entendu' ('The rapporteur having been heard'). 3. The considered legal arguments (sometimes structured with subtitles, sometimes not) are listed again as part of a long sentence ending with 'Décide' ('Decides'). The arguments are always introduced in a new line beginning with 'Considérant que' ('Considering that' or 'Whereas'). 4. The actual decision is then to be found under the heading 'Décide'. 5. At the end of the decision, the date and the judges taking part in the decision are listed.[26]

territories during the nineteenth century, see Matthias Miersch, *Der sogenannte référé legislatif*, Baden-Baden, Nomos 2000.

[23] For the situation in England in general see FH Lawson, Doctrinal Writing: A Foreign Element in English Law, in: Ernst von Caemmerer – Soia Mentschikoff – Max Rheinstein – Konrad Zweigert (eds.), *Ius privatum gentium. Festschrift für Max Rheinstein*. vol. I, Tübingen, Mohr Siebeck 1969, 191–210.

[24] Proven on the example of the *Cour de cassation* by Lasser (n. 3) 27–61.

[25] The obsessively strict French requirements on forms and style can be seen also in constitutional (or, in general, legal) scholarship: doctoral theses have to consist of two parts (A and B), each of them consisting of two sub-parts *(le plan)*; see in general for dissertations in law Pauline Türk – Isabelle Thumerel – Gilles Toulemonde, *Exercices corrigés. Théorie générale du droit constitutionnel*, Paris, Gualino 2010, 13–14 *(deux parties/quatre sous-parties)*. Any alteration of this structure has to be thoroughly justified. This seemingly logical structure results in the violation of the internal logic of topics and occasionally results in more effort being put into the structure than into the intellectual content. For foreigners, this structure makes it very difficult to make use of French constitutional literature, and it therefore contributes to the isolation of French constitutional scholarship.

[26] This style and structure of judgments is very similar to the ordinary court judgments. For a detailed analysis and a historical explanation with further references on the judgments of ordinary courts see Lasser (n. 3) 30–38; Hein Kötz, Über den Stil höchstrichterlicher Entscheidungen, *Rabels Zeitschrift für ausländisches und internationales Privatrecht* 1973, 245–263, especially 247–252; Pierre Mimin, *Le style des jugements. Vocabulaire – Construction – Dialectique – Formes juridiques*, Paris, Librairies techniques 1978.

In the UK, judgments are generally longer than in any other country in the world (with no predefined structure except for a usual beginning describing the facts, the procedural steps and the parties' submissions, the legal reasoning and the final decision), as the case load of judges is very low.[27] Traditionally, judges also considered one of their duties to be lecturing young lawyers sitting in court hearings; thus, they explained everything in detail, showing all the dilemmas to the future generation of judges sitting eagerly in the audience. The language is therefore much less technical than in France or even in Austria or Germany; the style is rather discursive.[28] Cases are just *ad hoc* solutions, no general conceptual system is meant to be built from them. In general, purposive interpretation was not particularly popular, because Parliament could easily change any law. If a legal solution was socially unacceptable, Parliament was meant to change it, not the courts. A purposive interpretation is becoming more and more popular, though, partly due to the influence of EU law and ECHR law (ECHR is the closest thing to a constitution that the UK has). In the UK, dissenting or parallel opinions are the default position, not a rarely used possibility as in Germany.

Interestingly, both in France and in the UK, some of the most recent developments in constitutional theory rely heavily on German, and to a lesser extent Austrian, background literature.[29] It is unlikely that the style of constitutional reasoning will become fully Germanised, but the influence is apparent and one-sided (as there is no similar French or UK influence in Germany).[30]

[27] Goutal (n. 3) 61–65.

[28] The style of constitutional scholarship literature is similar to the style of judgments: lengthy, essayistic style (sometimes rather an unstructured flow of text or collection of legal and non-legal information), building inductively on a series of examples explained in detail with an impressive eloquence (often with numerous proverbs and metaphors), but in a conceptually and methodologically rather undisciplined and unstructured manner. It reminds one, rather, of the speeches of barristers or judges in courts than of continental *Verfassungsdogmatik*. Large amounts of non-legal (factual political or political philosophical) information are also contained in the works (besides legal history, never or just not yet enacted draft statutes, or policy papers) which might be explained by the sporadic and unsystematic nature of British constitutional law itself (corrected in practice by non-legal constitutional conventions as a *modus vivendi*). On the latter point in general see Geoffrey Marshall, *Constitutional Conventions*, Oxford, Oxford University Press 1984. Consequently, the context of law seems to have sometimes even more emphasis than law itself, also in mainstream legal scholarship.

[29] Olivier Beaud, *La puissance de l'État*, Paris, Presses Universitaires de France 1994; Martin Loughlin, *Foundations of Public Law*, Oxford, Oxford University Press 2010.

[30] It is not the first time that European continental (more specifically: German) legal methodology has influenced its English counterpart. On Samuel Pufendorf's influence on Blackstone, see Jan Schröder, Zur gesamteuropäischen Tradition der juristischen

## 5.3 Hungary and Spain: copying the German model after the end of the dictatorship

After the end of dictatorships, both Spain and Hungary opted for the German constitutional model (with its accessories in constitutional reasoning, such as dissenting opinions). The UK model with no formal constitutional guarantees seemed to be a dangerous option; the decentralised American constitutional review looked chaotic (and ordinary judges were servants of the *ancien régime* who could not be trusted to be guardians of the new democratic constitution); and, in the absence of strong democratic traditions, a very strong president looked too much like a putative dictator. Basically, the choice was between the semi-presidential French system and the parliamentary German system (the unstable Italian parliamentary system looked less attractive, and there were no further major Western democracies to look at). Some European post-dictatorial countries opted for the French model, but most of them chose the German model.[31] The German constitutional system had been built up exactly as an intellectually sophisticated response to a former dictatorship, so (especially with its strong constitutional court) it seemed to fit such situations much more aptly than the French model (which originally was an answer to the inability of the executive branch to govern). The choice can partly be explained also by the generous German scholarship policy, which meant that a number of talented constitutional lawyers from the new democracies had already spent several months or years at a German university or at the Max Planck Institute for Comparative Public Law and International Law in Heidelberg. Accordingly, they all had learnt the 'democratic' style of constitutional law from German literature, and once they had a position at the constitutional court of their home country (either as a judge or as an advisor to a judge), they implemented what they had learned in Germany.

The style of constitutional reasoning in these relatively new democracies depended on how the legacy of the dictatorial past, and the few local innovations, merged with the new German transplants. During the

Methodenlehre, *Akademie-Journal* 2002/2, 37–41, 40. On Savigny's influence on John Austin, see HLA Hart, Introduction, in: John Austin, *The Province of Jurisprudence Determined and The Uses of the Study of Jurisprudence*, London, Weidenfeld and Nicolson 1971, vii–xviii, especially vii.

[31] The Portuguese and the Spanish constitutional courts are sometime called 'daughters' of the German Federal Constitutional Court (originally by Roman Herzog), the Hungarian and the Polish as 'grandchildren'; see discussion contribution by László Sólyom in: Jochen Abr. Frowein – Thilo Marauhn (eds.), *Grundfragen der Verfassungsgerichtsbarkeit in Mittel- und Osteuropa*, Berlin, Springer 1998, 83.

period of dictatorship, there were no constitutional courts in the dictatorships in socialist Eastern Europe (except for a very few constitutional courts with practically no activity whatsoever), so we cannot look for socialist case-law in order to identify the socialist elements in today's constitutional thought. We cannot use constitutional texts either, as the text of the constitutions has been almost entirely changed. Consequently, for the legacy of dictatorships we rather have to check the old constitutional scholarship and how it still influences today's constitutional reasoning, both in the constitutional courts and in the literature.

In Hungary, socialist constitutional law literature basically contained four elements: 1. explanations of how true the teachings of Marx and Lenin were, 2. descriptions of the factual political situation, 3. repetition of constitutional or (constitutionally relevant) statutory texts and 4. proposals for new laws. The traditional task of legal scholarship, that is, proposing a new interpretation of an old law, was almost entirely missing. Ad 1. The first element (naturally) died out after the end of socialism, but the three others remained. Ad 2. The description of the factual political situation resulted in textbooks, where political science merged with constitutional law.[32] Ad 3. The repetitive and intellectually timid style of analysing constitutional provisions and relevant statutes is reflected not only in the literature, but to some extent also in the constitutional court. Its reliance on literal methods of interpretation and the refusal of teleological (sometimes even systemic) arguments is typical.[33] Ad 4. A typical mistake of today's Hungarian *Verfassungsdogmatik* is to deliver meditations on what the text of the constitution should be instead of conceptual-doctrinal analysis of the existing text.[34] Legal scholars doing so do not help constitutional courts, they just dream about a better constitutional text, and instead of real lawyerly conceptual analysis they only provide futile future plans. This

[32] Some even proudly criticise, from this confused methodological point of view, the attempts at building a *Verfassungsdogmatik*. See György Müller, Kormányzati viszonyainkról az új alkotmánykommentár 'A Kormány' című fejezete kapcsán, *Jogelméleti Szemle* 2010/1, http://jesz.ajk.elte.hu/muller41.html. For a fitting response to that, see Vilmos Térey, Csodaváróknak, *Jogelméleti Szemle* 2010/2, http://jesz.ajk.elte.hu/terey42.html.

[33] The school of Hungarian textualists, as analysed in András Jakab, Wissenschaft und Lehre des Verfassungsrechts in Ungarn, in: Armin von Bogdandy – Pedro Cruz Villalón – Peter M Huber (eds.), *Ius Publicum Europaeum*, vol. 2, Heidelberg, C.F. Müller 2007, para 23–30, represent this symptom.

[34] This is particularly dangerous in the field of constitutional law, as it may lead the scholarly debate into one of political confessions. Arguments of constitutional law are (sometimes rightly) subject to 'ideological insinuation' anyway; see Hans Peter Ipsen, Die deutsche Staatsrechtswissenschaft im Spiegel der Lehrbücher, *Archiv des öffentlichen Rechts* 106 (1981) 161–204, especially 198.

type of legal scholarship dominated the landscape in socialist countries, where according to the official doctrine of 'socialist normativism', attempts were made to turn judges into law-applying machines (using rather literal interpretation), and law-making power only lay with Parliament. Parliament followed 'scientific' and modern socialist views in order to transform society into socialism and later into communism. For the great reform plan, they needed advisors about how to use law as an instrument of social transformation. These advisors were legal scholars suggesting amendments to the laws by the legislature.[35] If the legislature is legally omnipotent (i.e., there are no constitutional constraints, even the constitution can easily be amended),[36] then we do not have to deal with intricate doctrinal questions at all: instead we can concentrate on the instrumental character of law. Law was a means to change society, and lawyers were needed only to use this instrument. The socialist legacy is becoming weaker (newer generations are influenced primarily by German,[37] secondarily by American patterns), but probably for several decades its traces will remain strong in Hungary.

In Franco's Spain, the binding force of the constitution (Fundamental Laws of the Kingdom) was institutionally weak, as a constitutional court did not exist. As a consequence, *Verfassungsdogmatik* also remained unsophisticated as most constitutional lawyers understandably did not bother to work on it. The university subject and the title of textbooks was *derecho político* (political law), merging historical and ideological descriptions with the repetition of statutory provisions (very much like Hungary).[38] In the new democratic system, whole constructions of *Verfasungsdogmatik* have very often been borrowed *in extenso* from Germany, sometimes even original German words in German (e.g., *Drittwirkung*, i.e., the third-party effect or horizontal effect of fundamental rights) are used in Spanish texts. This doctrinal import is mostly well understood, but sometimes it is imprecise or cannot easily be reconciled with the text of the Spanish constitution.[39]

[35] See András Jakab, Surviving Socialist Legal Concepts and Methods, in: András Jakab – Péter Takács – Allan F Tatham (eds.), *The Transformation of the Hungarian Legal Order 1985–2005*, The Hague, Kluwer Law International 2007, 606–619, especially 607–608.

[36] At this point, the Westminster system and the socialist countries were very similar.

[37] Catherine Dupré, *Importing the Law in Post-Communist Transitions. The Hungarian Constitutional Court and the Right to Human Dignity*, Oxford, Hart 2003, 65–86; László Sólyom, Aufbau und dogmatische Fundierung der ungarischen Verfassungsgerichtsbarkeit, *Osteuropa Recht* 2000, 230–241.

[38] For an exception see Manuel García-Pelayo, *Derecho constitucional comparado*, Madrid, Revista Occidente 1950, but this was not a strictly doctrinal analysis, but rather an institutional and historical comparison. García-Pelayo left the country under Franco because of his political ideas and first returned after the regime change.

[39] Leonardo Álvarez, Die spanische Dogmatik der Verfassungstreue. Geschichte einer fehlgeschlagenen Rezeption des deutschen Verfassungsdenkens, *Zeitschrift für*

Thus, surprisingly, comparative law arguments sometimes prevail over all other methods of interpretation, breaching our normative methodological considerations.[40]

## 5.4 Is there a European style of constitutional reasoning?

To be able to talk about a 'European' style of constitutional reasoning, we should be able to name some features which are common to European constitutional cultures, but which do not characterise non-European (e. g., US) constitutional reasoning. Unfortunately (or fortunately), there are no such features. The most we can discern are different emphases. The average US Supreme Court judgment uses more substantive (moral, sociological or economic) reasons, than European counterparts since the general judicial style is more substantive in the United States.[41] In addition the conscious rejection of the use of comparative law arguments based on concerns of legitimacy is rather a US feature than a European one.[42] Radical originalism is also rather an American phenomenon (explained by the sacred and identity-building nature of the US Constitution),[43] even though questioned in the United States, too.[44]

*ausländisches öffentliches Recht und Völkerrecht* 2010, 433–458. For similar problems in Hungary concerning human dignity see Jakab (n. 33) n. 71.

40 See above p. 54.

41 Judges in the United States often behave like politicians (state judges are sometimes directly elected by the local population for a limited term; federal judges are appointed mostly because of party membership and loyalty, so their audience is much less the legal profession than the electing people or the appointing politicians), so non-legal (political, social, policy, moral) arguments are much more acceptable for them than for judges in other countries. Patrick S Atiyah – Robert S Summers, *Form and Substance in Anglo-American Law. A Comparative Study of Legal Reasoning, Legal Theory and Legal Institutions*, Oxford, Clarendon Press 1987, 342, 344, 350–351, 379.

42 According to Jeffrey Goldsworthy, Conclusions, in: Goldsworthy (n. 3) 342, the real reason for the low popularity of comparative law arguments in the United States is that the Constitution is old; thus there is a bigger pool of precedents to rely on for the solution of new cases. Comparative law is therefore rather used where guidance is needed because the Constitution is new. In Europe, the integration rather results in a growing use of comparative constitutional law in constitutional reasoning; see Ingolf Pernice, Europawissenschaft oder Staatsrechtslehre?, in: Helmuth Schulze-Fielitz (ed.), *Staatslehre als Wissenschaft*, Berlin, Duncker & Humblot 2007, 225–251, 239.

43 Robert C Post, Constitutional Scholarship in the United States, *International Journal of Constitutional Law* 7 (2009) 416–423, 418.

44 Michel Rosenfeld, Constitutional Adjudication in Europe and the United States: Paradoxes and Contrasts, in: Georg Nolte (ed.), *European and US Constitutionalism*, Strasbourg, Council of Europe Publishing 2005, 165–199, especially 187–194 with further references.

In Europe, neither the European Court of Justice (ECJ), nor the European Court of Human Rights (ECtHR), has unified the style of constitutional reasoning; only a stronger presence of teleological arguments can be attributed to them, at least in countries where formerly it was less common.[45] Also, the German style of constitutional reasoning is nearer to the American style, than to the French, even though Germany does have a strong influence on some European countries. It is clearly the most influential European constitutional culture, both intellectually in content and financially (especially via scholarship programmes in Germany for foreign constitutional scholars) promoting its own ideas. Until now, however, except for the emergence of the proportionality test, which came directly from the ECJ and the ECtHR but originally from Germany, the German style has been unable to alter significantly the style of constitutional reasoning in France or the UK. A phenomenon which is true also for the United States where, however, a similar indirect German influence can be shown.[46]

The differences in constitutional reasoning in European countries are partly based on historical and institutional coincidences, partly on implied theoretical presuppositions of a legal community and on general mentalities,[47] the latter of which are unlikely to converge in the near future. So, to put it briefly, there is currently no such thing as a

[45] On the teleological practices of the ECJ see Joxerammon Bengoetxea, *The Legal Reasoning of the European Court of Justice: Towards a European Jurisprudence*, Oxford, Clarendon Press 1993, 181–270; Anna Bredimas, *Methods of Interpretation and Community Law*, Amsterdam, North Holland Publishing 1978, 70–105 (calling it the 'functional method'); Giulio Itzcovich, The Interpretation of Community Law by the European Court of Justice, *German Law Journal* 10 (2009) 537–559, 557 (calling it the 'dynamic criteria of interpretation'); Gunnar Beck, *The Legal Reasoning of the Court of Justice of the EU*, Oxford, Hart 2012, 207–215. On the 'dynamic interpretation' of the ECtHR, see Hans-Joachim Cremer, Regeln der Konventionsinterpretation, in: Rainer Grote – Thilo Marauhn (eds.), *EMRK/GG. Konkordanzkommentar zum europäischen und deutschen Grundrechtsschutz*, Tübingen, Mohr Siebeck 2006, 155–230. On the influence of the EC (EU) on the British judicial style, see Jonathan E Levitsky, The Europeanization of the British Legal Style, *American Journal of Comparative Law* 42 (1994) 347–380. For recent normative accounts of how the ECJ and the ECHR *should* reason see Gerard Conway, *The Limits of Legal Reasoning of the European Court of Justice*, Cambridge, Cambridge University Press 2012; George Letsas, *A Theory of Interpretation of the European Court of Human Rights*, Oxford, Oxford University Press 2007.

[46] Alec Stone Sweet – Jud Mathews, Proportionality Balancing and Global Constitutionalism, *Columbia Journal of Transnational Law* 47 (2008–2009) 72–164 with further references to case-law and literature. On the differences between US and German concepts of balancing, see Jacco Bomhoff, *Balancing Constitutional Rights. The Origins and Meanings of Postwar Legal Discourse*, Cambridge, Cambridge University Press 2013.

[47] Jakab (n. 5) 933–955, especially 953–955.

'European' style of constitutional reasoning.[48] The question is rather whether we should, and whether one day we will, have such a common style in Europe.

For the combined purposes of constitutionalism and legal certainty, this style should converge, and it should be based on a sophisticated *Verfassungsdogmatik*. The present book has the ambition to contribute to this.

[48] For an opposite conclusion see Moshe Cohen-Eliya – Iddo Porat, *Proportionality and Constitutional Culture*, Cambridge, Cambridge University Press 2013. The authors, however, identify 'European' with German and thus ignore French, Italian etc. styles of constitutional reasoning in their otherwise excellent book.

# PART II

## Suggested vocabulary as a patchwork historical collection of responses to different challenges

> A szavaknak idejük van, vagy másképp: idő van a szavakban, a mi időnk, a használóké, a mi történelmünk, mi magunk.[1]

Key elements of constitutional vocabulary (i.e., key concepts of constitutional law, including the concept of the constitution itself) should be viewed as historical responses to different social challenges (see above 1.2.2).[2] There is thus no general historical masterplan behind these responses, and some of the responses are not even conscious responses (i.e., not all of them were *designed* to give a response; they just happen to be useful or serving as a response to a challenge). It is rather a series of historical, social and political circumstances which induced the invention and the application of these responses. Some of these circumstances still endure, others have slightly changed; while others have faded away entirely, either step by step, in an incremental manner, or in a sudden, revolutionary way.

Some of the responses were consciously designed, but they were *ad hoc* responses to very concrete challenges, like 'sovereignty' or 'the rule of law' (even if some of their users think that they have existed for time immemorial). Others, like 'nation' or 'democracy' are just partly so, and to a certain degree they are the result of social dynamics. These latter ones just happen to be able to serve as responses to certain important social challenges (like how to deal with ethnic diversity, or how to ensure loyalty and self-correction in a political system).

[1] 'Words have a time, or to put it differently: there is a time in the words, our time, the time of their users, our history, ourselves.' Péter Esterházy, *A szavak csodálatos életéből* (From the Beautiful Life of Words), Budapest, Magvető 2003, 14.

[2] For a similar approach to constitutional vocabulary of European integration, see Gráinne de Búrca, The Language of Rights and European Integration, in: Jo Shaw - Gillian More (eds.), *New Legal Dynamics of European Union*, Oxford, Clarendon 1995, 29–54, especially 40–43 explaining the usage of the 'language of rights' in EU law, rather sceptically, as a response to legitimacy concerns of European integration by strengthening its moral element.

Why and how exactly these happened, we will consider in the different chapters. We are also going to consider whether the changes in the original inducing circumstances or the side-effects of the original responses should lead us to emphasise, redefine or rather de-emphasise the key concepts which expressed these original responses. Some of these concepts should thus be used today in a different sense because the factual (social or political) situation is different,[3] the use of others should be minimised; or the opposite: they should be used more bravely, if we want to provide responses to today's social challenges. The best way to connect legal meaning and social challenges is to use objective teleological arguments which we have already discussed above (3.3.1).

Clarifying the historical, social and political context of the key concepts is especially necessary as lawyers often tend to refer in their reasoning to social facts as obvious truths (or just presuppose them without mentioning them explicitly) even if these are based on questionable sociological, psychological or historical knowledge. When we talk about key concepts of constitutional law, an additional problem appears: emotional-political or ideological preferences play an even bigger role than usual (lawyers love to sell these ideological preferences as purely legal-conceptual questions to conceal their actual influence on their constitutional reasoning).[4]

The following chapters may also be disappointing for some: they do not discover any unified moral explanation behind the key concepts of constitutional law (or just in a very indirect manner, if someone tries to conceptualise challenge-and-response as a moral scheme, which I do

[3] Constitutional lawyers always have to consider (even if they do not mention them explicitly) the social and political facts, see Heinrich Triepel, *Staatsrecht und Politik*, Berlin, de Gruyter 1927, 20 and 37.

[4] The abstract, evaluative, psychologically and sociologically influenced (where the participants of the debate are necessarily also personally affected to some degree), endlessly debated, through time slowly changing, variously describable and internally complex nature of constitutional key concepts which resist widely accepted definitions can probably be best characterised by what we call an 'essentially contested concept'; see WB Gallie, Essentially Contested Concepts, *Proceedings of the Aristotelian Society* 56 (1956) 167–198. Lawyers often shortcut such debates in an unreflective manner by referring to some kind of legal authority, typically constitutional court decisions (quoting from such decisions some arbitrarily chosen short theses), but this is a very weak method, as it does not give any answer to the question as to how the *legal* definition in these decisions relates to the actual sociological or political challenges societies face. In order to avoid this, I am first giving a sociological, political and historical explanation of the concepts, before I propose a legal definition for them.

not), as there is just no such master plan.[5] Our basic concepts of constitutional law are a patchwork historical collection of responses to different challenges, and rightly so. Great social achievements like modern constitutional systems are all based on an incremental, lengthy, trial-and-error development of human knowledge.[6]

In order to understand the different challenges and in order to find their fitting legal use, we are also going to engage in some comparative constitutional law.[7] This will, however, only be a corollary (or secondary) method of definition as to the just-described objective teleological one. Comparative constitutional law only serves as an inventory of ideas and as an occasion to test the results of our objective teleological method.

Before we begin to analyse the key concepts one by one, a table of the topics covered might be useful in order to gain a systematic overview.

Some usual key concepts of national constitutional laws are missing (e.g., republic or federalism), as some of the constitutional cultures of the EU explicitly reject them. Some other possible key concepts have been tried and rejected, and I have placed them in Part III (e.g., principles as logically distinct norms or the *Stufenbau*). I am not dealing with the concept of legitimacy as a separate concept, because either we define it in a very vague manner ('worthy to be followed'), which is difficult to operationalise in constitutional reasoning, or it is defined as some

5 For a very similar view, see Peter Häberle, Staatslehre als Verfassungsgeschichte, *Archiv des öffentlichen Rechts* 102 (1977) 284–297, 285: 'Obviously, it does not seem to be possible (any more) to explicate the theory of . . . constitution from *one* key concept or to reduce it to *one* . . . question, such as "integration", "decision", "Grundnorm" or Stufenbau, state/society, freedom' (translation of the present author). The rejection of a teleological masterplan (and consequently, the rejection of a unified conceptual explanation) does not mean, however, that constitutional theory could be written without a political vision (see above 1.2). The difference between the two is that the political vision is *not* referred to directly in constitutional reasoning, it is more pragmatic (i.e., it does not have the ambition to be applicable for eternity, it is more bound to the present) and it does not have to have the conceptual coherence that we would expect from a teleological masterplan. We can still work with different key concepts and with their *teloi* (and refer to them explicitly in constitutional reasoning), but they will not, and should not, form a unified conceptual system. And a final clarification: establishing the *telos* of these key concepts is *not* a lot more objective and only somewhat less political than the choice of a political vision; but the stakes are definitely smaller as the question itself is less general (see above 3.3.1).

6 On the limited intellectual and moral capacity of humans, see the classic by Anthony Quinton, *The Politics of Imperfection*, London, Faber & Faber 1978.

7 For an excellent general account of the methodological issues of comparing fundamental constitutional concepts in Europe see Diana Zacharias, Terminologie und Begrifflichkeit, in: Armin von Bogdandy e.a. (eds.), *Ius Publicum Europaeum*, vol. II, Heidelberg, CF Müller 2008, 843–891 (with further references).

Part II, Table 1. *Key concepts of European constitutional law*

| Key concept | Short legal definition | Date of origin | *Telos:* what is the purpose of the concept, to which type of social challenge was it originally supposed to provide a response? | Advice as to its use in today's European constitutional discourse |
|---|---|---|---|---|
| sovereignty | exclusive supreme power within a territory | 16th–17th centuries | how to justify absolutism in order to end religious civil wars | its use should be minimised, and it should be redefined as a mere *claim* of exclusive supreme power |
| the rule of law | prohibition of the arbitrary use of state power | 17th–18th centuries | how to avoid absolutism and the abuse of executive state power | the fight against terrorism does not justify a redefinition of the concept; it should be used in the same sense that it has been used until now |

| | | | | |
|---|---|---|---|---|
| constitution | man-made document to limit legally the legislator | 18th century (US), 20th century (Europe) | how to avoid absolutism and the abuse of legislative state power (secondary function: symbolic integration of the whole political community) | the Founding Treaties of the EU (including the Charter of Fundamental Rights of the EU) should also be referred to as constitutions |
| democracy | identity of the ruled and the rulers | 18th century | how to ensure loyalty and self-correction | democracy should be used in a sense which also makes EU political power accountable, e.g., which parliamentarises the EU |
| nation | homogenous political community of equal members | 18th–19th centuries | how to deal with ethnic diversity | the citizens of the EU should be referred to as the 'European Nation' |

combination of the above key concepts (especially 'democracy' and 'constitution'; see in their specific chapters).

But even without these, it would still be possible to have a more comprehensive, or at least another, list of key constitutional concepts (e.g., one also including as separate concepts social rights, equality, human dignity, freedom of religion, separation of powers, etc.). Every list would be a different narrative of European social history as told in constitutional concepts. The choice between these concepts is unavoidably political as described above (1.2.2), and expresses personal preferences and interests. But I hope that at the same time they do cover all major areas of contemporary European constitutional theory, and also those issues which are not explicitly covered might be better understood with the help of the areas covered.[8]

The key methodology in the following chapters will be objective teleology. We will try to discover the purpose behind the key concepts, and for that purpose we will analyse the type of social challenge it served to answer at the time of its origin. In light of this purpose, we will provide advice on how (in which sense) to use these concepts. Some of these key concepts are explicitly mentioned in constitutions (thus we will offer an objective teleological interpretation of such provisions, see above 3.6), others can only be abstracted and construed from concrete constitutional provisions and case-law, but also with a view to objective teleological considerations (see above 4.2).

[8] A newly emerging key concept in European constitutional law is 'sustainability' with its environmental, demographic and financial aspects. As it is still *in statu nascendi,* I did not include it in the present volume. For more details see András Jakab, Sustainability in European Constitutional Law (April 11, 2015). Available at SSRN: http://ssrn.com/abstract=2593371.

# 6

# Sovereignty and European integration

I know that prerogative is part of the law, but 'Sovereign Power' is no parliamentary word.[1]

This chapter aims to show first how the internal aspect of the originally radical concept of sovereignty was tamed in different constitutional laws by conceptual compromise strategies.[2] New challenges to the external aspect (i.e., international legal sovereignty) call, however, for new compromises. The chapter then examines whether the compromise strategies applied originally for the internal aspect can be used analogically for the problems of the external aspect posed by European integration, or whether there are other conceptual ways to go.

In order to understand the social function of sovereignty, we must have a look at the original challenges to which its invention gave a response.[3] The concept originated in the sixteenth–seventeenth centuries in Western Europe. The bloody anarchies caused by religious wars,

[1] Edward Coke, Speech on 17.05.1628, in: TC Hansard (ed.), *The Parliamentary History of England, from the Earliest Period to the Year 1803*, vol. 2, London, Hansard 1807, 357.

[2] An early version of this chapter was awarded the George Kassimatis Award (for the best conference paper) at the (quadrennial) VIIth World Congress of Constitutional Law Athens by the International Association of Constitutional Law, 11–15 June 2007, and published as 'Neutralizing the Sovereignty Question: Compromise Strategies in Constitutional Argumentations about the Concept of Sovereignty before European Integration and Since' in the *European Constitutional Law Review* 2 (2006) 375–397. For valuable remarks and insightful criticism, I am grateful to the participants of the Zlatibor Winter School of the University of Kragujevac (Serbia) on 24 February 2005, to the participants of the research seminar at the Max Planck Institute for Comparative Public Law and International Law (Heidelberg) on 6 July 2005, to the participants of the Interdisciplinary Symposium of the University of Aberdeen on 15 February 2006, further to Armin von Bogdandy, Irène Couzigou, Luc Heuschling, Niels Petersen, Pál Sonnevend, Péter Takács, Akos Toth, Neil Walker and Lorenzo Zucca.

[3] The expression *souverain* was also known before the sixteenth century, but it simply meant 'superior'; see Werner Conze e.a., Staat und Souveränität, in: Otto Brunner e.a. (eds.), *Geschichtliche Grundbegriffe*, vol. 6, Stuttgart, Klett-Cotta [1990] 2004, 1–154, especially 99–100.

emerging capitalism's need for predictability of rules and legal certainty, and the conflicts about absolutistic tendencies of monarchs called for a new doctrine ensuring a clear-cut, determinate solution to intrastate power relations. Because of secularisation it could no longer be a theological doctrine.[4] Further due to secularisation, the former divine legitimisation of monarchy was no longer current. So one had to face a new question: 'Why should one follow the law made by the monarch?' And the new answer was: 'because he is sovereign'.[5] By this we have exchanged God and divine natural law for the secularised doctrine of sovereignty.[6] And because of the need for a clear-cut solution, (monarchical) sovereignty – as described by Jean Bodin, the father of the concept, in his *Six livres de la République* (1576), later explicitly by Thomas Hobbes in his *Leviathan* (1651) and implicitly by Samuel von Pufendorf in his *De jure naturae et gentium* (1672) – was conceived to be 'all or nothing', that is, either unlimited or nonexistent. According to this doctrine, in a given territorial entity there is only one single final and unlimited decision-centre that cannot be questioned, neither from inside (internal aspect) nor from outside (external aspect).

In the following centuries, the discussion of the concept of sovereignty was about how to tame this unleashed concept, which was necessary to maintain peace and order in the time of the religious wars, but had itself become one of the major threats to peace and freedom in the new political context. Because, if there is such an absolutistic competence, then you have to possess it; otherwise your enemy will use it against you. Bodin, Hobbes and Pufendorf had invented the big gun, and in subsequent centuries a series of philosophers, politicians and lawyers worked on the problem of where to hide it, so nobody was hurt.

## 6.1 Taming the internal aspect of sovereignty: compromise strategies in national constitutional laws

The question of who possesses this unlimited sovereignty has led to or threatened to lead to bloody conflicts and civil wars in different European

4 We are going to return to the problem of secularisation in the chapter on democracy, see below 11.1.1.

5 On the usage of the concept during the times of sixteenth and seventeenth centuries' religious wars, see Michel Foucault, *'Society Must Be Defended': Lectures at the Collège de France 1975–1976*, New York, Picador 2003, 34–35.

6 On the theological origins of legal concepts, see Carl Schmitt, *Political Theology*, Cambridge, Mass., MIT Press 1985, 36.

countries. In England, the major scene of this long-lasting conflict was the Civil War of 1642–48.[7] The solution was found finally in the compromise formula 'King-in-Parliament' (currently: 'Queen-in-Parliament') by the Glorious Revolution (1688–1689).[8] As Blackstone formulated: 'In all States there is an absolute Supreme Power, to which the Right of Legislation belongs; and which, by the singular Constitution of these Kingdoms, is vested in the King, Lords, and Commons.'[9] Sovereignty (in the English perception: the highest law-making power) was given to the old enemies (King and Parliament) together, to their common custody.[10] We can call it the sharing strategy. 'King-in-Parliament' can make, amend and repeal any laws without restriction, as there is no constitution in the continental European sense. So sovereignty is still perceived as indivisible, unlimited,[11] but no longer as belonging to a single individual.

In France, the theory of Bodin on monarchical sovereignty received a new challenge: popular sovereignty *(souveraineté populaire)* as represented by Rousseau.[12] The unanswered question (besides other factors), whether the monarch or the people were sovereign, contributed to the

[7] Hans G Petersmann, *Die Souveränität des Britischen Parlaments in den Europäischen Gemeinschaften*, Baden-Baden, Nomos 1972, 233–239.

[8] The expression 'Parliamentary Sovereignty' is imprecise, as the highest law-making power does not lie with the Parliament but with 'King-in-Parliament' (by his royal assent); see Theo Langheid, *Souveränität und Verfassungsstaat. The Sovereignty of Parliament*, Köln, Köln Diss. 1984, 328–329 – even if the monarch did not refuse the royal assent to a bill in the last three centuries; see Christopher Hollis, *Parliament and Its Sovereignty*, London, Hollis & Carter 1973, 171. If we define Parliament as tripartite (monarch, House of Commons and House of Lords together), then the expression 'Parliamentary Sovereignty' can be accepted; see HT Dickinson – Michael Lynch, Introduction, in: HT Dickinson – Michael Lynch (eds.), *The Challenge to Westminster: Sovereignty, Devolution and Independence*, East Linton, Tuckwell 2000, 1–11, 1.

[9] William Blackstone, *An Analysis of the Laws of England*, Oxford, Clarendon Press [6]1771, 3. We should not confuse this legal problem ('legal sovereignty') with the question, the will of which organ or body prevails normally in the political practice ('political sovereignty' lying in England with the House of Commons or eventually rather with the electorate); see Albert Venn Dicey, *Introduction to the Study of the Law of the Constitution*, London & New York, Macmillan [10]1959, 73–74.

[10] The law-making by 'King-in-Parliament' is consistent both with the idea that law-making authority belongs to the monarch who chooses to exercise this right only with the consent of his subjects, and with the idea that authority belongs to the whole community; see Jeffrey Goldsworthy, The Development of Parliamentary Sovereignty, in: HT Dickinson – Michael Lynch (n. 8) 12 and 14.

[11] Cf. the failure of Sir Edward Coke to declare void a statute in *Doctor Bonham's* case (1610, 77 Eng. Rep. 638); Jeffrey Goldsworthy, *The Sovereignty of Parliament*, Oxford, Clarendon Press 1999, 111–112 and 122–123.

[12] Jean-Jacques Rousseau, *Du contrat social*, Amsterdam, Rey 1762.

outbreak of the French Revolution (1789). The structure of Rousseau's sovereignty theory was actually at some points very similar to that of Bodin, except that for Rousseau, sovereignty is the exercise of the general will *(volonté générale)* and not of the will of the monarch. It is still indivisible; it has simply a new bearer: the people.

The conflict was solved – as opposed to England – not by conferring sovereignty on monarch and people, but by creating an abstract spiritual subject, the nation, that can safeguard this dangerous weapon.[13] The idea of national sovereignty *(souveraineté nationale)* was born in 1789 in the French Revolution.[14] The invention of this very abstract concept was an attempt to reach a compromise between popular sovereignty and the sovereignty of the monarch, in order (1) to avoid general suffrage (which follows from popular sovereignty) and (2) to avoid monarchical absolutism as well, but (3) at the same time to prevent the partition of the state territory by emphasising its indivisibility.[15] The father of the concept, Sieyès, took part in the drafting both of the Declaration of the Rights of Man and of the Citizen (1789) and of the Constitution of the constitutional monarchy (1791), and his idea was received in both cases.[16] As the nation is not simply the aggregation of its citizens, but is rather a spiritual entity, this concept necessarily implies representative solutions as opposed to the directly democratic popular sovereignty. We will call this solution the *mystifying* strategy.

Today's French constitutional doctrine, though, was reached first with a further compromise: a compromise between the compromise formula of national sovereignty on the one hand, and popular sovereignty on the other hand.[17] Pure popular sovereignty was compromised by extensive

[13] Cf. Michel Troper, *La théorie du droit, le droit, l'État*, Paris, Presses Universitaires de France 2001, 302: 'la nation est distincte du peuple réel; c'est une entité abstraite'.

[14] Emmanuel-Joseph Sieyès, *Qu'est-ce que le Tiers État?* (1789; in English: Emmanuel-Joseph Sieyès, *Political Writings*, ed. Michael Sonenscher, Indianapolis, Hackett 2003, 92–162).

[15] On the origins of the concept of national sovereignty see Guillaume Bacot, *Carré de Malberg et l'origine de la distinction entre souveraineté du peuple et souveraineté nationale*, Paris, Édition du CNRS 1985.

[16] Art. 3 of the Declaration of Human and Citizen's Rights: 'The principle of all sovereignty lies essentially in the Nation. No body, no individual may exercise any authority that does not expressly emanate from it.' Title III Arts. 1 and 2 of France's first written Constitution of 3 September 1791: '(1) Sovereignty is one, and cannot be divided, alienated or extinguished. It belongs to the Nation, and no section of the people, nor any individual, may claim to exercise it. (2) The Nation, from which all powers stem, may only exercise them by delegation.'

[17] Jacques Ziller, Sovereignty in France: Getting Rid of the *Mal de Bodin*, in: Neil Walker (ed.), *Sovereignty in Transition*, Oxford, Hart 2003, 261–277.

abuse of referenda under Napoleon I and Napoleon III; pure national sovereignty was perceived as insufficient from a legitimacy point of view.[18] This 'compromise of compromise' can be found in Art. 3 of the Constitution of the Fifth Republic in the following form: 'National sovereignty belongs to the people. . . .'[19] It unifies the representative national sovereignty and directly democratic, republican popular sovereignty. This path permitted acceptance both of the indivisibility of territory, the inalienability of sovereignty, and the representation by Parliament or Head of State, on the one hand (national sovereignty), and on the other hand universal suffrage, referenda and the republican form (popular sovereignty).

The question still remained, whether this sovereignty had some kind of limits. The taming of sovereignty by accepting its limited nature was achieved by a decision of the Constitutional Council in 1985 on New Caledonia: 'The law once voted . . . is the expression of the general will, but only with due respect for the Constitution.'[20] One of the central ideas of continental European constitutionalism is that the sovereign beast is put in chains in the form of a constitution. Sovereignty can be used only in a specific (constitutional) manner.[21] We can call it the chaining strategy. Unlimited sovereignty has become limited: we have redefined it.

Germany in the nineteenth century went a different way. Sovereignty was not conferred on a spiritual entity like the French 'nation', but rather on an abstract institution possessing legal personality: on the state *(Staatssouveränität)*.[22] Since Hegel this concept was used to neutralise the conflict between monarchical sovereignty and popular sovereignty.[23]

[18] Florence Chaltiel, *La souveraineté de l'État et l'Union européenne, l'exemple français*, Paris, LGDJ 2000, 64–65. The French expression '*souveraineté de l'État*' corresponds to the external aspect, as opposed to the internal aspect, the '*souveraineté dans l'État*'; see Jean Gicquel, *Droit constitutionnel et institutions politiques*, Paris, Montchrestien [22]2008, 60–61.

[19] The very same formula was enacted already in Art. 3 of the 1946 Constitution (Fourth Republic).

[20] Decision 85–197 DC 23 August 1985, see Ziller (n. 17) 268.

[21] There remained, however, some rare exceptions: the Constitutional Council denied any review of amendments of the Constitution (either by the Parliament or by a referendum); see decision 2003–469 DC of 26 March 2003, and the review of any legislation approved in a referendum; see decision 92–313 DC of 23 September 1992 (*Maastricht III*). Or to put it simply: a 'loi votée' has to respect the Constitution only if it is not a constitutional amendment (by Parliament or by referendum) and if it is voted merely by Parliament (i.e., without a referendum).

[22] Michael Stolleis, *Public Law in Germany 1800–1914*, Oxford, Berghahn Books 2001, 343–347.

[23] Hermann Heller, *Die Souveränität*, Berlin - Leipzig, de Gruyter 1927, 59, 70–71.

Both the monarch and the people became mere organs of the state.[24] Let us call it the institutionalising strategy.[25] The concept of sovereignty was neutralised: nobody was able to operationalise this *ultima ratio* in intrastate conflicts, that is, to use it in concrete cases.[26] The big gun was hidden for some decades … until the Weimar Constitution conferred it on the people.[27] The reaction to this was given by the (in)famous constitutional theorist Carl Schmitt. He stated, 'sovereign is he who decides on the state of emergency', that is, the *Reichspräsident* (according to Art. 48 of the then valid Constitution of the Weimar Republic).[28] Sovereignty was again claimed to belong to one single person. And it was possessed by one single person, until the Allies ended the war in 1945. The new German Basic Law in 1949 (re-)enacted the popular sovereignty clause of the Weimar Constitution (*Grundgesetz* Art. 20(2) 'All state authority is derived from the people') but with a strong limitation. A referendum was (and is) not allowed.[29] The meaning of popular sovereignty became in that way just an abstract (emptied) formula about the legitimacy of Parliament(s). Sovereignty was given back to the people, but it became *verboten* for

24 Helmut Quaritsch, *Staat und Souveränität*, Frankfurt aM, Athenaeum 1970, 471–505.

25 This conceptual solution has led also to the current situation in German scholarship in which sovereignty as such is not really a topic, but rather 'statehood' serves as the central concept; see, e.g., Peter Badura, *Staatsrecht*, München, CH Beck $^{5}$2012, 1–9; Theodor Maunz – Reinhold Zippelius, *Deutsches Staatsrecht*, München, CH Beck $^{30}$1998, 1–3; Hartmut Maurer, *Staatsrecht I.*, München, CH Beck $^{6}$2010, 1–6.

26 Instead of the French 'general will' the German doctrine used the 'state will' as being behind the law-making process (*Staatswillenspositivismus*). The question of why the state has legitimacy for law-making, was answered in a very specific way, namely by the 'doctrine of state goals' (*Staatszwecklehre*), i.e., a doctrine explaining why and what a state as such has the immanent right to do in order to achieve specific aspects of the common good. By the emergence of popular sovereignty, the *Staatszwecklehre* had become outdated and useless (see Christoph Möllers, *Staat als Argument*, Tübingen, Mohr Siebeck $^{2}$2011, 192–198), but the state-centred conceptual framework (also in the traditional German genre of *Allgemeine Staatslehre* or 'general theory of the state' such as Karl Doehring, *Allgemeine Staatslehre*, Heidelberg, CF Müller $^{3}$2004) is still very influential in Germany's constitutional doctrine; see especially Josef Isensee, Staat und Verfassung, in: Josef Isensee – Paul Kirchhof (eds.), *Handbuch des Staatsrechts der Bundesrepublik Deutschland, Vol. II.: Verfassungsstaat*, Heidelberg, Müller $^{3}$2004, 3–106. Most constitutional law textbooks still have the title 'state law' (*Staatsrecht*); see, e.g., Ekkehart Stein – Götz Frank, *Staatsrecht*, Tübingen, Mohr Siebeck $^{21}$2010; Ulrich Battis – Christoph Gusy, *Einführung in das Staatsrecht*, Berlin, de Gruyter 2011; Dieter Schmalz, *Staatsrecht*, Baden-Baden, Nomos $^{4}$2000.

27 Art. 1(2): 'State authority derives from the people.'

28 Schmitt (n. 6) 5. For an account on past and present German constitutional topoi of state of emergency and their context see below 11.3.

29 The only exception is a referendum on new boundaries between two *Länder* according to Art. 29 of the *Grundgesetz*.

them to use it directly. It was hidden in a well-guarded (by the *Bundesverfassungsgericht*) bank vault, so the owner cannot jeopardise others and him- or herself by using it.[30] Only elected (chosen) agents, that is, the Parliament, are allowed to use it, and only under surveillance of the *Bundesverfassungsgericht*. We can call it the *(monitored) agent* strategy.

But some even feared that the owner would one day ask for that well-guarded property from the bank and nobody would be able to impede him. So the best way was to expropriate him or her, so we could secure the values of the constitution forever. But who should own the treasure? The answer followed from the goal of the expropriation: if we want to defend the constitution, then we should confer sovereignty on the constitution itself. And so the most abstract, most empty and most counter-intuitive formula was born: the sovereignty of the constitution.[31] The constitution is no longer the chain binding down the sovereign; it has become the sovereign itself. The sovereign was superseded by its own chains. We can call it the *substituting* strategy.

Instead of using the German style of overcomplicating formulas, the Austrian constitutional doctrine simply removed the concept. This was possible as the Constitution did not mention the term at all (as opposed, e.g., to the one in France). This approach can be traced back to Hans Kelsen, the famous Austrian constitutional and international lawyer who, as one of the drafters of the Federal Constitution (B-VG) of 1920, still has enormous influence. Kelsen in his *Reine Rechtslehre* (*Pure Theory of Law*, 1934) tried to evolve a legal theory without sociological, political and moral arguments (i.e., a pure theory) and also to fight the traditional doctrine of sovereignty. In earlier writings, he decidedly criticised the traditional concept of sovereignty, which he felt was based on a jumbled mixture of legal and sociological arguments, that is, a normative inference from facts (with the typical argument that from effective power stems a right to command).[32] Kelsen

[30] Sovereignty seems to be similar to the One Ring of the Lord of the Rings that is too dangerous for anybody to use, that mystifies and corrupts everybody bearing it. No moral stance is stronger than that, no will can resist it; it leads even the best to terrible actions. If you bear it, it is not you who possesses it, but it possesses you. You love it, you call it 'My Precious', and you cannot live without it. It becomes even more important than your life.

[31] Peter Häberle, *Verfassung als öffentlicher Prozeß*, Berlin, Duncker & Humblot 1978, 368, 395. Similar views from the past by Hugo Krabbe, *Lehre der Rechtssouveränität*, Groningen, Wolters 1906, 97; and the German Hugo Preuß, *Gemeinde, Staat und Reich*, Berlin, Springer 1889, 135.

[32] For a critique of the concept of fact-based sovereignty of the Hungarian legal theorist, Felix Somló, *Juristische Grundlehre*, Leipzig, Meiner 1917, 93, 97–98, 102, see Hans Kelsen, *Das Problem der Souveränität und die Theorie des Völkerrechts. Beitrag zu einer*

argued that, if the two types of argumentation were kept distinct, two possible categorisations of sovereignty would remain. First, one could define sovereignty as factual (sociological) sovereignty – though one must then confront the reality that complete independence does not factually exist.[33] In the alternative, if one were to define sovereignty as a legal term, two further definitions emerge. Either it is understood as a catalogue of state competences – which, however, become arbitrary and unjustifiable[34] – or it is simply a characteristic of the legal order. Kelsen advocated the latter. He conceived of sovereignty as a feature of the legal order, namely, as 'non-derivability.'[35] This means that 'sovereignty,' according to him, is a characteristic of a normative system. Thus, accepting both monism and the primacy of international law, which are other tenets of Kelsen's theory, the state (in his perception, the legal order) is not sovereign because it is derived from international law.[36] Only international law is sovereign. As a result of these complicated considerations, the term 'sovereignty' is banned from constitutional considerations.[37] The related problems are solved without this concept; for instance, instead of 'popular sovereignty' one speaks of 'democracy', instead of 'independence' one speaks of the 'international legal situation of Austria', and instead of 'defending sovereignty' rather of 'maintaining the basic principles of the Federal Constitution'. Austria did not go the way of complicated compromise formulas, but rather excluded the concept as such from argumentation. The big gun was not hidden; it was destroyed. We can call it the *disarmament* strategy.[38]

*reinen Rechtslehre*, Tübingen, Mohr 1920, 31. Somló's doctrine was inspired by Austin's theory of sovereignty in *The Province of Jurisprudence Determined*, London, John Murray 1832, see Somló, *ibid.* 32–37, 200–204, 248–291 and 353–359.

33 Kelsen (n. 32) 7.

34 Hans Kelsen, Der Wandel des Souveränitätsbegriffes, *Studi filosofico-giuridici dedicati a Giorgio del Vecchio*, vol. 2, Modena, Società Tipografica Modenese 1931, 1–11, 8–9.

35 Kelsen (n. 32) 10.

36 *Id.*, 13; Hans Kelsen, *Allgemeine Staatslehre*, Berlin, Springer 1925, 103; Hans Kelsen, Les rapports de système entre le droit interne et le droit international public, *Recueil des Cours* 1926, 231–329, 251, 256.

37 Later, though, Kelsen develops an understanding of sovereignty as directness in international law (Hans Kelsen, The Principle of Sovereign Equality of States as a Basis for International Organization, *Yale Law Journal* 53 (1944) 207–220, 208), meaning that a legal order is sovereign when its validity follows directly from international law. In this sense, the state can properly be called sovereign – as opposed to non-sovereign (sub-) states within a federal state. But at that time, Kelsen was already in the United States, and these thoughts were no longer received in Austrian constitutional scholarship.

38 For Kelsen, the grounds of the 'disarmament' were not political, but rather epistemological; see András Jakab, Kelsens Völkerrechtslehre zwischen Erkenntnistheorie und Politik, *Zeitschrift für ausländisches öffentliches Recht und Völkerrecht* 2004, 1045–1057,

In Hungary, for a long time sovereignty did not occur as a problem of constitutional law. Hungarian constitutional scholarship was inoculated against sovereignty by the vaccine named 'the doctrine of the Holy Crown', which was first described at the beginning of the sixteenth century.[39] It was an amalgam of medieval organic state theories and crown theories.[40] According to these, the estates and the king were 'partakers' of the Crown, and the king himself did not have power but only the Holy Crown (i.e., the object exhibited today in the Hungarian Parliament in Budapest), with which he is crowned.[41] The territory of the kingdom was owned by the Holy Crown; the king only had a mandate to exercise power for the Crown. In that form, the concept was already a compromise between estates and monarch. This mystical theory also allowed democratising in the sense that not only the estates but all citizens eventually became 'partakers of the Holy Crown'.[42] This compromise strategy is actually similar to the French mystifying strategy of *souveraineté nationale*: conflicts are conceptually prevented by merging the rivals in a mystical entity.

With the end of the Second World War the kingdom fell, and with the newly established popular republic the sovereignty of the 'working people' appeared in Hungary. In the decades of socialism, there was no need for a constitutional compromise, as dictatorships dislike admitting compromises (even if they sometimes make them) and the Constitution was just a façade anyway. The transformation to the rule of law has filled the doctrine of popular sovereignty with content: referendums became possible.[43] But this competence seemed to jeopardise the constitutional system, when a

1052–1053. This is, however, irrelevant from our point of view, because we are interested here in the practical political role of the concept. To put it in other words, Kelsen destroyed the (Austrian) big gun on technical and not on political grounds. The political consequences are the same, i.e., the neutralising of the concept has been done.

39 Stephanus Werbőczy, *Opus Tripartitum juris consuetudinarii inclyti regni Hungariae*, Wien, 1517.

40 András Gergely – Gábor Máthé (eds.), *The Hungarian State: Thousand Years in Europe*, Budapest, Korona 2000, 24–28.

41 The crown was holy because it was the crown of *Holy* Stephan (1000–1038), the first king of Hungary, who has Christianised the Hungarians. So the crown also objectified the idea of divine legitimacy that survived (despite of secularisation in civil and political life) until the end of the Second World War. The secular doctrine of sovereignty was not commensurable with it.

42 See, e.g., Stephan Csekey, *Die Verfassung Ungarns*, Budapest, Danubia 1944, 208–218.

43 A referendum on details of transformation in 1989 played an important role in the set-up of the new democratic system. Later on, other referenda decided both on NATO and EU accessions of Hungary.

referendum on a constitutional amendment was initiated in 1999 by an extra-parliamentary group. When the judges of the Constitutional Court, in spite of the lack of any explicit base for this approach in the constitution, pulled the brake and unanimously declared unconstitutional any binding referendum on a constitutional amendment on the ground that a referendum is only a subsidiary form of exercise of power beyond the parliamentary principle, they probably thought that the people might vote irresponsibly on the grounds of temporary passions and emotions without weighing consequences.[44] As Géza Kilényi points out, by this decision the referendum became 'mere silver jewellery on the gown of the nation'.[45] Hungary has put the big gun into a glass case, which can be shown proudly, but that should not be used. In fact, Hungary has ended up quite near to the German agent solution.

If we want to systematise the neutralising strategies, then we can differentiate between five different types. The simplest one is the sharing between different bodies (King and Parliament in England). The most used is the creation of a new unreal bearer of sovereignty (to which the claimants might belong), like state (Germany No. 1), nation (France), Crown (Hungary No 1.), or constitution (Germany No. 3). The third type is leaving the sovereignty itself untouched but forbidding the making use of it (Germany No. 2 and Hungary No. 2). The most radical solution is to abolish the concept (Austria). Finally, the typical lawyerly method of redefining the concept was used by the chaining strategy in the form of a constitution (here shown by the example of France).

These five abstract types cover, in my view, all the general strategies conceptually possible – even if the concrete national cases are not the only possible examples of them.

## 6.2 Taming the external aspect: challenges to international legal sovereignty

The idea of absolute sovereignty sketched in the introduction (i.e., in a given territorial entity there is only one final decision centre) became generally accepted in international relations by the Peace of Westphalia (1648).[46] Its

[44] 25/1999. (VII. 7.) AB hat.

[45] Géza Kilényi, A képviseleti és a közvetlen demokrácia viszonya a magyar államszervezetben, *Magyar Közigazgatás* 1999, 673–681, 681.

[46] Christopher Harding – CL Lim, The Significance of Westphalia: An Archaeology of the International Legal Order, in: Christopher Harding (ed.), *Renegotiating Westphalia*, The Hague, Kluwer Law International 1999, 1–23. Or at least later this date was chosen

main principle was non-intervention, applicable also to the Pope, which meant a secularisation in international relations. At that time, it seemed to be the best way to secure peace and stability in international relations—that is, for the same reasons put forth by Bodin, Hobbes and Pufendorf.

This Westphalian paradigm can be characterised as follows.[47] The world consists of, and is divided by, sovereign states which recognise no superior authority;[48] the process of law-making, the settlement of disputes and law enforcement are largely in the hands of individual states.[49] All states are internationally regarded as equal before the law; legal rules do not take account of asymmetries of power.[50] International law is orientated to the establishment of minimal rules of co-existence; the creation of enduring relationships amongst states is an aim, but only to the extent that it allows national political objectives to be met. Responsibility for wrongful cross-border acts is a 'private matter' concerning only those affected; differences amongst states are ultimately settled by force; the principle of effective power holds sway.[51] Virtually no legal fetters exist to curb the resort to force; international legal

as the milestone, even if at that time the doctrine was still counterfactual; see Stéphane Beaulac, *The Power of Language in the Making of International Law*, Leiden, Nijhoff 2004, 71–101.

[47] On the basis of Michael Keating, Sovereignty and Plurinational Democracy, in: Walker (n. 17) 191–208, 194 and David Held, *Democracy and Global Order*, Stanford, California, Stanford University Press 1995, 78.

[48] Emer de Vattel, *Le droit des gens*, Washington, Carnegie Institution of Washington 1916 [London, 1758], 7 states a nation is sovereign 'qui se gouverne elle-même sous quelque forme que ce soit sans dépendance d'aucune étranger' (that governs itself in whatever form but independently from anything foreign).

[49] The self subjection theory of Georg Jellinek, that says a state has international legal obligations only by subjecting itself to these, was founded in these presuppositions, Georg Jellinek, *Die rechtliche Natur der Staatenverträge*, Wien, Hoelder 1880. Alf Ross shows, though, how paradoxical this theory was: 'One either has to take seriously that the state is only limited by its own will; but in that case there will be no real limits, no real international law. Or one will have completely to embrace the restrictions of international law. However, in that case the state will be bound by things beyond its own free will, and will in that case not be "absolutely sovereign"', see Alf Ross, *International Law: An Introduction*, Copenhagen, Nyt Nordisk Forlag 1984, 44 (in Danish), cited by Marlene Wind, *Sovereignty and European Integration: Towards a Post-Hobbesian Order*, Basingstoke, Palgrave 2001, 9. Also the obvious problem, why new states are obliged by old international customary law (and by *jus cogens*), was never solved.

[50] See de Vattel (n. 48) 7: 'A dwarf is as much a man as a giant; a small Republic is no less a sovereign state than the most powerful kingdom.' The formulation is perceived as a sign of individualist philosophy at the inter-state level by Wilhelm G Grewe, *The Epochs of International Law*, Berlin, New York, de Gruyter 2000, 415.

[51] Until the Briand-Kellogg Pact (1928), which later also became customary international law, abolished the *ius ad bellum* in international law.

standards afford minimal protection. The minimisation of impediments to state freedom is the 'collective' priority.

The right definition or test for international legal sovereignty in order to find out whether a territorial entity is sovereign has always been contested. One attempt is to list the sovereign rights (competences), such as (1) the right to have international relations and make treaties, (2) the right to have one's currency, (3) the right to have an army and a police force, (4) non-intervention by other states, and (5) the competence-competence within a state (and its special original form, the *pouvoir constituant*).[52] The question of how to find out which rights are sovereign rights, and which are not, was never answered. So the list might not be exhaustive. Unfortunately, from the perspective of our interest to define the notion, sovereignty as such is not defined in any international treaty either (probably, because an agreement on it would be impossible); the concept of sovereign equality is simply presupposed by Art. 2(1) of the UN Charter: 'The Organization is based on the principle of the sovereign equality of all its Members.' Again unfortunately, the concept of 'sovereign equality' is not as obvious as the drafter of the UN Charter would have us believe. 'Equality' probably means equality in two basic rights: exclusion of any other state, that is, protection of a state's autonomy and independence (impermeability of territory, *par in parem non habet iurisdictionem* [immunity]) and, on the one hand, the state's equal membership in the international community, that is, in the United Nations (with the important infringement on equality in the Security Council), on the other hand.[53] But what could 'sovereignty' mean? By having a look at the *travaux préparatoires*, it becomes clear that 'sovereignty' was meant simply to exclude the legal superiority of any one state over another;[54] that is, sovereignty simply means equality in the enjoyment of the two 'sovereign' rights mentioned above.[55]

But the full acceptance of the first sovereign right – that is, the exclusivity – is not satisfactory in the light of new challenges, especially

[52] For a similar 'listing approach' in contemporaneous literature see Antonio Cassese, *International Law*, Oxford, Oxford University Press [2]2005, 89–90. For a critical view on listing approaches see Michel Troper, The Survival of Sovereignty, in: Hent Kalmo – Quentin Skinner (eds.), *Sovereignty in Fragments*, Cambridge, Cambridge University Press 2010, 132–150, 142.

[53] Bardo Fassbender, Sovereignty and Constitutionalism in International Law, in: Walker (n. 17) 132.

[54] Fassbender (n. 53) 128.

[55] There is a general view ('herrschende Meinung') that sovereign equality is not *jus cogens*, so every state can deviate from it by international treaty; see Fassbender (n. 53) 137.

of globalisation.[56] Its environmental,[57] economic[58] and criminal aspects make clear that we are facing a new kind of state interdependence with cross-border dangers. So it is becoming slowly recognised that for the same reasons for which Bodin and Hobbes invented their concept, that is, for security and stability, the traditional sovereignty concept should be weakened. More cooperation is needed between states, or even subordination. We are facing – to use an expression by Stephan Hobe – a time of open statehood *(offene Staatlichkeit)*.[59]

Another new phenomenon challenging the Westphalian paradigm is that after the demise of the Soviet Union, the Western World can force its morals (human rights, democracy) on the rest of the world.[60] It is leading to derogation of essential parts of sovereignty, such as immunity (Pinochet case) and non-intervention (Yugoslavia). It can be feared that this new approach may lead to wars similar to the religious wars of the sixteenth and seventeenth centuries.[61]

A third new challenge to traditional international legal sovereignty, forming the central part of this chapter, is European integration. With regard to EU Member States, it is no longer plausible to talk about the traditional sovereignty concept, as EU law obviously strongly intervenes in internal state relations of Member States, and as EU law perceives itself as original (not delegated) authority. This was clearly stated by the

[56] Charles W Kegley – Gregory A Raymond, *Exorcising the Ghost of Westphalia – Building World Order in the New Millennium*, Upper Saddle River, NJ, Prentice Hall 2002, 154–175; Maryann K Cusimano (ed.), *Beyond Sovereignty: Issues for a Global Agenda*, Boston, Bedford/St. Martin's 2000.

[57] For a detailed analysis see Cornelis Theunis van der Lugt, *State Sovereignty or Ecological Sovereignty?*, Baden-Baden, Nomos 2000.

[58] David A Smith – Dorothy J Solinger – Steven C Topik (eds.), *States and Sovereignty in the Global Economy*, London, Routledge 1999.

[59] Stephan Hobe, *Der offene Verfassungsstaat zwischen Souveränität und Interdependenz*, Berlin, Duncker & Humblot 1998, 380–443.

[60] Cf. Paul Williams, Fighting For Freetown: British Military Intervention in Sierra Leone, in: Colin McInnes – Nicholas J Wheeler (eds.), *Dimensions of Western Military Intervention*, London, Frank Cass 2002, 140–168; Robert H Jackson, International Community beyond the Cold War, in: Gene M Lyons – Michael Mastanduno (eds.), *Beyond Westphalia?*, Baltimore, Md., Johns Hopkins University Press 1995, 59–83; Mariano Aguirre – José Antonio Sanahuja, Haiti: Demokratie durch Einmischung?, in: Tobias Debiel – Franz Nuscheler (eds.), *Der neue Interventionismus*, Bonn, Dietz 1996, 155–184. An overview of the theoretical problems is given by Luis E Lugo (ed.), *Sovereignty at the Crossroads? Morality and International Politics in the Post-Cold War Era*, Lanham, Rowman Littlefield 1996.

[61] Cf. Jeremy A Rabkin, *The Case for Sovereignty*, Washington, AEI Press 2004, 110–111, 121.

European Court of Justice in *Costa v. ENEL*: 'the law stemming from the treaty, an independent source of law, could not because of its special and original nature, be overridden by domestic legal provisions, however framed, without being deprived of its character as Community law and without the legal basis of the Community itself being called into question'.[62] EU law is directly applicable and prevails over the national legal order, including constitutions (supremacy). This approach presupposes the European Union's sovereignty,[63] even if the Court of Justice drew the consequence rather moderately in *Van Gend en Loos* stating 'the Community constitutes a new legal order' for the benefit of which Member States 'have limited their sovereign rights'.[64] In fact, by accepting supremacy and direct effect, a new sovereign was born.

So we have a serious and explicit legal challenge as regards the sovereignty of EU Member States. The EU does seriously intervene in internal matters of these states; and the statement of non-intervention by outer decision centres is not plausible as regards these countries. These states have obviously not only one final decision centre but two. It is worthwhile having a look at the Member State (constitutional and doctrinal) answers to how they face this new challenge.

## 6.3 Member State answers to (and ignorance of) the constitutional challenge of EU membership

The main British solution for dealing with legal problems of EU membership was section 2(4) European Communities Act 1972: 'any enactment passed or to be passed . . . shall be construed and have effect subject to the foregoing provisions of this section'. The supremacy of EU law is based on it.[65] As EU law empowers both the courts and the executive, the only loser in the new situation is Parliament. So the question is how to deal with it in the light of the traditional British doctrine of parliamentary sovereignty (or more precisely: the sovereignty of 'King and

[62] ECJ 15 June 1964, Case 6/64, *Costa* v. *ENEL*, (1964) ECR 585 para 3. Cf. Hans Peter Ipsen, *Europäisches Gemeinschaftsrecht*, Tübingen, Mohr 1972, 58–62 on the *Gesamtakt* (common act) of the Member States creating a new legal order, not just pooling their competences.

[63] Gráinne de Búrca, Sovereignty and the Supremacy Doctrine of the European Court of Justice, in: Walker (n. 17) 449–460.

[64] ECJ 5 February 1963, Case 26/62, *Van Gend en Loos v. Administratie der Belastingen* (1963) ECR 1 para 3.

[65] Paul Craig – Graínne de Búrca, *EU Law*, Oxford, Oxford University Press $^{3}$2003, 301–312.

Parliament').[66] There are two main traditional approaches for this. The first one (the orthodox approach) argues that supremacy of EU law is based on the will of Parliament and that Parliament retains the right to repeal or amend an Act in a manner inconsistent with Treaty obligations.[67] The second one (the common law approach) argues that the authority of the courts is not derived from Parliament, but original. So the fact that the courts apply EU law instead of British law in case of conflict is not as revolutionary as it seems to be at the first sight, because 'King in Parliament' was never omnicompetent. Sedley has referred to it as a 'bi-polar sovereignty of the Crown in Parliament and the Crown in its courts, to each of which the Crown's ministers are answerable – politically to Parliament, legally to the courts'.[68] Or, in the words of Paul Craig, 'there is no a priori inexorable reason why Parliament, merely because of its very existence, must be regarded as legally omnicompetent.'[69] This common law approach is rather a legacy of the time before modern statehood, but it has something in common with the orthodox view: it is based on the idea of British sovereignty – the two approaches simply confer sovereignty onto (partly) different bodies. The European Union Act 2011 emphatically confirmed this by stating that EU law applies only by virtue of the European Communities Act 1972, that is, it is not applied in the UK as an autonomous legal order. The 2011 Act also prescribes that any amendment of the Treaty on the Functioning of the European Union (TFEU) and the Treaty on European Union (TEU) that transfers areas of power, or competences, is subject to a referendum on that amendment.[70] (In the absence of a legally binding formal Constitution, however, these new passages can all be amended by simple majority in the British Parliament.)[71]

66 Kenneth A Armstrong, United Kingdom – Divided on Sovereignty, in: Walker (n. 17) 327–350.

67 Continuing Dicey's and Austin's tradition today, Jeffrey Goldsworthy, *Parliamentary Sovereignty*, Cambridge, Cambridge University Press 2010. Embedding it into a rather Schmittian conceptual framework, Martin Loughlin, *The Idea of Public Law*, Oxford, Oxford University Press 2004, 33–37, 87, 95.

68 Sir Stephen Sedley, Human Rights: A Twenty First Century Agenda, *Public Law* 1995, 386–401, 386. On the concept of bi-polar sovereignty, see Alison L Young, Parliamentary Sovereignty Re-defined, in: Richard Rawlings – Peter Leyland – Alison Young (eds.), *Sovereignty and the Law*, Oxford, Oxford University Press 2013, 68–88.

69 Paul Craig, Britain in the EU, in: Jeffrey Jowell – Dawn Oliver (eds.), *The Changing Constitution*, Oxford, Oxford University Press [4]2000, 61–88, 79.

70 For details see Paul Craig, The European Union Act 2011: Locks, limits and legality, *Common Market Law Review* 2011, 1915–1944.

71 On further current issues of British parliamentary sovereignty (Human Rights Act 1998, *Jackson*) see below p. 148.

Similarly, the dominant view in French constitutional doctrine sees French sovereignty as still existing despite EU membership.[72] The three Maastricht decisions of the Constitutional Council did not deal directly with Member State sovereignty as endangered by European integration, but presupposed in the argumentations that it still exists.[73] In its *Maastricht II* decision, the Constitutional Council argued that 'constitution-making power is sovereign; it may repeal, modify or complement clauses that have constitutional value in the form it deems appropriate; and thus nothing opposes the introduction of new clauses in the Constitution which derogate from a constitutional rule or principle in the circumstances it refers to; such a derogation may be explicit as well implicit'.[74] So the French constitution-making power was able to allow membership in the EU by an explicit clause. In *Maastricht III* 92–313 DC of 23 September 1992, the Council had been asked by Members of Parliament if the Act, approved by referendum, that allowed for the ratification of the Maastricht Treaty was compatible with the Constitution. The Council found that it lacked any jurisdiction to review any act approved by referendum, since such acts 'constitute the direct expression of national sovereignty' because they 'have been adopted by the French People by referendum'.[75] So, in conclusion, the French answer is that (French) national sovereignty still belongs to the (French) people.[76] The French people can use this sovereignty towards any goal, even for an accession to the EU. At the most, we can talk about a temporary self-limitation of national sovereignty with the possibility remaining of revoking it.

[72] Cf. Olivier Beaud, *La puissance de l'État*, Paris, Presses Universitaires de France 1994, 457–491; Jacques Ziller, Sovereignty in France: Getting Rid of the *Mal de Bodin*, in: Walker (n. 17) 261–277.

[73] In *Maastricht I*, decision 92–308 DC of 9 April 1992, the Council had been asked by the President of the Republic whether the Maastricht Treaty could be ratified without prior amendment of the Constitution (cf. Art. 3 on sovereignty). The answer was no, so Art. 88 was amended for Maastricht ('transfer of necessary competences'). See Chaltiel (n. 18) 164–166 and 176–179.

[74] In *Maastricht II*, decision 92–312 DC of 2 September 1992, the Council was asked by members of Parliament if the Maastricht Treaty was compatible with the Constitution as it had been revised in the meantime. This time, the Council declared the Treaty in conformity with the Constitution.

[75] Paradoxically, due to the wording of Art. 3 of the Constitution, the Council had to quote this power of referendum as the direct expression of *national* sovereignty, whereas it is *de facto* clearly a triumph for *popular* sovereignty. See Ziller (n. 17) 273.

[76] Thus, also, the supremacy of EU law over French constitutional law can be based only on the French Constitution itself; see Jan Herman Reestman, *Conseil Constitutionnel* on the Status of (Secondary) Community Law in the French Internal Order. Decision of 10 June 2004, 2004–496 DC, *European Constitutional Law Review* 1 (2005) 302–317, 316–317.

In Germany, Art. 23 I *Grundgesetz* allows conferral of 'sovereign powers' on the European Union, under the precondition of safeguarding the principles of German constitutional law (democratic, social and federal principles and the rule of law), as well as subsidiarity.[77] The German Federal Constitutional Court, the *Bundesverfassungsgericht*, in a series of decisions (Solange I, Solange II, Maastricht, Banana Market, Lisbon) emphasised that (1) Member States are 'still masters of the Treaties' *(Herren der Verträge)* and (2) the German Federal Constitutional Court has the right to review EU measures (especially on their compatibility with fundamental rights of the *Grundgesetz*), although (3) it will not exercise this right because generally the protection of fundamental rights in the EU is on a high level. These arguments are also based on the continued existence of national sovereignty (or within the German conceptual framework: statehood)[78] in the European Union.[79]

In Austria, as we have already seen above, the concept of sovereignty is not used. The argumentation has, however, a similar structure. The dominant opinion states that, though EU law has supremacy over Austrian law, even over 'simple' constitutional law, the core constitution, that is, the 'basic principles' of the Federal Constitution (that can only be modified according to Art. 44(3) B-VG by a referendum), cannot be derogated from by EU integration (unless a referendum approves it).[80]

[77] 'To realise a unified Europe, Germany participates in the development of the European Union, which is bound to democratic, social, and federal principles and the rule of law as well as the principle of subsidiarity and provides a protection of human rights essentially equivalent to that of this Constitution [*Grundgesetz*]. The Federation can, for this purpose and with consent of the Senate [*Bundesrat*], delegate sovereign powers. . . . '

[78] E.g., Stefan Haack, *Verlust der Staatlichkeit*, Tübingen, Mohr Siebeck 2007 with further references.

[79] A recent decision of the Federal Constitutional Court on the Lisbon Treaty exemplifies the court's EC-*un*friendly adjudication. BVerfG, 2 BvR 2236/04 of June 30, 2009. See Christoph Schönberger, Lisbon in Karlsruhe: Maastricht's Epigones at Sea, *German Law Journal* 10 (2009) 1201–1218. But an even more recent one shows that the Federal Constitutional Court is (wisely) unlikely to go into direct and open conflict with the CJEU, see 2 BvR 2661/06 (6. July 2010, Mangold/Honeywell). For an analysis of the case-law, see Robert Chr. van Ooyen, *Die Staatstheorie des Bundesverfassungsgerichts und Europa*, Baden-Baden, Nomos [4]2011. On the last relevant judgment (2 BvR 1390/12 *et al.*, 12. Sept. 2012), which shows a similar approach, see Mattias Wendel, Judicial Restraint and the Return to Openness: The Decision of the German Federal Constitutional Court on the ESM and the Fiscal Treaty of 12 September 2012, *German Law Journal* 14 (2013) 21–52.

[80] Theo Öhlinger – Harald Eberhard, *Verfassungsrecht*, Wien, Facultas [9]2012, para. 158.

In Hungary, the integration clause of the Basic Law merely speaks about jointly exercising and not about conferring competences.[81] This strange formula seeks to ensure the defence of national sovereignty.[82] This has, however, only a rhetorical importance, as in practice the same will happen as when competences had been conferred. Similarly to other Eastern European Member States, it is often emphasised that sovereignty itself is not affected by EU accession, but only competences.[83] As Anneli Albi points out, this sovereigntist thinking also appears in the texts of constitutions, which are often characterised by a traditional ethno-cultural approach, by a series of provisions about sovereignty and independence and their safeguards, by the ethnically defined nation state and by national self-determination.[84] Constitutions often differentiate between independence and sovereignty: partial delegation of sovereignty is sometimes accepted (internal aspect, competences), but never a derogation of independence (statehood or external sovereignty).[85] These constitutions and their scholarship mostly do not speak the language of post-sovereignty but rather a pre-Soviet language of old-style, ethno-cultural sovereignty.[86] This can be explained by the fact that autonomous control or even statehood has just been (re)established, so the sensitivity of the question is much stronger.[87] In conclusion, these countries stick even more strongly and obviously to the rhetoric of national sovereignty than those in Western Europe.

81 Art. E '(2) In order to participate in the European Union as a Member State, and on the basis of an international treaty, Hungary may, to the extent necessary to exercise the rights and fulfil the obligations set out in the founding treaties, exercise some of its competences deriving from the Fundamental Law jointly with other Member States, through the institutions of the European Union.'

82 On the basis of the former (very similar) Art. 2/A of the 1949/1989 Constitution see László Kecskés, Indító tézisek a Magyar Köztársaság Alkotmánya EU-vonatkozású szabályainak továbbfejlesztéséhez, *Európai Jog* 2004, 3–11, 6.

83 E.g., in the Polish literature Cezary Mik, Sovereignty and European Integration in Poland, in: Walker (n. 17) 367–400, 398, as sovereignty is not mentioned in the text of the empowerment clause of Art. 90 Polish Constitution. It is worth mentioning that this Article is generally about conferring competences on international organisations. A special Europe-clause does not exist in Poland.

84 Anneli Albi, Postmodern versus Retrospective Sovereignty: Two Different Discourses in the EU and the Candidate Countries, in: Walker (n. 17) 401–422 with further references.

85 Anneli Albi, *EU Enlargement and the Constitutions of Central and Eastern Europe*, Cambridge, Cambridge University Press 2005, 122–130.

86 Albi (n. 85) 130–138. For a critique of the sovereigntist case-law of the Hungarian Constitutional Court, see András Sajó, Learning Co-Operative Constitutionalism the Hard Way: The Hungarian Constitutional Court Shying Away from EU Supremacy, *Zeitschrift für Staats- und Europawissenschaften* 2004, 351–371.

87 Cf. Albi (n. 85) 18–36.

### 6.4 Finding a new compromise formula between national sovereignty and European integration

The situation shortly sketched is that dominant views in the Member States' constitutional doctrines ignore the actual challenge of the European Union to national sovereignty and by some kind of self-deception believe that (almost) nothing has changed. Why is this so? Because the question of sovereignty is not a neutral, scientific one. It is a highly politicised concept, a politically highly sensitive area.[88] Nobody wants to see him- or herself giving up sovereignty to another entity (without feeling primarily a member of the latter), because it is linked to identity. 'We are sovereign', and simply the state is sovereign, in which we are living. There is a series of traditional criticisms of it, both for descriptive reasons[89] and for normative (moral) reasons,[90] and some recent ones based on the new internal state structure of multi-centred 'polyarchy',[91] but they all remain ineffective and unconvincing for all those who were touched by the identity spirit of sovereignty. These people would never give up 'Their Precious', either for epistemological reasons, or for moral ones.

But European integration calls at least for a compromise, as has happened on several occasions in the history of sovereignty. As a typical lawyerly task, we are called on to elaborate conceptual solutions that ensure that Members States' sovereignty does not endanger European integration (so that it can no longer be operationalised), but which does not frustrate the Member States by depriving them of their sovereignty.

[88] Hans Lindahl, Sovereignty and Representation in the European Union, in: Walker (n. 17) 87–114.

[89] Cf. Neil Walker, Late Sovereignty in the European Union, in: Walker (n. 17) 3–32, 6–8 on descriptive fallacy (redundancy and incoherence), and the criticism of Kelsen (see above at Austria).

[90] Jacques Maritain, *Man and the State*, Chicago, Chicago University Press 1951, 51–53 argues that sovereignty means *absolutism*, and *accountability* contradicts sovereignty, so we have to give up the concept on moral grounds. For a similar moral conclusion, see Bertrand de Jouvenel, *Souveraineté. Á la recherche du bien politique*, Paris, Génin 1955, 235, 251–252, 266–268, 360–371, who thinks sovereignty means power which is *above the rules*. For an attack in the name of individualism see Harold J Laski, *Studies in the Problem of Sovereignty*, New Haven, Yale University Press 1917, 5, 273.

[91] Horst Dreier, Souveränität, in: Görres-Gesellschaft (ed.), *Staatslexikon*, vol. 4., Freiburg, Herder $^{4}$1988, 1203–1209, 1207–1208 talks (on the trail of Harold Laski, Ernst Forsthoff and Werner Weber) about loss of internal state competences because of polyarchy, party statehood (i.e., when the actual state power lies with different political parties) and the rule of corporations, which is similar to the feudalism (i.e., the time before sovereignty and before modern statehood).

We need an argumentation strategy that satisfies both of these requirements.

So the time has come to look back at whether the compromises applied in Member State constitutional laws as shown above can be used here analogically. The five general strategies sketched at the end of Section 6.1 of the present chapter covering, in my view, all the strategies conceptually possible are (just to recall them) as follows: the sharing strategy, the creation of a new unreal bearer of sovereignty, leaving sovereignty itself untouched but forbidding the use of it, abolishing the concept and, finally, redefining the concept.

The sharing (British) way would be to give sovereignty to those rivals who claim it. In our case it would be a doctrine similar to the United States doctrine of shared (or divided) sovereignty.[92] At the end of the eighteenth century, when the American Union was founded, the United States were conceived as something 'sui generis', just like the European Union today.[93] Shared sovereignty would mean for us that sovereignty is divided between Brussels and the Member States.[94] This doctrine has, however, a dark history. As Donald Livingston points out:[95]

> The debate over the European Union today resembles the debate of 1787–89 between the Federalists and Antifederalists; the latter of which feared that the Constitution would end in a consolidated nationalism, and the former who assured them that such could never happen. One hopes that this will not degenerate into something like the shouting match between southerners who claimed that the Constitution was not a consolidated regime and northern unionists who declared that it was and always had been. But it could. One already hears from the left the claim that the European Union is

92 With references to James Madison and Alexis de Tocqueville, see Jeffrey Goldsworthy, The Debate About Sovereignty in the United States, in: Walker (n. 17) 440–441. For a similar solution in the EU, see Utz Schliesky, *Souveränität und Legitimität von Herrschaftsgewalt. Die Weiterentwicklung von Begriffen der Staatslehre und des Staatsrechts im europäischen Mehrebenensystem*, Tübingen, Mohr Siebeck 2004, 541–542 and 545–546, who proposes the concept 'common sovereignty' (*gemeinsame Souveränität*) of EU and Member States (instead of 'shared sovereignty') in order to preserve the indivisible character of sovereignty.

93 Goldsworthy (n. 92) 424.

94 For a similar view in French literature (i.e., Member State sovereignty has transformed, and some kind of European sovereignty has emerged), see Chaltiel (n. 18) 380–385 and Ziller (n. 17) 277. According to Chaltiel, this European sovereignty is, however, not autonomous, but rather a '*souveraineté collective*' of the Member States and a polyarchy (defined as a political system characterised by a plurality of decision centres) in the sense of Robert Dahl, see *ibid.* 467–469.

95 Donald W Livingston, The Secession Tradition in America, in: David Gordon (ed.), *Secession, State and Liberty*, New Brunswick, NJ, Transaction Publishers 1998, 1–33, 22–23.

> an instrument for achieving human rights and that the powers surrendered to the Union cannot be recalled. This was exactly Lincoln's doctrine. Unless the right of secession is thought through and faced squarely, one can imagine Europe re-enacting the melancholy history of the United States.

The mere doctrine of divided sovereignty without an explicit answer to the question of secession is not a stable compromise formula.[96] We can argue that it is already possible according to the general rules of public international law – so this problem does not seem to be unsolvable. But the major problem is rather that Member State constitutional rhetoric does not want to admit that its Precious is divided with anyone, so we should rather search for another solution.

After the sharing strategy, let us have a look at the strategies creating a new bearer. The French way would be to use a concept like the European nation or spirit bearing the sovereignty together with the people. The problem is to decide whether the people are the European people or the peoples of the Member States. The former (i.e., to base sovereignty partly on a European people) would not be consistent with the national popular sovereignties, and would thus be unacceptable from a Member State point of view. The latter would result in a solution similar to divided sovereignty. The 'European nation or spirit' would mean practically Brussels; the peoples of Member States would mean the national level. As we have noted above, this division of sovereignty is not a viable way.

The first German solution would be some kind of complicated abstract institution bearing sovereignty. Again, we can use US constitutional history to clarify the analogy. One of the conceptual solutions for that sovereignty problem was that sovereignty is vested in three-quarters of the States governments as forming one aggregate body (constitution-amending power).[97] In the European Union, this would mean sovereignty is vested in the whole of the Member States' legislatures as forming one aggregate body (treaty-amending power). The Member States still

[96] On the fact that sovereignty matters were not thought through thoroughly by the Founding Fathers, see Jack N Rakove, American Federalism: Was There an Original Understanding?, in: Mark R Killenbeck (ed.), *The Tenth Amendment and State Sovereignty*, Lanham Maryland, Rowman & Littlefield 2002, 107–129. For a conceptual criticism on 'divided sovereignty', see Bruno de Witte, Sovereignty and European Integration: The Weight of a Legal Tradition, in: Neil Walker (ed.), *Relocating Sovereignty*, Aldershot, Ashgate 2006, 491–520, 518.

[97] John C Hurd, *The Theory of our National Existence*, Boston, Little, Brown and Company 1881, 140, 374; Albert Venn Dicey, *Lectures Introductory to the Study of the Law of the Constitution*, London, Macmillan [2]1886, 135 and Lester Bernhard Orfield, *The Amending of the Federal Constitution*, Ann Arbor, University of Michigan Press 1942, 153–155.

have their sovereignty as members of that aggregate body; they simply exercise it together with the other Member States.[98] As opposed to the idea of shared sovereignty (quasi-British solution, see above), the Union itself would not gain sovereignty in this conception. This doctrine is one possible solution from a Member State point of view (sometimes referred to as 'pooled sovereignty'),[99] but not the only one. It is, however, doubtful whether this is in conformity with the self-perception of Community law as a supreme and autonomous legal order in the Union territory. This is namely a compromise rather amongst the Member State sovereignties and not between Member State sovereignty and European integration. Thus it would not be acceptable from an integrationist point of view.

The third German option would be to confer sovereignty on the Founding Treaties. But this is not only counter-intuitive, but also requires the Member States to give up their sovereignty. So this option stands no chance of success either.

The historical Hungarian solution would be to construe a community (though without the mystical idea of objectifying it in a Crown), the 'partaker' of which is everybody who claims original power. That would mean a jumbled community of 'European people', (British) 'King and Parliament', (French) 'nation and people', (Hungarian and German) 'peoples of member states' and so on bearing the sovereignty. But, as opposed to the idea of shared sovereignty, the partakers do not possess on their own any part of sovereignty; only the community as a whole bears the sovereignty (and it bears it in its entirety).[100] Even if this post-modern-like network idea might be seductive because of the interesting combination of popular sovereignty of different peoples, it would require the Member States to give up their sovereignty. So we have to decline this analogy as well. If, however, we suggest that in this jumbled aggregate body every part (both EU and Member States) retain their own sovereignties (a situation described by Samantha Besson as 'cooperative sovereignty'), then Member States should recognise that they are just one of the

[98] This idea is actually identical to the background theory of the Hungarian Europe-clause, see above note 81.

[99] Ingolf Pernice, Die Europäische Verfassung, *Walter Hallstein-Institut Papers* 12/01. 1–22, 5.

[100] This idea could be backed by the use of mixed agreements concluded jointly by EU and Member States; see Eleftheria Neframi, Mixed Agreements as a Source of European Union Law, in: Enzo Cannizzaro – Paolo Palchetti – Ramses A Wessel (eds.), *International Law as Law of the European Union*, Leiden, Martinus Nijhoff 2012, 325–349.

competing sovereignties even within their own territories.[101] Such a generous self-sacrifice seems rather unlikely either.

The next neutralising strategy to be examined is the 'leaving sovereignty itself untouched but forbidding the use of it' (Germany No. 2 and Hungary No. 2). This would mean that the argument of sovereignty becomes taboo except for mere rhetorical purposes. Member States are still sovereign, the EU might be sovereign (or might not be), but we do not use sovereignty as an argument for the solution of concrete conflicts.[102] Each side has its big gun, but nobody dares to use it, because the consequences are unforeseeable. To use the metaphor by Joseph Weiler we can call it the Cold War strategy.[103] The problem is that we would need a detailed competence regulation accepted by both sides solving all possible conflicts. Unfortunately, we do not have such a regulation: the European Court of Justice and the national constitutional courts are obviously working with partly different competence regulations.[104] So in the taut atmosphere there is a danger that war will break out at any moment; the two sides are not using their guns only because of fear.[105] One would rather wish for a less risky solution.

We can also try the Austrian abolishing (or disarmament) analogy. This means we have to get rid of the concept. This is the way Neil

[101] Samantha Besson, Sovereignty in Conflict, *European Integration online Papers (EIoP)* vol. 8 (2004) N°15, 1–50, 18.

[102] Similar solutions are known in public international law, e.g., by Art. IV of the Antarctic Treaty on the 'freezing' of sovereignty questions and on concentrating rather on concrete problems.

[103] Joseph HH Weiler, The Reformation of European Constitutionalism, *Journal of Common Market Studies* 1997, 97–131, 125 talks about 'cold war with its paradoxical guarantee of co-existence following the infamous MAD logic: Mutual Assured Destruction'. And he continues: 'For [a national constitutional court] ... to declare a Community norm unconstitutional, rather than simply threaten to do so, would be an extremely hazardous move so as to make its usage unlikely.' Such a declaration of unconstitutionality would include always (at least implied) references to national sovereignty.

[104] Josef Isensee, Vorrang des Europarechts und deutsche Verfassungsvorbehalte – offener Dissens, in: Joachim Burmeister (eds.), *Verfassungsstaatlichkeit. Festschrift Klaus Stern*, München, Beck 1997, 1239–1268.

[105] On an irresponsible attempt of the Czech Constitutional Court to launch a conflict (Slovak Pensions XVII case, 31 January 2012, Pl. ÚS 5/12), see Jan Komárek, Playing with Matches: The Czech Constitutional Court Declares a Judgment of the Court of Justice of the EU Ultra Vires, *European Constitutional Law Review* 8 (2012) 323–337. For a different interpretation of the judgment see Attila Vincze, Das tschechische Verfassungsgericht stoppt den EuGH – zum Urteil des tschechischen Verfassungsgerichts Pl. ÚS 5/12 vom 14.2.2012, *Europarecht* 2013/2, 194–204.

MacCormick goes in his *Questioning Sovereignty* (1999).[106] He finds that we have reached the era of post-sovereignty; sovereignty as such is outdated. According to him sovereignty is 'like virginity, something that can be lost by one without another's gaining it . . . ' – and we do not have to be sad about it (just as with losing virginity).[107] He recommends that we rather simply ignore and dismiss sovereignty. So conflicts between EU law and national law are to be decided by international law, without recurring to this concept. The obvious problem with this approach is that it expects national constitutional lawyers to give up the whole idea of national sovereignty. And it will not happen, because the question is beyond rational discussion since it is too politicised and strongly linked to identity.

And finally, we have to explore the possibility of redefinition. One solution could be to define Member State sovereignty in the EU as the right to secession (confirmed lately explicitly by the Treaty of Lisbon, see Art. 50 TEU). This means that Member States are still sovereign, but as long as they play the game called EU, they have to follow its rules. The option of secession is there, but no other way of resistance is lawful, and the supremacy of EU law should be accepted even over national constitutions. Unfortunately, national constitutional courts are not willing to accept this compromise.[108] So we need a more sophisticated solution that does not require explicitly accepting supremacy of EU law over national constitutions.

Exactly for this reason, the path taken by Neil Walker, in his *Late Sovereignty in the European Union* (2003), is very interesting.[109] He argues that we cannot get rid of this concept, because it is in the text of constitutions, and because everybody (lawyers, politicians) is using it. According to him, our task (as legal scholars) is to give a suitable meaning to it. His definition of sovereignty is a 'claim of exclusive supreme power'. In Walker's view this claim has to be (to some extent) effective, so it still

[106] For a similar suggestion in German literature, see Anne Peters, *Elemente einer Theorie der Verfassung Europas*, Berlin, Duncker & Humblot 2001, 148.

[107] Neil MacCormick, *Questioning Sovereignty*, Oxford, Oxford University Press 1999, 126. Similar suggestions with less radicalism by Arnaud Haquet, *Le concept de souveraineté en droit constitutionnel français*, Paris, Presses Universitaires de France 2004, 295–296.

[108] Just from the very newest Member State sovereigntist case-law, see the Judgment of the Polish Constitutional Tribunal of 11 May 2005, K 18/04, on Poland's Membership in the European Union (Accession Treaty); and the Judgement of the German Federal Constitutional Court of 18 July 2005, 2 BvR 2236/04, on the European Arrest Warrant Act.

[109] Walker (n. 89) 3–32.

has an objective component. But we could go even one step further and radicalise Walker's original idea by fully subjectivising this claim.

We could argue as follows. If sovereignty is just a subjective claim, then we have relativised and neutralised it without giving it up, because by introducing this claim-element into the definition, we have changed the 'Ought' concept (e.g., right of supreme law-making) to an 'Is' concept (a body or somebody is just claiming a right). If a body is sovereign, then it does not mean it has the 'exclusive supreme power', it simply thinks it has this power.[110] The question of who has in fact (objectively) that power, should rather not be addressed, as it is too sensitive and it is not necessary for our goal (i.e., to find a compromise formula keeping the idea of national sovereignty and ensuring at the same time that national sovereignty does not endanger European integration). In this way, the sharpness of a possible conflict has been reduced, but still it would be better to prevent conflicts between these 'claims'.

So how could we avoid possible conflicts? The answer is given by the theory of contrapunctual law of Miguel Poiares Maduro.[111] Counterpoint is the musical method of harmonising different melodies: if musicians obey some basic musical rules, then melodies played simultaneously do not have to be the same and still, on the whole, it will result in a musical harmony. According to Maduro, it is not impossible to reach harmony between two contradictory constitutional narratives in a similar way. The two narratives (national sovereignty and European integration) exclude each other mutually, but if we obey some basic rules, then we can avoid conflicts. These rules are (1) recognising the existence of other legal orders and at least the possibility of different viewpoints on the same norms (pluralism), (2) vertical and horizontal discourse amongst courts in order to achieve consistency in the system (i.e., at least considering the point of view of the respective court from the other legal order in the judgements) and (3) universalisablity (i.e., using only arguments that can

110 This conception also allows *parallel claims* (characteristic to our era of 'late sovereignty') without being forced immediately to decide between them. This new parallelism of claims also means we are facing from a political science perspective an era of post-sovereignty. If traditional sovereignty can be characterised by a homogenous demos, state-centrism, centralism, verticality, representation, command and monism, then post-sovereignty is distinguished by consensus on rights, multilevel solutions, decentralisation, horizontality, participation, deliberation, pluralism, directly deliberative polyarchy; see Richard Bellamy, Sovereignty, Post-Sovereignty and Pre-Sovereignty, in: Walker (n. 17) 167–190, 189 and Lindahl (n. 88) 90–92.

111 Miguel Poiares Maduro, Contrapunctual Law: Europe's Constitutional Pluralism in Action, in: Walker (n. 17) 501–537.

also be used by the 'other side'). These are the rules the sovereigns should bear as chains, similarly to the constitutions limiting how to use sovereignty in internal state-relations. Yet, this is a solution only for preventing conflicts, so there is no answer to the question of how to solve conflicts that have already arisen – because following on from the conflicting paradigms such a guaranteed prevention is not possible.

## 6.5 Conclusion as to how to use 'sovereignty' in today's European constitutional discourse

So, how can we solve on a legal level the conflict between European integration and national sovereignty? What should be our answer to the question concerning sovereignty in the EU? My point is exactly that it is a misunderstanding that we should answer the question. The real lawyerly task (as we have seen analogically in different constitutional laws) is to neutralise this question. There are times where straight answers are needed – as in the sixteenth and seventeenth centuries. And there are times where they are not – like now. Or to put it in a more cynical manner: our task is to avoid or to prevent the question, and if someone still poses it, then we should give a 'solution' that does not say anything practical for conflicts. Such a practical recommendation might seem disappointing from a scholarly point of view, but any other (straight) 'solution' would be unacceptable for at least one player of the game (as we have seen above), so it would just *strengthen* the possibility of conflicts outside of a common framework of argumentation that we are just trying to construct. If we do not want to strengthen the possibility of such conflicts, but rather to *prevent* them, then our paradoxical lawyerly task is to construe a legal uncertainty as to the legal outcome of a conflict (by developing complicated conceptual constructs which make virtually impossible the straight use of the sovereignty argument) and to provide practical methods on how to avoid the conflicts, so no one risks the conflict but everyone rather cooperates. Such a compromise strategy is of course useless if a conflict has already broken out. But at that time the final say will lie with the politicians anyway, and not with us, lawyers. *Inter arma silent musae.* If that time comes then we have already failed our task of neutralising the question.

# 7

# The rule of law, fundamental rights and the terrorist challenge in Europe and elsewhere

> There is always an easy solution to every human problem – neat, plausible, and wrong.[1]

In the present chapter, I am going to analyse the discourse about the conflict between the rule of law and the responses to the terrorist challenge in the European discourse (especially German) and elsewhere (especially in the United States).[2] First, I am going to explain how the concept of the rule of law originally served as a response to the social and political challenge of absolutism. In the second, main section of the chapter, I am going to show what kind of implied presuppositions explain disagreements in the recent constitutional debates on terrorism.

In accordance with the methodology of this volume (see above in Chapter 1), I am going to argue on a pragmatic[3] basis that a re-definition (or, rather, loosening our idea) of the rule of law and the protection of fundamental rights is unnecessary, even dangerous, since we might be unable to tackle the original challenge for which the rule of law was developed, namely the limitation of or fight against the arbitrary use of government power. Giving up this idea, especially an integral part of it, the prohibition of torture, would also endanger the identity of Western societies. In exceptional situations, on an *ad hoc* basis, the breach of constitutional requirements might, however, be morally justifiable in order to save lives or the constitution as a whole. But the illegality of

[1] Henry Louis Mencken, The Divine Afflatus, [New York] *Evening Mail*, November 16, 1917, in: *A Mencken Chrestomathy. His Own Selection of His Choicest Writings*, New York, AA Knopf 1949, 443.

[2] The expressions 'rule of law' and *Rechtsstaat* are used as synonymous in this chapter unless otherwise indicated.

[3] Richard A Posner, *The Problematics of Moral and Legal Theory*, Cambridge, Mass., London, Belknap Press of Harvard University Press 1999, 227–228.

these acts has to remain clear. I suggest therefore to keep our traditional definitions of both the rule of law and fundamental rights protection even in times of terrorist threats.[4]

## 7.1 The original challenge to which the response was the rule of law: absolutism

In the previous chapter we have seen that the concept of sovereignty was a secular response to the chaos of religious wars and to the challenges of emerging capitalism (especially its need for predictability of rules and legal certainty). But absolutism and its legal expression, the idea of sovereignty, themselves also became dangerous for the development of society. This (in theory) unlimited power can easily be abused, as tragic historical examples prove. Those societies which found the right response quickly to this new challenge (UK, France, Netherlands, certain German territories) were able to prosper and to use their resources efficiently. Those societies (like Spain, Portugal or Austria) which did not do so were declining (at least as compared to their counterparts), and followed the former countries later. The right response was the idea of the *rule of law*.[5]

The basic tenet behind it was to impede the arbitrary use of power. For this purpose, several (partly overlapping) methods were invented. Montesquieu's distrust of the monarchical executive (and distrust of

[4] Early versions of the present chapter have been presented at the *Societas Iuris Publici Europaei (SIPE)* conference on 'Rule of Law, Freedom and Security in Europe' in Budapest, 4–6 June 2009, at the 2 February 2010 research seminar of the Pompeu Fabra University (Barcelona), at the 2 March 2010 research seminar at the *Centro de Estudios Políticos y Constitucionales* (Madrid) and at the IACL World Congress in Mexico City, 5 December 2010, and an early version was published as 'Breaching Constitutional Law on Moral Grounds in the Fight against Terrorism: Implied Presuppositions and Proposed Solutions in the Discourse on 'the Rule of Law vs. Terrorism', *International Journal of Constitutional Law* 9 (2011) 58–78. For critical remarks I am grateful to the participants of these events, and also to Paul Behrens, John Bell, Mátyás Bódig, Thomas Bustamante, Tamás Győrfi, Pablo de Lora, Marta Simoncini, Péter Takács and Mark Tushnet.

[5] Similar ideas existed also before this time, but they were not central topics of state theory and public debates (only in antiquity, but the time gap is so big that any direct connection would be misleading). 'Rechtsstaat' as an answer by the bourgeoisie to absolutism and sovereignty doctrines; see Edin Šarčević, *Der Rechtsstaat*, Leipzig, Leipziger Universitätsverlag 1996, 47–48. In the Middle Ages, public power was conceived as consequence of immutable divine law. With secularisation, the need emerged to develop a new doctrine limiting public power. One of these (besides natural law theories including *universal* human rights) was the idea of *Rechtsstaat*. See Michael Stolleis, *Geschichte des öffentlichen Rechts in Deutschland*, vol. I, München, Beck 1988, 181–182.

the courts too) led to his theory of the separation of powers.[6] Locke rather concentrated on the independence of judges as protectors of individual freedom (as opposed to the corrupt and anti-reformist French judges, the English courts had always enjoyed greater prestige and trust).[7] In England law was identified with 'misty, murky but ages-old custom', which also limited the King (so legal certainty in today's sense was not part of it).[8] The English perception changed to the sovereign law-maker, but the American did not: 'In truth, the American Revolution, if understood from the development of the concept of rule of law in England and Great Britain should be seen as one of the last – if not the very last – constitutional stands for the old ideal of rule by customary, prescriptive, immutable, fundamental law'.[9] But nowadays the English idea of parliamentary sovereignty (i.e., 'rule of parliamentary statutes') is being softened up slightly by supremacy of EU law applied by judges and by the Human Rights Act 1998, which gives judges the competence to declare (without any further legal consequence) statutes incompatible with the European Convention on Human Rights and Fundamental Freedoms.[10] In US legal discourse, we find fewer references to the 'rule of law': the concept is substituted by the 'Constitution' reflecting the separation of powers and the protection of individual liberties.[11]

The traditional post-revolutionary French approach favoured the legislator and parliamentary statutes over acts of other branches of government (*principe de légalité*), as the generality of statutes excludes arbitrariness *per se.*[12] Carré de Malberg (inspired by the German doctrine) called this construction of the rule of law 'État légal' as opposed to 'État de droit', in

[6] On the much stronger prestige of statutes in France ('expression de la volonté générale') than in England (as a concept of mere legal technique), see Christoph Möllers, *Die drei Gewalten*, Göttingen, Velbrück 2008, 29–30.

[7] Later theorised by Albert Venn Dicey, *Lectures Introductory to the Study of the Law of the Constitution*, London, Macmillan ²1886, 195; and Alexander Hamilton ('the least dangerous branch' in *The Federalist*, No. 78). To the history of the concept of rule of law in the UK, see John Philip Reid, *Rule of Law. The Jurisprudence of Liberty in the Seventeenth and Eighteenth Centuries*, DeKalb, Northern Illinois University Press 2004.

[8] Martin Krygier, The Rule of Law: Legality, Teleology, Sociology, in: Gianluigi Palombella – Neil Walker (eds.), *Relocating the Rule of Law*, Oxford, Hart 2009, 45–69, 53.

[9] Reid (n. 7) 75. [10] On *Jackson* see below p. 148.

[11] Rainer Grote, Rule of Law, Rechtsstaat and État de droit, in: Christian Starck (ed.), *Constitutionalism, Universalism and Democracy – A Comparative Analysis*, Baden-Baden, Nomos 1999, 269–306, 301–302.

[12] Grote (n. 11) 282. For more details on the revolutionary ideal of the *règne de la loi* (which can be translated as 'rule of statutes' and not as 'rule of law'), see Eduardo García de Enterría, *Le lengua de los derechos. La formación del Derecho Público europeo tras la Revolución Francesa*, Madrid, Real Academia Española 1994, 123–170.

which the legislator is also guarded by a special court in order to enforce rights and liberties of the citizen.[13] The Constitutional Council, which was originally created to curtail the legislative competences in the fight between the legislative and the executive branch,[14] first assumed the task desired by Carré de Malberg in 1971 in a famous decision stating that the reference in the preamble of the 1958 Constitution to the 1789 Declaration of the Rights of Man and of the Citizen and to the Preamble of the 1946 Constitution allowed the Constitutional Council to review the constitutionality of statutes on the basic rights mentioned in these documents.[15]

The German concept 'Rechtsstaat' as opposed to 'Despotie' and 'Theokratie' appeared at the beginning of the nineteenth century (especially Theodor Welcker and Robert von Mohl) meaning the guarantee of basic freedoms (including property) and the separation of powers.[16] The latter meant not only the independence of judges, prevalence of statutes over the executive ('Gesetzmäßigkeit der Verwaltung'),[17] but also that statutes contained only general provisions as opposed to the individual decisions by the executive.[18] In the second half of the nineteenth century, the concept of 'Rechtsstaat' was slimmed down to a formal one (Friedrich Julius Stahl, Lorenz von Stein, Otto Mayer).[19] The opposite of 'Rechtsstaat' is no longer the 'Despotie', but rather the 'Polizeistaat' (meaning a state characterised by arbitrary decisions of the executive).[20] The idea of protecting basic rights is still there: in the form of judicial review of the acts by the executive (so not against the

[13] Raymond Carré de Malberg, *Contribution à la théorie générale de l'État*, vol. 1, Paris, Sirey 1920, 490–493.

[14] John Bell, *French Constitutional Law*, Oxford, Clarendon Press 1992, 78–80.

[15] Decision 71-44 DC 16 July 1971. On the latest extension of the competences of the Constitutional Council, see Federico Fabbrini, Kelsen in Paris: France's Constitutional Reform and the Introduction of a Posteriori Constitutional Review of Legislation, *German Law Journal* 9 (2008) 1297–1312.

[16] Ernst-Wolfgang Böckenförde, Rechtsstaat, in: Joachim Ritter – Karlfried Gründer (eds.), *Historisches Wörterbuch der Philosophie*, vol. 8, Darmstadt, Wissenschaftliche Buchgesellschaft 1992, 332–342, 332 with further references.

[17] A consequence of this is the judicial review of administrative acts; see András Patyi, *Közigazgatási bíráskodásunk modelljei*, Budapest, Logod 2012.

[18] Böckenförde (n. 16) 333. The English conception of rule of law did not contain the generality of laws; see Frederic William Maitland, *The Constitutional History of England*, Cambridge, Cambridge University Press 1908, 383.

[19] For opposite directions (Otto Bähr, Otto von Gierke), see Böckenförde (n. 16) 334.

[20] Böckenförde (n. 16) 335. For the contradiction between 'État de police' and 'État de droit' see Carré de Malberg (n. 13) 488–489. For the nineteenth-century German feature of using rule of law as a source of legitimacy (instead of democracy), see Möllers (n. 6) 37.

legislature). Freedom was not pre-legal, but is rather a product of statutes.[21] During Weimar, the concept of 'Rechtsstaat' became a material (or 'thick') one again, but every author had a different notion of it according to his idea of justice.[22] After 1945, the concept of human dignity (as a response to the experiences of the Second World War and the Holocaust) became a central part of the German understanding of 'Rechtsstaat' and this has influenced, in the second half of the twentieth century, several European constitutional cultures accordingly.[23] These legal cultures conceive 'Rechtsstaat' in a thick (or material sense), including also the protection of fundamental rights, but not in the sense of natural law theories but as they are codified in the respective constitutions (and interpreted by their respective constitutional courts).

As we have seen, definitions have changed over time.[24] The only core part which was never questioned remains the limitation of or fight against the arbitrary use of government power,[25] which can be justified both with moral arguments (and linked to this: the symbolic integrative force of the concept for a political community) and with economic efficiency arguments.[26] It definitely requires that enforceable legal rules bind government action ('formal or thin rule of law'), but also in today's dominant approach that fundamental rights limit government action ('substantive or thick rule of law').

21 Gianluigi Palombella, The Rule of Law and Its Core, in: Palombella – Walker (n. 8) 17–42, 19.

22 Böckenförde (n. 16) 335–336.

23 For a more detailed history of the relationship between security and freedom, see Winfried Brugger, *Freiheit und Sicherheit*, Baden-Baden, Nomos 2004, 12–38; and Gert-Joachim Glaeßner, *Sicherheit in Freiheit*, Opladen, Leske & Budrich 2003, 45–76.

24 'Rule of law' is often used in an expanded sense which includes the political ideology of the respective speaker or judge; cf. Joseph Raz, The Rule of Law and Its Virtue, in: *id.*, *The Authority of Law*, Oxford, Oxford University Press 1979, 210–229.

25 In the United States, this abuse means abuse in the interest of particular interests instead of the aggregated interest of all citizens; see Möllers (n. 6) 29–35. In France, the abuse was a danger from the monarchical executive. The legislature in the United States is conceived as representing lobbies or other particular interests, as opposed to France where the legislature is the people's voice. Möllers (n. 6) 32, 35. Rule of law as opposed to arbitrariness, Krygier (n. 8) 45–70. As restriction of government discretion, Brian Z Tamanaha, A Concise Guide to the Rule of Law, in: Palombella – Walker (n. 8) 3–15, 7–8.

26 For an empirical analysis of the effects of rule of law on human development, GDP and government efficiency, see Jan-Erik Lane, *Constitutions and Political Theory*, Manchester, Manchester University Press [2]2011, 87–128 with further references.

## 7.2 A challenge today: terrorism

In the following I am mainly going to analyse the question of how a *security challenge* (namely terrorism) can affect our understanding of the rule of law. The structure of the challenge is the following: (1) A new challenge to the security of our society appears (terrorism). (2) Society tries to tackle the security challenge through new measures. (3) These new measures are sometimes *conflicting* with parts of our traditional understanding of freedoms and the rule of law.[27] So it is not terrorism itself which directly endangers the rule of law (or at least not primarily), but the reaction to it. As the dilemma of how to solve the *conflict* as mentioned in (3) is usually conceptualised as a dilemma between 'security and the rule of law', we now have to clarify the concept of security for later parts of the chapter.

### *7.2.1 The concept of security*

Security can mean 'security from arbitrary state action (especially arrest)' (the expression is used in this sense, for instance, by Art. 5 ECHR or in Austria by the *BVG zum Schutz der persönlichen Freiheit*), but with this definition it would be difficult to differentiate it from the other concept (the rule of law including freedoms), so I refer rather to the concept as 'physical security (especially peace) to be assured by the state' (*Sicherheit als Staatsaufgabe*). Within this latter sense, we can differentiate between five types of approaches: (a) The first views security as a pre-legal purpose of the state or of the political community (*Sicherheit als vorverfassungsrechtlicher allgemeiner Staatszweck*).[28] (b) The second conceives security as a common interest recognised (at least implicitly) by the constitutions or as a purpose of the state prescribed by the constitution (*öffentliches Interesse Sicherheit, Sicherheit als Staatsziel*). (c) The third conceptualises

[27] On the zero sum game between security and liberty in the fight against terrorism, see Rudolf Wassermann, *Terrorismus contra Rechtsstaat*, Darmstadt, Luchterhand 1976, 133; Thomas Groß, Terrorbekämpfung und Grundrechte – Zur Operationalisierung des Verhältnismäßigkeitsgrundsatzes, *Kritische Justiz* 35 (2002) 1–17, especially 10. 'Liberty individualises state competences, security collectivises them', see Christoph Gusy, Gewährleistung von Freiheit und Sicherheit im Lichte unterschiedlicher Staats- und Verfassungsverständnisse, *Veröffentlichungen der Vereinigung der Deutschen Staatsrechtslehrer* 2004, 151–190, 155, 189.

[28] On this tradition by Hobbes and Hegel, see Wolfram Schwetzel, *Freiheit, Sicherheit, Terror*, München, Vahlen 2007, 5–7; Werner Conze, Sicherheit, Schutz, in: Otto Brunner – Werner Conze – Reinhart Koselleck (eds.), *Geschichtliche Grundbegriffe*, vol. 5, Stuttgart, Klett-Cotta 2004, 831–862.

it rather as an *objective* legal duty of the state to protect fundamental rights of its citizens by assuring their security (*grundrechtliche Schutzpflicht des Staates*).[29] (d) The fourth one tries to establish a (derived) *subjective* fundamental right of the citizen to be protected *(Grundrecht auf Sicherheit)*.[30] (e) The fifth one conceives security as also including the way of life to be protected, so eventually the freedoms of the citizens. Sometimes the different approaches are used together (one being derived from another),[31] and sometimes they are just mixed together. The actual difference in the nature of the legal argument is between (a) on the one hand, and (b)–(c)–(d) on the other, as the latter three are based on the constitution. If we weigh security against the freedoms of a(nother) citizen, then security in the sense of (d) seems to be the strongest, (c) weaker and (b) the weakest. The exact result of the balancing always depends on the concrete legal order, so I am not going to go into detail on that issue. Definition (e) is not used in literature, as it would expand the concept of security too far, and so the actual dilemmas (security vs. liberty) would be difficult to show.

In this sense, physical security stands on the one side, and the rule of law (including its material part, the protection of freedoms) on the other. The question in this situation is how we can effectively face the challenge, without running the danger of arbitrary use of power. The problem is

[29] Schwetzel (n. 28) 8–56. Christian Callies, Sicherheit im freiheitlichen Rechtsstaat. Eine verfassungsrechtliche Gratwanderung mit staatstheoretischem Kompass, *Zeitschrift für Rechtspolitik* 2002, 1–7, especially 5–6; Christian Callies, Gewährleistung von Freiheit und Sicherheit im Lichte unterschiedlicher Staats- und Verfassungsverständnisse, *Deutsches Verwaltungsblatt* 118 (2003) 1096–1105, especially 1100–1102. In some documents, it is codified (e.g., Art. 3 Virginia Bill of Rights 1776, preamble French Constitution 1947, preamble Polish Constitution 1997, Art. 6 EU Charter of Fundamental Rights), but mostly only implied or derived. For such documents, see Peter J Tettinger, Freiheit in Sicherheit, in: Landesvereinigung der Arbeitsverbände Nordrhein-Westfalen e.V. und Verband der Metall- und Elektro-Industrie Nordrhein-Westfalen (eds.), *Festschrift für Jochen F. Kirchhoff zum 75. Geburtstag*, Köln, Schmidt 2002, 281–296, 182–184.

[30] Josef Isensee, *Das Grundrecht auf Sicherheit*, Berlin, de Gruyter 1983 includes in his reasoning also (a) and (c). Similarly Gerhard Robbers, *Sicherheit als Menschenrecht*, Baden-Baden, Nomos 1987. According to Frankenberg, Isensee's 'fundamental right to security is a late birth of the fight against the RAF (*Rote Armee Fraktion*) terrorism' in Germany, and it also 'disavows the limiting function of freedoms and mutates the exception into the main rule'. See Günter Frankenberg, Folter, Feindstrafrecht und Sonderpolizeirecht. Anmerkungen zu Phänomenen des Bekämpfungsrechts, in: Gerhard Beestermöller – Hauke Brunkhorst (eds.), *Rückkehr der Folter. Rechtsstaat im Zwielicht?*, München, Beck 2006, 56–68, 57. Pros and contras with further references in the debate: Gusy (n. 27) 168–169.

[31] Markus Möstl, *Die staatliche Garantie für die öffentliche Sicherheit und Ordnung*, Tübingen, Mohr Siebeck 2002, 75–80.

similar to the problems of the state of emergency.[32] Only a few problems will be highlighted here, those which the author of these lines sees as the *theoretically* most interesting dilemmas.

### *7.2.2 The nature of the threat to security*

Terrorism is usually defined as an armed attack (or the threat thereof) on political or religious grounds in order to destabilise a political system or to awaken fear in the population. If the challenge called terrorism is not a serious challenge, then we have certainly no reason to change our understanding of the rule of law. The seriousness of the threat is usually defined by the following five elements.[33] (1) Today's terrorism is not necessarily limited to a small group of persons, but it can rather be considered as being used by a widespread extremist movement, (2) is not limited to geographical areas, (3) due to technical developments its damage can be immense, (4) the usual threat of punishment is useless against it (cf. suicide attacks) and (5) it has a systematic character (as it is directed generally against the Western way of life, not just against certain states or institutions). Even if some of the elements may not be considered as entirely new, the seriousness of the threat cannot be doubted. Thus the question will be whether the answer is appropriate or proportionate.

### *7.2.3 The dilemma*

The dilemma can be conceptualised as a *conflict* between fear of abuse (as expressed legally by the concept of the rule of law) on the one side, and effectiveness (to tackle the security issue indicated above) on the other. Or in other words, the question is: 'How can we effectively handle the challenge, without running the danger of arbitrary use of power?' In the following analysis, only two problems will be highlighted, those which the present author sees as the *theoretically* most interesting dilemmas. Our main goal is to reveal the structure of the discourse and to give a map of argumentation (and to explain certain features of it).

The first problem concerns how the formal rule of law can be questioned in the name of the fight against terrorism, the second an aspect of

[32] For a map of the German debate landscape on the state of emergency see below 11.3.

[33] Stefan Huster – Karsten Rudolph, Vom Rechtsstaat zum Präventionsstaat?, in: Stefan Huster – Karsten Rudolph (eds.), *Vom Rechtsstaat zum Präventionsstaat*, Frankfurt aM, Suhrkamp 2008, 9–22, 14–15 with further references.

the substantive rule of law (also including the protection of fundamental rights), the prohibition of torture.

#### 7.2.3.1 Formal rule of law vs. security: the constitution as a general constraint on the fight against terrorism

The first example where the dilemma can be shown concerns the nature of constitutional norms in the time of fight against terrorism. We have to differentiate between two different aspects of the problem in order to map the discourse: (1) the size or seriousness of the danger (big or just one of the usual ones), and (2) what we primarily protect (our lives and its main institutional guarantor, the state, or rather our freedom and its main guarantor, the constitution). The two objects of protection partly overlap with each other, but the former etatistic approach (in the tradition of Hobbes, Hegel and Schmitt) emphasises rather the protection of lives, whereas the latter constitution-centred approach emphasises rather the protection of our 'way of life'. According to the two times two aspects, we have four main possible positions:

**α. The danger is just one of the usual ones; our primary concern is our life.** In this case (as for now) we do not have to give up anything from our traditional understanding of the rule of law. However, in case this danger increases, we should reconsider our position. As far as I know, nobody currently represents this position explicitly in debates. The reason for this might be that those who prefer not to change anything in our understanding of the rule of law can build stronger arguments in a constitution-centred conceptualisation (as shown right below in point β).

**β. The danger is just one of the usual ones; our primary concern is our way of life.** The classic quote for this position stems from Lord Hoffmann in the Belmarsh case:[34]

> Of course the government has a duty to protect the lives and property of its citizens. But that is a duty which it owes all the time and which it must discharge without destroying our constitutional freedoms.... This is a nation which has been tested in adversity, which has survived physical destruction and catastrophic loss of life. I do not underestimate the ability of fanatical groups of terrorists to kill and destroy, but they do not threaten the life of the nation. Whether we would survive Hitler hung in the balance, but there is no doubt that we shall survive Al-Qaeda. The

[34] Lord Hoffmann in A (FC) and others (FC) (Appellants) v. Secretary of State for the Home Department (Respondent) X (FC) and another (FC) (Appellants) v. Secretary of State for the Home Department (Respondent) (the Belmarsh case) [2004] UKHL 56 para 95–97.

> Spanish people have not said that what happened in Madrid, hideous crime as it was, threatened the life of their nation. Their legendary pride would not allow it. Terrorist violence, serious as it is, does not threaten our institutions of government or our existence as a civil community. . . . The real threat to the life of the nation, in the sense of a people living in accordance with its traditional laws and political values, comes not from terrorism but from laws such as these. That is the true measure of what terrorism may achieve. It is for Parliament to decide whether to give the terrorists such a victory.

It is common in positions α and β that they both consider the danger of terrorism as exaggerated, and accordingly, certain reactions to it too. Consequently, there is no real dilemma where we have to balance the rule of law against security, and those who state such a dilemma simply misunderstand the factual situation. The danger these people see is that under the disguise of the fight against terrorism, the general guarantees of rule of law are losing weight.

**γ. The danger is great; our primary concern is our life and its main institutional guarantor, the state.** According to this position (as represented by Josef Isensee and Otto Depenheuer),[35] the constitution has to be interpreted in order to save our lives and the state. When presenting the security issue, these authors use the above analysed concept of security 'a' (i.e., security as a pre-legal purpose of the state or of the political community), in a way which basically avoids balancing against freedom or the rule of law, as security is their logical basis. According to this position, those who still stick to constitutional restraints, simply misunderstand the legal-conceptual nature of these norms and lose touch with common sense. One of their usual arguments is that the state is based on order and peace, that these are implied presuppositions of the pre-legal state, so also of the *Rechtsstaat*; accordingly, even if there are (constitutional) rules, they do not really matter in the case of a real emergency situation – otherwise our fight against terrorists would be asymmetric, as we would bind ourselves. This position is very German,[36] in other legal cultures the same practical result is reached through reasoning δ2 as described below.

[35] Otto Depenheuer, *Selbstbehauptung des Rechtsstaates*, Paderborn, Schöningh 2007; Josef Isensee, Der Verfassungsstaat als Friedensgarant, *Die politische Meinung* 2004, 66–72, 67. Similarly, Günther Jakobs, Bürgerstrafrecht und Feindstrafrecht, *HRRS-Online Zeitschrift für Höchstrichterliche Rechtsprechung zum Strafrecht* 3 (2004) 88–95.

[36] On the etatistic German public law tradition in more detail, see András Jakab, Two Opposing Paradigms of Continental European Constitutional Thinking: Austria and Germany, *International and Comparative Law Quarterly* 58 (2009) 933–955.

**δ. The danger is great; our primary concerns are our way of life and its main guarantor, the constitution.** This is the most interesting position as this shows the dilemma in its strongest form. Depending on the balancing between security and the rule of law, there are two possible (and existing) sub-positions with contradicting consequences.

**δ1. The danger is great, but we can never give up our freedoms.** This position is not really concerned with practical consequences (*fiat iustitia et pereat mundus* – let justice be done though the world perish); our way of life including our freedoms are considered to be part of our identity.[37] Only the traditional tests on fundamental rights restriction can be applied, there should be especially no political question doctrine used in this matter, and the burden of proof should remain on the state.[38] A key momentum behind this line of reasoning is the fear of arbitrariness and abuse of emergency powers.[39] Another usual *topos* is that once we allow greater restrictions on fundamental rights in the fight against terrorism, they will also become the norm in everyday life, as the line between the two is difficult to draw.[40] Some doubt even the efficiency of curtailing liberty in enhancing security, because an uncontrolled executive might base its decisions on untested (i.e., not cross-examined) witnesses, and also because guilt by association deters crime less likely than a system based on individual responsibility.[41] In situations where our lives could be protected only through a breach of the constitution, our only hope lies in someone who would dare make such a breach and accept the (risk of the) punishment for this.[42] In this

37 Michael Ignatieff, *The Lesser Evil: Political Ethics in an Age of Terror*, Edinburgh, Edinburgh University Press 2004, 144: 'we are fighting a war whose essential prize is preserving the identity of liberal society itself and preventing it from becoming what terrorists believe it to be. Terrorists seek to strip off the mask of law to reveal the nihilist heart of coercion within and we have to show ourselves and populations whose loyalty we seek that the rule of law is not a mask but the true image of our nature.'

38 Marta Simoncini, Risk Regulation Approach to EU Policy against Terrorism in the Light of ECJ / CFI Jurisprudence, *German Law Journal* 10 (2009) 1526–1549, especially 1545, 1549.

39 Under the disguise of 'war on terror', the opposition might be fought; see for examples in Latin America: Glaeßner (n. 23) 236. Or the new measures can be used against traditional criminality (which could be fought through traditional measures, but with a minor limitation of liberties); see Huster – Rudolph (n. 33) 10.

40 Aharon Barak, Human Rights in Times of Terror – A Judicial Point of View, *Legal Studies* 2008, 493–504, especially 494.

41 David Cole – James X Dempsey, *Terrorism and the Constitution*, New York, London, New Press [3]2006, 240–242.

42 For such a position concerning state of emergency in general see András Jakab, German Constitutional Law and Doctrine on State of Emergency – Paradigms and Dilemmas of a Traditional (Continental) Discourse, *German Law Journal* 5 (2006) 453–477, 472, 475.

position, security is defined in the relatively weak senses of 'b' (as a common interest recognised – at least implicitly – by constitutions or as a purpose of the state prescribed by the constitution) or 'c' (as a legal *duty* of the state to protect fundamental rights of its citizens by assuring their security). The German Federal Constitutional Court followed this approach;[43] in the UK, Lord Bingham published a successful monograph in this spirit;[44] amongst academics Oliver Lepsius or Ronald Dworkin should be mentioned.[45] Also the author of these lines belongs to this group.[46]

**δ2. The danger is great, so the constitution is to be interpreted (in a creative new way) in order to save the constitution.** This position emphasises the implied powers as conferred by the constitution on the legislature or the executive to uphold the constitution itself, typically supported by the *bons mots* 'the constitution is not a suicide pact'[47] or 'Silent enim leges inter arma (in battle, indeed, laws are silent)'.[48] In this approach, security is usually conceptualised in a relatively strong sense 'c' (as a legal *duty* of the state to protect the fundamental rights of its citizens by assuring their security) or 'd' (as a – derived – subjective fundamental

[43] The *Luftsicherheitsgesetz* case, see BVerfGE 115, 118–166.

[44] Tom Bingham, *The Rule of Law*, London, Allen Lane 2010, especially 158–159.

[45] Oliver Lepsius, Freiheit, Sicherheit und Terror. Die Rechtslage in Deutschland, *Leviathan* 2004, 64–88; Ronald Dworkin, Terror and the Attack on Civil Liberties, *New York Review of Books* 6 November 2003, 37–41; *id.*, What the Court really said, *New York Review of Books*, 12 August 2004, 26–29. Similarly the International Commission of Jurists, see *Assessing Damage, Urging Action: Report of the Eminent Jurists Panel on Terrorism, Counter-terrorism and Human Rights*, Geneva 2009; further, Richard C Leone – Greg Anrig Jr. (eds.), *The War on Our Freedoms*, New York, Public Affairs 2003; Oren Gross, Chaos and Rules: Should Responses to Violent Crises Always Be Constitutional?, *Yale Law Journal* 112 (2003) 1011–1034. Similarly in an anti-American Marxist terminology, Jean-Claude Paye, *La fin de l'État de droit. Lutte antiterrorist – de l'état d'exception à la dictature*, Paris, La Dispute 2004.

[46] Cf. Jakab (n. 42).

[47] Eric Posner – Adrian Vermeule, *Terror in the Balance: Security, Liberty, and the Courts*, Oxford, Oxford University Press 2007; Richard A Posner, *Not a Suicide Pact: The Constitution in a Time of National Emergency*, Oxford, Oxford University Press 2006; John Yoo, *War by Other Means*, New York, Atlantic Monthly Press 2006; *id.*, *The Powers of War and Peace*, Chicago, London, University of Chicago Press 2005. For an interesting position which is worried only about the separation of powers, but not about fundamental rights, see Benjamin Wittes, *Law and the Long War: The Future of Justice in the Age of Terror*, New York, Penguin Press 2008.

[48] After Cicero, *Pro Milone* (NH Watts transl.), Cambridge, Cambridge University Press $^{5}$1972, 16.

*right* of the citizen to be protected). In a painful choice, this approach accepts that in order to save our free society, we have to make concessions in freedom and the rule of law. In practice, the consequences of this δ2 position are very similar to the approach γ, the difference is only in the conceptualisation: in δ2 we reason with the tacit *implications* of the constitutional text, whereas in γ with something that is a logical *presupposition* of the existence of a constitution.

A special type of these δ2 theories is represented by Bruce Ackerman. He is ready to give up constitutional constraints (mainly concerning *habeas corpus*), but only for a limited time of the state of emergency (in the framework of an 'emergency constitution'). With this position he tries to show himself as a compromise solution between δ1 and δ2,[49] but in fact it is a temporally limited δ2 theory.[50]

The above positions can be shown in Table 7.1 on the next page.

#### 7.2.3.2 Substantive rule of law (freedoms) vs. security: the taboo of torture

Almost all fundamental rights can be affected, especially habeas corpus,[51] fair trial (due process of law), protection of privacy, freedom of religion, equality (Muslim citizens under stronger observation),[52] freedom of movement, right to life, right to human dignity.[53] Due to the lack of

[49] Bruce Ackerman, The Emergency Constitution, *Yale Law Journal* 113 (2003–2004) 1029–1091, 1032–1037 and *Before the Next Attack: Preserving Civil Liberties in an Age of Terrorism*, New Haven, London, Yale University Press 2006, 170. According to him, terrorism is not a 'crime' which could be prosecuted with ordinary measures (i.e., he denies δ1), but it is not a 'war' either which changes all old rules (so he also denies the main strand of δ2). On this issue, see also Bingham (n. 44) 137 with further references.

[50] Against which the usual δ1 objections can be raised, see especially David Cole, The Priority of Morality: The Emergency Constitution's Blind Spot, *Yale Law Journal* 113 (2003–2004) 1753–1800; and Lawrence H Tribe – Patrick O Gudridge, The Anti-Emergency Constitution, *ibid.* 1801–1870. For Ackerman's response, see This Is Not a War, *ibid.* 1871–1907.

[51] Johan Steyn, Guantanamo Bay: The Legal Black Hole, *International and Comparative Law Quarterly* 53 (2004) 1–15.

[52] Or discriminatory immigration policies, see Daniel Moeckli, *Human Rights and Non-Discrimination in the 'War on Terror'*, Oxford, Oxford University Press 2008.

[53] For a comparative overview, see Christian Walter – Silja Vöneky – Volker Röben – Frank Schorkopf (eds.), *Terrorism as a Challenge for National and International Law: Security versus Liberty?*, Berlin, Springer 2004, 49–785; Anna Oehmichen, *Terrorism and Anti-Terror Legislation: The Terrorised Legislator? A Comparison of Counter-Terrorism Legislation and Its Implications on Human Rights in the Legal Systems of the United Kingdom, Spain, Germany and France*, Antwerp, Intersentia 2009. For the German situation specifically, see, e.g., Schwetzel (n. 28) 131–229.

Table 7.1. *Positions on the legal nature of the constitution in the fight against terrorism*

| What do we protect? / How great is the threat/danger? | Our lives and its main institutional guarantor, the state (Hobbes, Hegel, Schmitt, etatistic tradition), so we protect primarily our *lives* | Our freedom and its main guarantor, the constitution (constitution-centred approaches), so we protect primarily our *way of life* |
|---|---|---|
| Not great (just a usual one) | α. *We do not have to give up much from our* Rechtsstaat *right now (but maybe later we do).* In case there is a danger, we could reinterpret the constitution, but as for right now, the terrorist danger is exaggerated. | β. *No reason to give up any part of our rule of law (we are happy not to have the dilemma of δ).* |
| Great | γ. *The state and our lives are in danger [security in the sense of (a)],* we are living in exceptional circumstances, so we have to make concessions as to the rule of law, the constitution is to be interpreted in order to save our lives and the state (efficiency to guarantee security, *salus rei publicae sumprema lex esto*). The state is based on order and peace, these are implied presuppositions of the pre-legal state, as well as the *Rechtsstaat*; even if there are rules, they do not matter, otherwise our fight would be asymmetric, as we would bind ourselves. | δ. *DIFFICULT DILEMMA*<br>δ1. *The danger is great [security is rather conceptualised as (b) or (c)], but* fiat iustitia et pereat mundus; our freedoms and our liberal constitutional order belong to our identity. Key moment: fear of abuse. Only hope: someone will sacrifice himself by breaching the law and accepting the sanctions, in order to save the constitution.<br>δ2. *The danger is great [security is rather conceptualised as (c) or (d)], so* the constitution is to be interpreted in a new creative way in order to save the constitution (implied powers). Key argument: 'The constitution is not a suicide pact.' In order to save our free society, we have to make concessions in freedom and the rule of law. |

time and space, we have to limit our inquiry to one concrete issue, and this will be the question of torture (as a violation of the human rights of the tortured person).

We do not concentrate here on the case-law of different courts on torture, but rather on showing some theoretical dilemmas which can emerge in a legal order, in which torture is absolutely prohibited. Either because (a/1) human dignity cannot be limited and in which (a/2) torture is perceived as a violation of human dignity (such legal orders are, e.g., Germany or Hungary), or because it would contradict privacy or the due process of law (United States).

In public debates, three issues are often mixed up: (1) whether torture is efficient, (2) whether torture can be moral in certain situations and (3) whether torture can be legal in certain situations. I am going to concentrate on the last issue; the first two are only used as means to reveal the legal issue (they will be seen as potential arguments for explaining the legal dilemma).

Unless otherwise indicated, I am going to conceptualise security in its strongest form (i.e., as a – derived – fundamental right), as this will reveal our dilemma in its most difficult form. By torture we mean the following: (1) causing severe pain or threat thereof,[54] (2) by a public official, (3) in order to obtain information, confession or as punishment, or to intimidate other persons.[55] Again, to heighten the dilemma, we will use a 'ticking bomb' scenario, in which a criminal (terrorist) who has hidden a (powerful, even nuclear) bomb in an unknown place is unwilling to give information on

[54] According to Gross, the differentiation between 'torture', on the one hand, and 'cruel, inhuman or degrading treatment', on the other hand, is simply a definitional wizardry. See Oren Gross, The Prohibition on Torture and the Limits of Law, in: Sanford Levinson (ed.), *Torture. A Collection*, Oxford, Oxford University Press 2004, 229–253, 232. Normally, governments communicate it as a success, if they are condemned by an international (quasi-)judicial body 'only' for inhuman treatment, even though it is prohibited as much as torture. For a morbid attempt to restrict the concept of torture only to those cases where the extreme pain is associated with death or organ failure, see the *Bybee Memorandum* quoted by Jeremy Waldron, Torture and Positive Law: Jurisprudence for the White House, *Columbia Law Review* 105 (2005) 1681–1750, 1685. Waldron suggests to concentrate on the intention to break the will of the interrogated person by pain, and not on the severity, see *ibid.* 1703.

[55] Art. 1 *UN Convention Against Torture and Other Cruel, Inhuman or Degrading Treatment or Punishment*, 1465 U.N.T.S. 85, 10 December 1984. For the absolute prohibition (excluding necessity defence), see David Luban, Liberalism, Torture and the Ticking Bomb, in: Karen J Greenberg (ed.), *The Torture Debate in America*, Cambridge, Cambridge University Press 2006, 35–83, 66.

the whereabouts of this ticking bomb.[56] So we do not consider the use of torture during the criminal procedure (this problem would be covered by the doctrine of the fruit of the poisonous tree),[57] but we consider only life-saving torture (*Rettungsfolter*). There are two usual objections against the ticking bomb example: (1) it is unrealistic, and (2) we can never be sure about what the terrorist really knows.[58] A convincing counter-objection to the first one is, however, that ticking bomb scenarios are able to test our conviction whether torture is or should *always* be prohibited.[59] So the issue is not to talk about real-life scenarios, but to question an absolute statement with a hypothetical case unlikely as it may be.[60] Whether the terrorist really knows anything about the bomb is already part of the dilemma, so we will return to it later.

In general, the usual argument for allowing torture would thus be its efficiency in obtaining information, which can then be used to save lives.[61]

[56] For such an example (from a rather moral philosophical perspective than from a legal one), see Michael Levin, The Case for Torture, *Newsweek*, 7 June 1982, who draws the consequences in the following way: 'Torturing the terrorist is unconstitutional? Probably. But millions of lives surely outweigh constitutionality. Torture is barbaric? Mass murder is far more barbaric. Indeed, letting millions of innocents die in defence to one who flaunts his guilt is moral cowardice, an unwillingness to dirty someone's hand. If you caught the terrorist, could you sleep nights knowing that millions die because you couldn't bring yourself to apply the electrodes?'

[57] Verena Murschetz, *Verwertungsverbote bei Zwangsmaßnahmen gegen den Beschuldigten im amerikanischen und österreichischen Strafprozess*, Innsbruck, Verlag Österreich 1999, 36.

[58] Emanuel Gross, Democracy in the War Against Terrorism – The Israeli Experience, *Loyola of Los Angeles Law Review* 35 (2002) 1161–1216, 1170–1171.

[59] Winfried Brugger, May Government Ever Use Torture? Two Responses From German Law, *American Journal of Comparative Law* 48 (2000) 661–678, 671.

[60] But for a real-life ticking bomb example (Daschner case), see Peter Finn, Police Torture Threat Sparks Painful Debate in Germany, *Washington Post*, 8 March 2003, A19; John Hooper, Germans wrestle with rights and wrongs of torture, *The Guardian*, 27 February 2003, 18. Deputy police chief Wolfgang Daschner was convicted by the Frankfurt Local Court for threatening with torture a criminal (Magnus Gäfgen) in order to save the life of an eleven-year-old boy who had been abducted (Daschner case, LG Frankfurt 5/27 KLs 7570 Js 203814/03 (4/04)). The threat was successful as to the location of the abducted person, but his life could not be saved. As a contrast in a very similar US case, the court found such police behaviour legally acceptable; see *Leon v. Wainwright*, 734 F.2d 770 11th Circuit 1984. This is a unique case, however, also in US legal history.

[61] Whether it is effective or not, is outside of the scope of this chapter. In case it is not, then there is no dilemma at all. So in the following (for the sake of the dilemma) we will presuppose that it is effective. For an opposing argument see John H Langbein, The Legal History of Torture, in: Levinson (n. 54) 93–103.

The usual arguments against it are:[62] (1) it makes police lazy and arrogant, and it can brutalise them; (2) it produces false information;[63] (3) it is likely to be used against political enemies or social outcast (prejudices confirmed); (4) it makes the state intimidating, and it lowers the tone of society; (5) incites disorder; (6) once done, mistakes cannot be corrected;[64] (7) is is impossible to find the right procedural guarantees;[65] (8) it is a slippery slope (e.g., the family members of the terrorist can also be tortured?);[66] and (9) it is a taboo. The last one means that it cannot be debated or doubted, it is forbidden to do so, it belongs to our identity,[67] and it is absolute (so there are no exceptions, and it is not based on instrumental rationality in a Weberian sense).[68] In this sense, torture is clearly a taboo in Germany, Austria and Hungary, and most European countries, slightly less in the United States (but it is also unaccepted there under the scope of the Constitution). This taboo, however, is being broken nowadays with reference to terrorism (the taboo-breakers are usually stigmatised, as it normally happens with taboo-breakers).

Four different questions should be differentiated when analysing the debate: (A) whether it is allowed constitutionally (in the respective national legal order); (B) whether it is allowed on a statutory level (in the respective national legal order); (C) whether it *should* be allowed by statutes; and (D) whether it is acceptable morally (in exceptional circumstances). If we test the participants of the debate with these four questions,[69] then we find five typical positions:

**I. Total ban forever.** This position is the traditional (and probably still majority) one.[70] It answers all of the questions with a clear 'No'. So,

[62] For most of the list, see Richard A Posner, *The Problematics of Moral and Legal Theory*, Cambridge, Mass., London, Belknap Press of Harvard University Press 105.

[63] Jeannine Bell, 'Behind this Mortal Bone': The (In)Effectiveness of Torture, *Indiana Law Journal* 83 (2008) 339–361.

[64] Marie-Luisa Frick, *Das Folterverbot im Rechtsstaat. Ethische Grundlagen und aktuelle Diskussion*, Saarbrücken, VDM 2007, 64.

[65] Cf. Frick (n. 64) 64. [66] Frick (n. 64) 65.

[67] With other identity elements like religion (secularisation) or nation (globalisation, supranational integration) losing ground, constitutional values gain in relevance, as the self-definition of communities tends to include these.

[68] Ralf Poscher, Menschenwürde als Tabu. Die verdeckte Rationalität eines absoluten Rechtsverbots der Folter, in: Beestermöller – Brunkhorst (n. 30) 75–87, 80–81.

[69] It is not always easy to categorise the authors as some of them do not answer all the four questions explicitly, so we have to guess what they imply in their respective reasoning.

[70] E.g., Waldron (n. 54); Ignatieff (n. 37) 137; Aufruf zur Verteidigung des Folterverbotes, 23. Mai 2005; Ernst Wolfgang Böckenförde, Die Würde des Menschen war unantastbar, *Frankfurter Allgemeine Zeitung*, 3 September 2003, 33; Florian Lamprecht, *Darf der Staat foltern um Leben zu retten?*, Paderborn, Mentis-Verlag 2009; Mathias Hong, Das

according to this position, torture is absolutely prohibited both by the constitution and statutes, it should also remain like this, and torture is also to be rejected morally in all circumstances.[71] This absolute prohibition is considered to be a cultural achievement, which belongs to the identity of Western civilised nations.[72] We have 'to fight with one hand tied behind our back' because 'only then will our society truly show that we maintain the upper hand in the fight against terrorism'.[73] Or in emotionally stronger words: 'Any polity that endorses torture has incorporated into its DNA a totalitarian mutation.'[74] Even terrorists (as human beings) deserve the protection of their dignity.[75] Any taboo-breaking attempt should be stigmatised, and at the end of the slippery slope the frightening doom of liberal democracies is waiting.

Beyond the identity or value issue, some authors also doubt the long-term usefulness of torture. Whereas there is little doubt that in a concrete case torture can deliver useful (though never entirely reliable) information about future terror attacks, its use alienates the local population and results in an even greater loss of civil cooperation (i.e., greater difficulty in obtaining intelligence from locals).[76] In addition, the ticking bomb

grundgesetzliche Folterverbot und der Menschenwürdegehalt der Grundrechte – eine verfassungsjuristische Betrachtung, in: Beestermöller – Brunkhorst (n. 30) 24–35; Klaus Günther, Darf der Staat foltern, um Menschenleben zu retten?, *ibid.* 101–108; Heiner Bielefeldt, Die Absolutheit des Folterverbots. Über die Unabwägbarkeit der Menschenwürde, *ibid.* 109–114; Gerhard Beestmöller, Folter – Daumenschrauben an der Würde des Menschen. Zur Ausnahmelosigkeit eines Absoluten Verbotes, *ibid.* 115–129; Felix Hanschmann, Kalkulation des Unverfügbaren; Das Folterverbot in der Neu-Kommentierung von Art. 1 Abs. 1 GG im Maunz-Dürig, *ibid.* 130–141; Laurel L Fletcher – Eric Stover, *Guantánamo and Its Aftermath: U.S. Detention and Interrogation Practices and Their Impact on Former Detainees*, Berkeley, University of California Press 2008.

71 Jan Philipp Reemtsma, *Folter im Rechtsstaat?*, Hamburg, ]Hamburger Edition 2005, 125: 'Torture contradicts the rule of law, as it attacks . . . the legal personality of a citizen or, in the extreme case, even destroys him or her as an autonomous individual.'

72 Hartmut Brenneisen, Grenzlinie Folter, in: Heribert Ostendorf (ed.), *Folter. Praxis, Verbot, Verantwortlichkeit*, Münster, LIT Verlag 2005, 53–80, 79–80.

73 By Aharon Barak, HCJ 5100/94, Public Committee Against Torture in Israel v. Government of Israel, Tak-El 458 (3) 99, para 39. In a former passage (para 38) of the judgment, the court allowed, however, in a cryptic (and in the light of its reasoning rather surprising) manner the necessity defence – probably to avoid any accusation for the future that the cause of any terrorist attack would have been the court's prohibition of torture.

74 Andrew Sullivan, The Abolition of Torture, in: Levinson (n. 54) 317–327, 320.

75 *Chahal v. United Kingdom* (Application no. 22414/93), Judgment of 15 November 1996; (1997) 23 EHRR 413, para 80. For a similar logic, see Fionnuala Ni Aoláin, Truth Telling, Accountability and the Right to Life, *European Human Rights Law Review* 5 (2002) 572–590.

76 Sullivan (n. 74) 325–326; Darius Rejali, *Torture and Democracy*, Princeton, Oxford, Princeton University Press 2007, 459–460.

situation (especially its last assumption according to which we certainly know of a person that he or she knows where the bomb is located) is often blamed as an almost impossible scenario, on the basis of which we should not construct rules. Even during the Inquisition there were also strict rules about proportionality and procedural restraints, which indeed made it to a degree more humane than contemporary secular (state-run) criminal procedures; but the Inquisition still became, and with good grounds, almost a synonym for cruelty, abuse and torture.[77]

**II. Tragic choice.** This position basically gives up solving the problem. While recognising that it is prohibited both by the constitution and statutes, it finds the question of whether we should introduce it legally, and whether as *life-saving* torture it would be acceptable, as unanswerable. The most well-known representative of this approach is Niklas Luhmann.[78]

**III. Heroes needed.** This position maintains that torture is prohibited both by the constitution and statutes, and that this legal situation should not be changed (because of the above-mentioned identity function). It accepts, however, that in certain situations (namely when it is necessary to save innocent lives) it is morally acceptable, or even required.[79] It means that there has to be someone who – by a heroic self-sacrificial act – accepts the (risk of) punishment by law in order to save (by obtaining information through torture) the lives of innocent people. These heroes either have to accept the punishment (with a Socratic gesture, to uphold the legal order and the taboos of the political community), or they simply should hope for mercy by the respective head of state. The heroic element lies in bearing the risk, as she or he has strict (objective) liability in the question: if, for example, we actually find no ticking bomb at all, then she or he has to go to prison; but if, with the help of the information acquired via torture, we find the bomb and we manage to defuse it, then she or he might be granted mercy.

**IV. We could/should introduce it.** This position also views the current legal situation as prohibiting torture, but it differs from the former one in

77 Langbein (n. 61) 93–103.

78 Niklas Luhmann, *Gibt es in unserer Gesellschaft noch unverzichtbare Normen?*, Heidelberg, Müller 1993, 2.

79 Poscher (n. 68) 75–87; Hauke Brunkhorst, Folter, Würde und repressive Liberalismus, in: Beestermöller – Brunkhorst (n. 30) 88–100; John McCain, Torture's Terrible Toll, *Newsweek*, 21 November 2005; Slavoj Žižek, Der Körper des Feindes, *Die Zeit*, 6 December 2001; Sanford H Kadish, Torture, the State, and the Individual, *Israel Law Review* 23 (1989) 345–356; Gross (n. 54) 229–253, especially 231; Elaine Scarry, Five Errors in the Reasoning of Alan Dershowitz, in: Levinson (n. 54) 281–290, especially 283; Richard A Posner, Torture, Terrorism, and Interrogation, *ibid.* 291–298, especially 298.

two points: Here the prohibition is only on a statutory level (so there is no constitutional prohibition),[80] and it also proposes or at least allows for the introduction of the exceptional possibility of life-saving torture (with precise procedural safeguards).[81] A possible additional argument is here, that in practice it is happening anyway, so at least we should cover it by (transparent) legal controls, for instance, by a 'torture warrant' issued by judges.[82]

**V. It is already allowed (or even obligatory).**[83] This position is the real taboo-breaking one: it states that life-saving torture is already allowed (as the protection of life is more valuable than the protection of dignity, because life is a logical precondition of human dignity).[84] Sometimes the ticking bomb scenarios are modified including a bomb which causes a painful death by torture, so we should torture only one terrorist to save maybe millions of people from death by torture. Criminal lawyers usually conceptualise the problem as the 'defence of others',[85] whereas constitutional lawyers argue with concurring fundamental rights (either the right to life, or in the modified ticking bomb scenario with the right to human dignity of those threatened with death by torture).[86] If there is an explicit or implicit general prohibition of torture in the respective legal order, then its scope should be interpreted in a restrictive way (*teleologische Reduktion*), so allowing for the narrow

80 Dignity is no longer untouchable, but can be balanced against other constitutional principles (like the protection of dignity of others), see Matthias Herdegen, Art. 1 Abs. 1, in: Theodor Maunz – Günter Dürig (eds.), *Grundgesetz. Kommentar* (München, Beck, loose-leaf edition since 1958, state of August 2005) para 43, 45, 90.

81 Frick (n. 64) 113–114; Alan M Dershowitz, *Why Terrorism Works – Understanding the Threat, Responding to the Challenge*, New Haven, London, Yale University Press 2002; Charles Krauthammer, The Truth about Torture, in: Levinson (n. 54) 307–316, 313.

82 Alan M Dershowitz, Tortured Reasoning, in: Levinson (n. 54) 266.

83 The radical position of an obligation to torture is represented by Winfried Brugger, Vom unbedingten Verbot der Folter zum bedingten Recht auf Folter?, *JuristenZeitung* 2000, 165–173. For the US position (incl. official documents by the Bush administration) on softening up the prohibition of torture, see Greenberg (n. 55).

84 Christian Starck, Art. 1 Abs. 1, in: Hermann von Mangoldt – Friedrich Klein – Christian Starck (eds.), *Kommentar zum Grundgesetz*, München, Vahlen $^{6}$2010, 61–62.

85 Volker Erb, Folterverbot und Notwehrrecht, in: Peter Nitschke (ed.), *Rettungsfolter im modernen Rechtsstaat*, Bochum, Kamp 2005, 149–167 referring to 'Notwehr' or 'Nothilfe'; Wolfgang Schild, Folter einst und jetzt, *ibid.* 69–93 to 'rechtfertigender Notstand'. The usual counter-argument is that the 'defence of others' or 'necessity' can be applied only if it is 'an ad hoc endeavour, in reaction to an event' or an 'improvisation given the unpredictable character of the events', which is not the case in the ticking bomb scenarios; see HCJ 5100/94, Public Committee Against Torture in Israel v. Government of Israel, Tak-El 458 (3) 99, para 36.

86 On the dignity vs. dignity problem, see Fabian Wittreck, Menschenwürde und Folterverbot, *Die öffentliche Verwaltung* 2003, 873–882 with further references.

exception of life-saving torture.[87] Torture is considered by these authors as a necessary evil to avoid an even greater evil. According to Zippelius and Würtenberger, torture can never be an obligation of any policeman, but if she or he wants to save an innocent person from death by torture, then torturing the perpetrator might be justified. Whether the policeman will actually do that, should be left to his or her conscience.[88]

Before we move on to draw consequences from the above described landscape of the debate, it is useful to show the different positions in Table 7.2.

It was not possible to use the former Table 7.1 to map the debate, as (1) a few of the authors in the torture debate do not make clear whether they base their reasoning on the pre-legal duty of the state to protect life or on an implied constitutional duty; and (2) the actually interesting differences (which go beyond the simplistic 'yes' or 'no' concerning torture) do not lie at the frontiers between the above Greek letters categories (but *within* the whole area of γ, δ1 and δ2, and the front lines are not simply within each of them, but these partly also cross them). We can still point out the tendency that positions I, II and III are usually held by those sympathetic towards the δ1 approach, whereas positions IV and V are preferred by those who use the γ or the δ2 approach. A stronger correlation between the respective positions of the two templates is impossible to state.

The two extremes in the template are No. I with four cases of no (most traditional) and No. V with four yeses (most radical). There could be many (precisely $2^4-2=14$) intermediate combinations, but we actually have only Nos. III and IV as real combinations (No. II abandons solving the problem, so it is outside of the counting). Therefore, the interesting question at this point is, why these intermediate positions are missing from the landscape, that is, why they do not exist (in countries where the traditional majority position in law is the total prohibition). The missing positions are the following:

**1. Constitutionally prohibited (A no), but on a statutory level allowed (B yes).** It is missing because (a) if you want to soften up the prohibition of

[87] Winfried Brugger, Darf der Staat ausnahmweise foltern?, *Der Staat* 35 (1996) 67–97, especially 84; Brugger (n. 83), especially 169. According to Brugger (n. 59) 671, 673, this scope-narrowing-interpretation can be applied also to the international law prohibitions of torture.

[88] Reinhold Zippelius – Thomas Würtenberger, *Deutsches Staatsrecht*, München, Beck [31]2005, 209. It remains unclear what should happen according to them, if after the torture we find out that the policeman was wrong and the person tortured in custody actually does not have anything to do with the person to be saved.

Table 7.2. *Positions on the acceptability of life-saving torture*

| Is life-saving torture (*Rettungsfolter*) allowed? / Name of the position and representatives | A. Is it allowed on a constitutional level (in the respective national legal order)? (*de constitutione lata*) | B. Is it allowed on a statutory level (in the respective national legal order)? (*de lege lata*) | C. Should we change the statutes? (*de lege ferenda*) | D. Is it allowed morally (in exceptional circumstances)? |
|---|---|---|---|---|
| I. Total ban forever (Aufruf zur Verteidigung des Folterverbotes, 23. Mai 2005, Florian Lamprecht, Michael Ignatieff, Jeremy Waldron) | NO, the constitution prohibits it (or even an *Ewigkeitsklausel*). | NO, statutes also prohibit it (either explicitly or because they do not give an empowerment to torture). | NO, we should keep it illegal, it is our cultural achievement, it belongs to our identity. | NO, it is never allowed morally. |
| II. Tragic choice (concentrated on C and D) (Niklas Luhmann) | NO. | NO. | ? (it is impossible to give an answer) | ? (it is impossible to give an answer) |
| III. Heroes needed (Ralf Poscher, Hauke Brunkhorst; John McCain, Slavoj Žižek, Sanford H Kadish, Oren Gross, Richard A Posner, Elaine Scarry) | NO, it would be unconstitutional. | NO, it is also prohibited by statutes. | NO, we should keep it illegal (as to change it would break a taboo), but let us hope that there will be someone who ventures the breach of law if it is really necessary and accepts the risk of punishment. | YES, in exceptional circumstances it is morally allowed. |

| | | | | |
|---|---|---|---|---|
| IV. We could/should introduce it (Marie-Luisa Frick, Alan Dershowitz, Charles Krauthammer) | YES, constitutionally it would be allowed (in exceptional circumstances). | NO, statutory prohibitions. | YES, the statutory prohibition should cease, and a detailed procedure should be introduced. | YES, in exceptional circumstances it is morally allowed. |
| V. It is already allowed (or even obligatory in certain situations) (Winfried Brugger, Volker Erb, Wolfgang Schild, Christian Starck) | YES, the constitution allows it (variations: life *vs.* dignity; dignity *vs.* dignity). | YES, there is no clear statutory prohibition (defence of others, or *teleologische Reduktion*). | YES, but a more detailed statutory procedure would be useful and it would make things clearer. | YES, in exceptional circumstances it is morally allowed. |

torture, then logically the first step is to set aside constitutional constraints (first you have to do this, as the other way around it does not work legally); (b) it is also easier to state that it is constitutionally allowed (as it is more abstract, there is more possibility for creative reasoning). So a position with 'A no, but B yes' would be logically problematic.

**2. Constitutionally prohibited (A no), but we should introduce it (C yes).** The *de lege ferenda* positions (C) cannot be fully separated from A: a 'yes' on the *de lege ferenda* question (as I formulated it only as changing statutes – in the debates too, it is formulated like this) is only possible if it is constitutionally allowed. So to say a 'yes' to C, but to say no to A would be logically problematic. The *de lege ferenda* question is formulated in the debates only as statute changing, because changing the constitution (especially if there is an *Ewigkeitsklausel*) is practically difficult, and because instead of formal change a reinterpretation can have the same effect.

**3. Allowed on statutory level (B yes), and we should introduce it (C yes).** This position would not make much sense: if it is already allowed by statute, then we cannot introduce it anymore.

**4. Constitutionally it is allowed (A yes), statutory prohibition (B no), but we should introduce it (C yes).** This position is missing because why would you argue for a (debatable) constitutional possibility if you do not want to make use of it in your reasoning? If someone does it, than she or he could only be stigmatised by group No. I (they stigmatise namely Nos. IV and V) without actually giving any useful contribution to the discussion. So such a position would be logically possible, but practically useless.

**5. It is morally unacceptable (D no), but there is a variation in A–B–C (i.e., at least one of them is yes).** It is missing because the question is emotionally and ideologically so heavily burdened (identity, taboos), that a clear 'no' in D will make us say, that A–B–C are also clear 'noes', even if they are not. A position 'no' in D, but 'yes' in some of the other questions would contradict the nature of interpretation which contains the more personal value judgements, the more abstract the legal question is. A 'yes' in D does not mean automatically a 'yes' in all the other parameters, though, as some of the 'yeses' are more radical than the others. A 'yes' in D shows only the possibility of a change of the traditional *four 'noes'*, but not the exact position.

**6. It is allowed both on a constitutional and statutory level (A and B yes), and there is no need for new legislation (C no).** This position is missing because even the promoters of life-saving torture agree that because of the danger of abuse detailed statutory rules should be introduced.

The personal preference of the present author is for position III ('Heroes needed'), for the above-mentioned reasons: the identity elements of the prohibition and the dangers of abuse are so strong that a legal authorisation seems to be unacceptable. But in certain situations, people are needed who are willing to sacrifice themselves (by accepting the punishment) for the values (and taboos) of a liberal society. We usually accept that law and morality differ in a dictatorship, but we are unwilling to accept the same for liberal democracies. And we are right to do so . . . mostly. In a dictatorship the separation (or even contradiction) of law and morality is a structural feature, whereas in a liberal democracy it is a condemnable exception. These exceptions should be minimised, but in this very concrete situation of life-saving torture we cannot eliminate the contradiction without paying an even greater price for it.

## 7.3 Old challenges vs. new challenges: rejecting the redefinition of the 'rule of law'

We have seen that the questions in the fight against terrorism cannot be answered with a simplistic 'yes' or 'no', the possible arguments and counter-arguments require a much more structured and sophisticated position whichever solution we go for. I have argued that the terrorist challenge does not justify a new paradigm of the rule of law and that we should stick to our old legal concepts in this respect. We should not consider the terrorist challenge as reason to overrule constitutional constraints in general, and we should stick to the absolute legal prohibition of torture. The reasons for that are twofold: danger of abuse and (especially concerning torture) the identity role of the prohibition of torture in modern Western societies,[89] amongst which the former weighs more. In other words, my approach was rather pragmatic (or utilitarian), even though my legal results are near to deontological (or absolutist) point of views.[90] The difference is that while I propose

[89] The argument about the identity element of the prohibition of torture would be stronger, if we had empirical sociological data about the identity of several Western countries' population rejecting the formal legalisation of torture. The nearest empirical research on the issue is Timothy M Jones – Penelope Sheets, Torture in the Eye of the Beholder: Social Identity, News Coverage, and Abu Ghraib, *Political Communication* 2009, 278–295 which shows that journalists of leading dailies in Australia, Britain, Canada, Italy, Spain, Germany and the United States describe what has happened in Abu Ghraib depending on how far their own nation is affected. US (and allied Anglo-Saxon) journalists mostly avoided the term 'torture', as their sense of identity did not tolerate describing their own community/nation as a torturer.

[90] On utilitarian and deontological theories of torture, see William Twining, Torture and Philosophy, *Proceedings of the Aristotelian Society*, supplementary volumes (52) 1978, 143–195, 144–168.

to stick to our old *legal* paradigm of rule of law (as a constitutional tenet of our society), I allow for breaching it in exceptional situations on *moral* reasons without saying that it would make that breach lawful. Most utilitarians would not agree with the former, and probably no deontologist would ever agree with the latter. So I do not claim to have found a compromise. Rather the opposite: I think that both are wrong because they simplify the problems to a monotonous 'yes' or 'no'.

Terrorism is by its nature an exceptional (even if occasionally devastating) phenomenon as opposed to the exercise of state authority in our everyday life. If we seriously weaken the concept of the rule of law for fighting this new challenge (terrorism), we risk failing to answer to a traditional major challenge (limitation of our fight against the arbitrary use of government power). We should not think that when the time of action comes, nobody will dare to use his or her common moral sense to breach the law in order to save lives or to save the constitution as a whole. But if she or he does so, it should remain her or his risk whether he or she is right or not, and we can honour his or her illegal act (beyond the possible moral recognition) only by grace and not by making it legal. As we have seen above, any other solution would either be dogmatic and suicidal, or dangerous for abuse and consequently also suicidal.

But independently of how exactly we argue in this matter, we should definitely avoid a usual lawyerly trick (often also used in this discourse), namely to pretend that the problem is a primarily conceptual-juridical one.[91] Throughout history, old legal concepts have always been redefined according to changing *Weltbilder* and according to the necessary responses to social challenges (instead of introducing new concepts). If we do so, we should not place the burden of responsibility on concepts, however heavy it may be.

[91] Expressing ideological conflicts in (or concealing them as) constitutional-legal dilemmas does have a (useful) taming function within modern societies by diminishing the disintegrative effect of intra-societal conflicts when reshaping their discourse in an emotionally less burdened manner. So if within the society, the question is 'what separates us', then we should formulate it in the most technical-juridical manner. But in the case of the 'fight against terrorism', the actual (primary) conflict is not within the society but between society and terrorists, so the question is rather 'what keeps us together (against the terrorists)'. In the latter case, concealing the ideological-emotional components would weaken the identity of society, which would be self-destructive to allow. So during the 'fight against terrorism' we have to be open about the non-legal part of our constitutional reasoning.

# 8

# The constitution of Europe

> First she tells us to beware of the song the heavenly Sirens sing . . . you must tie me with ropes pulled painfully tight, so that I stay fast where I am, upright against the mast-holder with the ropes attached to the mast itself. And if I beg you and order you to release me, then you are to tighten yet further ropes on me.[1]

Constitutions are generally expected to do two things: (1) to be a means of legal self-restraint on the political power (as expressed by the protection of fundamental rights and the idea of the separation of powers); and (2) to be symbols that bind the community together.[2] This chapter examines these two requirements, arguing that any constitution that fulfils these may be regarded as legitimate (i.e., worthy of being obeyed). After some remarks on the typical content and structure (3), the closing section of the chapter contends that we should refer to the founding treaties of the EU as the 'Constitution of Europe' (or somewhat more precisely as the 'Constitution of the European Union') (4).[3]

## 8.1 The primary function: legal self-restraint or a list of taboos

The modern idea of constitutionalism appeared as a response to absolutism.[4] Its most important element was, and still is, that even political

[1] Homer, *The Odyssey* [tr. Martin Hammond], London, Duckworth 2000, (XII.159–164) 123.

[2] Jürgen Gebhardt, Die Idee der Verfassung. Symbol und Instrument, in: Adolf Kimmel (ed.), *Verfassungen als Fundament und Instrument der Politik*, Baden-Baden, Nomos 1995, 9–23; Edward S Corwin, The Constitution as Instrument and as Symbol, *American Political Science Review* 30 (1936) 1071–1085.

[3] For questions and critical remarks I am grateful to the participants of the conference 'What Is a Constitution Good For? Between National Differences and European Consensus' in Fehérvárcsurgó, Hungary on 9 March 2013, and to the participants of the workshop 'Verfassunggebung in konsolidierten Demokratien' at the Andrássy University Budapest on 15 April 2013, especially to Kálmán Pócza.

[4] For more details on this question see also above 7.1.

power possesses limits; that is, it cannot be exerted in an arbitrary manner.[5] Thus, it is not power that makes law, but on the contrary: power has to be based upon law *(lex facit regem)*.[6] This idea was shaped by historical predecessors, such as medieval and ancient theories of natural law. According to the natural law theories, there exists a higher law (that originates from God or nature),[7] which sets limits on the power of the monarch (and on that of the estates). Nevertheless, the idea of constitutionalism is actually rather a modern invention: the idea of a 'human-made constitution' or a 'codified natural law' emerged in response to absolutism and as a result of secularisation (i.e., the decline of religious power in the social and political domain). This kind of constitution is a human-made legal norm that sets limits on those currently in power.

This idea was formulated during the French Revolution, in Art. 16 of the *Declaration of the Rights of Man and of the Citizen* (1789): 'A society in which rights are not guaranteed, nor the separation of powers defined, has no constitution at all.'[8] The bloodstained events of the revolution soon demonstrated that it is not enough to formulate the limits of power in such a lofty declaration, for they are easily circumvented (with reference to popular sovereignty, justice or other concurring noble ideas).

A more promising legal technique was developed (not long before the French Revolution) in the United States. This technique is comprised of two elements. (a) A special procedure is prescribed for amending the constitution. Not only must both houses of the federal legislature (Congress) pass the amendments (with a two-thirds majority), but they

[5] On the *telos* of constitutions as the limitation of power see Karl Löwenstein, *Verfassungslehre*, Tübingen, Mohr [4]2000, 127–129.

[6] Martin Kriele, *Einführung in die Staatslehre*, Stuttgart, Kohlhammer [6]2003, 81.

[7] One may mention, e.g., Augustine, Thomas Aquinas or Hugo Grotius. On further antecedents, see Görg Haverkate, *Verfassungslehre*, München, Beck 1992, 13–14 with further references.

[8] Modern constitutions are also different from medieval freedom charters, such as the English Magna Carta (1215) or the Hungarian Golden Bull (1222), even if there are some similarities. These are as follows. (1) Modern constitutions use the language of human rights, whereas the medieval documents only refer to the rights of certain (legally defined) social groups. Those who did not belong to these groups lacked any protection. (2) The medieval documents only confirmed 'old' rights; they were not meant to set up a new regime. (3) The rights were conceived as privileges, rather than as objective norms. Thus the modern constitutions (both in the United States and France) do not stem from these documents, but rather from the interplay of rationalist system-building efforts and hearsay about legal reality in England. (4) Modern constitutions are adopted in a special procedure that distinguishes them from ordinary laws. For the first three differences, see Manuel García-Pelayo, *Obras completas*, Madrid, Centro de Estudios Políticos y Constitucionales [2]2009, 346–347.

also have to be accepted in at least three-quarters of the federal states, either by special constitution-making assemblies or by the ordinary legislative organs.[9] This way, a legal norm is created which has greater legal power than ordinary acts of the legislature, as it is more difficult to amend.[10] The French also tried this technique shortly after the 1789 Declaration, namely in the 1791 Constitution (Title VII, an even more cumbersome procedure than the US one), but without the second legal technique (to be described next) it was not effective. (b) This second legal technique came in the United States not from those drafting the Constitution, but from its interpreters. In 1803, in what may be the most celebrated legal case of all time, Chief Justice John Marshall declared that laws contrary to the Constitution could not be applied,[11] for otherwise the Constitution would be a mere declaration without legal power.[12] In the American model, it is still the regular courts that perform constitutional adjudication, that is, the constitutional review of laws. Constitutions that are not applied by the judiciary are merely political declarations:[13] what makes them real legal documents is that the courts base their decisions on them.

In the legal culture of continental Europe, the idea of constitutional adjudication has faced strong opposition for a long time.[14] The reason for

9 Constitution of the United States of America (1787), Art. 5.

10 On the formal constitution as a law that has 'a higher degree of formal legal power' (*erhöhte formelle Gesetzeskraft*); see Georg Jellinek, *Verfassungsänderung und Verfassungswandlung*, Berlin, Häring 1906, 8.

11 *Marbury v. Madison*, 5 U.S. (1 Cranch) 137 (1803). For the few cases in which even before *Marbury v. Madison* statutes were invalidated by US courts (directly after the adoption of the US Constitution), see William Michael Treanor, Judicial Review Before Marbury, *Stanford Law Review* 58 (2005) 455–562. The fact that *Marbury v. Madison* became iconic owes probably much to the high political profile of its litigants.

12 A similar idea also appeared in France during the Revolution (in 1795), but it was never realised. Sieyès proposed to set up a *jury constitutionnaire* (a lay body with the power to annul statutes for their unconstitutionality; besides the *locus standi* of certain organs also the possibility of *actio popularis* would have been included), see Pasquale Pasquino, *Sieyès et l'invention de la Constitution en France*, Paris, Odile Jacob 1998, especially 193–196.

13 Alibi constitutions, or as Karl Löwenstein put it, *semantische Verfassungen*. See Löwenstein (n. 5) 153–157. These just follow political reality, without the ambition to influence it; they therefore can only have a symbolic function. For a different terminology ('camouflage constitutions') see Jan-Erik Lane, *Constitutions and Political Theory*, Manchester, Manchester University Press [2]2011, 44.

14 As an emblematic (and highly influential) work, see Édouard Lambert, *Le gouvernement des juges et la lutte contre la législation sociale aux États-Unis. L'expérience américaine du contrôle judiciaire de la constitutionnalité des lois*, Paris, M. Giard & Cie 1921. On the influence of Lambert's work, see Alec Stone Sweet, Why Europe Rejected American Judicial Review: And Why It May Not Matter, *Michigan Law Review* 101 (2003)

this was that Europeans regarded the executive power (the monarch and his government) as the primary threat to freedom; the legislature, in turn, was taken to be the defender of freedom against the executive. After the First World War, constitutional courts with the power to annul laws were established in Austria (along the ideas of Georg Jellinek and Hans Kelsen) and Czechoslovakia (following, again, Georg Jellinek and Jiří Hoetzel), but these were soon abolished and for a while had no influence on other European countries.[15] The first attempt to introduce constitutional courts in Europe basically failed. The interwar period and the Second World War, however, proved that the legislature may also pose a threat to freedom. In other words, even a democratically elected legislature may establish a dictatorship.[16]

After the Second World War, all democracies that replaced national socialist or fascist regimes established their own constitutional courts (immediately after the war in Italy and Germany, and later also in Spain and Portugal). By far the most influential of these was the Federal Constitutional Court of the German Federal Republic: in most ex-socialist countries (including Hungary), the new institutions admittedly followed German patterns. By today, even the French Constitutional Council, originally conceived as a body resolving disputes between the legislature and the executive, has become a real constitutional court as it has the power to annul laws that have already been passed that violate constitutionally protected fundamental rights.[17] European countries in which there are no separate constitutional courts have either adopted the American model of decentralised constitutional review (Scandinavian countries, Ireland), or the same function is fulfilled by international treaties on human rights that are directly applicable by regular courts (the Netherlands).[18] There are two notable, but partial, exceptions in Europe

2744–2780, especially 2758–2760. On similar worries about contemporary phenomena, see Ran Hirschl, Towards Juristocracy, Cambridge, Mass., Harvard University Press 2004.

15 Jana Osterkamp, *Verfassungsgerichtsbarkeit in der Tschechoslowakei (1920–1939)*, Frankfurt aM, Vittorio Klostermann 2009.

16 Democratic procedures have to be protected against the legislature itself; see John Hart Ely, *Democracy and Distrust*, Cambridge, Mass., Harvard University Press 1981.

17 Federico Fabbrini, Kelsen in Paris: France's Constitutional Reform and the Introduction of *a posteriori* Constitutional Review of Legislation, *German Law Journal* 9 (2008) 1297–1312.

18 Bernd Wieser, *Vergleichendes Verfassungsrecht*, Wien, Springer 2005, 121–123. For more details on the topic, see CDL-AD(2010)039rev Study on individual access to constitutional justice – Adopted by the Venice Commission at its 85th Plenary Session (Venice, 17–18 December 2010). For a worldwide comparative overview of different political motivations behind the establishment of constitutional courts, see Francisco Ramos

from the general rule of constitutional review of statutes: (a) the UK and (b) Switzerland.

Ad (a). In the UK, there is no constitution in the formal sense, that is, no legal document (or set of legal documents) that had to be passed in a procedure different from that of ordinary statutes.[19] The system is similar to what was known in Hungary before the Second World War as 'the historical constitution': all laws were passed with a simple majority, but some were regarded as particularly important ('cardinal laws') and therefore as part of the Constitution.

The lack of a formal constitution represents a primitive stage in terms of legal technique.[20] This suggests that the given political community cannot distinguish certain issues as being of particular importance, legal or otherwise, and therefore cannot structure its legal system (i.e., differentiate between statutes and the constitution), so its legal provisions make a homogeneous mass. This also means that a future government can abolish all the measures of its predecessor.

It should be noted, however, that even the legal system of the UK is somewhat different from how it is often described in continental debates on these issues. Since the adoption of the Human Rights Act 1998, the highest judicial body (until October 2009 it was the Appellate Committee of the House of Lords; since then it has been a separate institution: the Supreme Court of the UK) can declare any law to be contrary to the rights guaranteed by the European Convention on Human Rights

Romeu, The Establishment of Constitutional Courts: A Study of 128 Democratic Constitutions, *Review of Law and Economics* 2 (2006) 103–135.

[19] FF Ridley, There is no British Constitution: A Dangerous Case of the Emperor's Clothes, *Parliamentary Affairs* 41 (1988) 340–361.

[20] British authors call this, with some euphemism, an expression of flexibility. See, e.g., Hilaire Barnett, *Constitutional & Administrative Law*, London, New York, Routledge [9]2011, 7–10. For the lack of constitutional rules and their unstructured character, 'constitutional conventions' (stating, e.g., that the monarch has to appoint the PM from amongst the MPs of the House of Commons; legally speaking, the monarch could appoint anyone, even the author of these lines) are no real substitute, these latter ones being rather like rules of morality or constitutional politeness, at least according to continental terminology (no formal codification, no legal sanction in case they are breached). Yet these conventions are strongly culture-bound (in the UK they do function, even if sometimes they are breached, just as legal rules are breached too, but the culturally bound political and social pressure still keeps them alive), and cannot therefore be transplanted as such into a continental legal system. Consequently, it is not without hypocrisy to refer to a 'British model' of lacking constitutional guarantees (i.e., to justify the erosion of constitutional review with these examples), since in the UK there are other limits instead, which cannot be established (at least within a reasonable time) in post-dictatorial societies.

*(declaration of incompatibility)*. To make it clear, this does not mean annulment, but the tendency is clearly of a judicial overview of statutes.[21] In 2005, even the Appellate Committee of the House of Lords considered *obiter dicta* the possibility of declaring parliamentary acts invalid,[22] provoking a lively debate in British constitutional scholarship.[23]

Two further, non-European, countries are generally mentioned as not having formal constitutions: Israel and New Zealand. In fact, this is not quite true in the case of Israel anymore, as in 1992 the Knesset passed two 'basic laws' on human rights, and following this, Aharon Barak, Justice (later Chief Justice) of the Supreme Court of Israel, declared a 'constitutional revolution'. He repeated his earlier ideas, according to which the Supreme Court had the power to annul laws that violated fundamental rights (even in the absence of an explicit authorisation by any law), in his official capacity (in judgments), and there were also annulments.[24]

21 Those theorists who oppose any further advancement of this judicialisation of politics are purporting a so-called 'political constitutionalism' as opposed to 'legal constitutionalism'. For such views from the UK, see, e.g., Richard Bellamy, *Political Constitutionalism*, Cambridge, Cambridge University Press 2007; and Adam Tomkins, *Our Republican Constitution*, Oxford, Hart 2005; from the United States, e.g., Jeremy Waldron, *Law and Disagreement*, Oxford, Clarendon Press 1999. These authors state that the democratic political process, besides being more accountable and more transparent, is also apt to guarantee fundamental rights. This view, however, presupposes that *all* relevant political players share a democratic culture, which, unfortunately, is untrue in many countries, especially in countries that have just recently transitioned from a dictatorship to democracy. In many countries, even the democratic process would fail without a judicial guarantee thereof, let alone the protection of fundamental rights (especially minority rights).

22 *R (Jackson) v .Attorney General* [2005] UKHL 56.

23 See e.g., Cosmo Graham, A Very British Affair – Jackson v. Attorney General, *European Public Law* 12 (2006) 501–513; Tom Mullen, Reflections on Jackson v. Attorney General: Questioning Sovereignty, *Legal Studies* 27 (2007) 1–25; Stuart Lakin, Debunking the Idea of Parliamentary Sovereignty: The Controlling Factor of Legality in the British Constitution, *Oxford Journal of Legal Studies* 28 (2008) 709–734; Lord Bingham of Cornhill, The Rule of Law and the Sovereignty of Parliament, *King's Law Journal* 19 (2008) 223–234; see also the contributions in the special issue of the *International Journal of Constitutional Law* 9 (2011) 79–273 on the 'Changing Landscape of British Constitutionalism'.

24 HCJ 6821/93 *United Mizrachi Bank Ltd v. Migdal Cooperative Village* 49 (4) PD 221. For a general narrative, see Yoseph M Edrey, The Israeli constitutional revolution/evolution, *American Journal of Comparative Law* 53 (2005) 77–123. For a full list of annulments up to date, see Suzie Navot, Israel, in: Dawn Oliver – Carlo Fusaro (eds.), *How Constitutions Change*, Oxford, Portland, Hart 2011, 191–209, 199, n. 16. For an early (failed) attempt of judicial constitution-creation in the UK, see Dr Bonham's Case [*Thomas Bonham v. College of Physicians*, 8. Co. Rep. 114 (1610)], discussed in detail in Theodore FT Plucknett, Bonham's Case and Judicial Review, *Harvard Law Review* 40 (1926–1927) 30–70.

This means that the last (democratic) state today where there is a clearly historical constitution is New Zealand. There are some parts in the Constitution Act 1986 which can only be amended with a 75 per cent parliamentary majority (provisions on the three years parliamentary term and on elections), but the provision which prescribes this is not entrenched itself (thus eventually it can be amended by a simple majority). The Treaty of Waitangi 1840 (between the British Crown and the Maori Chiefs) is considered to be above the normal legislative procedure, but it is not the Constitution itself, rather just an international treaty founding New Zealand. There is no judicial review of statutes in New Zealand either.[25] The only measure that is slightly similar to *a priori* judicial review is the competence of the Attorney-General under Section 7 of New Zealand Bill of Rights Act 1990 to submit a report which draws the attention of the Parliament to any draft legislation that would be inconsistent with the Bill of Rights. Once a bill has been made into a statute though, the Bill of Rights is simply an interpretive tool (cf. Section 6 of the same Act).[26]

Ad (b). In Switzerland, there is no constitutional review of federal laws. This function, however, is fulfilled by referenda, which are very easy to initiate in the Swiss system. This is to say, where there is no constitutional adjudication, there is the possibility of referendum as a limit to federal legislation. This corresponds to the logic of constitutional democracy, according to which if a state organ is not controlled by one of the possible supervisory organs (in this case that would be the *Bundesgericht* of Switzerland), there should be some other kind of control. This substitute is the referendum in Switzerland, and to a lesser extent international human rights law which is considered by the *Bundesgericht* to be a general limit of Swiss legislation, and even a limit on constitutional amendments.[27]

One of the key elements of modern democracies based on the separation of powers is that no legally unlimited power should be accepted. The reason for this is that unlimited power would have to be based on a high degree of confidence in politicians, and historical experience shows that such confidence is just too risky (in any human being in general, not just

25 Paul Rishworth, New Zealand, in: Oliver – Fusaro (n. 24) 235–260.

26 Stephen Gardbaum, *The New Commonwealth Model of Constitutionalism*, Cambridge, Cambridge University Press 2013, 129–155.

27 BGer Urteil 2C_828/2011 vom 12. 10. 12 Ausschaffungsinitiative. See Rafael Häcki, Im Westen nichts Neues, *juwiss* 21. February 2013 http://www.juwiss.de/im-westen-nichts-neues/.

in politicians).[28] Therefore, no matter how strong the electoral authorisation the legislation receives, its power cannot be unlimited in a constitutional democracy.[29] We have to protect politicians from the inebriating or hypnotising effects of power. Wiser ones recognise this and have tied themselves to the mast, like Odysseus in the quote at the beginning of this chapter who knew he would not be able to resist the Sirens.[30] Less wise politicians will have to be tied down by the passengers on the vessel.

Besides these two partial exceptions, European legal systems seem to be equivocal in supporting constitutional review of statutes (whether conducted by ordinary judges or by constitutional court judges). This seems to be necessary to give legal weight to constitutions. The role model that judges take when exercising the constitutional review of statutes is, however, different from country to country (or to a smaller degree even from judge to judge), and these role models also explain differences in the applied methods of constitutional interpretation (see above Chapter 3). If judges perceive their roles only as agents of the constitution-maker, then their task is just to enforce the choices of the constitution-makers over legislative majorities. If judges, however, see themselves as trustees of the political system, then their task is to ensure that the legislative process produces the 'best' policy outcomes.[31] The former model is unable to explain judicial activism, cannot deal with incomplete constitutions and social changes, but it is nearer to the usual judicial rhetoric. The latter model is somewhat nearer to reality, but it is

[28] Political freedom is based on distrust of politicians. Since the end of the eighteenth century, a number of (promising) revolutionaries who became dictators demonstrates that such suspicions are, regrettably, well-founded.

[29] The British solution placed the balances within a tripartite Parliament: the monarch, the upper house and the lower house counterbalanced one another in the late seventeenth-century scenario. For a more detailed analysis of related conceptual manipulation, see above 6.1. By today, the roles of the monarch and the upper house have lost their importance: it is for this reason that the system has moved towards judicial review through the passing of the *Human Rights Act 1998* mentioned above.

[30] Jon Elster, *Ulysses and the Sirens: Studies in Rationality and Irrationality*, Cambridge, Melbourne, Cambridge University Press, Paris, Maison des Sciences de l'Homme 1984, 36–37, 87–96. Or to use another metaphor by Stephen Holmes: 'A constitution is Peter sober while the electorate is Peter drunk,' quoted by Ulrich R Haltern, *Verfassungsgerichtsbarkeit, Demokratie und Mißtrauen*, Berlin, Duncker & Humblot 1998, 173.

[31] For an excellent analysis of the topic with further references and empirical analysis, see Arthur Dyevre, Technocracy and Distrust: Revisiting the Rationale for Constitutional Review, *International Journal of Constitutional Law* 13 (2015) 30–60.

uncomfortable because it does not allow judges to hide behind the rhetoric of the agent model and it requires them to give a more complete justification (including social consequences). The two models are, of course, Weberian ideal types and consequently, nowhere fully realised, but they do help to conceptualise the role of constitutional courts on a simple scale.

### 8.1.1 *Different material concepts of the constitution*

Besides the above ('formal') concept of the constitution, there are also so-called 'material' ones.[32]

(1) These can have the most diverging, only halfway legal definitions like fundamental decisions on the form of political existence,[33] the continuing process of integration which holds the state together (i.e., the everyday acceptance of the state by its citizens)[34] or the political-social reality.[35] The danger of such re-conceptualisation is that it weakens the normative-legal force of the real ('formal' or 'legal') constitution, as theories using these material-political concepts mostly proffer them as logically superior to the formal Constitution.[36] If the political reality is the constitution, then the constitution is (conceptually) unable to

[32] For an overview, see Peter Badura, Verfassung und Verfassungsgesetz, in: Horst Ehmke (ed.), *Festschrift für Ulrich Scheuner zum 70. Geburtstag*, Berlin, Duncker & Humblot 1973, 19–39. For such a concept in the context of the EU, see Leonard Besselink, The Notion and Nature of the European Constitution after the Lisbon Treaty, in: Jan Wouters – Luc Verhey – Philipp Kiiver (eds.), *European Constitutionalism beyond Lisbon*, Antwerp, Intersentia 2009, 261–281.

[33] Carl Schmitt, *Verfassungslehre*, München, Leipzig, Duncker & Humblot 1928, 23–25; Peter Badura, *Staatsrecht*, München, Beck [5]2012, 12–13; Hartmut Maurer, *Staatsrecht I*, München, CH Beck [6]2010, 10–11.

[34] Rudolf Smend, *Verfassung und Verfassungsrecht*, München, Leipzig, Duncker & Humblot 1928, 78. For application of Smend to the EU, see Marco Dani, Economic and Social Conflicts, Integration and Constitutionalism in Contemporary Europe, LSE 'Europe in Question' Discussion Paper Series 13/2009, available at http://www2.lse.ac.uk/europeanInstitute/LEQS/LEQSPaper13b.pdf.

[35] Hermann Heller, *Staatslehre* [ed. Gerhart Niemeyer], Leiden, Sijthoff 1934, 249–259; Louis Favoreu – Patrick Gaïa – Richard Ghevontian – Jean-Louis Mestre – Otto Pfersmann – André Roux – Guy Scoffoni, *Droit constitutionnel*, Paris, Dalloz [14]2011, 57 (calling it the 'political concept' of the constitution).

[36] Christoph Möllers, *Der vermisste Leviathan*, Frankfurt aM, Suhrkamp 2008, 54. For references to Carl Schmitt and Ernst Rudolf Huber during the national socialist regime in Germany, showing how easily these material concepts can be abused, see Dieter Grimm, Verfassung II, in: Otto Brunner – Werner Conze – Reinhart Koselleck (eds.), *Geschichtliche Grundbegriffe*, vol. 6, Stuttgart, Klett-Cotta [1990] 2004, 863–899, 897.

regulate politics; it is just 'what happens'.[37] The consequence is, of course, that a constitution cannot limit politics, it can only follow or abide by politics, which contradicts the whole idea of constitutionalism.

(2) A second type of 'material constitutions' is strictly legal, meaning the 'rules of law-making'.[38] In this case, there is no such danger of relativisation, but this terminology implies the acceptance of the Pure Theory of Law, which we find doubtful (see below Chapter 12).

(3) A third type of 'material constitution' just means 'the most important legal rules' of a given legal order.[39] This concept has vague borders: there is always a grey zone as to which legal rules belong to it and which do not.

(4) And finally, a material concept of the constitution can also include substantive elements, like democracy[40] or rule of law (see above Art. 16 of the 1789 Declaration).[41] When British authors talk about their constitution (and analyse, in fact, statutes and case-law), they have a mixture of meanings (3) and (4) of the constitution.[42]

The common core in all these material definitions might be seen in showing the 'basis of the legal order'. But their use, unfortunately, is rather confusing; for the sake of terminological clarity, we should restrict the use of the concept of the constitution to the formal constitution.

[37] The 'Constitution is what happens', see JAG Griffith, The Political Constitution, *Modern Law Review* 42 (1979) 1–21. For a similar view see Ferdinand Lassalle, Über Verfassungswesen [1862], in: *id.*, *Gesammelte Reden*, vol. 2, Berlin, Paul Cassirer 1919, 59–60.

[38] Hans Kelsen, *Allgemeine Staatslehre*, Berlin, Springer 1925, 98, 234; Robert Walter, *Der Aufbau der Rechtsordnung*, Graz, Leykam 1964, 30–31 and 35–36; Robert Walter – Heinz Mayer – Gabriele Kucsko-Stadlmayer, *Grundriss des österreichischen Bundesverfassungsrechts*, Wien, Manz [10]2007, para 4; Favoreu (n. 35) 78.

[39] Theo Öhlinger – Harald Eberhard, *Verfassungsrecht*, Wien, Facultas [9]2012, para 14.

[40] Dieter Grimm, *Braucht Europa eine Verfassung?*, München, Carl Friedrich von Siemens Stiftung 1995, 31.

[41] Or in a more general form, a document which confers legitimacy, see, e.g., JJ Solozábal Echavarría, Constitución, in: Manuel Aragón Reyes (ed.), *Temas básicos de derecho constitucional*, vol 1., Madrid, Civitas 2001, 21.

[42] For a classic account, see Edmund Burke, Speech on the Representation of the Commons in Parliaments (1782), in: PJ Stanlis (ed.), *Selected Writings and Speeches of Edmund Burke*, Garden City, NJ, Doubleday 1963, 330–331. The 'historical constitution' in the Spanish and in the Hungarian terminology had the same meaning; see Joaquín Varela Suanzes-Carpegna, La doctrina de la Constitución histórica de España, in: Fernández Sarasola – Joaquín Varela Suanzes-Carpegna (eds.), *Conceptos de Constitución en la historia*, Oviedo, Junta General del Principado de Asturias 2010, 307–359; Zoltán Szente, A historizáló alkotmányozás problémái – a történeti alkotmány és a Szent Korona az új Alaptörvényben, *Közjogi Szemle* 2011/3, 1–13.

### 8.1.2 Constituting vs. restraining?

Besides their self-restraining function, the other task constitutions should perform is to organise, that is, *to constitute* political power.[43] Hence the etymology of the expressions *constitution, constitución, alkotmány, Verfassung* and so on.[44] As power could also be constituted through ordinary legislation (as it is done in the UK), this is not a specificity of constitutions.

As a matter of fact, however, constituting the power in the constitution is also part of the self-restraining function: if power is constituted by the constitution, then no other power can be accepted as legitimate. In the words of Thomas Paine, 'A constitution is a thing antecedent to a government, and a government is only the creature of a constitution. The constitution of a country is not the act of its government, but of the people constituting a government.'[45] We are going to return to this point in more detail when discussing the state of emergency in Chapter 11 (11.3).

### 8.1.3 Rules of rationality and default responses

Legal self-restraint is important not only in order to avoid a dictatorship (with older terminology: a tyranny), but also to force decision-makers to consider certain aspects (interdependencies and externalities) which they otherwise would not (for reasons of self-interest or for lack of intellectual-cognitive capacity). James Buchanan calls them the 'rules of rationality'.[46]

If these rules of rationality narrow down the possible options to one single choice, then we can call it the 'default option':[47] constitutions can somctimes provide for default responses to usual social challenges. As there

[43] Constitutions both enable and disable political decision making; see Stephen Holmes, *Passions and Constraint: On the Theory of Liberal Democracy*, Chicago, University of Chicago Press 1995, 271–272; Graham Maddox, A Note on the Meaning of 'Constitution', *American Political Science Review* 56 (1982) 805–809.

[44] On the ancient Roman etymology *(rem publicam constituere)*, see Georg Jellinek, *Allgemeine Staatslehre*, Berlin, Häring $^{3}$1914, 652. The pre-modern uses of 'constitutio' simply meaning fundamental laws, form of government or form of state, but not the limitation of power. It was first used by Emer de Vattel in 1758 *(Le droit des gens, ou principes de la loi naturelle)* in the modern sense (as man-made law of higher rank); see Dieter Grimm, Verfassung II, in: Brunner (n. 36) vol. 6, 863–899, 897–898.

[45] Thomas Paine, The Rights of Man (1791), in: Moncure Daniel Conway (ed.), *Writings of Thomas Paine*, vol. 2, New York, AMS Press 1967, 265–523, 309–310.

[46] James M Buchanan, Why Do Constitutions Matter?, in: Niclas Berggren – Nils Karlson – Joakim Nergelius (eds.), *Why Constitutions Matter*, Stockholm, City University Press 2000, 1–16, especially 5–8.

[47] Buchanan (n. 46) 9–12.

are always several remaining options, though, it seems more accurate to depict constitutions as rules of rationality than as default responses.

## 8.2 A secondary function: a symbol of the community

A constitution is not just a legal document, but a symbol as well.[48] It expresses the aspirations of the political community (the nation).[49] Actually, most key concepts ('sovereignty', 'the rule of law', 'democracy' and 'nation') have an emotional-integrative role, which we will discuss in the specific chapters (on constitutional patriotism, see below 10.2.6).[50]

Some constitutions consciously take on this role with an emotionally loaded rhetoric about goals and values; others, however, remain technical and sober like a phone book.[51] We are going to concentrate here on two issues concerning the symbolic power of constitutions: the preambles and the procedure for constitution-making.

[48] André Brodocz, *Die symbolische Dimension der Verfassung*, Wiesbaden, Westdeutscher Verlag 2003; Max Lerner, Constitution and Court as Symbols, *Yale Law Journal* 46 (1937) 1290–1319; Geoffrey Brennan – Alan Hamlin, Constitutions as Expressive Documents, in: Barry R Weingast – Donald A Wittman (eds.), *The Oxford Handbook of Political Economy*, Oxford, Oxford University Press 2006, 329–341.

[49] Therefore, drafting a new constitution can be important especially at the birth of a new political community (or when regaining their independence); see Ernst-Wolfgang Böckenförde, Geschichtliche Entwicklung und Bedeutungswandel der Verfassung, in: *id., Staat, Verfassung, Demokratie*, Frankfurt aM, Suhrkamp 1991, 29–52, 42–43. On this tradition see Christoph Möllers, Pouvoir Constituant – Constitution – Constitutionalism, in: Armin von Bogdandy – Jürgen Bast (eds.), *Principles of European Constitutional Law*, Oxford, Hart $^{2}$2010, 169–205, 171–173; Nico Krisch, *Beyond Constitutionalism: The Pluralist Structure of Postnational Law*, Oxford, Oxford University Press 2010, 47–52, all with further references.

[50] For the latest general attempt to explain constitutional concepts with sentiments, see András Sajó, *Constitutional Sentiments*, New Haven, Yale University Press 2010.

[51] For an opposing view, conceiving of constitutions simply as 'rules of the (political) game', see James M Buchanan, The Domain of Constitutional Economics, *Constitutional Political Economy* 1990, 1–18; Friedrich Koja, Die Verfassung, in: Heinz Mayer – Clemens Jabloner, Kucsko-Stadlmayer – Rene Laurer – Kurt Ringhofer – Rudolf Thienel (eds.), *Staatsrecht in Theorie und Praxis: Festschrift für Robert Walter*, Wien, Manz 1991, 349–361 (*Verfassung als Spielregel*); Hans Kelsen, *Vom Wesen und Wert der Demokratie*, Tübingen, Mohr $^{2}$1929, 53–58. The Austrian B-VG is not programmatically oriented, nor does it have a preamble. One reason for this is the fact that Kelsen (as one of the experts who drafted it) wanted to draft it as non-ideologically as possible. See Heinz Schäffer, *Verfassungsinterpretation in Österreich*, Wien, Springer 1971, 64 n.19 (citing further references). Another reason was the inability of the parties to find common ground on ideological elements. Thus, Austria's central constitutional text was construed as a model for lawmaking and the necessary oversight of legal conformity, but not as a symbol of the political community. See *id.*, at 64.

### 8.2.1 *Preambles*

Debates surrounding preambles can be understood mainly in the light of the symbolic power of constitutions, and it is for the same reason that the preamble has to be formulated in a way that allows for an emotional identification on the part of as many citizens as possible.[52] Certainly, the legal content itself can partially fulfil such a role of community identity binding (as, e.g., 'we do not violate human rights, so we are the good boys; those who are against us do violate human rights, so they are the bad boys').[53] Yet it is still the rhetoric of the preamble where this function comes mostly to the fore.

Preambles have a peculiar legal character. In most European legal cultures, they only have a reduced legal power, as they do not assign obligations to anybody by themselves, and may be used as an aid to the interpretation of the documents to which they serve as preambles (here: of the constitutions).[54] Their actual legal importance is therefore a rather limited one. However, their pride of place (right at the beginning of the document) increases their symbolic importance. If the primary function of the preamble is to express the togetherness of the political community, then it has to be formulated in a way that allows for an emotional identification on the part of as many citizens as possible. If we ignore this, then a proportion of the citizens will view the constitution as one that has been forced upon them, regardless of its actual content, and as a symbol of resentment rather than of identification. This is not to say that certain historical narratives[55] or certain values cannot or should not

[52] Sanford Levinson, Do Constitutions Have a Point? Reflections on 'Parchment Barriers' and Preambles, in: Ellen Frankel Paul – Fred D Miller, Jr. – Jeffrey Paul (eds.), *What Should Constitutions Do?*, Cambridge, Cambridge University Press 2011, 150–178.

[53] On related dilemmas concerning the prohibition of torture in the fight against terrorism, see above p. 141.

[54] On German debates concerning the legal force of the preambles of the 1871 and the 1919 constitutions, see Peter Schoepke, *Die rechtliche Bedeutung der Präambel des Grundgesetzes für die Bundesrepublik Deutschland. Eine Grundlegung mit rechtshistorischer Einführung und Abhandlung der Präambeln zu den Verfassungen der Länder in der Bundesrepublik Deutschland* [Diss. Tübingen], Bamberg, Bamberger Fotodruck 1965, 1–47. For recent exceptions which consider the preambles as having full legal power, see Décision no 71–44 DC du 16 juillet 1971 concernant la loi du 1er juillet 1901 relative au contrat d'association; BVerfGE 5, 85 (127f) – 'KPD-Verbotsurteil'. On the legal nature of preambles in general, see Liav Orgad, The preamble in constitutional interpretation, *International Journal of Constitutional Law* 8 (2010) 714–738.

[55] On the role of historical narratives in constitutional law (especially in case-law), see Renáta Uitz, *Constitutions, Courts and History: Historical Narratives in Constitutional Adjudication*, Budapest, CEU Press 2005.

receive more emphasis in the preamble than others. Yet this has to be done in a way which makes these values orientating rather than compulsory, that is, to make no one feel threatened in any way.

In light of all this, if a preamble of a constitution (written in the twenty-first century) contains any reference to God, it also has to contain an *additional* phrase that makes the document acceptable for non-believers as well. We find unfortunate a formulation similar to that of the German *Grundgesetz* of 1949, which says 'being aware of our responsibility to God and man', for it would suggest that we all believe in God.[56] The Polish way ('we who believe that God is the Lord of history, and we who seek to understand the course of history from other sources ... '), however, seems to be a suitable solution.[57]

The references in the preamble to the *pouvoir constituant*[58] should follow a similar logic.[59] Their role is not to explain where the empowerment came from (who had the empowerment first turns out anyway after

[56] Similarly problematic is the preamble of the new Hungarian Basic Law, because it is not inclusive or integrative towards atheist citizens; see Balázs Schanda, Considerations on the Place of Religion in Constitutional Law, in: Zoltán Csehi – Balázs Schanda – Pál Sonnevend (eds.), *Viva Vox Iuris Civilis. Tanulmányok Sólyom László tiszteletére*, Budapest, Szent István Társulat 2012, 278–285, 285.

[57] On debates concerning *vocatio dei* in the preamble of the German constitution, see Andreas Vogt, *Der Gottesbezug in der Präambel des Grundgesetzes*, Hamburg, Kovač 2007. On the debates concerning the preamble of the (now defunct) EU Constitutional Treaty, see Alfonso Mattera, L'européanité est-elle chrétienne?, *Revue du droit de l'Union européenne* 2003, 352–342; Joseph HH Weiler, *Ein christliches Europa* [introd. Ernst-Wolfgang Böckenförde], Salzburg, München, Pustet 2004; Heinrich Hoffschulte, *Christliches Menschenbild und Gottesbezug in der Verfassung der Europäischen Union*, Münster, Akademie Franz Hitze Haus 2004; Helmut Goerlich – Wolfgang Huber – Karl Lehrmann, *Verfassung ohne Gottesbezug?*, Leipzig, Evangelische Verlagsanstalt 2004; Srdjan Cvijic – Lorenzo Zucca, Does the European Constitution Need Christian Values?, *Oxford Journal of Legal Studies* 24 (2004) 739–748; Norbert K Riedel, Gott in der Europäischen Verfassung?, *Europarecht* 2005. 676–683; Agustín José Menéndez, A pious Europe? Why Europe Should Not Define Itself as Christian, *European Law Review* 30 (2005) 133–148; Agustín José Menéndez, A Christian or a Laic Europe? Christian Values and European Identity, *Ratio Juris* 18 (2005) 179–205.

[58] The term first appeared during the French Revolution in 1789 (Abbé Sieyès, *Qu'est-ce que le Tiers Etat?;* Chapter 5) as the opposite of *pouvoir constitué* (a power constituted by the constitution), i.e., as the counter-concept of all other branches of power. See Claude Klein, *Théorie et pratique du pouvoir constituant*, Paris, Presses Universitaires de France 1996, 7–18; and Egon Zweig, *Die Lehre vom Pouvoir Constituant. Ein Beitrag zum Staatsrecht der französischen Revolution*, Tübingen, Mohr Siebeck 1909. The concept (but not the term) seems to have origins pre-dating the French Revolution; see Joel Colón-Ríos, Five conceptions of constituent power, *Law Quarterly Review* 130 (2014) 306–336, esp. 306–307.

[59] The concept stems from Sieyès; we are going to discuss it later in Chapter 10.

the event),[60] but to express symbolic unity and to give an integrating narrative to the political unity.

### 8.2.2 *The procedure of constitution-making?*

The procedure of constitution-making even if not completely unimportant, is at any rate a question of secondary importance when we enquire as to whether a document can fulfil the symbolic function of a constitution.[61] Besides, there are no general rules for such procedures, not even trends. Some countries follow one procedure of constitution-making, others another (see the table below at p.160). The reason for this is that the fulfilment of the symbolic function of a constitution does not primarily depend on the procedure of constitution-making, or at least not in the long run. Certain procedures are more likely to contribute to the symbolic function,[62] but this function can also be acquired *ex post*, after a long(er) period of time.

Should there be any immediate link of causality between the formal procedure and fulfilment of the symbolic function, every rational constitution-maker would choose the procedure that is most rewarding in terms of these functions. Yet there is no such procedure (and consequently the procedures are manifold), since there is just no such causal link.

This may be well illustrated by picking two of the contemporary constitutions that seem to play exemplary roles (the US Constitution and the German *Grundgesetz*). In 1787, the new US Constitution was made through a conspicuous and grave violation of the democratic procedure prescribed in exact legal terms by the former constitution, the so-called Articles of Confederation:

> 'We the People of the United States. . . . ' Begin with the remarkable act involved in writing these opening words. Only six years before, all thirteen

[60] On the *ex post* nature of the concept (in the context of the EU), see Möllers (n. 49) 185. Its nature is thus similar to the concept of the 'right to secession', see below 10.4. If the procedural rules for the making of the new constitution are breached, then we might view it as a revolutionary *creatio ex nihilo*, but for the fulfilment of its two functions it is not of primary relevance whether this was the case. See below 11.2.7.

[61] On the topic in general, see Claude Klein – András Sajó, Constitution-making: Process and Substance, in: Michel Rosenfeld – András Sajó (eds.), *The Oxford Handbook of Comparative Constitutional Law*, Oxford, Oxford University Press 2012, 419–441 with further references.

[62] On the role of participatory procedures making acceptance more likely, see Justin Blount, Participation in Constitutional Design, in: Tom Ginsburg – Rosalind Dixon, *Comparative Constitutional Law*, Cheltenham, Edward Elgar 2011, 38–56.

> states had unanimously agreed on the Articles of Confederation, which they solemnly proclaimed the basis of 'perpetual Union.' Now, after a short summer of top secret meetings, thirty-nine 'patriots' at the Convention were not only proposing to destroy this initial hard-won effort. They were also claiming authority, in the name of the People, to ignore the rules that the Articles themselves laid out to govern their own revision. The Articles explicitly required the agreement of all thirteen states before any constitutional change was enacted; yet the Founders declared that their new Constitution spoke for 'We the People' if only nine states give their assent. This revolutionary redefinition of the rules of the game extended further – to the manner in which the nine states were to signify their approval. As the Convention looked ahead to the struggle over ratification, it refused to permit existing state governments to veto its authority to speak for the People. Only special 'constitutional conventions' would be allowed to determine the fate of the new Constitution. What [in the world] justified the Federalists in asserting that this end run around legal forms gave them a *better* claim to represent the People than the standing government of the day?[63]

The German *Grundgesetz* of 1949, which may well be the most influential and (at least in Europe) the most often copied constitution,[64] has a similarly dubious pedigree. Here, even the military pressure of foreign countries (viz. the occupying Western allied forces) can be proven.[65] The frameworks for constitution-making (also in terms of substance) were

[63] Quoted from Bruce Ackerman, *We the People. 1: Foundations*, Cambridge, Mass., Belknap Press of Harvard University Press 1991, 167–168. On the problem of the lacking mandate to draft a constitution, see James Madison: *The Federalist Papers No. 40.*

[64] For more details on this question, see David S Law – Mila Versteeg, The Declining Influence of the United States Constitution, *New York University Law Review* 87 (2012) 762–858.

[65] Carlo Schmid, *Erinnerungen*, Bern, München, Scherz 1979, 370; Chris Thornhill, *A Sociology of Constitutions: Constitutions and State Legitimacy in Historical-Sociological Perspective*, Cambridge, Cambridge University Press 2011, 335–337; Christian Winterhoff, *Verfassung – Verfassunggebung – Verfassungsänderung*, Tübingen, Mohr Siebeck 2007, 1–2 *(Geburtsmakeltheorie)* with further references. The Japanese constitution of 1947 was not merely influenced by the occupying (American) forces, but virtually drafted by American lawyers in its entirety, and forced on the country by military threat (see Frederick Schauer, On the Migration of Constitutional Ideas, *Connecticut Law Review* 37 (2004–2005) 907–919, 908, with further references). Still, no one today would doubt its legitimacy, as it meets the expectations in terms of rule of law, democracy and symbolic community. Symbolic suitability means that those drafting the constitution tried not to offend the traditions and national sentiments of the defeated country (e.g., the institution of the Emperor was not abolished). This way, the constitution did not become the constitution of humiliation, and could not be used as a negative symbol, because despite its total victory, the occupying American power aimed at a compromise. Another factor that strengthened the legitimacy of the constitution was that Japan became one of the most successful powers of the world economy under this constitution.

determined by the occupying forces, and even the final draft had to be approved by them. Once the final version had been drafted, US generals 'persuaded' the *Länder* (notably Bavaria which seemed to have had enough of 'Northern Protestant rule' and planned to opt for a more Catholic vision) that were unwilling to accept the *Grundgesetz.*

Initially, the *Grundgesetz* was not held in high esteem by (West) German citizens, either. Yet it soon became the symbol of post-war economic prosperity and of the new regime in general. The current respect for democratic values and the rule of law in Germany is due to the fact that the *Grundgesetz*, which works as a positive symbol because it seemed to make Germany successful, is based upon these. Thus, strengthening the symbolic function has at the same time contributed to the acceptance of its content. No doubt, one might also argue that the democratic establishment and the rule of law partly contributed to Germany's economic prosperity, but at the end of the day the general respect for these values amongst Germans was still just a consequence, rather than the cause, of this success.

After two positive examples, let us briefly note a negative one. In Hungary, the content of the 1949/1989 Constitution conformed to all usual expectations of constitutionalism, but it was rather unpopular, *because* the country did not achieve much success (either economically, or morally, i.e., dealing with injustices of the past) during the two decades after 1989. This (amongst other political factors) led to the adoption of a new Basic Law in 2010/2011.[66] See Table 8.1 for a summary of procedures for making constitutions.

## 8.3 Consequences of the two functions

The two functions (limitation and symbolic integration) have important consequences as to the usual (and ideal) amendment procedure and the typical content of constitutions.

### *8.3.1 The amendment procedure and stability*

If we want a legal document which serves as a limitation of politics, then it should not be possible to modify (amend) it in the normal political

[66] See András Jakab, On the Legitimacy of a New Constitution: Remarks on the Occasion of the New Hungarian Basic Law of 2011, in: Miodrag Jovanović – Đorđe Pavićević (eds.), *Crisis and Quality of Democracy in Eastern Europe*, The Hague, Eleven 2012, 61–76.

Table 8.1. *Procedures of constitution-making*[67]

| | Special conventional assembly | | Ordinary parliament | | |
|---|---|---|---|---|---|
| | direct democratic legitimacy | indirect democratic legitimacy | democratic legitimacy (newly elected) | no democratic legitimacy (old Parliament) | Highest executive organ (prime minister, president) |
| without referendum | Austria, Portugal, Norway, Bulgaria | | Slovenia, Croatia, Macedonia, Montenegro, Ukraine, Czech Republic, Slovakia, Latvia [the old constitution of 1922 revived] | Serbia 1990; Hungary 1989 | |
| with referendum | Romania, Estonia | | Lithuania, Albania 1998 | | France 1958; Russia 1993 |
| further participants in the procedure | | USA (separate conventions in the Member States); German *Grundgesetz* (drafted by a convention, the members of which were delegated by the parliaments of the *Länder* + ratification by the parliaments of the *Länder* + approved by the occupying forces) | | | |

[67] Following Wieser (n. 18) 58–66. Years are given only where it was necessary for identifying the constitution that was meant.

process.[68] Amendments that happen too often also endanger the symbolic function of constitutions. There are different legal techniques to achieve it: special (usually two-thirds, but sometimes three- or four-fifths, or three-quarters) majority requirements in the legislature, special additional organs (or the people itself via referendum) which should consent, the requirement of explicit amendment,[69] prohibition of frequent modifications, requirement of the consent of two or more subsequent parliaments, or the technique of *Ewigkeitsklausel* (i.e., the prohibition of the amendment of certain principles).[70] Choosing the right type of special procedures depends on the one hand on the institutional setting and the legal context (in a first-past-the-vote electoral system, a two-thirds majority might be easily achieved by one party, and consequently, a two-thirds majority rule cannot limit this party's power), and on the other hand on the political context (if a grand coalition with constitution-amending majority is frequent, then the constitution cannot serve as a limit of the grand coalition's power).[71]

[68] The codificatory technique of the modification is normally a rewriting of certain passages of the text (or inserting new articles where it seems most logical). In some countries, however, modification is done through amendment, i.e., by adding new parts called 'amendments' at the end of the constitution. This technique makes the text structurally nontransparent, and consequently is mostly avoided. Traditionally, the US Constitution follows the amendment technique, and so does the Constitution of Macedonia amongst the newer constitutions (as an exception).

[69] Without such a requirement, the temptation is bigger to make exceptions from the constitution, as the symbolic force is not endangered in lack of a formal amendment. One consequence of the German *Inkorporationsgebot* [Art. 79(1) GG] is exactly the prohibition of this, as it accepts constitutional amendments only as an explicit amendment of the *Grundgesetz* [for a different, but in the literature minority opinion, see Ulrich Hufeld, *Die Verfassungsdurchbrechung*, Berlin, Duncker & Humblot 1997, which views it only as a limitation but not as a total prohibition]. The other consequence is that no separate legal acts can acquire constitutional rank (not even explicitly). This impedes a structurally nontransparent constitutional law, like the Austrian one, which is a hodgepodge of statutes, international treaties and individual provisions in otherwise ordinary statutes (all explicitly designated as being of constitutional rank). This is harmful both as to its symbolic function, and to its legal function (the actual limits become unclear and legally unintelligible).

[70] By 'principles' I mean '*important* norms', see below 13.1.4.

[71] During the periods of the grand parliamentary coalition in Austria, federal constitutional statutes were also passed to 'correct' the Constitutional Court's judgments. Peter Pernthaler, *Der Verfassungskern*, Wien, Manz 1998, VI, 85 (describing this practice as offhand violation of the constitution and abuse of the constitution making). Thus, when a statutory provision was struck down for unconstitutionality, the grand coalition had a majority sufficient to amend the constitution and simply readopted the provision with constitutional rank. When the grand coalition broke apart, this practice thankfully also ended and could not further fragment the constitutional law.

A constitution needs stability, if it wants to serve as a limitation of politics.[72] But stability does not only mean the above described special amendment procedures. You can make it impossible to amend a constitution, but this does not make it stable. Political reality will simply wipe it away if a change is needed. So, paradoxically, for stability you also need flexibility; that is, it has to be possible to amend it (the amendment procedure has to be more difficult than ordinary legislation, but it has to be easy enough to make it worth trying to follow the amendment procedure instead of a legal revolution). It also has to be acceptable for the political actors (especially for the majority of citizens); that is, it has to have an integrating character. And finally, it has to be sufficiently detailed, so the political players can discover their particular interest which is worth protecting. The necessity of these three factors (flexibility, integrating character and sufficient details) has been proven by empirical studies.[73]

The US Constitution is interesting from this point of view. On the one hand, it is extremely stable (since 1787 only 27 amendments have been made, but the first ten in 1791, thus only 17 amendments since 1791),[74] which can be explained by its extreme rigidity. The amendment procedure is just so cumbersome[75] that it seems hopeless for most issues. It also contains relatively few details; the text is extremely short. But both flexibility and details are ensured by the case-law of the Supreme Court, which has hugely expanded the lapidary text. Thus the text has

72 It is true even if constitutions are used – in a perverted manner – to support authoritarian attempts which limit future democratic political changes. For recent examples, see David Landau, Abusive Constitutionalism, 47 *UC Davis Law Review* 2013, 189–260.

73 Zachary Elkins – Tom Ginsburg – James Melton, *The Endurance of National Constitutions*, Cambridge, Cambridge University Press 2009, 65. In order to achieve the integrating character, public involvement in the procedure and the explicit mentioning of rights are relevant; see Tom Ginsburg – Justin Blount – Zachary Elkins, Does the Process of Constitution-Making Matter?, in: Tom Ginsburg (ed.), *Comparative Constitutional Design*, Cambridge, Cambridge University Press 2012, 31–65.

74 The other extreme is probably the Austrian constitution, which has been amended 900 (!) times since 1920, even though the constitution consists of a series statutes and special provisions in ordinary statutes (which rank equally as constitutional).

75 It is a combination of special majority requirements and additional consenting organs; see Art. 5 U.S. Constitution: 'The Congress, whenever two thirds of both Houses shall deem it necessary, shall propose Amendments to this Constitution, or, on the Application of the Legislatures of two thirds of the several States, shall call a Convention for proposing Amendments, which, in either Case, shall be valid to all Intents and Purposes, as part of this Constitution, when ratified by the Legislatures of three fourths of the several States, or by Conventions in three fourths thereof, as the one or the other Mode of Ratification may be proposed by the Congress . . .'.

hardly been amended, but the constitution has still changed considerably.[76]

The stability of the constitution can also be protected as a combination of different procedures: a relatively easy procedure for 'ordinary' constitutional amendments and a very difficult one for the basic tenets of a constitution (or even the prohibition of the amendment of the latter ones in the form of an *Ewigkeitsklausel*).[77] The advantage of this twofold procedure is that it establishes what is most important amongst the constitutional provisions (helping the symbolic function, see below), and it can ensure a combination of flexibility and stability. The danger is, however, that an *Ewigkeitsklausel* is prone to be hijacked by constitutional court judges, and there is no legal way to circumvent this. Once a mistaken interpretation of the *Ewigkeitsklausel* is chosen, it is basically impossible for a constitutional court to withdraw from it without a loss of face.[78]

The introduction of new levels in the hierarchy of norms can happen also in the opposing direction; that is. directly below 'ordinary' constitutional law but above ordinary laws: this is the institution of organic laws (e.g., in France, Hungary, Romania, Moldova, Spain and Portugal). These have the legal function of constitutional laws (as they cannot be amended in ordinary legislation, that is, they limit the simple legislative majority), but their amendment procedure does not reach the difficulty of constitutional amendments. These have a rank between the constitution and the ordinary laws. This can have two purposes: either (1) the symbolic role is protected by keeping the constitution short (thus every word of the constitution will relatively be more important); or (2) some details are not felt apt for the constitution as they should often be amended; and (2/a) the

[76] This (i.e., the change of the constitution through interpretation) is called 'constitutional alteration' or 'implicit constitutional change' [*Verfassungswandlung* or *Verfassungswandel*]. See Jellinek (n. 10) especially 9, 21, 26–27. For a modern and convincing account of the phenomenon, with the conceptual tools of constitutional economics, see Stefan Voigt, *Explaining Constitutional Change*, Cheltenham, Edward Elgar 1999, 145–179.

[77] Ordinary constitutional amendments can thus be struck down by constitutional courts ('unconstitutional constitutional law'). For an Austrian example to strike down 'ordinary' constitutional law, see VfGH 11.10.2001, G 12/00. In countries with a one-layer constitution, constitutional amendments can only be struck down for procedural reasons. On the judicial review of constitutional amendments in general, see Sabrina Ragone, *El control judicial de la reforma constitucional. Aspectos teóricos y comparativos*, Porrúa, Instituto Mexicano de Derecho Procesal Constitucional 2012.

[78] This interesting dilemma is shown by the case-law of the German BVerfG on European integration; see Robert Chr van Ooyen, *Die Staatstheorie des Bundesverfassungsgerichts und Europa. Von Solange über Maastricht zu Lissabon – und zurück mit Mangold/Honeywell?*, Baden-Baden, Nomos $^{4}$2011.

necessary majority might not be there to do that; or (2/b) frequent modification would endanger the symbolic function of the constitution. The danger of such organic laws is that if they cover too many issues, the democratically elected majority in the legislature will not be able to pass the legislation for which it received the electorate's mandate.[79]

### 8.3.2 *Typical content*

What is usually contained in constitutions[80] can be explained by two of the above-mentioned functions. The limitation of power means on the one hand separation of powers (i.e., you need provisions on organs, competences, law-making procedures), on the other hand protection of fundamental rights (i.e., you need a catalogue of fundamental rights). For the symbolic function, you need preambles and provisions on symbols (coat of arms, flag, capital and anthem). And finally, some basic principles (rule of law, democracy) can serve both the limitation and the symbolic functions. They can be in different documents (symbolically it is better to have them in one single document), but normally their regulation is in legal acts enjoying constitutional rank.[81]

Some of these elements can, however, be missing. In the long run, however, if it is an enduring constitution, they normally all appear, or if they do not, then it is a constant point of debate and cause for worry. In 1920 in Austria, political parties were unable to reach compromises on issues concerning the legal relationships between state and church, state and education, and state and family, the function of property and the role of labour, thus the easiest solution was not to draft a (new) catalogue of

[79] This, in turn, may raise further issues in light of Protocol 1 to the European Convention on Human Rights, which guarantees the possibility for the democratic majority to govern. Opinion no. 618/2011. of 17–18 June 2011 of the European Commission for Democracy through Law (CDL-AD(2011)016.) para. 24. We also have to remark that this objection applies to the majority rules of the legislation in the European Parliament. There is a similar danger if a constitutional court expands the meaning of the constitutional text to a degree which leaves no room for the executive and the legislature to change policies; see Oliver Lepsius, Rechtswissenschaft in der Demokratie, *Der Staat* 2013, 157–186.

[80] Ruth Gavison, What Belongs in a Constitution?, in: Stefan Voigt (ed.), *Constitutions, Markets and Law: Recent Experiences in Transition Economies*, Cheltenham, Edward Elgar 2002, 1–25; Markus Möstl, Regelungsfelder der Verfassung, in: Otto Depenheuer – Christoph Grabenwarter (eds.), *Verfassungstheorie*, Tübingen, Mohr Siebeck 2010, 569–597, especially 587–589.

[81] Examples for legal orders with several legal documents of constitutional rank range from Denmark and Sweden through the Czech Republic to Italy.

fundamental rights, but to keep the Basic Law of 1867 *(StGG)* in force.[82] Without a new catalogue of fundamental rights, the Austrian Constitution thus remained a mere torso.[83] As political parties remained unable to reach a compromise, an international treaty, the ECHR was adopted in constitutional rank in order to have a modern catalogue of fundamental rights.[84]

In France, a somewhat similar development can be seen: the 1958 Constitution did not contain a catalogue of fundamental rights, only a reference in its Preamble to the Preamble of the 1946 Constitution and to the 1789 Declaration which contained a catalogue of fundamental rights. Here, the Constitutional Council ventured into creating a catalogue of fundamental rights by declaring that this reference gives the two other documents a constitutional rank.[85] For shorter periods after the end of socialism, the Polish Constitution (between 1992 and 1997) also lacked a catalogue of fundamental rights.[86] The only European constitution which currently lacks a catalogue of fundamental rights is the highly lapidary Constitution of the Vatican.[87]

[82] See Felix Ermacora, Die Grundrechte in der Verfassungsfrage 1919/1920, in: Rudolf Neck - Adam Wandruszka (eds.), *Die österreichische Verfassung von 1918 bis 1938*, München, Oldenburg 1980, 53–61, 53–55. The 1867 Basic Law (*StGG*), even today, has the force of binding constitutional law.

[83] See Felix Ermacora (ed.), *Die österreichische Bundesverfassung und Hans Kelsen*, Wien, Braumueller 1982, 37–38.

[84] Austria ratified the ECHR in 1958 but elevated it to constitutional rank only in 1964. See BGBl 59/1964. The ECHR is today directly applicable constitutional law in Austria.

[85] Décision no 71-44 DC du 16 juillet 1971 concernant la loi du 1er juillet 1901 relative au contrat d'association. The 1958 Constitution and the two other historical documents are called in the French doctrine *bloc de constitutionnalité*, because all these can be used as standards of the constitutionality of statutes. Francis Hammon - Michel Troper, *Droit constitutionnel*, Paris, LGDJ [29]2005, 838–841. The preamble of the 1958 Constitution contains since 2005 a new reference, to the Charter of Environment of 2004 *(Charte de l'environment de 2004, Loi constitutionnelle n° 2005-205 du 1er mars 2005, JO du 2 mars 2005)*, thus yet another (fourth) document gained constitutional rank.

[86] Bogusław Banaszak - Tomasz Milej, *Polnisches Staatsrecht*, Warszawa, Beck 2009, 11–12.

[87] *Legge fondamentale dello Stato della Città del Vaticano*, 26.11.2000. Art. 1(1) declares that the Pope as 'the Sovereign of Vatican City State, has the fullness of legislative, executive and judicial powers'. This document is formally a constitution (as its adoption is more difficult than that of ordinary legislation: the constitution is adopted by the Pope, the statutes by a commission consisting of cardinals designated by him), but it does not fulfil the actual function of a constitution, as it cannot serve as a limitation of power by its own self-definition. The idea of a constitution was directed against absolutism, but the Vatican is an absolute monarchy (the last one in Europe).

Some typical symbolic provisions, like rules on national anthems, are also sometimes missing from constitutions.[88] For example, the Austrian anthem is legally established by a 1946 cabinet decision,[89] the Dutch by a 1932 cabinet decision[90] and the German just by a letter exchange (!) between the Federal President and the Federal Chancellor.[91] But flags and coats of arms are to be found in all modern European constitutions (as far as the present author is aware).[92]

Sometimes, constitutions also determine specific policies. This is, however, a dangerous thing, as those political forces that do not agree with these policies will see themselves forced to campaign against the constitution.[93] Consequently, the constitution will be less able to play its symbolic integrative function, and the engraved policies (even if they prove to be detrimental to the political community) will be more difficult to change.

## 8.4 Shall we use the expression the 'constitution of the European Union'?

The Treaty establishing a Constitution for Europe (TCE) seems to have failed in 2005 in the Dutch and French referenda. Thus we are unlikely to have a legal document officially called 'constitution' in the foreseeable future. But the designation is not decisive on its own (cf. the German Grundgesetz or the Hungarian Basic Law). Treaties can also be constitutions, as the examples of Cyprus (1960, Treaty of Establishment),[94]

[88] For a general overview on how and in which rank anthems are regulated, see Peter Häberle, *Nationalhymnen als kulturelle Identitätselemente des Verfassungsstaates*, Berlin, Duncker & Humblot 2007, 12–48.

[89] Bernd Wieser, Das Rechtsphänomen Bundeshymne, *Juristische Blätter* 111 (1989) 496–508, especially 503–507.

[90] Harry D Schurdel, *Nationalhymnen der Welt. Entstehung und Gehalt*, Zürich, Atlantis Musikbuch-Verlag 2006, 145.

[91] Christian Tünnesen-Harmes – Jörn Westhoff, Hymne kraft Briefwechsels?, *Neue Justiz* 1993, 60–62.

[92] For a comparative overview of constitutional rules on flags, see Peter Häberle, *Nationalflaggen. Bürgerdemokratische Identitätselemente und internationale Erkennungssymbole*, Berlin, Duncker & Humblot 2008, 16–109. On the rules on capitals, see Peter Häberle, Die Hauptstadtfrage als Verfassungsproblem, *Die öffentliche Verwaltung* 1990, 989–999.

[93] On the example of Italy see Carlo Fusaro, Italy, in: Oliver – Fusaro (n. 24) 211–234, especially 233.

[94] Karl Doehring, Staat und Verfassung in einem zusammenwachsenden Europa, *Zeitschrift für Rechtspolitik* 1993/3, 98–103; Alecos Markides, The Republic of Cyprus, in: Constantijn AJM Kortmann – Joseph Fleuren – Wim Voermans (eds.), *Constitutional Law of 10 EU Member States*, Deventer, Kluwer 2006, I–3.

the Constitution of Württemberg (1819), the Constitution of Saxony (1831)[95] or the Norddeutscher Bund (1867) show this.[96] And the fact, that there was no (successful) constitution-making procedure (or that the treaty draftings and amendments were not meant to be a constitution-making) is also of secondary importance: in Israel, for example, as we have seen above, there was no constitution-making procedure at all, as the formal constitution was created by judicial case-law out of ordinary statutes.

It seems that the EU does have a constitution; the founding treaties serve as a constitution (in the formal sense).[97] According to our definition (i.e., one or several legal documents which are more difficult to amend than 'ordinary' laws, and on which one can measure the validity of the 'ordinary' laws), the founding treaties can be qualified as the Constitution of the European Union. These treaties are procedurally more difficult to amend, than 'ordinary' laws (regulations, directives); and the validity of these ordinary measures is measured on the founding treaties (Art. 263 TFEU).

This Constitution is more rigid than constitutions usually are, but on the one hand since the Treaty of Lisbon we also have simplified treaty revision procedures (Art. 48(6)–(7) TEU);[98] on the other hand EU primary law was more frequently amended than the US Constitution during the same period. And flexibility can be and has successfully been assured in both entities through (creative objective teleological) judicial interpretation of the respective Constitution.

Consequently, the treaties serve the function of limiting the power of EU institutions (including the European Council) and of the Member States.[99] As to the symbolic function, the EU Constitution

[95] Böckenförde (n. 49) 38 with further references. [96] Möllers (n. 49) 176.

[97] In this sense, referring to the Founding Treaties the ECJ already in Case 294/83 Les Verts v Parliament [1986] ECR 1339, para 23; Opinion EEA I [1991] I-6079, para 21; 'constitutional principle' and 'constitutional guarantee' Cases C-402/05 P and C415/05 P Kadi et al. v. Council and Commission [2008] ECR I-6351 paras 285 and 290. For a sceptical view on this terminology of the ECJ, see Alexander Somek, Constitutional Treaty: A Comment on the Legal Language of the European Union, *Annual of German & European Law* 1 (2003) 310–322.

[98] As a very last resort, if one single country is blocking the amendment, a legal option to overcome this is for all other Member States to withdraw and to re-found the EU. As this would bring up some issues of succession of international organisations under general public international law, it can only be used as last resort. This option (because it basically re-founds the entity) does not help or harm the use of the expression 'constitution'; it is a legal, but extra-constitutional option.

[99] They can serve even as a limitation of the constitutional autonomy of the Members States; see Armin von Bogdandy – Matthias Kottmann – Carlino Antpöhler – Johanna Dickschen – Simon Hentrei – Maja Smrkolj, Reverse Solange – Protecting the essence of fundamental rights against EU Member States, *Common Market Law Review* 2012/2,

seems deficient, however. On the one hand, numerous acts (most of them called protocols) enjoy the same rank as the treaties (making primary law almost as nontransparent as Austrian constitutional law). On the other hand, the symbolic content of the Constitution is rather slim. Values of modern constitutionalism and constitutional principles (mentioned in the preamble, e.g., rule of law, democracy) can have symbolic force, but no explicit references are made to the anthem, flag or coat of arms.[100] The failure of the TCE is partly to be explained by the rejection of this symbolic content (the Lisbon Treaty is more or less the TCE without the symbolic content of and the designation as a constitution).[101] This is not unique either, some national constitutions also lack these elements, but it is still a deficiency, if we expect a constitution to be a symbol of a political community.

As legal scholars, we cannot entirely substitute the symbolic side. But if we call the founding treaties (including the Charter of Fundamental Rights of the European Union) as the 'Constitution of Europe'[102] (or somewhat more precisely, but less enthusiastically the 'Constitution of the European Union'), and if we conceptualise legal issues as constitutional issues,[103] then we are forming the public discourse by vesting some symbolic force into these documents.[104] Consequently, the

489–519; Gil Carlos Rodríguez Iglesias, Zur 'Verfassung' der Europäischen Gemeinschaft, *Europäische Grundrechte-Zeitschrift* 1996, 125–131, 125–126.

100 On the symbols of the EU and their (sometimes questionable) legal base, see Moritz Röttinger, Die Hoheitszeichen der Europäischen Union – ein paar vielleicht nicht nur theoretische Rechtsfragen, *Europarecht* 2003, 1095–1108; Falco Federmann, *Die Konstitutionalisierung der Europäischen Union*, Lohmar, Josef Eul 2007, 217–218.

101 Only as the rejection of the *symbolism* of a constitution can be understood the Presidency Conclusions of the European Council, 21/22 June 2007 (11177/1/07 REV 1), Annex I: IGC Mandate, para 3: 'The TEU and the Treaty on the Functioning of the Union will not have a constitutional character.' But it cannot bind legal scholars as to their terminology; see Armin von Bogdandy – Jürgen Bast, The Constitutional Approach to EU Law – From Taming Intergovernmental Relationships to Framing Political Processes, in: von Bogdandy – Bast (n. 49) 1.

102 E.g., Jürgen Habermas, *Zur Verfassung Europas*, Berlin, Suhrkamp 2011.

103 For a missed opportunity where the ECJ did not conceptualise a legal issue as a constitutional issue see C-364/10, Hungary v. Slovakia (not yet published).

104 Cf. the numerous handbooks and textbooks having in their title the 'constitutional law' of the European Union. From the latest ones, see, e.g., Robert Schütze, *European Constitutional Law*, Cambridge, Cambridge University Press 2012; von Bogdandy – Bast (n. 49); Dimitris Th Tsatsos (ed.), *Die Unionsgrundordnung*, Berlin, BWV 2010; Allan Rosas – Lorna Armati, *EU Constitutional Law*, Oxford, Oregon, Hart 2012, especially 1–6 with further references.

decoupling of state and constitution,[105] and expressions like 'postnational constitutionalism',[106] 'unity of European and national constitutional law',[107] 'transnational constitutionalism',[108] 'multilevel constitutionalism',[109] 'constitutional pluralism'[110] are all to be welcomed, as they soften up the traditional national-state-centred paradigm (even if they seem somewhat confused).[111] They all contribute to constitutionalising the legal terminology of the European Union, which (through implied connotations, besides the legal situation which is directly not influenced by the terminology) (1) can help in strengthening the European Union in public discourse (the constitutional language can enhance public attention, which leads to better political accountability;

[105] Fabian Amtenbrink - Peter AJ van den Berg (eds.), *The Constitutional Intergrity of the European Union*, The Hague, TMC Asser 2010; Giuseppe Martinico, *The Tangled Complexity of the EU Constitutional Process: The Frustrating Knot of Europe*, London, Routledge 2012; Ulrich K Preuß, Disconnecting Constitutions from Statehood, in: Petra Dobner - Martin Loughlin (eds.), *The Twilight of Constitutionalism?*, Oxford, Oxford University Press 2010, 23–46; JHH Weiler - M Wind (eds.), *European Constitutionalism Beyond the State*, Cambridge, Cambridge University Press 2003; Paul Craig, Constitutions, Constitutionalism, and the European Union, *European Law Journal* 7 (2001) 125–150; Anne Peters, *Elemente einer Theorie der Verfassung Europas*, Berlin, Duncker & Humblot 2001, with further references; Albrecht Weber, *Europäische Verfassungsvergleichung*, München, Beck 2010, 17–18.

[106] Anneli Albi, Introduction: The European Constitution and National Constitutions in the Context of 'Post-national Constitutionalism', in: Anneli Albi - Jacques Ziller (eds.), *The European Constitution and National Constitutions: Ratification and Beyond*, Alphen aan den Rijn, Kluwer Law International 2007, 1–14; Jo Shaw, 'Postnational Constitutionalism' in the European Union, *European Public Policy* 6 (1999) 579–597.

[107] Ingolf Pernice, Europäisches und nationales Verfassungsrecht, *Veröffentlichungen der Vereinigung der Deutschen Staatsrechtslehrer* 2001, 149–193, especially 172–176.

[108] Nicholas Tsagourias (ed.), *Transnational Constitutionalism: International and European Models*, Cambridge, Cambridge University Press 2007.

[109] Ingolf Pernice, Multilevel Constitutionalism in the European Union, *European Law Review* 2002, 511–529.

[110] Nicholas William Barber, *The Constitutional State*, Oxford, Oxford University Press 2010, 172–183; Matej Avbelj - Jan Komárek (eds.), Four Visions of Constitutional Pluralism, *EUI Working Papers Law* 2008/21; Matej Avbelj - Jan Komárek (eds.), *Constitutional Pluralism in the European Union and Beyond*, Oxford, Hart 2012, with further references.

[111] For opposing views, using mainly arguments based on the historical origins and on the inherent meaning of the word 'constitution', see Olivier Beaud, *La puissance de l'État*, Paris, Presses Universitaires de France 1994, 209; Dieter Grimm, Does Europe Need a Constitution? *European Law Journal* 1 (1995) 282–302, 292; Martin Loughlin, What Is Constitutionalisation?, in: Petra Dobner - Martin Loughlin (eds.), *The Twilight of Constitutionalism?*, Oxford, Oxford University Press 2010, 47–70, especially 69–70.

the new language can also contribute to European polity formation);[112] and (2) even more importantly, this can help to stop constitutional changes in Member States, if these changes contradict the principles of the Constitution of the European Union (both by forming EU discourse and awakening responsibility at EU level, and by forming domestic discourses and making clear that not everything can be done that is a procedurally possible constitutional amendment).[113]

[112] Cf. Miguel Poiares Maduro, The Importance of Being Called a Constitution, *International Journal of Constitutional Law* 3 (2005) 332–356, 354–355.

[113] See especially von Bogdandy (n. 99).

# 9

# Democracy in Europe through parliamentarisation

> La démocratie est aujourd'hui une philosophie, une manière de vivre, une religion et, presque accessoirement, une forme de gouvernement.[1]

This chapter deals with the question what we should mean by the concept of democracy, and how we can apply this to the European Union.[2] After setting out some theoretical premises on the virtues of democracy and explaining its historical success in the first section, the second section of this chapter tests the usual arguments in the political and scholarly discourse about the well-functioning of democracy in the European Union (EU). We are also going to show how in practice the problem of the EU democratic deficit could be solved. Based on these results, in the final section, we are going to make some suggestions as to the usage of the concept of democracy in the EU constitutional discourse.

The chapter's main thesis is that if we want to enjoy the two virtues of democracy (i.e., its capacity to generate loyalty and its self-correction potential), then a direct connection between the act of electing Members of Parliament (MPs) to the European Parliament and the formation of the Commission has to be established. For this purpose,

[1] 'Democracy is today a philosophy, a way of life, a religion, and – almost accessorily – a form of government.' Georges Burdeau, *La démocratie*, Paris, Le Seuil 1956, 8.

[2] For valuable criticism and useful remarks I am grateful to Krisztina Arató, Armin von Bogdandy, Jürgen Bast, Paul Behrens, András Bozóki, Carlos Closa, Philipp Dann, Sergio Dellavalle, Zsolt Enyedi, Gábor Hamza, Ferenc Hörcher, Elena Jileva, Miodrag A Jovanović, Stephan Kirste, János Kis, András Körösényi, Mária Ludassy, Enric Martinez Herrera, Tamás Meszerics, Zoltán Pállinger, Theodor Schilling, Allan F Tatham, Szilárd Tattay, Ingo Venzke, Robert Zbíral, and to the participants of the research seminars held on 20–21 May 2010 in Oñati (Spain), on 24 August 2010 in Heidelberg (Germany), on 12 October 2010 in Budapest (Hungary), on 8 December 2010 in Mexico City (IACL World Congress workshop) and on 26 January 2012 at CEU (Budapest). A very early version of this chapter was published as 'Full Parliamentarisation of the EU without Changing the Treaties. Why We Should Aim for It and How Easily It Can be Achieved', *Jean Monnet Working Papers* 2012/3.

no treaty amendment is necessary, as the European Parliament already has the legal means to decide alone on the composition of the Commission.

## 9.1 Why does a successful EU have to be democratic?

There are two main strategies to justify democracy. One is to try to show that it is superior to contending theories because it fits better to the *moral* nature of human beings, as, for instance, it is based on equal dignity or equal freedom of the people. Iranian religious fundamentalists or European xenophobic-fascist parties, however, definitely have a different view on what is the moral nature of human beings, and beyond the mere assertion that they are wrong it is difficult to argue against them. They simply have a different source of legitimacy (a divine one, or the 'nation' as defined by culture, history and language), which can be internally as coherent as the best democratic theories (even if they are scary in some elements to our sensitive democratic ears).[3] A moral justification for democracy is thus mostly unable to convince anyone who is not a democrat anyway.

The other option is to choose a more neutral language (even if we know that it is never fully neutral, but at least less directly value-laden), and to concentrate on *why* democracy won the contest for the leading source of legitimacy in the modern world (and why it changed its *precise* meaning in political discourse in a Proteus-like manner). So we look at democracy's story from a more realistic, outsider or even pragmatic perspective. In this way, its virtues will become more convincing (for non-democrats) and its dead-ends more instructive (for democrats).[4] Such an approach has fewer normative (moral philosophical) assumptions as a starting point (in this sense it is a minimalistic approach and is thus less vulnerable to competing normative theories); it looks rather for explanations for the success of the democratic legitimacy claim. The

[3] Cf. Karl Doehring, *Allgemeine Staatslehre*, Heidelberg, CF Müller [3]2004, 143 pointing to the fact that democracy is based on the fiction that citizens are both morally (except for criminals) and intellectually (except for minors and insane people) qualified to decide about the country's future. But factually untrue starting points are not necessarily a problem for political philosophies. Similarly to ancient gods, people (and politicians) adhere to political philosophies primarily *not* for their intellectual coherence ('intellectual potency'), but for their capability of emotional identification and for their long-term practical achievements in society ('political potency'). Cf. John Dunn, *Setting the People Free: The Story of Democracy*, London, Atlantic Books 2005, 17.

[4] Cf. Friedrich August von Hayek, *Die Verfassung der Freiheit*, Tübingen, Mohr 1971 (1960), 129 on the issue that democracy is not an end in itself but a means to achieve goals.

*explanatory* starting point of this chapter is that the success can be explained by two features of democracy: namely (a) its capability to induce loyalty and (b) its potential for self-correction. The chapter becomes normative only in its second part, when it shows that *if we want to enjoy these two features* (the normative presupposition will be that we do), then we have to have a certain understanding and institutional structure, namely a parliamentary system at the EU level.

### *9.1.1 Genealogy: birth in the eighteenth century*

There is a nice myth, which traces today's democracy back to ancient Greece.[5] As a matter of fact, the Athenians themselves borrowed it from Asia: its origins are to be found rather in today's Syria, Iraq and Iran where the 'inhabitants' (in Sumerian: the *dumu*) decided the important issues in assemblies. The idea had been carried to the West, to Phoenician cities (Byblos, Sidon) which set up similar governmental systems, and then picked up by the Athenians (who were in intensive maritime commercial contact with the Phoenicians).[6] As for its survival after ancient Greece, we have to differentiate between three different issues: (A) the survival of the word 'democracy', (B) the institutional setting of ancient Athens and today's democracies, (C) the idea of popular self-rule or the idea that 'it ought to be ordinary people (the adult citizen) and not extra-ordinary people who rule'.[7]

Ad (A). We still use the Greek word (*δημοκρατία* or *demokratia*), simply because we know this form of government from the (translated)[8] descriptions by Plato, Aristotle, Aeschylus or Demosthenes, and not because they invented it. As in Athens the system miserably failed (i.e., it led to the military catastrophe of the Peloponnesian War similar to the German catastrophe in the Second World War and occasionally also, again similarly, to the persecution of its own elite, the most notable case of which

[5] E.g., Robert A Dahl, *Democracy and its Critics*, New Haven, London, Yale University Press 1989, 1.

[6] John Keane, *The Life and Death of Democracy*, London, Simon & Schuster 2009, xi; Simon Hornblower, Democratic Institutions in Ancient Greece, in: John Dunn (ed.), *Democracy. The Unfinished Journey 508* BC *to* AD *1993*, Oxford, Oxford University Press 1994, 1–16, 4.

[7] Dunn (n. 6) Preface, v. The definition of who are 'ordinary people' has gone through several changes in the history of democracy.

[8] In his Latin translation of Aristotle's *Politics*, William of Moerbecke in the middle of thirteenth century did not translate the Greek word to 'populi potentia', but rather kept the original word *demokratia*, and so determined today's terminology. See Quentin Skinner, The Italian City-Republics, in: Dunn (n. 6) 57–69, 59.

was the death penalty being given to one of its leading intellectuals, Socrates); over the next two thousand years 'democracy' was used in a strongly pejorative sense.[9] The Greek 'democracy' (meant as direct democracy for everybody, or at least all male adult citizens) was rather explicitly rejected in the name of the 'republic' (in today's terminology: 'representative democracy' for the white, male and rich electorate).[10] In the United States, the term was not used to describe their own system of government (only as a party-political direction, often in a pejorative sense) until a foreigner, the French aristocrat Alexis de Tocqueville, used it for the American form of government.[11] In Europe, it appeared earlier as self-description by certain political forces (first in today's Netherlands and Belgium, in the 1780s),[12] not, however, because these forces happened to be fascinated by the Greeks, but out of rhetorical reasons. We will come back to this later.

Ad (B). The core institution of modern representative democracy, the parliament, has its institutional origins in feudal Europe, in which the estates were represented. In some countries on a careful step-by-step basis, in others rather abruptly, the general suffrage was widened to today's size comprising all (in cases limited to sane and non-criminal) adult citizens, which is neither Greek, nor feudal in origin. It is simply new.

Ad (C). Today's idea of popular self-rule is indeed similar to the ancient Greek one, but also to old European (German) tribal traditions.[13] Sporadic Greek inspirations are possible (e.g., through Marsilius of Padua, though even these cases are rather debatable),[14] but none of these can actually be proven to have essentially influenced the

[9] The good and successful example from the antiquity was rather Rome. Partly with its imperial tradition; partly with its republican tradition, where the unit of political authority was *Senatus Populusque Romanus* in which notably the Senate came first. Dunn (n. 3) 54.

[10] James Madison, *The Federalist Papers* No. 61, 63 and 65. Also the Italian city-republics in the twelfth to the eighteenth centuries never described themselves as democracies, and when the first Italian city-republics began to exist, the relevant Greek classics had not yet even been translated into Latin. See Skinner (n. 8) 57–59. Italian city-republics all failed and were often (similarly to their Greek predecessors) referred to as an example of chaos, see *ibid.* 59, 63.

[11] Dunn (n. 3) 72–73. Alexis de Tocqueville, *De la démocratie en Amérique*, vols. I–II, Paris, Gosselin 1835–40 (the first volume was translated into English as early as 1839 by Henry Reeve).

[12] Dunn (n. 3) 84–88; John Markoff, *Waves of Democracy: Social Movements and Political Change*, London, Pine Forge 1996, 2.

[13] Reinhold Zippelius, *Geschichte der Staatsideen*, München, Beck [10]2003, 97; Dahl (n. 5) 32.

[14] For a convincing critique of the view that Marsilius was an early 'democrat', see Hans Leo Reimann, Überlieferung und Rezeption im Mittelalter [der Demokratie], in: Otto Brunner – Werner Conze – Reinhart Koselleck (eds.), *Geschichtliche Grundbegriffe*, vol. 1, Stuttgart, Klett-Cotta 2004, 835–839, 836–837 with further references.

eighteenth-century re-emergence of popular self-rule. As an idea, it was based rather on eventually secularised but originally biblical Christian ideas of equality in their Protestant interpretation,[15] and on the feudal idea of basing authority on contract (between the liege lord and his vassals).[16] To emphasise these origins would have, however, been unwise, as the idea of popular self-rule as a source of legitimacy was directed against the divine legitimacy of feudal monarchs. To mask it *ex post facto* as a revival of some old Ancient Greek truth (which was prestigious enough but evidently different from the rejected feudalism) was rhetorically much more effective. And so it happened: they began to call it democracy – after they invented it without the Greeks.

But even if we see that the idea is based on a certain interpretation of Christianity and on feudalistic contractualism, it still remains unclear: (1) *why* it emerged exactly in the eighteenth century (and not, e.g., in the fourteenth), and (2) *why* it became stronger than the traditional hierarchical conceptions of (monarchical) authority, which were equally based in (a different interpretation of) the very same ideas.

Let us examine now the first, genealogical question. The social and political situation for successful democratic claims became ripe first in the eighteenth century. (a) The main reason for that was *secularisation* (not to be confused with atheism, which remained rare even during this period), meaning here the declining explanatory and justificatory force of

[15] David Wootton, The Levellers, in: Dunn (n. 6) 71–90. The leveller idea of giving suffrage to *every* male adult proved to be too radical in the seventeenth century and was successfully oppressed. Even though democratic claims were not totally unknown in Catholic theology (Francisco Suárez, 1548–1617), in practice Catholicism stood for a long time clearly on the traditionalist hierarchic anti-democratic side. The American Revolution in the eighteenth century later used similar justifications (with eventually tamed claims on suffrage); see the *Declaration of Independence* 1776: 'all men are created equal, that they are endowed by their Creator with certain unalienable Rights'. The French *Declaration of the Rights of Man and of the Citizen* (1789) became slightly less directly Christian, but the origins are obvious even here: 'the National Assembly recognises and proclaims, in the presence and under the auspices of the Supreme Being, the following rights of man and of the citizen: Article 1. Men are born and remain free and equal in rights.' Besides the biblical equality idea, the institution of medieval towns (*universitas civium*) in which the community members (city-members, or 'citizens') were free and equal should be mentioned as a predecessor of modern citizens' equality. Randall Lesaffer, *European Legal History*, Cambridge, Cambridge University Press 2009, 226.

[16] The feudal contract was developed from Germanic tribal traditions, and included *mutual* rights and obligations. See Lesaffer (n. 15) 151. Also the *Magna Carta* of 1215 was contractual in nature, even if the text seems a one-sided grant of freedoms: the barons (who were vassals of the King) were expected to be loyal and to accept royal authority in exchange for the King's signing (or rather: sealing) of the document.

religion in politics. Secularisation also meant a growing acceptance of social changes: the static nature of law and society of the Middle Ages was based on the pre-ordained order by the infallible divine will, and as the order was losing its religious side, it was also losing its unchangeable and sacred nature.[17] In the language of politics, theological divine will was replaced by the legal will of the sovereign or by the will of the legislator.[18] It was caused by a unique constellation of European developments. (a/1) Early feudal monarchs used the church as a legitimacy-supporting organisation for the kingdom or the empire, which was in theory ('spiritually') subordinated to an independent Pope, but in practice served the stability of the respective monarchy.[19] The Investiture Controversy (eleventh–twelfth centuries) as an independence struggle of the church against secular authority or even as a fight for taking over the leading role in the Christian world led, however, to a certain distance between religious and political authority (Concordat of Worms, 1122).[20] The ongoing legal quest between the pope and the emperor and the attempt of these powers to strengthen their internal hierarchical administration by legal rules made more lawyers necessary on both sides: canonists (or decretists, experts in church laws) and legists (experts in secular Roman law).[21] This growing amount of legal knowledge and the finding of a remaining copy of Justinian's *Digesta* (i.e., a vast secular but extremely prestigious body of law) at the end of the eleventh century also eventually contributed to the autonomy of legal science from theology (so resulting in separate faculties of law at the early

[17] António Manuel Hespanha, *Cultura jurídica europea. Síntesis de un milenio*, Madrid, Tecnos 2002, 59–66.

[18] Hespanha (n. 17) 71, 105–106.

[19] For the justification of this situation, the 'two swords doctrine' of Pope Gelasius I (492–96) was used, according to which the secular ('temporal') sword also stems from the church (the pope), but it is used by secular monarchs (the emperor) for secular government, but the spiritual sword remains with the pope. Gerhard Köbler, *Deutsche Rechtsgeschichte*, München, Franz Vahlen [6]2005, 109–110. It is based on Luke 22:38, where the disciples tell the arrested Jesus: 'Lord, behold, here are two swords.' The re-interpretation of this passage and of this doctrine was itself part of the Investiture Controversy.

[20] Lesaffer (n. 15) 212–216.

[21] Roman law was especially used by the secular side as a pool of argument, especially the phrases by Ulpian 'quod principi placuit, legis habet vigorem' ('what pleases the emperor, has the force of law') and 'princeps legibus solutus est' ('the emperor is not bound by the law'). D. 1.4.1 and D. 1.3.31. It was used later by other secular powers (kings, princes) against the emperor himself. For more detail, see Piper Gilmore, *Arguments from Roman Law in Political Thought, 1220–1600*, Cambridge, Mass., Harvard University Press 1941; Jacques Krynen – Albert Rigaudière (eds.), *Droits savants et pratiques françaises du pouvoir, 11e–15e siècles*, Bordeaux, Presses Universitaires de Bordeaux 1992.

universities).[22] (a/2) Based on the actual political practice of Italian city-republics in the fifteenth and sixteenth centuries (which did not claim any divine legitimacy), Machiavelli described the internal logic of politics in his *Il principe* and the *Discorsi*. Even though it outraged most of Europe, it also contributed considerably to thinking about politics in a secular way.[23] (a/3) Even more importantly, the Reformation and the following religious wars in the sixteenth and seventeenth centuries shook the force of the Church (or from then on: the churches) even in the spiritual arena. The struggle between Catholicism and Protestantism ended undecided (Peace of Augsburg, 1555; Peace of Westphalia, 1648): both continued to exist in a Europe, which from then on was recognised to consist of equally sovereign states. The co-existence of Protestants and Catholics in Europe and sometimes even within individual states required a new language for the political discourse, a secular language. The horrific results of religious (civil) wars in the seventeenth century further strengthened the feeling of the elites in many countries that a new non-religious conceptual framework might be a more fruitful way to secure stable peace. At the same time, the Peace of Westphalia also meant that claims for universal (papal or imperial) authority had been rejected. But by shaking the unified religious authority, monarchical (divine) legitimacy was also weakened, and needed additional (secular) support. Because basing their authority on the assent of aristocrats (which would actually have been a historically more appropriate explanation of the original emergence of their power) would have weakened their internal situation, it was not an attractive option. A new doctrine was needed: the doctrine of sovereignty.[24] As one of the leading figures of the sovereignty doctrine, Hobbes explained monarchical power by two contracts: the people first made a contract with each other and then with the monarch, making him sovereign. From this, it was only a small (but important) intellectual step to leave aside the second contract, that is, to keep sovereignty with the people itself (Locke, Rousseau).

(b) Another reason for the success of the democratic idea based on equal freedom of individuals was *individualism*.[25] The corporatist (in which rights and duties depended on belonging to a social-juridical group, like

[22] Lesaffer (n. 15) 236, 243, 253–254. On the role of Justinian's *Digesta* and its first teacher in Bologna, Irnerius, see Aulis Aarnio, *Essays on the Doctrinal Study of Law*, Dordrecht, Springer 2011, 1–2 with further references.

[23] Lesaffer (n. 15) 313. [24] For more details see above the introduction to Chapter 6.

[25] Some authors trace back individualism to John Duns Scotus (1266–1308) or to William of Ockham (1300–c.1350). Hespanha (n. 17) 70. It might be true as a germinal anticipation of the epistemological individualism, but definitely untrue as a political idea.

an estate) and hierarchical picture of society faded away. (b/1) European states chased each other through constant wars into becoming more centralised, militarily and financially more efficient states (those which were unable to follow this path, like Poland, disappeared). The new absolute states subdued traditional aristocracies, which led people living on the territory of the aristocrats to consider themselves as direct subjects of the king, rather than belonging to the aristocrat. Instead of following group or collectivistic logic, in the new constellation people became simply *individual* subjects of the central monarchical power.[26] (b/2) Self-governing commercial city-republics in Italy with their necessarily more open mentality and social structure were also more open to new ideas, to critical thinking and to reasoning instead of authority, thus preparing the landscape for renaissance humanism (instead of scholasticism) which then spread throughout Europe. (b/3) Johannes Guttenberg's inventing the printing machine around 1440 not only contributed to the success of the Reformation, but it also made possible the development of printed newspapers. During the eighteenth century, in England, France, certain parts of the Holy Roman Empire, the Netherlands and the British colonies of North America (today's US East Coast), the number of literate people and the connecting journalism reached a critical mass. Public opinion was considerably formed by newspapers, and for a printed text it became less important as to who had said it in which ostentatious palace. The argument itself became more important, about which each reader formed his opinion *individually*.[27] (b/4) To a certain extent, the weakening of general religious spiritual authority (i.e., secularisation) led to intellectual 'loneliness', since there were no longer unquestionable truths. One had to believe in his or her own (individual) reason, which served as the epistemological starting point for the Enlightenment, which on the political level eventually promoted equality and freedom.

(c) Due to developing trade and demographic growth, commercialised agriculture gained ground. In countries where there was also a strong bourgeoisie (and, due to political contingencies, a balance between the monarch and the land-owning aristocracy), hierarchical feudal social structures were more likely to grow weaker and to give way to democratisation.[28] Capitalism also meant relatively autonomous firms and economic growth, the latter of which had the consequence that politics was

[26] Markoff (n. 12) 43–45. [27] Markoff (n. 12) 46.

[28] Barrington Moore, Jr., *Social Origins of Dictatorship and Democracy*, Boston, Beacon Press 1966, especially 3–155, 413–422.

no longer a zero-sum game, so that it was in the interest of different social groups within the state to agree to compromise solutions with political opponents.[29]

(d) Changes in military organisation and technique made the sheer number of foot soldiers with relatively cheap equipment the decisive factor in winning wars in the seventeenth century.[30] Much later, of course, with the appearance of heavy artillery, mortars, machine guns, tanks and air power, this factor was no longer so important, but at the birth of modern political democracy it did play an essential role.[31]

All these factors (but none of them decisively alone) contributed to the structural probability for the success of democratic arguments. It did not make the re-emergence of the democratic idea a 'historical necessity', but it made concrete democratic actions and movements likelier to succeed.

### *9.1.2 The success story of democracy or the strength of the claim for democracy*

After having outlined the circumstances of its birth, we should now turn to the question of *why* democracy became so successful in the following 250 years? *Why* has this legitimacy claim proved stronger in practice than other claims? The strength of the democratic argument lies in its capacity to widen the circle of political actors. So whoever needs 'outsider' support in a political chess game, new figures can be placed on the chess-board with reference to democracy.[32] This is why intellectually different social movements fought under the banner of democracy, and this is why the democrats of the eighteenth or even of the nineteenth century would be counted today as blatant anti-democrats.[33] In the name of democracy, the suffrage was eventually broadened from rich white males to the poor

[29] Dahl (n. 5) 252.

[30] Dahl (n. 5) 245–248. One of the factors in democratising ancient Athens was also the change in military technique (instead of expensive cavalrymen hoplites and rowers in the galleys became prominent). On the topic in general, see Stanislav Andreski, *Military Organization and Society*, Berkeley, University of California Press 1968.

[31] Dahl (n. 5) 248.

[32] It is extremely difficult (mostly possible only through violence) to reverse democratisation: with the exception of some short-lived and tragic exceptions, it is a one-way street. Dunn (n. 3) 154 talks about 'the political logic of ever-widening representation'. Any claim to narrow democracy would automatically make the claimer into an open enemy of all those who would lose their political rights, so it is a risk which a rational politician is normally not willing to take.

[33] Markoff (n. 12) 3–4.

and to women. In the name of democracy, slavery and feudal dependencies were abolished. In the name of democracy, the power of the elected representative body (parliament) gained competences and control over the executive. In the name of democracy, a struggle was fought for honest electoral counts and secret voting in order to obtain the real will of the electorate. And in the name of democracy, organised political parties gained acceptance as legitimate social actors. It was not obvious at all that whoever fought for one of these goals also agreed with the others.

Through these struggles with respectively different stakeholders and with considerably different political ideas, democracy has been redefined again and again, either by the people challenging power holders in the streets and fields, or by the powerholders themselves writing new laws and constitutional documents.[34] Whether a specific struggle was motivated cynically by self-interest,[35] or whether it happened out of a deep and honest moral conviction, varied. The two motivations could even reinforce each other, as in the case of women's right to vote. After the First World War, the suffragette movement received support from arch-conservative circles who wanted to have some counterweight after the right to vote was broadened to the poor male (due to the need for their support as soldiers in that War or due to fear from the returning veterans after it), as conservatives hoped that the females being rather religious would impede or at least slow down a radical left turn in politics.[36] Similarly, for the nineteenth-century incremental broadening of the suffrage in Britain, the main motive of the elite was to divide the poorer, in order to avoid a revolutionary explosion similar to France.[37] The social (financial, human resources or popular support) costs of counterbalancing a democratic claim with another one seemed to be smaller than the costs of oppressing all democratic claims.

[34] Markoff (n. 12) xvi.

[35] According to Herodotus, even the Athenian origins can be explained rather by the self-interest of a certain part of the elite: Kleisthenes adopted democracy not because of personal conviction, but because he needed help for his fight against rival aristocrats and their Spartan supporters. Herodotus, *History*, tr. AD Godley, Cambridge, Mass., Harvard University Press 1922, V,66,2: 72–73. Cf. Mogens H Hansen, *The Athenian Democracy in the Age of Demosthenes*, Oxford, Blackwell 1991, 33–34.

[36] Markoff (n. 12) 86. For a more nuanced picture, also including bottom-up elements in the explanation, with country-specific differences, see Blanca Rodríguez-Ruiz – Ruth Rubio-Marín (eds.), *The Struggle for Female Suffrage in Europe: Voting to Become Citizens*, Leiden, Brill 2012.

[37] Thomas Babington Macaulay, speech of 2 March 1831, in: James B Conacher, *The Emergence of British Parliamentary Democracy in the Nineteenth Century*, New York, Wiley 1971, 25.

If democratic claims emerge, even anti-democrats tend to be forced to pay at least lip-service to democracy. As the political sociologist John Markoff convincingly puts it:[38]

> Before the end of the [eighteenth] century, the future Pope Pius VII, in his Christmas talk, was saying that 'democratic government' was compatible with the Gospel.[39] Such developments were to a significant degree stimulated by the French events. But even after the French defeat, countries that had experienced French rule could not restore the previous divine-right hierarchy. To match the French achievement, France's enemies had to build enormous armies. To do so, many of them needed to court the ordinary people who would fill the ranks and supply the armies. Even governments with no wish to give real power to those below were beginning to find essential the claim to be doing so.

And once you open up the gates rhetorically, you make it more difficult to oppress democratic claims than before.

But democratic movements not only proved to be successful for the power contest within a state; in addition already-established democratic states showed impressive power in international conflicts. So democracy was not simply an epidemic which unavoidably caught some countries and then doomed them, but rather the opposite: it helped them to become considerably stronger. This was for two main reasons: (a) it was able to produce loyalty; and (b) it had a remarkable capacity for self-correction.

Ad (a). On the one hand, it strengthened the loyalty of their respective political-community members by giving them a voice in what was happening (or at least it gave them the impression that they had it).[40] This was especially important during times of crisis or even war.[41]

Ad (b). On the other hand, it seemed to be an efficient procedural solution to promote the citizens' interests through the possibility of making elected officials responsible if they did not promote these interests (by not re-electing them, i.e., by making them compete on the basis of who could promote the citizens' interests best).[42] Governments could

[38] Markoff (n. 12) 49 (footnote in original).

[39] Robert R Palmer, *The Age of Democratic Revolution: A Political History of Europe and America, 1760–1800*, vol. 1, Princeton, NJ, Princeton University Press 1959, 18.

[40] Robert C Cooter, *The Strategic Constitution*, Princeton, NJ, Princeton University Press 2000, 144.

[41] Albert O Hirschman, *Exit, Voice, and Loyalty: Responses to Decline in Firms, Organizations, and States*, Cambridge, Mass., Harvard University Press 1970.

[42] Cooter (n. 40) 4, 11, 13, 17, 359–360, 373–374. Cf. Amartya Sen, *Development as Freedom*, New York, Knopf 1999, 152: 'no substantial famine has ever occurred in any independent country with a democratic form of government and a relatively free press.'

be forced by their electorate to change measures harmful to its interests (trial and error).[43] This eventually also made these communities economically stronger, which was necessary for successfully fighting international conflicts.[44] Empirical studies have confirmed that (except for extremely poor countries) democracy makes economic growth more likely (all other factors being equal).[45]

Since the end of the eighteenth century, democratisation has succeeded in its above-mentioned struggles in the world through different transnational or even multicontinental waves, in which one country's experience often helped the other ones, resulting in 'democratic waves' – the latest one after the fall of communism.[46] Sometimes democracy (in its then understood form) was directly imposed by an army (the French in the 1790s in Europe, the United States after the Second World War, or lately in Haiti and Iraq), sometimes it was followed by respective elites as a model of success (especially after winning major international conflicts, like the First and Second World Wars or the Cold War),[47] sometimes by power contenders as a strong tool to challenge existing power structures, or sometimes simply by offering students fellowships after which they returned to their home country to spread their newly learned ideas (all major Western democracies followed this latter practice).[48] These mechanisms contribute to the fact that generally only a limited number of political models are followed in the world, and that changes in the

[43] Karl Raimund Popper, *The Open Society and Its Enemies*, London, Routledge 2006, vol. I, 163, 167, vol. II, 90, 143, 434; Christoph Möllers, *Demokratie. Zumutungen und Versprechen*, Berlin, Klaus Wagenbach 2008, 11, 13.

[44] The idea of equal freedom itself has also economic implications, as it helps competition. Non-discrimination means that the most capable should do the job, only his or her individual achievements count. Protection of private property is necessary for capitalist economic growth. Protection of privacy and freedom of thought contribute to a fearless and creative working environment. Political freedoms ensure democracy, so their economic impact is more indirect than the any of the latter. For a deep analysis of these questions with further references, see Cooter (n. 40) 241–357.

[45] Elias Papaioannou – Gregorios Siourounis, Democratization and Growth, *CEDI Working Papers* 2007–13.

[46] Improving communication and transportation contributed to the spreading of broad ideas, forms of public action (e.g., strike, demonstration, non-violent resistance), organisational vehicles, symbols or slogans. Waves became in this manner faster and more effective. Markoff (n. 12) 25–28.

[47] The US and the French revolutions proved also the power of democratic states and their ability to mobilise masses. Markoff (n. 12) 50; Dunn (n. 3) 91.

[48] Markoff (n. 12) 32–34.

political model are rather wave-like than sporadic.[49] As for now, neither a new major democratic wave (not many countries remain to be democratised with our current concept of democracy, only a few island-like countries resist accepting the democratic claim) nor anti-democratic waves are to be seen. Democracy seems to have acquired a quasi-monopoly as today's claim to political legitimacy.[50]

Further the EU itself claims democratic legitimacy in the Preamble, further in Arts. 2 and 10 Treaty on European Union (TEU). The question is, however, whether it has any other choice, or whether it could base itself on another form of legitimacy. In the light of the above, the answer seems to be in the negative, but as in the literature the alternative option of 'output legitimacy' is sometimes mentioned,[51] we have to deal with it here too.

### *9.1.3 Is output legitimacy an alternative?*

Output legitimacy means that an authority has to be obeyed because its decisions lead to good (acceptable) results.[52] So the main issue is not about the source of the authority but about its use and result. To a certain degree, this enlightened technocratic idea served historically as the basis of the EU.[53] A similar argument is, when the EU (formerly European

[49] Through these mechanisms, anti-democratic waves are also possible: in the 1920s and 1930s, most of the newly established European democracies swapped side to authoritarian or even totalitarian regimes.

[50] Cf. Francis Fukuyama, *The End of History and the Last Man*, New York, Free Press 1992. When communism fell, also the justification for some right-wing dictatorships fell, as they could not point at the enemy anymore, so it also accelerated their democratisation. Markoff (n. 12) 97.

[51] E.g., Fritz W Scharpf, *Demokratietheorie zwischen Utopie und Anpassung*, Konstanz, Konstanz University Press 1970, 21–28; Giandomenico Majone, *Regulating Europe*, London, Routledge 1996; Daniel Wincott, Does the European Union Pervert Democracy? Questions of Democracy in New Constitutionalist Thought on the Future of Europe, *European Law Journal* 4 (1998) 411–428, 414.

[52] Fritz W Scharpf, *Regieren in Europa*, Frankfurt aM, Campus Verlag 1999, 16–28; Marcus Höreth, *Die Europäische Union im Legitimationstrilemma*, Baden-Baden, Nomos 1999, 82–87.

[53] On Jean Monnet's approach, see Ernst Haas, *The Uniting of Europe*, Stanford, Stanford University Press 1958, 456; Kevin Featherstone, Jean Monnet and the democratic deficit in the European Union, *Journal of Common Market Studies* 1994, 149–170. For further details on neo-functionalist approaches of legitimacy (i.e., concentrating on economic, rationality-driven integration instead of political identity), see Amaryllis Verhoeven, *The European Union in Search of a* Democratic *and Constitutional* Theory, The Hague, Kluwer Law International 2002, 14, 65.

Communities) is described as exercising a rather technical-regulatory expert type of legislation, than a political one, which for this reason does not even need a democratic legitimacy.[54] The latter (i.e., non-political) argument is becoming weaker by every revision of the founding treaties, but even from the beginning there was potential for a democratic institutional system in European integration.[55]

The above explanation of the success of democracy was itself partly output-oriented, as its success (besides structural features of politics) was partly explained by its results. But it is quite a different thing to rely explicitly and directly in the discourse on the output without the bridging element of a moralistic or emotional rhetoric. That is happening, however, in the case of what we call 'output legitimacy'.

Output legitimacy has two main weaknesses. (1) The first is that such an approach is unlikely to survive crisis situations. If the reason for obeying an authority is that it is successful, then in the absence of success the political community dissolves very quickly. As opposed to the emotional loyalty produced by democratic procedures ('voice'), there is no motivation to stand up for a struggling authority based on output legitimacy. Output legitimacy's survival probability is thus lower than that of democratic legitimacy. (2) The second is that output legitimacy does not counterbalance democratic claims. Democratic claims (as we have seen in its history) can be counterbalanced only by other democratic claims. So what output legitimacy claims do, is simply postpone the question to a later occasion, when a democratic claim turns up. To sum up, output legitimacy is simply fragile, and due to its too concrete promises it cannot guarantee to keep communities emotionally together in crisis situations.

Today, both in political scientific and legal analysis, the requirement of democratic legitimacy for the EU is absolutely dominant. So the question

[54] Hans Peter Ipsen, *Europäisches Gemeinschaftsrecht,* Tübingen, Mohr 1972, 1044; Hans Peter Ipsen, *Fusionsverfassung Europäische Gemeinschaften,* Bad Homburg, Gehlen 1969, 64–66. Cf. Giandomenico Majone, Europe's 'Democratic Deficit'. The Question of Standards, *European Law Journal* 4 (1998) 5–28, 8–10; Andrew Moravcsik, The Myth of Europe's 'Democratic Deficit', *Intereconomics: Journal of European Economic Policy* November-December 2008, 331–340. The danger of legitimacy based on expert knowledge is that it does not possess a well-defined procedural solution of self-correction; see Dahl (n. 5) 76. On self-interest of experts, on necessary moral implications of expert-decisions and on disagreement amongst experts, see *ibid.* 61–62, 74, 76.

[55] 'Indeed, it made little sense to provide for the future elections of a Common Assembly responsible under the terms of the ECSC Treaty only for debating coal and steel policy, unless such a body were to evolve into something more far reaching.' Richard Corbett – Francis Jacobs – Michael Shackleton, *The European Parliament,* London, Catermill $^{3}$1995, 8.

is not whether the authority of the EU has to be democratically legitimised, but *how* we achieve it; that is, what kind of conceptual, procedural and infrastructural solution we need to achieve it.

## 9.2 Criteria for the well-functioning of democracy and their fulfilment in the EU

In the first section of the chapter we have seen how democracy can be approached by looking at its history in a rather pragmatic way, and we have also seen which two virtues explain its success. In the second part, we are going to elaborate this picture in order to gain a more accurate view of the kind of democracy that we could aim for in the EU. We need this more sophisticated view because the concrete implementation of the general idea of democracy (i.e., popular self-rule) can blatantly contradict the moral aspirations of the framers and devastate political unity;[56] it can even economically ruin the country.[57] If we want to run a well-functioning democracy, that is, if we want to achieve or keep the competitive advantages of democracy (loyalty and economic growth through self-correction of mistaken decisions), then we have to fulfil some further criteria.

### *9.2.1 A technical-procedural issue: direct or representative democracy*

If we conceive the virtue of democracy as expressing the will of the people (the 'general will'), then direct democracy seems superior to representative democracy.[58] But if we think of democracy as an instrument to achieve loyalty and economic growth through self-correction of mistaken decisions, as we did above, then the choice seems to be a mere technical one, as representative democracy can ensure these achievements.

In large democracies (nation-states), it is physically impossible to let the people vote on all important questions (even with the use of Internet, it would be at least impractical for citizens because of the constant research for the information needed for the decisions).

[56] On the fear from 'elective despotism', see Thomas Jefferson, *Notes on the State of Virginia*, New York, Harper 1964, 113–124.

[57] On populist welfare states see Markoff (n. 12) 93, Dunn (n. 3) 149–150.

[58] Following Rousseau, e.g., Carl Schmitt, *Verfassungslehre*, München, Leipzig, Duncker & Humblot 1928, 221–359.

Citizens cannot devote all their time to public affairs (in the absence of slaves working for them), so they have to elect representatives.[59] In modern times, political decisions have become complicated, for which we need full-time expert politicians (or even teams of politicians); the task of the voter will be to choose the right person(s) who will make the right substantive decisions for him or her.[60] Even if we have referenda, they are normally under the influence of party politics, as the necessary financial and infrastructural background for successful referendum campaigns lies with political parties.[61] With the exotic *half*-exemptions of Switzerland (or as a US state, California) today's political democracies are representative democracies, where referenda are rarely or even never used.

The EU itself makes the right choice in this matter when Art. 10(1) TEU states: 'The functioning of the Union shall be founded on representative democracy.'[62] As a nice jewel with limited practical relevance, in Art. 11(4) TEU, the direct democratic institution of the citizens' initiative has also been introduced by the Treaty of Lisbon, with no legal binding force concerning the actual decision.[63]

59 Benjamin Constant, De la liberté des Anciens comparée à celle des Modernes [1819], in: id., *Écrits politiques*, Paris, Gallimard/Folio, 1997, 591–619.

60 Joseph A Schumpeter, *Capitalism, Socialism, and Democracy*, London, Allen & Unwin [3]1950, 269–283. This structural feature necessarily leads to campaign-financing issues. See Cooter (n. 40) 15: 'Politics has a large effect on citizens, whereas each individual citizen has a small effect on politics. Since ordinary citizens gain little for themselves by participating in democracy, few citizens invest the time and energy needed to obtain detailed information about electoral candidates and issues. When citizens remain rationally ignorant, politicians need costly campaigns to influence citizens and win votes. To finance campaigns, politicians trade political influence for money from lobbyists.'

61 Ernst-Wolfgang Böckenförde, Mittelbare/repräsentative Demokratie als eigentliche Form der Demokratie. Bemerkungen zu Begriff und Verwirklichungsproblemen der Demokratie als Staats- und Regierungsfrom, in: Georg Müller e.a. (eds.), *Staatsorganisation und Staatsfunktion im Wandel. Festschrift für Kurt Eichenberger*, Basel, Frankfurt aM, Helbing & Lichtenhahn 1982, 301–328.

62 The principle of democracy (as many other later treaty provisions) came up first in the case-law of the European Court of Justice (ECJ). See Case 138/79, Roquette Frères v. Council 1980 ECR 3333, para 33: 'the fundamental democratic principle that the peoples should take part in the exercise of power through the intermediary of a representative assembly'; similarly in Case 139/79, Maïzena v. Council [1980] ECR 3393 para 34.

63 'Not less than one million citizens who are nationals of a significant number of Member States may take the initiative of inviting the European Commission, within the framework of its powers, to submit any appropriate proposal on matters where citizens consider that a legal act of the Union is required for the purpose of implementing the Treaties . . .'

### *9.2.2 Political freedoms and access to information on government*

Democracy without political freedoms is unlikely to sustain itself. The institutional system of even voting procedures (i.e., regular elections) might be similar to functioning democracies, but once someone gets into power (either democratically or through violence) he or she is unlikely to get voted out of it. So self-correction mechanisms cannot work efficiently;[64] textbook examples of this were formerly the socialist states (democratic centralism); today such states are called in literature 'illiberal democracies'.[65] Even though in every country there might be doubts about certain parts or aspects of some political freedoms, this is probably one of the least problematic issues in the EU as a whole, not only because the Charter of Fundamental Rights of the European Union has full legal binding force after the Treaty of Lisbon, but also because the constitutional systems of the Member States all ensure these rights.

But political freedoms can be used effectively only if we know what the government did: that is, if its work is transparent enough. Otherwise we cannot measure whether politicians deserve to be voted out of power; that is, the self-correction mechanism cannot work either. Traditionally, the EU was criticised much more (and for good reasons) on this basis.[66] After the Treaty of Lisbon, the situation is, however, probably no worse than in most European states:[67] both the meetings of the Council and the European Parliament are now open, and a general right to access to EU documents is also enshrined in Art. 15 Treaty on the Functioning of the European Union (TFEU). A further general clause on the principle of transparency is now contained in Art. 11 TEU.

[64] Oppression and the lack of political freedoms can even lead to the loss of loyalty (i.e., the other virtue of democracies besides the self-correction capacity), especially in those parts of society (e.g., minorities) which suffer from it.

[65] Fareed Zakaria, *The Future of Freedom: Illiberal Democracy at Home and Abroad*, New York, W. W. Norton & Company 2007.

[66] E.g., Fiona Hayes-Renshaw – Helen Wallace, Executive Power in the European Union: The Functions and Limits of the Council of Ministers, *Journal of European Public Policy* 2 (1995) 559–582; Michael Newman, *Democracy, Sovereignty and the European Union*, London, C Hurst and Co. Publishing 1996, 198; Kieran St C Bradley, La transparence de l'Union Européenne, *Cahiers de droit* européen, N° 3–4 (1999) 285–362.

[67] Stephen C Sieberson, The Treaty of Lisbon and Its Impact on the European Union's Democratic Deficit, *Columbia Journal of European Law* 2007–2008, 445–465, 453–454.

### 9.2.3 *Statehood*

Traditionally, democracy has been conceived as the form of government within the state.[68] One of the usual objections against the EU is that it cannot be democratic as it is not a state, so EU competences are not simply opposed to national sovereignty, but they are opposed (conceptually) to popular sovereignty and democracy.[69] On its own, the statement is a mere assertion without much power to convince,[70] but sometimes these objections arise mixed together with the arguments that 'there is no homogeneous European *demos*' or that 'there is no European national identity'. Without these non-legal factors – say the critics – a democracy on the EU level can have similar legal institutions as on national level, but it will not really work. In the following we turn to address these criticisms.

### 9.2.4 *Non-legal political and social infrastructure*

#### 9.2.4.1 A homogeneous *demos*

A usual topic in the debate on EU democracy is whether there is a European *demos* which could be the bearer of EU popular

68 Verhoeven (n. 53) xi.

69 Dieter Grimm, Does Europe Need a Constitution?, *European Law Journal* 1 (1995) 282–302; Jean-Marie Guéhenno, *La fin de la démocratie*, Paris, Flammarion 1993; Fritz W Scharpf, Democratic Polity in Europe, *European Law Journal* 2 (1996) 136–155; Claus Offe, Homogeneity and Constitutional Democracy: Coping with Identity Conflicts through Group Rights, *Journal of Political Philosophy* 6 (1998) 113–141; Paul Kirchhof, Der deutsche Staat im Prozeß der europäischen Integration, in: Josef Isensee – Paul Kirchhof (eds.), *Handbuch des Staatsrechts der Bundesrepublik Deutschland, Vol.* VII: *Normativität und Schutz der Verfassung – Internationale Beziehungen*, Heidelberg, CF Müller 1992, 855–887, para 33, 53; Udo Di Fabio, Der neue Art. 23 des Grundgesetzes, *Der Staat* 32 (1993) 191–217, 200–201, 206. The argument is especially strong in Germany, with its etatistic public law scholarship tradition. Cf. András Jakab, Two Opposing Paradigms of Continental European Constitutional Thinking: Austria and Germany, *International and Comparative Law Quarterly* 58 (2009) 933–955; Marcel Kaufmann, The Legitimation of the European Union – Democracy versus Integration, in: Hermann Pünder – Christian Waldhoff (eds.), *Debates in German Public Law*, Oxford, Hart 2014, 263–281.

70 For an impressive demonstration, see Deirdre M Curtin, *Postnational Democracy: The European Union in Search of a Political Philosophy*, The Hague, Kluwer Law International 1997. Cf. Robert A Dahl – Edward R Tufte, *Size and Democracy*, Stanford, Stanford University Press 1973, 135: 'Today and in the foreseeable future, people will live in a multiplicity of political units. . . Rather than conceiving democracy as located in a particular kind of inclusive, sovereign unit, we must learn to conceive of democracy spreading through a set of interrelated political systems, sometimes though not always arranged like Chinese boxes, the smaller nesting in the larger. The central theoretical problem is no longer to find suitable rules, like the majority principle, to apply within a sovereign unit, but to find suitable rules to apply among a variety of units, none of which is sovereign.'

sovereignty.[71] The argument has two forms: (1) it can concern the factual homogeneity of the EU; and (2) it can concern the feeling of togetherness (national identity) of European citizens.[72] The latter will be dealt with in the next subsection; here we are analysing only the former.

The worry about the value and the survival capacity of democracy in view of social inequalities is a well-known classic topic (Thomas Jefferson, Anatole France), and in the light of some recent South American or African developments still an appropriate one, but in the EU the homogeneity concern is of a different nature. It is about *cultural homogeneity*.[73]

There are numerous counter-arguments against this approach. (1) According to a well-known classic argument, it is not homogeneity, but rather the opposite *heterogeneity* that is necessary for democracy. In Madison's faction theory (*Federalist Papers* No. 10) different social factions are the guarantee that none of them will have full power and none of them will be oppressed. (2) Another argument goes along the line that it is not heterogeneity itself that can be the problem, but only if the heterogeneous groups are fixed (e.g., along national or religious lines).[74] In this case, elections are not elections, but only population censuses. But European elections have not seemed so far to move towards this dead-end, so a fear of it would be premature. (3) A third counter-argument emphasises the point that even European nation-

[71] Answering in the positive: Verhoeven (n. 53) 159–189. Opposing the idea of a European *demos*: Winfried Veil, *Volkssouveränität und Völkersouveränität in der EU*, Baden-Baden, Nomos 2007, 77–104; Marcel Kaufmann, *Europäische Integration und Demokratieprinzip*, Baden-Baden, Nomos 1997; Joseph HH Weiler, European Democracy and Its Critics: Polity and System, in: id., *The Constitution of Europe*, Cambridge, Cambridge University Press 1999, 264–285, 265; Albrecht Randelzhofer, Souveränität und Rechtsstaat: Anforderungen an eine Europäische Verfassung, in: Heiner Noske (ed.), *Der Rechtsstaat am Ende?*, München, Olzog 1995, 130–131; Fritz Ossenbühl, Maastricht und das Grundgesetz, *Deutsches Verwaltungsblatt* 108 (1993) 629–637, 634; Grimm (n. 69) 295.

[72] Both arguments have a soft ('not yet') and a radical ('there will never be a European *demos*') version. Cf. Carlos Closa, Some Foundations for the Normative Discussion on Supranational Citizenship and Democracy, in: Ulrich K Preuß – Ferrán Requejo (eds.), *European Citizenship, Multiculturalism and the State*, Baden-Baden, Nomos 1998, 113.

[73] Linguistic heterogeneity will be dealt with below at *9.2.4.4 Interested public opinion and media coverage*. The question of exactly how much homogeneity is necessary (and of how we actually measure it), is mostly not explained. What is mostly stated is simply that 'it is not homogeneous enough (yet)'. A modified argument is also possible by stating the EU can*not* ever be homogeneous enough, because it is just too big. The last argument can easily be countered by a reference to the United States or to India. See Dahl (n. 5) 217.

[74] Christoph Gusy, Demokratiedefizite postnationaler Gemeinschaften unter Berücksichtigung der EU, *Zeitschrift für Politik* 1998, 279, Anne Peters, *Elemente einer Theorie der Verfassung Europas*, Berlin, Duncker & Humblot 2001, 712.

states are no longer as homogeneous as some would like to see them. We are currently living in multicultural societies (not only in the United States or in Switzerland, but in most EU Member States).[75] The requirement of homogeneity (if it goes further than the requirement to accept the rule of law and democracy) would bring up the danger of assimilation and exclusion, or even a friend-enemy distinction within society.[76] (4) A fourth argument is based on history stating that most of today's nation states were not formed along ethnic lines: it was rather the other way around. First there was the political unit, and it formed the population into one cultural and linguistic unit.[77] At the time of the French Revolution (1789) half of the population of France did not speak French (but Italian, German, Breton, English, Occitan, Catalan, Basque, Dutch), and only 12–13 per cent spoke it correctly. At the time of Italian unification (1861) only 2.5 per cent (!) of the population spoke the Italian that we know today.[78] (5) A fifth argument concentrates on the logic of democracy: it is based on *individuals* (and not on collectivist units) and the popular unity will be formed first by the democratic procedure itself.[79] So *ethnos* and *demos* are analytically different.[80]

In the light of the above arguments, it is very difficult to say that it is conceptually impossible to have a democracy on the EU level because of cultural differences.[81] But we can still state that practically it would not work . . . the main reason being that the European peoples just do not want it; they do not have the feeling of togetherness with other European peoples.

[75] Verhoeven (n. 53) xi. [76] Peters (n. 74) 704.

[77] The traditional opposing idea originates, e.g., from Herder, Savigny, Meinecke based on the rather peculiar German case, where actually common identity was first and then came the political unity. See Peters (n. 74) 653. In public law scholarship for an early formulation of the necessity of a pre-legal cultural unit of people for the state-forming, see Georg Jellinek, *Die Lehre von den Staatenverbindungen*, Wien, Hoelder 1882, 263. For a contemporary formulation in the context of the EU see Ernst-Wolfgang Böckenförde, *Welchen Weg geht Europa?*, München, Carl-Friedrich-von-Siemens-Stiftung 1997, 40–41.

[78] Eric J Hobsbawm, *Nations and Nationalism since 1780. Programme: Myth, Reality*, Cambridge, Cambridge University Press 1990, 60–61. For more details, see below 10.1.2.

[79] Peters (n. 74) 649 n. 86, 704, 707. A classic form of this idea is to be found in Emmanuel-Joseph Sieyès, *Qu'est-ce que le Tiers État?* (1789, in English: Emmanuel Joseph Sieyès, *Political Writings*, Indianapolis, Hackett 2003) and remained strong in the French republican tradition.

[80] Emerich K Francis, *Ethnos und Demos*, Berlin, Duncker & Humblot 1965, 77.

[81] We can reason, though, that a simple Westminster-style majoritarian parliamentarism would not be the right choice for the pluralist EU, but a consensual coalition style parliamentarism is better. On the difference between majoritarian and consensus government, see Arend Lijphart, *Democracies*, New Haven, London, Yale University Press 1984, especially 1–36.

#### 9.2.4.2 Political identity or the European 'nation'

The critics of the idea of a European *demos* as formed by procedures can easily point out that separatist Catalan or Scottish nationalists were not impressed by the Spanish or British procedures either, and national identity in general does not necessarily flow from procedures. So the problem is not factual similarity or dissimilarity, but rather the identity.[82] And identity still primarily belongs to the nation states.[83]

It is all very true. (1) One possible counter-argument is that national identity is fading in general in the world,[84] so in time the feeling of togetherness will lose its relevance. This would, however, be a weak counter-argument. We do not have exact and convincing empirical data about fading national identities, and examples of the opposite can also be presented. But even if we had data for it, it would be very difficult to project a certain level of fading to the future as a continuous development. (2) A more convincing argument says that even in the United States, when the famous words 'We the people' have been put on paper, it was nothing more than wishful thinking, or rather political manipulation. So we could similarly attempt it in the EU.[85] We can also point out that nations are imagined or even mythical communities, so it is not a fixed fact; it can even change in time (as it happens when an ethnic minority assimilates into the majority).[86] Peaceful methods of identity building are possible (like having EU sport teams competing against the Americans or the Chinese), which could be used in the future. I have some doubts whether it could work in the foreseeable future. But it is less relevant here, as my actual point would be that national identity in this strong substantive sense is not absolutely necessary. (3) What we need is only a loyalty towards the system, towards the procedures of democracy (such a loyalty is possible only, of course, if the procedures work).[87] It helps the effectiveness of law (so the rule of law), and

[82] Grimm (n. 69) 297.

[83] For an empirical survey proving this, see Mathieu Deflem – Fred C Pampel, The myth of postnational identity: popular support for European unification, *Social Forces* 75 (1996) 119–143.

[84] Michael Sandel, *Democracy's Discontent*, Cambridge, Mass., Belknap Press of Harvard University Press 1996, 344.

[85] Manfred Zuleeg, What Holds a Nation Together? Cohesion and Democracy in the United States of America and in the European Union, *American Journal of Comparative Law* 45 (1997) 505–526, 526.

[86] Shown on the example of France by Eugen Weber, *From Peasants into Frenchmen: The Modernization of Rural France, 1880–1914*, Stanford, Stanford University Press 1976.

[87] To name national identity as a precondition for democracy is methodologically biased, as it reconstructs the concept of democracy along the concrete sociological features of some

with the adherence to these basic constitutional values (and the connecting emotional identification) it can survive crisis situations too. Nationalism can indeed be a centrifugal force in integration, but it did not so far lead to any secession in Western Europe. As a matter of fact, one of the reasons it did not happen so far is exactly the fear of secessionists that they might get rid of the oppressive (normally majority) nation, but then find themselves outside of the EU, which none of them really wants. As for now, independence of these countries (Flanders, Scotland, Catalonia or the Basque Country) is unsure, but even if they were to achieve it, it would be likely to happen within the framework of the EU. Nationalism can rather lead to explosions if a basic democratic mentality is missing (as we have seen in former socialist countries).

Therefore, the existence of a unified and dominant European political identity is not necessary in order to have a functioning European democracy. There is no doubt that it is useful, but it is not necessary. We are going to return to this problem in Chapter 10 (10.5).

#### 9.2.4.3 Democratic mentality

If citizens talk about politics, they very often switch into an irrational and emotional way of arguing.[88] It is more or less natural, as (in the absence of expertise and time) we cannot precisely judge the actions of politicians (we have only sporadic factual impressions, which do not however have to be underestimated either); we can only promote our own mentality (i.e., vote for politicians with a similar mentality), which is necessarily based partly on emotions. So to a certain extent, it is rational for citizens to be emotional. Citizens are not political philosophers.

But we have a real problem from the point of view of democracy only if the democratic struggle for power evolves into a general distinction between friend and enemy ('cold civil war' or 'life or death fight'), and if the struggle steps over the limits of law. In a democracy we need a minimum level of brotherhood[89] where we suppose that the other party is not going to devastate deliberately (or betray) the country or to destroy

democracies. See Jürgen Habermas, Remarks on Dieter Grimm's 'Does Europe need a Constitution?' *European Law Journal*, 1995, 303–307.

[88] Schumpeter (n. 60) 262 'Thus the typical citizen drops down to a lower level of mental performance as soon as he enters the political field. He argues and analyzes in a way which he would readily recognize as infantile within the sphere of his real interests. He becomes a primitive again. His thinking becomes associative and affective.'

[89] Möllers (n. 43) 19.

our basic values.[90] We need citizens who are able and willing to accept that they can lose in elections. A democracy needs democrats.[91]

We can have doubts about the democratic nature of the EU, but it would be farfetched to think in general terms that European citizens living under domestic democracies are lacking this mentality. Democratic procedures formed their mentality, in some fortunate countries for centuries, in others for decades.[92] What the problem in the EU as a whole could be is not really overheated anti-democratic politics, but rather the opposite: the lack of interest.[93]

#### 9.2.4.4 Interested public opinion and media coverage

The lack of interest can be explained by different factors. One is that there is no unified media coverage due to linguistic heterogeneity. Consequently, public opinion focuses predominantly on domestic issues.[94]

The real problem is, however, not the linguistic heterogeneity. It is possible to have relevant public opinion in multilingual societies (even if more difficult in practice than in a monolingual society),[95] as shown in Finland, Canada, Switzerland or India.[96] And also the other way around: the same language does not result automatically in unified media coverage either; Austrian and German newspapers write about very different issues. So the link between language and unified media coverage (which is the current problem from the point of view of building a relevant public opinion)[97] is not automatic. But if we want to have a unified discourse

[90] Dahl (n. 5) 255.

[91] Martin Kriele, *Einführung in die Staatslehre*, Stuttgart, Kohlhammer [6]2003, 268. For an explanation of the failure of the Weimar Republic on these grounds see Georg Lukács, *Die Zerstörung der Vernunft*, Berlin, Aufbau Verlag 1955, 61: 'Thus the Weimar Republic was basically a republic without republicans, a democracy without democrats' (translation mine). In the long run, however, institutions form mentalities, see Daron Acemoglu – James Robinson, *Why Nations Fail: The Origins of Power, Prosperity and Poverty*, New York, Crown Publishers, 2012, 302–334 and 404–427.

[92] Institutions form mentalities; see Kriele (n. 91) 268.

[93] As further non-legal preconditions, we can name non-tribal social structure, the lack of a dominant theocratic religion and the existence of a developed school system. See Ernst-Wolfgang Böckenförde, Demokratie als Verfassungsprinzip, in: id., *Staat, Verfassung, Demokratie*, Frankfurt aM, Suhrkamp 1991, 345–346, 351–352. All these seem to be given in the whole of the EU.

[94] Alexander von Brünneck, Die öffentliche Meinung in der EG als Verfassungsproblem, *Europarecht* 1989, 249–261, 251–252.

[95] Elisabeth Bakke, Towards a European Identity?, *ARENA Working Paper* 10/95, Oslo.

[96] Peters (n. 74) 706.

[97] Ingolf Pernice, Maastricht, Staat und Demokratie, *Die Verwaltung* 1993, 449–488, 479–481; Manfred Zuleeg, Demokratie in der Europäischen Gemeinschaft, *Juristen-Zeitung* 1993,

space forming a public opinion,[98] we need questions that might be relevant for all the readers as voters. We do not even need exactly the same information (e.g., in the form of translated news, like Euronews) reaching readers. We just need more or less overlapping relevant information potentially reaching them, which is arguably happening even now. But the electorate are just not really interested in such news (with the notable exceptions when the EU is in a serious crisis, like the euro crisis).

So the real issue is rather that readers (as voters) have to see that they will be able to decide about the direction of (EU) government power at the next European Parliament (EP) elections, so they will need information for that decision. The EU would thus no longer be a necessary evil, some kind of *vis maior,* which we cannot influence, but rather our (democratically elected) government. It is the case if there is a direct link between election and political responsibility of the EU government, that is, the Commission.[99]

### 9.2.5 *The direct link between election and responsibility: the effectiveness of popular will*

Where the actual problem lies, is rather what Anne Peters calls 'the missing correlation between election and responsibility'.[100] In other words, there are elections, and also a new government (Commission)

1069–1074, 1073–1074; Claus Dieter Classen, Europäische Integration und demokratische Legitimation, *Archiv des öffentlichen Rechts* 119 (1994) 238–260; Jochen Abr Frowein, Die Verfassung der Europäischen Union aus der Sicht der Mitgliedstaaten, *Europarecht* 1995, 315–333, 324; Siegfried Magiera, Das Europäische Parlament als Garant der demokratischen Legitimation in der Europäischen Union, in: Ole Due – Marcus Lutter – Jürgen Schwarze (eds.), *Festschrift für Ulrich Everling*, vol. 1, Baden-Baden, Nomos 1995, 789–801, 797–798; Christian Tomuschat, Das Endziel der europäischen Integration, *Deutsches Verwaltungsblatt* 1996, 1073–1082, 1079 n. 29.

98 It is debatable how far discourse spaces are entirely unified, even within one country. Readers of the *Sun* and of the *Guardian* might have indeed very different perceptions what is happening in the UK, but their discourse space is at least partly the same.

99 The Commission can be conceptualised as the government of the EU, the European Parliament as the lower chamber, the Council as the upper chamber of the legislative branch (even if the latter has some limited executive functions). See Simon Hix, Legislative Behaviour and Party Competition in the European Parliament, *Journal of Common Market Studies* 2001, 663–688; Andreas Maurer – Wolfgang Wessels, *Das Europäische Parlament nach Amsterdam und Nizza: Akteur, Arena oder Alibi?*, Baden-Baden, Nomos 2003, 213. For a different conceptualisation, see Philipp Dann, *Parlamente im Exekutivföderalismus*, Berlin, Springer 2004, 316–321.

100 Peters (n. 74) 627: 'mangelnde Korrelation zwischen Wahl und Verantwortung'.

will be set up, but the direct link between the two acts is missing.[101] There seem to be only two institutional solutions to ensure the virtues of democracy (both loyalty and self-correction): one possibility would be to transform the EU into a presidential system (similar to the United States); the other would be to parliamentarise it.[102] The latter seems to be a more viable option, as the current system is much nearer to the parliamentary system; that is, only minor institutional changes would be necessary to achieve it.[103] The solution would thus be to make only the European Parliament responsible for the election of the Commission, whereas the European Council could have a ceremonial role similar to monarchs or presidents in parliamentary systems.[104] The possible answers to counter this idea are fourfold. In the following we are going to analyse them.

#### 9.2.5.1 'The current system is democratic enough, as we have democratic empowerment chains leading to the people'

This answer, according to which the Commission has a dual democratic legitimacy,[105] as the European Council is democratically legitimised on a

[101] Some authors criticise not only the election of the Commission, but also that a complicated regulatory network with independent (i.e., not accountable) authorities have the power. See András Sajó, EU Networks under the New Constitution, Impact on Domestic Constitutional Structures, in: Ingolf Pernice – Jiri Zemanek (eds.), *A Constitution for Europe: The IGC, the Ratification Process and Beyond*, Baden-Baden, Nomos 2005, 183–197; Joseph HH Weiler, To Be a European Citizen: Eros and Civilization, in: *id.* (n. 71) 324–357, 349. This is a general problem of supranational influence in domestic affairs (OECD, WTO, World Bank), which we cannot deal with in this chapter.

[102] Different institutional sub- and in-between types are considered with their advantages by Werner van Gerven, *The European Union: A Polity of States and Peoples*, Oxford, Portland, Hart 2005, 318–332.

[103] See van Gerven (n. 102) 344–345.

[104] For a similar approach see Francesca E Bignami, The Democratic Deficit in European Community Rulemaking: A Call for Notice and Comment in Comitology, *Harvard International Law Journal* 40 (1999) 415–515, 463; van Gerven (n. 102) 350. The idea goes back almost to the beginning of the EEC, see Walter Hallstein, the first president of the Commission on this issue: 'As a parliamentary democracy, the Community is still imperfect . . . because the European Parliament has not yet acquired its full role.' Walter Hallstein, *Europe in the Making*, London, Allen & Unwin 1972, 40–41. Jean Monnet had a different (functionalist) view on the issue, see above n. 53.

[105] On the idea of dual democratic legitimacy of EU institutions and legislation, see Winfried Kluth, *Die demokratische Legitimation der Europäischen Union*, Berlin, Duncker & Humblot 1995, 87; Karl-Peter Sommermann, Verfassungsperspektiven für die Demokratie in der erweiterten Europäischen Union: Gefahr der Entdemokratisierung oder Fortentwicklung im Rahmen europäischer Supranationalität?, *Die öffentliche Verwaltung* 2003, 1009–1017. The idea has even been codified in Art. 10(2) TEU. There is a third option (besides dual legitimacy and purely European legitimacy): legitimacy based

national level, and the European Parliament is legitimised on a European level, misses the point. We can, of course, trace back in a long chain (or rather on separate several chains)[106] the Commission's authority over ordinary citizens. But the nice metaphysical picture about the 'source of power' being the people is simply a metaphor, which cuts short the debate about the reasons for having a democracy. This shortcut works normally pretty well, except if we take the metaphor itself too seriously and try to analyse it too much. This is happening, however, unfortunately often in the discourse about democracy in the EU. We should concentrate rather on the two keys for its international success mentioned above: (1) loyalty and (2) self-correction.

What we need for that (at this point) is to have a system where the citizens (in our case, the European citizens) can vote out one government and vote in another (the Commission). The Lisbon Treaty did not change much on this issue either (cf. Art. 17(7) TEU).[107] In the current situation, the European Parliament has only a veto as to the President and the other members of the Commission. This is probably one of the major reasons for having a low turnout at European polls and for having in general low level of interest amongst citizens in EU politics.[108]

#### 9.2.5.2 'The EU has democratic origins, so its functioning must be democratic'

We could refer to the fact that the founding treaties and all their modifications were democratically legitimised, as they have been ratified by their respective democratically elected bodies or organs.[109] This is very true. But

purely on national parliaments. In an old-fashioned etatistic and radical reasoning, in a surprising manner of *Begriffsjurisprudenz*, the German Federal Constitutional Court followed this approach in its Lisbon Decision. BVerfG, 2 BvE 2/08, of June 30, 2009. For one of the many convincing criticisms on the judgments, see Christoph Schönberger, Lisbon in Karlsruhe: Maastricht's Epigones at Sea, *German Law Journal* 10 (2009) 1201–1218.

[106] The chain theory is especially vivid in German constitutional doctrine. See Böckenförde (n. 93) 300–311; also BVerfGE 83, 60, 72; 93, 37, 66–67.

[107] The only relevant change is a vague statement in Art. 17(7) that the European Council has to take 'into account the elections to the European Parliament' when choosing the candidate for the President of the Commission.

[108] Cf. Mattias Kumm, Why Europeans Will Not Embrace Constitutional Patriotism, *International Journal of Constitutional Law* 6 (2008) 117–136, 130: 'The fact that citizens turn out for [European Parliament] elections at all, knowing that their vote is practically not to change anything, has long puzzled public choice theorists.'

[109] Peter Badura, Bewahrung und Veränderung demokratischer und rechtsstaatlicher Verfassungsstruktur in den internationalen Gemeinschaften, *Veröffentlichungen der Vereinigung der Deutschen Staatsrechtslehrer* 1966, 34–104, 72; Pierre Pescatore, Les exigences de la démocratie et la legitimité de la Communauté européenne, *Cahiers de*

this is unfortunately not the issue here. The actual issue is whether *currently* the EU is functioning democratically. The origin of a system does not say much of its current functioning. As a matter of fact, democracies are normally born non-democratically.[110] We have seen in Chapter 8 (8.2.2), with the examples of the US Constitution and the German Constitution, even a clear breach of the democratic procedures of the then constitution is not a hindrance for subsequently accepting those constitutions as 'democratic'. So the democratic origin of the EU cannot satisfy the requirement for its *current* democratic running. The question about the democratic origins is a different and clearly secondary one.

#### 9.2.5.3 'We should rather make national parliaments stronger'

A usual claim is that the EU can be made more democratic by making national parliaments stronger. Even Art. 12 TEU emphasises the role of national parliaments in the EU. This is a serious misunderstanding and definitely the wrong direction to take. The definition of fundamental legal concepts, such as that of democracy, is a conceptual game which should be played out in a manner which leads to practically (morally or economically) acceptable results.

Efficient control by national parliaments is primarily possible, if decisions in the Council are made by unanimity.[111] But this is less and less the case. Democratic control through a bunch of national parliaments is not only inefficient,[112] but it also misses the point, which would be to have a

*droit européen* 1974, 499–514, 508–509; Joseph HH Weiler, The Transformation of Europe, *Yale Law Journal* 100 (1991) 2403–2483, 2472; Hans Heinrich Rupp, Europäische 'Verfassung' und demokratische Legitimation, *Archiv des öffentlichen Rechts* 120 (1995) 269–275, 271; Armin von Bogdandy, *Supranationaler Föderalismus als Wirklichkeit und Idee einer neuen Herrschaftsform*, Baden-Baden, Nomos 1999, 56; Thomas W Pogge, How to Create Supra-National Institutions Democratically, in: Andreas Føllesdahl - Peter Koslowski (eds.), *Democracy and the European Union*, Berlin, Springer 1998, 160–185.

110 Möllers (n. 43) 20.

111 Closa (n. 72) 109. National parliaments controlling European institutions (i.e., not their own government) would be either procedurally cumbersome (why not the European Parliament?), or it would invite national veto players to block EU legislation. Cf. for (fortunately shy) misplaced attempts in this direction *Protocol on the Role of National Parliaments in the European Union* and *Protocol on the Application of the Principles of Subsidiarity and Proportionality*.

112 Joseph HH Weiler, Does Europe Need a Constitution?, *European Law Journal* 1 (1995) 219–258, 232: 'national procedures to ensure democratic control over international treaties of the State are clearly ill-suited and woefully inadequate to address the problems posited by the European Union'. EU negotiations force national governments to act

clear and efficient procedure whereby voters can vote out one and vote in another government. This self-correction mechanism can work efficiently *only* if voters receive the direct question whether they want to keep a team of politicians (a Commission) in power or not. But the question cannot be put in this direct way right now, as the European Parliament just does not have the right to choose (on its own) the members of the Commission.

Emphasising the role of national parliaments is simply a civilised (because democratic) rhetorical form of expressing nationalism.[113] It is the strongest argument to counter the claim for a parliamentary system on EU level,[114] or to counter European integration in general.[115]

But the question is no longer whether we would like to have a deep European integration, or whether we want to see decisions made in Brussels about policy issues in Europe. It is already there. The question is rather whether we want to use those democratic mechanisms to run it,[116] which made democratic countries so powerful. If we decide that a parliamentary system is not desirable on an EU level, we are still going to deal with the EU's authority, but this authority will be less efficient and useful for us in the long term.[117] If we think, however, that in the light of

quickly (to accept or to refuse unforeseeable compromises) in the Council, and afterwards their actions will simply be accepted by national parliaments, where they normally have the majority anyway.

113 Those who stick to the idea of national states, normally see the democratic deficit in the weakness of national parliaments; those who support a European federal state see the democratic deficit in the weakness of the European Parliament. Sieberson (n. 67) 447.

114 It makes sense only as long as there is a possibility of veto in the Council. 'So long as each Member Government can veto a Council decision, if it wants to, there is a sense in which each Member Government [can] be held to account for them by its Parliament. If national vetoes disappear this will no longer be true. . . . The resulting "democratic deficit" would not be acceptable in a Community committed to democratic principles. Yet such a deficit would be inevitable unless the gap were somehow to be filled by the European Parliament.' David Marquand, *Parliament for Europe*, London, Jonathan Cape Ltd 1979, 65. For a similar argument (the turn to majority voting unleashed legitimacy problems, veto is democratic), see Joseph HH Weiler, Problems of Legitimacy in post-1992 Europe, *Außenwirtschaft* 1991, 411–437.

115 Cf. the heavily criticised Lisbon decision of the German Federal Constitutional Court: BVerfG, 2 BvE 2/08, of June 30, 2009. See Schönberger (n. 105).

116 On the dilemma, see Thomas D Zweifel, Democratic Deficit; Institutions and Regulation in the European Union, Switzerland and the United States, Lanham, Md., Lexington 2002, 142.

117 Intergovernmental package deals tend to favour partial bureaucratic interests in a nontransparent and uncontrollable way; see Stefan Oeter, Souveränität und Demokratie in der 'Verfassungsentwicklung' der Europäischen Union, *Zeitschrift für ausländisches öffentliches Recht und Völkerrecht* 1995, 659–712, 699.

the above a parliamentary system is desirable (as I do), then we have to answer the practical question of how to introduce it.

#### 9.2.5.4 'It is practically impossible, as Member State politicians would not allow it'

The claim for introducing a parliamentary system can be countered by saying that it would be nice, but it is an unrealistic dream, as Member State governments (or at least some of them) would never give up such a power (i.e., to choose the members of the Commission).[118] It is all very true. But if they have to follow rules which tell them to do so, then they will be forced to do so. We can think of three different types of rules: (a) explicit treaty rules; (b) a tricky lawyerly interpretation of some treaty rules which implies an obligation to leave the choice of Commission members to the European Parliament and to have simply a ceremonial role by the European Council; or (c) constitutional conventions.

Ad (a). If we want to have explicit treaty rules, then we have to modify the TEU. For that purpose we need the ratification by all Member States. Having seen the miserable struggle with the Draft Constitutional Treaty and then with the Lisbon Treaty, it is unlikely that in the foreseeable future such an attempt could be successful.[119] So this is not an option.

Ad (b). We could try to argue that the passage introduced by the Lisbon Treaty saying that the candidate for the president of the Commission has to be chosen by the European Parliament 'taking into account the elections to the European Parliament and after having held the appropriate consultations' (Art. 17(7) TEU) actually means (in the light of the general democratic principle underlying the EU), that *legally* the decisive organ in choosing the Commission members *is* the European Parliament and the European Council actually has only a ceremonial role. Such an interpretation would clearly contradict the text of TEU, which in itself does not make it impossible that the ECJ (in a procedure of Art. 263(1) TEU when the 'act' would be the appointment of the president and other members of the Commission) would venture such a

[118] Simon Hix, *The Political System of the European Union*, New York, Palgrave Macmillan $^{2}$2005, 62.

[119] On this problem, see Julio Baquero Cruz, Alternativas a las condiciones de revisión y entrada en vigor, in: Iñigo Méndez de Vigo (ed.), *¿Qué fue de la Constitución Europea?*, Barcelona, Planeta 2007, 293–306; Bruno de Witte, The Rules of Change in the European Union: The Lost Balance between Rigidity and Flexibility, in: Catherine Moury – Luís de Sousa (eds.), *Institutional Challenges in Post-Constitutional Europe*, London, New York, Routledge 2009, 33–42.

revolutionary move. Such *contra legem* move already happened when the ECJ introduced direct effect for provisions of directives. But to do the same on so politically sensitive an issue would probably go too far even for the ECJ. So we have to go for another option to parliamentarise the EU.

Ad (c). The solution I am proposing is the following: we have to accept that the EU legally cannot become a parliamentary system, but the non-legal political structure can still be changed. For that purpose we first have to have a look at the concept of constitutional conventions as used in British constitutional doctrine and at one of its examples being the most relevant for us: the appointment of the PM.

Constitutional conventions can be defined as 'understandings and practices that are not legally binding',[120] as rules of 'political morality'[121] or as 'rules of constitutional morality'.[122] They are something like constitutional soft law, but they are not: there was no law-making procedure.[123] It is rather a habit, which is considered to be obligatory but not in a strict legal sense.[124] It is a certain type of self-restriction, but it can also be forced by other actors onto a constitutional organ.[125] Conventions cannot be enforced directly in a court,[126] but they have an indirect legal effect in interpreting legal rules.[127] Conventions may arise through a series of precedents, but they may arise much more quickly than this, without any previous history as usage.[128] 'A single precedent with a good reason may be enough to establish the rule.'[129]

Conventions are obeyed because they are part of a shared system of values[130] and because their breach would result in political consequences

[120] John Alder, *Constitutional and Administrative Law*, New York, Palgrave Macmillan [5]2005, 43.

[121] Geoffrey Marshall, *Constitutional Theory*, Oxford, Clarendon Press 1971, 9.

[122] Frederick William Maitland, *The Constitutional History of England*, Cambridge, Cambridge University Press 1908, 398.

[123] Geoffrey Marshall, *Constitutional Conventions*, Oxford, Oxford University Press 1984, 216.

[124] Kenneth Wheare, *Modern Constitutions*, London, Oxford University Press 1951, 179. On the legal or non-legal nature of conventions in detail, see Joseph Jaconelli, Do Constitutional Conventions Bind?, *Cambridge Law Journal* 64 (2005) 149–176.

[125] Colin Turpin, *British Government and the Constitution*, London Butterworths [5]2002, 115.

[126] Albert Venn Dicey, *Introduction to the Study of the Law of the Constitution*, London, New York, Macmillan [10]1959, 24.

[127] Marshall (n. 123) 14.

[128] Wheare (n. 124) 180.

[129] Ivor Jennings, *The Law and the Constitution*, London, University of London Press [5]1959, 136.

[130] Colin R Munro, *Studies in Constitutional Law*, London, Butterworths [2]1999, 61.

(such as the political blame of anti-democratic or unconstitutional behaviour). For our current topic, the most relevant example is that from a *legal* point of view, the Queen could choose anyone for the position of PM, but by *convention* she should choose as PM the person who can command a majority support in the House of Commons.[131] She does not breach any law by obeying this convention; she just uses her powers in a way which *also* fits the conventions.[132]

This is exactly what we need now. The election of Commission members should depend on which EP faction(s) have the most seats, and who they (in coalition) want to see in the seats of Commission members. But how can the European Council be forced to such a practice? The mere accusations of anti-democratic behaviour can probably not force them, as they would refer to the literal interpretation of TEU, which favours a non-parliamentary solution. So the solution would simply be that the European Parliament, by using its veto possibilities (or to put it more bluntly: blackmailing capacity), only accepts those concretely (and before the relevant meeting of the European Council already) defined persons as candidates by the European Council, whom the majority of the European Parliament supports.[133] All other candidates will be refused.

The logic of such a change is not unknown to the EU institutions: before Mr Barroso became President of the Commission for the first time (2004), the European Council intended to propose a person from the political left, even though the elections to the European Parliament had been won by the political right. The European Parliament vetoed the idea, and the European Council had to choose someone from the political right. It would only be one step in the same direction (an important and big step, though), if the European Parliament announced that they would accept only one

[131] As a matter of fact, the office of PM itself is also based on constitutional convention; see Andrew Le Sueur – Maurice Sunkin, *Public Law*, London, New York, Longman 1997, 56.

[132] Conventions in this sense exist also in other countries, but they have their most prominent role in British constitutional life due to the rudimentary legal framework of the British constitution. Cf. James G Wilson, American Constitutional Conventions, *Buffalo Law Review* 40 (1992) 645–738; Andrew Heard, *Canadian Constitutional Conventions: The Marriage of Law and Politics*, Toronto, Oxford University Press 1991; Giuseppe Ugo Rescigno, *Le convenzioni costituzionali*, Padua, Cedam 1972.

[133] This would not transform the EU into a majoritarian system (in Lijphart's terminology, see above n. 81) similar to the UK, as the majority support in the EU would still mean a party coalition, and the quasi-constitutional court control of the European Court of Justice (ECJ) (based on the treaties) would strongly limit the Commission. It would become a parliamentary system similar to Germany.

particular person for that position. Such a revolt by the European Parliament would be most likely if the political colour of the European Council and of the European Parliament were to differ, as happened in Mr Barroso's case.[134] In 2004, a second event during the formation of the European Commission also showed that the European Parliament had the strength to influence substantially the composition of the Commission: criticism from the European Parliament on one of the candidates for Commissioner (Rocco Buttiglione) led Barroso to change its membership and to alter the distribution of portfolios. But what we also need is the EU electorate knowing before the European Parliament elections the candidate Commissioners (and their programmes), so they can choose their parties in light of this.[135] Some might even argue that the *Spitzenkandidat* debate in 2014, and the success of Jean-Claude Juncker, was the Rubicon and that the EU actually already did become a parliamentary system.[136] What is still missing, however, is the same system for all members of the Commission, that is, knowing not only the *Spitzenkandidat* but all candidate Commissioners (and their programmes) before the elections. Unfortunately, the formation of the Juncker Commission seems to go along the traditional Member State dominated (and consequently, in the conceptual frame of European constitutionalism: anti-democratic) way.

After 2014, however, all upcoming elections to the European Parliament are going to be with a much higher probability about concrete persons to be elected at least to the position of the President of the European Commission, who hopefully will even work out some understandable and concrete policies to campaign for votes.[137] These policies could be checked on at the following elections, and if unfulfilled, the Commission could be voted out. With such a transparent and direct link between

[134] The differing political colour is the default position as voters of domestic opposition parties are more likely to vote at European Parliament elections; see Philip Manow – Holger Döring, Electoral and Mechanical Causes of Divided Government in the European Union, *Comparative Political Studies* 2008, 1349–1370.

[135] Simon Hix – Bjørn Høyland, *The Political System of the European Union*, London, Palgrave Macmillan [3]2011, 152.

[136] For the usual arguments in the Spitzenkandidat debate, see András Jakab, Why the Debate between Kumm and Armstrong is about the Wrong Question, *verfassungsblog.de* 20. June 2014, available at http://www.verfassungsblog.de/debate-kumm-armstrong-wrong-question/#.U6RIbfl_uqg.

[137] The first time it happens, we probably would not call it as a convention, but the second or third time it will become convention. See above n. 129 and the relevant main text.

election and responsibility, that is, with an effectiveness of popular will, the turnout at European Parliament elections would very probably rise,[138] the respective campaign would be much more about EU policies and with the growth of public interest the media would also cover EU affairs more thoroughly,[139] and most likely the popularity of the European Union would also grow.[140] The possible counter-argument that MEPs cannot initiate legislation is not central from a democratic point of view. If their trustees are sitting in the Commission (which has the competence to initiate legislation), then the question who initiates legislation is merely a technical one. Also the fact that the Commission can be dismissed only by a two-thirds majority is secondary (a simple majority would probably be healthier though), because democracy's self-correction mechanism can work efficiently at the latest at the next EP elections: for the new Commission only a simple majority is needed (Art. 17(7) TEU).

If it were to happen, then the EU government system would become similar to some extent to today's German system, where a party coalition in the lower chamber supports the government, and the upper chamber takes part substantively only in the legislation but not in the formation of the government.[141]

## 9.3 Conclusion as to how to conceptualise democracy in Europe

The above is a nice plan, but what should actually be done right now? First of all, future MEPs have to be convinced that this is a viable way.

[138] Dana Spinant, How to Make Elections Sexy: Give Voters a Say in Europe's Top Jobs, *European Voice* 5-11.02.2004, 12. Turnout at elections is primarily *not* influenced by the public esteem of the institutions concerned; see Mark N Franklin, How Structural Factors Cause Turnout Variations at European Parliament Elections, *European Union Politics* 2001, 309–328. But turnout is influenced by the stakes of the election; that is why domestic turnout is usually higher than the European Parliament turnout, and this is why in countries where EU subsidies are higher European Parliament turnout is also higher; see Mikko Mattila, Why bother? Determinants of Turnout in the European Elections, *Electoral Studies* 2003, 449–468.

[139] For a mostly similar view see Hix (n. 118) 179–180, 203–204.

[140] Peter Mair, Political Opposition and the European Union, *Government and Opposition* 2007, 1–17, especially 12: 'because we are denied an appropriate political arena in which to hold European governance accountable, we are almost pushed into organizing opposition to Europe.'

[141] The voting rules, especially the weights of different countries, in the Council and the number of MEPs from the different Member States would remain, of course, the same (any change of these would require a treaty amendment anyway, which is almost impossible).

Strong, willing and able politicians are needed in the European Parliament, who will have enough ambition to make this change. As politicians are mostly not lacking ambition, I am optimistic that sooner or later they will take the steps as described above, and that this tendency will not stop at the position of the President of the European Commission (as it unfortunately did in 2014) but will include all Commissioners in the future. The right moment when the political colour of the European Parliament and that of the Council will be different in order to play out this conflict will arrive sooner or later.

In the words of John Markoff, 'One might anticipate a recapitulation of Europe's nineteenth-century struggles over democratisation on a larger scale, in which the power of the European Parliament in Strasbourg in relation to the European bureaucracy becomes a central point of contention.'[142] It is happening here and now, and the outcome is likely to be the same as in the nineteenth century. The sooner, the better.

As legal scholars, we can contribute to this in one way: by using 'democracy' and 'democratic' in the EU context in a sense which helps the realisation of the purpose of this concept, that is, which helps the improvement of the self-correction capacity and the induction of loyalty. The EU's political power is a fact, and if we want to run it in the most useful way for its citizens, then accountability has to be improved. The most viable way to this end seems to be the parliamentarisation of the EU. Conceptualisations which inhibit this, should thus be rejected; conceptualisations which help this should be embraced.

[142] Markoff (n. 12) 135.

# 10

# Constitutional visions of the nation and multi-ethnic societies in Europe

> 'Nation' is a category of 'practice', not (in the first instance) a category of analysis. To understand nationalism, we have to understand the practical uses of the category 'nation', the ways it can structure the perception, to inform thought and experience, to organise discourse and political action.[1]

The nature of the political community (often vaguely called the 'nation') is mainly an unexplained presupposition in constitutional reasoning.[2] Some constitutions allow for different visions, and the constitutional or supreme courts can choose; other constitutions suggest very specific ones, but even in these cases, interpretation can transform one vision into another.

Before we go into detail about the different visions and their constitutional consequences, we should, however, following our general methodological considerations (see above in Chapter 1), clarify the general political and social nature of the definitional debate so we can see the actual issues at stake. In the second section, we are then going to analyse the constitutional visions of the (often just implied) borders of the political community. The different visions will be the following: (I) one state – one ethnic nation: assimilation or exclusion (classical ethnic

[1] Rogers Brubaker, *Nationalism Reframed: Nationhood and the National Question in the New Europe*, Cambridge, Cambridge University Press 1996, 10.

[2] For valuable criticism and useful remarks I am grateful to Leonardo Álvarez Álvarez, Alfons Aragoneses, Balázs Ablonczy, Miklós Bakk, Zoltán Balázs, Armin von Bogdandy, György Csepeli, Arthur Dyevre, Thomas Fleiner, Balázs Fekete, Victor Ferreres Comella, Péter Hahner, Kristin Henrard, György Hunyady, Zoltán Kántor, Viktor Koska, Herbert Küpper, Enric Martínez-Herrera, Jacob T Levy, Zoran Oklopcic, Antal Örkény, Csaba Pákozdi, András László Pap, Kálmán Pócza, Ferran Requejo, Alex Saiz Arnaiz, George Schöpflin, Markku Suksi, Márton Sulyok, Gábor Zoltán Szűcs, Péter Takács and András Zs Varga, as wells as to the participants of the multiculturalism workshop on 23 March 2012 in Belgrade, the MTA PTI workshop on 10 May 2012 and the ELTE TáTK workshop on 16 May 2012 in Budapest, the MPI Dienstagsrunde on 29 May 2012 in Heidelberg, the Pompeu Fabra Seminar on 26 June 2012 in Barcelona, and the CEU Citizenship Summer University on 9 July 2012 in Budapest.

nationalist vision); (II) one state – one multi-ethnic nation: the nation as an emotional alliance of different ethnies (Switzerland); (III) one state – several equal ethnic nations: the state as an empty shell which does not claim an emotional connection between the ethnic communities (Belgium); (IV) one state – a dominant ethnic nation and different minority ethnic groups (most European states); (V) one state – no ethnic nation: the concept of a civic nation (United States). After discussing borderline cases and secession from this perspective, the chapter closes by looking at the possible future scenarios faced by the European Union as to the constitutional vision of its national nature.

As to the concepts used, I am going to explain 'nation/national' and 'ethnie/ethnic' throughout the first (sociological, historical) section of the chapter, but I am not going to define them (see the quote by Brubaker in the motto above). For the later (constitutional) parts of the chapter, however, I am compelled to define these concepts at the beginning of the second section for the purposes of the analysis, as otherwise a transparent and understandable conceptual typology of constitutional visions would not be possible (which would be my primary purpose). During the analysis, I am going to concentrate on Europe and include examples from countries on other continents (especially the United States) only rarely and mainly for contrast purposes.

## 10.1 How ethnic diversity becomes a challenge: the nation as a political and social phenomenon

In the first section of the present chapter, we are going to see how and why ethnic diversity is a challenge for the state: on its own, it does not pose a challenge, but with the idea of nation and nationalism it does become a potential problem. Thus first, we are going to analyse the factors which led to the breakthrough of nationalism in the eighteenth century. Second, some antinomies about the nature of modern nations will be dealt with, using the term in a Kantian sense as equally rational but contradictory statements.

### *10.1.1 Factors helping the formation of modern nations*

The factors which led to the formation of modern nations and which we are discussing in this section should be considered as being only conducive towards that formation.[3] This means that no individual factor is a sufficient ground for nation formation on its own; and, conversely, the lack of any of them did not make modern nation formation impossible, but only less likely. As we will see, these factors have also partly influenced (mostly reinforced) each other; thus the following explanation of social-political mechanisms is rather similar to a network than to a series of individual, neat and parallel grounds. The order of the different factors does not mean any ranking in importance, it simply seemed the most logical way to explain in a concise manner the complexity of the issue.

##### 10.1.1.1 Nationalism itself as a political ideology helping the formation of nations

'Nationalism is primarily' a political principle, which holds that the political and national unit should be congruent;[4] thus, (1) a nation should have a state (national self-determination), and (2) states should be nation-states (nation-building).[5] As nations are not biological or physical entities, their political existence can be explained to a great extent by the emergence of the political idea behind them, that is, by nationalism.[6] Or to put it more bluntly: nations did not create nationalism; it was rather the other way around.[7] Ethnic/cultural communities became nations by means of the idea of nationalism, that is, by the claim to render the boundaries of the nation congruent with those of its

[3] Miroslav Hroch, From National Movement to the Fully-Formed Nation: The Nation-Building Process in Europe, *New Left Review* 198 (1993) 3–20, 8–9 on the fact that any account has to be multi-causal.

[4] Ernest Gellner, *Nations and Nationalism*, Oxford, Blackwell [2]2006, 1. The term 'nationalism' first appeared in a text by Herder in 1774; see Isaiah Berlin, *Vico and Herder*, London, Hogarth 1976, 181.

[5] As a matter of fact though, they are and were mostly not congruent, see William H McNeill, *Polyethnicity and National Unity in World History*, Toronto, Toronto University Press 1986.

[6] We are not going to analyse what did *not* have a direct influence on the emergence of nationalism. Because of its well-known and widespread nature, only one of such factors should be mentioned here. As opposed to some Marxist accounts, it is *not* possible to establish a causal link between capitalism and nationalism, except at the most general level; the bourgeoisie was *not* the inventor of nationalism: if we look for a specific social group behind nationalism, then in modern times its first mover was rather the intelligentsia. See Josep R Llobera, *The God of Modernity: The Development of Nationalism in Western Europe*, Oxford, Berg 1994, 220.

[7] Eric Hobsbawm, *Nations and Nationalism since 1780*, Cambridge, Cambridge University Press [2]1992, 10; Eugen Lemberg, *Nationalismus*, vol. II, Reinbek bei Hamburg, Rowohlt 1964, 250.

governance unit.[8] The main normative argument usually employed for nationalism ('nations should have a state') is thus necessarily circular, as nations become nations exactly through believing in the idea of nationalism.[9] The other usual nationalist argument ('states should be nation-states') contradicts the former; consequently, nationalist politics is not simply about reinforcing or establishing the belonging to a national community, but a bitter struggle between nationalising states and state-seeking national minorities for the loyalty of the members and for the political rights to self-government.[10]

For the success of this political idea, however, some of the structural social factors which are detailed below were helpful, and the presence of at least some of them indispensable. In the words of Miroslav Hroch:[11]

> The diffusion of national ideas could only occur in specific social settings. Nation-building was never a mere project of ambitious or narcissistic intellectuals.... Intellectuals can invent national communities only if certain objective preconditions for the formation of a nation exist.

These social preconditions are succinctly summarised by Paul Brass (we are going to deal with them one by one in later parts of the present chapter):[12]

> Nationalism is most likely to develop when new elites arise to challenge a system of ethnic stratification in the cities or an existing pattern of distribution of economic resources and political power between ethnically distinct urban and rural groups or ethnically diverse regions. One moment at which such challenges tend to arise most forcefully is when industrial development and political centralization have led to concentrations of job opportunities in key urban centers and to the need for trained personnel to fill the new positions. It is also at this point in pluralistic societies that the issue of language becomes critical because the choice of the official language and the medium of education determines which groups have favored access to the best jobs.

It is difficult to consider nationalism as a usual political philosophy: as opposed to conservatism or liberalism; it just does not claim to be a

[8] Michael Hechter, *Containing Nationalism*, Oxford, New York, Oxford University Press 2000, 7.

[9] Jacob T Levy, National Minorities without Nationalism, in: Alain Dieckhoff (ed.), *The Politics of Belonging*, Lanham, Md., Lexington Press 2004, 155–174, 160.

[10] Levy (n. 9) 161. [11] Hroch (n. 3) 4.

[12] Paul R Brass, *Ethnicity and Nationalism: Theory and Comparison*, New Delhi, Sage 1991, 43–44.

philosophically sophisticated system.[13] It is rather an emotional alliance and a *mass* movement.[14] It does have some clearly identifiable tenets, though, which, according to Smith, are the following:[15]

> 1. The world is divided into nations, each with its own peculiar character, history and destiny. 2. The nation is the source of all political and social power, and loyalty to the nation has priority over all other allegiances. 3. Human beings must identify with a nation if they want to be free and realize themselves. 4. Nations must be free and secure if peace is to prevail in the world.

Therefore, nationalism is not simply a claim of ethnic/cultural similarity, but a claim that ethnic/cultural similarity should count as *the* definition of the political community.[16] Nationalism also refers to a specific way of thinking and talking about the people, that is, a nationalist discourse. One of the reasons why it is difficult to understand the features of this discourse is partly due to the fact that it is a discourse systematically forming the object of which it speaks.[17] This discourse can be characterised by the following typical elements:[18]

> 1. boundaries of territory or population, or both, 2. indivisibility, 3. sovereignty or the aspiration of sovereignty, usually through an autonomous or a putatively self-sufficient state, 4. an 'ascending' notion of legitimacy, or the idea that government is just only when it is supported by popular will, 5. popular participation in collective affairs, 6. direct membership, where each individual is a part of the nation and is categorically equal to all others, 7. culture which includes some combination of language, values and shared beliefs, 8. temporal depth, the idea of a nation extending from the past to the future, 9. common descent or racial

[13] Cf. Bernard Yack as cited in Ronald Beiner, Introduction: Nationalism's Challenge to Political Philosophy, in: Ronald Beiner (ed.), *Theorizing Nationalism*, New York, State University of New York Press 1999, 1–25, 2: 'there are no great theoretical texts outlining and defending nationalism. No Marx, no Mill, no Machiavelli. Only minor texts by first rate thinkers, like Fichte, or major texts by second rate thinkers, like Mazzini.'

[14] According to Erica Benner, Is there a core national doctrine?, *Nations and Nationalism* 2001, 155–174, its nature is rather similar to doctrines on the placement of the political community, like imperialism, regionalism or globalism.

[15] Anthony D Smith, *National Identity*, London, Penguin 1991 74.

[16] Craig Calhoun, *Nationalism*, Buckingham, Open University Press 1997, 9; and Craig Calhoun, Nationalism and Ethnicity, *Annual Review of Sociology* 19 (1993) 211–239, especially 229.

[17] For such a concept of discourse, see Michel Foucault, *The Archaeology of Knowledge*, London, New York, Routledge 2002, 54.

[18] Calhoun 1997 (n. 16) 4–5. The features are to be understood only as family resemblances in the sense of Wittgenstein.

characteristics, 10. special historical, sometimes sacred connections to a territory.

Though some philosophical precursors can be found in Rousseau or in Herder, neither of them can actually be identified as being a nationalist thinker, using the fully fledged arguments as shown above which have been used by nationalist politicians.[19] Nationalism as a political ideology is a modern phenomenon (even if some elements of nations and even of national identity can be traced back to pre-modern times, but nationalism as a mass movement claiming that the nation should have a right of self-determination, and consequently also its own state, stems from the end of the eighteenth century, see below *10.1.2.1 Old vs. modern*).

#### 10.1.1.2 The socio-psychological needs of individuals

During the eighteenth century in Europe, the nation became a substitute for social cohesion both through royal families (or other cohesive traditions and allegiances) and through religion and national churches.[20] First, we will take a look at secularisation as a force behind nationalism; then we will analyse the influence of the breakdown of traditional social structures.

**10.1.1.2.1 The need to give a meaning to life after secularisation** Modern national identity appeared in Western Europe at a time when religion itself was losing its grip on the masses.[21] How identity-building based primarily on (universal Catholic) religion failed in Europe is shown by the slow but unstoppable demise of the Habsburg Empire beginning with the Dutch wars in the sixteenth century and ending in 1918 with the dissolution of Austria-Hungary.[22] The emergence of nationalism came hand in hand with secularisation (meaning here the declining explanatory and justificatory force of religion in politics), which we already analysed in the chapter on democracy (see above 9.1.1).

But religion was a ready-made model for nationalism in rituals and schemes of thought, and in many cases it was a substitute for religion; in

[19] On the consciousness of belonging together and on patriotism: Frederick M Barnard, National Culture and Political Legitimacy: Herder and Rousseau, *Journal of the History of Political Ideas* 1983, 231–253; Frederick M Barnard, Patriotism and Citizenship in Rousseau, *Review of Politics* 46 (1984) 244–265.

[20] Eric Hobsbawm, Mass-Producing Traditions: Europe, 1870–1914, in: Eric Hobsbawm – Terence Ranger (eds.), *The Invention of Tradition*, Cambridge, Cambridge University Press 1983, 263–307, 303.

[21] Hobsbawm (n. 20) 269. [22] Llobera (n. 6) 140.

others it became a powerful ally, reinforcing emerging (but in its nature actually secular) nationalism.[23] The former happened during the French Revolution in the form of a new anti-Christian religion in which abstract concepts such as Fatherland *(Patrie)*, Reason *(Raison)*, Liberty *(Liberté)*, and so on became deified and were worshipped as gods (or rather goddesses),[24] the latter in the form of national Christian churches supporting nationalist movements (as in Poland or Ireland).[25]

Symbols and semi-ritual practices, such as flags, singing national anthems, election days, images (icons) and ceremonies (feasts, processions, pilgrimages, holy days), all resembled older religious practices.[26] Instead of saints, patriotic heroes and national geniuses were (and are) worshipped.[27] In the words of Llobera:[28]

> [N]ationalism has become a religion – a secular religion where god is the nation. What is meant by that is not only that modern nationalism has all the trappings and rituals of a religion, but also that, like religion, it has tapped into the emotional reservoir of human beings. Religion . . . operates at the same level as nationalism: the level of deep elementary emotions.

A new answer has been given to the question of fear from death, probably the most important psychological factor behind religions, stating that the meaning of individual life is to be part of a larger community which lives forever,[29] for which entity it is consequently worth sacrificing our own individual lives.[30] Accordingly, being a member of a nation often acquired a missionary zeal, its anonymous war martyrs were worshipped in ceremonies of national holidays, which used as their scene the Tomb of the Unknown Soldier.[31] Instead of religious martyrs, our public events began

[23] Llobera (n. 6) x, 144; Heinrich August Winkler, Einleitung: Der Nationalismus und seine Funktionen, in: *id.* (ed.), *Nationalismus*, Königstein, Athenaeum 1978, 5–46, 6; Peter Alter, *Nationalismus*, Frankfurt aM, Suhrkamp 1985, 15–16.

[24] Llobera (n. 6) 139, 145. Also the home-land often became sacralised, like the 'holy Russian land' or 'Holy Ireland'; see Hobsbawm (n. 7) 49. Sometimes old sacralised expressions achieved new emphasis: for instance, in Hungary the expression 'countries of the [Hungarian] Holy Crown' gained a more ethnic connotation than before.

[25] James G Kellas, *The Politics of Nationalism and Ethnicity*, London, Macmillan 1991, 48.

[26] Hobsbawm (n. 7) 72; Carlton JH Hayes, *Nationalism: A Religion*, New York, Macmillan 1960, 164–168.

[27] Rogers Brubaker, Religion and nationalism, *Nations and Nationalism* 2012, 2–20, 3.

[28] Llobera (n. 6) 143.

[29] Bruce Kapferer, Nationalist Ideology and Comparative Anthropology, *Ethnos* 54 (1989) 161–199.

[30] Benedict Anderson, *Imagined Communities*, London, New York, Verso $^{2}$2006, 11.

[31] Anderson (n. 30) 9–10.

to worship the historical founding fathers of our nation, or even more its anonymous member, the Unknown Soldier, that is, potentially ourselves.

**10.1.1.2.2 The need for social cohesion in a dynamically changing world** Even though members of nations are actually not relatives in a biological sense, we still often use metaphors based on family ('mother country', 'fatherland', 'founding fathers of the nation', 'our brothers on the front').[32] From the nation, we not only expect (mutual) actual help in case of need, but it also gives the feeling of togetherness which, in modern individualised times, is so much needed.

Modern nations, even though by definition collective entities, emerge under the precondition of individualism in society (meaning not the philosophical idea, but the sociological fact). Nationalism is actually balancing out social individualism by giving an identity anchor to individuals. Individualism as a social phenomenon can be explained on the basis of different grounds, such as absolutism, printing machines, the Reformation, and urbanisation and industrialisation. As to the first three (absolutism, printing machines and the Reformation), we would refer back to the detailed explanation in the chapter on democracy (9.1.1). The latter two, however, should be detailed at this point.

*Urbanisation and industrialisation* contributed to the breakdown of traditional (extended) family and clan ties, and the social and cultural vacuum left by this was filled by the nation. In large-scale industrial societies, people moved between many positions, migrating and changing jobs; thus people did not have to be prepared for unique jobs that would last a lifetime and furnish them with an identity (priest, guildsman, aristocrat, peasant, king).[33] They also worked in specialised jobs, resulting in the loss of the feeling of unity of their living environment.[34] Modern society is not mobile because it is egalitarian; it is egalitarian because it is mobile.[35]

All these led in turn to social alienation *(Entfremdung)*. Because of this alienation and because of the gradually diminishing role of old traditions, new traditions had to be invented which gave common political identities to societies.[36] These social and political identities

[32] Thomas Hylland Eriksen, *Ethnicity and Nationalism*, London, Pluto $^{3}$2010, 130.

[33] John Breuilly, Introduction, in: Gellner (n. 4) xxiv.

[34] Heinrich August Winkler, *Nationalismus*, Königstein, Athenaeum 1978, 26.

[35] Gellner (n. 4) 24.

[36] Eric Hobsbawm, Introduction, in: Hobsbawm – Ranger (n. 20) 1–14, 12 on the need for stable identification points in a changing and dynamic world. Cf. Llobera (n. 6) x on the

could no longer be overwhelmingly religious ones because of the *secularisation* (as described above). Accordingly, the nineteenth century became the century for inventing new national traditions or for transforming local or dynastic traditions into national ones. New public holidays emerged, monuments and buildings were built that tried to look ancient, national anthems were written, the national flag was raised at every ceremony (wedding, election day) and on public buildings,[37] huge national festivities were celebrated (where the nation worshipped itself and its own culture).[38] Folk tales and folk songs were collected (sometimes partly even invented, such as the Finnish Kalevala in 1835). All this happened in the name of a *conscious* effort to build nations.[39]

Competing identities like that of class (with its own festive day, 1 May, with its own symbols and mythology), proved to be doomed to fail in the long run.[40] To use the words of Hobsbawm:[41]

> What is clear is that nationalism became a substitute for social cohesion through a national church, a royal family or other cohesive traditions, or collective self-representations, a new secular religion, and that the class which required such a mode of cohesion most was the growing middle class, or rather that large intermediate mass which so signally lacked other forms of cohesion.

#### 10.1.1.3 Political and cultural compartmentalisation

Political compartmentalisation beginning in the sixteenth century had different elements. On the one hand, universalist structures *(Imperium* and *Ecclesia)* had been fragmented; on the other hand, the centralised modern administrative state was born. Both have been helped by a third factor, namely by linguistic unification in vernacular tongues (and vice versa, the first two factors had themselves also helped this unification). The fuzzy picture of the Middle Ages where universalist structures

need for roots, and *ibid.* 153: 'The nation was a family (tribe) writ large.' Similarly John Breuilly, *Nationalism and the State*, Manchester, Manchester University Press ²1993, 418–419.

37 An extreme form of respect for national flags is to be to the present day in the United States, where the flag is worshipped every day (since the 1880s); see Raymond Firth, *Symbols, Public and Private*, London, Allen & Unwin 1973, 358–359.

38 Gellner (n. 4)135; Hobsbawm (n. 20) 263, 264, 273, 278.

39 Cf. Hobsbawm (n. 20) 267 quoting Massimo d'Azeglio 'We have made Italy: now we must make Italians.' (1861). According to David Laven, Italy, in: Timothy Baycroft – Mark Hewitson (eds.), *What Is a Nation? Europe 1789–1914*, Oxford, Oxford University Press 2006, 256 (with further references) the phrase actually stems from Ferdinando Martini (1896).

40 Hobsbawm (n. 7) 173. 41 Hobsbawm (n. 20) 303.

claimed authority over heterogeneous political units slowly faded away: it broke up into strictly separated units, and these became more homogenous inside than before.

In the Middle Ages, cultural differentiation was a means of hierarchisation, thus a protected stabilising factor of existing power structures.[42] Privileged groups such as dynasties, the clergy and the nobility shared identities which transcended political boundaries.[43] By contrast, immobile peasant communities could identify neither with higher social groups (social division) nor with other peasant groups (absence of communication).[44] In the modern era, however, cultural (especially linguistic) homogenisation was necessary for a functioning capitalist society that could provide the financial support and the human resources needed for international conflicts with other states. Modern nations are thus anonymous,[45] fluid and mobile: they are unmediated; that is, individuals belong to them directly, by virtue of their cultural style (this even applies to the so-called civic nations, see below *10.1.2.2 Natural (ethnic, that is, based on ancestry or culture) vs. artificial (based on elite manipulation; or civic, that is, based on law and deliberate choice)*), and not by virtue of membership of nested groups.[46] The key conceptual elements of modern nations are thus a certain minimal size (being able to run a full educational system), homogeneity and literacy. All this was missing in the Middle Ages.

In this section, we are first going to analyse this last issue of country-wide linguistic unification, and then the emergence of modern bureaucratic states, followed by the fragmentation of universalist structures.

**10.1.1.3.1 Country-wide communication in the vernacular through linguistic unification** At the time of the French Revolution (1789), half of the population of France did not speak French (but Italian, German, Breton, English, Occitan, Catalan, Basque, Dutch), and only 12–13 per cent spoke it correctly. At the time of the Italian unification (1861), only 2.5 per cent, according to more generous estimates 9.5 per cent, of the

[42] Gellner (n. 4) 9–10.

[43] John Breuilly, Approaches to Nationalism, in: Gopal Balakrishnan (ed.), *Mapping the Nation*, London, Verso 1996, 146–174, 150–151.

[44] Gellner (n. 4) 10.

[45] Linguistic unification meant internal interchangeability of men and documents, thus anonymity. Anderson (n. 30) 55.

[46] Gellner (n. 4) 132.

population spoke the Italian we today call Italian.[47] Ignorance of another group's language constitutes the most obvious barrier to communication,[48] and thus the most obvious defining line which separates groups.[49] Therefore, for the emergence of nations, a linguistic unification of different dialects was an extremely important component.

This unification happened through different mechanisms. On the one hand, in order to be able to recruit the expanding number of bureaucrats, modern bureaucracies switched from Latin to the vernacular.[50] The origins of the modern school system are partly to be found in the educational institutions set up in order to supply the state with the necessary number of bureaucrats. On the other hand, the new and mobile industrial societal structure also required both a mobile division of labour, and sustained, frequent and precise communication between strangers who could share an explicit meaning, transmitted in a standard idiom and in writing when required.[51] As labour became more complex, communication became more important for production. In addition, because of continuous technical inventions, knowledge could not be passed on within the family or within corporations, and instead larger, organised professional educational units were needed. To reproduce its own personnel, such societies needed a pyramidal educational system, which could only be afforded by larger entities, nowadays called nation-states.[52]

The educational system allowed not only for linguistic unification *(cuius regio, eius lingua)*, but also for the dispersion of national historical narratives and identities. The monopoly of legitimate education became from this point of view even more important, more central than the monopoly of legitimate violence.[53] Education was one of the major means of turning the population of a country into a nation.[54] Both

47 Tullio De Mauro, *Storia linguistica dell'Italia unita*, Bari, Laterza 1970, 43; Arrigo Castellani, Quanti erano gl'italofoni nel 1861?, *Studi linguistici italiani* 1982, 3–26.

48 On the role of communication in the formation of nations, see Karl W Deutsch, *Nationalism and Social Communication. An Inquiry into the Foundations of Nationalism*, Cambridge, Mass., Technology Press 1953.

49 Hobsbawm (n. 7) 51. 50 Anderson (n. 30) 39–40. 51 Gellner (n. 4) 33.

52 Gellner (n. 4) 31. 'A viable higher culture-sustaining modern state cannot fall below a certain minimal size (unless in effect parasitic on its neighbours); and there is only room for a limited number of such states on this earth.' Gellner (n. 4) 47.

53 Gellner (n. 4) 33.

54 Michael Mann, The Emergence of Modern European Nationalism, in: John Hall – Ian Jarvie (eds.), *The Social Philosophy of Ernest Gellner*, Amsterdam and Atlanta, Rodopi 1996, 147–170; Charles Tilly, States and Nationalism in Europe 1492–1992, in: John L Comaroff – Paul C Stern (eds.), *Perspectives on Nationalism and War*, Amsterdam, Gordon and Breach 1995, 187–204.

cultural homogenisation within the political unit and differentiation from external political units were sometimes helped by national Protestant churches using a vernacular translation of the scripturalist God.[55] Printed languages laid the ground for geographically large-scale national consciousness (in unwritten languages, speakers of different dialects often do not understand each other),[56] it unified communication and it also made linguistic changes more difficult.[57]

In addition, industrial inventions indirectly led to circumstances favouring linguistic unification. One is the train, which opened up formerly closed rural areas, broke up these small social communities and integrated them into the whole of country and facilitated countrywide communication.[58] But even more importantly, the invention of printing machines should be mentioned here. Printing machines resulted in cheap books which could be afforded by a large proportion of society (and a large proportion of society achieved literacy due to the educational system just mentioned); thus a whole industry could be built up on publishing books. The market for Latin and ancient Greek books was quickly filled up; thus new markets were needed. Vernacular books entered into the market, but it would not have been economically efficient to print books in every dialect. Thus certain dialects became the standard (printed) ones; others were downgraded to merely oral ones (even before any centralised academic institution could have decided about it). Linguistic unification in the vernacular (sometimes even beyond state boundaries), so useful for nation-building, was thus much of a result of print-capitalism.[59]

Print-capitalism could, however, only influence the literate members of society. Protestantism and the Counter-Reformation did extend literacy,[60] but the decisive step was the introduction of mass schooling (required for jobs both in the private economy and as a state bureaucrat)[61] combined with the emergence of newspapers (through which the news in

55 Gellner (n. 4) 40, 136; Adrian Hastings, *The Construction of Nationhood*, Cambridge, Cambridge University Press 1997, 12–13.

56 Hobsbawm (n. 7) 52. 57 Anderson (n. 30) 44.

58 József Eötvös, *A XIX. század uralkodó eszméinek befolyása az államra I.*, Budapest, Magyar Helikon 1981, 248.

59 Anderson (n. 30) 43.

60 Michael Mann, A Political Theory of Nationalism and Its Excesses, in: Sukumar Periwal (ed.), *Notions of Nationalism*, Budapest, Central University Press 1995, 42–64, 45–46.

61 National languages emerged through mass schooling; see Hobsbawm (n. 7) 52, 81, 96. On the literate civil service middle class as the basis of nationalism, see Anderson (n. 30) 76.

the vernacular bound the reading audience together).[62] Its main audience were socially modest, but educated middle strata (provincial journalists, schoolteachers, aspiring subaltern officials, the lower echelons of the nobility, low-ranking clergy), and nationalism was socially based on precisely these activists.[63] Not only the language itself, but its script could also be identity-building, but only for the literate strata: the demand of Albanian nationalists that their language should be written neither in Arabic nor in Greek script, but in the Latin alphabet, which implied inferiority to neither Greeks or Turks, was obviously irrelevant to people who could not read.[64]

For the less educated (mostly rural, often analphabetic) strata of society, the rise of modern mass media (radio, cinema, television) made it possible for them to be involved in linguistic unification.[65] The evolution of the British royal family into a domestic as well as a public icon of national identification would have been impossible but for the modern mass media, and its most deliberate ritual expression was actually devised specifically for the radio (later adapted to the television): the royal Christmas broadcast, instituted in 1932.[66] Democratic changes, especially the extension of suffrage also boosted linguistic unification, as nationwide electoral campaigns were conducted in a unified vernacular (and not in dialects).[67] The importance of language in the office and in school was obvious for the nationalists themselves, and they often even insisted with an exclusionary logic on the linguistic purity of the national vocabulary.[68]

Though the state machinery (national/royal academies setting linguistic standards, schooling system, public administration) was very useful for linguistic unification (cf. the 'King's English'), such unification was also possible in the absence of state standards (as in Germany, with Luther and the theatres), if there were no deliberate state policy fighting against it.[69]

Linguistic compartmentalisation is not absolutely necessary for the formation of nations, though; it is rather just a factor which makes it more likely to happen. Nations having distinct identities, but not having

[62] Anderson (n. 30) 62. Only in countries, like Switzerland, where the schooling system always remained highly decentralised, could multilingualism be sustained.

[63] Hobsbawm (n. 7) 117, 104. [64] Hobsbawm (n. 7) 115. [65] Anderson (n. 30) 54.

[66] Hobsbawm (n. 7) 142. [67] Hobsbawm (n. 7) 94.

[68] Hobsbawm (n. 7) 96. The fight against foreign words as 'philological nationalism'; see *ibid.* 56.

[69] Hobsbawm (n. 7) 61.

their own language (South America, to a certain extent Ireland, or see the Zionists unable to speak Hebrew), or the opposite, having several languages (Switzerland), are possible.

It is not too bold, though, to predict that the probability of the end of national identity will be higher if automated portable translating machines with earphones instantaneously translating foreign languages into the user's native tongue become available for the masses. Such a technological invention could have a similarly huge effect on indirectly influencing the political landscape as the invention of the printing machines by Gutenberg did.[70] In the meantime, universal linguistic unification is restricted to the widening use of English, used in most countries only by the intellectual elite in its international communications, which does not seem to affect the identity of the masses.

**10.1.1.3.2 The modern bureaucratic state** The modern bureaucratic state means an institutionalised organisation with continuous territory connected through infrastructure (highways, railways, canals, telegraph lines), administering the inhabitants directly, having the same laws in all its territory, directing a growing number of public servants (such as postmen, tax officers, policemen, gendarmes and schoolteachers), conducting military conscription and introducing personal documentation and registration (births, marriages, deaths) for each of its citizens. All these new phenomena in the eighteenth and nineteenth centuries led to a new situation in which not just the growing number of public servants and the government, but the government and *all* citizens were inevitably linked as never before by daily bonds.[71] This modern 'direct rule' not only gave rise to state-building nationalism, but also provoked counter-nationalisms of local ethnic groups.[72]

There is a certain mutual gravitation between modern bureaucratic states and nations:[73] it is probable that they converge, but no necessary connection can be proven (as a matter of fact, there are quite a few counter-examples).[74] Nations claimed a right to a state, and states often

[70] On the effect of printing machines on individualism, Protestantism and the democratic idea in general, see above 9.1.1.

[71] Hobsbawm (n. 7) 80–82. [72] Hechter (n. 8) 24–33, 113–133.

[73] On the 'tendency' of nations 'to become states', see Leopold von Ranke, *Sämtliche Werke*, vols. 49–50, Leipzig, Duncker & Humblot 1887, 326.

[74] Llobera (n. 6) 121.

required a quasi-religious loyalty (civic religion in the form of 'patriotism'), which was especially necessary in international conflicts.[75]

The modern bureaucratic state is an expensive machine, though; one which not all states could afford in its full efficiency. For example, as opposed to France, Spain in the nineteenth century was a state void of particularly good natural resources and fertile land, and continually on the verge of bankruptcy. Statesmen lacked the money, and consequently also the will and the vision, to 'nationalise' the country around a centralised system of education, a tight network of internal communications, a defined set of public holidays, a patriotic history or even a single language or uniform code of civil laws.[76] Thus ethnic diversity (which was actually similar in France and Spain in the eighteenth century) has survived until the present day in Spain, but exists only in a very weak form in France.

Nationalism was also suited to the military tactics of the modern mass armies of bureaucratic states.[77] Three factors should be considered from this point of view, which characterised wars between the eighteenth and the twentieth centuries. Firstly, due to increases in population and wealth, armies of previously unseen sizes marched across Europe, especially during the French Revolution and the Napoleonic wars. Secondly, due to improved artillery techniques, it was no longer advisable to use large numbers of foot soldiers in disciplined formations, since they were too vulnerable to distant cannons. And thirdly, due to improved firearms, infantrymen became potent killers on their own. These three factors resulted in a new military tactic: huge numbers of soldiers fought as dispersed, lonely individual skirmishers cooperating to take the lives of others (as opposed to former disciplined military formations, for the success of such cooperation a common language as a shared vernacular proved to be extremely useful for solving unexpected situations creatively and quickly).[78] This made

[75] Arthur Schlesinger, Nationalism in the Modern World, in: Michael Palumbo – William Oswald Shanahan (eds.), *Nationalism: Essays in Honour of Louis L Snyder*, Westport, Conn., Greenwood 1981, ix.

[76] Stephen Jacobson, Spain, in: Timothy Baycroft – Mark Hewitson (eds.), *What Is a Nation? Europe 1789–1914*, Oxford, Oxford University Press 2006, 210–227, 211; Juan J Linz, Early State Building and Late Peripheral Nationalism against the State: The Case of Spain, in: Stein Rokkan (ed.), *Building States and Nations*, vol. 2, Beverly Hills, Calif., Sage 1973, 32–116; José Álvarez Junco, El nacionalismo español: las insuficiencias en la acción estatal, *Historia social* 40 (2001) 29–51.

[77] The paragraph is based on Barry R Posen, Nationalism, Mass Army, and Military Power, *International Security* 18 (1993) 80–124.

[78] For similar arguments by Max Weber, see David Beetham, *Max Weber and the Theory of Modern Politics*, Cambridge, Polity Press 1985, 129 with further references.

command and control very difficult; thus, if officers wanted to prevent their troops from deserting, they needed to motivate them (and not by simple force or threat, as due to the dispersed tactics it was no longer possible). Nationalism fit this need, and also the other way around: because nationalism was useful in wars, wars contributed to the success of nationalism. In historical sources, it is now well documented that after a while, even military strategists consciously advised the enhancement of patriotic feelings in education in order to create better motivated soldiers for their armies: the spread of mass education itself was partly motivated by the needs of the army; manpower was needed with a basic level of literacy (so they could read the official government propaganda, training manuals, technical guides, and could understand written orders) and with a nationalist predisposition.[79] The former strategy of training fewer soldiers but to a higher standard was no longer applicable, as the efficiency of new firearms resulted in high losses, which could only be replaced if only a short period of training were needed. Such a short period of training was only possible if citizens were already educated to the level of general primary education.[80]

**10.1.1.3.3 Fragmentation of universalist structures** The man of the Middle Ages was mesmerised by the memory of Ancient Rome, and everything that reminded him of this: the idea of *Imperium*, Roman law, the Latin language or the universal church *(Ecclesia)*.[81] As to the *Imperium*, Europe proved to be a failed Empire:[82] instead nation-states emerged. National laws also fragmented any idea of legal unity. As already shown, instead of the Latin language, vernaculars took over. And the universalist Catholic Church also fractured into smaller units (this not only meant national Protestant churches, but also movements of national Catholic churches, such as French Gallicanism).[83] National churches have played a significant role in the development of many nationalisms, as in modernity, the national sentiment was often a reaction against the cosmopolitan pretension of the Enlightenment.[84] These factors also strengthened each other: the major protector of the universalist Catholic church, the Habsburg Imperium, slowly lost ground. The growing importance of vernaculars contributed to the

79 Posen (n. 77) 85, 98, 111–115.
80 According to Posen (n. 77) 124, if mass armies become outdated for technical reasons, one of the driving forces of nationalism will also cease.
81 Llobera (n. 6) 5. 82 Llobera (n. 6) 113.
83 Anderson (n. 30) 17 on the territorialisation of faiths as the forerunner of 'nation'.
84 Llobera (n. 6) 221.

impression that the imagined community of Christendom seemed less real.[85] With the demise of Latin, the universalist community-building role of universities also declined.[86] In the centre of the fading universalist structures, the birth of nation-states was delayed (Germany, Italy), but medieval structures were also eventually defeated there.[87]

The explorations of other continents broadened horizons and strengthened the perception that other forms of human life were also possible.[88] Scholars discovered that Sanskrit and the Indic cultures developed independently from Europe and that they were actually much more ancient than Greek or Hebrew.[89] All this meant that the traditional universalist claims became less plausible than before.[90]

#### 10.1.1.4 Political struggles and wars

National feeling means a strong emotional bond, which can be important in political struggles. Article 3 of the 1789 Declaration (adopted by the *National* Constituent Assembly) stated: 'The principle of all sovereignty resides in the *nation*'. The French Revolution made everything *royal* into *national*: the national navy, the national police, the national estates.[91] By heating up nationalistic feelings during the revolutionary wars, the French were able to use their mobilisation capacity *(levée en masse)*,[92] but at the same time they both irritated the population in occupied territories and gave them a behavioural example. Spanish and German nationalisms were, to some extent, triggered by the French Revolution and the following Napoleonic wars.[93]

85 Anderson (n. 30) 42. 86 Anderson (n. 30) 54. 87 Hastings (n. 55) 8.

88 Erich Auerbach, *Mimesis: The Representation of Reality in Western Literature*, Princeton, Princeton University Press 1957, 282; Anderson (n. 30) 16, 69.

89 Anderson (n. 30) 70.

90 Whether new universalist, or at least European, continental structures are now being rebuilt and whether this can affect the national idea will be dealt with below, see *10.5. The European Union and the Visions of a European political community.*

91 Jacques Godechot, The New Concept of the Nation, in: Otto Dann and John Dinwiddy (eds.), *Nationalism in the Age of the French Revolution*, London, Hambledon 1988, 13–26, 15.

92 Stephen Tierney, *Constitutional Law and National Pluralism*, Oxford, Oxford University Press 2004, 25. National wars also strengthened the state's legitimacy as *the* dominating institution which could provide for the financial and military means of warfare; see Jörn Leonhard, Nation-States and Warfare, in: Baycroft – Hewitson (n. 76) 231–254, 236.

93 Mikulás Teich – Roy Porter, Introduction, in: Mikulás Teich – Roy Porter (eds.), *The National Question in Europe in Historical Context*, Cambridge, Cambridge University Press 1993, xix.

But revolution had an effect not only on those who had direct contact with the French Revolution: the French and the American Revolutions also served as successful examples worldwide, namely in South America for Creole nationalists. Those locals who led anti-colonial wars were mostly educated in Europe or in the United States and learned the logic of nationalism and the rhetoric of liberation there and took it back home and turned it against their educators.[94] The 'nation' proved to be an invention on which it was impossible to secure a patent: it became available for pirating by widely different, and sometimes unexpected, hands.[95]

Nationalism was also easy to combine with democracy (both the idea of a national community and democracy opposed serfdom; the doctrine of popular sovereignty can easily be interpreted as implying the idea of a pre-state community),[96] or nationalism could sometimes even take the place of democracy (cf. nationalist autocratic regimes).[97] Nationalism gave the *feeling* of equality, and it aimed at unity, making it a useful tool for both secessionist and unification movements (depending on the definition of nation).[98] Its (military) mobilisation capacity was even stronger than that of democracy, and in some cases it was used against international democratic movements (or against democratising occupational forces) by old-style anti-democratic monarchies.[99] Democracy *on its own* proved to be too abstract a political community to be able to gain a strong emotional attachment and to command the loyalty of its citizens.[100] The best answer to the nation was just another nation. In the course of the nineteenth and twentieth centuries, most states thus became

[94] Anderson (n. 30) 51, 118.

[95] Anderson (n. 30) 67. On how Hungarian, English and Japanese nationalism triggered as a reaction Slovak, Indian and Korean nationalism, see Anderson (n. 30) 109–110.

[96] Jürgen Habermas, Citizenship and National Identity: Some Reflections on the Future of Europe, in: Ronald Beiner (ed.), *Theorizing Citizenship*, Albany, University of New York Press 1995, 255–282, 257: 'The nation-state and democracy are the twins born of the French Revolution. From a cultural point of view, both have been growing in the shadow of nationalism.' Similarly Montserrat Guibernau, *Nationalisms: The Nation-State and Nationalism in the Twentieth Century*, London, Polity 1996, 3. For many liberals of the nineteenth century, 'nation-state' meant 'democratic state'; see Lothar Gall, Liberalismus und Nationalstaat. Der deutsche Liberalismus und die Reichsgründung, in: Helmut Berding – Kurt Düwell – Lothar Gall – Wolfgang J Mommsen – Hans-Ulrich Wehler (eds.), *Vom Staat des Ancien régime zum modernen Parteienstaat. Festschrift für Theodor Schieder*, München, Oldenbourg 1978, 287–300, 287–291.

[97] Anderson (n. 30) 47–50 on Creole nationalism without democratisation.

[98] Michael Jeismann, Nation, Identity, and Ethnicity, in: Baycroft – Hewitson (n. 76) 25.

[99] Hobsbawm (n. 7) 84. [100] Hobsbawm (n. 20) 264–265.

nation-states (at least in their ambitions),[101] expressed in the titles 'League of *Nations*' and 'United *Nations*' actually consisting of states.

#### 10.1.1.5 Side-effects of scientific and cultural advancements: census (statistics), maps (geography), bilingual dictionaries (linguistics), museums (scientific history), sport (Olympic games)

Statistics and census seem to be neutral with respect to nationalism. As a matter of fact, however, the question itself to a citizen concerning his or her ethnicity/cultural background strengthens his or her national feeling. Before this question was put to people, they did not have to choose. Once the choice was made, national identities were frozen.[102]

Geographical maps were not new inventions. But geographical maps showing every country in a different colour and using them in schools of mass education were new. Children learned in classes to identify the 'us' with the area of their state. This strengthened the identity-building capacity of the home country, and maps often have been (and are) used as logos expressing national feelings.[103]

The linguistic and philological research of the eighteenth and nineteenth centuries and the discovery of proto-languages showed that there was no ontological difference between the Jewish/Greek/Latin and the vernacular tongues.[104] The appearance of bilingual dictionaries also implied the equality of languages.[105] All this meant that a side-effect of linguistic achievements was that universalist claims became less plausible (meaning compartmentalisation as described above), and one's own vernacular became more valuable.

Scientific history itself was often used for the purposes of nationalism. Or to put it even more boldly, the early figures of scientific history (Leopold von Ranke, Heinrich von Treitschke, Jules Michelet, Mihály Horváth) wrote their works partly in order to support nationalistic claims.[106] Without historians, there is no national mythology, or as

[101] Anderson (n. 30) 86 on the official nationalism of Russification as 'stretching the short, tight skin of the nation over the gigantic body of the empire'.

[102] Anderson (n. 30) 164, Hobsbawm (n. 7) 100 on this effect of the census in the Habsburg Empire beginning the 1880s. On the durability of national identities once they have been formed see Anthony D Smith, *The Ethnic Origins of Nations*, Oxford, Blackwell 1986, 16–18 and Llobera (n. 6) 5.

[103] Anderson (n. 30) 175. [104] Anderson (n. 30) 70. [105] Anderson (n. 30) 71.

[106] Patrick J Geary, *The Myth of Nations: The Medieval Origins of Europe*, Princeton, Princeton University Press 2002, 16; Monika Baár, *Historians and Nationalism*, Oxford, Oxford University Press 2010, 167–194.

Hobsbawm put it: 'historians are to nationalism what poppy-growers in Pakistan are to heroin addicts: we supply the essential raw material for the market'.[107] And a new genre of public buildings helped to spread the consciously narrated past amongst the population: the museum.[108]

Finally, one of the most efficient ways to bolster nationalist feelings (national pride) is through good sporting results.[109] The most institutionalised form of sport is the Olympic Games (since 1896) in which – since 1904 – 'nations' are ranked in medal tables, even though nations as such obviously cannot box, weightlift or play football. Every single day, national feelings are being reconfirmed by sports news, in which the gladiators of our nation (symbolising the whole nation) also fight for our honour and prestige.[110]

### *10.1.2 Antinomies of the nature of modern nations*

The problem with the definition of 'nation' is that no list of objective criteria has ever been written which would fit all nations. Even if we write a list containing elements as family resemblances in the sense of Wittgenstein, it would be a very loose list: not a list of elements from which *most* should be fulfilled but rather a list from which *some* elements should be fulfilled.[111] This would not be particularly helpful. The key element is, a subjective one: national identity (for the emergence of which certain objective factors are of course useful).

[107] Eric Hobsbawm, Ethnicity and Nationalism in Europe Today, in: Balakrishnan (n. 43) 255–266.

[108] Anderson (n. 30) 178; Anne-Marie Thiesse, *La création des identités nationales*, Paris, Seuil 2001, 204–210. On this point in the Scottish context, in: J Magnus Fladmark (ed.), *Heritage and Museums: Shaping National Identity*, Shaftesbury, Donhead 2000. On the relationship between archaeology and nationalism, see Margarita Díaz-Andreu – Timothy C Champion, *Nationalism and Archaeology in Europe*, London, UCL Press 1996; Philip L Kohl – Clare P Fawcett (eds.), *Nationalism, Politics and the Practice of Archaeology*?, Cambridge, Cambridge University Press 1995.

[109] Maurice Roche, Nations, Mega-events and International Culture, in: Gerard Delanty – Krishan Kumar (eds.), *The SAGE Handbook of Nations and Nationalism*, London, Sage 2006, 260–272.

[110] Hobsbawm (n. 7) 132. On the relationship between nationalism and football, see Vic Duke – Liz Crolley, *Football, Nationality and the State*, Harlow, Longman 1996.

[111] Neither language nor religion is differentiating; also border referenda often showed results of national identity differing from these criteria; see Hobsbawm (n. 7) 70, 134. Some even claim that there is no definitional way of distinguishing ethnicity from other types of collective identity; see John A Armstrong, *Nations before Nationalism*, Chapel Hill, University of North Carolina Press 1982, 6–7.

It is an imagined community, a deep, horizontal comradeship.[112] It is a spiritual community, a 'community of fate' having the sentiment of the community's own shared destiny.[113] It is a community of solidarity based on trust towards each other.[114] It is a community which expresses its will to continue a common life everyday (to use Renan's *bon mot*, a 'daily plebiscite').[115] It is the denial of membership to another nation.[116] It is the claimed or hoped-for community, the community of all those who *ought to be* citizens of our political community.

Members' consciousness of belonging to it provides, however, only an *a posteriori* guide to what a nation is:[117] we can at best guess about whether a new nation emerges in the presence of certain objective factors. But once it has emerged, national identity seems to be quite resistant to historical storms.

The difficulty of any description of its nature is that it is not meant to be a concept of analysis, but a category of 'practice' (see the epigraph at the start of this chapter). When we talk about 'the nation', the features we emphasise in our description depend (often subconsciously) on whether we sympathise with the general idea (for philosophical reasons) or how it effects us in our concrete politico-geographical situation. Consequently, different, equally convincing descriptions of *what* and *how* 'the nation' is can consist of contradicting elements. In the following, we are going to detail these antinomies.

#### 10.1.2.1 Old vs. modern

It is undeniable that certain feelings of togetherness in a political community also existed in pre-modern eras.[118] It is less clear, however, how far these feelings concerned the whole of the population or rather just a slim elite. It seems that nationalism as a *mass movement* is a rather

[112] Anderson (n. 30) 6.

[113] Otto Bauer, The Nation [1924], in: Balakrishnan (n. 43) 39–77, 43–50.

[114] Umut Özkirimli, *Theories of Nationalism*, Basingstoke, Palgrave Macmillan $^{2}$2010, 215.

[115] Ernest Renan, What Is a Nation? [1882], in: Homi K Bhabha (ed.), *Nation and Narration*, London, Routledge 1990, 8–22, 19.

[116] Armstrong (n. 111) 5 on the fact that groups tend to define themselves not by reference to their own characteristics but by exclusion, that is, by comparison to 'strangers'.

[117] Hobsbawm (n. 7) 8.

[118] See, e.g., Jenő Szűcs, *Nation und Geschichte*, Budapest, Corvina 1981, 161–243. As the present work is an analysis of constitutional theory, we will be less interested in pre-modern issues, as the constitution (i.e., a man-made law that is higher in rank than simple statutes) itself is a modern invention. See above 8.1.

modern phenomenon; its breakthrough is mostly attributed to the end of the eighteenth century.[119]

Hard-core nationalists are mostly convinced that nations (or at least their own nation) have existed for ever, whereas hard-core anti-nationalists all state nations are a modern invention. And there is a big grey zone of opinions in between (to which the present work also belongs), with different shades, especially if we begin to talk about the nature of former identities and about the relative number of people believing in them.

A more or less balanced opinion would be to say that nations as shared (1) *political* identities of (2) the *masses* are rather new in modern Europe.[120] Amongst the less-educated strata, national consciousness was missing even during the nineteenth century. When Garibaldi spoke to southern Italian peasants about 'Italia', they thought he was talking about his mistress.[121] When the cry 'Viva Italia!' was raised during Victor Emmanuel's entry into Naples, some natives thought it must refer to his wife.[122] In 1864, a French school inspector in Lozère was terrified to find out that at one school he visited not a single child was able to answer questions like 'Are you English or Russian?' or 'What country is the department of Lozère in?'[123]

When the expression *natio* was used in the Middle Ages, it meant the population of another (foreign) country,[124] a state or a society.[125] At universities, students were divided into *nationes*, but it did not mean either any specific country nor did it have any political significance: small

119 Anthony D Smith, *Nationalism and Modernism: A Critical Survey of Recent Theories of Nations and Nationalism*, London, New York, Routledge 1998, 1.

120 Walter Bagehot, *Physics and Politics*, London, King 1887, chs III and IV: 'nation-making' was the essential content of nineteenth-century evolution.

121 Ralph Gibson, The Intensification of Nationalist Consciousness in Modern Europe, in: Claus Bjørn e.a. (eds.), *Nations, Nationalism and Patriotism in the European Past*, Copenhagen, Academic Press Copenhagen 1994, 177–197, 179.

122 Breuilly (n. 36) 113.

123 Eugen Weber, *Peasants into Frenchmen*, Stanford, Stanford University Press 1976, 110.

124 Ulrich Scheuner, Nationalstaatsprinzip und Staatenordnung, in: Theodor Schieder (ed.), *Staatsgründungen und Nationalitätsprinzip*, Wien, München, Oldenbourg, 1974, 17. See also Hobsbawm (n. 7) 14–17 on 'nation' as a geographical category.

125 Aira Kemiläinen, *Nationalism*, Jyväskylä, Kustantajat 1964, 48–49: when Adam Smith talked about the wealth of nations, he just meant 'societies' or 'states'. On the uses of *natio* in Roman antiquity mostly in the sense of *gens* ('barbarian people') as opposed to *populus* ('Roman citizens'), see Fritz Gschnitzer – Reinhart Koselleck – Bernd Schönemann – Karl Ferdinand Werner, Volk, Nation, Nationalismus, Masse, in: Otto Brunner – Werner Conze – Reinhart Koselleck (eds.), *Geschichtliche Grundbegriffe*, vol. 7, Stuttgart, Klett-Cotta 2004, 141–431, 168–170 (quoting Reinhart Koselleck ).

universities divided the world into a few nations, big universities into many (*natio* meant then rather 'people/students stemming from a certain region').[126] The tendency of some historical sources to differentiate between 'native of the land' and 'foreigner' is not enough to talk about pre-modern nations.[127] In those few cases where *natio* in the pre-modern era meant the politically relevant population (as in Poland or in Hungary of the Middle Ages), then ethnicity was irrelevant; it was used as synonymous with the 'estates'; and vice versa, ethnic Hungarian and Polish populations in serfdom did not belong to the pre-modern Hungarian or Polish nation.[128] Local aristocracies actually preferred foreign (thus ethnically different) rulers, because they did not take sides in their internal rivalries.[129] We also have to note that this political *natio* of the Middle Ages was different too from modern civic nations, as it did not contain the idea of legal homogeneity and equality, even amongst those who belonged to the *natio* (some belonged by birth to the Upper Chamber of Parliament or had by birth other *legal* privileges etc.). Modern national(istic) feelings are also similar to the ancient Greco-Roman forms of patriotism,[130] but that tradition broke down and re-emerged first in early modern times; thus it cannot prove the old age of nations either.

But on the other hand, in some cases, ethnic identity also existed in pre-modern times.[131] Nations did not emerge *ex nihilo*.[132] But before the modern era, it was not the primary element of defining *political* identity. Instead, political identity was defined in terms of personal allegiance (to a monarch) and religion. As these two faded (due to secularisation and democratic ideas), ethnicity gained strength; and combined with the factors as described in the first section of the chapter, nationalism and modern nations emerged.[133] Nations became

126 Koselleck (n. 125) 231–233. 127 Özkirimli (n. 114) 70.

128 Szűcs (n. 118) 84–85. Similarly the 'deutsche Nation' as used by Luther in the 16th century only meant the noblemen; see Koselleck (n. 125) 235. On modern nations as 'ethnically narrow[er]', but 'socially deep[er]' phenomenon than the (Polish) *natio* of the Middle Ages see Brubaker (n. 1) 84–86.

129 Ernest Gellner, *Thought and Change*, London, Weidenfeld and Nicolson 1964, 136.

130 Llobera (n. 6) 151.

131 Smith (n. 102) 16, 17; Hastings (n. 55) 1–34. According to Johan Huizinga, *Men and Ideas*, Cambridge, Cambridge University Press 1984 (orig. 1940) 107, national feelings existed at the beginning of the twelfth century in Europe. Cf. Özkirimli (n. 114) 68 on Sri Lanka, Israel, Japan (Armenia and Korea could have been added) showing signs of national identities even before that time.

132 On the importance of *longue durée* when explaining nations see Llobera (n. 6) xii, 3.

133 Reinhard Wittram, *Nationalismus und Säkularisation*, Lüneburg, Heliand Verlag 1949, 6.

to be perceived as 'active political agents, the bearers of the ultimate powers of sovereignty'.[134]

The other key issue is that before modernity, political identities were identities of small privileged groups, not of *masses*, as politics itself was the privilege of only such groups.[135] These small groups have been widened into nations by mass schooling, conscription, democratisation and mass media.

The mere fact that certain population names have continuously been used does not mean continuity in identity.[136] As Geary appositely described:[137]

> Whatever a Goth was in the third century kingdom of Cniva, the reality of a Goth in a sixteenth-century Spain was far different, in language, religion, political and social organization, even ancestry. . . . With the constant shifting of allegiances, intermarriages, transformations, and appropriations, it appears that all that remained constant were names, and these were vessels that could hold different contents at different times.

Names were renewable resources, old names could be reclaimed,[138] and to explain the past from the political (national) structure of today is no more than a presentist illusion.[139] Or to put our finding in a rather tautological way: modern nations emerged in modernity.[140]

#### 10.1.2.2 Natural (ethnic, that is, based on ancestry or culture) vs. artificial (based on elite manipulation; or civic, that is, based on law and deliberate choice)

Hugh Seton-Watson famously stated that 'a nation exists when a significant number of people in a community consider themselves to form a nation, or behave as if they formed one.'[141] But this formulation

[134] David Miller, *On Nationality*, Oxford, Clarendon Press 1995, 31.

[135] See Llobera (n. 6) 81, 120, Özkirimli (n. 114) 199–200. As a matter of fact, we just do not know much about the identity of the masses, as the written sources normally concentrate on the elites; see Walker Connor, The Timelessness of Nations, in: Montserrat Guibernau – John Hutchinson (eds.), *History and National Destiny: Ethnosymbolism and Its Critics*, Oxford, Blackwell 2004, 35–47, 40–41. But because of the structural features of pre-modern politics, our guess would be that they did not have a strong political identity based on ethnicity.

[136] John Breuilly, Dating the Nation: How Old Is an Old Nation?, in: Atsuko Ichijo – Gordana Uzelac (eds.), *When Is the Nation?*, London, Routledge 2005, 15–39, 19.

[137] Geary (n. 106) 118. [138] Özkirimli (n. 114) 64. [139] Llobera (n. 6) 21.

[140] Anthony D Smith, *The Cultural Foundations of Nations*, Oxford, Blackwell 2008, 13–14. Cf. Llobera (n. 6) 96: 'Whether we can or cannot talk about nationalism in the medieval period is . . . a definitional matter.'

[141] Hugh Seton-Watson, *Nations and States*, London, Methuen 1977, 5.

actually begs the question of when and why these people consider themselves a nation. Is it because they recognise their 'natural' status, or because they voluntarily choose to do so? (And if it is a choice, is this choice a rational and well-considered one, or is it just the result of elite manipulation?) The dichotomy 'fate vs. choice' was conceptualised by Friedrich Meinecke when he spoke of *Kulturnation* and *Staatsnation*, meaning what we call nowadays ethnic nation and civic nation.[142]

Most (but not all)[143] nationalists want to see nations (or at least their own nation) as something natural;[144] whereas anti-nationalists try to show that nations are artificial. As soon as we begin to analyse what 'natural' and 'artificial' mean, the question becomes really complicated. If 'natural' means some kind of sociobiological approach (common descent maintained by endogamy, nations as superfamilies of distant relatives),[145] then almost in every case nations can in fact be proved to be artificial, and common descent can be proved to be historically falsified (except for a very small fraction of nations, e.g., those living on islands).[146]

But if 'natural' just means a cultural community, that is, if *ethnic* means 'cultural' (sometimes including the *belief* in a common ancestry), then the statement defining nation as a natural unit is more difficult to criticise.[147] Deliberate manipulations of national identity (even if supported by the state) often fail if they do not fit the feelings of the population. In the words of Miroslav Hroch:[148]

142 Friedrich Meinecke, *Weltbürgertum und Nationalstaat*, München, Oldenbourg ²1969 [1907]. On the dichotomy civic vs. ethnic, see Rogers Brubaker, *Citizenship and Nationhood in France and Germany*, Cambridge, Mass., Harvard University Press 1992.

143 Besides the classic account of Renan, see also Yael Tamir, *Liberal Nationalism*, Princeton, Princeton University Press 1993, 87.

144 Cf. the description of the liberal Swiss constitutional lawyer Johann Caspar Bluntschli, *Die schweizerische Nationalität*, Zürich, Rascher und Cie. 1915 [1875], 11: 'The Swiss homeland constitutes such a coherent a richly structured natural whole, one that enables the evolution on its soil of a peculiar feeling of a common homeland which unites its inhabitants as sons of the same fatherland, even though they live in different valleys and speak different languages.'

145 Pierre L van den Berghe, Sociobiological Theory of Nationalism, in: Athena S Leoussi (ed.), *Encyclopaedia of Nationalism*, New Brunswick, London, Transaction 2001, 274.

146 Özkirimli (n. 114) 62.

147 Fredrik Barth, *Ethnic Groups and Boundaries*, Boston, Little, Brown and Co. 1969, on ethnic groups as cultural groups, as opposed to biological ones.

148 Miroslav Hroch, Real and Constructed: The Nature of the Nation, in: John Hall (ed.), *The State of the Nation: Ernest Gellner and the Theory of Nationalism*, Cambridge, Cambridge University Press 1998, 91–106, 99. For a concrete example, see David Svoboda, Nations under Siege: Interview with Historian Miroslav Hroch, *New Presence* 2004/4, 24–27, 26:

> The basic condition for the success of any agitation . . . is that its argument at least roughly corresponds to reality as perceived by those to whom it is directed. National agitation thereby had to (and normally did) begin with the fact that, quite independently of the will of the 'patriots', certain relations and ties had developed over centuries which united those people towards whom the agitation is directed.

Once national identities have been formed, elite manipulations work only within their frameworks (except for extreme oppression, but even then sometimes they do not work).[149] But how these original identities form and which cultural features they pick as the decisive ones, are partly due to elite (meaning not only the political elite, but often also the intelligentsia) manipulation.[150] Cultural (ethnic) features are not absolute facts and are also not simply intellectual categories: people often refer to them in order to acquire identities which legitimate their claim for certain rights.[151] Ethnicity is thus not about facts of common descent; it is about *belief* in such common descent,[152] or *belief* in the existence of other binding facts. Identity in general is less about trails from the past and more about maps for the future; it is about what we want to become and about how we want to see ourselves, and much less about what we were.[153] With the words of Stuart Hall:[154]

'Czechoslovakia is a perfect example of how a national identity cannot be invented. The failure of Czechoslovakia shows how people – which in this instance pertains to the Slovaks – won't accept the concept of a nation that doesn't conform to reality.'

149 Anthony D Smith, The Nation: Invented, Imagined, Reconstructed?, *Millennium: Journal of International Studies* 20 (1991) 353–368, 357.

150 Barth (n. 147) 14–15. According to Breuilly (n. 36) 46, 131, 157, 294 nationalism is often a form of politics used by subordinate elites attempting to seize power. On the role of intelligentsia, see Hugh Seton-Watson, Intelligentsia und Nationalismus in Osteuropa 1948–1918, *Historische Zeitschrift* 1962, 331–345; Otto Dann, Nationalismus und Sozialer Wandel in Deutschland 1806–1850, in: *id.* (ed.), *Nationalismus und sozialer Wandel*, Hamburg, Hoffmann und Campe 1978, 113; Lewis Namier, *1848: The Revolution of Intellectuals*, Oxford, Oxford University Press 1992. The moment when the intelligentsia mobilises the masses is called 'national awakening'; see Miroslav Hroch, *Die Vorkämpfer der nationalen Bewegung bei den kleinen Völkern Europas*, Prague, Univerzita Karlova 1968, 24–25.

151 Or they express fears; see Michael Ignatieff, Nationalism and Narcissism of Minor Differences, in: Beiner (n. 13) 91–102, 96: 'The differences between Serb and Croat are tiny – when seen from the outside – but from the inside they are worth dying for *because* someone will kill you for them.'

152 Emerich K Francis, *Interethnic Relations: An Essay in Sociological Theory*, New York, Elsevier 1976, 382.

153 David McCrone, *The Sociology of Nationalism*, London, New York, Routledge 1998, 34.

154 Stuart Hall, Introduction: Who Needs 'Identity'?, in: Stuart Hall – Paul du Gay (eds.), *Questions of Cultural Identity*, London, Sage, 1996, 1–17, 4.

> Though they seem to invoke an origin in a historical past with which they continue to correspond, actually identities are about using the resources of history, language and culture in the process of becoming rather than being; not 'who we are' or 'where have we come from' so much as what we might become, how we have been represented and how that bears on how we might represent ourselves.

The instrumentalisation of ethnic categorisation does not exclude, though, the fact that the persons affected deeply, genuinely and honestly believe in it, and through a spillover effect they are even ready to make extreme sacrifices:[155]

> When members of a categorically bounded network acquire access to a resource that is valuable, renewable, subject to monopoly, supportive of network activities, and enhanced by the network's modus operandi, network members regularly hoard their access to the resource, creating beliefs and practices that sustain their control.

Ethnic categorisations (the emphases on certain cultural features as a means of differentiation in order to conceptualise cultural differences as ethnic differences) are thus strategies or weapons in the struggle for scarce social resources (or sometimes weapons of revenge for oppressed groups against centuries of discrimination),[156] even if they can live their own lives for shorter periods.[157] Nationalism itself is 'a language game that takes the facts of difference and turns them into a narrative justifying political self-determination.'[158]

The American and the French nations were formed based on the revolutionary idea of choice: the concept of the nation was recognised as having been constituted by the deliberate political choice of its potential citizens because they had accepted the tenets of the revolution (enshrined in the 1789 Declaration or in the US Constitution), whereby ethnic bonds or linguistic features remained secondary.[159] The French Republic saw no difficulty in electing the Anglo-American Thomas Paine to its National Convention.[160] Political freedom and nationality fused

155 Charles Tilly, *Durable Inequality*, Berkeley, University of California Press 1998, 91.

156 Alberto Melucci, *Nomads of the Present: Social Movements and Individual Needs in Contemporary Society*, London, Hutchinson, 1989, 90.

157 Peter Worsley, *The Three Worlds: Culture and World Development*, London, Weidenfeld and Nicholson 1984, 249.

158 Ignatieff (n. 151) 96.

159 Cf. Emmanuel-Joseph Sieyès, *Political Writings*, Indianapolis, Hackett, 2003, 94–97, 99, stating in 1789 that belonging to the 'Nation' does not depend on ethnic or linguistic features.

160 Hobsbawm (n. 7) 20.

together, giving an optimistic taste of universal development to these nations (as opposed to many 'ethnic' nations).[161] Formal ethnic exclusion would anyway have excluded a large part of the French and American populations (the state was just much bigger than the central ethnic community); thus it would have contradicted the democratic idea promoted by these revolutions.[162] Informally and in practice, of course, the French and American 'civic' nations are also based on a particular inherited culture and language, but at least the idea would be ethnic-neutral (and consequently, the assimilation for those who want to join the community, is easier).[163] This ideal of deliberate choice has survived in French and US republican traditions until the present day, a remarkable moment of which is Renan's famous definition of the existence of a nation as a 'plébiscite de tous les jours' from 1882.[164]

In German territories, however, the ethnic community was much greater than Prussia or Austria. Thus by defining nation through ethnicity, especially by language ('Soweit die deutsche Zunge klingt'),[165] political influence could rather increase it. The choice between civic and ethnic nationalism thus depended on the political goals: a future Germany awaiting unification of ethnically tied states needed a different concept than the multi-ethnic already-existing state of France.[166] A nation defined by state boundaries would have contradicted the interests of both the German intelligentsia and politicians; thus more emphasis was placed on the ethnic element.[167] Definers of nations made use of

[161] Hans Rothfels, Grundsätzliches zum Problem der Nationalität, in: *id.*, *Zeitgeschichtliche Betrachtungen*, Göttingen, Vandenhoeck & Ruprecht ²1963, 89–111, 97.

[162] Weber (n. 123) on the fact that the building of an ethnic French nation as a *mass* phenomenon (through compulsory schooling, military conscription and the development of communications) had not been finished by as late as the First World War.

[163] For a criticism of the concept of civic nation as 'a mixture of self-congratulation and wishful thinking', see Bernard Yack, The Myth of the Civic Nation, in: Beiner (n. 13) 103–118, 105.

[164] Renan (n. 115) 19.

[165] 'As far as the German tongue sounds', a formula used by liberal German nationalists in 1848; see Günter Wollstein, *Das Großdeutschland der Paulskirche*, Düsseldorf, Droste 1977, 316.

[166] André Lecours, Ethnic and Civic Nationalism: Towards a New Dimension, *Space & Polity* 4 (2000) 153–165.

[167] Brendan O'Leary, Instrumentalist Theories of Nationalism, in: Leoussi (n. 145) 148 on nationalism as an instrument in the hands of competing elites in order to achieve power, wealth and prestige. Eventually, though, even nineteenth-century German nationalism contained civic elements and its depiction as a *purely* ethnic one is just a projection of the twentieth century; see Stefan Berger, Ethnic Nationalism Par Excellence? Germany 1789–1914, in: Baycroft – Hewitson (n. 76) 42–62, 58–60.

some ties, ignored others, and transformed them beyond recognition to suit their current (political) needs.[168]

As a matter of fact, even within one nation, the definitions changed according to the current interest: German politicians mostly emphasised the cultural/linguistic moments, but in the case of Eastern Prussia the Mazurian people having a dialect of Polish as a mother tongue but feeling German, 'obviously' considered themselves as German.[169] Similarly, Hungarian noblemen did not become nationalists in the first half of the nineteenth century because they suddenly felt that they had much in common with their serfs (some of whom were Hungarian ethnics, others non-Hungarians), but because it seemed a rhetorically and emotionally convincing new tool in their centuries-long quest against Habsburg centralisation. As Breuilly put it more generally: 'Nationalism has little to do with the existence of a nation. . . . Rather there were circumstances . . . when nationalism was the most appropriate form political opposition could take.'[170] Once, however, the idea spread (even amongst Hungarian non-noblemen), it also brought consequences that noblemen did not necessarily favour (especially the end of serfdom). Or to mention yet another Hungarian example: the country before the First World War presented itself as a civic nation integrating its many national minorities under the symbol of the Holy Crown (a pre-modern, religious and inherently non-ethnic institutional symbol), whereas after having lost two-thirds of its territory in the 1920 Trianon Peace Treaty and having ethnic Hungarians on the other side of its surrounding borders, it redefined the role of the Holy Crown and used it as an ethno-nationalist symbol reinforcing claims of national self-determination for neighbouring territories inhabited by ethnic Hungarians.

From the potentially many nations, only a few make it: those where conscious nation building takes place.[171] 'Why is Holland a nation, when Hannover, or the Grand Duchy of Parma, are not?' famously asked

[168] Özkirimli (n. 114) 137. Cf. Katherine Verdery, Whither 'Nation' and 'Nationalism'?, *Daedalus* 122 (1993) 37–46, 39, stating that the nation is a symbol with multiple meanings, competed over by different groups manoeuvring to capture its definition and its legitimating effects. On the 'nation' as a source of legitimacy, see John Breuilly, Approaches to Nationalism, in: Balakrishnan (n. 43) 166.

[169] Hans Rothfels, Die Nationalidee in westlicher und ostlicher Sicht, in: Hans Rothfels – Theodor Schieder (eds.), *Osteuropa und der deutsche Osten*, Köln, Rudolf Müller 1956, 7–18.

[170] Breuilly (n. 36) 397.

[171] Sinisa Malesevic, *Identity as Ideology*, Basingstoke, New York, Palgrave Macmillan, 2006.

Ernest Renan almost 150 years ago.[172] But similar questions could be asked about why Austrians are a nation and Bavarians not, and so on. Modern nations can thus be defined as a combination of ethnic and civic elements; in some nations there is a major emphasis on the first, in others on the second, but never as a full realisation of any of these Weberian ideal types.[173]

To redefine such identities later for whatever reason is extremely difficult, as shown by the failure of Habermas's theory to redefine German identity through the *Grundgesetz* ('constitutional patriotism'), which rather fits to the American identity situation and which never actually had any real influence in Germany except for some leftist intellectuals.[174] Such redefinitions could work if ethnic situations seriously change, but other identity factors (such as the constitution) do not. If Germany kept the *Grundgesetz* for another hundred years and if the proportion of ethnic Germans decreased considerably, then constitutional patriotism would be a logical identity anchor, but it would still be a question how far the population could actually internalise it in practice. Similarly, an American concept of nation in the absence of permanent immigration could in theory differ from the present non-ethnic one, but it would be questionable how far such a sharp switch (i.e., an ethnicisation) could be internalised by US citizens who have been socialised for generations to a differing one.

#### 10.1.2.3 Based on historical facts vs. based on fabricated myths

Of course, nationalism itself is partly based on counter-factual presuppositions (e.g. 'the world is and has always been divided into nations'), as political ideologies often are. This, though, is less of a problem, as political ideologies become successful not because of their truth, but because they match the social and political landscape where they occur, and thus they can effectively influence this landscape (by changing or stabilising it).[175] Nationalism as a civil religion is naturally supported by myths which try to idealise reality and in so doing bring 'moral and

[172] Renan (n. 115) 12.

[173] Brian Vick, Language and Nation, in: Baycroft – Hewitson (n. 76) 155–170, 169–170.

[174] See, e.g., Habermas (n. 96). On Habermas and his critics, see Jan-Werner Müller, *Verfassungspatriotismus*, Berlin, Suhrkamp 2010. The concept stems originally from Dolf Sternberger, Aspekte des bürgerlichen Charakters [1946] in: *id.*, *Ich wünschte ein Bürger zu sein*, Frankfurt aM, Suhrkamp 1995, 10–27.

[175] Breuilly (n. 33) xv, xx.

spiritual meaning to individuals or societies'.[176] The historical truth is secondary (though not entirely unimportant) in this function.[177]

The invention of traditions in the nineteenth century was obviously easier if there was some historical truth in them (thus statehood and a viable high culture from the Middle Ages was an advantage),[178] but truth was never a necessary component of national mythology (cf. the still official Romanian theory of Daco-Romanian continuity).[179] Even on the base of historical facts, the building of actual national narratives seems mostly quite arbitrary. Whether something in the Middle Ages was a civil war, a struggle for independence or just an unjustified revolt will be clear first through the narrative given *ex post facto* by historians. Even without actual lies or mistakes, you can distort historical truth by leaving some details out, implying others, and emphasising yet others, as Benedict Anderson put it in an amusing example:[180]

> English history textbooks offer the diverting spectacle of a great Founding Father whom every schoolchild is taught to call William the Conqueror. The same child is not informed that William spoke no English, indeed could not have done so, since the English language did not exist in his epoch; nor is he or she told 'Conqueror of what?'. For the only intelligible modern answer would have to be 'Conqueror of the English', which would turn the old Norman predator into a more successful precursor of Napoleon and Hitler.

Identity does not draw its sustenance from facts but from subjective perceptions; not from chronological or factual history but from sentiment or felt history.[181] Whatever new results come up in the research of

176 Robert N Bellah, *The Broken Covenant*, New York, Seabury 1975, 2.

177 Renan (n. 115) 11: certain events have to be forgotten, others have to be invented.

178 Gellner (n. 4) 83. Michael Keating, *Nations against the State: The New Politics of Nationalism in Quebec, Catalonia and Scotland*, London, Palgrave Macmillan [2]2001, 9 calls it 'usable past'. Even recent past and recent institutions could serve as identity-building; see John McGarry – Brendan O'Leary – Richard Simeon, Integration or Accommodation?, in: Sujit Choudhry (ed.), *Constitutional Design for Divided Societies: Integration or Accommodation?*, Oxford, Oxford University Press 2008, 41–88, 72: 'In the Soviet Union, Yugoslavia, and Czechoslovakia, pluralist or ethnofederal institutions are alleged to have created identities and divisions where none had existed previously, and to have done so needlessly.'

179 Karl Strobel, Die Frage der rumänischen Ethnogenese. Kontinuität – Diskontinuität im unteren Donauraum in Antike und Frühmittelalter, *Balkan-Archiv* 30/32 (2005–2007) 59–166; Catherine Durandin, *Histoire des Roumains*, Paris, Fayard 1995, chapter 2; Gottfried Schramm, *Ein Damm bricht. Die römische Donaugrenze und die Invasion des 5.–7. Jahrhunderts im Lichte von Namen und Wörtern*, München, Oldenbourg 1997, 275–368.

180 Anderson (n. 30) 201. 181 Connor (n. 135) 45.

historians, in popular perceptions nations are eternal. Nobody ever denied the actual multinationality or multilinguality or multiethnicity of the oldest and most unquestioned nation-states, such as Britain, France and Spain.[182] Italian linguistic unity was first achieved in the 1970s.[183] But all this is irrelevant for the public perception. A national mythology has to be coherent,[184] but (as mythology) does not have to be true. Its emotive and convincing power is stronger, however, if at least *some* historical facts support it.[185] As Schöpflin put it:[186]

> there has to be some factor, some event, some incident in the collective identity to which (national) myth makes an appeal; it is only at that point that the reinterpretation can vary very radically from a closer historical assessment. It is hard to see how the Czechs and Slovaks, say, could define their mythopoeias by inventing a strong seafaring tradition.

#### 10.1.2.4 Growing vs. fading

Anti-nationalist liberals or Marxists often predicted or even saw the end of nations and nationalism.[187] Similar predictions have already failed once, when Marxists had to realise with disappointment that during the First World War workers were fighting in the ditches and trenches, because national solidarity was so much stronger than any competing international labour solidarity. And after the war, nationalist veterans of the losing nations did not give up nationalism, but rather the opposite: many of them joined nationalistic organisations propagating an even stronger nationalistic and militaristic worldview justifying exceptional (totalitarian) measures with the exceptional new circumstances. Losing the war did not mean the failure of the national idea for them, but it meant that the hinterland was not nationalistic, disciplined and militaristic enough to support them. This, combined with a general feeling of the downfall of liberal Western societies (Spengler, etc.), made a fascist reorganisation of society seem a necessity for many. Thus nationalism retained its position not only in the winning countries (which is logical after winning a war in which nationalistic rhetoric was used), but

182 Hobsbawm (n. 7) 33. 183 Llobera (n. 6) 200. 184 Smith (n. 15) 41.

185 Anthony D Smith, Opening Statement: Nations and Their Past, *Nations and Nationalism* 1996, 358–365, 362.

186 George Schöpflin, The Functions of Myth and a Taxonomy of Myths, in: Geoffrey Hosking – George Schöpflin (eds.), *Myth and Nationhood*, London, Christopher Hurst 1997, 19–35, 26.

187 Francis Fukuyama, *The End of History and the Last Man*, New York, Free Press 1992; Thomas M Franck, *The Empowered Self: Law and Society in the Age of Individualism*, Oxford, Oxford University Press 1999, 1.

paradoxically it even grew stronger and more powerful in the losing countries.[188]

The end of nationalism seemed and seems to be no more than wishful thinking by cosmopolitan thinkers.[189] It recently gained power not only in Central and Eastern Europe after the end of socialism (which could be explained by the failure of old social and legitimacy structures),[190] but also in Scotland and in Catalonia (where such explanations based on failure do not fit). The consciously anti-nationalist language of multiculturalism also seems to be in decline in Western Europe.[191]

Every single day, national feelings are being confirmed and reconfirmed by political speeches referring to patriotism, referring to our nation as 'us', and referring to foreigners as 'them'.[192] These feelings are confirmed every day by the newspapers when domestic and foreign news are separated, or when sports news gives rise to national pride.[193] Streets and squares, awards and prizes all reflect national(ist) narratives of history.

But on the other hand, an overheated national feeling in an economically and partly also politically integrated world, especially in Europe seems less likely than ever before. It would also be difficult to imagine that young conscripts would be as enthusiastic (or willing at all) to go to war in the same way as at the beginning of the First World War. The role of national languages seems to have declined in the scientific elites (meaning the pervasive use of English).

Thus any simplistic thesis about either growing or fading nationalism would be difficult to prove, as parallel contradicting developments can be seen.

188 Nationalism can even become stronger in the people's hearts after losing a nationalist struggle, as George Bernard Shaw expressed it: 'A healthy nation is as unconscious of its nationality as a healthy man of his bones. But if you break a nation's nationality, it will think of nothing else but getting it set again.' Shaw, *John Bull's Other Island* (preface).

189 Craig Calhoun, *Nations Matter: Culture, History, and the Cosmopolitan Dream*, London, New York, Routledge 2007, 1.

190 See Hobsbawm (n. 7) 173 quoting an unpublished paper by Miroslav Hroch stating that after the fall of communism the nation was 'a substitute for factors of integration in a disintegrating society. When society fails, the nation appears as the ultimate guarantee.'

191 Steven Vertovec – Susanne Wessendorf (eds.), *The Multiculturalism Backlash: European Discourses, Policies and Practices*, London, New York, Routledge 2010.

192 Michael Billig, *Banal Nationalism*, London, Sage 1995, 16–17, 55, 99–101, 106–109.

193 Billig (n. 192) 119.

#### 10.1.2.5 Constructive vs. destructive

Nations are *not* held together by rational calculation:[194] most individuals do not desert their nations even if it is in their interest.[195] Some people were or are ready to die for their nations, which by definition cannot be a rational choice. In this sense, it is definitely 'irrational' which, however, does not say much about whether it is a useful or a harmful, a morally good or a morally bad, phenomenon.[196] Hobsbawm famously denoted nationalism as 'self-destructive' and as necessarily leading to bloodshed:[197]

> The logical implication of trying to create a continent neatly divided into coherent territorial states each inhabited by a separate ethnically and linguistically homogenous population, was the mass expulsion or extermination of minorities.

Some even assert a contradiction between constitutionalism and nationalism: Nationalism generates power, provides a basis for political mobilisation and encourages the ambition of elites, whereas constitutionalism tames power, channels it through formal institutions and often brings to an end the populist impulse of nationalist movements.[198]

Some characterise nationalistic logic primarily as *autistic* (and only as a consequence thereof as destructive): you are so much enclosed in your own circle of self-righteous victimhood that you cannot listen to anybody outside.[199] Nationalism – so the argument goes – means intolerance, and intolerant groups are unable or unwilling to perceive those they despise as individuals, because intolerant individuals are unable or unwilling to perceive themselves as such. Their own identities are too insecure to permit individualisation: they cannot see themselves as the makers of their individualities, and hence they cannot see others as the makers of theirs either.[200] Nationalists thus find anything, even violence, – so the

[194] Hobsbawm (n. 20) 269. [195] Özkirimli (n. 114) 124.

[196] For more details on the moral debates on nationalism, see Margaret Moore, *The Ethics of Nationalism*, Oxford, Oxford University Press 2001.

[197] Hobsbawm (n. 7) 133, 186, referring in this respect to Adolf Hitler as a 'logical Wilsonian nationalist'. Similarly: Sanford Levinson, Is liberal Nationalism an Oxymoron? An Essay for Judith Shklar, *Ethics* 1995/3, 626–645; Brian Barry, Nationalism, in: David Miller (ed.), *The Blackwell Encyclopaedia of Political Thought*, Oxford, Blackwell 1987, 352–354.

[198] Bill Kissane – Nick Sitter, National Identity and Constitutionalism in Europe, *Nations and Nationalism* 2010, 1–5, 2. For an opposite view stating that liberalism (the idea of freedom, especially the right to culture) and nationalism are complementary, see Tamir (n. 143).

[199] Ignatieff (n. 151) 97. [200] Ignatieff (n. 151) 99.

argument goes – as justified and natural if it is the interest of their nation (especially making the territory of the country as large as it ever was in history, even if it was just for a short period of time, even if it was many centuries ago or even if today's ethnic maps do not coincide with their claims).

Quantitative research, however, proved that nationalism *on its own* does not lead to any violence.[201] As a matter of fact, nationalism can be combined with universal ideals such as liberalism and democracy.[202] Present-day nationalisms in Scotland, Belgium, Catalonia, Wales and Quebec are peaceful and democratic, fitting in well with a liberal concept of society.[203] Moderate nationalists like Neil MacCormick rather blame different ideas coupled with nationalism:[204]

> [t]he problems associated with nationalism lie more with the state and with statism than with the nation. . . . The principle of national self-determination becomes morally and practically problematic because (or when) it is coupled to the concept of doctrine of the absolutely sovereign state.

Others even go further, and claim the nation to be a guarantor of freedom.[205] This on its own is neither useful nor harmful, but when combined with other factors, it can have different effects ranging from violence (towards other nations' members) to altruistic sacrifices (towards one's own nation).[206] Or to put it differently: for

[201] David D Laitin, *Nations, States and Violence*, Oxford, Oxford University Press 2007, 10–11, 22.

[202] Margaret Moore, Globalization, Cosmopolitanism, and Minority Nationalism, in: Michael Keating – John McGarry (eds.), *Minority Nationalism and the Changing International Order*, Oxford, Oxford University Press 2001, 44–60, 58. Cf. Anderson (n. 30) 103 on the twin stars of 'nationalism' and 'liberalism' during the revolutions of 1848: both were based on the rhetoric of 'liberation'. For an opposite view (i.e., the antagonism of liberalism and nationalism), see Elie Kedourie, *Nationalism*, Oxford, Blackwell [4]1993, 104. On the combination of nationalism and communism in Asia, however, see Stein Tønnesson, Globalising National States, *Nations and Nationalism* 2004, 179–194, 185.

[203] Kain Nielsen, Cultural Nationalism, Neither Ethnic nor Civic, in: Beiner (n. 13) 119–130, 121.

[204] Neil MacCormick, *Questioning Sovereignty*, Oxford, Oxford University Press 1999, 190.

[205] Anthony D Smith, *Nations and Nationalism in a Global Era*, Cambridge, Polity Press 1995, 155: 'the only safeguard against imperial tyranny'.

[206] Lorenz Khazaleh (interview), Benedict Anderson – I like Nationalism's Utopian Elements, 2005 www.culcom.uio.no/english/news/2005/: 'Nationalism encourages good behaviour. . . . [N]ationalism is like the human body. Sometimes it is healthy, but occasionally it might become sick, feverous and do ill things. But normal body temperature is not 41 degrees Celsius but 36.5 degrees Celsius.' For a similar view, see Carlton JH Hayes, *Essays on Nationalism*, New York, Macmillan 1926, 245–275.

nationalists morality ends at the borders of the (targeted) political community.[207]

This is not to deny that even non-violent nationalism may also be harmful to one's own nation: nationalist rhetoric is often used to divert the attention of the public from the corruption or incompetence of the elite; and even without such deliberate manipulations, it often causes the public (and politicians) not to think about socially more pressing and more important, but emotionally less straightforward questions such as pensions, social or health care reforms.[208] Once nationalist passions are awakened, it is very difficult to exert full control over them, even by those who formerly worked on heightening them; and even if they can be tamed at the end of the day, the efforts spent on taming them also use up necessarily limited time and intellectual resources of any society from the mentioned pressing social issues. Politicians, though, do like to use both nationalist and (emotionally emphatic) anti-nationalist arguments, as their use and understanding do not require either from the politicians themselves, or from the electorate, major intellectual efforts, having thus a considerable, easy-to-reach and consequently cheap mobilising capacity.

Nevertheless on the other hand, we also have to recognise that without having the feeling of large-scale solidarity awoken by nationalism, it is difficult to run a democracy and gain the agreement of the citizens for redistributive policies which do not benefit them. The mutual trust eases not only redistributive policies, but deliberative forms of democracy in general.[209]

'Our' nationalism is considered to be normal, and it is always seen as moderate and called patriotism anyway, whereas 'their' nationalism is by definition exaggerated and called chauvinism. 'Our' nationalism helps us feel as though we are members of an overarching community, it supports the 'social duties to act for the common good of that community, to help out members when they are in need etc. [It] is *de facto* the main source of such solidarity.'[210] Thus the positive effects are also plausible, *if* it does not happen in an emotionally overheated way and if it respects the

[207] Raymond Aron, *Peace and War*, Malabar, Krieger 1962, 781.

[208] On this perspective during the Hungarian constitution-making process of 2010/11, see András Jakab, Az alkotmányozás előkérdéseiről, *Iustum Aequum Salutare* 2010/4, 11–17.

[209] Miller (n. 134) 98.

[210] David Miller, In Defence of Nationality, in: Paul Gilbert – Paul Gregory (eds.), *Nations, Cultures, and Markets*, Abingdon, Avebury 1994, 22.

principles of democracy and the rule of law, and especially if it respects those who do not (want to) belong to that community.

##### 10.1.2.6 Universal vs. local

Nations are by definition limited.[211] If the whole world belonged to our nation, then the concept would not make any sense. Without 'them' there is no 'us'.[212] Therefore, nations are by definition local. But the idea is universalist: the whole world consists of nations; every person has a nationality (if not, then it is a sad handicap similar to a person lacking ears or a nose).[213] It is thus a universalist idea of everybody being a local of his own nation.

## 10.2 Five different responses: constitutional visions of the nation

As we have seen, ethnicity and nations are facts of social and political reality (even if socially constructed ones, and even if this concept is an essentially contested one); constitutional law has to respond to the challenges it potentially poses. There is no unified response in the world and not even in Europe.[214] In the following, we are going to see the different constitutional strategies to come to terms with such challenges. For this purpose, we are going to draw up constitutional visions as shown by constitutional preambles and other provisions, and also by citizenship laws (especially provisions on naturalisation) and immigration laws. Different visions deal in different ways with the fact that the actual legal political community might not be the same as the emotional ethnic (cultural) community. The borders between the visions can be blurred in real examples, but for the purposes of analysis, they still seem useful.

The aspects of analysis we are going to apply to each vision are the following: 1. supporting theories, 2. main constitutional features, 3. the relationship between constitution and nation, 4. the relationship between the 'people' (the body of electorate) and the 'nation', 5. what are the relevant political communities and what is their respective purpose?, 6. recognition of group rights,[215] 7. minority protection (through specific

[211] Anderson (n. 30) 7. [212] Billig (n. 192) 78–79. [213] Gellner (n. 4) 2, 6.

[214] See the Council of Europe Parliamentary Assembly's *Recommendation 1735 (2006) on the concept of 'nation'*, adopted on 26 January 2006 (7th Sitting) para 3.

[215] Group rights can include very different claims: 1. exemptions from laws which penalise cultural practices (no motorcycle helmet for Sikhs, no mandatory schooling for Amish), 2. assistance for those things the majority can do unassisted (multilingual ballots, funding ethnic associations), 3. self-government (Slovenian secession, Catalonian and

minority rights), 8. the legal status of ethnic belonging, 9. institutional support for ethnic identity (education etc.), 10. relative complexity of constitutional design (as to the ethnic element), 11. naturalisation rules,[216] 12. nearest real-life examples, 13. to what type of challenge does it provide an answer?, 14. advantages (pros), 15. disadvantages (contras), 16. chances of a development in the EU in this direction.

The different visions are the following: (I) one state – one ethnic nation: assimilation or exclusion (classical ethnic nationalist vision); (II) one state – one multi-ethnic nation: the nation as an emotional alliance of different ethnies (Switzerland); (III) one state – several equal ethnic nations: the state as an empty shell which does not claim an emotional connection between the ethnic communities (Belgium); (IV) one state – a dominant ethnic nation and different minority ethnic groups (most European states); (V) one state – no ethnic nation: the concept of a civic nation (United States). This division into five categories seems more subtle and more apt to constitutional consideration than the dichotomy of integration and accommodation originating from political science and is also often used in constitutional literature dealing with such issues.[217] The visions should rather be understood as ideal types developed for the purposes of analysis in the sense of Max Weber. Thus some features of the countries which I am going to name as nearest real-life examples will not fit into them entirely nice and neatly.

Based on the considerations in the first section of this chapter, by ethnies (or ethnic communities, *Nationalitäten*) I mean in the following cultural communities which are constitutionally conceptualised as political actors; whereas by a nation I mean a (cultural or legal) community which is constitutionally conceptualised as a political actor with the

Scottish autonomy), 4. restricting non-members in order to protect members' culture (restrictions on English language in Quebec, restrictions on voting and property rights of whites in US Indian territories), 5. exclusion of members if they do not follow cultural practices (Mennonite shunning), 6. enforcement of traditional laws (aboriginal land rights, traditional family law), 7. representation of minorities in government bodies (Maori voting roll for Parliament), 8. symbolic claims (disputes over the name of the polity, national holidays). See Jacob T Levy, *The Multiculturalism of Fear*, Oxford, Oxford University Press 2000, 127–156.

216 For the most thorough comparative analysis see Rainer Bauböck – Eva Ersbøll – Kees Groenendijk – Harald Waldrauch (eds.), *Acquisition and Loss of Nationality*, vols. v1–2, Amsterdam, Amsterdam University Press 2006.

217 For an overview of the literature and the terminology, see McGarry – O'Leary – Simeon (n. 178) 41–88, especially 70–71.

(constitutionally respected, but not necessarily supported) ambition of having its own state.

### *10.2.1 One state – one ethnic nation: assimilation or exclusion (vision no. I: classical ethnic nationalist vision)*

Classical ethnic nationalism meant that every citizen of the country should also be a member of the cultural community. Every nation is a state, and every state is a nation.[218] The rather liberal method of achieving this is assimilation; the tougher illiberal method is exclusion (expulsion or even genocide).[219] The borders between the two are not straightforward, though, as even liberal states use exclusion (cf. the Russian minority born in the Baltic states who today often lack local citizenship because of discriminatory citizenship laws; the official 'White Australia' immigration policy up to 1972).[220] But in general we can say that nowadays the dominant method of unifying political and cultural elements within a country is assimilation, as it is the less intrusive of the two.

In the nineteenth century, this was the vision behind most nation-states,[221] some still share certain of its features (especially in Central and Eastern Europe). Not only classical ethnic nationalist theorists had this vision (Mazzini, Fichte, Korais), but also the liberal John Stuart Mill, who stated that it is in the interest of the assimilated to become members of a larger political community.[222] And on the other hand, the cultural

[218] Johann Caspar Bluntschli, Die nationale Staatenbildung und der moderne deutsche Staat, in: *id.*, *Gesammelte kleine Schriften*, vol. 2, Nördlingen, Beck 1881, 70–113, 90: 'Jede Nation ist ein Staat. Jeder Staat ein nationales Wesen.'

[219] Similar ideas existed even before the time of nationalism: after the *reconquista*, Spanish Jews and Muslims had the choice to either convert or to leave the country. The identity of Spain was then not linguistic or ethnic, but religious (Catholic), and every subject had to either assimilate or to leave. On analogies between modern nationalism and the crown-led (and often violent) early modern exclusions of Catholics in England and Protestants in France, see Anthony W Marx, *Faith in Nation: Exclusionary Origins of Nationalism*, Oxford, Oxford University Press 2003.

[220] Graham Smith – Andrew Wilson – Annette Bohr – Edward Allworth, *Nation-Building in the Post-Soviet Borderlands*, Cambridge, Cambridge University Press 1998, 94–97; Joseph H Carens, Nationalism and the Exclusion of Immigrants: Lessons from Australian Immigration Policy, in: Mark Gibney (ed.), *Open Borders? Closed Societies*, Westport, Conn., Greenwood 1988, 41–60, 45.

[221] Ferran Requejo, Introduction, in: *id.* (ed.), *Democracy and National Pluralism*, London, Routledge 2001, 1–11, 4: 'practically speaking, all liberal democracies have acted as nationalising agencies for specific cultural particularisms'.

[222] John Stuart Mill, *Utilitarianism, Liberty and Representative Government*, Everyman, London 1910, 363–364: 'Nobody can suppose that it is not more beneficial for a

homogenisation *(ceteris paribus)* of the population makes it more likely that the political community will survive crisis situations,[223] and even in peace situations, common identity makes obedience to laws more likely.[224]

Here, the ethnic nation is *the* political community; it has its own existence which is independent of (and more important than) that of the individuals. The purpose of the political community is to promote the *interests* of the respective ethnic nation (human rights might limit the fulfilment of these interests, but it is not necessary that they do).

The vision is characterised by ethnic blindness, in the sense of considering everyone as belonging to one ethnic nation, even if the facts contradict this assertion; equality is bound to assimilation; assimilation is open to anyone (if not, then apartheid). The nation conceptually predates the constitution: the nation (as the *pouvoir constituant)* gives itself the constitution. The 'people' (the body of the electorate) and the 'nation' ought to coincide; if they do not, then measures have to be taken to achieve the coincidence of the two concepts (either through assimilation/exclusion or through territorial enlargement). Consequently, (ethnic/national) minority protection does not fit into this vision, and the constitutional architecture (as to the ethnic element) is accordingly very simple. Ethnic belonging is here a public affair, and only the ethnie of the state-nation is recognised (i.e., belonging to the state-nation means the maximum extent of rights). Naturalisation is mostly conditional either on ethnic identity or on the plausibility of promising ethnic

Breton or a Basque of French Navarre to be ... a member of the French nationality, admitted on equal terms to all the privileges of French citizenship ... than sulk on his own rocks, the half-savage relic of past times, revolving in his own little mental orbit, without participation or interest in the general movement of the world. The same remark applies to the Welshman or the Scottish highlander as members of the British nation.' For a defence of Mill's theory of nationalism, see Georgios Varouxakis, *Mill on Nationality*, London, Routledge 2002. For similar ideas in recent literature, but concentrating on the incentives of the individual, see Russell Hardin, *One for All: The Logic of Group Conflict*, Princeton, Princeton University Press 1995, 70: 'Individuals identify with such groups because it is in their interest to do so.'; Karl W Deutsch e.a., *Political Community and the North Atlantic Arena*, New York, Greenwood 1957, 85: 'political habits of loyalty to a particular unit could be more easily shifted to a political unit of another size, either larger or smaller, if this seemed to offer a more promising framework within which this attractive way of life could be developed'.

223 Charles Tilly (ed.), *The Formation of National States in Western Europe*, Princeton, Princeton University Press 1975, 632–633.

224 Peter Graf Kielmansegg, Integration und Demokratie, in: Markus Jachtenfuchs – Beate Kohler-Koch (eds.), *Europäische Integration*, Opladen, Leske & Budrich 1996, 49–84, 50.

assimilation or integration (cultural, linguistic, racial, religious or ancestry requirements).

It is a viable solution if the ethnic minorities within the country are not bound to a specific geographic area, but are dispersed (relationship towards diaspora minorities). Its greatest advantage is that it is a theoretically clear-cut, easily understandable solution. It is also easy to combine with the radical democratic approach of Rousseau.[225] The latter leaves open the question of who 'the people' are, which would be especially pressing in moments of drastic political changes (end of monarchy, end of dictatorship).

The vision is, however, currently under growing pressure for various reasons. The first and most obvious objection is that this vision is strongly counter-factual: the reality of modern states is multi-ethnic.[226] Another group of problems is rather pragmatic. Exclusion and assimilation both lead to resentment from the side of the excluded,[227] or from the ones who are supposed to be assimilated. Due to immigration, which is necessary for the demographic sustainability of developed countries (see above 9.4), these concerns grow even larger.[228] Doubts even arise concerning the utility of cultural homogenisation for the political community: cultural differences might strengthen the adaptation capabilities.[229] The other group of objections is normative (moral or legal). Human rights and moral concerns towards both groups (autochthon and immigrant minorities, the difference being whether or not ancestors lived in the territory for several generations) limit the full application of this vision.[230] Most European countries show this attitude towards immigrants (sometimes aggressively like the prohibition on Islamic veils in French state schools

225 Cf. Bernard Yack, Popular sovereignty and nationalism, *Political Theory* 25 (2001) 517–536. For the tacit presupposition of 'nation' in contemporary (liberal) political theories, see the following revealing study: Margaret Canovan, *Nationhood and Political Theory*, Cheltenham, Edward Elgar 1996, 3, 101–113.

226 H Patrick Glenn, *The Cosmopolitan State*, Oxford, Oxford University Press 2013, 86–107.

227 Anderson (n. 30) 51, 57, 60, on the exclusion of Creoles from Spanish positions leading to the formation of Creole nationalisms.

228 Hobsbawm (n. 7) 157.

229 John Hutchinson, *Nations as Zones of Conflict*, London, Sage 2005, 5.

230 The argument is an old one; Lord Acton already used it in 1862 against JS Mill; see Vincent P Pecora (ed.), *Nations and Identities. Classic Readings*, Oxford, Blackwell 2001, 153–154. Cf. also Art. 27 ICCPR and further international legal instruments in Péter Kovács, *International Law and Minority Protection*, Budapest, Akadémiai 2000 and Will Kymlicka, The Internationalization of Minority Rights, in: Choudhry (n. 217) 111–140.

as an expression of civic nationalism;[231] sometimes in a more subtle way like subsidising the language courses of immigrants in order to facilitate assimilation or through extremely cumbersome naturalisation rules aiming at exclusion),[232] whereas they are more tolerant towards autochthon minorities (see vision No. IV below).

Amongst the old (pre-2004) Member States of the EU, Greece and Ireland probably come the closest to this vision. The Greek Constitution has been adopted '[i]n the name of the Holy and Con-substantial and Indivisible Trinity'; it does not recognise any minority rights, according to Art. 1(3) 'All powers are derived from the People, exist for the benefit of the People and the *Nation'*. Most notable from this perspective is Art. 120(4) according to which '[o]bservance of the Constitution shall be committed to the patriotism of the Greeks'. The Irish Constitution opens with a concise credo of Irish nationalism, showing in a textbook-like manner all the above-mentioned features of classic nationalism:

> **Article 1**
> The Irish nation hereby affirms its inalienable, indefeasible, and sovereign right to choose its own form of Government, to determine its relations with other nations, and to develop its life, political, economic and cultural, in accordance with its own genius and traditions.
>
> **Article 2**
> It is the entitlement and birthright of every person born in the island of Ireland, which includes its islands and seas, to be part of the Irish Nation. That is also the entitlement of all persons otherwise qualified in accordance with law to be citizens of Ireland. Furthermore, the Irish nation cherishes its special affinity with people of Irish ancestry living abroad who share its cultural identity and heritage.
>
> **Article 3**
> 1. It is the firm will of the Irish Nation, in harmony and friendship, to unite all the people who share the territory of the island of Ireland, in all the diversity of their identities and traditions, recognising that a united Ireland shall be brought about only by peaceful means with the consent of a majority of the people, democratically expressed, in both jurisdictions in

231 John R Bowen, Why the French Don't Like Headscarves: Islam, the State, and Public Space, Princeton, Princeton University Press 2006.

232 See Enric Martínez Herrera – Djaouida Moualhi, Predispositions to Discriminatory Immigration Policies in Western Europe: An Exploration of Political Causes, *Portuguese Journal of Social Sciences* 2007/3, 215–233. The tolerant attitude towards immigrants was shaken in the 2000s by different Islamic terror attacks in Europe and in the United States, the killing of Dutch film director Theo van Gogh (2004) and the Mohammed cartoons affair (2005). See Jytte Klausen, *The Cartoons That Shook the World*, New Haven, Yale University Press 2009.

the island. Until then, the laws enacted by the Parliament established by this Constitution shall have the like area and extent of application as the laws enacted by the Parliament that existed immediately before the coming into operation of this Constitution.

2. Institutions with executive powers and functions that are shared between those jurisdictions may be established by their respective responsible authorities for stated purposes and may exercise powers and functions in respect of all or any part of the island.

### *10.2.2 One state – one multi-ethnic nation: the nation as an emotional alliance of different ethnies (vision no. II: Switzerland)*

A different vision is when a multi-ethnic nation is the political community behind the state. What we call a consociational regime, either refers to this vision or to the next (Belgian) one.[233] Here it is recognised that citizens belong to different ethnic groups, there are several ethnic groups and all of them form an emotional alliance (based on common history and political values).[234] The typical territorial organisation for this vision is federalism; an example is Switzerland (the Constitution uses only the expression 'linguistic community', the word 'ethnic' is not a legal term). This vision is half-way between the former and the next vision: the emotional (identity) attachment is divided here between the federal and the sub-state level (with a clear primacy for the federal level).[235] The ethnic groups can be bound to well-defined territories (cantons), as opposed to the United States belonging to the last category as described below. Another difference from the US vision is that it actively supports ethnic (linguistic, cultural) differences (see Swiss Constitution Art. 2.2, Art. 4 and Art. 70), rejecting any idea of a melting pot.

[233] E.g., Arend Lijphart, Constitutional Design for Divided Societies, *Journal of Democracy* 2004/2, 96–109. The terminology is not entirely coherent in the literature as to my categories; thus I am going to avoid the use of this term.

[234] Thomas Fleiner – Lidija R Basta Fleiner, *Allgemeine Staatslehre*, Berlin, Springer [3]2004, 636: Switzerland as a '*Willensnation*'. The term was coined by a nineteenth-century Swiss constitutional lawyer; see Carl Hilty, *Die schweizerische Nationalität*, Bern, Max Fiala 1875.

[235] Paolo Dardanelli – Nenad Stojanovic, The Acid Test: Competing Theses on Nationality-Democracy Nexus and the Case of Switzerland, *Nations and Nationalism* 2011, 357–376, 372; Andreas Wimmer, A Swiss anomaly?, *Nations and Nationalism* 2011, 718–737, 718–719; Miller (n. 134) 94–95.

Here, the multi-ethnic nation is the primary political community; the ethnic communities are only secondary political communities. The purpose of all these communities is to promote their group *interests* (human rights might limit this, but they do not necessarily do that). As long as it existed, the constitutional vision of the former Soviet Union was similar to the one in Switzerland from this point of view (cf. Art. 1 of the 1977 Soviet Constitution: 'The Union of Soviet Socialist Republics is a socialist state of the whole people, expressing the will and interests of . . . the working people of all the nations and nationalities of the country.').[236]

In this vision, both the ethnic communities and the nation pre-date the constitution; the latter happens to coincide with the 'people' (electorate). Group rights are recognised, but if someone does not belong to one of the co-ethnies, then minority protection might however be missing (cf. especially Art. 72(3) Swiss Constitution: 'The building of minarets is prohibited.'). Ethnic belonging is a public affair; belonging to a co-ethnie means the maximum extent of rights. The constitutional architecture (as to the ethnic element) is consequently more complex than that of the former vision. The naturalisation rules normally combine the ethnic and the civic elements (often favouring the co-ethnies). This vision can be recommended if the state is multi-ethnic, and the geographic concentration might otherwise lead to secession. The advantage is that it smooths conflicts; the ethnic vision is near to reality (thus it faces reality).

Such constitutional constructions can, however, suddenly become unstable, unless based on long historical traditions (dating back before the emergence of modern nations),[237] as shown in the examples of Yugoslavia and Soviet Union.[238]

[236] For more details on the 'official myth', see Walker Connor, *The National Question in Marxist-Leninist Theory and Strategy*, Princeton, Princeton University Press 1984, 45–61, especially 61. On building a common identity in spite of officially recognised ethnic diversity, see John M Hazard, Socialism and Federation, *Michigan Law Review* 1984, 1182–1194, 1185.

[237] Fleiner – Basta Fleiner (n. 234) 603.

[238] Czechoslovakia showed during its existence different features (from a unitary state in 1920 to an eventually federal state of 'two fraternal nations' in 1968); thus it would fit according to the categorisation of the present chapter into different visions (namely either no. II or no. III). Elisabeth Bakke, The principle of national self-determination in Czechoslovak constitutions 1920–1992, *Central European Political Science Review* 3 (2002) no. 10, 173–198.

### *10.2.3 One state – several equal ethnic nations: the state as an empty shell without claiming an emotional connection between the ethnic communities (vision no. III: Belgium)*

The typical example for this vision is Belgium. There are two equal (painstakingly equal) ethnic nations behind the state: the Flemish and the Walloon.[239] The Belgian Constitution divides the country into a double federal system by establishing 'communities' and 'regions', both being territorial units. The word 'nation' is reserved for the federal level; the Constitution even states in Art. 33 that 'All powers emanate from the Nation', but the actual detailed constitutional and statutory rules disperse this power almost fully to the two ethnic groups and regions, which consequently are rather to be considered as the actual political communities (i.e., nations). The Belgian federal level aims to accommodate these two ethnic groups; as a matter of fact, the whole constitutional system is built around this division (either through rotations or through painstakingly precisely defined divisions of positions). Emotional alliance is presumed to lie only with the ethnic groups; the federal level is just an empty shell enabling cooperation.[240] The federal level is neither Flemish, nor Walloon: it is Belgian (in a country where there are no ethnic Belgians). This is shown in the legal rules on official languages, on separated institutions, on rotation and division of seats in common institutions, and also on election laws. Belgium is a legal community, not a cultural one, where the *demos* is constituted only by the Constitution.[241]

As opposed to the last vision (United States, see below), ethnic differences are explicitly recognised by the Constitution, *territorially* accounted for; for the full enjoyment of rights (in Brussels) you even have to join one of the ethnic groups. As opposed to the Swiss vision (see below), the Constitution expresses a deep mistrust of ethnic groups

[239] The German community is also recognised by Belgian constitutional law (with fewer rights than the two others), but for the purposes of model-building, it will be left aside here.

[240] Cf. the famous open letter by the Walloon socialist Jules Destrée to the Belgian King Albert I: 'Sire, you reign over two peoples. In Belgium there are Walloons and Flemings; there are no Belgians as such' (*Revue de Belgique* 15 August 1912). Nowadays, second- or third-generation immigrants could be considered as 'ethnic Belgians', but despite of their high number, Belgian constitutional law did not take notice of them.

[241] Sujit Choudhry, Bridging comparative politics and comparative constitutional law, in: Choudhry (n. 178) 3–40, 6.

both towards each other and towards the federal level (through establishing many veto possibilities).

Here, the constituent nations are the primary political communities; the multi-national state-entity community is only the secondary political community. The purpose of these communities is to promote their group *interests* (human rights might, though, limit the fulfilment of these interests).

This vision is rare behind a state (besides Belgium, Bosnia and Herzegovina could be named as another European example) as it is unstable: often it is just a preliminary stop on the way towards the dissolution of the state. A typical legal consequence of this vision is the lack of language requirements for naturalisation (in Belgium), as it would be too difficult to require two languages for new citizens, and a preference for either of the two would defy the whole vision (another option, also officially considered, would be to make the choice alternative: either of the two official languages could be enough for naturalisation). Similarly indicative is the lack of any cultural knowledge requirements in Belgian citizenship laws, as the history and the current social situation of the country would have two contradicting narratives anyway.[242] Ethnic/national belonging is here a public affair; belonging to a co-nation means the maximum extent of rights.

A very similar (but internationally less well known) constitutional vision stands behind the Cypriot Constitution of 1960.[243] The most telling (and sometimes astonishing) provisions showing the lack of a common identity and reflecting the centrifugal national forces shall be quoted here:

> **Article 1**
>
> The State of Cyprus is an independent and sovereign Republic with a presidential regime, the President being Greek and the Vice-President being Turk elected by the Greek and the Turkish Communities of Cyprus respectively as hereinafter in this Constitution provided.

[242] Sara Wallace Goodman, Naturalisation Policies in Europe, *Eudo* 2010, 14, available at http://eudo-citizenship.eu/docs/7-Naturalisation%20Policies%20in%20Europe.pdf.

[243] Costas Constantinou, Aporias of Identity: Bicommunalism, Hybridity and the 'Cyprus Problem', *Cooperation and Conflict* 2007, 247–270, 248. Recently, the short-lived 2001 Constitution of Serbia and Montenegro had similar features; see András Jakab, Die Verfassungscharta von Serbien und Montenegro, *Heidelberg Journal of International Law* 2003/3, 101–115. As examples from outside of Europe, Lebanon or Iraq could be mentioned.

**Article 2**

For the purposes of this Constitution:

(1) the Greek Community comprises all citizens of the Republic who are of Greek origin and whose mother tongue is Greek or who share the Greek cultural traditions or who are members of the Greek-Orthodox Church;

(2) the Turkish Community comprises all citizens of the Republic who are of Turkish origin and whose mother tongue is Turkish or who share the Turkish cultural traditions or who are Moslems;

(3) citizens of the Republic who do not come within the provisions of paragraph (1) or (2) of this Article shall, within three months of the date of the coming into operation of this Constitution, opt to belong to either the Greek or the Turkish Community as individuals. . . .

(7) (a) a married woman shall belong to the Community to which her husband belongs. . . .

**Article 3**

1.The official languages of the Republic are Greek and Turkish. . . .

7. The two official languages shall be used on coins, currency notes and stamps. . . .

**Article 4**

1. The Republic shall have its own flag of neutral design and colour, chosen jointly by the President and the Vice-President of the Republic.

2. The authorities of the Republic . . . shall fly the flag of the Republic and they shall have the right to fly on holidays together with the flag of the Republic both the Greek and the Turkish flags at the same time.

3. The Communal authorities and institutions shall have the right to fly on holidays together with the flag of the Republic either the Greek or the Turkish flag at the same time.

4. Any citizen of the Republic . . . shall have the right to fly on their premises the flag of the Republic or the Greek or the Turkish flag without any restriction

**Article 5**

The Greek and the Turkish Communities shall have the right to celebrate respectively the Greek and the Turkish national holidays.

Co-nations predate the constitution, they do not coincide with the 'people' (the electorate) and the constitutional arrangements are meant to come to terms with this. This is achieved by recognising the group rights of co-nations and the different rules of minority protection for the co-nations, which make the constitutional architecture often very complex (except if only minimal common institutions exist). An apposite critique is given by van den Berghe:[244]

244 Pierre L van den Berghe, Multicultural Democracy: Can It Work?, *Nations and Nationalism* 2002, 433–449, 437–438.

> The high cost, fragility and limiting conditions [of this vision] have also been demonstrated. . . . [This] is a clumsy, inflexible, conservative model that benefits mostly the ruling elites. It works best, even then not very well, in relatively affluent countries with stable, highly territorialised, indigenous ethnies of approximately equal socio-economic status, and in the absence of a history of conquest between the constituent ethnies. Belgium is a typical example of the limiting conditions for [this vision], and of its high cost. Even under favourable conditions, consociation makes for wasteful duplication of governing bodies, continuous renegotiation of territorial boundaries and proportionality to reflect any demographic changes, and perennial, albeit low-intensity, conflict over trivial and often purely symbolic issues (such as the language of road signs).

As to the philosophical background, it can either be a communitarian view (stating in a metaphysically demanding way that 'human nature' requires a national belonging), or a classical ethnic nationalist vision (in which the conflicts could not be resolved and this vision is just a pragmatic *modus vivendi*), pragmatic liberalism trying to avoid ethnic violence,[245] or it can also be based on individualist tenets (on the liberal 'right to be different').[246] Therefore, it should not necessarily be considered as a backslide to nineteenth-century nationalism, but often rather as a further element of a fully fledged modern approach, in which 'people want the opportunity for cosmopolitan lifestyles, but they want this *within the context of their own national societies*'.[247]

Similar ideas for dealing with the nationalities problem have also been proposed by the Austro-Marxists who were inspired by the situation in Austria-Hungary at the end of the nineteenth and the beginning of the twentieth century.[248] Co-nationalities, according to the regulation

[245] Levy (n. 215).

[246] Will Kymlicka (interview with Ruth Rubio-Marín), Liberalism and Minority Rights, *Ratio Juris* 12 (1999) 133–152, especially 138–139. Tierney (n. 92) 49: 'The seemingly contrasting notions of personal autonomy and communal belonging are in fact complementary rather than conflicting.' For similar views, see Joseph Raz, *Ethics in the Public Domain*, Oxford, Clarendon Press 1994, 160–163. These authors seem to presuppose that nationality or ethnicity justify political autonomy more than any other (e.g., religious or sexual) identities.

[247] Tierney (n. 92) 65.

[248] See especially Ephraim J Nimni, Introduction for the English-Reading Audience, in: Otto Bauer, *The Questions of Nationalities and Social Democracy*, Minneapolis, University of Minnesota Press [1924] 2000, xvii–xviii. To many, though, Austria-Hungary looked after the emergence of nationalism like a dinosaur doomed to die out; see Theodor Schieder, *Nationale und übernationale Gestaltungskräfte in der Geschichte des europäischen Ostens,* Krefeld, Scherpe 1954, 5 with further references.

proposed by Karl Renner in 1899, were supposed to be built on the personality principle (like that of churches) rather than on the territorial principle; that is, they should be similar to associations (and not to federal Member States).[249] His co-thinker, Otto Bauer, though, recognised rightly that such a model is possible only with some territorial-federal elements:[250]

> [Renner's] system does not represent the pure application of the personality principle. This is possible in the case of the legal regulation of the religious communities, but the national cultural community has an incomparably stronger hold on the modern individual than do the ties of religion. For this reason the religious communities appear to the citizenry to be amply protected once the independent administration of their affairs without any intrusion by the public administrative apparatus has been guaranteed. Such a guarantee does not suffice for the national associations. They require autonomous administration; but it is only when public administration is also based on this self-administration that the nations are protected from the state. Only then is state power founded just as firmly on the power of the nations as the power of the nations is on the instruments of the power of the state.

The realisation of such a vision can help, as a last resort, to avoid secession if mutual trust cannot be built up (e.g. in post-civil-war situations or following a long history of unequal treatment resulting in resentment). It thus smoothes conflicts, and it is a guarantee for avoiding the oppression of the recognised ethnic communities. The problem is, however, that emotional loyalty is owed in this vision only to the ethnic nations, and not to the central state; thus the latter is politically unstable and in crisis situations may fall apart (a living example of this is Bosnia and Herzegovina, which is only held together by international force).[251] Also governing might become difficult because of ethnic veto players; and individuals belonging to non-recognised ethnic nations may be deprived of certain political rights.[252]

[249] Karl Renner, State and Nation, in: Ephraim Nimni (ed.), *National Cultural Autonomy and Its Contemporary Critics*, London, Routledge 2005 [1899], 15–47, 29. For a contemporary proponent of this idea, see Stéphane Pierré-Caps, Karl Renner et l'État multinational, *Droit et Société* 27 (1994) 421–441.

[250] Bauer (n. 248) 85.

[251] For a plea to accept the possibility of the dissolution of Bosnia and Herzegovina, see Robert L Ivie – Timothy W Waters, Discursive Democracy and the Challenge of State Building in Divided Societies: Reckoning with Symbolic Capital in Bosnia and Herzegovina, *Nationalities Papers* 2010/4. 449–468.

[252] On the latter issue in Bosnia and Herzegovina, see Constance Grewe – Michael Riegner, Internationalised Constitutionalism in Ethnically Divided Societies, *Max Planck Yearbook of UN Law* 2011, 1–64, 19 with further references.

### *10.2.4 One state – a dominant ethnic nation and different minority ethnic groups (vision no. IV: most European states)*

This vision is the modernised and liberalised version of vision no. I. It takes into account that ethnically different citizens also have to feel at home and that in the twenty-first century they have *a right to be ethnically different* (thus neither assimilation nor exclusion is possible).[253] After the Second World War, most countries realised that a homogenous nation-state could only be constructed through barbaric methods,[254] but at the same time constitutions continue to recognise the dominant nature of a certain ethnic community.[255] Tolerance and minority protection (even through collective rights) are thus the key concepts in this constitutional vision, which is characteristic of most European countries (e.g., Austria, Denmark, Poland, Italy, Germany).[256] In this way, one's own ethnic identity can be adhered to, without violating the rights of others.

This vision can have two versions as to the nature of the political community and its purpose. (1) In the first version, both the ethnic/national communities and the electorate are relevant political communities, and it is not decided constitutionally which is primary. The

[253] Or to be more precise: only entirely voluntary assimilation is possible; see on the freedom to assimilate (i.e., to change identity): Art 3.1 Framework Convention for the Protection of National Minorities, Council of Europe, ETS no. 157, Strasbourg 1.II.1995.

[254] Hobsbawm (n. 7) 134. The dissolution of multinational empires did not help either, as the nationalism of the newly born small nation-states was not better at all; see *ibid*.

[255] For a thorough analysis of the German *Grundgesetz* from this perspective, see Arnd Uhle, *Freiheitlicher Verfassungsstaat und kulturelle Identität*, Tübingen, Mohr Siebeck 2004.

[256] The expression *Nation* is not used in the German *Grundgesetz*; it is not even a legal concept in Germany (only the *Volk* is used in legal norms mostly meaning the 'people' as the population on which democracy is based, rarely meaning a culturally defined 'nation'), but the constitutional vision concerning the nation still can be identified on the basis of naturalisation rules (especially before 1999) and other provisions (cf. Art. 116 *Grundgesetz*, §§ 1–6 *Bundesvertriebenengesetz*). See Koselleck (n. 125) 420–430. It is partly due to the German 'allergy' against the use of the term *Nation* since the end of the Second World War; see Tilman Mayer, *Prinzip Nation*, Opladen, Leske & Budrich 1986, 48–49 for further references. Partly, though, already before the Second World War, the German term *Volk* traditionally substituted for the *Nation*, which was perceived as being very French and thus by definition something to avoid; see, e.g., the preambles of the 1867 and 1871 German constitutions (in connection with Art. 79 of the 1867 Constitution). Nowadays, the references to the necessary cultural 'homogeneity' of the *Volk* in German constitutional law literature and case-law (most notably in the Maastricht decision of the FCC) in relation to European integration is the expression of the classical ethnic nationalism (vision no. I) disguised in a constitutionally tamed language; see Holger Hestermeyer, *Staatsvolk and Homogeneity* (manuscript on file with the author) with further references.

purpose of these communities is here to promote their group *interests* (human rights might limit the fulfilment of these interests, but they do not necessarily do). (2) In the second version, the relevant political community is defined as the electorate, but its members also have a 'right to be ethnically different'. The purpose of the community is in this version to promote/support these human rights, including cultural rights.

Both the (minority) ethnic communities and the (majority ethnic) nation pre-date the constitution. The 'people' (the electorate) do not coincide with the 'nation', and the constitutional rules are meant to come to terms with this. They do it through the recognition of group rights and through minority protection. Even though there are plausible arguments stating that, in some cases, putting minorities into separate legal categories and granting them special rights entrenches the borderline between them and the majority, or it can contribute to their social disadvantage through the negative reactions from the rest of the society,[257] the idea of special group rights is nowadays difficult to refuse in light of the piecemeal, step-by-step success of the constitutional and political quests for them.[258] They are not just political wishes, but in most European countries also codified constitutional law; the idea of group rights is widely accepted in political discourses.[259]

Ethnic belonging is a public affair; belonging to a minority means the maximum extent of rights (as there are special minority rights and privileges).[260] The constitutional architecture (as to the ethnic element) is less complex than that of the Belgian model, but more complex than the classical ethnic nationalist or the US one. Naturalisation rules

[257] Juha Räikkä, Is a Membership-Blind Model of Justice False by Definition?, in: *id.* (ed.), *Do We Need Minority Rights? Conceptual Issues*, The Hague, Nijhoff 1996, 3–19, 7–8.

[258] Cf. Susanna Mancini, Rethinking the boundaries of democratic secession. Liberalism, Nationalism, and the Right of Minorities to Self-Determination, *International Journal of Constitutional Law* 6 (2008) 553–584, especially 562 n. 31 with a long list of special minority rights in European constitutions. This is not to deny the possible human rights issues within minorities; see especially Avigail Eisenberg – Jeff Spinner-Halev (eds.), *Minorities within Minorities*, Cambridge, Cambridge University Press 2005.

[259] Even though the doctrinal elaboration of group rights is still in its germinal phase. For an impressive doctrinal attempt, see Miodrag Jovanović, *Collective Rights: A Legal Theory*, Cambridge, Cambridge University Press 2011.

[260] I am not treating countries in which ethnic minority groups enjoy some special rights, but this amounts to a lesser level of rights protection than that accorded to the ethnic majority. Sammy Smooha, Type of Democracy and Modes of Conflict Management in Ethnically Divided Societies, *Nations and Nationalism* 2002, 423–431 calls this type 'ethnic democracy' and refers with it mainly to Israel.

combine ethnic and civic elements (normally favouring the main ethnic nation, especially concerning linguistic knowledge).

According to this vision, the state necessarily privileges one of the ethnic communities (by choosing a vernacular official language, public holidays, official symbols, sometimes official religion etc., or in cases even the name of the country reflects its dominant ethnic community);[261] thus the other ethnic communities have to be compensated through minority protection. The arguments for this version (and against the others) are the following. Most countries are in fact multi-ethnic, and the classical ethnic nationalist vision ignores this; the Belgian vision is on the one hand unstable; on the other hand you also need certain ethnic ratios which are missing in some countries; the Swiss vision seems too ethnic-neutral (even though in some countries the direction of liberalisation shows similar features, like the introduction of Swedish as an official language in Finland); and the US vision seems to be too ethnic-blind and not applicable to the ethnically bound European states. This is thus the vision recommended for most states as a main rule (the other visions are the exceptions). Its disadvantage, however, is that it can facilitate the assimilation of ethnic minorities (despite minority protection), or, even without that, the openly ethnic character of the state can alienate minorities from the public sphere.[262]

In order to be able to take part in democratic politics, even minorities have to command the majority language, as democratic politics is 'politics in the vernacular', which requires a better knowledge of the language and of the connected linguistic rituals than what is needed for business or tourism.[263] Thus linguistic requirements can be posed both towards autochthon minorities as well as towards immigrants (e.g., in naturalisation rules).

A collateral consequence of admitting the actual ethnic nature of the state is not only the protection of its own minorities within the borders, but also a protective role of kin-ethnics in other countries (often provided

[261] Cf. Art. 2 French Constitution on the official language; s. 4 Danish Constitution, Art. 62 Icelandic Constitution and Art. 2(2) Norwegian Constitution on establishing the Evangelical Lutheran Church as the official state religion (based on the fact that the majority of the population is traditionally Lutheran); Art. 103(2) Ukrainian Constitution on the requirement that the President shall have command of the Ukrainian language.

[262] Geneviève Nootens, Liberal Nationalism and the Sovereign Territorial Ideal, *Nations and Nationalism* 2006, 35–50, 39.

[263] Will Kymlicka, Citizenship in the Era of Globalization, in: Ian Shapiro – Casiano Hacker-Cordón (eds.), *Democracy's Edge*, London, New York, Cambridge University Press 1999, 112–126, 121.

for by the constitution)[264] and the facilitated naturalisation for ethnics immigrating to their kin-state.[265] This does not necessarily mean a coherent approach: for instance, Romania has asserted its kin-state role vis-à-vis Moldova while rejecting Hungary's assumption of a kin-state role vis-à-vis the Hungarian minority in Romania.[266] But Germany also fit into this extraterritorial scheme after the Second World War, where the 'reunification of the German Nation' (an expression also used by the German Federal Constitutional Court) was the duty of all state organs.[267]

Through autonomy, ethnic minorities receive by definition *collective rights* (either personal or territorial).[268] Political fights become legal ones through the constitutional conceptualisation of autonomy,[269] a concept which will always be re-defined according to the different ethnic interests.[270]

This vision can be combined with the Belgian and the Swiss vision, if there are several dominant ethnic nations (either with the claim of emotional alliance or without it) and several ethnic minorities. Towards different minorities, different constitutional visions can co-exist: immigrants normally are not treated according to vision II or III, and often not even according to vision IV.[271]

264 On issues of international and EU law of such rules, see Peter Hilpold – Christoph Perathoner, *Die Schutzfunktion des Mutterstaates im Minderheitenrecht (the 'kin-state'). Eine völkerrechtliche und europarechtliche Untersuchung unter besonderer Berücksichtigung der Schutzfunktion Österreichs gegenüber der deutsch- und ladinischsprachigen Volksgruppe in Südtirol sowie der Diskussion um das ungarische Statusgesetz*, Wien, Neuer Wissenschaftlicher Verlag 2006.

265 Szabolcs Pogonyi – Mária M Kovács – Zsolt Körtvélyesi, The Politics of External Kin-State Citizenship in East Central Europe, *Eudo* 2010, 2–3, available at http://eudo-citizenship.eu/docs/ECEcompreport.pdf; Goodman (n. 242) 13–18.

266 Brigid Fowler, Fuzzing Citizenship, Nationalising Political Space, *ESRC 'One Europe or Several' Programme Working Paper* 2002, 40/02, 26.

267 BVerfGE 36, 1, 16ff (31.7.1973). Cf. *ibid.* 'Zwei Staaten in einer Nation' ('Two States in One Nation'). For further references to the case-law of the German FCC and relevant commentary literature, see Irène Couzigou, *L'évolution du statut international de l'Allemagne depuis 1945*, Bruxelles, Bruylant 2011, 564–565.

268 Cf. Balázs Majtényi, *A nemzetállam új ruhája*, Budapest, Gondolat 2007, 17 on the fact that territorial autonomy is in fact just a different form of majority rule, which serves the nation-building of the minority (which becomes the majority within the autonomous territory); thus the new minorities within the territorial autonomy also need minority protection.

269 For autonomy, citizens need to be legally categorised (and often also registered) according to their ethnicity, which would be impossible in the last (US) vision.

270 Tierney (n. 92) ix.

271 Will Kymlicka, Misunderstanding Nationalism, in: Beiner (n. 13) 131–140, 131–132. Immigrants are expected 'to speak the common language', 'feel loyalty to national

### *10.2.5 One state – no ethnic nation: the concept of a civic nation (vision no. V: United States)*

This vision simply tries to ignore the concept of the ethnic nation, which does not mean that it would not reflect a certain type of nationalism. Like fish unaware of the water they swim in (as long as nothing muddies the otherwise transparent water, especially the spilling of their own blood by an outsider force), citizens, constitutional lawyers and even public intellectuals both in France and in the United States tend *not* to see their political and constitutional cultures as nationalist.[272] It is nationalist, though, but in a different way: it reflects 'civic' nationalism.

In the European (revolutionary French) version of this vision, state and nation are interchangeable concepts,[273] a key concept of this constitutional vocabulary is 'national sovereignty',[274] the typical territorial organisation for this vision is a unitary centralised state. A classic account of this approach stems from the time of the French Revolution:[275]

> To the Jews as a Nation, nothing; to the Jews as individuals, everything. . . . They must not form a political corps or an Order in the state; they must be citizens individually.

And if we want to read a classic American quote reflecting a similar inclusive nationalist strategy (expressing the official motto included also

institutions' and 'share a commitment to maintaining the nation as a single, self-governing community into the indefinite future'; see Will Kymlicka, New Forms of Citizenship, in: Thomas J Courchene – Donald J Savoie (eds.), *The Art of the State*, Montréal, IRPP 2003, 265–309, 273.

272 Wayne Norman, *Negotiating Nationalism: Nation-Building, Federalism, and Secession in the Multinational State*, Oxford, Oxford University Press 2006, xiii–xiv.

273 Michael Sonenscher, Introduction, in: Sieyès (n. 159) xxv on the fact that Sieyès replaced the word 'state' with 'nation'. It still has consequences on today's French terminology, even if Sieyès' ideas do not entirely correspond to the current French constitutional vision (cf. below *10.3.5 France and Poland (IV and V, but historically also I)*); see Michael Keating, *Plurinational Democracy, stateless nations in a post-sovereignty era*, Oxford, Oxford University Press 2001, 7: the French words *État* and *nation* are largely interchangeable. In the United States, 'state' means the subnational unit, that is, a Member State of the United States, and 'national' is used as synonymous with 'federal'; see Mark Tushnet, *The Constitution of the United States*, Oxford, Hart 2009, 161.

274 For more details on the concept see above 6.1.

275 'Opinion de M le Comte Stanislas de Clermont-Tonnerre, député de Paris, 23 décembre 1789', quoted in Paula Hyman, *The Jews of Modern France*, Berkeley, University of California Press 1998, 27.

in the US coat of arms 'e pluribus unum'), then we can to turn to Theodore Roosevelt:[276]

> We welcome the German or the Irishman who becomes an American. We have no use for the German or Irishman who remains such. We do not wish German-Americans and Irish-Americans who figure as such in our social and political life; we want only Americans, and, provided they are such, we do not care whether they are of native or of Irish or of German ancestry.

This (US or revolutionary French) vision equates *demos* with the nation. It is a viable option, if something *fully* substitutes the integrative force of the ethnic nation, which can typically be nowadays fundamental rights.[277] It should not be confused with classical republicanism, which is more concentrated on warlike virtues, the readiness to bring sacrifices, and it is more local, than this vision.[278]

As a real-life example today, the United States could be named; and, as an influential contemporary European theory, Habermas's theory on *Verfassungspatriotismus*.[279] In this vision, one's own country is the representative of universal ideals (something like a large-size Vatican of human rights),[280] thus, it is open by definition to anybody who is willing to accept these ideals, and the nation is created by the Constitution itself.[281] The nation does not possess any ontological status in this vision:

[276] Theodore Roosevelt, *True Americanism* [1894], in: *Works of Theodore Roosevelt*, vol. 1, New York, Collier 1897, 42. For very similar legal arguments in recent American literature, see Cynthia Ward, The Limits of 'Liberal Republicanism': Why Group-Based Remedies and Republican Citizenship Don't Mix, *Columbia Law Review* 91 (1991) 581–607.

[277] Theoretically, another option would be religion as an integrative force (e.g., Vatican), but following secularisation it is normally no longer an option. See above *10.1.1.2.1 The need to give a meaning to life after secularisation*. For the conceptualisation of American nationalism as a secularised religion, see Robert N Bellah, Civil Religion in America, *Daedalus* 1967, 1–21.

[278] Müller (n. 174) 10.

[279] Jürgen Habermas, *Between Facts and Norms*, Cambridge, Mass., MIT 1996, 491–515. A former example could be Sieyès (n. 159) and the French tradition of civic nation. Timothy Baycroft, Ethnicity and Revolutionary Tradition in France, in: Baycroft – Hewitson (n. 76) 28–41, 34–38 with further references shows convincingly, however, that in real life this French tradition mostly functioned just like any other ethnic nationalism; only the rhetoric was different.

[280] Even though in practice these ideals might be overruled in the interest of the concrete community, see Beau Breslin, *The Communitarian Constitution*, Baltimore, Johns Hopkins University Press 2004, ix–xii.

[281] Samuel H Beer, *To Make a Nation: The Rediscovery of American Federalism*, Cambridge, Mass., Harvard University Press 1994, 4; Hans Vorländer, Verfassungsverehrung in

it is just the nearest empirical approximation of humanity as a whole, the universal values of which (especially human rights) a smaller-size political community (the 'civic nation') is supposed to represent.[282]

According to its proponents, it expresses a 'post-nationalistic culture', in which ethnic belonging becomes part of the private sphere (instead of the public sphere) just as this has already happened with religion some time ago.[283] In real life, ethnic belonging can, of course, be discussed in politics (and voters can know and even be influenced in their choice at elections by such factors), but no *legal* consequence can be drawn from it. Naturalisation is conditional here on explicitly accepting the non-ethnic (civic) values of the constitution; living on the territory (or being born on the territory); working or contributing to GDP otherwise.

There are two usual ways to criticise this vision: a pragmatic and a normative.[284] On the one hand, this vision can seem to be just a 'pale academic thought',[285] or a 'nice idea that does not work because people do not feel like this'.[286] On the other hand, the seemingly non-ethnic and neutral character can be doubted.[287] The latter means that a cultural and value community is unavoidable, independently from one's ancestry:

Amerika, *Amerikastudien* 34 (1989) 69–82. The conception of Sieyès is different, as he views constitution-making as a voluntary act of the 'nation', which itself is constituted by the will to unite; see Stéphane Pierré-Caps, Le constitutionnalisme et la nation, in: Jean-Claude Colliard – Yves Jegouzo (eds.), *Le nouveau constitutionnalisme. Mélanges en l'honneur de Gérard Conac*, Paris, Economica 2001, 67–86, 70–74.

282 On the French revolutionary approach, see Louis Dumont, *Essais sur l'individualisme*, Paris, Seuil 1983, 129.

283 Müller (n. 174) 16; Majtényi (n. 268) 27.

284 Zoran Oklopcic, The Territorial Challenge: From Constitutional Patriotism to Unencumbered Agonism in Bosnia and Herzegovina, *German Law Journal* 13 (2012) 23–50, 24.

285 By Ernst-Wolfgang Böckenförde ('blasser Seminargedanke') quoted by Müller (n. 174) 14. For a similar view, see Miller (n. 134) 163.

286 By Joachim Fest ('Eine schöne Idee – aber sie funktioniert nicht, weil die Menschen nicht so fühlen.') quoted by Müller (n. 174) 14. For a similar view, see Smith (n. 119) 195: 'To date, we cannot discern a serious rival [including any idea of human rights – AJ] to the nation for the affections and loyalties of most human beings.'

287 Will Kymlicka, The New Debate over Minority Rights, in: Requejo (n. 221) 15–39, especially 21: 'the idea that liberal-democratic states (or "civic nations") are ethnoculturally neutral is manifestly false, both historically and conceptually'. Ferran Requejo, Political Liberalism in Multinational States, in: Alain-G. Gagnon – James Tully (eds.), *Multinational Democracies*, Cambridge, Cambridge University Press 2001, 110–132, 110–111: 'Despite the usual liberal defence of a laissez faire approach to cultural matters, experience indicates that the state has not been, nor can it be, culturally neutral.' Tierney (n. 92) 55: 'The purported neutrality of liberalism in many ways masks the unification of the state around a set of political values and the prioritisation of a set of specific cultural practices or societal policies.' Will Kymlicka, The New Debate on Minority Rights, in:

in this sense, Barack Obama and John Fitzgerald Kennedy were equally white Protestant Americans. Critics also claim that shared political values do not mean that different people want to share the same state.[288] Some countries with a relatively new constitution, but with a political community dating back for centuries are just not plausible candidates for such a vision. By remaining blind to ethnic belongings (which do exist, independently from the fact of whether or not we want to see them), the state wastes a valuable pool of loyalty of its citizens, instead of using it. Even for the proper functioning of liberal democracies, certain *cultural preconditions* are needed, which do have certain ethnic connections.[289] As a matter of fact, most constitutions contain references to the dominant ethnic community anyway (flags, anthems, official languages,[290] holidays), thus 'constitutional' patriotism also necessarily means ethnic loyalty too.[291] The difference to 'ethnic nations' can rather be seen in *an inclusive rhetoric*, which welcomes the voluntary efforts of assimilation: in an 'ethnic nation' the different ethnicity of people's ancestors is something which is normally not a particular reason for pride (even though factually very common), or sometimes it is even kept as a shameful secret (if it is not too obvious for anthropological reasons), whereas in a 'civic nation' it can be openly professed. The founding myths of civic nations are rather ideological, whereas the founding myths of ethnic nations are genealogical.[292] Voluntary assimilation is consequently often easier in a civic nation. But the nature of nations is – in

Ronald Beiner – Wayne Norman (eds.), *Canadian Political Philosophy: Contemporary Reflections*, Oxford, Oxford University Press 2001, 159–176, 170.

288 Neil MacCormick, Nations and Nationalism, in: Beiner (n. 13) 189–204, especially 202.

289 Cf. the understandable upheaval about the light-headed remark by the Archbishop of Canterbury on the possible introduction of Sharia in the UK, or the picture shown by Timothy Garton Ash on 'Eurabia'. On the cultural preconditions of liberal democracies in general, see Ernst-Wolfgang Böckenförde, *Staat, Verfassung, Demokratie*, Frankfurt aM, Suhrkamp 1991, 345–346, 351–352. For an opposing view see Arash Abizadeh, Does Democracy Presuppose a Cultural Nation?, *American Political Science Review* 96 (2002) 495–509.

290 A good example for the symbolic character of constitutional provisions on official languages is Art. 8 Irish Constitution according to which the '(1) The Irish language as the national language is the first official language. (2) The English language is recognised as a second official language.' As a matter of fact, most Irish cannot use Irish as their mother tongue (they either learn it in school, or sometimes not even that), and the drafters of the Constitution knew this fact very well.

291 Peter Häberle, *Nationalflaggen. Bürgerdemokratische Identitätselemente und internationale Erkennungssymbole*, Berlin, Duncker & Humblot 2008, 215.

292 Cf. Anthony D Smith, *Myths and Memories of the Nation*, Oxford, New York, Oxford University Press 1999, 70–82 on the different mixtures of myths.

both types – partly culturally defined, and thus ethnic; the matters which are different are merely the emphasis in rhetoric (civic inclusive vs. ethnic, emphasising common ancestry), the weight of ethnic elements in the constitutional arrangements and the relative importance of constitutional issues in ethnic/cultural identity.

A further criticism is that proponents of constitutional patriotism are unable to give a plausible answer within this conceptual framework to the question of what ethnic minorities should do if their oppression is codified in the constitution. Or in general, what happens if ideas contradicting the (or their) approach of constitutionalism appear in the text of the constitution? If they can resist in such cases, then constitutional patriotism cannot be differentiated from universalist cosmopolitanism, or to be more precise it will just be the same in disguise or a theoretically unnecessary outgrowth on any (otherwise possibly coherent) cosmopolitan theory. Thus this theory works only if the constitution is in conformity with the ideals of constitutionalism.

This vision can be recommended mainly if the birth of the nation is bound to a constitution and it has been continuous ever since; otherwise the traditional national loyalty ties will remain outside of its reach (meaning both that these loyalty resources will be wasted, and that by ignoring these loyalties, ethnic conflicts are more likely to arise). The fact that a nation is an immigrant nation is also an argument for choosing this vision, as this makes integration and assimilation easier and faster.[293] Its main advantage is its theoretical elegance and the offered protection of fundamental rights. The disadvantages have already been mentioned above.

When we talk about multiculturalism, we either refer to this difference-blind model or to the difference-supportive Belgian one.[294] As a matter of fact, the classical difference-blind US model does no longer even fully apply in the United States either; ethnic (racial) quotas and affirmative actions deviate from the model at certain points (towards vision no. IV). Such deviations are often justified with reference to balancing the former oppression of ethnic minorities (notably slavery

[293] Donald Ipperciel, Constitutional Democracy and Civic Nationalism, *Nations and Nationalism* 2007, 397.

[294] As the word 'multiculturalism' cuts thus across the different visions I am establishing, I try to avoid its use in this book. For a notable legal expression of this multifaceted concept, see the Canadian Multiculturalism Act of 1988 containing measures ranging from non-discrimination through recognition to the promotion of cultural diversity.

and long-lasting discrimination even after the end of slavery in the case of the United States).[295]

A final remark, or rather disclaimer is necessary on indigenous peoples in the United States: for the sake of model- (or vision-)building they have not been considered.[296] Already in the original 1787 version of the US Constitution, Indian tribes were conceptualised as entities outside states, federal government or foreign states. Nowadays, they are officially referred to as 'domestic dependent nations', possessing their own constitutions and having original (i.e., non-delegated, but by Congress revocable) authority for self-government (sometimes even called 'tribal sovereignty').[297]

### 10.2.6 *Schedule on the constitutional visions of the nation*

It might be useful at this point to present an overview of the five different responses in a schedule, in order enhance contrast and transparency (Table 10.1).

## 10.3 Debated or borderline cases

A few European countries cannot be classified according to the above models.[298] On the one hand, it is a usual phenomenon in social sciences that categorisations do not entirely fit, on the other hand, the categorisation itself is often a political action that is highly debated (cf. the motto of the present chapter).

[295] Even though not all blacks were slaves, not all slaves were black, most whites were never slaveowners, and not all slaveowners were whites. Affirmative action is also inefficient in integrating society as it rather reconfirms and entrenches social cleavages; see van den Berghe (n. 244) 440, 444.

[296] For a notable argument from the hero of modern constitutionalism, CJ Marshall, see *Johnson and Graham's Lessee v. William McIntosh*, U.S. 1823, 523 stating that native Americans were not members of civilised nations, but rather wild savages. See Blake A Watson, John Marshall and Indian Land Rights, *Seton Hall Law Review* 2006, 481–549.

[297] *United States v. Mazurie*, 419 U.S. 544 (1975); *Santa Clara Pueblo v. Martinez*, 436 U.S. 49, 56, 63 (1978). For more details, see Philip P Frickey, The Status and Rights of Indigenous Peoples in the United States, *Heidelberg Journal of International Law* 1999, 383–404.

[298] There are, of course, also strong classification problems outside of Europe; see especially the case of Canada. Sujit Choudhry, Does the World Need More Canada?, in: Choudhry (n. 178) 141–172 with further references and Norman (n. 272) 131–138.

Table 10.1. *Constitutional visions of the nation*

| | I. one state – one ethnic nation | II. one state – one multi-ethnic nation | III. one state – several equal ethnic nations | IV. one state – a dominant ethnic nation and different minority ethnic groups | V. one state – no ethnic nation |
|---|---|---|---|---|---|
| 1. supporting theories | classical ethnic nationalism, Mazzini, Fichte, Korais | theories of Swiss federalism; Leninism | communitarian theories, certain types of liberal nationalism, Austro-Marxism (Otto Bauer, Karl Renner) | certain types of liberal nationalism (especially Will Kymlicka), communitarian theories | French theories of civic citizenship (Renan, Sieyès), *The Federalist Papers*, *Verfassungspatriotismus* (Habermas) |
| 2. main constitutional features | ethnic blindness in the sense of considering everyone as belonging to one ethnic nation, even if facts contradict; equality bound to assimilation; assimilation is open to anyone (if not, then apartheid) | the state is not ethnic blind: it recognises the different ethnic communities; the nation is an emotional alliance of the different ethnies | equally supporting identity of all (recognised) nations, none of them is dominant; rotation systems or painstakingly precise division of competences amongst the ethnic co-nations | constitutional symbols (holidays) bound to one particular ethnie; institutionalised minority protection (sometimes with extraterritorial features) | ethnic blindness (except if former ethnic repression has to be compensated) |

| | | | | | |
|---|---|---|---|---|---|
| 3. the relationship between constitution and nation | the nation predates the constitution | both the ethnic communities and the nation pre-date the constitution | co-nations predate the constitution | both the ethnic communities and the nation pre-date the constitution | the constitution constitutes the nation (liberal procedural approach), or a pre-constitutional *voluntary* act does it (Sieyès) |
| 4. the relationship between the 'people' (the body of the electorate) and the 'nation' | they ought to coincide (through assimilation, exclusion or expansion) | they happen to coincide for historical reasons | they do not coincide, and we have to come to terms with this | they do not coincide, and we have to come to terms with this | they necessarily (conceptually) coincide |
| 5. what are the relevant political communities and what is their respective purpose? | the ethnic nation is *the* political community; it has its own existence, which is independent (and more important) than that of the individuals; the purpose of the political community is to promote the *interests* of the | the multi-ethnic nation is the primary political community; the ethnic communities are secondary political communities; the purpose of these communities is to promote their group *interests* | the constituent nations are the primary political communities; the multi-national state entity community is the secondary political community; the purpose of these communities is to promote their group *interests* | 1. both the ethnic/national communities and the electorate are relevant political communities; it is not decided constitutionally which is primary; the purpose of these communities is to promote their group *interests* | the political community is the civic nation (i.e., the electorate), which is just the representative of universal *ideals* (especially human rights); the main purpose of the political community is to promote these ideals in the world |

Table 10.1. (*cont.*)

| | I. one state – one ethnic nation | II. one state – one multi-ethnic nation | III. one state – several equal ethnic nations | IV. one state – a dominant ethnic nation and different minority ethnic groups | V. one state – no ethnic nation |
|---|---|---|---|---|---|
| | respective ethnic nation (human rights might limit it) | (human rights might limit it) | (human rights might limit it) | (human rights might limit it)<br>or<br>2. the relevant political community is defined as the electorate, but their members also have a 'right to be ethnically different' (the purpose of the community is to promote/support these human rights, including cultural rights) | |

| | | | | | |
|---|---|---|---|---|---|
| 6. recognition of group rights | only individual rights (but minorities might even openly be discriminated against) | recognition of the group rights of co-ethnies | recognition of the group rights of co-nations | recognition of the group rights of ethnic minorities | fundamental rights perceived only as individual rights |
| 7. minority protection (through specific minority rights) | no | possibly (if not in the rank of a co-ethnie, then sometimes missing, though) | possibly (if not in the rank of a co-nation, then sometimes missing, though) | yes | no, only as anti-discrimination |
| 8. the legal status of ethnic belonging | public affair, and only the ethnie of the state-nation is recognised (belonging to the state-nation means the maximum of rights) | public affair, belonging to a co-ethnie means the maximum of rights | public affair, belonging to a co-nation means the maximum of rights | public affair, belonging to a recognised minority means the maximum of rights (as there are special minority rights and privileges) | private matter |
| 9. institutional support for ethnic identity (education etc.) | only the official ethnic identity is supported; the minority ethnic identity is oppressed | the ethnic identity of the co-ethnies is supported, otherwise accidental (mostly missing) | the ethnic identity of the co-nations is supported, otherwise accidental (mostly missing) | both the official ethnic identity and the ethnic identity of the recognised minorities are supported | ethnic identities are neither supported nor oppressed by the state |

Table 10.1. (*cont.*)

| | I. one state – one ethnic nation | II. one state – one multi-ethnic nation | III. one state – several equal ethnic nations | IV. one state – a dominant ethnic nation and different minority ethnic groups | V. one state – no ethnic nation |
|---|---|---|---|---|---|
| 10. relative complexity of constitutional design (as to the ethnic element) | simple | moderately complex | either very complex, or only minimal common institutions | moderately complex | simple |
| 11. naturalisation rules | conditional on the plausibility of promising ethnic assimilation or integration (cultural, linguistic, racial, religious or ancestry requirements) | combination of ethnic and civic elements (often favouring the co-ethnies) | combination of ethnic and civic elements (often favouring the co-nations) | combination of ethnic and civic elements (normally favouring the main nation, especially concerning linguistic knowledge) | conditional on explicitly accepting the non-ethnic (civic) values of the constitution; living on the territory; working or contributing to GDP otherwise |
| 12. nearest real-life examples | towards immigrants most European states (but normally not towards autochthon minorities); also | Switzerland (formerly Soviet-Union, Yugoslavia) | Belgium, Cyprus, Bosnia and Herzegovina (formerly part of Austria-Hungary) | most European states (in relation to their autochthon minorities) | United States (except for Indian tribes) |

| | | | | | |
|---|---|---|---|---|---|
| | towards autochthon minorities in some Central and Eastern European states and in Greece | | | | |
| 13. to what type of challenge does it provide an answer? | integration of ethnic minorities within the country if they are not bound to a specific geographic area, but they are dispersed (like most immigrants); if there are major groups of kin-ethnics abroad (justifying even military expansion) | if the state is multi-ethnic, and the geographic concentration would otherwise threaten with secession | as a last resort to avoid secession, if mutual trust cannot be built up (after-civil-war situations or after a long history of unequal treatment resulting in resentment) | in most cases as a main rule nowadays (the other visions are the exceptions) in order to integrate and accommodate autochthon minorities; especially if there are also major groups of kin-ethnics abroad (justifying kin-protection laws, and thus the expansion of emotional-political influence) | how to integrate a multi-ethnic society under the conditions of liberal constitutionalism, if minorities are not concentrated in any specific area; it can also be applied in situations in which there is no clear majority ethnie |

Table 10.1. (*cont.*)

| | I. one state – one ethnic nation | II. one state – one multi-ethnic nation | III. one state – several equal ethnic nations | IV. one state – a dominant ethnic nation and different minority ethnic groups | V. one state – no ethnic nation |
|---|---|---|---|---|---|
| 14. advantages (pros) | theoretically clear-cut, easily understandable solution | smooths conflicts (avoids oppression and secession); the ethnic vision is near to reality (thus it faces the reality of ethnic diversity); it protects the cultural rights of the recognised co-ethnies | smooths conflicts (avoids oppression and secession); the ethnic vision is near to reality (thus it faces the reality of ethnic diversity); it protects the cultural rights of the recognised co-nations | smooths conflicts (avoids oppression and secession); the ethnic vision is near to reality (thus it faces the reality of ethnic diversity); it protects the cultural rights of the recognised minorities; the openly ethnic character of the state can alienate even the recognised minorities from the public sphere | theoretical elegance; protection of fundamental rights |

|  |  |  |  |  |  |
| --- | --- | --- | --- | --- | --- |
| 15. disadvantages (contras) | in fact there are almost always national minorities; the lack of recognition can lead to animosity of ethnic minorities towards the state | it is difficult to build up such a state in a way that would be stable, unless oppression helps it or historical tradition supports it; individuals belonging to non-recognised ethnies might be deprived of certain rights | emotional loyalty owed the ethnic nations, and not to the central state, thus unstable; governing might become difficult because of veto players; individuals belonging to non-recognised ethnic nations might be deprived of certain rights | it can facilitate the assimilation of ethnic minorities (in spite of minority protection); individuals belonging to non-recognised ethnic minorities might be deprived of certain rights; it cannot by applied if there is no majority ethnic nation | it is actually ethnic in nature, at least understood as a thin ethnicity (its ethnic-neutrality is thus a lie); under the circumstances of human rights protection it can be efficiently applied for integration only in geographically evenly divided immigrant multi-ethnic societies (otherwise the competing emotional force of ethnic belonging will be in conflict and will likely prevail); it is not a plausible option where the nation is older than its Constitution |
| 16. chances of a development in the EU in this direction | demographically impossible in the foreseeable future (and also | common European identity as an alliance of different ethnic | this is the current situation (the EU as an alliance of different nations, | demographically impossible in the foreseeable future | European constitutional patriotism (common identity formed by European constitutional |

Table 10.1. (*cont.*)

| | I. one state – one ethnic nation | II. one state – one multi-ethnic nation | III. one state – several equal ethnic nations | IV. one state – a dominant ethnic nation and different minority ethnic groups | V. one state – no ethnic nation |
|---|---|---|---|---|---|
| | undesirable for reasons of minority protection) | communities: unlikely to be realised, even though a slight shift towards this direction is possible and advisable | sometimes coinciding with the Member States, sometimes not) | | values): the rhetoric is already there, but it is unlikely to be fully realised, even though a slight shift towards this direction is possible and advisable |

### *10.3.1 Spain (mainly IV with elements of II and III, but historically also I)*

The Spanish case shows basically all possible visions. The text of the Spanish Constitution seems to leave the question of ethnic vision open (being deliberately ambiguous):[299]

> [Preamble] The Spanish Nation ... in the exercise of its sovereignty proclaims its will to: ... protect all Spaniards and peoples of Spain in the exercise of human rights, their cultures and traditions, languages, and institutions; ... Therefore, the Parliament approves, and the Spanish people ratify the following Constitution:
>
> Article 2. The Constitution is based on the indissoluble unity of the Spanish nation, the common and indivisible homeland of all Spaniards, and recognises and guarantees the right to autonomy of the nationalities and regions which make it up and the solidarity among all of them.

The beginning of the Preamble shows signs of the majority European vision, in which the subject of the constitution-making (the *pouvoir constituant*) lies with the Spanish nation to which other nationalities (as collectives: 'peoples of Spain') also adhere. But the final sentence of the Preamble hints at a civic approach: Spanish citizens ('the Spanish people') were to approve the text by referendum. Article 2 is similarly contradictory (or to be more 'precise': ambiguous): on the one hand it mentions the 'indissoluble unity of Spain'; on the other hand it 'recognises' the autonomy of nationalities and regions. The word 'recognise' ('reconoce') means that it already exists before the Constitution; thus nationalities are collective subjects of the Constitution (thereby contradicting the last sentence of the Preamble). All this is not a result of unskilled drafting, but rather of complex compromises in the careful wording from 1978, which had to be accepted both by partisans of a unitary state and of a federal solution.[300]

[299] On leaving constitutional questions deliberately open, see Michael Foley, *The Silence of Constitutions: Gaps, Abeyances and Political Temperament in the Maintenance of Government*, London, New York, Routledge 1989, 9–10 ('constitutional abeyance'); Carl Schmitt, *Verfassungslehre*, München, Leipzig, Duncker & Humblot 1928, 31–32 ('dilatorischer Formelkompromiss').

[300] Enric Martínez-Herrera – Thomas Jeffrey Miley, The Constitution and the Politics of National Identity in Spain, *Nations and Nationalism* 2010, 6–30, 8–10. Title VIII of the Constitution contains similarly ambiguous provisions.

Some right-wing Spanish politicians, however, still adhere to the classical ethnic nationalist vision (even if not codified),[301] whereas Catalan nationalists would opt for the Belgian plurinational model,[302] and the Spanish Constitutional Court seems to favour the Swiss model in which the Spanish nation consists of Basques, Catalans, Castilians and others. Lately, the Spanish Constitutional Court had to decide whether the new Autonomy Statute of Catalonia, which states in its Preamble the existence of a 'Catalan nation', is in conformity with Art. 2 of the Spanish Constitution, which refers only to the 'Spanish nation'.[303] It confirmed that there is only one nation in Spain (and it is the bearer of sovereignty), which, however, consists of different ethnies ('nationalities').[304] The reality is, however, that the state level is not ethnic-neutral, but Castilian both in linguistic and symbolic terms. Thus despite some elements of vision no. II, Spain dominantly belongs to constitutional vision no. IV.

The only missing model is the classical US one, the difference-blind one, as taking into account the heart of the topic, it would not be plausible to ignore the issue. The dilemma is well-described by Resina:[305]

301 Josep M Vallès, Catalonia 1979–2001: A Self-Government Experience in the Globalisation Age, *Scottish Affairs* 2001, Special Issue: Stateless Nations in the 21st Century: Scotland, Catalonia, Quebec, 156–161, 160.

302 Kenneth McRoberts, *Catalonia: Nation Building without a State*, Toronto, University of Toronto Press 2001, 79. Representing the Catalan nationalist opinion: Ferran Requejo, *Multinational Federalism and Value Pluralism: The Spanish Case*, London, Routledge 2005, 93–102. This even means possible future independence; see Albert Balcells, *Catalan Nationalism: Past and Present*, London, Macmillan 1995, 193 on the resolution of 12 December 1989 of the Catalan Parliament stating that 'observance of the Constitution does not imply the Catalan people's renunciation of self-determination'.

303 STC 31/2010. For positive reviews of the judgment, see Oscar Alzaga Villaamil, La Nación como Poder Constituyente en los preambulos de las *leges superiores*. El Estatut de 2006 y la STC 31/2010, *Teoría y Realidad Constitucional* n. 27 (2011/1) 131–176; Javier Tajadura Tejada, El pronunciamiento del Tribunal Constitucional sobre el preámbulo del Estatuto de Autonomía de Cataluña: nación, realidad nacional y derechos históricos, *ibid.* 423–447. For critical commentaries concentrating on the concept of nation (pleading mostly for a Belgian vision), see Alberto López Basaguren, Nación y lengua en el Estatuto de Autonomía de Cataluña. Consideraciones sobre la STC 31/2010, *Revista General de Derecho Constitucional* 13 (2011) 1–26; Joaquim Ferret Jacas, Nació, símbols i drets històrics, *Revista d'Estudis Autonòmics i Federals* 12 (2011) 44–60.

304 The legal definition of 'nationalities' is, however, far from clear; see Xavier Arbós Marín – Fernando Domínguez García, Cataluña como nación y los símbolos nacionales, *Revista catalana de dret públic* [Especial Sentencia 31/2010] 2010, 101–114.

305 Joan Ramon Resina, Post-National Spain? Post-Spanish Spain? *Nations and Nationalism* 8 (2002) 377–396, 394.

Rather than in cut-throat competition among the various national constituencies, opportunities for a stronger democracy exist in the admission that national realities cannot be suppressed or stemmed without generating violence and pain, and that, in order to take the full measure of their potential, these historical collectivities require guarantees that only states can offer. Hence the state needs to adapt to the shape of its nations rather than the other way around. If that proves impossible, then nations will naturally try to grow a state inside out from their emancipation, like a new tail from a lizard's wriggling body.

### *10.3.2 Slovakia, Croatia and Romania (I and IV)*

The Preamble of the Constitution of Slovakia expresses the 'ethnonational ideological foundation of the Slovak Republic':[306]

> *We, the Slovak nation,* mindful of the political and cultural heritage of our forebears, and of the centuries of experience from the struggle for national existence and our own statehood, in the sense of the spiritual heritage of Cyril and Methodius and the historical legacy of the Great Moravian Empire, proceeding from the natural right of nations to self-determination, *together with members of national minorities and ethnic groups living on the territory of the Slovak Republic,* in the interest of lasting peaceful cooperation with other democratic states, seeking the application of the democratic form of government and the guarantees of a free life and the development of spiritual culture and economic prosperity, that is, *we, citizens of the Slovak Republic,* adopt through our representatives the following Constitution: [emphasis added]

Seemingly, the Constitution also recognises ethnic minorities, but it is worth paying attention to the exact wording: ethnic minorities as such are not recognised, only their 'members' as individuals can join the Slovak nation.[307] According to Smooha, this means that '[a]ccording to the preamble of the constitution, both ethnic Slovaks and other citizens ought to develop Slovakia as an ethnic nation-state for the benefit of ethnic Slovaks'.[308] Similarly the oath of the President of the Republic according to Art. 104 para 1 of the Constitution: 'I swear on my honour and conscience allegiance to the Slovak Republic. I will attend to the welfare of the Slovak people, and members of national minorities and ethnic groups living in the

306 Pieter van Duin, Is National Mobilization in Slovakia on the Decline?, *Slovak Foreign Policy Affairs* 2001/Spring 121–128, 123.

307 Moshe Berent, The Ethnic Democracy Debate, *Nations and Nationalism* 2010, 657–674, 667.

308 Sammy Smooha, The Model of Ethnic Democracy, *ECMI (European Center for Minority Issues, Flensburg) Working Papers* No. 13 (2001), 66.

Slovak Republic. I will perform my duties in the interest of citizens, uphold and defend the Constitution and other laws.'

Thus, under the facade of vision No. IV (one state – a dominant ethnic nation and different minority ethnic groups), we actually find a real-life example of model No. I (one state – one ethnic nation), at least on the basis of the Preamble of the Constitution. Other provisions of the Constitution, however, do ensure certain group rights to ethnic and national minorities (especially language rights), with a notable limit as mentioned in Art. 34(3) of the Constitution, stating that '[t]he exercise of the rights of citizens belonging to national minorities and ethnic groups guaranteed by this Constitution must not lead to jeopardising the sovereignty and territorial integrity of the Slovak Republic and to discrimination against its other inhabitants.'

A similar solution is chosen by the preamble of the Croatian Constitution ('the Republic of Croatia is established as the national state of the Croatian nation and the state of the members of autochthonous national minorities').[309] Even then, other parts of the Constitution (especially Art. 15) seem more open to group rights than the Preamble of the Constitution.

Article 1(1) of the Romanian Constitution states that 'Romania is a sovereign, independent, unitary, and indivisible Nation State'. In a similarly nationalistic vein, Art. 3(4) provides that '[n]o foreign populations may be displaced or colonised in the territory of the Romanian State' (a rather unlikely scenario nowadays); Art. 4(1) proclaims that '[t]he State foundation is laid on the unity of the Romanian people'; and in Art. 7 we find the principle of protecting (ethnic) Romanians abroad. All these show a rhetorically strong version of vision no. I (classical ethnic nationalism in its essence).[310] But on the other hand, the Constitution also contains a sophisticated system of minority protection including group rights in Arts. 4(2), 6, 32(3), 59 and 127(2), which are clear signs of vision no. IV.

### *10.3.3 The United Kingdom (II, IV and V)*

The UK and the British nation could probably be best categorised as belonging to vision No. II (Switzerland, in which the British nation would

[309] SJ Roth, The effects of ethno-nationalism on citizens' rights in the former communist countries, in: András Sajó (ed.), *Western Rights? Post-Communist Application*, Leiden, Kluwer 1996, 273–290, 277–281; Robert M Hayden, Constitutional Nationalism in the Former Yugoslav Republics, *Slavic Review* 51 (1992) 654–673.

[310] Ioana Lungu, Romanian Constitutional Nationalism, *Polish Sociological Review* 2002 (140) 397–412, especially 402.

consist of English, Scottish, Welsh and Irish ethnies – also expressed by the Union Flag (popularly known as the 'Union Jack') unifying the historical flags of Scotland, Ireland and England), even though it also shows features of the European vision, as there is clearly a dominant ethnic community, namely the English (more so than in Switzerland; cf. the officially used languages).[311] Within British political discourse, traditionally a civic vision (now, after devolution rather a Swiss vision) is attributed to Labour and a European vision to the Conservatives.[312] Traditional British citizenship law was based on the *ius soli* principle (which is characteristic of vision no. V), but it was rather an old legacy of the 'common law doctrine of monarchical allegiance, which labelled as British subjects anyone perchance born within the king's dominions'.[313] Thirty years ago, the situation became fuzzier though: the Nationality Act 1981 introduced *ius sanguinis,* and kept *ius soli* only for cases in which at least one of the parents had permanent residence.[314]

In the British legal terminology, autochton non-English ethnic communities are recognised as 'nations' (in our terminology 'ethnies', as the Parliament in London has the right to revoke devolution at any time which thereby excludes a constitutional respect for any ambition on the part of the Scots or Welsh to have their own states) with their historical and territorial characteristics (without 'nationality' in the sense of public international law though),[315] after devolution even in a strongly institutionalised form in domestic constitutional law. Devolution means a strong (ethnic) decentralisation without formally federalising the

[311] And formally, it is not a federal state in spite of the devolution. The unitary and federal dichotomy does not describe precisely, however, the newer developments in this area anyway; see Tierney (n. 92) ix.

[312] McCrone (n. 153) 37; Stephen Haseler, *The English Tribe*, London, New York, Macmillan 1996, 30: 'Great Britain was always a misnomer; "Greater England" would have been better.'

[313] Michelle Everson, 'Subjects' or 'Citizens of Erewhon'? Law and Non-Law in the Development of 'British Citizenship', *Citizenship Studies* 2003/1, 57–85, 61.

[314] Albert Kraler, The Legal Status of Immigrants and Their Access to Nationality, in: Rainer Bauböck (ed.), *Migration and Citizenship*, Amsterdam, Amsterdam University Press 2006, 33–65, 45.

[315] '"Nation" and "national" in their popular . . . sense are also vague terms. They do not necessarily imply statehood. For example, there were many submerged nations in the former Hapsburg Empire. Scotland is not a nation in the eye of international law; but Scotsmen constitute a nation by reason of those most powerful elements in the creation of a national spirit–tradition, folk memory, a sentiment of community. . . . By the Act of Union English and Scots lost their separate nationalities, but they retained their separate nationhoods.' Lord Simon of Glaisdale in *London Borough of Ealing v. Race Relations Board* [1972] Appeal Court 342 at 364.

country. But the central authority is itself of a contractual nature, as it is based on the 1707 Treaty of Union between Scotland and England.[316] The classification dilemmas are well expressed by Neil MacCormick: 'There is no doubt that we have a single state, but it is at least possible that we have two interpretations, two conceptions, two understandings, of the constitution of that state.'[317] The UK is one single unified subject in international law and there does exist a purportedly British nation (as opposed to the Belgian situation), but at many sporting events different English, Scottish, Welsh and Northern Irish teams compete: a theoretically confusing, but practically well-functioning (one could say, typically British) solution.

### *10.3.4 Hungary (mainly IV, with elements of I and V)*

There is an interesting division in the approach to the Hungarian nation taken by Hungarian legal sources: internally – that is, within the territory of Hungary – the term 'nation' seems to be understood either as a civic/political or as an ethnic/cultural nation (whereas the substantive constitutional vision is clearly No. IV: the political community consists of one dominant ethnic nation and some ethnic minorities);[318] externally – that is, beyond the territory of Hungary – it seems to be conceived as a clear-cut ethnic/cultural nation (nearing to the logic of vision no. I).[319]

This logical inconsistency conforms to our former result (see above *10.1.2.2 Natural (ethnic, that is, based on ancestry or culture) vs. artificial (based on elite manipulation; or civic, that is, based on law and deliberate choice)*): the use of the concept of nation depends on which one claims

[316] *MacCormick v. Lord Advocate* [1953] SC 396 [1953] SLT 255. Lord Justice Cooper stated that parliamentary sovereignty is unknown in Scotland and it cannot be used to override the union settlement. But he also added that if it still happened then the courts could do nothing about it.

[317] Neil MacCormick, Is There a Constitutional Path to Scottish Independence?, *Parliamentary Affairs* 53 (2000) 721–736, 727.

[318] In Hungary, the legal order has expressed vision No. IV since 1989 (in a rhetorically more ethnic form since the enactment of the new Basic Law in 2011), even though the vision of the political left is rather the civic (US) model; see Agnes Batory, Kin-State Identity in the European Context: Citizenship, Nationalism and Constitutionalism in Hungary, *Nations and Nationalism* 2010, 31–48, 42. The difference is also expressed in naming the country: the political left prefers 'the Republic of Hungary', whereas the political right just 'Hungary' (without actually intending to change the state form).

[319] Cf. Helge Hornburg, The Concept of Nation in the Hungarian Legal Order, in: András Jakab – Péter Takács – Allan F Tatham (eds.), *The Transformation of the Hungarian Legal Order 1985–2005*, The Hague, Kluwer Law International 2007, 507–520.

more political influence for its user. As there are many ethnic Hungarians abroad, an ethnic concept seems to be more apt to keep their connection with the kin state; but also to include the ethnic minorities of Hungary, a civic (No. V) or a traditional European (No. IV) vision seems better. For the academic mind, a choice would be necessary, but drafters of constitutions are not bothered by internal inconsistencies if these seem purposeful (like the Spanish example already indicated).

This fuzzy picture did not change with the approval of the new Constitution in 2011 (called the Basic Law).[320] For internal purposes, the concept is sometimes civic, sometimes ethnic/cultural. For example, when Art. J Basic Law mentions '*national* holidays' then it means 'state holidays' (the most important national holiday even bears the name '*official* state holiday'), and 'the family as the basis of the *nation's* survival' in Art. L refers to the general demographic situation (and not to its ethnic ratio). Similarly, the 'the *nation's* common heritage' in Art. P Basic Law also includes the culture of the ethnic minorities; and when the President of the Republic 'embodies the unity of the *nation*' according to Art. 9, by that is meant all citizens of the country. And also when Art. 38 declares state property '*national* assets', or when issues of '*national* security' are regulated, then the concept of nation is ethnic-neutral.

The Preamble of the new Constitution begins with the words: 'We, the members of the Hungarian *Nation*'.[321] Whether it uses the term 'nation' in an ethnic or cultural sense as the *pouvoir constituant* is not entirely clear, but there are probably stronger arguments for an ethnic/cultural interpretation. An argument for the ethnic nature of the term is the following paragraph of the Preamble:

> We [i.e., the 'Hungarian Nation' – A.J.] promise to preserve the intellectual and spiritual unity of our *nation* torn apart in the storms of the past

[320] For a general analysis of the changes brought by the new Basic Law, see András Jakab – Pál Sonnevend, Kontinuität mit Mängeln: Das neue ungarische Grundgesetz, *Zeitschrift für ausländisches öffentliches Recht und Völkerrecht* 2012, 79–102.

[321] The preamble is called 'National Avowal of Faith' giving a quasi-religious sense to the self-description of the nation (confirming our thesis on the similar nature of religion and nationalism, see above *10.1.1.2.1 The need to give a meaning to life after secularisation*). On the English and Hungarian terminology in more detail, see Ferenc Horkay Hörcher, The National Avowal, in: Lóránt Csink – Balázs Schanda – András Zs Varga (eds.), *The Basic Law of Hungary*, Dublin, Budapest, Clarus, NIPA 2012, 25–45, 26–27. Other religious elements in the new Basic Law are the motto, which is in fact the first line of the national anthem written in 1823 ('*God* bless the Hungarians') and references to the *Holy* Crown as a symbol of Hungarian historical statehood (not adopting the Doctrine of the Holy Crown though, on this traditional doctrine see above 6.1).

> century. The nationalities living with us *form part of the Hungarian political community* and are constituent parts of the State.

The first sentence refers to ethnic Hungarians living abroad (note that they are part of the nation), the second to ethnic non-Hungarians living in Hungary (note that the nationalities are not part of the 'Nation' but of the 'State'). But on the other hand, the last sentence of the Preamble refers to a civic concept of the nation ('We, the citizens of Hungary' used now as synonymous with 'We, the members of the Hungarian Nation', italics mine):

> Our Basic Law ... is a living framework expressing the *nation's* will and the form in which we wish to live. *We, the citizens of Hungary,* are ready to found the order of our country upon the cooperation of the *nation.*

Thus the picture about the use of the term 'nation' is unclear, possibly even deliberately contradictory. The Preamble confirms, on the one hand, that the concept of nation is an ethnic one ('We promise to preserve the intellectual and spiritual unity of our nation torn apart in the storms of the past century.'),[322] but at the same time, right in the next sentence we find a non-ethnic inclusive definition of the political community conceived as a group of ethnic groups ('The nationalities living with us form part of the Hungarian political community and are constituent parts of the State.').

The actual rules about ethnic/national minorities living in Hungary reflect, however, vision No. IV, in which a dominant ethnic majority recognises the ethnic minorities. These minorities are recognised as cultural entities with special constitutional privileges (autonomies, language rights, seats in Parliament to be won with lower thresholds than otherwise required).

It seems that the new Hungarian Basic Law of 2011 differs from its predecessor through a stronger rhetorical emphasis on ethnic Hungarians (not only in the Preamble but also, for instance, in a new Art. *H)* on the state's duty to protect the Hungarian language, which does not seem to bear any concrete legal relevance;[323] in Art. *D)* with a more detailed

[322] The nation 'torn apart' is an implied reference to the Trianon Peace Treaty which meant that territories inhabited by several millions of ethnic Hungarians (amongst other ethnies) became parts of Hungary's neighbouring countries. On the topic, see András Jakab, Trianon Peace Treaty (1920), in: Rüdiger Wolfrum (ed.), *Max Planck Encyclopedia of Public International Law*, Oxford, Oxford University Press 2011 [electronically available at http://www.mpepil.com/].

[323] András Jakab, *Az új Alaptörvény keletkezése és gyakorlati következményei*, Budapest, HVG Orac 2011, 190.

description of the state's responsibility for ethnic Hungarians abroad than in the former Constitution),[324] but also – maybe as something balancing out the latter – a stronger emphasis on the group rights of ethnic minorities within Hungary.

### *10.3.5 France and Poland (IV and V, but historically also I)*

Revolutionary France has already been mentioned as an example of the civic nation (vision no. V). Elements of this approach have survived until the present day in French legal thought. A clear example of this is the 1991 decision of the Constitutional Council on the Statute of Corsica in which the Council confirmed that only one 'people' can exist in France, and that the Statute cannot mention a 'Corsican people'.[325] Pluralism is considered to be a threat to the unity of the Republic, and the concept of equality is often instrumentalised to achieve this unity.[326] Ethnic differences are dealt with in the private sphere.[327] But since the Second World War, state-subsidised schools teaching Alsatian have muddied this picture slightly (as this would resemble vision no. IV, cf. also the 2008 amendment of the French Constitution which now states in Art. 75-1 that 'the regional languages belong to the heritage of France'), even if the main features are still the civic ones.

And we also have to mention that the treatment of immigrants basically conforms to vision no. I (see especially the prohibition of Muslim veils). In the nineteenth century, vision no. I (classical ethnic nationalism) applied even to autochthon minorities, as Eugen Weber describes it in his classic *Peasants into Frenchmen*:[328]

324 Art. D. 'Bearing in mind that there is one single Hungarian nation that belongs together, Hungary shall bear responsibility for the fate of Hungarians living beyond its borders, shall facilitate the survival and development of their communities, shall support their efforts to preserve their Hungarian identity, the application of their individual and collective rights, the establishment of their community self-governments, and their prosperity in their native lands, and shall promote their cooperation with each other and with Hungary.'

325 CC, 9 May 1991, para 11 (*Revue universelle des droits de l'homme* 1991, 183).

326 Norbert Rouland, La tradition juridique française et la diversité culturelle, *Droit et société* 1994, 381–419, especially 385; Gérard Marcou, Le principe d'indivisibilité de la République, *Pouvoirs* 100 (2002) 45–65.

327 Luc Heuschling, Die Struktur der demokratischen Legitimität im französischen Recht: zwischen Monismus und Pluralismus, zwischen Subjekt Symbolik und Gewaltenmechanik, *Europäische Grundrechte-Zeitschrift* 33 (2006) 338–353, 344.

328 Weber (n. 123) 313. Also the Dreyfus Affair and the *État Français* of Pétain fit into this vision nr I, which considers as its historical predecessor not the French revolutionary past but the medieval French Catholic monarchy.

> Breton was hunted out of the schools. Children caught using it were systematically punished – put on dry bread and water or sent to clean out the school latrine. . . . A favourite punishment . . . was the token of shame to be displayed by the child caught using his native tongue. The token varied. . . . A child saddled with such a 'symbol' kept it until he caught another child not speaking French, denounced him and passed it on. The pupil left with the token at the end of the day received a punishment.

The 1997 Polish Constitution shows similar features. On the one hand, the Preamble identifies 'Nation' with the sum of citizens (civic nation: 'We, the Polish Nation – all citizens of the Republic'), and consequently, Art. 4 places sovereignty in the hands of the 'Nation'.[329]

But on the other hand, Art. 6 refers to a Nation which is rather a cultural entity: cultural goods are 'the source of the Nation's identity, continuity and development' and it also mentions 'national cultural heritage'. And finally, Art. 52(5) declares that those having Polish ancestry (but not necessarily citizenship) have the right to settle in Poland. The current Polish regime definitely cannot be qualified, though as an ethnic (No. I) vision, since in Art. 35 it guarantees minority group rights. The Preamble itself contains a compromise formula when referring at the same time to the ethno-religious (Catholic-Polish) cultural concept of the nation when it mentions 'our culture rooted in the Christian heritage of the Nation', but it also emphasises civic elements like 'universal human values', or when the citizens are mentioned as 'Both those who believe in God as the source of truth, justice, good and beauty, As well as those not sharing such faith but respecting those universal values as arising from other sources'.

Thus the Constitution seems to have two parallel visions of the nation: a civic (No. V) and a dominant European (No. IV) one.

[329] Art. 4: '(1) Supreme power in the Republic of Poland shall be vested in the Nation. (2) The Nation shall exercise such power directly or through their representatives.' On the civic nature of this nation concept, see Leszek Garlicki, *Polskie prawo konstytucyjne. Zarys wykładu*, Warszawa, Liber 1999, 53 quoted by Iván Halász, A nemzetfogalom nyelvi-kulturális elemei a modern kelet- és közép-európai demokratikus alkotmányokban, in: Iván Halász – Balázs Majtényi – László Szarka (eds.), *Ami összeköt?*, Budapest, Gondolat 2004, 27–41, 33. On the debates of how to (re)define nation in ethnic or civic terms during the constitutional drafting process, see Geneviève Zubrycki, 'We, the Polish Nation': Ethnic and Civic Visions of nationhood in Post-Communist Constitutional Debates, *Theory and Society* 2001, 629–688.

## 10.4 Excursus on secession: giving up the constitutional vision

Until now, we have discussed different constitutional visions of the nation. In certain situations, however, the constitutional nature of the vision will be given up, and a part of the old nation leaves the political community: a new nation will be formed in the name of the principle of self-determination. We call it secession.

At the end of the First World War, national self-determination became one of the main tenets of the new international order (at least at the level of rhetoric).[330] The people (meaning here the nation) of a country are supposed to have the right to independence, but the problem is that 'the people cannot decide until someone decides who are the people'.[331] Depending on the conceptualisation, either the population of the territory seeking independence or the whole country's population can be the *demos*.[332] If you approve the right to secede in some form,[333] then necessarily you override the right of the 'sovereign' people of the whole country to preserve the country's territorial integrity.[334] It also leaves it unclear as to what is to be done if majorities come and go: should borders immediately follow the changing preferences of citizens?

Most states have faced secession in their histories, and most of them tried (and try) to prevent it. Some constitutions explicitly commit to territorial integrity in their text. Some, though, are open to the possibility of secession, for which we know three ways.[335] (1) A classic example was Art. 72 of the 1977 Soviet Constitution and Art. 17 of the 1936 Soviet Constitution, both of which stated: 'Each Union Republic shall retain the right freely to secede from the USSR.' Thus it was a mere declaration, without any further procedural details. The reason for the lack of procedural details is that it was never meant to be used, but with the

[330] Cf. Woodrow Wilson's Fourteen Points, 8. January 1918, Point V; Lenin's Declaration of the Rights of the People of Russia, 15. November 1917. For a concise overview with further references to contemporary sources of international law, see Daniel Thürer – Thomas Burri, Self-Determination, in: Wolfrum (n. 322) 113–128.

[331] Ivor Jennings, *The Approach of Self-Government*, Cambridge, Cambridge University Press 1956, 56.

[332] Gregory Millard, The Secession Reference and National Reconciliation: A Critical View, *Canadian Journal of Law and Society* 14 (1999) 1–19, 3.

[333] E.g., the Canadian Supreme Court in the Secession Reference opinion (20 August 1998, (1998) 2 SCR 217) stating that Quebec does have a *prima facie* right to secede which the rest of Canada may not frustrate if Quebec negotiates the details of that secession in good faith.

[334] Tierney (n. 92) 267.

[335] On the three ways with more details, see Norman (n. 272) 176–177.

end of the dictatorship constitutional provisions originally intended only for PR purposes became shockingly alive. The lack of procedural rules, however, caused many grave conflicts. (2) A second and extremely rare solution, trying to remedy the problem of the former, is a procedurally detailed constitutional regulation on the secession process. Such provisions are to be found in s. 113 of the 1983 Constitution of Saint Christopher and Nevis (St Kitts and Nevis, both names are official) and in Art. 39 of the 1994 Constitution of Ethiopia.[336] (3) And finally, a third solution is if the text of the Constitution does not contain any possibility of secession (or even refers to the unity and integrity of the country, as in France),[337] but the constitutional court or the supreme court accepts the right to secede. This happened in France with the 'Overseas Departments'[338] and in Canada with Quebec.[339] Even though most commentators argue against secession, some still welcome a constitutional entrenchment of the right to secede. Most notably, Wayne Norman argues as follows:[340]

> in some states, particularly multination states in which there is a distinct possibility of secessionist politics, it would often be appropriate to have provisions for secession entrenched in the constitution. My principal reasons for this derive not from any enthusiasm for secession but rather because, first, secessionist politics in such states are likely to arise with or without such a clause; second, when they do arise they invite political turmoil and violence, squeeze the amount of political time and energy available for other urgent public concerns, and are unlikely to be resolved in as fair a manner as they would have been with prior ground rules; and third, it is reasonable to think that a fair secession clause could actually serve, in some cases at least, as a deterrent to the formation of secessionist politics rather than as a source of encouragement.

I rather argue with Cass Sunstein, who emphasises the dangers of such entrenchments, as this would open up the imagination to secession and

[336] Miodrag Jovanović, *Constitutionalizing Secession in Federalized States: A Procedural Approach*, Utrecht, Eleven 2007, 137–143. On a statutory level, in Russia we find similarly detailed rules; see the Law on Secession of 1990.

[337] See Art. 1(1) 'France shall be an indivisible . . . Republic.' and Art. 3(2) 'No section of the people nor any individual may arrogate to itself, or to himself, the exercise [of national sovereignty].'

[338] Alain Moyrand – Tony Angelo, International Law Perspectives on the Evolution in Status of the French Overseas Territories, *La Revue Juridique Polynésienne* 5 (1999) 49–69, http://www.upf.pf/Revue-no-5-1999.html?lang=fr.

[339] See above n. 333.

[340] Wayne Norman, Secession and (constitutional) democracy, in: Requejo (n. 221) 84–102, 98.

would probably lead to blackmailing strategies in a constitutional system.[341]

In international law, barring extreme brutality, secession is normally permitted only by mutual agreement between a central government and a regional minority.[342] Otherwise there is no 'right to secede' in public international law.[343] International practice is, however, entirely inconsistent: decisions about when to recognise a newly born (seceded) state do not depend on former human rights violations, ethnic homogeneity or successful referenda, but on political considerations.[344] As Thomas Franck rightly put it, 'Why should the international community approve the formal right of Croatia to secede from the Yugoslav Federation while denying a similar right to the Serbian regions of Croatia?'[345] Thus the right to self-determination basically never establishes an actual right *before* the event; it only gives an explanation (or legal excuse) *after* the successful secession.

Besides the legal problems, secession has quite a few practical disadvantages. First of all, it is a high-cost strategy (emotionally and economically) for both sides; therefore it is used mostly only as an *ultima ratio.*[346] Secondly, it does not solve minority problems, as in 'nine out of ten' cases it results in new minorities (often the old majorities become new minorities, facing similar or even graver minority protection issues).[347] One possible solution could be the method applied within Switzerland, when the French-speaking Canton Jura seceded from the German-speaking Canton Bern in 1979, in which not simply the potentially new canton could decide via referendum on its independence

341 Cass R Sunstein, Constitutionalism and Secession, *University of Chicago Law Review* 58 (1991) 633–670, 634.

342 Norman (n. 272) 172.

343 James R Crawford, State Practice and International Law in Relation to Unilateral Secession, in: Anne F Bayefsky (ed.), *Self-Determination in International Law: Quebec and Lessons Learned*, The Hague, Kluwer 2000, 31–61 with further references.

344 For a concise overview of law and state practice with further references, see Daniel Thürer - Thomas Burri, Secession, in: Wolfrum (n. 322).

345 Thomas Franck, *Fairness in International Law and Institutions*, Oxford, Clarendon Press 1995, 160. For a similarly sceptical view, see Zoran Oklopcic, Populus Interruptus, *Leiden Journal of International Law* 22 (2009) 677–702, especially 679–680 with further references.

346 Paul R Brass, *Ethnicity and Nationalism: Theory and Comparison*, New Delhi, Sage 1991, 61.

347 Donald L Horowitz, Self-Determination: Politics, Philosophy, and Law, in: Margaret Moore (ed.), *National Self-Determination and Secession*, Oxford, Oxford University Press 1998, 181–214, 199.

(within Switzerland), but also every village (municipality) in the future border area. It does not solve, of course, all problems, and new minorities will exist, but it does alleviate the problem of 'new minorities'.[348] Thirdly, if secession is too easy, then there is no incentive to solve issues through negotiation and to make compromises.[349] It can also subvert majority rule, so important in democracies.[350] Fourthly, sometimes it is just practically not viable:[351]

> secession is not always possible or desirable. Some national minorities, particularly indigenous people, would have trouble forming viable independent states. In other cases, competing claims over land and resources would make peaceful secession virtually impossible. In general, there are more nations in the world than possible states, and since we cannot simply wish national consciousness away, we need to find some way to keep multinational states together.

There seem to be basically three ways to contain nationalist independence movements: 1. increase the cost of collective action, 2. reduce the importance of national identity, 3. decrease the demand for national identity. The first one is possible only in repressive regimes. The second is just not happening; national identity still remains important. And the third one means some kind of autonomy (devolution, indirect rule, decentralised decision-making, federalism), which consequently remains the only viable option.[352] The possibility of sharing power gives all ethnic (national) parties a stake in the survival of the constitutional system as a whole.[353]

348 For more details see John R Jenkins, *Jura Separatism in Switzerland*, Oxford, Clarendon Press 1986. Art. 53 of the Swiss Constitution entrenches the right to secession within the country, if all parties (the population affected, the cantons affected, further the two chambers Federal Parliament and the majority of the Cantons) assent.

349 Allen Buchanan, *Secession: The Morality of Political Divorce from Sumter to Lithuania and Quebec*, Boulder, Colo., Westview 1991, 134.

350 Buchanan (n. 349) 98–99.

351 Will Kymlicka, *Multicultural Citizenship*, Oxford, Oxford University Press 1995, 186. For a similar opinion, see David Miller, In Defence of Nationality, in: Paul Gilbert – Paul Gregory (eds.), *Nations, Cultures, and Markets*, Abingdon, Avebury 1994, 15–32.

352 Hechter (n. 8) 134–136. With a special emphasis on federalism for taming ethnic conflicts, see Will Kymlicka, *Politics in the Vernacular*, Oxford, Oxford University Press 2001, 92–93; Richard Simeon – Daniel-Patrick Conway, Federalism and Management of Conflict in Multinational Societies, in: Alain Gagnon – James Tully (eds.), *Multinational Democracies*, Cambridge, Cambridge University Press 2001, 338–365, 364.

353 Choudhry (n. 178) 19.

If we want to avoid these problems of secession, self-determination as a legal concept has to be defined as empowering only autonomy *within* a state rather than secession.[354] Thus, we have to turn the concept of self-determination from an international law concept into a constitutional law one.[355] If we cannot manage this redefinition, the Cassandra-like prophecy of Robert Lansing, Wilson's Secretary of State, will sadly continue to contain an element of truth:[356]

> The phrase [on self-determination by Wilson] is simply loaded with dynamite. It will raise hopes which can never be realized. It will, I fear, cost thousand of lives. In the end it is bound to be discredited, to be called the dream of an idealist who failed to realize the danger until too late to check those who attempt to put the principle into force. What a calamity the phrase was ever uttered! What misery it will cause!

## 10.5 The European Union and the visions of a European political community

The question arises as to what the national nature of the EU could be, or which of the above models it should follow; that is, *if* we conceptualise the EU as a nation, then which of the visions can be applied now and which in the future.

There is currently no linguistically defined dominant ethnic group in Europe (even the largest group as defined by native tongue, that is, German speaking people, are well below 50 per cent of European citizens, and even this group consisting of Austrians and Germans can hardly be defined as one single ethnic group), and the attempt to give European-ness a religious content also failed during the (otherwise also failed) European constitution-making process.[357] Consequently, vision Nos. I and IV seem to be excluded.

The EU is nowadays most similar to the Belgian model: it is not conceived as *the* political community (except for some intellectuals) in

354 For such approaches see s. 235 of the Constitution of the Republic of South Africa Act (No. 108 of 1996) stating: 'The right of the South African people as a whole to self-determination, as manifested in this Constitution, does not preclude, within the framework of this right, recognition of the notion of the right of self-determination of any community sharing a common cultural and language heritage; within a territorial entity in the Republic or in any other way, determined by national legislation.'

355 Tierney (n. 92) viii.

356 Robert Lansing, *The Peace Negotiations: A Personal Narrative*, Orlando, Houghton Mifflin 1921, 97–98.

357 On the debate, see above p. 156 n. 57.

which we live; thus it cannot be conceived as a nation.[358] Also, the constitutional design is similarly both complex and inefficient. The future options are either a Swiss type (that is, having also an overarching identity as the alliance of European ethnic communities) or some kind of European multilingual[359] constitutional patriotism.[360] As for now, however, the socialising effects of the EU institutions are very weak.[361] The current (mostly Belgian, consisting of co-nations: 'The Union shall respect … the national identities [of its Member States]', Art. 4(2) TEU) vision already shows some elements of constitutional patriotism (cf. especially preamble and Art. 2 TEU), but a full realisation of this model is also unlikely (cf. the many legal rules about the cultural and constitutional identities of Member States, which do not fit to a difference-blind political entity; or the lack of meaningful electoral politics).[362] The debates about the limits on future enlargement also show resistance towards a fully civic type of EU nation (cf. the provisions on future enlargement – justified on cultural/ethnic/national grounds – contradicting the concept of a civic nation in the *Grundgesetz* or in the German Constitution of 1867). Thus, besides the current Belgian option, the strongest possibility is some kind of Swiss direction with minor elements of the US vision, but whether, when and how far we move, in which direction, is so far unclear. Recent case-law of the European Court of Justice (ECJ) strengthens the impression that EU citizenship is beginning to move away from the Belgian empty shell model towards a more substantive (rights-based) civic model, decoupling it from cross-border elements.[363]

358 For a sceptical tone, see, e.g., Smith (n. 205) 139: 'In short, who will die for Europe?'

359 It is doubtful whether English can serve as a common political language, as you need to do it your vernacular; see Philippe van Parijs, Europe's Linguistic Challenge, *Archives Européennes de Sociologie* 2004 (XLV/1), 113–154.

360 The latter is proposed by Justine Lacroix, For a European Constitutional Patriotism, *Political Studies* 2002, 944–958; Jan-Werner Müller, A European Constitutional Patriotism? The Case Restated, *European Law Journal* 14 (2008) 542–557; Jean-Marc Ferry, *La question de l'État européen*, Paris, Gallimard 2000.

361 Jeffrey Checkel, International Institutions and Socialization in Europe, *International Organization* 2005, 801–826, 815.

362 Mattias Kumm, Why Europeans Will Not Embrace Constitutional Patriotism, *International Journal of Constitutional Law* 6 (2008) 117–136.

363 Koen Lenaerts, Civis Europaeus Sum: From the Cross-Border Link to the Status of Citizen of the Union, *Online Journal on Free Movement of Workers within the European Union* 3 (2011) 6–18; Dimitry Kochenov, The Essence of EU Citizenship Emerging from the Last Ten Years of Academic Debate: Beyond the Cherry Blossoms and the Moon, *International and Comparative Law Quarterly* 62 (2013) 97–136, quoting the cases

Having some nationally defined (Belgian- or Swiss-type) elements is probably necessary, because a democratic federation without a clear and secure *Staatsvolk* (like the EU) must also adopt such practices in order to ensure that national minorities do not feel threatened or systematically outvoted.[364]

The most likely scenario seems to be some kind of multiple identity, and *not* a clear choice of any of the above models.[365] The strength and nature of European identity is already, and will also be, different from country to country, as the different national and sub-national identities filter it.[366] European-ness is mostly already part of national identities in the Member States.[367] It is also possible to strengthen the European elements of such an identity by introducing in the regular census the possibility of dividing identity (either by percentage, that is, one person could claim to be 60 per cent German, 30 per cent French and 10 per cent European, the latter either in Swiss or US style; or in order to avoid a zero-sum game marking his or her identity on a 1 to 10 scale, that is, one person could claim to have a level 8 Spanish identity, a level 7 Catalan identity and a level 3 European identity),[368] by having EU sports teams

C–135/08 *Rottmann v. Freistaat Bayern* [2010] ECR I–1449 and C–34/09 *Gerardo Ruiz Zambrano v. Office National de l'emploi (Onem)* [2011] I–1177.

364 Brendan O'Leary, An Iron Law of Nationalism and Federation? A (neo-Diceyan) theory of the necessity of a federal *Staatsvolk*, and of consociational rescue, *Nations and Nationalism* 2001, 273–296, 291–292.

365 Carl F Graumann, Soziale Identitäten, in: Reinhold Viehoff – Rien T Segers (eds.), *Kultur, Identität, Europa*, Frankfurt am Main, Suhrkamp 1999, 59–74, 67. For empirical evidence on the possibility of multiple identities see Luis Moreno, Multiple Identities in Decentralized Spain, *Regional and Federal Studies* 8 (1998) 65–88; for a theoretical plea for multiple loyalties, see Jacob T Levy, Federalism, Liberalism, and the Separation of Loyalties, *American Political Science Review* 101 (2007) 459–477. As we have seen, the different visions mingle even on the domestic level. For a theoretical amalgam of (what I called) the Belgian and the US model, see Alex Schwartz, Patriotism or Integrity? Constitutional Community in Divided Societies, *Oxford Journal of Legal Studies* 2011, 503–526.

366 Stephen Tierney, Beyond the Ontological Question: Liberal Nationalism and the Task of Constitution-Building, *European Law Journal* 14 (2008) 128–137, 133.

367 Laura Cram, Identity and European integration, *Nations and Nationalism* 2009, 109–128, 116; Armin von Bogdandy, Europäische und nationale Identität: Integration durch Verfassungsrecht?, *Veröffentlichungen der Vereinigung der Deutschen Staatsrechtslehrer* 62 (2003) 156–193, 171.

368 This would also fit the actual identity situation on the sub-national level; see McCrone (n. 153), 138: 'If a single and homogenous national identity is a key feature of classical nationalism, then plural and shifting identities characterise neo-nationalism.' It is also in the interest of the EU to support minority nationalism in Europe, as this could help to break up the traditional nation-state level identities; see John McGarry – Michael Keating – Margaret Moore, Introduction: European Integration and the Nationalities

stepping up against Chinese or US ones, by also opening up domestic political positions for all EU citizens, by founding a fully fledged network of institutions in Europe similar to the European University Institute in Florence in order to form the common identity of social science intellectuals (who tend to be influential both in national public discourses and in educating future generations of politicians at domestic universities), or by changing the EU government system into a parliamentary one.[369] Also the sociological fact of workers' mobility and the subsequent mixed marriages show the possibility of such gradual changes in the future.[370] Banal everyday experiences confirm the EU identity of the citizens, such as carrying passports and driving licences with EU symbols, seeing EU flags on domestic buildings, paying with the Euro, and so on. But it is unlikely that some kind of EU national identity could take over from the domestic national one; for this to happen an enormous social and cultural (educational) reorganisation would be necessary, which does not seem possible because of financial, political identity and competence issues,[371] even though the legal framework of the EU is becoming more and more similar to domestic concepts of the political community.[372] Any attempt to force a European identity from above would most likely be counterproductive;[373] thus conscious European identity-building has to understand itself as an addition to, and not as a substitution for, national identities. Substitution, though not necessarily a bad outcome, should only be an accidental by-product and never the actual purpose.

Such a development would be useful for Europe, as a common (even if just partial) Swiss-type identity would make human

Question, in: John McGarry – Michael Keating (eds.), *European Integration and the Nationalities Question*, New York, Routledge 2006, 1–20.

369 For the latter possibility see 9.3.

370 Dora Kostakopoulou, European Union Citizenship: Writing the Future, *European Law Journal* 13 (2007) 623–646, especially 646.

371 Smith (n. 205) 143. For similar doubts see Llobera (n. 6) 207.

372 See especially CJEU Case C–34/09, *Ruiz Zambrano*, [2011] ECR I–01177 protecting EU citizens against their own mother countries. Also the TEU mentions 'European identity' in several places with the (sometimes explicit) purpose of strengthening it. For a thorough and theoretically well-founded analysis of EU citizenship from a legal perspective, see Christoph Schönberger, *Unionsbürger. Europas föderales Bürgerrecht in vergleichender Sicht*, Tübingen, Mohr Siebeck 2005.

373 Cf. more generally Arend Lijphart, *Democracy in Plural Societies*, New Haven, Yale University Press 1977, 24.

resources management more efficient (e.g., larger pool for choosing politicians); it could enhance social mobility and use economies of scale; and it would thus make Europe as a great deal stronger in the global playground.[374] But it seems that Ernest Renan's prediction about Europe's future from 1882 has still not been entirely fulfilled:[375] 'Nations are not something eternal. They had their beginnings and they will end. A European confederation will very probably replace them.' It seems, though, that we are at least somewhere at the beginning or probably rather more ahead in that process.

## 10.6 Conclusions as to the use of 'nation' in the European constitutional discourse

In the first section of the present chapter, we saw how and why ethnic diversity is a challenge for the state: on its own, it does not pose a challenge, but with the idea of nation and nationalism it does become a potential problem. The second section of the chapter showed the different types of responses given by constitutions (conceptualised as visions). Our result is that there is no *generally* recommendable solution. As to immigrants, the classical ethnic assimilationist nationalist approach seems to be the usual one, but as to autochthon minorities the recognition of group rights with the acceptance of the ethnic nature of the state (vision No. IV) is advisable.[376] All other visions are exceptions, which are meaningful only under very special (historical and sociological) circumstances.

The European Union is currently nearest to the Belgian (No. III) constitutional vision, but a parallel shift towards the Swiss (No. II) and towards the US (No. V) visions is both possible and advisable, even though a *full* realisation of either of these is not possible in the foreseeable future. If, as legal scholars, we want to help this shift, we should refer to the population of the EU as the 'European Nation' in our writings (but we also use 'nation' in the domestic Member State

[374] Cf. Tierney (n. 92) 24 on the advantages of national feelings for the political community.

[375] Renan (n. 115) 20.

[376] The question of how to differentiate between autochthon minorities and immigrants is not an easy one, as there is no predetermined period (50, 100 or 200 years; second, third or fourth generation) which would make immigrants into autochthons. This is rather a question of local political context than an abstract issue.

context).[377] Such terminological changes can, first of all, have an effect on the constitutional discourse, but it can also influence (slowly, step-by-step) the general political discourse, making contradictions between the Member States and the EU more difficult to conceptualise.

[377] Without such a shift, European culture could face the same problems of fragmentation as the ancient Greek city states, which were unable to unite, and went down unavoidably in history, see Arnold J Toynbee, *A Study of History*, vol. VI, London, Oxford University Press 1939, 208. See also Othmar Anderle, *Das universalhistorische System Arnold Joseph Toynbees*, Frankfurt aM, Humboldt 1955, 340; Joseph Vogt, *Wege zum historischen Universum*, Stuttgart, Kohlhammer 1961, 101.

# PART III

## Redundant vocabulary

> The difficulty lies not so much in developing new ideas, as in escaping from old ones.[1]

In this Part of the book, I will analyse a few analytical frameworks (or terminologies) which often come up in the discourse on European constitutional theory, but which I believe to be erroneous. In the following, I am going to explain why I consider them as conceptual dead-ends, that is, why they should not be incorporated in constitutional reasoning.

The following chapters are also a personal history of intellectual failures. I actually intended to use them as key concepts (in different stages of this project), and I failed. I documented the failures, and began to consider them as (negative) results. Most of these dead-ends (2.5 from the 4) stem from the German-speaking discourse(s), more precisely from Austria and Germany, which can be explained by the traditionally rich production of *Verfassungsdogmatik* in these countries (i.e., the more you work and the more innovations you make, the greater the chance that you make mistakes).

The survival of these concepts has different reasons. The most important is probably sheer habit: we always used them (our PhD supervisor also used them). Also, the search for their 'true' meaning has never ceased, in the same way that there are still people searching for Eldorado in the rain forest (instead of admitting that there is nothing to search for). However, it is more than just that: these concepts acquired identity-building functions in some cases, although in a different sense from the identity-building function of my proposed key concepts. These conceptual dead-ends serve as group-building factors only within the scholarly community, and they are not used by the political discourse.

The use of the *Stufenbaulehre* means (except for Austria where it belongs to the general constitutional folklore) a rejection of the conservative

[1] John Maynard Keynes, *The General Theory of Employment, Interest and Money*, London, Palgrave Macmillan 1936, vii.

Part III, Table 1. *Redundant concepts in European constitutional law*

| | Nature of the concept or theory | Short *legal* definition or explanation | Date of origin | The question which it tries to answer | Advice as to its use in today's European constitutional discourse |
|---|---|---|---|---|---|
| *Staatslehre* | Partly analytical, partly political | The state is a pre-legal entity (the central state administration) which has primacy against the constitution; the constitution does not create it legally, but just limits its pre-legal powers | Second half of 19th century | How to theorise the constitutional law of the constitutional monarchies of the 19th century, which lacked both democracy and a fully fledged judicial review of government acts | It should possibly be avoided, as it has implications which contradict to the primacy of constitutions |
| *Stufenbaulehre* | Primarily analytical | The validity of every norm in the legal order can logically be traced back to a (hypothetical) *Grundnorm* | First half of 20th century | How to explain the validity of the legal order; how to show the possibility of judicial review of statutes to Europeans | The use of the terminology of the *Stufenbaulehre* (especially the expression *Grundnorm*) should be avoided |

| | | | | | |
|---|---|---|---|---|---|
| Principles | Purely analytical | Norms that are logically distinct from rules | Second half of 20th century | How to conceptualise the limitation of fundamental rights | Not to be used in a logically distinct sense, only as 'important norms' |
| Public law | Partly analytical, partly political | The legal system has a special part, called 'public law' which has special features | 16th and17th century (earlier references have only a didactic function) | How to help absolutism and how to get rid of medieval privileges in the interest of economic prosperity at the same time | It should be understood only as a branch of legal scholarship (i.e., as a concept of the sociology of legal scholarship), but not as a special part of law (i.e., not as a concept of *Verfassungsdogmatik*) |

etatistic traditions of one's own country;[2] and using the traditional terminology of *Staatslehre* mostly means in Germany a eurosceptic political affiliation. The use of the terminology of 'principles' often serves amongst non-German scholars to show (off) intellectual superiority and to demonstrate that you know the German doctrine (even though, paradoxically, the Alexian doctrine of principles is actually much less influential in Germany than abroad). So you belong to an 'intellectual elite club', if you are able to use this conceptual framework (even if it is actually unnecessary for any part of your research). Sometimes the same applies to non-German-speaking countries to the uses of *Stufenbaulehre* and *Staatslehre* as well (using German words, often even in the original as I do, seems to be very much in vogue in many European constitutional discourses, sometimes even by those who do not speak German). And the emphasis on the 'public law–private law' divide often serves as a rhetorical emancipation of constitutional lawyers from private lawyers, who tend to see constitutionalists as parvenus (which historically, to be fair, does have some truth in it, and for a long time it was also sadly true concerning conceptual sophistication): 'we are not secondary, we are just different from private lawyers, as we are dealing with public law, which has a different nature from private law'. So, the use of these concepts does have a symbolic force, but I am going to ignore this, because this symbolic force works only within the scholarly community and this is a book about constitutional theory and not about the sociology of constitutional scholars. Symbolic force is only considered in this book if it (potentially) works for the whole political community.

[2] Helmuth Schulze-Fielitz, Konjunkturen der Klassiker-Rezeption in der deutschen Staatsrechtslehre – Vermutungen auch im Blick auf Hans Kelsen, in: Matthias Jestaedt (ed.), *Hans Kelsen und die deutsche Staatsrechtslehre*, Tübingen, Mohr Siebeck 2013, 147–174, especially 170–172.

# 11

# *Staatslehre* as constitutional theory?

> Für den Staatsbegriff der deutschen staatstheoretischen Tradition bleibt es bei der Feststellung, dass er zu stark einer spezifisch deutschen vordemokratischen Tradition verhangen bleibt, um als wissenschaftliche Kategorie taugen zu können.[1]

*Staatslehre* (lit. 'state theory') has always been a very German discipline, with a long-standing tradition since the nineteenth century,[2] even though lately this conceptual framework is losing ground even in Germany; amongst the younger generation it probably has already done so.[3] The fact that we still deal with it in this book is due both to the general preeminence of German scholarship in European constitutional discourse and to the recent dissemination of the conceptual framework of *Staatslehre* in France and the UK.[4]

In the first section of this chapter, I will show how its key concept *Staat* (literally 'state', but meaning rather 'pre-legal state administration') was forged in nineteenth-century Germany. I will analyse the differences, in the political and scholarly context, to other countries in order to explain why in other constitutional discourses this concept never became the dominant one. In the second section, I will weigh the pros and cons about

1 Christoph Möllers, *Staat als Argument*, Tübingen, Mohr ²2011, xlix: 'As to the concept of state of the German tradition of state theory we have to come to the conclusion that it remains too much bound to a specifically German pre-democratic tradition to be used as a scholarly category.'

2 Christoph Schönberger, Der 'Staat' der Allgemeinen Staatslehre: Anmerkungen zu einer eigenwilligen deutschen Disziplin im Vergleich mit Frankreich, in: Olivier Beaud - Erik Volkmar Heyen (eds.), *Eine deutsch-französische Rechtswissenschaft?*, Baden-Baden, Nomos 1999, 111–137, especially 116.

3 For remarks on earlier versions of this chapter, I am grateful to Andreas Anter, Jürgen Bast, Armin von Bogdandy, Isabel Feichtner, Matthias Goldmann, Oliver Lepsius, Christoph Möllers, Stephan Schill, Markus Wagner and to the participants of the *Dienstagsrunde* at the Max Planck Institute for Comparative Public Law and International Law in Heidelberg on 12 February 2013.

4 See, e.g., Olivier Beaud, *La puissance de l'État*, Paris, Presses Universitaires de France 1994; Martin Loughlin, *Foundations of Public Law*, Oxford, Oxford University Press 2010.

the usage of the *Staatslehre* conceptual framework, including its methodology and importance, both from a legal and a non-legal perspective. I will then, in the third section, as a decisive argument against its usage, show the practical application of its key concept *Staat* on the state of emergency and how it can disable any constitutional restraints on political power in these situations. My conclusion in the fourth section will be that *Staatslehre* does *not* offer a conceptual framework which can meaningfully be used in European constitutional discourse as it does not suit modern democracy and constitutionalism.

## 11.1 The key concept of the *Staatslehre* tradition: the *Staat*

If we want to understand the German *Staatslehre* tradition; it is probably best to trace it back to its origins in the nineteenth century, and to analyse the political and scholarly context in which it was forged. We will see to what kind of political and scholarly, and indirectly social, challenges and dilemmas it was supposed to provide a response.

### *11.1.1 The German* Staatslehre *tradition*

The intellectual position of *Staatslehre* in Germany can be explained by a peculiar political and scholarly situation of the end of the nineteenth century. Paul Laband and Carl Friedrich von Gerber, two prominent figures in the history of German legal scholarship, introduced a new legalistic method into public law scholarship in that period:[5] they deliberately excluded from legal analysis all historical, sociological and political considerations.[6] They did so for two reasons.[7] (1) On the one hand, they could become in this way more similar to the conceptually more

[5] Paul Laband, Die *Wandlungen der deutschen Reichsverfassung*, Dresden, Zahn & Jaensch 1895; Paul Laband, Das Budgetrecht nach den Bestimmungen der Preußischen Verfassungsurkunde unter Berücksichtigung der Verfassung des Norddeutschen Bundes, *Zeitschrift für Gesetzgebung und Rechtspflege in Preußen* 4 (1870) 619–707; Paul Laband, *Staatsrechtliche Vorlesungen [ed. Bernd Schlüter]*, Berlin, Duncker & Humblot 2004; Carl Friedrich von Gerber, *Über öffentliche Rechte*, Tübingen, Laupp 1852; Carl Friedrich von Gerber, *Grundzuege eines Systems des deutschen Staatsrechts*, Leipzig, Tauschnitz 1865.

[6] Walter Pauly, *Methodenwandel im deutschen Spätkonstitutionalismus*, Tübingen, Mohr 1993, 177–208.

[7] Bernd Schlüter, *Reichswissenschaft, Staatsrechtslehre, Staatstheorie und Wissenschaftspolitik im Deutschen Kaiserreich am Beispiel der Reichsuniversität Straßburg*, Frankfurt aM, Klostermann 2004.

systematic private law (especially Roman law) scholarship and that fitted better to the scientific ideal of the end of the nineteenth century than the traditional anecdotal, sociological and unsystematic German public law scholarship (e.g., Robert von Mohl, Lorenz von Stein).[8] (2) On the other hand, in this way they could exclude legitimacy questions from the analysis since these were 'politically incorrect' and embarrassing questions, as the German constitutional system (just like most European ones) suffered from a serious democratic deficit at the time.[9] The executive was unelected and basically independent from the legislature, and, both at a federal level and in most of its constituent states, the executive justified its power by stating that it served the public interest. There was also no effective judicial review of statutes, even certain executive acts (especially in the area of foreign and defence policies) were excluded from judicial review. This all resulted in a proceduralistic and legalistic approach in German public law doctrine; the substantive (value) questions all basically remained un-analysed (in the absence of judicial review they were not legally relevant, and because of the political situation it was also politically incorrect for anyone to mention them, at least anyone who harboured the ambition to become an officially recognised public lawyer).

Before German unification in 1871, talking about the state in German public law discourse expressed a wish for national unity. But even after 1871, the most puzzling question remained that of the state, as the German Empire was on the one hand a very complex entity, consisting of city republics, principalities, duchies, grand duchies and kingdoms, and also because full German unity (with Austria) had not been realised.[10] Consequently, the state remained probably the most important key concept of German public law discourse, even after 1871.

The legal conceptual system *(Rechtsdogmatik)* of this state-centred legalistic scholarship was called *Staatsrechtslehre*, whereas *Staatsrecht* was used to describe the actual legal material (constitutions, statutes, and case-law).[11]

[8] Walter Wilhelm, *Zur juristischen Methodenlehre im 19. Jahrhundert. Die Herkunft der Methode Paul Labands aus der Privatrechtswissenschaft*, Frankfurt aM, Klostermann 1958, especially 13–16.

[9] Wilhelm (n. 8) 152–159.

[10] Oliver Lepsius, Rechtswissenschaft in der Demokratie, *Der Staat* 2013, 157–186, 159–160.

[11] Ernst-Wolfgang Böckenförde, Die Eigenart des Staatsrechts und der Staatsrechtswissenschaft, in: *id.*, *Staat, Verfassung, Demokratie*, Frankfurt aM, Suhrkamp 1991, 11–28, especially 23. For an interesting and unusual attempt to separate *Staatslehre* and *Staatsrechtslehre*, approving the former but rejecting the latter, see Oliver

All the substantive, sociological and historical questions which remained un-answered in the *Staatsrechtslehre* were collected under the heading *Allgemeine Staatslehre* (literally, General Theory of State; a discipline which was not new but which reached its peak of popularity due to this situation).[12] This discipline tried to present a complex (legal, sociological, historical) picture of the fundamental concepts of public law scholarship,[13] the most important being the *Staat*,[14] which is not simply the state in English, but rather a 'pre-legal state administration'.[15] This pre-legal state administration has some residual powers by its very nature which cannot be limited by law; as a matter of fact, the pre-legal state administration ensures the existence of the legal order; that is, the state logically comes first. The complex (legal and non-legal) method and the

Lepsius, Funktion und Wandel von Staatsverständnissen, in: Andreas Voßkuhle – Christian Bumke – Florian Meinel (eds.), *Verabschiedung und Wiederentdeckung des Staates im Spannungsfeld der Disziplinen*, Berlin, Duncker & Humblot 2013, 37–58.

12 Schönberger (n. 2) 117 characterising *Allgemeine Staatslehre* as a collection of everything that did not fit into the new Labandian picture of public law scholarship. For similar accounts of the origins of *Staatslehre*, see Carl Schmitt, *Verfassungslehre*, München, Leipzig, Duncker & Humblot 1928, ix; and Martin Morlok, *Was heißt und zu welchem Ende studiert man Verfassungstheorie?*, Berlin, Duncker & Humblot 1988, 24. The expression *Allgemeine Staatslehre* stems from Robert von Mohl, *Geschichte und Literatur der Staatswissenschaften*, vol. 1, Erlangen, Enke 1855, 125–126, but the genre has its origins in the literature of *ius publicum universale* (a philosophical subject taught in Latin at some German law faculties of the eighteenth century). See Hans Boldt, *Deutsche Staatslehre im Vormärz*, Düsseldorf, Droste 1975.

13 David Dyzenhaus, Introduction: Why Carl Schmitt?, in: *id.* (ed.), *Law as Politics: Carl Schmitt's Critique of Liberalism*, Durham, Duke University Press 1998, 1–20. Carl Schmitt misleadingly called his main work *Verfassungslehre* (literally, constitutional theory) (1929), even though his work and his complex method were very much embedded in the *Staatslehre* tradition.

14 On the history of the concept in different European languages, see Werner Conze Hans Boldt – Werner Conze – Görg Haverkate – Diethelm Klippel – Reinhart Koselleck, Staat und Souveränität, in: Otto Brunner – Werner Conze – Reinhart Koselleck (eds.), *Geschichtliche Grundbegriffe*, vol. 6, Stuttgart, Klett-Cotta [1990] 2004, 1–154.

15 Christoph Möllers, Staat, in: Werner Heun – Martin Honecker – Martin Morlok – Joachim Wieland (eds.), *Evangelisches Staatslexikon*, Stuttgart, Kohlhammer, $^{2}$2006, 2272–2283, especially 2278. On the German identification of 'state' and 'central state administration', see Schönberger (n. 2) 124. This type of state is also called *Anstaltsstaat*. See Christoph Schönberger, *Das Parlament im Anstaltsstaat. Zur Theorie der parlamentarischen Repräsentation in der Staatsrechtslehre des Kaiserreichs*, Frankfurt aM, Klostermann 1997, 369 on *inter alia* Kelsen's and Krabbe's criticism on the Jellinekian premise of the state pre-existing the law; and citing further references. For a contemporary proponent, see Udo Di Fabio, *Die Staatsrechtslehre und der Staat*, Paderborn, Ferdinand Schöningh 2003, especially 63–64, 73; for an explicit thesis in this spirit see *ibid.* 35, 'The state administration seems thus to be the substance of the institutions [of the state]' (my translation).

choice of the key concept (the choice of the discipline itself) are not independent from the political environment: a pre-legal state having residual powers can only be conceptualised with partly non-legal arguments. But this discipline is also complex in another sense: it is partly descriptive, partly prescriptive. It 'describes' the political situation (i.e., the pre-eminence of the executive over the legislature) and then takes it as the basis of legal-prescriptive reasoning, making the factual situation into the legal situation. The *Staatslehre* is what we call in this volume the language of this legal discourse using the 'pre-legal state administration' (*Staat*) as its primary key concept.

There were different attempts to redefine the methodological starting points of this discipline. One direction was to turn it into a purely descriptive sociological discipline.[16] The opposing direction was to have a purely legal discipline in which even the state was redefined as the legal order itself (proposed by Austrian authors).[17] But eventually, it seems that, in Germany, the original complex approach survived all attempts of methodological purification of the Weimar period.[18] *Staatslehre* had its own journal, *Der Staat. Zeitschrift für Staatslehre und Verfassungsgeschichte,* founded in 1962 by the third generation of Schmittian disciples;[19] even though lately, the newly elected

[16] Hermann Heller, *Staatslehre* [ed. Gerhart Niemeyer], Leiden, Sijthoff 1934. Another change Heller introduced is to call it just *Staatslehre* and not *Allgemeine Staatslehre*, as he had doubts whether it was possible to have a (geographically) general state theory. His words remained, however, unheard.

[17] Hans Kelsen, *Allgemeine Staatslehre*, Berlin, Springer 1925; Friedrich Koja, *Allgemeine Staatslehre*, Wien, Manz 1993; Friedrich Koja, Der Begriff der *Allgemeinen Staatslehre*, in: Bernd-Christian Funk (ed.), *Staatsrecht und Staatswissenschaft in Zeiten des Wandels. Festschrift für Ludwig Adamovich*, Wien, Springer 1992, 244–252. On this Austrian school, see also Ewald Wiederin, Denken vom Recht her. Über den modus austriacus in der Staatsrechtslehre, in: Helmuth Schulze-Fielitz (ed.), *Staatsrechtslehre als Wissenschaft*, Berlin, Duncker & Humblot 2007, 293–318.

[18] From the latest literature, see Thomas Fleiner – Lidija R Basta Fleiner, *Allgemeine Staatslehre*, Berlin, Springer $^{3}$2004; Reinhold Zippelius, *Allgemeine Staatslehre*, München, Beck $^{15}$2007; Burkhard Schöbener, *Allgemeine Staatslehre*, München, Beck 2009. Some authors write *Staatslehre* under the heading [*Neue*] *Staatswissenschaft*; see Andreas Voßkuhle, Die Renaissance der 'Allgemeinen Staatslehre' im Zeitalter der Europäisierung und Internationalisierung, *Juristische Schulung* 2004, 1–7, especially 7 on Gunnar Folke Schuppert, *Staatswissenschaft*, Baden-Baden, Nomos 2003. The complex German approach even conquered Austria; see the latest textbook Anna Gamper, *Staat und Verfassung*, Wien, Facultas $^{3}$2014. On the inability of methodological innovation in *Staatslehre*, see Michel Troper, Sur la théorie juridique de l'État, in: *id. Pour une théorie juridique de l'État*, Presses Universitaires de France 1994, 5–22, 6, n. 4.

[19] Christoph Möllers, *Der vermisste Leviathan*, Frankfurt aM, Suhrkamp 2008, 110.

(relatively young) editors paradoxically represent a new generation of pro-European and fundamental-rights-centred constitutional lawyers and explicitly oppose the *Staat* tradition.[20] The largest work in German constitutional law ever, the *Handbuch des Staatsrechts* is also oriented towards this conceptual framework; as a matter of fact its very title indicates its programme (reinforcing the concept of *Staat* in German constitutional doctrine).[21] The recent counter-project, the *Ius Publicum Europaeum,* already expressing in its title the new research programme, started only a couple of years ago, but it is most likely to overshadow the *Handbuch des Staatsrechts* in the near future.[22] Thus the *Staat* tradition seems to fade in constitutional discourse.

### *11.1.2* Staatslehre *and the concept of state in other countries*

The term 'state' seldom appears in any reasoning used in Austrian constitutional law,[23] nor does 'statehood'.[24] Even in the context of the extent of European integration, one speaks of an 'integration-proof constitutional core' instead of an old-school German-type 'preservation of statehood'. Equally seldom does one come across the notion of the *Willensbildung* of the state, or the state's intent. At most, discussion about 'legislative intent' can be found.

[20] Esp. Armin von Bogdandy, Christoph Möllers, Oliver Lepsius.

[21] Hasso Hofmann, Von der Staatssoziologie zur Soziologie der Verfassung *JuristenZeitung* 1999, 1065–1074, especially 1066 on Josef Isensee – Paul Kirchhof (eds.), *Handbuch des Staatsrechts der Bundesrepublik Deutschland.* vols. I–X, Heidelberg, CF Müller 1987–2001 (since then in several new editions). For similar views, see Helmuth Schulze-Fielitz, Grundsatzkontroversen in der deutschen Staatsrechtslehre, *Die Verwaltung* 1999, 241–282, especially 248; and Peter Häberle, Ein 'Zwischenruf' zum Diskussionsstand in der deutschen Staatsrechtslehre, in: Theo Stammen – Heinrich Oberreuter – Paul Mikat (eds.), *Politik – Bildung – Religion. Festschrift Hans Maier*, Padeborn, Schöningh 1996, 327–339, especially 331–332.

[22] Armin von Bogdandy – Peter M Huber (eds.), *Ius Publicum Europaeum*, vols. I–VII, Heidelberg, CF Müller 2007–2015. For more details on the project, see Armin von Bogdandy – Stephan Hinghofer-Szalkay, Das etwas unheimliche Ius Publicum Europaeum, *Zeitschrift für ausländisches öffentliches Recht und Völkerrecht* 2013, 209–248, 216–220.

[23] There are occasional exceptions, especially in more recent literature. See, e.g., Walter Berka, *Die Grundrechte*, Wien, Springer 1999, para 186–187 framing the state as bearer of the duties flowing from fundamental rights.

[24] In the treatise by Ludwig K Adamovich – Bernd-Christian Funk – Gerhart Holzinger, *Österreichisches Staatsrecht*, vol. 1, Wien, Springer 1997, not a single passage deals with the 'state', although its title, *Österreichisches Staatsrecht* (Austrian state law), might lead one to expect otherwise.

Explaining these differences turns attention initially to Hans Kelsen. In his normativistic theory of the state, the state as such becomes the legal order, which is to say that, in law, it only makes sense to speak of the constitution. The German literature makes frequent use of the idea of a pre-legal state, an institutionalised authority distinct from the people and with its own decision-making capacity.[25] Such a conceptualisation, however, is foreign to the Austrian literature. There, the state as a personification of the legal order cannot form intent in order to make decisions; at most, state institutions (e.g., the legislature) might be thus personified. This disembodiment of a sociological concept of the state may be a result of the experience with the political reality of the Austro-Hungarian monarchy. As a highly multiethnic state, it had a constitution (and an army which held the state together in crisis situations) but obviously lacked other integrative factors, such as a common culture, language and civic solidarity.[26]

Traditional Austrian doctrine has, however, to face a difficulty: the word 'state' does appear in the wording of statutes with a sense that cannot be understood as 'legal order'. To manage this difficulty, Adolf Merkl, one of Kelsen's disciples, developed the theory of a threefold definition of the state, according to which 'state' can mean: (1) the sum of institutions (whether public or private) serving to implement the legal order (thus comprising not only law-making, adjudicative and administrative agencies, but also private parties to a commercial or employment contract); (2) a narrower concept: that part of the first definition which is typically characterised by *enforcement institutions* authorised to issue mandatory instructions (that is, mostly executive bodies or organs); or (3) an institutional complex, functionally maintained by centralised funds from legally regulated sources of revenue (that is, central administrative agencies excluding any autonomously administered institutions like local authorities).[27] The three definitions form concentric circles, with the first as the widest circle and the third as the narrowest. Obviously, none of the three definitions corresponds to the German concept of the state, which approximates most closely to the Austrian term 'republic', itself a legal term contained in the Constitution.[28]

[25] On the different perceptions of sovereignty (and of the bearer of sovereignty) in European countries see above 6.1.

[26] Rudolf Aladár Métall, *Hans Kelsen: Leben und Werk*, Wien, Deuticke 1969, 22.

[27] Adolf Merkl, *Allgemeines Verwaltungsrecht*, Berlin, Springer 1927, 291–294; Koja (n. 17) 24–29.

[28] E.g., Art. 6(1) and Art. 8(1) of the Austrian Constitution. For the sake of convenience, the primary constitutional document in Austria, the *Bundes-Verfassungsgesetz* (abbreviated

Thus traditional Austrian doctrine does know the term *Staat*, but it does not mean the 'pre-legal state administration'. And traditional Austrian *Staatslehre* has also fully redefined its own object, dealing only with positive law and the theory thereof, that is, stripping it off from its most important original feature.

You cannot find the German type of *Staatslehre* in France either. The reasons for this are manifold. First of all, *Staatslehre* seemed (as indeed it was) terribly German, which by definition made it eminently rejectable by their arch-enemy, the French.[29] Secondly, French public law scholarship never experienced such a methodological purification as Laband and Gerber did to German public law scholarship, so constitutional lawyers did not feel the urge to express their sociological and historical thoughts outside of their own discipline.[30] Moreover, sociology and political science appeared relatively early (earlier than in Germany); thus specialised 'professionals' (some of them originally lawyers who changed profession and founded the new disciplines) took over the topics before constitutional lawyers of the establishment could acquire a taste for it.[31] And finally, in France statehood was an important topic in legal scholarship (during and after the First World War sometimes even as a pre-legal state, similar to the German concept of *Staat*),[32] but it was never a primary issue of public debates.[33] In Germany, however, 'statehood' as such was a hot topic of public debates, precisely because for a long time (until 1871) Germans did not have the institutional framework of statehood they wished for; and then after the Second World War because

'B-VG'), is referred to as the Austrian Constitution, although strictly speaking the constitution comprises numerous texts and statutes.

29 Olivier Jouanjan, Braucht das Verfassungsrecht eine Staatslehre? Eine französische Perspektive, *Europäische Grundrechte-Zeitschrift* 31 (2004) 362–370, especially 363–365. The only major work in French in the *Staatslehre* tradition was Raymond Carré de Malberg, *Contribution à la théorie générale de l'État*, vols. 1–2, Paris, Sirey 1920–1922, written by a French professor in Strasbourg who was oriented very much towards the German literature. Nobody in France continued the genre in this form.

30 Schönberger (n. 2) 126–127. On the use of sociological arguments in French constitutional scholarship, see Oliver Lepsius, L'influence du droit public français sur la doctrine juridique allemande de la République Fédérale, *Revue d'histoire des facultés de droit et de la science juridique* 24 (2004) 205–227, 216.

31 Schönberger (n. 2) 126–127.

32 David Bates, Political Unity and the Spirit of the Law: Juridical Concepts of the State in the Late Third Republic, *French Historical Studies* 28 (2005) 69–101; HS Jones, *The French State in Question: Public Law and Political Argument in the Third Republic*, Cambridge, Cambridge University Press 1993, 29–54 and 149–204 with further references.

33 Schönberger (n. 2) 123.

there were two German states, but according to the official West German position only one nation and also because continuity with the *Reich* was widely discussed.[34]

In the UK the 'state' is not a key concept in constitutional scholarship,[35] the somewhat similar concept of the Crown[36] is much more personified than the state,[37] and no 'sovereignty' is bound to it (as sovereignty lies in the British tradition not with the 'state', but with the 'Crown-in-Parliament', see above 6.1). In German, one tends to append '*staat*' to many constitutional concepts, which more or less equate to English words lacking the component 'state': *Rechtsstaat* ('rule of law'), *Verfassungsstaat* ('constitionalism'), *Sozialstaat* ('social justice'), *Bundesstaat* ('federation' or 'federalism').[38] In Britain, the state was rarely seen as the bearer of national identity (even though as an institution it was stronger than its continental counterparts, it was also less activist in domestic matters); its role in public debate was much smaller than in Germany or in France; and constitutional lawyers tended to neglect the concept.[39]

There have been (and there are) in most European countries, however, attempts to import the German *Staatslehre*.[40] But in none of these

[34] Möllers (n. 1) 136–149.

[35] Nevil Johnson, Law as the articulation of the state in Western Germany: A German Tradition from a British Perspective, *West European Politics* 1 (1978) 177–192, especially 179; Dieter Grimm, Der Staat in der kontinentaleuropäischen Tradition, in: *id.*, *Recht und Staat der bürgerlichen Gesellschaft*, Frankfurt aM, Suhrkamp 1987, 54–81, especially 61–62. For a comprehensive analysis of the occurrences of the concept of state in British legal thought, see Janet McLean, *Searching for the State in British Legal Thought*, Cambridge, Cambridge University Press 2012.

[36] Florian Becker, Staat und Krone im Vereinigten Königreich, in Otto Depenheuer – Markus Heintzen – Matthias Jestaedt – Peter Axer (eds.), *Staat um Wort. Festschrift für Josef Isensee*, Heidelberg, CF Müller 2007, 471–488, especially 484 on reminiscent monarchical powers as the key function of the concept of 'Crown'. On the similarity of the two concepts, see also Martin Loughlin, The State, the Crown and the Law, in: Maurice Sunkin – Sebastian Payne (eds.), *The Nature of the Crown*, Oxford, Oxford University Press 1999, 33–76.

[37] Jones (n. 32) 9.

[38] Brun-Otto Bryde, Konstitutionalisierung des Völkerrechts und Internationalisierung des Verfassungsrechts, *Der Staat* 42 (2003) 61–75, especially 62–63 suggests getting rid of the German expressions containing 'staat'.

[39] Jones (n. 32) 15; José Harris, Society and the State in Twentieth-Century Britain, in: FML Thompson (ed.), *The Cambridge Social History of Britain 1750–1950*, vol. 3, Cambridge, Cambridge University Press 1990, 63–118, 67–68.

[40] See above n. 4, further Andrés de Blas Guerrero (ed.), *Teoria del Estado*, Madrid, UNED 2010; Péter Takács, *Allamtan*, Budapest, Corvinus 2011; Christian Behrendt – Frédéric Bouhon, *Introduction à la théorie générale de l'État*, Bruxelles, Larcier ²2011. Martin Loughlin (UK) sometimes uses the expression 'public law' in the sense of *Staatslehre*; see Martin Loughlin, *The Idea of Public Law*, Oxford, Oxford University Press 2004, 157 on the complex (not only juridic nature) of the questions of 'public law'. Cf. *ibid.* 155 on

countries has it become the dominant conceptual framework. Despite of its usual name (*Allgemeine Staatslehre* or General Theory of State) it is geographically not general at all, even though there were different more or less successful export attempts; it remains a specifically German (but even within Germany, a weakening and fading) way of approaching problems of constitutional law.[41]

## 11.2 Arguments about the usefulness of *Staatslehre* today

After having seen what *Staatslehre* is in Germany and elsewhere, let us turn to the topic of whether *Staatslehre* (i.e., a constitutional theory using a 'pre-legal administrative state' as its primary key concept) is a conceptual framework which one should use in European constitutional discourse.

### *11.2.1 An object-defined discipline with a complex method*

The first possible argument that comes up when discussing the usefulness of *Staatslehre* is its complex method: it analyses the state from legal, sociological and so on perspectives. It is not a legal discipline; neither is it a social science, but instead a mixture of these. It is not its method, but rather its object (i.e., the state) which defines this discipline. One could question whether it is acceptable at all to have such disciplines. This is, however, not a convincing way to criticise this discipline as there are many others nowadays (e.g., regional, cultural, nationalism studies) which all are object-defined and which work with a complex method.[42]

One could argue that the fact that the methodological debates and doubts of Weimar survived means that the methodological issues cannot be resolved.[43] This rightly arouses some suspicion, but the mere fact of an endless, ongoing debate (repeating the same arguments) on its own is not enough to dismiss a question. A debate lasting several generations about the right answer is likely to be the symptom of a

'public law' including the description of political practices (his approach fits better to the UK, which lacks a formal constitution, than to Germany, by the way).

41 Schönberger (n. 2) 127. 42 Möllers (n. 15) 2321.

43 Oliver Lepsius, Braucht das Verfassungsrecht eine Theorie des Staates? *Europäische Grundrechte-Zeitschrift* 31 (2004) 370–381, especially 375.

wrongly asked question, but this is definitely not the reason itself why a question is bad.

And finally, one could object to *Staatslehre* that it necessarily implies some kind of metaphysical essentialism,[44] as it implies that there is such a thing as a state which can be observed from different angles with different methods. The truth is, so the argument goes, that when lawyers talk about the state they mean something different from political scientists, and when economists talk about the state they use yet another concept. Different disciplines are different languages, and to mix up the methods would be just as meaningless as putting words from random languages after each other in the same sentence. This is a powerful objection, as in fact many writers on *Staatslehre* commit this mistake when they do 'multidisciplinary' analysis (see below *11.2.2 Staatslehre as methodologically uncontrolled social science by lawyers*). Nevertheless, the objection is not decisive as multidisciplinary research *is* possible, if we carefully define which discipline can do what and if we are very careful when importing the results from one discipline into another. In order to realise meaningful interdisciplinary research, we have to conform with the internal discourse rules and proof requirements of the affected disciplines, or to reject them explicitly if we provide sufficient reasons to do so; and most importantly, we should not mix up concepts from different disciplines randomly, as is sadly often done under the pretext of interdisciplinarity.

This is, therefore, not a conclusive argument about the usefulness of *Staatslehre*.

### *11.2.2* Staatslehre *as methodologically uncontrolled social science by lawyers*

Another usual objection is that *Staatslehre* is in fact just a discipline created by lawyers for their own fun to discuss questions of political science and sociology, without the rigorous methodological control of real social scientists (armchair sociology and anecdotal political science).[45] *Staatslehre* as a university subject, so the argument goes, serves only as an introduction to social sciences for law students,[46]

[44] Cf. Harry Eckstein, On the 'Science' of State, *Daedalus* 1979/4, 1–20, especially 15 criticising the German *Staatslehre* tradition as methodologically flawed from a political science perspective and referring to it as 'hazy Germanic metaphysics'.

[45] Lepsius (n. 43) 376; Möllers (n. 19) 54; Karsten Plog, *Die Krise der Allgemeinen Staatslehre in der Wissenschaftsgeschichte der Politik*, München, Schön 1969, 156.

[46] Möllers (n. 15) 2320

which could probably be done better by properly trained social scientists. Precisely because of the lack of social science methodological rigour, none of the results of *Staatslehre* are accepted by (rather: not even known to) social scientists, and consequently it does not serve any real interdisciplinary dialogue.[47] Rather the opposite: it contributes to the disciplinary isolation of legal scholarship, because we can pretend to be interdisciplinary without actually saying anything which could be useful for non-lawyers. Instead of interdisciplinarity (or multidisciplinarity), we sadly often face universal-dilettantism.[48] The main genre of *Staatslehre* is the university textbook, which is a mostly repetitive compilation of social science results and key concepts of constitutional law.[49]

These are all valid objections, since the current literature of *Staatslehre* does suffer from all these problems. But this does not mean that *Staatslehre* as such should be dismissed; rather, it only means that well-trained social scientists should do it (they might or they might not have a law degree). Therefore, this too is not a conclusive argument about the usefulness of *Staatslehre*.

### *11.2.3 Confusion about the key concept: the* Staat

The next possible objection against *Staatslehre* could be that its key concept is unclear, or different in different disciplines at the best.[50] Even proponents of *Staatslehre* recognise this difficulty, but they consider it as a proof of the complicated nature of the question.[51] The lack of clarity of the concept of the state has even led some commentators – maybe just to anger the traditionalist *Staatslehre* authors, who are mostly eurosceptics to assert – that even the EU is now a state.[52] As mentioned above, however, the mere fact that a question remains debated for a long time, is not clear evidence of an implied mistake in the question; even in

[47] Lepsius (n. 43) 376. [48] I am grateful to Ewald Wiederin for this expression.

[49] For a similar view see Schönberger (n. 2) 117.

[50] Cf. Peter Badura, *Methoden der neueren Allgemeinen Staatslehre*, Goldbach, Keip $^{2}$1998, 99.

[51] Josef Isensee – Paul Mikat – Martin Honecker – Ernst Chr Suttner, Staat, in: Görres-Gesellschaft (ed.), *Staatslexikon*, vol. 5, Freiburg, Herder $^{7}$1989, 133–170, especially 134. Cf. Paul Kirchhof, Die Identität der Verfassung, in: Josef Isensee – Paul Kirchhof (eds.), *Handbuch des Staatsrechts der Bundesrepublik Deutschland. vol. II: Verfassungsstaat*, Heidelberg CF Müller $^{3}$2004, 261–316, especially 277 on the concept of state, which is both a source of law and, partly, also a creation of law.

[52] Cf. Rainer Wahl, Erklären staatstheoretische Leitbegriffe die Europäische Union?, *JuristenZeitung* 2005, 916–925, 920.

nationalism studies, the concept of nation is likewise endlessly debated (and most authors of that discipline find this natural).

One specific state definition should be mentioned here because of its prestige and popularity. Georg Jellinek defined 'state' as having three conceptual elements: state power, people and territory.[53] An objection can, however, be raised against this definition, as listing the three conceptual elements after each other is like putting apples and oranges into the same line. It does not clarify the relationship between the conceptual elements, that is, that it is about power and then power's personal and territorial scope.[54] It is a valid objection, but the Jellinekian definition can be reformulated to avoid this objection: we can say that 'state' should be defined as physical (political) power over a territory and over a population.

This is, as Badura rightly noted, however, actually a sociological definition: it defines 'state' as the factual situation of actual power.[55] And then, from the fact of a (sociological) state it infers the legal personality of the state,[56] and this pre-legal state can then be bound by legal measures (constitutions or international treaties).[57] Here is the trick. If it is not the constitution which defines 'state' in this way and gives it a legal relevance (and constitutions do not contain the Jellinekian definition), then it is the scholar who does so, and if the scholar does so then he or she should clarify (justify) where this definition comes from. This clarification is, however, normally missing. What we find is a short reference to Jellinek (or to any other defunct scholar),[58] or a reference to public international law.[59]

[53] Georg Jellinek, *Allgemeine Staatslehre*, Berlin, Häring $^{3}$1914, 180–181. See also BVerfGE 123, 267 (Lisbon Treaty), 340–349 with an explicit reference to Jellinek. For scholarly literature in this spirit with further references, see Josef Isensee, Staat und Verfassung, in: Isensee – Kirchhof (n. 51) 3–106, 34–37.

[54] Möllers (n. 15) 2274.

[55] Badura (n. 50) 208–209. For a different interpretation of Jellinek, see Möllers (n. 1) 34.

[56] On the normative force of facts, see Jellinek (n. 53) 338–342. On Kelsen's criticism on this type of reasoning see above 6.1. Following from the factual situation to the legal one had the 'advantage' that legitimacy questions could simply be avoided; see Möllers (n. 1) 21.

[57] According to Jellinek, any limitation of states can only be a self-limitation (theory of auto-limitation or *Selbstverpflichtungslehre*); see Georg Jellinek, *Die rechtliche Natur der Staatenverträge*, Wien, Hoelder 1880. The question is, of course, whether such self-limitation can be undone by the state itself, and if yes whether it still qualifies as a proper legal obligation; see Hans Kelsen, *Das Problem der Souveränität und die Theorie des Völkerrechts*, Tübingen, Mohr $^{2}$1928, 168–174.

[58] On the influence of Jellinek on today's German constitutional discourse, see Jens Kersten, *Georg Jellinek und die klassische Staatslehre*, Tübingen, Mohr 2000, 1–2.

[59] Karl Doehring, Allgemeine Staatslehre aus der Sicht des Völkerrechts, in: Herbert Haller e.a. (eds.), *Festschrift für Günther Winkler. Staat und Recht*, Wien, Springer 1997, 179–192.

The latter reference poses an interesting problem. In public international law, we have a definition of the 'state', and it is the Jellinekian definition (sometimes called the Montevideo test of statehood, which, however, adds one more element concerning the capacity to enter into relations with the other states).[60] One could even say, to define 'state' in constitutional law in the Jellinekian manner is just the consequence of the principle which says that domestic law should be interpreted in conformity with international law. This very last argument would, however, be mistaken. International law does not require domestic legal orders to accept legal concepts, but only to make changes concerning its legal consequences in domestic law.[61] I have not seen any analysis which would have shown that the presupposition of a pre-legal state in domestic constitutional reasoning has legal consequences required by international law which can only be reached through this presupposition. Consequently, from the mere definition of state in international law the definition of 'state' in domestic law does not follow.

So what remains is the necessity of a justification of the (Jellinekian) pre-legal state definition. In the following, we are going to show possible justifications for the use of this *Staat* concept.

### *11.2.4 Sociological importance or unimportance of the state in the age of globalisation*

A common justification on both sides of the argument concerns the (political or sociological) importance of the institution of state nowadays. Some assert that the role of the state is declining, especially because of globalisation and in Europe because of the EU; consequently, the traditional state-centred concepts of *Staatslehre* are no longer able to explain what is happening.[62] Others, however, assert that the state is still an

[60] Art. 1 of the Montevideo Convention on Rights and Duties of States (26 December 1933, (165) LNTS 19): 'The state as a person of international law should possess the following qualifications: *a)* a permanent population; *b)* a defined territory; *c)* government; and *d)* capacity to enter into relations with the other states.' The listed criteria of statehood are, however, not seen as a fully exhaustive list; see James R Crawford, State, in: Rüdiger Wolfrum (ed.): *Max Planck Encyclopedia of Public International Law*, Oxford, Oxford University Press 2011 [electronically available at http://www.mpepil.com/].

[61] On interpretation of domestic constitutions in light of international law in general see above 3.2.1.

[62] Wahl (n. 52); Jo Eric Khushal Murkens, The Future of Staatsrecht: Dominance, Demise or Demystification?, *Modern Law Review* 2007, 731–758, especially 758.

important actor in political life, and consequently the state-centred terminology still applies.[63] Yet others view the diminishing institutional force of the state caused by European integration as a series of new questions, which could actually be answered by *Staatslehre.*[64]

Besides the fact that there is an ongoing debate about the concept of the state (so we cannot be entirely sure how to measure whether or not its role is diminishing),[65] the main problem is with both sides of the argument, that their relevance is unclear for our question. It is a debatable issue whether or not and then to what extent the influence of the state (on what?) is declining. But it is unclear how exactly we can make a legal argument from it. The use of a legal argument and the institutional importance are two issues.[66] The explanation of how these two issues connect is missing from the above-mentioned assertions.

This type of argument is therefore inconclusive about the usefulness of *Staatslehre.*

### 11.2.5 *Legal relevance or irrelevance*

One could refer to constitutional texts in which the word 'state' is mentioned in order to justify a *Staatslehre:* if the word is mentioned in a constitution, then it has to be defined; thus we need a *Staatslehre* which can deliver the definition – so the argument goes.[67] This is, however, quite a weak argument. There are many customary words in constitutions, but we do not have specific scholarly disciplines for (most of) them, and/or we do not treat all these concepts as key concepts. So we would need something else to justify the existence of *Staatslehre* and the use of *Staat* as a key concept.

One could object to *Staatslehre* as being legally irrelevant, as it is mostly just a potpourri of sociological and historical information about the state.[68] This is definitely true for a large part of *Staatslehre* literature,

[63] Martin Loughlin, In Defence of Staatslehre, *Der Staat* 48 (2009) 1–28. On the importance of the state in general, see the classic work Peter B Evans – Dietrich Rueschemeyer – Theda Skocpol (eds.), *Bringing the State Back In*, Cambridge, Cambridge University Press 1985. For a more nuanced general (historical) view see Martin von Creveld, *Aufstieg und Untergang des Staates*, München, Gerling 1999.

[64] Voßkuhle (n. 18) 6–7. [65] Voßkuhle (n. 18) 3. [66] Möllers (n. 1) xiii–xiv.

[67] Christoph Gusy, Brauchen wir eine juristische Staatslehre? *Jahrbuch des öffentlichen Rechts der Gegenwart* 55 (2007) 41–71, especially 48–51. Gusy uses further arguments to support his point (especially the logical primacy, but in a very tamed version), which we reject elsewhere in this chapter.

[68] Against some parts of Jellinek's work with such arguments Möllers (n. 1) 35.

but not always: the pre-legal state can be used as a doctrinal concept (a concept of *Verfassungsdogmatik*) in constitutional reasoning; it can have legal consequences. In the following, we are going to try to discern such legal consequences.

#### 11.2.5.1 *Staatslehre* as a conceptualisation of the separation of state and society

We could argue that the separation of state and society is necessary in constitutional reasoning, as it is the precondition of individual liberty (i.e., the state should keep out of the sphere of society).[69] This doctrinal reasoning uses the concept of the state; *ergo* the concept of state has to be central in the constitutional doctrine of a liberal democracy – so the argument goes. Sometimes the separation of state and society is connected to the separation of public law ('law of state') and private law ('law of society'), to which problem we are going to return in Chapter 14 (14.3).[70]

This approach would, however, be mistaken. There are constitutional doctrines which work without the concept of the state (let alone pre-legal state), and which can ensure a high level of fundamental rights protection, most notably in the United States.[71] Moreover, the separation of state and society implies that the state has its own standing against society, which was a correct characterisation of Bismarck's government, but which is not (and should not) be a feature of a democratic state.[72]

[69] Ernst-Wolfgang Böckenförde, *Die verfassungstheoretische Unterscheidung von Staat und Gesellschaft als Bedingung der individuellen Freiheit*, Opladen, Westdeutscher Verlag 1973. For an opposing view, showing the necessary political connection between 'state' and 'society' in order to protect freedoms (i.e., the 'state' should not become independent of 'society', as it might step up against the society then), see Christian Graf von Krockow, Staat, Gesellschaft, Freiheitsbewahrung, in: Ernst-Wolfgang Böckenförde (ed.), *Staat und Gesellschaft*, Darmstadt, Wissenschaftliche Buchgesellschaft 1976, 432–483.

[70] Horst Ehmke, Staat und Gesellschaft als verfassungstheoretisches Problem, in: Konrad Hesse – Siegfried Reicke – Ulrich Scheuner (eds.), *Festgabe für Rudolf Smend*, Tübingen, Mohr 1962, 23–49.

[71] The French republican tradition does not know a separation of 'state' and 'society' either; see Olivier Jouanjan, Synthese, in: Constance Grewe – Christoph Gusy (eds.), *Französisches Staatsdenken*, Baden-Baden, Nomos 2002, 242–252, 252 n. 27. But considering the serious lacunae of French constitutional review before 2008, the example of the United States seems more convincing here to prove that a high level of fundamental rights protection is possible without this German dichotomy.

[72] Otto Hintze, Das monarchische Prinzip und die konstitutionelle Verfassung (1911), in: *id.*, *Staat und Verfassung. Gesammelte Abhandlungen*, vol. 1, Göttingen, Vandenhoeck & Ruprecht $^{2}$1962, 359–389, 365–366. The separation also implies the *Impermeablitätstheorie*, i.e., a doctrine according to which internal acts of the state administration cannot be subject to judicial review. For more details about this, see below 12.3.2.

The separation of state and society is therefore not a necessary element of modern constitutional doctrine. Consequently, we cannot gain any argument from this as to whether we should use the concept of (pre-legal) state as a key concept in constitutional reasoning.

#### 11.2.5.2 Primacy of the state against the constitution

The primary way in which authors of *Staatslehre* justify why the state (as a pre-legal institution) is used as a key constitutional concept refers to its logical primacy against the constitution:[73]

> The state comes before the Constitution. The priority is ontological, (with reservation) legal and mostly also historical... The Constitution does not create the state, it only develops the state in more detail. The Constitution grows from it. A new Constitution is not *creatio ex nihilo*, but it is attached to already existing statal structures.

It is true that in most European countries the state existed historically well before the first constitution was adopted. But the assertion goes further: it concerns 'logical primacy', that is, that the state is a logical precondition of a constitution.[74] And then it draws arguments from logical primacy to weaken the legal force of the constitution. The concrete legal consequence could be that constitutions can be revoked by the state (as the constitution is also just an act of the pre-existing state),[75] or that the constitutional court cannot review all state acts,[76] or that during the state of emergency the government can override the constitution in the interest of the state *(salus rei publicae suprema lex esto).*[77] We are going to analyse the last issue in more detail below (*11.3 'Pre-legal state' vs. 'constitution' as a key concept: the example of the state of emergency*).

There are several problems with this reasoning: (1) it introduces (invents) an etatistic supra-constitution, which can then be used against the actual constitution.[78] It remains unclear where the legal nature of this

[73] Isensee (n. 51) 150–151. Similar views: Beaud (n. 4) 208; Ernst-Wolfgang Böckenförde, Begriff und Probleme des Verfassungsstaates, in: *id.*, *Staat, Nation, Europa*, Frankfurt aM, Suhrkamp 1999, 127–140, 136.

[74] Herbert Krüger, Verfassungsvoraussetzungen und Verfassungserwartungen, in: Horst Ehmke (ed.), *Festschrift für Ulrich Scheuner zum 70. Geburtstag*, Berlin, Duncker & Humblot 1973, 285–306, especially 293–297; Isensee (n. 53) 4, 24, 102. For an early argument, see Phillip Karl Ludwig Zorn, *Das Staatsrecht des Deutschen Reiches*, vol. 1, Berlin, Guttentag 1880, 26.

[75] Paul Laband, *Das Staatsrecht des Deutschen Reiches*, vol. II, Tübingen, Mohr $^{5}$1911, 39–40.

[76] Hans H Klein, *Bundesverfassungsgericht und Staatsraison*, Frankfurt aM, Metzner 1968.

[77] Martin Loughlin, *The Idea of Public Law*, Oxford, Oxford University Press 2004, 154.

[78] Möllers (n. 15) 2280.

supra-constitution comes from. (2) In a constitutional state, only as much state is possible as the constitution constitutes (see above 8.1).[79] This approach rejects this basic assumption of constitutionalism. (3) There is a logical mistake (or a missing step) in the reasoning: somehow, suddenly and miraculously, the empirical-historical primacy of states becomes a conceptual-logical primacy.[80] We can, of course, argue that an effective state organisation is the precondition for the healthy running of a legal order and consequently also of the effectiveness of a constitution. In addition to this, there are, nevertheless, several other (social, political) preconditions in a state to have a constitution.[81]

As this seems to be a decisive blow for *Staatslehre*, we should look into more detail on what the concrete legal consequences of this argument are.

## 11.3 'Pre-legal state' vs. 'constitution' as a key concept: the example of the state of emergency

After the former, rather abstract conceptual explanations we should see the probably most illustrative example about the consequences of the use of the concept of a pre-legal state in constitutional reasoning: the conceptualisation of the state of emergency.[82] We are going to analyse two types of conceptualisation: (1) state-centred theories and (2) constitution-centred theories.

### *11.3.1 State-centred theories*

Supporters of state-centred theories presume that the state has a pre-legal right, or non-positive right of natural law, to act for its own

[79] Peter Häberle, *Verfassungslehre als Kulturwissenschaft*, Berlin, Duncker & Humblot $^{2}$1998, 620.

[80] Anne Peters, *Elemente einer Theorie der Verfassung Europas*, Berlin, Duncker & Humblot 2001, 101.

[81] Thomas Kleinlein, *Konstitutionalisierung im Völkerrecht*, Heidelberg, Springer 2012, 141–142 with further references. On the topic in general, see the volume Ute Sacksofsky e.a., Erosion von Verfassungsvoraussetzungen, *Veröffentlichungen der Vereinigung der deutschen Staatsrechtslehrer* 68 (2008).

[82] We could also use other examples to show the difference between the 'pre-legal state' *(Staatslehre)* tradition and the constitutionalist tradition like their approach to European integration, see above 6.1 and Murkens (n. 62). For an excellent comprehensive analysis of the uses of 'pre-legal state' arguments in German constitutional law, see Möllers (n. 1). For further references on the German debates on the state of emergency after the Second World War, see Michael Stolleis, *Geschichte des öffentlichen Rechts in Deutschland*, vol. IV, München, Beck 2012, 308, 457, 568.

preservation.[83] In contrast to the classical version, a moderated version sees this power as subject(able) to positive law.

#### 11.3.1.1 Classical state-centrism

Tracing back to pre-constitutional times, the best-known contemporary proponent of classical state-centrism in a state of emergency is Klaus Stern. According to him, the state always has an unwritten, supra-positive right of necessity, which positive law cannot limit.[84] Similar approaches are advanced by Herbert Krüger, Hans Nawiasky, Carl Schmitt, Paul Kirchhof and Ulrich Scheuner.[85]

The argumentation of these jurists is that *normativity presumes normality* of circumstances.[86] This implies 'that norms only apply in normal situations and that the presumption of situational normality is a positive-law precondition of their applicability'.[87] Thus, norms cannot bind the

[83] Friedrich Koja would trace these concepts back to the Hegelian idea of the state as preeminent institution. See Friedrich Koja, *Der Staatsnotstand als Rechtsbegriff*, Salzburg, Pustet 1979, 12. Koja is partially correct, although one must also bear in mind that these ideas predate even Hegel. See Ernst Rudolf Huber, *Deutsche Verfassungsgeschichte*, vol. 1, Stuttgart, Kohlhammer 1960, 654.

[84] See Klaus Stern, Das Staatsrecht der Bundesrepublik Deutschland, Vol. 2: Staatsorgane, Staatsfunktionen, Finanz- und Haushaltsverfassungen, Notstandsverfassung, München, Beck 1980, 1337.

[85] See Carl Schmitt, *Die Diktatur: Von den Anfängen des modernen Souveränitätsgedankens bis zum proletarischen Klassenkampf*, München, Duncker & Humblot 1921, ix. Cf. Stern (n. 84) 1337 (rejecting Schmitt in formulation, but not in essence). See also Meinhard Schröder, *Staatsrecht an den Grenzen des Rechtsstaates, Archiv des öffentlichen Rechts* 103 (1978) 121–148, 134; Georg Flor, Staatsnotstand und rechtliche Bindung, *Deutsches Verwaltungsblatt* 73 (1958) 149–152; Paul Kirchhof, Die Zulässigkeit des Einsatzes staatlicher Gewalt in Ausnahmesituationen, in: William Birtles e.a., *Die Zulässigkeit des Einsatzes staatlicher Gewalt in Ausnahmesituationen*, Karlsruhe, Müller 1976, 83–118, 98, 100; Ulrich Scheuner, Der Verfassungsschutz im Bonner Grundgesetz, in: Hermann Jahrreiss e.a. (eds.), *Um Recht und Gerechtigkeit: Festgabe für Erich Kaufmann*, Stuttgart, Kohlhammer 1950, 313–330, 318–319; Hans Nawiasky, *Allgemeine Staatslehre*, vol. 2/2, Einsiedeln, Benziger 1955, 108; Hanns Kurz, *Volkssouveränität und Volksrepräsentation*, Köln, Heymanns 1965, 317; Rudolf Zihlmann, *Legitimität und Legalität des Notrechts*, Bern, Stämpfli 1950, 72.

[86] See Herbert Krüger, *Allgemeine Staatslehre*, Stuttgart, Kohlhammer [2]1966, 31; Carl Schmitt, *Politische Theologie*, München, Duncker & Humblot [2]1934, 19. This is also recognised by the moderated state-centred theories, discussed below. See Ernst-Wolfgang Böckenförde, Der verdrängte Ausnahmezustand, *Neue Juristische Wochenschrift* 1978, 1881–1890, 1884 (stating that, when the presumed normality falls away, the reference point for a norm's normativity falls with it); Hermann Heller, *Staatslehre*, Leiden, Sijthoff 1934, 255.

[87] Carl Schmitt, Legalität und Legitimität, in: *id.*, *Verfassungsrechtliche Aufsätze aus den Jahren 1924–1954*, Berlin, Duncker & Humblot 1958, 303–350, 321.

state in exceptional situations in which instead, the state, by necessity, has a right to its self-preservation. And a norm cannot dispense with this necessary right of the state due to the very abnormality of exceptional situations.[88]

It is apparent that this line of reasoning has its basis in natural law, which provides for the state's pre-positive right to existence[89] (*jus eminens*[90]). This right is not merely alongside the constitution, but even against it,[91] since the constitution cannot apply, by definition, in an abnormal, emergency situation. Some assert this openly,[92] others are more reserved.[93] In this sense, Herbert Krüger speaks openly, stating that it is impossible to institutionalise this emergency right at all.[94] Stern formulates it more reservedly, although, ultimately with the same result. While not openly asserting the pointlessness of any and all emergency regulation, he nonetheless develops a system of restraints on emergency powers, a system separate from the given constitution.[95]

[88] The state is viewed as a pre-legal institution, whose power is originally unlimited, and only tamed by the law. Even moderate state-centred theorists display this Schmittian viewpoint. See, e.g., Böckenförde (n. 86) 1885; Kirchhof (n. 85) 117–118.

[89] See Carl Friedrich von Gerber, *Grundzüge des deutschen Staatsrechts*, Leipzig, Tauschnitz [3]1880, 42 n. 2 ('The recognition of emergency powers contains the idea of the state's right of existence beyond its usual constitutional life, a right that appears in abnormal emergency circumstances'); Erich Kaufmann, *Zur Problematik des Volkswillens*, Berlin, de Gruyter 1931, 14 ('For the extreme case, an ultimate right of necessity exists, alongside standardized and formalized exceptional rights, in the unwritten, natural-law content of every body of constitutional law'). See also Rudolf von Jhering, *Der Zweck im Recht*, Leipzig, Breitkopf & Haertel [8]1923, 330 ('As the individual human being, so too the state has a right of necessity when its existence is threatened'). Or from antiquity, see Cicero, *De Legibus* III, 3 ('Salus populi suprema lex esto').

[90] See Schröder (n. 85) 132 (detailing the history of the term *jus eminens* and citing further references).

[91] See Krüger (n. 86) 31 ('Emergency law, by its very concept, implies recourse to natural law as against positive law'). See also Stern (n. 84) 1336 (reasoning identically).

[92] E.g., Georg Meyer - Gerhard Anschütz, *Lehrbuch des deutschen Staatsrechts*, München, Duncker & Humblot [7]1919, 906 ('Only one thing is sure: the constitution does not intend, cannot intend . . . for the life of the state to stand still. . . Here, constitutional law ceases, and the inquiry . . . is no longer a legal inquiry'). See also Schmitt (n. 86) 11 (describing the supremacy of this right to existence over positive law: 'Sovereign is whoever decides in the exceptional state'). Schmitt claims that positive law cannot bind this sovereign decision-making and this state of emergency. See Schmitt (n. 85) ix.

[93] Nawiasky (n. 85) 108. [94] See Krüger (n. 86) 31.

[95] The restraints are meant to show that unwritten emergency law does not imply an 'open general empowerment'. See Stern (n. 84) 1337. For a similar opinion, see Böckenförde (n. 86) 1883.

These restraints are (1) the protection of essential constitutional interests; (2) that emergency powers should only be triggered as *ultima ratio*; (3) a balancing of conflicting legal interests; (4) a prohibition on excessiveness; and (5) the intention to return to the normal situation. At first glance, Stern seemingly argues himself back into the positive constitutional law protection of essential constitutional interests as restraint on the exercise of pre-positive emergency powers. But appearances here are deceptive. In and of itself, this restraint is not further clarified. Furthermore, such widely interpretable 'essential constitutional interests' cannot replace detailed regulation, which constitutes the true heart of the current German law on emergencies. Thus, positive constitutional law is not rehabilitated; instead, only its primary principles are made over into points of reference.

According to Stern, positive law cannot displace the state's natural law right to existence.[96] But instead, he offers a system of non-positive restraints on the exercise of this right.[97] However, it remains unclear as to exactly for what purpose the positive law on state of emergency still serves.

Klaus Stern's reasoning, therefore, demands compliance with this positive law only insofar as it is consistent with the state's right of existence. Thus, positive law's normativity must be recognised *only within* the limits of this right of existence. This is generally the case with positive law ('statutes'), which is only to be recognised within the limits of natural law ('the law').[98] The right of existence, although possibly contradictory to the positive law, always continues to be directly exercisable, according to Stern.[99] Thus, in this conceptualisation, the normativity of constitutional regulation of the state of emergency always depends on pre-legal rules governing emergencies. As a result, the constitutional law on the state of emergency devolves into a *non-justiciable, intra-administrative plan of action* or mere guidelines, and natural law ascends to become the actual law on the state of emergency. This is because violations, usually by the executive, of the positive constitutional law on the state of emergency always have a 'good legal excuse,' namely, their having occurred on the basis of unwritten

[96] See Stern (n. 84) 1337. [97] Stern (n. 84) 1337. [98] See Stern (n. 84) 1334, 1337.
[99] Stern (n. 84) 1337.

pre-positive emergency powers. This disallows any effective legal review.

#### 11.3.1.2 Moderate state-centred theories

In contrast to the above-discussed classically state-centred theories, the moderate theories presume that *positive* constitutional law *can* override the state's pre-positive right to existence.[100] This overriding occurs in the form of detailed regulation.

First, Ernst-Wolfgang Böckenförde, a well-known proponent of this approach, sees an 'open general empowerment' for every state institution in unwritten emergency law, limited only by proportionality, but *not* limited according to the bearer, extent, or scope. Such an open general empowerment, he continues, would breach the structural basis of a constitution grounded in the rule of law.[101] This general empowerment can be displaced only by a sufficiently detailed constitutional regulation. Böckenförde, however, considers the current German regulation of the state of emergency to be *insufficiently detailed* to replace those emergency powers superior to constitutional law.[102] His conclusions, therefore, strikingly resemble those of classical state-centrism, notwithstanding his criticism of how state-centrism lays the theoretical foundation of the state. According to him, supra-positive emergency law is presently in force in Germany, precisely for the reason that detailed emergency regulation should be adopted in order to displace it.

Second, in contrast, others follow the will of the constitution-making body.[103] As a consequence, the emergency regulations introduced in Germany in 1968 rule out the exercise of supra-

[100] See Theodor Maunz – Reinhold Zippelius, *Deutsches Staatsrecht*, München, Beck [30]1998, 415 (referring only to the theoretical situation where regulation is lacking); Karl Doehring, *Das Staatsrecht der Bundesrepublik Deutschland*, Frankfurt aM, Metzner [3]1984, 270–275; Karl Doehring, *Allgemeine Staatslehre*, Heidelberg, CF Müller [3]2004, 204–213; Markus Trotter, *Der Ausnahmezustand im historischen und europäischen Rechtsvergleich* (1997) 99 (dissertation, University of Heidelberg) (on file at the Max Planck Institute for International Law, Heidelberg); Günter Dürig, Artikel 87a, in: Theodor Maunz – Günter Dürig (eds.), *Das Grundgesetz* (loose-leaf edition, update of 1971) para 128, especially n.5.

[101] See Böckenförde (n. 86) 1883.

[102] For his *de lege ferenda* constitutional regulatory text, see Ernst-Wolfgang Böckenförde, Ausnahmerecht und demokratischer Rechtsstaat, in: Hans-Jochen Vogel (ed.), *Die Freiheit des Anderen: Festschrift für Martin Hirsch*, Baden-Baden, Nomos 1981, 259–272, especially 264–272.

[103] See above n. 100.

constitutional powers, which otherwise would exist in the background.[104]

### *11.3.2 Constitution-centred theories*

Constitution-centred theories dispute the existence of pre-legal state powers. The positive (fixed) constitution always serves as a starting point for argumentation.

#### 11.3.2.1 The classical constitution-centrism

The classical or radical version of this viewpoint limits the state's emergency powers to those explicitly named in constitutional law.[105]

More strongly than state-centred theories, constitution-centrism underscores the danger of abuse stemming from unwritten emergency

[104] Thus, the objective of emergency legislation in 1968 was precisely to make recourse to unwritten constitutional principles unnecessary by way of explicit regulation. See *Schriftlicher Bericht des Rechtsauschusses, Bundestags-Drucksache* V/2873 (quoted by Stern (n. 84) 1329).

[105] See Richard Thoma, Der Vorbehalt der Legislative und das Prinzip der Gesetzmäßigkeit von Verwaltung und Rechtsprechung, in: Gerhard Anschütz – Richard Thoma (eds.), *Handbuch des deutschen Staatsrechts*, vol. 2, Tübingen, Mohr 1932, 221–236, 232 ('In a structured, republican constitutional state, there can be no state's right of necessity beyond what is constitutionally foreseen'); Alfred Voigt, Ungeschriebenes Verfassungsrecht, *Veröffentlichungen der Vereinigung der Deutschen Staatsrechtslehrer* 1952, 33–45, 44; Adolf Arndt, Der Rechtsstaat und sein polizeilicher Verfassungsschutz, *Neue Juristische Wochenschrift* 1961, 897–902, 900; Hans M Parche, *Der Einsatz von Streitkräften im inneren Notstand. Zugleich ein Beitrag zur Lehre vom rechtsstaatlichen Handeln der Exekutive und seiner Kontrolle* (1974) 3, 179 (dissertation, University of Münster) (on file at the Max Planck Institute for International Law, Heidelberg); Möllers (n. 1) 267; Heinrich Oberreuter, *Notstand und Demokratie*, München, Vögel 1978, 113, 120–121; Werner Kägi, *Die Verfassung als rechtliche Grundordnung des Staates*, Zürich, Polygraph 1945, 118; Michael Krenzler, *An den Grenzen der Notstandsverfassung. Ausnahmezustand und Staatsnotrecht im Verfassungssystem des Grundgesetzes*, Berlin, Duncker & Humblot 1974, 74; Frank-Bodo von Wehrs, *Zur Anwendbarkeit des Notstandsrechts der Bundesrepublik Deutschland* (1971) 116–117 (dissertation, University of Mainz) (on file at the Max Planck Institute for International Law, Heidelberg). Surprisingly, the approach taken by the anti-Kelsenian Konrad Hesse is similar to the Kelsenian approach. See Konrad Hesse, *Die normative Kraft der Verfassung*, Tübingen, Mohr 1959, 24; Konrad Hesse, *Grundzüge des Verfassungsrechts der Bundesrepublik Deutschland*, Heidelberg, CF Müller [20]1999, 300–317. According to Hesse, one cannot call upon supra-positive emergency law, but one should keep in mind that state institutions will indeed do so, where regulation on state of emergency is lacking.

empowerments.[106] Adolf Arndt formulates the standpoint eloquently: 'All speculation about a "supra-constitutional state of emergency", permitting measures not justified by the documentary constitution, is nothing but a deplorable glossing-over of unconstitutionality, of constitutional treason.'[107]

Such an approach, therefore, views the state of emergency not as an extra-constitutional situation, but simply as constitutional *lex specialis.*[108]

And it rejects the argument for a constitutional law subject to the state's superior right to existence.[109] Kelsen formulates and exposes this by saying: 'Behind the naïve assurance that the state must "live", there usually lurks the reckless desire that it live exactly as those who avail themselves of the justification of an "emergency right" consider it appropriate for it to live.'[110]

However, this does not imply that this group would punish *every* violation of the positive provisions of emergency law, even where the violation, for instance, occurred in the interests of re-establishing the constitutional order. Subsequently, the competent institution, for example, the parliament, could approve an order of indemnity for such a violation. The violation as such, though in opposition to the position of state-centred theories, could not be denied.[111] In this conceptualisation, a moral duty to violate the law, in the interests of preserving the constitutional state, may exist; however, one must strictly distinguish between such a duty and the legal analysis of the case.

#### 11.3.2.2 The open version of constitutional-centrism

Eckart Klein advances a more open version of the constitution-centred theory. Specifically, while all the state's emergency powers must indeed derive from the positive constitution, these powers can also include *implied*

[106] Aside from this, the natural-law viewpoint as such is criticised as unscholarly in the Kelsenian tradition. See, e.g., Koja (n. 17) 398; Koja (n. 83) 10.

[107] Adolf Arndt, Demokratie: Wertsystem des Rechts, in: Adolf Arndt – Michael Freund (eds.), *Notstandsgesetz – aber wie?*, Köln, Verlag Wissenschaft und Politik 1962, 7–66, 13. Cf. also Merkl (n. 27) 166 (stating that supra-positive emergency law is the last refuge of those who advocate freedom of the executive from the law, to some degree).

[108] Koja (n. 17) 399. See also Koja (n. 83) 14 ('State of emergency, understood thus, becomes—and this is important—a constitutional state, and not a state of constitutionlessness').

[109] See Adolf Arndt, Der Rechtsstaat und sein polizeilicher Verfassungsschutz, *Neue Juristische Wochenschrift* 1961, 897–902, 899 ('A constitutional state has no other *raison* than its constitution'); Konrad Hesse, Ausnahmezustand und Grundgesetz, *Die öffentliche Verwaltung* (1955) 741.

[110] Kelsen (n. 17) 157. [111] See Koja (n. 83) 17.

*powers*, since the constitution inherently contains a general obligation to sustain itself.[112] The fundamental flaw in this viewpoint is its contradiction, based only on the positive constitution, of the well-known intent of the constitution-making body, whose will in 1968 was namely the exclusion of any unwritten emergency powers.[113]

### *11.3.3 Conclusions about the conceptualisation of state of emergency*

One can arrange the various viewpoints as follows. The first organising criterion is the theoretical basis, that is, the recognition of pre-positive emergency powers. Constitution-centred theories deny this basis, whereas state-centred theories affirm it. The other organising criterion is more practical, namely, whether the respective author allows for emergency powers not explicit in the *Grundgesetz* in Germany's constitutional order. According to this, a differentiation can be made between theories bound and not bound to the constitutional text.[114]

State-centred and textually not bound theories (lower left part of the table) focus on effectiveness as the key moment in the state of emergency, while constitution-centred and textually bound theories (upper right part of the table) focus on fear of abuse of emergency powers. Those who combine the two legal doctrines (e.g., constitution-centred but textually not bound, like E Klein), try to find a compromise between effectiveness and fear. These compromises are, however, dead ends. If a person like Klein refers to the constitution, but does not seem to be bound by its text, then the legal constraints, in the text of the constitution, on emergency powers cannot fulfil their functions, and the compromise mentioned is going to be lost for the sake of effectiveness. The other compromise

[112] Eckart Klein, Der innere Notstand, in: Josef Isensee – Paul Kirchhof (eds.), *Handbuch des Staatsrechts der Bundesrepublik Deutschland. Vol. 7: Normativität und Schutz der Verfassung – internationale Beziehungen*, Heidelberg, CF Müller 1992, 387–414, 412. This is similar to the doctrine of implied powers; see Karl Doehring, Das Staatsnotrecht in den Vereinigten Staaten von Amerika, in: Hans Ballreich e.a., *Das Staatsnotrecht in Belgien, Frankreich, Großbritannien, Italien, den Niederlanden, der Schweiz und den Vereinigten Staaten von Amerika*, Köln, Heymann 1955, 209–247, 212–222.

[113] See above note 104.

[114] Those who do not concretely address the current legal situation of the Federal Republic of Germany are in parentheses.

Table 11.1. *Conceptualisations of state of emergency*

| Do pre-legal emergency powers exist? (theoretical basis) / Can only those emergency powers which are explicitly mentioned in the *Grundgesetz* be exercised? (practical consequence) | Yes (state-centred) | No (constittion-centred) |
|---|---|---|
| Yes (textually bound) | Maunz, Zippelius, Doehring, Dürig, Trotter | Hesse, Möllers, Wehrs, Krenzler, Oberreuter, Parche (Kägi, Arndt, Voigt, Koja, Kelsen, Merkl) |
| No (textually not bound) | Böckenförde, Stern, Schröder, Kirchhof (Schmitt, Krüger, Flor, Jhering, Zihlmann, Meyer, Anschütz, Gerber, Kaufmann, Scheuner, Kurz, Nawiasky) | E. Klein |

(upper left, e.g., Zippelius) stating that supra-constitutional powers still exist in the background, but cannot be exercised because of positive law is simply useless in current German constitutional law, because it could be applied only if the relevant articles of the *Grundgesetz* were abolished. This is highly hypothetical, or rather very unlikely, which does not make this theory harmful, rather simply useless in today's German constitutional law. And, finally, the traditional and radical 'state-centred, textually not bound' approach does not recognise any compromises; it simply opens the gates of abuse and practically denies the legal-normative nature of relevant constitutional provisions.

Therefore, the right solution seems to be a constitution-centred, textually bound approach with a moral complement.[115] It addresses the dangers of abuse, without raising problems of effectiveness. That is also why it most closely resembles the approach of the present author. This also means the rejection of the use of a pre-legal state concept in constitutional reasoning when talking about the state of emergency.

## 11.4 Conclusion on the use of the conceptual framework of *Staatslehre*

The use of the concept of a 'pre-legal administrative state' *(Staat)* in constitutional reasoning does not suit modern democracy and constitutionalism. It partly implies pre-democratic ideas (separation of state and society) which were well suited to Germany before the First World War, but which are unacceptable today. Similarly, the idea of primacy of the state being primary to the constitution is a questionable idea, as it contradicts the prevalence of the constitution. Consequently, building a language for European constitutional discourse based on this presupposition (i.e., to write a *Staatslehre*) is not advisable.[116]

As opposed to sovereignty, pre-legal statehood cannot be reformulated into a 'claim' either (cf. above 6.5). But fortunately, it has less emotional value than sovereignty, except maybe for Germany where in the absence of democracy after the foundation of the

[115] See above *11.3.2.1 The classical constitution-centrism.*
[116] For a similar conclusion, see Möllers (n. 1) 418–425; Möllers (n. 19) 17 and 69.

*Reich* in 1871 emotional identification was bound to the state.[117] The state also had the advantage in Germany that it was not discredited as was the nation (or *Volk*) after the Second World War; and it offered a language of rich intellectual history which could express national feelings in public debates in an inoffensive way until German re-unification in 1990. But by now, it has lost all its meaningful functions, it has become no more than a coded language of German eurosceptic constitutional lawyers,[118] and its pre-democratic and anti-constitutionalist elements seriously bring into question whether even within Germany, let alone European constitutional discourse, it should have a place in the future.[119]

117 Kenneth HF Dyson, Die Ideen des Staates und der Demokratie. Ein Vergleich 'staatlich verfaßter' und 'nicht staatlich verfaßter' Gesellschaften, *Der Staat* 19 (1980) 485–515, especially 490–491.

118 See, e.g., Josef Isensee, Die Staatlichkeit der Verfassung, in: Otto Depenheuer – Christoph Grabenwarter (eds.), *Verfassungstheorie*, Tübingen, Mohr Siebeck 2010, 199–270, 263–269 with further references. For a critical view on this *Staat* terminology, see JHH Weiler, The State 'über alles'. Demos, Telos and the German Maastricht Decision, *Jean Monnet Working Papers* 1995/6.

119 For similar sceptical conclusions concerning the compatibility of this conceptual frame with either European integration or modern constitutionalism, see Jo Eric Khushal Murkens, *From Empire to Union: Conceptions of German Constitutional Law since 1871*, Oxford, Oxford University Press 2013.

12

# The *Stufenbaulehre* as a basis for a constitutional theory?

> C'est l'*ordre* que nous réclamons, c'est la *hiérarchie* la plus unitaire, la plus ferme, que nous appelons pour l'avenir.[1]

In the last two decades, several attempts have been made to conceptualise European integration (especially the issues regarding the hierarchy between EU law and national constitutional laws) with the help of the *Stufenbaulehre*.[2] In the following I will show why the theoretical background of these attempts is questionable, that is, why this conceptualisation of European constitutional law is futile.

The *Stufenbaulehre* (doctrine on the hierarchical structure of the legal order, or literally 'step structure doctrine') is perhaps the most characteristic feature of the *Pure Theory of Law*.[3] In the present chapter, this

[1] 'It is *order* that we ask for, it is the most unitary and most closed *hierarchy* that we call for for the future.' [Saint-Amand Bazard – Barthélémy Prosper Enfantin], *Doctrine de Saint-Simon, Exposition première année (1828–1829)*, Paris, Bureau de l'organisateur [3]1831, 218 (emphasis in original).

[2] Theodor Schilling, *Rang und Geltung von Normen in gestuften Rechtsordnungen*, Berlin, Spitz 1994, especially 199–206, 213–215; Franz C Mayer, *Kompetenzüberschreitung und Letztentscheidung*, Munchen, Beck 2000, 3, 48–49 with further references, Theodor Schilling, The Autonomy of the Community Legal Order, *Harvard International Law Journal* 37 (1996) 389–409; Alec Stone Sweet, The Juridical Coup d'Etat and the Problem of Authority, *German Law Journal* 8 (2007) 915–927, Theo Öhlinger, Unity of the Legal System or Legal Pluralism: The Stufenbau Doctrine in Present-Day Europe, in: Antero Jyränki (ed.), *National Constitutions in the Era of Integration*, The Hague, Kluwer Law International 1999, 163–174; Hans René Laurer, Europarecht und österreichische Rechtsordnung: Rechtsnormen in einem einheitlichen Stufenbau?, *Österreichische Juristen-Zeitung* 52 (1997) 801–810; Christoph Grabenwarter, Die Verfassung in der Hierarchie der Rechtsordnung, in: Otto Depenheuer – Christoph Grabenwarter (eds.), *Verfassungstheorie*, Tübingen, Mohr Siebeck 2010, 391–413, especially 411–413; Theodor Schilling, Justizrevolutionen, *Der Staat* 51 (2012) 525–558.

[3] I am grateful to Anne van Aaken, Michael Anderheiden, Jürgen Bast, Mátyás Bódig, Péter Cserne, Stefan Häußler, Cristina Hoss, Jörg Kammerhofer, András Karácsony, Stephan Kirste, Jana Lachmund, Nele Matz, Otto Pfersmann, Theodor Schilling, Silja Vöneky and Robert Walter for their thoughtful criticism and valuable comments. A very early version of this chapter was published as 'Problems of the *Stufenbaulehre*. Kelsen's Failure to Derive

construction and the criticism of it are sketched (1), followed by an account of the attempt of Robert Walter, a contemporary exponent of the Vienna School of legal theory, to structure the legal system in a way different from the *Stufenbaulehre* (2). Finally, the chapter shows what ideological background of the *Stufenbaulehre* is often alleged to have and examines if it is justified (3), then the results of the present survey are summarised (4).

## 12.1 The hierarchy of the legal order

Although the *Stufenbaulehre* is known as a part of the Kelsenian *Pure Theory of Law*,[4] the idea does not come from him, but from one of his disciples,[5] Adolf Merkl. Merkl first developed his doctrine in his article *Das doppelte Rechtsantlitz*,[6] then in his book *Die Lehre von der Rechtskraft*,[7] but in its full form in the *Prolegomena einer Theorie des rechtlichen Stufenbaues*.[8]

Kelsen adopted the argumentation of Merkl[9] first in the second edition of the *Hauptprobleme der Staatsrechtslehre* (more precisely, in the preface

the Validity of a Norm from Another Norm' in the *Canadian Journal of Law and Jurisprudence* 20 (2007) 35–68.

[4] *Pure Theory of Law* refers here not to Kelsen's book with the same title, but to the whole Vienna School and its doctrine. For the same terminology, see Robert Walter, Der gegenwärtige Stand der Reinen Rechtslehre, *Rechtstheorie* 1970, 69–75; and the founding document of the Hans Kelsen-Institut (Vienna), see Walter Antoniolli e.a., *Hans Kelsen zum Gedenken*, Wien, Europaverlag 1974, 77. Kelsen has first called his doctrine *'reine Rechtslehre'* (with a small 'r') in the subtitle of his *Das Problem der Souveränität und die Theorie des Völkerrechts. Beitrag zu einer reinen Rechtslehre*, Tübingen, Mohr 1920.

[5] Gabriele Kucsko-Stadlmayer, Der Beitrag Adolf Merkls zur Reinen Rechtslehre, in: Robert Walter (ed.), *Schwerpunkte der Reinen Rechtslehre*, Wien, Manz 1992, 107–121; Wolf-Dietrich Grussmann, *Adolf Julius Merkl. Leben und Werk*, Wien, Manz 1989, 14 and 18–21 with further references.

[6] Adolf Merkl, Das doppelte Rechtsantlitz [1918], in: Hans R Klecatsky – René Marcic – Herbert Schambeck (eds.), *Hans Kelsen – Adolf Merkl – Alfred Verdross: Die Wiener Rechtstheoretische Schule*, Wien, Europa-Verlag 1968, [henceforth *WRS*] 1091–1113.

[7] Adolf Merkl, *Die Lehre von der Rechtskraft entwickelt aus dem Rechtsbegriff*, Leipzig, Deuticke 1923.

[8] Adolf Merkl, Prolegomena einer Theorie des rechtlichen Stufenbaues [1931], in: *WRS*, 1311–1361. It was, however, as indicated in the title (*Prolegomena* = preface), only an introductory article, and Merkl planned, as it is mentioned by himself (cf. *op. cit.* 1361, n. 1), to write a whole monograph on this topic. This announced major work was never written.

[9] It has to be mentioned, that the *Stufenbaulehre* of Merkl (particularly in its methodological premises) draws strongly on Hans Kelsen's *Hauptprobleme der Staatsrechtslehre entwickelt aus der Lehre vom Rechtssatze*, Tübingen, Mohr 1911. Hence one speaks best of a 'cross-fertilisation'. Similarly Jürgen Behrend, *Untersuchungen zur Stufenbaulehre Adolf Merkls und Hans Kelsens*, Berlin, Duncker & Humblot 1977, 49.

of this otherwise unchanged edition).[10] He made this doctrine known worldwide in his *Reine Rechtslehre*.[11] Kelsen himself considered the *Stufenbaulehre* as a central element of the *Pure Theory of Law*, and therefore regarded Merkl as a co-founder of the Vienna School of legal theory.[12]

### 12.1.1 *The* Stufenbaulehre *as a construction of legal theory*

The starting question is this: What is the unity of the legal system based on? The answer, according to the *Pure Theory of Law*, is that it is the so-called basic norm (*Grundnorm*) from which every norm in the legal system derives its validity.[13] Validity can never be based on social facts ('is', *Sein*), since an 'ought' (*Sollen*) may only come from another 'ought'. The validity of a norm can stem only from another norm. In this case, an 'ancestral norm' (*Urnorm*) has to exist there, from which the validity of all other norms can be derived.[14] If one does not intend to construct a metaphysical, natural-law theory, then one has to choose a formal basic norm (i.e., lacking in substantive content) in order to prove the validity.[15]

10 Hans Kelsen, *Hauptprobleme der Staatsrechtslehre entwickelt aus der Lehre vom Rechtssatze*, Tübingen, Mohr $^{2}$1923, xv–xvi acknowledges the contribution of Merkl to the development of the *Pure Theory of Law* explicitly.

11 Hans Kelsen, *Introduction to the Problems of Legal Theory*, Oxford, Clarendon Press 1992 (transl. by Bonnie Litschewski Paulson and Stanley L Paulson) [*Reine Rechtslehre*, 1934] (henceforth Kelsen, *Introduction*), 55–75.

12 As Kelsen writes in a letter to Merkl, 'if only there is a "Vienna School of legal theory", it is, in a very great part, due you', cited by Wolf-Dietrich Grussmann, in: Robert Walter (ed.), *Adolf J. Merkl. Werk und Wirksamkeit*, Wien, Manz 1990, 142; see also Hans Kelsen, Adolf Merkl zu seinem 70. Geburtstag, *Zeitschrift für öffentliches Recht* 10 (1959–1960) 313–323. Cf. also Kelsen's letter to Merkl, where he acknowledges 'most gratefully the great importance of this scholarly work for the Pure Theory of Law', published in: Max Imboden e.a. (eds.), *Festschrift für Adolf J. Merkl zum 80. Geburtstag*, München, Funk 1970, 11.

13 As Merkl (n. 7), 210 states: 'If one wants to be able to present the chaos of legal forms as a sum of coherent phenomena, in a word as a legal system, as a cosmos of law, . . . it has to be . . . acknowledged as the outcome of a common origin'. Thus, unity of the legal order is to be found in the chain of delegations (*Delegationszusammenhang*). For this, cf. Merkl (n. 8), 1336; Hans Kelsen, Der Begriff der Rechtsordnung [1958], in: *ibid.* 1395–1416.

14 Cf. Christian Dahlmann, The Trinity in Kelsen's Basic Norm Unravelled, *Archiv für Rechts- und Sozialphilosophie* (2004) 147–162, 149.

15 Behrend (n. 9) 68. On the double case of the *Pure Theory of Law* against the role of 1. causal sciences, e.g., sociology and 2. of natural law in legal science, see Horst Dreier, *Rechtslehre, Staatssoziologie und Demokratietheorie bei Hans Kelsen*, Baden-Baden, Nomos 1986, 42.

But what does derivation mean? It is not equal to the assumption that the content of legal norms could be derived by deduction from the basic norm (it would be characteristic for moral systems of norms or for Natural Law). Derivation means that an act of will (i.e., not a mere act of thought) '*A*' is to be regarded as an act of law creation (*Rechtserzeugungsakt*), if it is an act of law creation according to a norm '*B*' regulating the creation of law. It means that validity of the norm '*A*' that came into existence by the law-creating act '*A*' is to be derived from the validity of the norm '*B*', since if the creation of the norm '*A*' does not correspond to the process of law creation as described in the norm '*B*', then the norm '*A*' is not valid. Thus, the *Stufenbaulehre* gives an answer to the question concerning the origin of validity ('Where does the validity of a legal norm come from?') as well.

The next step of the argument is that derivation is also connected to the question of forms of law (*Rechtsform*). In different law-creating processes, different forms of law (according to the current terminology 'sources of law', e.g., statute, ordinance) are created. The number of possible forms (sources) of law is limited within a certain legal system; the possible content of law (i.e., the actual content of the regulation) is, however, infinite.[16] These forms have a hierarchical relation to each other, according to which a certain form of law derives its validity from another. Thus, an individual norm (e.g., an administrative act) is subordinate to the ordnance according to the *Stufenbaulehre*; the former derives its validity from the latter.

Therefore, an individual norm is valid only because its validity can be derived from a valid ordinance, which is, in turn, only valid because its validity is derived from statutes; and a statute derives its validity from the constitution; the constitution itself – if it were produced legally (i.e., according to the law) – from the previous constitution, and so on until the historically first constitution. The *historically first constitution* can be recognised by its illegal (i.e., unlawful) way of production. The question is, then, where the validity of this historically first constitution comes from. The answer of the *Pure Theory of Law* comprises the rather idiosyncratic solution of the *hypothetical basic norm (hypothetische*

[16] Merkl, Prolegomena (n. 13) 1311. Every form may have an arbitrary content; see Merkl, *op.cit.*, 1313; Hans Kelsen, *The Pure Theory of Law* (transl. by Max Knight), Clark, New Jersey, Lawbook Exchange 1970 [*Reine Rechtslehre*, $^{2}$1960] (henceforth Kelsen, *PTL2*), 201. Thus, every topic may *theoretically* (i.e., if the concrete legal system does not impose something else, e.g., in the constitution) be regulated by any kind of sources of law; see Behrend (n. 9) 54 n. 191.

*Grundnorm).*[17] According to that, one has to presuppose that there exists such a hypothetical basic norm that is the condition of every kind of legislation. Otherwise the 'ought' that is characteristic of law could not be derived. This basic norm says: 'Coercion is to be applied under certain conditions and in a certain way, namely, as determined by the framers of the first constitution or by the authorities to whom they have delegated appropriate powers.'[18] The validity of the hypothetical basic norm can be recognised inasmuch as the legal order based on it is *by and large* effective (i.e., it is obeyed). It does not mean that effectiveness and validity are identical, only that 'effectiveness of the legal order' is a (necessary) condition of the validity of the legal order.[19]

The hierarchy in the *Stufenbaulehre* is thus constructed as follows: hypothetical basic norm (or synonymously: constitution in terms of legal logic[20]) – constitution (constitution in terms of positive law) – statutes – ordinances – judicial decisions, administrative acts, private legal transactions (e.g., contracts) – physical executive acts (acts of compulsion or

[17] With the terminology of Merkl: original norm (*Ursprungsnorm*); see, e.g., Merkl (n. 7) 209 n. 1. Kelsen himself uses the expression 'original norm' sometimes; e.g., in his *Allgemeinen Staatslehre*, Berlin, Springer 1925 (henceforth *AStL*), 99. The idea of the basic norm (*Grundnorm*) (but not the expression) appears in Kelsen's works before the *Stufenbaulehre*; first in his article 'Reichsgesetz und Landesgesetz nach österreichischer Verfassung', *Archiv des öffentlichen Rechts* 32 (1914) 202–245, especially 216–220, but the article of Alfred Verdross, Zum Problem der Rechtsunterworfenheit des Gesetzgebers, *Juristische Blätter* 45 (1916) 471–473 contributed to its final elaboration (the distinction between the constitution of positive law and the basic norm as constitution in a legal logical sense), as it was explicitly acknowledged by Kelsen (n. 10) xv–xvi. Perhaps this is why Kelsen dedicated the second edition of the *Hauptprobleme* to Merkl and Verdross (*op.cit.*, iii).

The expression 'basic norm' comes from Edmund Husserl, *Logische Untersuchungen. 1. Prolegomena zur reinen Logik*, Halle aS, Niemeyer 1900, 45; see Helmut Holzhey, Kelsens Rechts- und Staatslehre in ihrem Verhältnis zum Neukantianismus, in: Stanley L Paulson – Robert Walter (eds.), *Untersuchungen zur Reinen Rechtslehre. Ergebnisse eines Wiener Rechtstheoretischen Seminars 1985/86*, Wien, Manz 1986, 167–192, especially 177–181. Cf. also Werner Krawietz, Grundnorm, in: Joachim Ritter (ed.), *Historisches Wörterbuch der Philosophie*, vol. 3, Darmstadt, Wissenschaftliche Buchhandlung 1974, 918–922, 921–922. Just to be sure, the basic norm of the valid US legal system is not the Constitution (1787) (which is the constitution of positive law), but the norm that says: 'The Constitution (1787) ought to be obeyed'.

[18] Kelsen *Introduction* (n. 11) 57.

[19] Kelsen *Introduction* (n. 11) 61: 'while the law cannot exist without power, neither is it identical to power'.

[20] Kelsen *AStL* (n. 17) 248–255. Another synonym is 'the constitution in the transcendental-logical sense'; see Hans Kelsen, Naturrechtslehre und Rechtspositivismus [1961], in: *WRS* (n. 13) 817–832, 827. On synonymity, see Uta Bindreiter, *Why Grundnorm? A Treatise on the Implications of Kelsen's Doctrine*, The Hague, Kluwer Law International 2002, 18.

coercive acts).[21] The latter (i.e., coercive acts) are not considered as part of the legal order, since they do not comprise norms, only the execution of a norm (i.e., an 'is').

But this is an account of the hierarchy *(Stufenbau)* of an ideal typical, parliamentary legal order. A valid legal order is not necessarily constructed according to this scheme. But there are, according to Merkl, at least two necessary levels: 1. the one of the *basic norm* and 2. the one of norms with the threat of immediate coercion.[22]

Some theoretical implications and characteristics of the *Stufenbaulehre* are to be mentioned here: 1. First, a high level of autonomy inherent in the legal order that is obtained in the way that law regulates its own creation and validity ('self-creation of law', *Selbsterzeugung des Rechts*). 2. Second, every level of the hierarchy comprises creation and application of law at the same time (except for the levels of the basic norm and physical execution, since the former means only legislation, while the latter means only application); that is, all legal acts have a *double legal appearance (doppeltes Rechtsantlitz)*. They are Janus-faced.[23] Legal acts are thus, to a certain extent, always objectively determined by law, but they also depend, to a certain degree, on the subject of the law-creating/law-applying organ.[24] This freedom of the law-creating/law-applying organ becomes increasingly less on the way from the hypothetical basic norm to

[21] Single levels can also be skipped (an individual act may also, for example, be based directly on the statute and not have to gain its validity by the ordinance as an intermediate) as Hans Nawiasky rightly reminds in his Kritische Bemerkungen zur Lehre vom Stufenbau des Rechtes, *Zeitschrift für öffentliches Recht* 6 (1926/27) 488–496, 495. In the same way, Joseph Raz, *The Concept of a Legal System: An Introduction to the Theory of Legal System*, Oxford, Clarendon Press [2]1980, 99 n. 1, who therefore prefers the metaphor of a tree to the usual image of a pyramid. This is, however, only a slight addition to the *Stufenbaulehre*, and cannot refute it at all.

[22] Adolf Merkl, Gesetzesrecht und Richterrecht [1922], in: *WRS* (n. 13) 1615–1624, 1618; on relevant modifications in the work of Merkl, see Behrend (n. 9), 19–27. Moreover, according to Behrend, one needs at least three levels to make a legal order: the two mentioned by Merkl and the norm of competence for the creation of the coercive norm; see Behrend (n. 9), 26. The argument of Behrend assumes, however, that one wants to maintain the possibility of a later modification of coercive norms. It is – although rational – not conceptually necessary; or, in the words of the *Pure Theory of Law*, not essential to law (*rechtswesentlich*).

[23] Merkl (n. 7), 216; Adolf Merkl, Das doppelte Rechtsantlitz [1918], in: *WRS* (n. 13) 1091–1113, 1097 (henceforth Merkl, *Rechtsantlitz*).

[24] The reason for it is not the explicitly approved discretion, but the fact that linguistic expressions are themselves indefinite to a certain extent; see Merkl, Rechtsantlitz (n. 23) 1111: '*Every word* has, along with a definite *core* of meaning, more or less wavering *peripheral* meanings' (my italics) – in the year 1918, a long time before Hart.

the physical coercive act, as the acts become increasingly more concrete and individualised,[25] but the freedom of decision (even if increasingly less) still remains. The *autonomous* and *heteronomous determinants* are, then, present in both creation and application of law at the same time.[26] Therefore, an absolute opposition of creation and application of law is inadequate, since they differ in degree but not in kind. 3. Third, it has to be mentioned that the *Stufenbaulehre* explains more than do traditional conceptions of the hierarchy of norms, as it explains not only the general norms but also the individual acts (individual norms in the terminology of the *Pure Theory of Law*)[27] such as judicial decisions and the physical executive acts.[28] 4. Fourth, it is a new feature of the *Stufenbaulehre*, as opposed to previous[29] conceptions of the hierarchy of norms, that it not only identifies the hierarchy, but also furnishes criteria ('a test') for its identification.[30] 5. And lastly, its most important feature (its virtue, according to some)[31] is that it gives a dynamic approach to the legal order instead of a static one ('In what system do the norms exist?'); that is, it answers the question of how norms are created.[32]

### *12.1.2 Points of criticism*

In the following, an account is given of the points where objections are or could be made to the *Stufenbaulehre*: (1) the indefensibility of the *basic norm*, (2) blurring the difference between individual and normative acts,

[25] Adolf Merkl, *Allgemeines Verwaltungsrecht*, Berlin, Springer 1927, 142 and 146. Norbert Achterberg, Hans Kelsens Bedeutung in der gegenwärtigen deutschen Staatslehre, *Die öffentliche Verwaltung* 1974, 445–454, 454 explains that the pyramid of norms corresponds to an opposite pyramid showing the role of extra-legal factors: it is the broadest in the constitution, and the narrowest in the coercive act.

[26] Merkl (n. 25) 142.

[27] Behrend (n. 9) 51. In this aspect, Ernst Rudolf Bierling, *Juristische Prinzipienlehre*, vol. II, Freiburg, Mohr 1898, 117–134, especially 119 and 127 may be mentioned as one of the predecessors.

[28] Theo Öhlinger, *Der Stufenbau der Rechtsordnung. Rechtstheoretische und ideologische Aspekte*, Wien, Manz 1975, 10.

[29] Particularly Binding, Bierling and Thon. Cf. Wolfram Müller-Freienfels, Zur Rangstufung rechtlicher Normen, in: Institute of Comparative Law Waseda University (ed.), *Law in East and West. Recht in Ost und West*, Tokyo, Waseda University Press 1988, 3–39, 19 (with further references) and 21.

[30] Öhlinger (n. 28) 11.

[31] Stanley L Paulson, Zur Stufenbaulehre Merkls in ihrer Bedeutung für die Allgemeine Rechtslehre, in: Walter (n. 12) 93–105.

[32] Merkl, Prolegomena (n. 13) 1314. Kelsen himself emphasises this advantage, see Kelsen (n. 10) xii.

(3) the defeasibility of monism, (4) the derivation of the validity of a norm from *one single* other norm, and last (5) the derivation of validity itself. It is necessary to examine, to what extent the respective criticism is correct, and what answer was or would have been given by exponents of the *Pure Theory of Law.*

#### 12.1.2.1 The basic norm

Criticism of the *basic norm* has almost become a custom in legal theory: there is hardly any comprehensive work on legal theory that does not – routinely – attack it.[33] This criticism has five main grounds: that is, the *basic norm* seems to be assailable in five different aspects: (a) first, as the failure of disparity between 'is' and 'ought'; (b) second, as a metaphysical construct; (c) third, as fiction; (d) fourth, as a logical *circulus vitiosus*; and (e) fifth, as a redundant notion. In addition to that, general methodological objections (the elimination of morals in particular)[34] can be made to the *Pure Theory of Law,* but they are not elaborated on here,[35] since they concern some underlying assumptions of the *Pure Theory of Law* (e.g., value-relativism or normativism), whose assessment would need a general analysis of the *Pure Theory of Law* that is not possible here. The present examination of the *basic norm* is limited to the points of criticism that can (also) be made while accepting the methodical starting points of the *Pure Theory of Law.*

(a) The first point of criticism, that is, the failure of the 'is'–'ought' disparity, basically means that the *basic norm* actually depends on

[33] Kelsen's inconsequence occasionally gives another ground for criticism, especially the fact that sometimes he refers to the legal order as a condition of the *basic norm*, but sometimes he does its inverse. See Dreier (n. 15) 45 n. 117 with further references.

[34] Such criticism, e.g., Ralf Dreier, Bemerkungen zur Theorie der Grundnorm, in: Hans-Kelsen-Institut (ed.), *Die Reine Rechtslehre in wissenschaftlicher Diskussion*, Wien, Manz 1982, 38–46, especially 45.

[35] We do not have to discuss here the criticism of Herbert Hart, *The Concept of Law*, Oxford, Clarendon $^{2}$1994, 292–293 (ch. VI, endnote 1), who challenges Kelsen's basic methodological approach and therefore states – amongst other points – that the *basic norm* is simply 'redundant'. The criticism of Werner Krawietz, Die Lehre vom Stufenbau des Rechts – eine säkularisierte politische Theologie?, in: Werner Krawietz – Helmut Schelsky (eds.), *Rechtssystem und gesellschaftliche Basis bei Hans Kelsen*, Rechtstheorie, Beiheft 5, Berlin, Duncker & Humblot 1984, 255–271, especially 264–268 remains outside the scope of this chapter, who claims that the *Stufenbaulehre* cannot grasp 'social reality', since it pretends that decisions are determined from the top to the bottom – although there is another, inverse way of influence, is also omitted, because this criticism points to a problem of sociology (of law), while the *Stufenbaulehre* (as a purely normative theory) says nothing about it.

effectiveness, that is to say, on social facts. This would mean that the source of legal order ('ought') could still be found in 'is'.[36]

(b) According to the second possible point of criticism, the basic norm is in fact a hollow construction of Natural Law, that is, a metaphysical relic in the *Pure Theory of Law*.[37] Kelsen himself, as a matter of fact, also admits this, as he considers the *basic norm* as a relic of Natural Law.[38]

(c) According to the third possible objection, the *basic norm* is a (redundant) fiction; that is, it has nothing to do with the objective description of law as announced by the *Pure Theory of Law*, since – strictly speaking – it does not even exist. This objection is supported by Kelsen himself, who refers to the basic norms in his later works as fiction.[39]

(d) According to the fourth possible objection, the idea of the basic norm is based on a *circulus vitiosus*, as it is deduced from legal order, and the legal order is deduced from it.[40] A plausible compound of the third and fourth objection was developed by Roman Herzog and says that the *basic norm* is either *circulus vitiosus* (if derived

[36] E.g., Ernst von Hippel, *Allgemeine Staatslehre*, Berlin, Vahlen 1963, 146; Hans-Ludwig Schreiber, *Der Begriff der Rechtspflicht*, Berlin, de Gruyter 1966, 144; Aleksander Peczenik, Two Sides of Grundnorm, in: Hans-Kelsen-Institut (n. 34) 58–62, 61.

[37] See Stefan Hammer, Kelsens Grundnormkonzeption als neukantische Erkenntnistheorie des Rechts?, in: Paulson – Walter (n. 17) 210–231, 225; Dreier (n. 15) 51 n. 138 with further references. For similar reasons (namely because of the supposition of a non-empirical, transcendental *basic norm*), Norbert Hoerster, Kritischer Vergleich der Theorien der Rechtsgeltung von Hans Kelsen und HLA Hart, in: Paulson – Walter (n. 61) 1–19, especially 18 finds Kelsen's theory less plausible than that of Hart. I think that the argument of Hoerster is a strong one; however, I am not going to discuss it here, since (as is emphasised by Hoerster himself) it cannot finally refute the *Stufenbaulehre*, but only weakens it.

[38] Hans Kelsen, Die philosophischen Grundlagen der Naturrechtslehre und des Rechtspositivismus [1928], in: *WRS* (n. 13) 281–350, 294; Hans Kelsen, *General Theory of Law and State*, Cambridge, Mass., Harvard University Press 1949 (hereafter: Kelsen, *GTL*), 437. The idea of the *basic norm* does, so to say, offer itself to be rewritten in the spirit of Natural Law. For such an attempt, see, e.g., René Marcic, Das Naturrecht als Grundnorm der Verfassung, in: Franz-Martin Schmölz (ed.), *Das Naturrecht in der politischen Theorie*, Wien, Springer 1963, 69–90.

[39] Hans Kelsen, Die Funktion der Verfassung, *Forum* 11 (1964) 583–586. He puts it in the same way in his posthumously published work: Hans Kelsen, *General Theory of Norms*, Oxford, Clarendon Press 1991 (transl. by Michael Hartney) [Hans Kelsen, *Allgemeine Theorie der Normen*, eds. Kurt Ringhofer – Robert Walter, Wien, Manz 1979] (henceforth *GTN*), 256.

[40] Joseph Raz, Kelsen's Theory of the Basic Norm, *American Journal of Jurisprudence* 19 (1974) 99–111.

inductively from the existing legal order), or a fiction (if it is not derived from the valid legal order but simply postulated).[41]

(e) According to the fifth possible objection, the *basic norm* is a redundant notion, since the question about the validity of the legal order or the constitution does not make any sense, as validity implies empowering; validity is a 'concept of relation' ('does the norm correspond to the constitution?'); therefore no question can be asked meaningfully about the validity of the legal order or the constitution.[42]

To give an answer to these questions (objections) is even harder, since Kelsen elaborated his views about the basic norm in different places, in different ways, and partially contradicts himself in his argumentation.[43] In the following, an attempt is made to reconstruct how one can meaningfully advocate the idea of the basic norm, even if some explanations of Kelsen have thereby to be rejected.[44]

The most important point is that the basic norm has an exclusively epistemological ('transcendental-logical')[45] function,[46] that is, the *basic norm* does not ground any claim for obeying,[47] and it does not even ground the objective existence of the legal order. It only serves the purpose of regarding a coercive order that claims to be law *as* an objective legal order. An objective object of knowledge is an implication of scientific survey, Kelsen says.[48] 'In different words: the Pure Theory of Law does not say that law *is* an objectively valid order, because one presupposes the norm, according to which one has to abide by the historically first constitution; but: law can only be regarded as an objectively valid

[41] Roman Herzog, *Allgemeine Staatslehre*, Frankfurt aM, Athenaeum 1971, 90.

[42] Cf. Rainer Lippold, *Recht und Ordnung. Statik und Dynamik der Rechtsordnung*, Wien, Manz 2000, 499–506, especially 505.

[43] Dreier (n. 15) 45 n. 117. Because of this contradictory nature, Priester calls the *basic norm* a chimera, i.e., something that has features, at the same time, that are not compatible with each other. Cf. Jens-Michael Priester, Die Grundnorm als Chimäre, in: Krawietz – Schelsky (n. 35) 211–244, 238. The chimera has the head of a lion, the back of a dragon, and the trunk of a goat. According to Priester, Kelsen's arguments about the *basic norm* are similarly 'manifold'.

[44] Here I follow principally Dreier (n. 15) 42–43.

[45] According to Kant (and the neo-Kantian Kelsen), 'transcendental' refers to the epistemological method (i.e., *a priori*) and 'transcendent' to the knowledge that is beyond experience. See Immanuel Kant, *Kritik der reinen Vernunft*, Hamburg, Meiner 1956, 69.

[46] Kelsen, *PTL2* (n. 16) 218; Behrend (n. 9) 65.

[47] Dreier (n. 15) 49.

[48] Hoerster (n. 37) 2.

order, *if* one assumes that one has to abide by the historically first constitution, that is, by *presupposing* the basic norm.'[49]

Therefore, any question of whether the *basic norm* is derived from the legal order or *vice versa*, is already wrong in itself. The only thing that exists temporally and logically before the *basic law* is the effective coercive order. The *basic norm* is not 'before' or 'after' the legal order, but renders it possible to conceive an effective coercive order – claiming to be law – *as* a legal order.[50] As Kelsen puts it: 'an anarchist, for instance, who denied the validity of the hypothetical basic norm of positive law . . ., will view its positive regulation of human relationships (such as property, the hiring contract) as mere power relations'.[51]

What is this all about, then? If one thinks of an action as accomplishing or violating a norm (norm as a schema of meaning), one presupposes the existence of a norm as well. Thus, the next question is why this norm exists, that is, where its validity comes from. As it cannot come from an 'is', one can only think of another norm (i.e., of another 'ought').[52] But this latter 'ought' also has its origins somewhere, and so on . . . – until one can no longer find a (man-made) norm, to deduce the norm from – then we are at the historically first constitution. Having once arrived at this point, one has to assume the existence of a basic norm and from this presupposed basic norm, the validity (the existence) of the historically first constitution is to be derived.[53] The basic norm is thus not part of the positive legal order, since it is not set, only supposed. It is therefore necessary to assume the existence of the basic norm in order that one be able to consider an act as accomplishing or violating a norm – and without that, any legal science is unthinkable.[54]

This argument (i.e., assuming the basic norm) is, of course, no use for the citizen or legal practice. But the basic norm of Kelsen was developed for legal science and not for the citizen.[55] Thus, the *basic norm* is essentially a

[49] Hans Kelsen, Recht, Rechtswissenschaft und Logik, *Archiv für Rechts- und Sozialphilosophie* 52 (1966) 545–552, 547 (italics in the original).

[50] Dreier (n. 15) 47 n. 119. [51] Kelsen, *GTLS* (n. 38) 413.

[52] Kelsen, *GTN* (n. 39) 255: 'Only a norm can be the reason for the validity of another norm.'

[53] On the identification of existence, validity and binding force in Kelsen, see below, n. 125.

[54] I.e., a non-proved supposition becomes *sine qua non* of scientific knowledge. It seems at first paradoxical, but a great deal of epistemological considerations work this way. See, e.g., Willard VO Quine, On Empirically Equivalent Systems of the World, *Erkenntnis* 9 (1975) 313–328.

[55] Raz (n. 40) 94–111, especially 107 and 109; JW Harris, When and Why Does the Grundnorm Change?, *Cambridge Law Journal* 29 (1971) 103–133, 117 n. 57a: 'The grundnorm is postulated by Kelsen as something logically essential to explain the practice of legal scientific discourse.'

useful postulate of legal scientific work.[56] What is the meaning of this? The *Pure Theory of Law* (as opposed to more old-fashioned positivism) does not say anything about the validity of norms in concrete legal orders; it regards its object of knowledge simply 'as if' it were valid law.[57] The basic norm is therefore only an epistemological postulate:[58] 'It allows us to show, to describe effective coercive orders as normative ones, or, more precisely, *as if* they were normative orders, although a science cannot decide this.'[59]

From the fact that the existence (validity) of the basic norm is hypothetical, it follows that the existence (validity) of the whole legal order is hypothetical, since the latter is derived from the former. If the legal order is based on an assumption (or presupposition) that is not proven and cannot be proven, it is obvious that one cannot prove its existence (and its synonym, according to Kelsen: its validity or legally binding power) either.[60]

A possible objection against this view could be that in this way the 'historically existing' legal order is based on uncertain ground, since the validity of the 'historically existing' legal order is based only on a postulate of legal scholars. This counter-argument, however, stems from a misunderstanding, since Kelsen did not say anything about the 'historically existing' legal order, so the question of its validity remains open. Kelsen makes use 1. of a concept of legal order that is consequent in terms of the theory of science (in a neo-Kantian sense) only for the purposes of legal scientific work, and he constructs, for that reason, a system of 'ought' for himself, that 2. is compatible with the everyday legal work/experience (i.e., with the generally effective coercive order experienced by him). This system of 'ought' (constructed from the point of view of a legal scholar) is, at the same time, not perceptible to the senses (thus transcendent): it is the 'price' to pay for the neo-Kantian method (especially the disparity of 'is' and 'ought').

After clarifying the function of the *basic* norm, we now turn to the question of the proper terminology. The problem with the '*hypothesis*' is that it is used in natural sciences only for assumptions that can be proven to be true or false. In the case of the basic norm, however, the question cannot be whether it is true or false. The problem with the notion of '*fiction*' is that what its purpose really is, is not explained.[61] Moreover,

[56] Robert Walter, Wirksamkeit und Geltung, *Zeitschrift für öffentliches Recht* 11 (1961) 532–541, 539–540.

[57] Cf. Walter (n. 4) 73.

[58] Walter (n. 4) 81; Behrend (n. 9) 71.

[59] Walter (n. 4) 80 (my italics).

[60] See also below, n. 127.

[61] Robert Walter, Entstehung und Entwicklung des Gedankens der Grundnorm, in: Walter (n. 5) 56–57.

one could make a similar objection to it as to the hypothesis, since it is characteristic for a fiction that it is not in accordance with reality. In the case of the *basic norm*, however, one cannot verify the truth; that is, one can never be sure that the *basic norm* does not exist 'in reality', because it is not perceptible to the senses (i.e., transcendent).

Consequently, the terminology of '*assumption*' (*'Annahme'*) – according to the suggestion of Walter Robert – seems to be the most appropriate.[62]

Basically, this terminology also gives an answer to the third ('fiction') and fourth ('*circulus vitiosus*') objections, since what is concerned is not a simple invention (fiction), nor the deduction of its existence from the legal order. As a matter of fact, it is about an epistemological assumption that allows us to conceive coercive orders that claim to be legal orders *as* (objective) legal orders, and allows them thereby to be examined by legal science.

What answer, then, can be given to the first ('effectiveness) and second ('metaphysics') objections?

The simplest – but relatively weak – answer could be that although for Kelsen effectiveness means a (necessary) condition of validity, it is not the ground of validity, and even less validity itself.[63] This answer would namely contradict the *Stufenbaulehre*, according to which a norm is to be considered as the ground of the validity of another norm, even because it is the condition of its creation (ground and condition are thus taken to be the same; that is, the argument of the *Stufenbaulehre* draws on the identification of both concepts). It is obvious that one cannot equate validity with effectiveness, since it is only about a 'conditional relation', but one could say that the hypothetical (assumed) validity has its origins in effectiveness. And in this way, the attempt to make a sharp distinction between 'is' and 'ought' would be a failure. What is, then, the proper answer that saves the *basic norm*? It is, in fact, the same that was said above, but from a different perspective.

Given the fact that the matter here is an epistemological assumption, one has to presuppose a basic norm, that serves the purpose of gaining the desired knowledge. Hence if the valid legal order has to be examined as well, one has to presuppose a basic norm that catches the examination of the valid legal order, that is, that allows legal science to examine the order supported by coercion. In this case, one cannot dispense with the element of effectiveness. This does not mean, however, that the basic norm is based on effectiveness, only that from the variety of possible basic norms, one has to choose the one which is the most useful for a legal

[62] Walter (n. 4) 80–81. [63] Behrend (n. 9) 70.

scientific examination, that is, the one supported by effective power.[64] In this way, redundant arguments can be avoided *(economy of thought [Denkökonomie]).*[65]

As for the (second) error, admitted by Kelsen, that is, the error of metaphysics, in the case of the basic norm it is not about metaphysics. In this aspect, Kelsen has made an admission of a charge that could not have been brought against him at all. He did not claim that the *basic norm* really exists, only that it has to be presupposed for the sake of legal scientific work, or, more precisely, one should pretend that it exists.[66] And an epistemological assumption that has its origins in pragmatics of science cannot be equated with the declaration of a transcendent existence. Kelsen does not claim the existence of any norm, not even of the basic norm: he only says that if one wants to conduct legal scientific work, one has to suppose that there are objectively existing norms.[67] Whether there are *in fact* norms can never be found out, as norms are transcendent (parts of the 'ought'), and so not perceptible to the senses.

The last objection, according to which the *basic norm* is a redundant notion, since any question about the validity of a constitution or a legal system is meaningless, would be adequate only if Kelsen understood validity as a concept of relation (i.e., a norm is valid only if it corresponds to the constitution). But validity is, according to Kelsen, a modus of existence (*Existenzmodus*) and not a concept of relation. In this sense, one may meaningfully ask questions about the validity of the constitution that originates from the basic norm.

Thus, objections to the *basic norm* are answered; that is, it has been defended (sometimes even against Kelsen).

[64] This means that, for example, the scientific analysis of the valid German legal order, one does not choose a *basic norm* that refers to the legal order of the Weimar republic. Thus, if one wants to work scientifically with the valid German legal order, one should not suppose the basic norm to be 'The Weimar constitution is valid.' See also n. 17.

[65] Cf. Leonidas Pitamic, Denkökonomische Voraussetzungen der Rechtswissenschaft, *Zeitschrift für öffentliches Recht* 3 (1916–1918) 339–367, 347. On the role of Pitamic in the development of the idea of the *basic norm*, see Kelsen (n. 10) xv; Walter (n. 61) 52.

[66] Hans Kelsen, Die philosophischen Grundlagen der Naturrechtslehre und des Rechtspositivismus [1928], in: *WRS* (n. 13) 294.

[67] This means that it is not necessary for the existence of the legal order to suppose the *basic norm* (to put it somewhat sharply: there also have been legal orders before the *Pure Theory of Law*), only for its scientific analysis. A scientific analysis does not give an answer to the question about the existence of the legal order anyway, but only presupposes it. In fact, the methodical starting points (e.g., moral relativism) are in general of metaphysical nature – but this is a general characteristic of all epistemological starting points. Cf. above n. 54.

A feature of the *Pure Theory of Law* has to be shown here which has so far not been mentioned, and which follows from the function discussed above. According to this theory, there is no legal order that is objectively obligatory *per se*. Supposition of the *basic norm* is in fact an *act of legal self-obligation* by the legal scholar,[68] i.e., normativity is not grounded as generally obligatory, but it depends on individual decisions. Individuals can reject or accept the claim of effective coercive orders to be legal orders. In the first case, they only regard norms as conglomerates of structures of power, as mere expressions of the factual situation; their objective validity is recognised only in the second case.[69] According to Kelsen, every legal approach is based on this latter hypothesis.[70]

The final conclusion is that objections to the basic norm are based on misinterpretations or can be eliminated by correcting the description of the basic norm.[71]

[68] Dreier (n. 15) 54 n. 160. This juristic self-obligation, however, does not mean that a given legal order is somehow morally justified, and lawyers are morally obliged to abide by it, since this is a moral question, and thus definitely eliminated by Kelsen from his theory of law.

[69] Objective validity means here a validity that is independent from the subjective will of the norm-poser.

[70] Dreier (n. 15) 55. Cf. Kelsen *Introduction* (n. 11) 58; Kelsen, *PTL2* (n. 16) 204–205, that the basic norm expresses only what positivists have always thought.

[71] But only if the methodological starting points are accepted (so especially the elimination of sociological and natural-law elements, and the objectivity of science). We cannot examine here the question if they resist.

The defence is a conditional one also in the sense that not all (possible) objections have been answered. (1) In particular, the sophisticated anti-Kelsenian example of Raz (n. 40) 98 was not discussed. Raz mentions a colony that becomes independent in peace, its constitution of independence being given by its mother country. In this case, the new constitution can be derived from the legal order of the mother country, i.e., from the basic norm of the mother country – although the former colony considers itself (as every other country, including its mother-country considers it) as an independent country that should thus have an independent basic norm. I.e. it is not an autonomous legal order after all. The objection of Raz can be overcome if one adopts the monism of international law – as does Kelsen himself – and hence considers all legal norms to be parts of a single huge legal order: in this way, arguments based on the 'independence of a legal order' are neutralised. This solution may, however, be problematic from other aspects, see also *12.1.2.3 The indefensibility of monism* below. (On the other anti-Kelsenian example of Raz, see n. 107.) (2) The criticism of Ilmar Tammelo, Von der reinen zu einer reineren Rechtslehre, in: Krawietz – Schelsky (n. 35) 245–252, 252, is also worth of mentioning, who says that a plurality of *basic norms* could also be logically imagined, as several logical systems exist with more axioms. Tammelo is undoubtedly right on this point. But if it is not about previously given *basic norm*(s), but constructions assumed by legal scholars themselves, then it is much more elegant to minimise the number of (epistemological) assumptions. Therefore, the objection of Tammelo is not very persuasive.

#### 12.1.2.2 Blurring the difference between individual and general acts

An important characteristic of the *Stufenbaulehre* in its original form is that it relativises the difference between general and individual acts, as it says that this difference is only one of degree.[72] The lower the level in the *Stufenbau*, the more concrete and individual the norm is. It precludes the perception of any sharp logical difference between general acts and individual acts.[73] The original argument may be, however, modified in order that the *Stufenbaulehre* survive the recognition of the difference between the individual and the general.

This amendment was made by Robert Walter, who is, after Kelsen, the most well-known exponent of the *Pure Theory of Law*. He holds the view that concretisation and individualisation are not interchangeable,[74] since a general norm (like a statute) may well be concrete, and an individual norm (like a command) may be general. So, for example, the disposition that 'the President of the United States ought to take a look at the White House from the south every morning at 8:15' is obviously a general one (as it is valid for every US President), even if it is completely concrete.[75] On the contrary, the disposition that 'Mr John Abraham Schmitt ought to do something good' is, without any doubt, an individual one, but not concrete at all.

A disposition is either individual or not. There are no transitional levels, no 'more' or 'less individual' norms. A transition in degree is possible only in terms of 'concreteness'. Therefore an amendment to the *Stufenbaulehre* has to be made; that is, the lower the level in the *Stufenbau*, the more concrete a norm is. But whether it is an individual one or not, is not explained by the *Stufenbaulehre*.

In this way, the *Stufenbaulehre* is not destroyed, only corrected to some extent. Both starting questions (1. where does the validity of law come from?; 2. what is the unity of legal order based on?) are therefore still answered by it.

72 Kelsen, *AStL* (n. 17) 235.

73 On the logical difference in Hungarian legal order see András Jakab, *A jogszabálytan főbb kérdéseiről* [On the Main Questions of a Theory of Legal Rules], Budapest, Unió 2003, 21–25.

74 Robert Walter, *Der Aufbau der Rechtsordnung*, Graz, Leykam 1964, 40–41.

75 'Concrete' means *specialis*, therefore its sphere of validity is a narrower one, see Jakab (n. 73) 43.

#### 12.1.2.3 The indefensibility of monism

In terms of the relation between national and international law, the *Pure Theory of Law* advocates monism.[76] Its grounds are of an epistemological origin; as Kelsen puts it: '*The unity of the epistemological position calls authoritatively for a monistic approach.*'[77] If one works with a unitary legal method, the object of knowledge also has to be unitary, since it is the method, according to neo-Kantian epistemology, that produces its object.[78]

It means that one has to accept monism – either with the primacy of international law, or with the primacy of national law.[79] The choice between the two is not a question of law but one of *Weltanschauung* and politics. The primacy of international law may be advocated by pacifists, the primacy of national law by imperialists.[80] Kelsen, being a pacifist, makes a stand for international law.

The question is, then, what this all has to do with the *Stufenbaulehre*. If there is only one legal order, there is only one basic norm. The *basic norm* of international law explains not only the validity of international law, but also the validity of national legal orders.[81] The national legal order (or the state itself) is therefore only a *partial legal order*.

[76] On the debates about the question, cf. Josef L Kunz, *Völkerrechtswissenschaft und reine Rechtslehre*, Leipzig, Deuticke 1923, 69–83. On Kelsen's theory of international law in general, see Alfred Rub, *Hans Kelsens Völkerrechtslehre. Versuch einer Würdigung*, Zürich, Schulthess 1995.

[77] Kelsen (n. 4) 123. Cf. also Jochen von Bernstorff, *Der Glaube an das universale Recht. Zur Völkerrechtstheorie Hans Kelsens und seiner Schüler*, Baden-Baden, Nomos 2001, 70–71. For a detailed criticism of Bernstorff, see András Jakab, Kelsen's Doctrine of International Law between Epistemology and Politics, *Austrian Review of International and European Law* (ARIEL) 2004, 49–62.

[78] See also Jürgen Mittelstraß, *Enzyklopädie Philosophie und Wissenschaftstheorie*, vol. 2, Mannheim, Bibliographisches Institut 1984, 989: the typically neo-Kantian claim of the '*unity of the object of knowledge*'.

[79] Kelsen, *AStL* (n. 17) 121: 'the necessary unity of the normative system. Two orders, as legal orders, cannot be declared as valid, unless their validity is somehow derived from a unitary reason of validity.'

[80] See, e.g., Hans Kelsen, *Principles of International Law*, New York, Rinehart 1952, 446–447. Cf. Bernstorff (n. 77) 93. For a detailed presentation of this argument, see Alfred Verdross, Völkerrecht und einheitliches Rechtssystem. Kritische Studie zu den Völkerrechtstheorien von Max Wenzel, Hans Kelsen und Fritz Sander, *Zeitschrift für Völkerrecht* 1923, 405–438, especially 415–416.

[81] On the changes of formulation of the basic norm of international law in Kelsen's *oeuvre*, see François Rigaux, Hans Kelsen on International Law, *European Journal of International Law* 9 (1998) 325–343, 328.

This argument and – in more general terms – monism is assailable at various points,[82] but the critique of monism is not discussed here, since monism and *Stufenbaulehre* are – despite of their connection by Kelsen – not necessarily connected to one another. Even Kelsen contradicts himself in this case, as in some places he speaks of monism and the basic norm of international law, while in others of the basic norm of a national legal order.[83] The contradiction between these two constructs is obvious, but it is not of importance here.

A suitable solution may be that monism is not a necessary consequence of the *Stufenbaulehre*: one could work without any problem with the basic norms of single national legal orders and still give an answer to the starting questions (1. where does the validity of law come from?; 2. what is the unity of legal order based on?). Thus, a dualist view may well be compatible with the *Stufenbaulehre.*[84]

Monism does not have to be discussed here, since if it is untenable, it can be separated from the *Stufenbaulehre* (hence the *Stufenbaulehre* may not be rejected in this way). On the other hand, if it is tenable, it simply cannot endanger the *Stufenbaulehre.*

#### 12.1.2.4 The validity of a norm conditioned by one single other norm

According to the *Stufenbaulehre*, the validity of a norm ('conditioned norm', *bedingte Norm*) stems always from one single other norm ('conditioning norm', *bedingende Norm*). The problem with this idea is – according to Öhlinger – twofold: 1. it is never *one single other* norm that is the condition of the validity of another norm, and 2. sometimes it is not *another* but the same norm that is the condition of its creation (procedural condition). Therefore, validity does not have to stem from *one single other* norm.[85]

For example, the procedural conditions of a statute are always the constitution, the standing orders of the parliament, or the Act on Promulgation (e.g., in Austria).[86] Thus, the case is anything but that

[82] As shown by Albert Bleckmann, Monismus mit Primat des Völkerrechts. Zur Kelsenschen Konstruktion des Verhältnisses von Völkerrecht und Landesrecht, in: Krawietz – Schelsky (n. 35) 337–347, especially 340.

[83] Bleckmann (n. 82) 339 with further references.

[84] A plurality of *basic norms* is used by Theodor Schilling, Zum Verhältnis von Gemeinschafts- und nationalem Recht, *Zeitschrift für Rechtsvergleichung, Internationales Privatrecht und Europarecht* 1998, 149–151.

[85] Öhlinger (n. 28) 17.

[86] Federal Act on the Federal Official Journal of 1996 (BGBl 1996/660).

*one single* other norm is the condition of setting a norm. Sometimes it is not even *another* norm. In making an amendment to parliamentary standing orders, the parliamentary standing orders themselves have to be followed and are therefore the conditions of their own creation. If one would like to draw the hierarchy according to the condition of creation, it would be a failure, since the result can only be an infinitely complex network—the descriptive potential of a metaphor of *Stufenbau* would be strongly limited.[87]

One can only say that the condition of setting a new norm is a part of the legal order (i.e., some of the norms). But this would also mean that there is no hierarchy anymore, always only two respective levels.[88]

The standard answer to such objections given by exponents of the *Pure Theory of* Law is that in the case of the *Stufenbaulehre* it is about an ideal type, and hence it cannot be denied by giving counter-examples.[89] This, however, contradicts the objective of the *Pure Theory of Law* that claims to be 'a general theory of dogmatics of positive law'.[90] If this theory does not fit to positive legal orders, the objective is obviously not achieved. Moreover, these are not simple counter-examples (exceptions) here, but general functional mechanisms of legal order(s) departing 'regularly' from the model of the *Stufenbaulehre*.

Thus, the problem seems to be even more complicated than Öhlinger or Walter saw it. It may be illustrated with a simple example of the amended regulation of procedure of parliament. The problem is the following: if a regulation of parliament was (in accordance with its own dispositions) already modified, its validity is based partially on itself, and

[87] Öhlinger (n. 28) 17.

[88] It is also acknowledged by Walter (n. 74), 63. A radical claim of Öhlinger (n. 28) 17–18. is based on this. According to Öhlinger, the hierarchy of legal order according to the legal conditioning (i.e., the original form of the *Stufenbaulehre*) is useless for legal theory. After this, Robert Walter, Die Lehre vom Stufenbau der Rechtsordnung, *Archivum Iuridicum Cracoviense* 13 (1980) 5–16, 9 refined his view: 'What I have told is that there are regularly only two different levels of conditions in law-making; it does not preclude the possibility of further levels. Would there be any of them, then Öhlinger too should consequently acknowledge a "hierarchy" according to the conditions of law-making.' To the argument of Walter, the following answer could be given, according to Öhlinger's logic. Even if one assumes that validity of a norm stems from one single norm in some cases, no hierarchy emerges there, since the next level is probably (in Walter's words: 'regularly') again an infinitely complicated network. This means that we have only one moment of sanity (a level of sanity) before going back to the jungle again.

[89] Bettina Stoitzner, Die Lehre vom Stufenbau der Rechtsordnung, in: Paulson – Walter (n. 17) 51–90, 58; Heinz Mayer, Die Theorie des rechtlichen Stufenbaues, in: Walter (n. 5) 37–46, especially 40–41.

[90] Robert Walter, *Hans Kelsens Rechtslehre*, Baden-Baden, Nomos 1999, 8.

the cat catches its own tail. There are two possible argumentative counter-tactics:

1. A possible solution could be to regard the amended regulation as a completely new one, whose validity can be derived from the former regulation (so one makes use of the fiction that a completely new regulation was set). The problem with this solution is not only that (a) it is not true (being a fiction); but also that (b) it is not compatible with lawyerly *common sense*. Do we have to regard an amended regulation as a new one just in order to save the *Stufenbaulehre*? Only this absurd answer seems to be possible – therefore this possibility is to be rejected.

2. Another solution could claim that only the validity of the amended dispositions (i.e., not the validity of the whole regulation) has to be derived from the regulation, thus not from the regulation 'in general', but from its previous state. In this way, circularity could be avoided, but a high price has to be paid for it: one cannot speak of validity of legal acts as a whole but only of validity of single dispositions (i.e., provisions). But if questions can be made only of single dispositions, it is not the whole legal act that *carries validity*, but only the single dispositions, and thus also the answer is to be found is single dispositions: therefore the validity of a disposition does not stem from another legal act but from the dispositions regulating its production (that are to be found in legal acts). And there are a great number of these.

The (historically first) constitution also comprises many dispositions; that is, the question would not be: 'Where does the validity of a concrete last positive valid normative unit come from?' (the answer for it was the *basic norm*). But there would be a number of last positive valid normative units (in this case dispositions). The *basic norm* would not, then, speak of the 'constitution' (or of obeying it), but about the 'dispositions of the constitution'.

Thus, the question is whether one can eliminate the objection of Öhlinger with this disposition-based and temporarily differentiated[91] *Stufenbaulehre*. The answer is yes. The validity of a disposition could in this way be derived from a number of other dispositions (this obvious 'complicatedness'[92] is the 'price' for such an amendment to the *Stufenbaulehre*), but it is, at least, never circular. The various lines of derivation ('chains of validity', using an expression of Raz)[93] do not come

[91] 'Temporally differentiated' refers to the distinction between the states of the norm in different moments.

[92] Therefore, there are not only a few lines of derivation (as one could imagine after Öhlinger), but hundreds (!).

[93] Raz (n. 40) 97.

together into a single disposition: there are more original starting points in positive law. The ensemble of these original starting points is called the historically first constitution.[94] Validity (or supposed/hypothetical validity) of these starting points is derived from the *basic norm*.

The originally elegant and simple *Stufenbaulehre* thus becomes an overcomplicated monster, but it is still alive. It still gives an answer to the questions about 1. the unity of the legal order, and 2. the origin of validity. It is the next point which gives it the *coup de grâce*.

#### 12.1.2.5 Derivation of validity (existence) of a norm in extreme examples

According to the next point of criticism, the basic idea that claims the validity of a norm to stem from the norm that regulates its creation is wrong in itself.

1. In order to understand this objection, one has to call forth the idea of the basic norm that was already discussed. According to this idea, the basic norm is only an assumption.[95] But since the validity (= existence in Kelsen's theory) of the whole legal order stems from the basic norm, the whole legal order is also only an assumption. This assumed legal order is used as a schema of meaning (*Deutungsschema*) to interpret different 'is'-events as violating or fulfilling the law.

This assumption has to be made by the individual himself or herself, it cannot be enforced. An anarchist will not share this assumption and will never use legal order as a scheme of meaning: experienced coercive acts will remain for him mere abuse of power and will never be interpreted as violating or fulfilling the law.[96]

There is a consequence of the assumptive character of the basic norm (and thereby of the whole legal order) that could best be described as *jurisprudential solipsism*: every legal scholar has a legal order in his mind and uses it as a scheme of meaning.[97]

[94] Cf. Walter (n. 74) 62, who rightly sees that the hierarchy of the legal order according to the conditions of law-making is independent from the traditional levels of the hierarchy of norms (e.g., constitution, statute), as the latter is the hierarchy of the legal order according to the derogatory power. See section 12.1.3 below for a more detailed account.

[95] See section *12.1.2.1* above.

[96] Therefore, one can always consider international affairs as an anarchy that is only subject to the principle of power; see Hans Kelsen, *Law and Peace in International Relations*, Cambridge, Mass., Harvard University Press 1942, 48 and 54.

[97] One may well ask whether these schemes of meanings (i.e., legal orders) are the same at all (at least in their content). There are good reasons for claiming that this is not exactly the case, since interpretation of law, according to Kelsen, always includes a subjective

2. But from the very *constructivist* nature of law described above (i.e., that the legal scholar assumes or constructs it in his mind) also follows the point that one cannot speak of automatic (logical) derivations. The validity of every single norm is constructed in the mind of the legal scholar. In an individual case, it always depends on him whether he carries out this construction: he follows the principle of economy of thought (*Denkökonomie*) here.

3. To avoid dangerous pathways of constructivist and solipsist structures of thought, Kelsen makes use of the principle of *Denkökonomie.*[98] According to that, redundant arguments have to be avoided, and one has to follow only those compatible with the objective of knowledge. The first consequence of this is that one has to assume a basic norm that is useful for legal scientific work.[99] Second, the *one-level* basic norm follows from the principle of *Denkökonomie*, since, in order to avoid *regressus ad infinitum*, a basic norm is assumed that immediately gives validity to the historically first (positive) constitution (without any intermediate levels through merely hypothetical quasi-basic norms).[100] Third, in the second edition of his *Pure Theory of Law,*[101] Kelsen takes for valid only those norms that are effective.[102] Kelsen's opting for this latter (and often ignored) amendment to his theory of law was perhaps motivated by the argument that assuming the validity of an ineffective norm would not lead to new legal knowledge; hence it was not worth assuming its validity (existence).

Without such a 'braking principle' like *Denkökonomie*, every constructivistic theory is haunted by scholastic metaphysics, in which it is unclear what knowledge can be gained from an argument. Therefore it is wholly justifiable that Kelsen makes use of it.

element; see Kelsen, *PTL2* (n. 16) 348–349. It means, then, that every legal scholar has a partially different scheme of meaning in his mind. These general problems of the *Pure Theory of Law* cannot, however, be discussed here at length.

98 Kelsen has adopted this from Pitamic (n. 66) 339–367, as he confirms it in his work: Kelsen (n. 10) xv.

99 Cf. n. 64 above.

100 Cf. Kelsen, *GTLS* (n. 38) 111, adopted from Achterberg (n. 25) 453; Behrend (n. 9) 77.

101 Kelsen, *PTL2* (n. 16) 211–212.

102 As opposed to the first edition, Kelsen, *Introduction* (n. 11) 60–61, where only the validity of the legal order as a whole was dependent on the effectiveness of the legal order as a whole, but not validity of every single norm from the effectiveness of that single norm. For a different perspective on this problem, see Robert Walter, Bemerkungen zu Kelsen, Geltung und Wirksamkeit des Rechts, in: *id.* (eds.), *Hans Kelsens stete Aktualität. Zum 30. Todestag Kelsens*, Wien, Manz 2003, 31–41, 35.

4. But if one follows the principle of *Denkökonomie*, the basic idea of the *Stufenbaulehre* also consequently falls, according to which validity can be derived. I am going to mention here two examples where the idea of derivation obviously does not work.

4/1. Let us assume that an administrative organ issues a norm 'A' according to the rules, but *nobody* regards it as existent (valid). In the following, the government or the legislative issues a number of other norms ('B', 'C') that are considered as valid by *everyone*.[103] In this case, the statement that 'norm *A* is a valid norm' is not necessarily false, but contradicts in any case the demand of *Denkökonomie*, and is therefore untenable. Of course, this example is not very probable, particularly in a state under the rule of law. But this improbability does not mean impossibility. It makes clear that validity is not 'derived' but 'emerges' (or does 'not emerge'), even because a norm is regarded as valid by those concerned with law.[104] The influence of norms (in our case the *norm regulating the creation of norms [Erzeugungsnorm]*) in this regard (belief) is, normally, a total one; but one can also think of 'abnormal cases' that make clear that this influence is not a conceptual necessity.

4/2. On the other hand, a norm may well be set without any *norm of creation*. In such a case, validity is not derived: its original emergence shows itself. A typical example for this is customary law. A flexible Kelsenian could answer: there is also a norm of creation in the case of customary law, but it is a tacit (implicit) one.[105] This tacit norm of creation has, however, a nature similar to that of the basic norm – in the sense that one has to presuppose it for the sake of legal scientific explanation.[106] The only difference is that the *basic norm* is a mere presupposition, but the tacit norm of creation is just an implicit appendix of a positive norm (or the constitution): that is, it is connected to a concrete (explicit) legislative act. Thus, the construction of Kelsen is to be saved with the help of this tacit *norm of creation*. The *Stufenbaulehre* would be confronted with an unsolvable problem only if a legal order that does not recognise customary law changes gradually (peacefully, without

[103] Thus, it is not about the *desuetudo* of the norm empowering to setting of norms.

[104] Any other theoretical construction of explanation would contradict the *Denkökonomie*.

[105] For a different perspective (as a strict Kelsenian, rejecting such implicit rules), see Robert Walter, Die Gewohnheit als rechtserzeugender Tatbestand, *Österreichische Juristen-Zeitung* 18 (1963) 225–232.

[106] It is underlined by Jorge A Bacqué, Stufenbau der Rechtsordnung oder Einebnung der Normenpyramide, in: Eugenio Bulygin – Ernesto Garzón Valdés (eds.), *Argentinische Rechtstheorie und Rechtsphilosophie heute*, Berlin, Duncker & Humblot 1987, 111–116, 115.

a revolution) to a legal order that recognises it. This new customary law can obviously not be 'derived': it has simply emerged.[107] It is not even possible to postulate a tacit *norm of creation*, since at first there was obviously no authorisation to set this customary law, and whoever (e.g., the legislator) could have given this authorisation to the courts (i.e., he could have set the norm of creation of customary law *[Gewohnheitsrechtserzeugungsregel]*), has not done it, not even implicitly, since he did not recognise customary law. In the legal orders where customary law is recognised, one can argue that the legislator implicitly attaches a *norm of creation of customary law* to every statute. But where customary law is not recognised, one cannot argue this, and if later (in applying previous laws) customary law actually becomes recognised, the *Pure Theory of Law* faces this phenomenon completely helplessly – as it cannot explain the origin of the new customary law.[108] For the *Pure Theory of Law*, it would be a completely new legal order, but this is seen, from the point of view of *Denkökonomie*, as an implausible reduplication (or construction).

If one, however, makes use of the principle of *Denkökonomie*, one could say that the validity of the new *norm of creation of customary law* does not have to be derived; it simply has to be assumed, since legal scientific work is made easier in this way.

5. As was shown, the idea of derivation fails in some cases. One should therefore rather accept that validity is not derived but assumed, according to the principle of *Denkökonomie* – and it is supposed for every single norm. In this way, not only usual acts of legislation but also the above-mentioned extreme cases could be explained.

One could say, however, that the examples mentioned here are so extreme (or even absurd), that failure of the *Stufenbaulehre* in these

[107] This sophisticated anti-Kelsenian example can be found in Raz (n. 40) 99. (On another anti-Kelsenian example by Raz – challenging its plausibility – see n. 71).

[108] One cannot defend the *Pure Theory of Law* either with the argument that the rule regulating the creation of norms in the new customary law came into existence slowly by evolution, since this slow evolution would mean that the rule regulating the creation of customary law was posed by way of customary law. This is, however, impossible, since customary law was not acknowledged (i.e., did not exist) before its rule of creation came into existence in the country of our example.

It would also be implausible to consider the legal order, which acknowledges the customary law, as a new legal order, as the great majority of norms (i.e., all but the rules of customary law) are to be derived from the historically first constitution of the 'old' legal order. To assume the existence of a new legal order, would be then, to a certain extent, a duplication of legal reality, and hence contradictory to the principle of *Denkökonomie*.

cases is not a serious problem, since in cases of normal (usual) legislation the idea of derivation still works. In the following, it will be shown that the idea of derivation does not work even in the case of the simplest legislation.

#### 12.1.2.6 Derivation of validity (existence) of a norm in the case of simple legislation

The idea of derivation does not work even in the case of the simplest legislation, since it implies a logical error that concludes with an 'is' from an 'ought'. Let us now turn to this point.

Kelsen holds – rightly – that one cannot conclude from an 'is' to an 'ought'.[109] The problem, however, is that it means, according to Kelsen, that an 'ought' may be derived only from another 'ought'.[110] Kelsen takes thus into account only two possibilities: the 'ought' is derived either (1) from an 'is', or (2) from another 'ought'. *Tertium non datur*. And since he – rightly – excludes the first one, only the second one remains. But there is still a third possibility, that is *law-making*. In the case of law-making, there is no derivation – not even in terms of validity. By law-making, a new norm is created. Its validity does not stem from the validity of another norm, but is autonomous and original: it is always just an assumption in the mind of the legal scholar. From the point of view of norm logic, it is created from nothing. In the following, this problem is analysed more thoroughly.

Further, Kelsen admitted that the content of the created norm could not be derived from the content of the norm regulating its creation.[111] But at least – as Kelsen probably thought – its validity should be derived from this other norm, or else one should derive it from an 'is'. The derivation from the 'is' is, however, (really) impossible. Therefore, the derivation of validity from another norm is, for Kelsen, necessary. Kelsen was puzzled by this problem from the beginning,[112] and Merkl's

[109] It is persuasively proven by Ulrich Klug, Die Reine Rechtslehre von Hans Kelsen und die formallogische Rechtfertigung der Kritik an dem Pseudoschluss vom Sein auf Sollen, in: Salo Engel (ed.), *Law, State, and International Legal Order: Essays in Honor of Hans Kelsen*, Knoxville, University of Tennessee Press 1964, 153–169, especially 156. He shows, without any doubt, that if one would like to have an 'ought' in the conclusion (of a syllogism), one also has to have an 'ought' in one of the premises.

[110] Kelsen, *GTN* (n. 39) 255: 'Only a norm can be the reason for the validity of another norm.'

[111] This is an important difference between the legal order and the norms of a moral system, see Kelsen, *Introduction* (n. 11) 55–56.

[112] Kelsen (n. 10) 411: 'This is the great mystery of law and state, that takes place in the act of legislation.'

*Stufenbaulehre* offered a – seemingly – good solution: it fit right into his theory; it was, so to say, the missing piece of the puzzle, which explained legislation in such a way that the strong disparity of 'is' and 'ought' could be still maintained.

But why is this conception of the validity of a norm so plausible at first sight? Since the setting of norms is regulated by norms, creation of a valid norm is regulated by another valid norm. One can thus easily have the delusion that validity of a produced (valid) norm stems from the norm regulating its creation *(rule of creation [Erzeugungsregel])*. But what does, then, the real situation look like?

The rule of creation only sets out under which conditions a new valid norm is created.[113] The mere fact, that the *rule of creation* prescribes how under certain conditions (law-making actions) a new valid norm is created, does not mean that under these conditions this norm is really created. It is only a rule that has to be abided by – but this abiding is not conceptually necessary. The basic logical error committed by Kelsen is the following: from that 'A' ought to be (the new norm ought to exist), he concludes that 'A' is the case (the new norm exists). But it is nothing other than the logical error condemned by Kelsen himself, the *naturalist fallacy*, only in the reverse direction. The error might have had its origins in the fact that the *rule of creation* does not prescribe any physical conduct (where any conduct departing from the norm, being visible, can easily show the fallacy of concluding from an 'ought' to an 'is'), but the existence of a norm. And it easily leads to the false simplification that this norm really exists. The structure of Kelsen's error may be formulated more clearly as follows:

(a) [rule of creation] 'If (performance of law-making actions), then (the law $ought_c$ to exist).'[114]
(b) [content of the concrete *l*aw] '*A* $ought_l$ to be.'

[113] Thus, it is not only a simple descriptive definition that defines the notion of 'valid norm'. In fact, it is a real 'ought' that prescribes which norm ought to be valid. In law, one often uses descriptive language, even if it is obviously a prescription. E.g., Art. 46(3) of the B-VG: 'The Federal President announces the national referendum.' It is only a simplification in style.

[114] It is very important to see that the rule of creation itself is a norm too. It is not merely a description like 'If (performance of law-making actions), then (the law exists)' or like 'If parliament enacts the law (B $ought_l$ to be done), then (B $ought_l$ to be done)'. The latter seems to be a prescription because it contains an 'ought' (precisely: '$ought_l$'), but its actual form would be 'If parliament enacts the law (B $ought_l$ to be done), then the law (B $ought_l$ to be done) *is* valid', which would be merely a description and not a norm.

Law-making according to *K*elsen:

(k1) 'If (performance of law-making actions), then (the law $ought_c$ to exist).'

(k2) Performance of law-making actions.

(k3) The law exists.

Law-making *r*ightly:

(r1) 'If (performance of law-making actions), then (the law $ought_c$ to exist).'

(r2) Performance of law-making actions.

(r3) The law $ought_c$ to exist.

It has to be made clear first that the 'ought' of the rule of creation ($ought_c$) and the 'ought' as content of the law thus created ($ought_l$) are not the same. If one does not confuse these two 'oughts', then the content of the law (b) is henceforth irrelevant. The rule of creation is a norm like other norms: it is thus not a descriptive rule like 'if (performance of law-making actions), then (the law exists)', but as a rule (norm) it also contains an 'ought'-element (as expressed by '$ought_c$').

As lawyer and as law-abiding man, one abides by this prescription *r3* ('Law $ought_c$ to exist.'); that is, one 'pretends/believes that' the respective norm really came into existence. And if all who are concerned with law believe it, one can suppose, for reasons of *Denkökonomie*, that this norm came into existence. Therefore, this *r3* rule is almost totally accomplished. This, however, does not mean any conceptual necessity (thus no derivation or deduction), only a very high degree of probability (even if this contradicts at first sight our legal intuition). From the aspect of the *Stufenbaulehre*, this is a hard problem, since it is based on the idea of derivation of validity. The two examples (4/1 and 4/2) above were intended to show that it is only about accomplishment of norms[115]

[115] To be sure: in a Kelsenian way, this 'abnormal exception' may not be explained by saying that the legal order is only 'by and large' effective anyway, and that this is also true for the derivation of validity. Effectiveness 'by and large' only refers to the accomplishment in the 'is' and not to the accomplishment in the 'ought'. But as it was just shown, even the accomplishment in the *Sollen* is not an automatic (logical) necessity: only a high level of probability. This means that validity, in fact, *cannot be derived*. Such a moment of probability that refers to the world of 'ought' is very far from the ideas of the *Stufenbaulehre*: derivation (deduction) of validity excludes this kind of validity based on probability. But validity is actually based on probability. And to add something more: this accomplishment of norms does not refer to the physical 'is', but to the existence of norms in the 'ought' (thus, this is not the usual sociological objection).

(and therefore only about a high probability) since, in these examples, the idea of derivation of validity failed, hence the improbable but possible distance between the creation of norms and the regulation of this creation could be observed here. In the first example, the new law does not come into existence, although the rule of creation was followed. In the second example, in turn, a new norm came to existence without any rule of creation. The error of Kelsen was that he replaced *r3* ('The law ought$_c$ to exist.') with *k3* ('The law exists.'), and thereby concluded implicitly from an 'ought' (*r3*) to an 'is' (*k3*).[116]

The final conclusion of the above argument is that in the case of law-making, the validity of a norm cannot be derived from the validity of another norm.[117]

What are the consequences for the *Stufenbaulehre*? Essentially, it means complete collapse, since the idea, according to which the validity of a legal norm stems from the validity of another legal norm, is a failure. Thereby the hierarchy of legal order according to legal conditioning and also the idea of the *basic norm* become untenable (redundant). One does not even reach the point where the question, to which the *basic norm* would be the answer, would arise.

Before turning to the effects of such a collapse of the *Stufenbaulehre* to the *Pure Theory of Law*, three problems should be examined more thoroughly: 1. another hierarchy of the legal order, 2. another attempt of the *Pure Theory of Law* to structure the legal order and 3. the alleged ideological background of the *Stufenbaulehre*.

116 This was an exclusively logical error and not an ontological one, since the law as well as the disposition 'Law ought$_c$ to exist' are in the sphere of 'ought'.

117 One could clearly refute the previous arguments by showing, with the means of symbolic logic, how validity can be derived in legislation in a way that content is not derived at the same time. There was, until now, no such attempt, which is, in itself, not a proof but rather a call for discussion.

It is worth mentioning that, at the end of his life, Kelsen also rejected the derivation of validity of norms from norms (for other reasons than those considered in our argument). Cf. his posthumously published theory of norms, according to which the validity of the individual norm cannot be derived from the validity of the general norm, as an act of will is also needed; see Kelsen, *GTN* (n. 39) 237–238. More generally: validity of a norm cannot be derived from another norm; see *ibid.* 423–424, endnote 179; Priester (n. 43) 238. Kelsen, however, did not revise the *Stufenbaulehre* (what would follow from this); see especially Kelsen, *GTN* (n. 39) 258 for his usual old content text.

On how logic became less and less important in the *oeuvre* of Kelsen, see Hendrik J van Eikema Hommes, The Development of Hans Kelsen's Concept of Legal Norms, in: Krawietz – Schelsky (n. 35) 159–178, 159–160.

### 12.1.3 An(?)other hierarchy of legal order

Merkl in his *Prolegomena* also mentions another hierarchy of legal order. It is the hierarchy according to the derogatory power (*derogatorische Kraft*). In the *hierarchy of legal order according to the derogatory power*, any norm 'A' is superior to norm 'B', if norm 'A' can derogate norm 'B', but the inverse is not possible. This method can be seen as a test of the *Stufenbau* according to the derogatory power; that is, in the case of two given norms one can decide, in this way, which one is superior to the other. This hierarchy is not identical with the hierarchy mentioned above as *Stufenbaulehre*, the *hierarchy of legal order according to the conditions of law-making (Stufenbau der Rechtsordnung nach der rechtlichen Bedingtheit)*, since the criterion of the hierarchy was, which norm regulates the creation of another norm.[118] Parliamentary standing orders, for example, are (in the case of an amendment to the constitution) superior to the act of amendments to the constitution in the *hierarchy of legal order according to the conditions of law-making*, since the latter has to be enacted according to the dispositions of the standing orders. In the hierarchy of legal order according to the derogatory power, however, an amendment to the constitution is superior to parliamentary standing orders, since the former can abolish (put out of force) the latter (and the reverse is not possible).

According to Merkl, norms as a default position are not derogable. The possibility of derogation is created only by positive law.[119] If positive law would not allow that, every small modification to a norm would lead to a completely new legal order. Thus, the necessity of the derogation stems from the fact that the identity of the legal order can be ensured only in this way.[120] The existence of derogation is, however, not a necessity of norm *logic*, only a question of expedience. Therefore, the hierarchy of the legal order according to the derogatory power is only a question of positive law, and not one of legal logic or of legal-logical necessity.[121] This may be the reason why Kelsen does not discuss this question more thoroughly and does not adopt this part of Merkl's argument.[122] This problem is re-introduced into the *Pure*

[118] Merkl, Prolegomena (n. 13) 1350; Friedrich Koja, *Allgemeine Staatslehre*, Wien, Manz 1993, 20.

[119] Adolf Merkl, Die Unveränderlichkeit von Gesetzen – ein normlogisches Prinzip [1917], in: *WRS* (n. 13) 1079–1090, 1088.

[120] Merkl (n. 7) 259. [121] Öhlinger (n. 28) 18. [122] Behrend (n. 9) 42.

*Theory of Law* only by Robert Walter in 1964,[123] and has since then been a topic frequently discussed in the writings of the Vienna School of legal theory.

The most puzzling question of the hierarchy of the legal order according to the derogatory power is, of course, the concept of derogation itself. According to the most widely used definition, derogatory power is 'the ability of a legal norm to abolish or at least confine the validity of another legal norm.'[124] Derogatory power basically depends on the law-making process (i.e., on the *rule of creation*). Thus, if another step in the process is needed to set a norm, it is superior to a norm that can be set in a more simple way.[125] If the law-making process is the same for both, they are at the same level.[126]

On the ground of derogatory force, another weak point of the current *Pure Theory of Law* becomes clear: validity is understood as existence but also as binding force. The expression 'to abolish validity' means namely the (peremptory) end of existence, while 'to confine validity' means 'lack of applicability'.[127] Applicability and existence do not have a relation of 'more-or-less', but are simply different concepts.[128] The most important difference is that if derogation means the end of existence, after the derogation of norm 'A' that has derogated

[123] Walter (n. 74) 55–56. See Robert Walter, Die Reine Rechtslehre – eine Theorie in steter Entwicklung. Einige Klarstellungen, *Juristische Blätter* 116 (1994) 493–495, 494. Cf. in terms of EU-law Jürgen Bast, Handlungsformen, in: Armin von Bogdandy (ed.), *Europäisches Verfassungsrecht*, Berlin, Springer 2003, 497–537, 505–506.

[124] Öhlinger (n. 28) 22; in the same way as Walter (n. 74) 57–58, but with different words ('complete annulment (*vollständige Vernichtung*)', 'to annul completely (*gänzlich vernichten*)' and 'to repeal irreversibly (*unwiederbringlich beseitigen*)' on the one hand, and 'limited repeal (*beschränkte Beseitigung*)' on the other hand; Mayer (n. 89), 43 with another different terminology ('peremptory [*endgültige*]' vs. 'temporal [*vorläufige*] derogation').

[125] Walter (n. 74) 59.

[126] Walter (n. 74) 55. But not necessarily *vice versa*: they may well stand on the same level, in spite of the different legislative processes. E.g., this may be the case with a statutory decree of former socialist countries or statutory instruments according to Henry VIII clauses in England, both of which are able to amend statutes, even though issued by the executive (thus not in a statute-making process).

[127] See 'validity' as the mere existence of a norm: Kelsen, *Introduction* (n. 11) 12 and 71–72 on the validity of unconstitutional statutes. On the other hand, as binding force, see *ibid.* 56–57. Normally, Kelsen uses the words *'Geltung'* and *'Gültigkeit'* as synonyms; see Hoerster (n. 37) 8.

[128] For a clear conceptual distinction, see also Ewald Wiederin, *Bundesrecht und Landesrecht*, Wien, Springer 1995, 51–52.

norm 'B', norm 'B' does not return but has to be set again. If, however, derogation means only the end of applicability, then after the derogation of norm 'A' derogating norm 'B', norm 'B' does return and become applicable again (since it existed continuously, but was not applicable, its applicability being suspended). Confusion of both conceptions is particularly problematic in terms of the relation of EU law to the law of Member States (priority in validity vs. priority in application). A striking example for the difference between the two is offered by the relationship of EU law and Member States law. The former does not affect the validity of national norms but has a priority of application (normally called supremacy of EU law) against them. Supremacy of EU law means that the legal order of a Member State can be applied only if the question is not regulated otherwise by EU law. EU law cannot, however, repeal the law of a Member State. Consequently, this priority of application is not more and not less than derogation (which is based on the concept of scope) but is simply of another nature.

In fact, legal orders can be hierarchised in more aspects.[129] 1. There is a hierarchy according to the power to put out of force (abolish) a norm.[130] In terms of the Hungarian legal system, for example, the hierarchy of sources of law is understood as this kind of hierarchy: a statute is thus superior to an ordinance, since the former can abolish the latter, while the reverse is impossible.[131] 2. Hierarchy according to priority in application is most characteristic of the US legal system, in which an act contrary to the Constitution is simply not applied (without being formally abolished) by the courts. This means that in the case of collision, the constitution has priority in application over statutes.[132] 3. And finally, one can speak of hierarchy according to 'annulment because of collision'.[133]

[129] This is indicated by the question mark in the title of this section after 'an', see *12.1.3 An(?) other hierarchy*.

[130] A particular form of abolition is the abolition of existence, which is a kind of abolition that has a retroactive effect on the beginning of the temporal sphere of validity.

[131] Jakab (n. 73) 71–72. According to that, one can go further into details. Abolition is in some legal orders (e.g., in Hungary, according to Art. 10(1) of the Act No. CXXX. of 2010 on legislation) only possible explicitly (formally), while in others also implicitly (materially) (e.g., in England, implied repeal doctrine), i.e., in the case of a contradiction, the former norm of the same level is to be considered automatically as abolished.

[132] See *Marbury v. Madison* 1 Cranch 137 (U.S. 1803).

[133] Annulment is actually a kind of abolition, i.e., because of some violation of the law. It may happen for substantive as well as procedural reasons. It is the former that is of importance here, i.e., annulment because of a contradiction with the content of another norm, since – as it was shown above – the hierarchy based on the process (i.e., the *Stufenbaulehre*) offers no clear and tenable structure for the legal order.

A superior norm can be recognised in the case of collision: if another norm is contrary to it, then it is annulled by an authority (mostly by the constitutional court).[134] The hierarchy according to annulment and the hierarchy according to the power to put out of force (abolish) a norm may be connected to each other. (In the current Hungarian legal system, for example, an infringement of the hierarchy according to derogation – that is, the hierarchy of sources of law – has the legal consequence of annulment by the Constitutional Court).[135] But this is not necessary: in a legal order without a constitutional court (or without a court having the power to annul norms) there is no hierarchy according to annulment, only one according to derogation or according to priority of application.

One may, of course, attempt to describe each legal order with each form of hierarchy. The question is, however, by which description the most transparent and complete picture of the respective legal system can be obtained. If there is a contradiction between the two criteria, one has to deliberate.

The now undifferentiated concept of derogation is, however, not able to describe hierarchies adequately.[136] Therefore, some Austrian attempts to explain the relation of EU law and Member State law with the help of this undifferentiated concept of derogation, by including EU law into the hierarchy of Austrian law, are doomed

[134] In my view, this is the best way to give an account of the hierarchy of norms in the Austrian legal order, since the hierarchy according to abolition cannot handle the fact that the federal constitution (*Bundesverfassung*) cannot entirely abolish the constitution of Member States (*Landesverfassung*) – although it is described by the accounts of the hierarchy of Austrian legal order as superior to them; see, e.g., Theo Öhlinger – Harald Eberhard, *Verfassungsrecht*, Wien, Facultas [9]2012, para 9. This derogation would be contrary to the fundamental principles of the federal constitution (which are, according to the accounts of the hierarchy, superior to the federal constitution); see Öhlinger (n. 28) 25 with further references. Another special feature of the Austrian hierarchy of norms is that single dispositions may also have a hierarchic relation to each other (e.g., in certain statutes there are dispositions that are explicitly defined as having a constitutional status – see Art. 1 of the *Datenschutzgesetz*). In most other countries, on the contrary, only legal acts (e.g., statutes, ordinances) can have a hierarchic relation (and the criterion for the hierarchy is the derogatory power, but not the annulment by the constitutional court).

[135] Cf. Jakab (n. 73) 74 n. 159.

[136] There are two possible solutions: (1) Either one always expresses unequivocally, which kind of derogation is spoken of (e.g., *derogation as abolition* or *derogation as priority in application*), (2) or one uses the notion of 'derogation' only for *abolition*.

to fail as well,[137] since in this way different relations of subordination are confused.[138]

This does not mean to say that the search for hierarchy is useless for describing legal orders. But one should work with a more differentiated concept of hierarchy than was the case until now.

First, it needs to be mentioned that these hierarchies do not amend the *Stufenbaulehre* but make use only of another (new) concept of hierarchy.[139] The *Stufenbaulehre* (i.e., hierarchy of the legal order according to the conditions of law-making) answered two questions: 1. where does the validity of law come from?, and 2. what is the unity of legal order based on? As the hierarchies sketched above fail to answer these questions, they therefore cannot be accepted as substitutes for the collapsed *Stufenbaulehre*.[140]

## 12.2 Another attempt of the *Pure Theory of Law* to structure legal order

Here we have to make an excursus to present briefly an attempt to structure the legal order, made by Robert Walter, the most eminent exponent of the

[137] One of the advocates of this approach is Theo Öhlinger, a sharp critic of the *Stufenbaulehre (the hierachy of legal order according to condition of law-making)* (see above, *12.1.2.4 The validity of a norm conditioned by one single other norm*); Theo Öhlinger, Unity of the Legal System or Legal Pluralism: The Stufenbau Doctrine in Present-Day Europe, in: Antero Jyränki (ed.), *National Constitutions in the Era of Integration*, The Hague, Kluwer Law International 1999, 163–173. For further discussion of this approach, see Alfred Schramm, Zweistufige Rechtsakte – oder: Über Richtlinien und Grundsatzgesetze, *Zeitschrift für öffentliches Recht* 56 (2001) 65–96, 69 n. 11. These objections are surprising particularly because also (a part of) Austrian literature sees clearly that the word 'derogation' nowadays refers to more concepts; see Stoitzner (n. 89), 64, 67–68; Öhlinger (n. 28), 22. I would like to add that the problem here is not that the use of notions is discussed on another level. In that case, Austrian literature should speak of two different 'hierarchies of the legal order according to derogatory power'. One speaks, however, of a single hierarchy of legal order according to the derogatory power, although two completely different phenomena are meant by 'derogation'.

[138] See my more detailed criticism: András Jakab, Az osztrák EU-csatlakozás alkotmányjogi szempontból [Austrian EU Accession from the Perspective of Constitutional Law], *Jogelméleti Szemle* (http://jesz.ajk.elte.hu/) (2002/1) II./1.3.2.

[139] A different view: Mayer (n. 89), 41–42.

[140] This hierarchy (these hierarchies) is (are) 'weaker' also in the sense that individual norms (*Einzelakte*) are not included; see Stoitzner (n. 89), 71; a particular survey is needed in the case of every legal order to elaborate on this question.

*Pure Theory of Law* since Kelsen.[141] His structuring suggestion has some points in common with that of Hart ('primary rules' – 'secondary rules'). The success of Walter's theory may show that the *Pure Theory of Law* is to be considered as living legal theory (not simply an interesting moment in the history of ideas), even without the *Stufenbaulehre*.

Walter's argument begins with criticism of Kelsen:[142] it shows that Kelsen, in his *Pure Theory of Law*, makes use of two different concepts of norm, a dynamic – as Walter puts it – and a static one, not keeping them strictly separate.[143] The first one is working with a 'norm' that is so large that it is unmanageable, meaning the whole condition of the application of sanctions (beginning with the constitution, through the statutes and ordinances relevant for the case, to the concrete judicial decision); the latter describes a norm, that makes the individual levels in the hierarchy.[144] If one speaks of norm in the dynamic sense, then norms cannot form a hierarchy, and one can speak of a hierarchy at most inside of a norm. The norm is dynamic, because it comprises the whole line of *creation* that leads to the use of coercion.

The advantage of the static norm is that one can easily work with it;[145] it is, however, less suitable for explaining the dynamics of the legal order. Walter calls this static norm *legal disposition* (*Rechtsvorschrift*).[146] The hierarchy of the legal order according to the derogatory power is built on these *legal dispositions*.[147] One has to consider *'legal disposition'* in legal theory because collisions emerge between concrete *legal dispositions*.[148]

The advantage of the dynamic norm is that every legal phenomenon can be described as part of the dynamic norm.[149] Its disadvantage is that

[141] At which points Walter developed the view of Kelsen (and differed from his master); see Wolfgang Schild, *Die Reinen Rechtslehren. Gedanken zu Hans Kelsen und Robert Walter*, 1975, 33–35.

[142] Contemporary *Pure Theory of Law* often claims that it not only reconstructs and applies the doctrines of Kelsen, but also criticises and develops them. See Robert Walter, Die Reine Rechtslehre – eine Theorie in steter Entwicklung. Einige Klarstellungen, *Juristische Blätter* 116 (1994) 493–496.

[143] Walter (n. 74) 16–17.

[144] Raz (n. 21) 109 actually points out the same thing. According to him, the following Kelsenian theses contradict each other: 1. every norm is supported by a sanction; 2. some norms are only empowering to the setting of norms, but are not directly supported by sanctions. The reason for this contradiction is that Kelsen makes use of two different concepts of norm, but not explicitly. Raz shows the difference as one between static and dynamic points of view; see Raz (n. 21) 110–112.

[145] Walter (n. 74) 19. [146] Walter (n. 74) 46–47.

[147] Walter is interpreted in this way by Stoitzner (n. 89) 56. [148] Walter (n. 74) 51.

[149] Walter (n. 74) 18.

it is too broad[150] and therefore difficult to work with;[151] this is why Walter modifies it. Then it is basically a renewal of the hierarchy according to the legal condition. In Walter's view, the positive legal order consists of three kinds of norms: 1. rules of creation of coercive norms (*Zwangsnormerzeugungsregeln*), 2. coercive norms (*Zwangsnormen*) and 3. rules of execution of coercive norms (*Zwangsnormvollzugsregeln*).[152] Walter basically adheres to the original idea that validity of coercive norms stems from the validity of rules of creation of coercive norms.[153] The respective objections have already been developed above.[154]

In fact, Kelsen does not regard the norm called *rule of creation of coercive norms* by Walter as (completely) autonomous, but only as part of the 'great norm' called dynamic norm by Walter *(incomplete legal norm [unvollständige Rechtsnorm])*.[155] According to Walter, this is problematic, since the idea of Kelsen would be possible only if the coercive norm has already been created. Until then, however, the existence of the rule of creation of coercive norms is unmanageable in the system of Kelsen (as being just an incomplete norm).[156] Hence, it also has to be considered – according to Walter – as an autonomous norm.

This makes clear why the *rule of creation of coercive norms* is considered to be autonomous. The next question is, then, what is the difference between *Zwangsnorm* and *Zwangsnormvollzugsregel* based on. In Walter's view, this differentiation is necessary, because in this way one can also explain the difference between formal law (*Zwangsnormvollzugsregel*) and material or substantive law (*Zwangsnorm*) in this theory.[157] The rule of execution of coercive norms regulates the way from the coercive norm to the physical coercive act. Traditionally, it is the task of the legislature to set

150 In the same way Raz (n. 21) 115: the dynamic norm is counter-intuitive (it does not correspond to lawyerly *'common sense'*) and over-complicated.

151 Walter (n. 74) 18.

152 Consequently, the *basic norm* is not part of the positive legal order, and therefore he does not deal with it here. Hence the fact that Walter does not explicitly discuss the *basic norm* in this work, is – in my opinion – exclusively due to the fact that he only describes the structure of positive law. On Walter's view about the *basic norm* in details, see Robert Walter, Die Grundnorm im System der Reinen Rechtslehre, in: Aulis Aarnio e.a. (eds.) *Rechtsnorm und Rechtswirklichkeit. Festschrift für Werner Krawietz zum 60. Geburtstag*, Berlin, Duncker & Humblot 1993, 85–99.

153 Walter (n. 74) 26.

154 See above: *12.1.2.6 Derivation of validity (existence) of a norm in the case of simple legislation.*

155 Kelsen, *Introduction* (n. 11) 52–53.

156 Walter (n. 74) 26–27. This is the reason why Raz criticises Kelsen; cf. Raz (n. 21) 117.

157 Walter (n. 74) 28.

the coercive norm, whereas setting the rules of execution of coercive norms is accomplished by the executive.[158] The rule of creation of coercive norms is essentially the constitution in a material sense, that is, the rules of law-making.[159]

All three kinds of norms comprise a number of legal dispositions.[160] A legal disposition may be part of more *coercive norms* at the same time: *legal dispositions* of the general part of the Criminal Code are, for example, part of every coercive norm in criminal law (i.e., of the special part of the Criminal Code).[161] A *legal disposition* may even be simultaneously part of a *Zwangsnormerzeugungsregel* and a *Zwangsnorm*, or of a *Zwangsnorm* and a *Zwangsnormvollzugsregel*, or of all the three.[162] A *legal disposition* creating an organ that participates in the creation of coercive norms as well as in the execution of coercive norms is at the same time part of the rule of creation of coercive norms and the rule of execution of coercive norms. A *coercive norm* as a whole is part of a *rule of creation of coercive norms* if it is superior to the norm (to be produced) regulated by the *rule of creation of coercive norms*, and thus the new norm cannot contradict to it.

According to Walter it is important to emphasise that the execution of the coercive norm is not mere execution but also specification. There are three kinds of specification:[163] 1. if the description of facts is inaccurate, 2. if the sanction is unclear and if 3. the description of facts and the sanction are not connected unconditionally (so-called real discretion).

Let us now turn to the assessment of Walter's theory. A comparison with the similar structure of the legal order suggested by Herbert Hart seems to be a useful starting point. In this respect, the following can be stated: 1. as a first step, Hart's 'primary rules' can be equated with Walter's *Zwangsnormen*, and Hart's 'secondary rules' with Walter's *Zwangsnormerzeugungsregeln* and *Zwangsnormvollzugsregeln* (and with the basic norm that is not part of the positive legal order). 2. It is, however, an important difference (in addition to the epistemological differences that are not analysed here) that according to Hart, coercion is not a conceptual element of law and therefore his structure of the legal order is not based on this. This may be seen as a slight advantage of Hart, since the theory of Walter cannot handle legal orders not based on

[158] Walter (n. 74) 31. To what extent Walter is right in this particular question is not discussed here.

[159] Walter (n. 74) 30–31 and 35–36.

[160] Walter (n. 74) 48.

[161] Walter (n. 74) 48. Cf. Jakab (n. 73) 60.

[162] Walter (n. 74) 51–52.

[163] Walter (n. 74) 39.

physical coercion (e.g., canon law). 3. And finally, they also have different backgrounds of legal traditions. Walter tries to adopt traditional German or Austrian legal concepts (e.g., the difference between formal and material law) in a new framework of legal theory.[164]

This new attempt of the *Pure Theory of Law* to structure the legal order cannot be regarded as a successful one for three reasons. First, Walter also commits the 'error of derivation'; that is, he tries to derive the validity of a norm from another norm. On the other hand, he does not make a clear distinction between legal provision (e.g., a section or an article of a statute) and legal act (e.g., a statute) but includes both in the concept of *legal disposition*. And finally, the conservation of coercion as a conceptual element of law excludes non-coercive legal orders (e.g., canon law) from the analysis. The so-called error of derivation is the most difficult to solve of all problems mentioned above. It is another reason why this structure of legal order cannot count as a substitute for the collapsed *Stufenbaulehre* (12.1.2.6).

## 12.3 Excursus: the underlying ideology of the *Stufenbaulehre*

In the following, I will examine what ideological background of the *Stufenbaulehre* is often alleged to have and whether it is justified. Three typical problems are to be discussed from this aspect: 1. the inherent autonomy of law, 2. the effect of acknowledging the legal nature of general internal orders of the administration on the doctrine of the separation of powers and 3. the role of theological conceptions of hierarchy.

These underlying ideologies are not homogeneous, but this does not exclude the point that they have really exercised some influence over the *Stufenbaulehre*. We have to emphasise in advance, however, that such an unveiling of underlying ideologies cannot prove the *Stufenbaulehre* erroneous.[165]

[164] Moreover, Walter's theory also includes a striking criticism of Hart: the distinction between *primary rules* and *secondary rules* (and their 'sub-classes') is actually not as easy to make as one could think at first sight after Hart.

[165] To unveil the underlying ideology of a legal theory would refute it only in the case that legal theory would be considered as pure ideology, i.e., if one denied any autonomy of it whatsoever. This approach is characteristic of Marxism. Without discussing this question here at length, it has to be stated that the above analysis of the underlying ideologies of the *Stufenbaulehre* is not intended to do that. Examining the ideological background may only be an interesting excursus in a legal theoretical analysis, but it belongs to another dimension. To show this background, in my opinion, does not mean supporting (or rejecting) a theory of law, only explaining it (from the perspective of the sociology of science).

### 12.3.1 Autonomy of law

An important feature of the *Stufenbaulehre* (and of the *Pure Theory of Law* in general) is the emphasis on the autonomy of modern law *(Selbsterzeugung des Rechts)*.[166] In terms of sociology of science, this idea may have its origins in the experience of reality in the Austro-Hungarian Monarchy, a state of four nations, where other integrative factors (a common culture, language, national mentality) were obviously absent. Therefore, only law remained as the factor of convergence.[167]

One may ask two questions concerning autonomy: 1. Is modern law really autonomous?; 2. Is it socially desirable and useful to believe that it is autonomous? Ad 1. Modern law is, without any doubt, more autonomous than former laws were; that is, it is more independent of social morality than were pre-modern ones. The answer to the question whether the high degree of autonomy that is asserted by the *Pure Theory of Law* is present in reality, would, however, lead too far away and over-extend the scope of this chapter.

Ad 2. The answer to the question if it is useful for the society to believe that law is autonomous depends on the social context, since the belief in the autonomy of law may be confirmed by the belief in its autonomy. Thus, if there is a social morality that does not allow society to develop efficiently (e.g., lack of respect for property), it may be helpful to regard (and describe) law as autonomous, since arguments like 'but according to the morality of society . . . ', that inhibit the development of society may in this way be rejected as possessing legal utility. But if social morality works for an efficient social structure, as is the case in the United States, this could be used for a more efficient achievement. Scholars of legal theory are, however, not always aware of that, and in this case – depending on the conception of ideology used – even the ideological character of the respective legal theory may be challenged. This argument, however, is not one of legal science. It is mentioned here as an often forgotten point of view, but its more thorough discussion would lead us too far away from the focus of the present discussion.

[166] Öhlinger (n. 28) 10. The autonomy of law in Kelsen's system is emphasised in the same way by Raz (n. 40) 96.

[167] Walter (n. 90) 19; Rudolf Aladár Métall, *Hans Kelsen. Leben und Werk*, Wien, Deuticke 1969, 22. I do not mean by this that, beside the above-mentioned factors, only law can play an integrative role. However, the lack of other factors has shaped the autonomous idea of law in the *Pure Theory of Law*.

### 12.3.2 Separation of powers and acknowledging the legal nature of general internal policies of the administration

The two most important virtues of the *Pure Theory of Law* are, in terms of legal policy are as follows: 1. the theoretic ground for constitutional control and 2. acknowledging the legal nature of general internal policies of the administration.[168]

Ad 1. Emphasising the applicative character (*Rechtsanwendungscharakter*) of the setting of norms (and of the legislation in particular), the *Stufenbaulehre* also supported the possibility of judicial control of the legislative power. It has thereby set the theoretical grounds for constitutional control[169] and thus contributed to the development of the rule of law (*Rechtsstaatlichkeit*).

Ad 2. By acknowledging the legal nature of general internal policies of the state administration, *Stufenbaulehre* was of great assistance to democracy and particularly to a democratic administration.[170] 'Democratic administration' means administration bound by statutes,[171] since statutes are expressions of the will of the people.[172] If we acknowledge the legal nature of general internal policies of the state administration, then we make a judicial review of these policies possible, so we can more efficiently force the state administration to abide by the laws of the legislature.

*Stufenbaulehre* also means the rejection of traditional theories of separation of powers, where there are three powers of equal position. According to the *Stufenbaulehre*, the two other powers (executive and judiciary) are similarly subordinates to the legislative power that expresses democracy. This finally means that there are only two powers (legislative and implementing powers; but within the latter, the executive and judiciary act separately).[173] The *Stufenbaulehre* thereby provided the conceptual

[168] Öhlinger (n. 28) 28.

[169] Hans Kelsen, Wesen und Entwicklung der Staatsgerichtsbarkeit, *Veröffentlichungen der Vereinigung der Deutschen Staatsrechtslehrer* 1929, 30–88; Kelsen, *Introduction* (n. 11) 71–73; Verdross (n. 17).

[170] Behrend (n. 9) 18. On the legal nature of general internal orders of the administration, see also Hans Heinrich Rupp, *Grundfragen der heutigen Verwaltungsrechtslehre*, Tübingen, Mohr 1965, 11–13; Norbert Achterberg, Kriterien des Gesetzesbegriffs unter dem Grundgesetz, *Die öffentliche Verwaltung* 1973, 289–298, 298; Christoph Möllers, *Staat als Argument*, Tübingen, Mohr [2]2011, 154–156; Jakab (n. 73) 83, especially n. 172.

[171] Öhlinger (n. 28) 31; Hans Kelsen, *Vom Wesen und Wert der Demokratie*, Tübingen, Mohr [2]1929, 69–70.

[172] Merkl (n. 25) 339; Kelsen (n. 171) 70–71.

[173] Öhlinger (n. 28) 29.

framework and a legal legitimacy for parliamentary democracy.[174] This new configuration of powers may be called – in the words of Öhlinger – *the hierarchy of the branches of powers (Stufenbau der Staatsfunktionen).*[175]

*Stufenbaulehre* thus served the idea of democracy (democratic administration) as well as that of the rule of law (judicial review of statutes).[176]

### 12.3.3 Secularised theological conceptions of hierarchy

According to one well-known argument, the *Stufenbaulehre* is the secularised form of theological conceptions of hierarchy.[177] The idea of the hierarchy of norms has, without doubt, its origins in the Middle Ages, or even in antiquity *(lex divina, lex aeterna, lex naturalis* and *positiva).*[178] Knowledge of these conceptions has probably had an impact on the views of contemporary lawyers. But the hierarchy of norms is a construct so general that it cannot be connected exclusively to theology. It is not hard to imagine that these conceptions of hierarchy had a real influence on the authors of the *Stufenbaulehre*; it is, however, difficult to prove and – to my knowledge – this has hitherto not been attempted by anyone on the basis of concrete texts. But *Stufenbaulehre* itself is not necessarily connected to – perhaps doubtful – theological conceptions of hierarchy.

According to another – maybe more interesting – argument, one of the questions that the *Stufenbaulehre* is intended to answer is of theological nature: the question about the origin of the validity of law,[179] that is, the assumption that there is a starting point from which validity may be derived. This argument again seems to be plausible, but it is not an argument of legal theory against the *Stufenbaulehre*, and may therefore only be considered as a suggestion for the explanation of its genesis.

[174] Öhlinger (n. 28) 32.

[175] Öhlinger (n. 28) 30. Although some – e.g. Stoitzner (n. 89), 73–75 and Öhlinger (n. 28) 30 – regard this as a special *Stufenbaulehre*, it is, in my opinion, something different, since it gives (similarly to the hierarchy according to derogatory power) no answer to the starting questions (1. origin of validity, 2. unity of legal order). It is, therefore, only an underlying ideology and the political consequence of the *Stufenbaulehre*.

[176] Öhlinger (n. 28) 32. [177] Krawietz (n. 35) 255–257.

[178] Öhlinger (n. 28) 9 n. 1. According to Werner Krawietz, Reinheit der Rechtslehre als Ideologie?, in: Werner Krawietz – Ernst Topitsch – Peter Koller (eds.), *Ideologiekritik und Demokratietheorie bei Hans Kelsen*, Rechstheorie, Beiheft 4, Berlin, Duncker & Humblot 1982, 345–421, 413 this is why its influence is so strong. It may certainly have contributed to the success of the *Stufenbaulehre*, but it was perhaps even more important that it could give an answer to a number of complicated questions of legal theory with the help of a surprisingly simple construction.

[179] Krawietz (n. 35) 258.

## 12.4 Is the *Pure Theory of Law* still alive?

### 12.4.1 *Summary of the argument*

After reconstructing the *Stufenbaulehre* (12.1.1), the most important objections to it have been discussed (12.1.2). Most of the objections (especially those against the *basic norm* and the statement that the validity of a norm is conditioned by one single other norm) could be refuted, except for one: this 'lethal' thrust was given the *Pure Theory of Law* by the basic doubt as to the derivation of validity (existence) of a norm from another norm. It has, in fact, also made the previous defence of the *basic norm* pointless, as the question of the basic norm is not at all reached in this way.

This was followed by an analysis of the hierarchy according to the derogatory power (12.1.3). It was shown that it is, unlike the former hierarchy (according to legal condition), useful for legal theory (or even for black-letter legal science), and that it has a certain explanatory potential, but the concept of derogation should be used in a more differentiated way than is currently the case. As criteria of the hierarchy of norms, priority in application (*Anwendungsvorrang*), abolition (*Aufhebung*) and annulment (*Vernichtung*) should be distinguished. These hierarchies, however, cannot replace the collapsed (12.1.2) hierarchy according to the condition of law-making (i.e., the *Stufenbaulehre*) in the system of the *Pure Theory of Law*, as they cannot answer the starting questions of the *Stufenbaulehre* (i.e., 1. what is the unity of legal order based on?, and 2. where does the validity of law come from?).

After that, another attempt for structuring the legal order, made by Robert Walter, the most eminent contemporary exponent of the *Pure Theory of Law*, was sketched. His theory has some common features with the theory of Hart (12.2). It was, however, shown that also the theory of Walter suffers from the 'error of derivation' and has therefore also to be rejected.

An analysis of the alleged ideological background made clear that these ideologies may well have had an impact on the shape of the *Stufenbaulehre* (12.3). But these arguments (i.e., 'unveiling' the backgrounds) cannot refute the *Stufenbaulehre* as a construct of legal theory; refutation is only possible by way of legal theoretical arguments (as it was done e.g., above in 12.1.2.6).

### 12.4.2 *Perspectives of the* Pure Theory of Law

If observations have to be made on the perspectives of the *Pure Theory of Law*, one could state the following. The *Stufenbaulehre* was a central, important part of the *Pure Theory of Law* (it was not by coincidence that Kelsen mentioned Merkl as co-founder of the Vienna School of legal theory). By its failure, the *Pure Theory of Law* is also doomed to fail. In the system of the *Pure Theory of Law*, the *Stufenbaulehre* was intended to answer two questions: 1. what is the unity of legal order based on?, and 2. where does the validity of law come from?[180] Even the notion of legal norm is defined in this way: a coercive norm of the state differs from the threat of sanction made by a gangster inasmuch as the former may be included in the hierarchy of the legal order.[181] Without the *Stufenbaulehre*, the *Pure Theory of Law* cannot solve this problem.

The *Pure Theory of Law* narrowed its field of examination rather strongly anyway (no sociology, no moral deliberations). Therefore, if it can no longer answer the abovementioned questions, not much of the world of law remains that could be explained by it.[182] Hence the *Pure Theory of Law* no longer has perspectives.

### 12.4.3 *The virtues of the* Pure Theory of Law *and whether they can be saved*

This does not mean, however, that the *Pure Theory of Law* has no virtues and achievements for legal theory that are worth saving. These conservable theses or features could not all be thoroughly discussed in the present chapter, and are only briefly mentioned here:

[180] Behrend (n. 9) 54; Dreier (n. 15) 43.

[181] Andreas Trupp, Zur Kritik der Stufenbautheorie und wissenschaftstheoretischen Konzeption der Reinen Rechtslehre, in: Krawietz – Schelsky (n. 35) 299–317, 300. Cf. Kelsen, *GTN* (n. 39) 27–29.

[182] The only way remaining is the one that leads back to the state of 1911, see Kelsen (n. 9) 10: 'Here it is shown unequivocally that any question about the formation and destruction of the "is" is beyond the perception of the "is" (*Seinsbetrachtung*) and its particular (causal) epistemological method of explication, in the same way as any question about the formation and destruction of the "ought" is not at the level of observation focused on the "ought", nor in the scope of a normative epistemological method.'; or even 411: 'This is the great mystery of law and state, that takes place in the act of legislation, and this might be the reason why its essence is represented only in images which are far from being satisfactory.' I.e. one can no longer explain law-making in the Pure Theory of Law.

1. In terms of methods
1.1. conscious selection of applicable arguments in legal science (methodological purity),
1.2. logical and clear ('true') arguments, clarification of the premises,
1.3. from an 'is' one cannot logically conclude an 'ought'; if you conclude an 'ought' from an 'is', then you necessarily imply some further premises which should be openly admitted for the sake of transparency of the reasoning,
1.4. rejection of redundant concepts (i.e., those lacking explanatory potential).
2. In terms of achievements:
2.1. the subjective factor cannot be avoided in the application of law,
2.2. also individual legal decisions (e.g., judicial decisions) are part of the legal order,
2.3. it is not the 'State that creates legal order'; the state itself is of a legal nature,
2.4. the distinction between public and private law is pointless for legal theory,[183]
2.5. the concept of person is basically a complex of norms,
2.6. subjective right (*subjektives Recht*) is to be derived from objective law (*objektives Recht*).

These elements are, however, only 'organs to be transplanted' from the dead body of the *Pure Theory of Law*, whose heart – the *Stufenbaulehre* – is no longer capable of keeping the body alive. The monumental prepared corpse of the *Pure Theory of Law* can only serve as a spectacle in the museum of futile efforts of legal theory. Any attempt at reanimation, be it for the purposes of a European constitutional theory[184] or for any other reason, would be hopeless.

[183] For more details see below Chapter 14.

[184] Cf. a list of such attempts above in n. 2.

# 13

# Principles as norms logically distinct from rules?

Frustra fit per plura quod potest fieri per pauciora.[1]

## 13.1 What are principles?

In recent decades, various theories have postulated that principles have a structure distinct from that of rules (or norms).[2] Some of the authors developed their theories specifically for the purposes of constitutional law (Dworkin and Alexy), and the idea was well-received and applied throughout the world.[3] This chapter introduces and critically analyses these theories (especially the one of Robert Alexy) in order to develop a new approach to the concept and function of principles.[4] Its main thesis is that 'principles' should not be conceived as structurally different from

[1] 'It is futile to do with more things that which can be done with fewer' (William of Ockham, *Summa Totius Logicae*, i. 12).

[2] Josef Esser, *Grundsatz und Norm in der richterlichen Fortbildung des Privatrechts*, Tübingen, Mohr 1956; Ronald Dworkin, Taking Rights Seriously, London, Duckworth 1977; Robert Alexy, Zum Begriff des Rechtsprinzips, in: Werner Krawietz - Kazimierz Opalek - Aleksander Peczenik - Alfred Schramm (eds.), *Argumentation und Hermeneutik in der Jurisprudenz*, Rechtstheorie, Beiheft 1, Berlin, Duncker & Humblot 1979, 59–87 [hereinafter Alexy, *Zum Begriff*]; Alexy, Robert, *Theorie der Grundrechte*, Frankfurt aM, Suhrkamp 2001 [hereinafter Alexy, Theorie]; Robert Alexy, Zur Struktur der Rechtsprinzipien, in: Bernd Schilcher - Peter Koller - Bernd-Christian Funk (eds.), *Regeln, Prinzipien und Elemente im System des Rechts*, Wien, Verlag Österreich 2000, 31–52 [hereinafter Alexy, *Zur Struktur*].

[3] Just to name a few, see e.g. Lorenzo Zucca, *Constitutional Dilemmas: Conflicts of Fundamental Legal Rights in Europe and the USA*, Oxford, Oxford University Press 2007; Martin Borowski, *Grundrechte als Prinzipien*, Baden-Baden, Nomos 2007. The numerous translations of Dworkin and Alexy also contributed to the success of their ideas.

[4] I am very grateful to Matthias Goldmann, Tamás Győrfi, Stefan Häußler, Robert Stelzer and Grégoire Webber, and also to the participants of the Theory of Principles workshop at the XXIII World Congress of Philosophy of Law and Social Philosophy in (IVR) in Cracòw (Poland, 1-6. August 2007), especially to Robert Alexy, Carsten Bäcker, Mátyás Bódig, Martin Borowski, David Duarte and Jan-Reinard Sieckmann for their valuable criticism and comments.

'rules'; a 'principle' means simply a 'very *important* rule', so the differentiation is only of a rhetorical nature. This result does not deny, however, the existence of special functions bound to 'principles'. It simply wants to remove a superfluous commonplace on the distinct logical structure of principles. It is superfluous because the phenomena explained by it can also be otherwise (i.e., by the traditional rule paradigm) explained. Its introduction, thus, only superfluously, unnecessarily complicates the explanation.

### *13.1.1 Alexy's theory*

One of the most influential, German-language works on the problematic of principles is Josef Esser's book, *Grundsatz und Norm in der richterlichen Fortbildung des Privatrechts* (1956).[5] As a point of origin, then, a similarly influential book in the English-speaking constitutional scholarship, namely, Ronald Dworkin's *Taking Rights Seriously* (1977), may be instructive.[6]

Both authors stress that, in a legal order, principles (*Grundsätze*) and rules (*Normen*) exhibit differing logical structures, not with a merely gradual differentiation but with a strict separation. What according to the authors is the difference between principles and rules? To answer this question, we now turn to Robert Alexy, who elaborates on the distinction in more theoretical detail and with more analytical sensitivity than Dworkin or Esser.[7] Another advantage of choosing Alexy as the main target of my criticism is that he escapes from the Dworkinian problems of moral and/or legal nature of principles. This aspect of the Dworkinian principles theory has already been convincingly criticised.[8] But my point is rather, whether there is a structural difference between *legal* principles

[5] Esser (n. 2). As a predecessor to Esser, the Austrian Walter Wilburg comes to mind. Under 'elements', he understood fundamental principles of a legal subject-matter or of a legal concept. Elements, according to him, have a more-or-less structure and play an orienting and systemising role. See Walter Wilburg, *Elemente des Schadensrechts*, Marburg an der Lahn, Elwert 1941; Walter Wilburg, *Entwicklung eines beweglichen Systems im bürgerlichen Recht*, Graz, Kienreich 1950.

[6] We are not dealing with later changes in Dworkin's point of view concerning principles, cf., e.g., Larry Alexander, Striking Back at the Empire: A Brief Survey of Problems in Dworkin's Theory of Law, *Law and Philosophy* 6 (1987) 419–438, 422–423.

[7] See Alexy, *Zum Begriff* (n. 2) 67; Alexy, *Zur Struktur* (n. 2) 31. On Dworkin's and Esser's theory of principles in more detail see below *13.1.4 So What Are Principles?*. See also above n. 2.

[8] Larry Alexander – Ken Kress, Against Legal Principles, in: Andrei Marmor (ed.), *Law and Interpretation*, Oxford, Clarendon Press 1995, 279–327. For a criticism of Dworkin's claim that principles are non-legal, see Rolf Sartorius, Hart's Concept of Law, in: Robert S Summers (ed.), *More Essays in Legal Philosophy*, Oxford, Blackwell 1971, 131–161, 156.

and *legal* rules – something that has been accepted even by Dworkin's critics.[9] I contest it. The strongest and most sophisticated of the theories on *legal* principles seems to be Alexy's, so we are rather going to concentrate on that.

Alexy dismisses as unsound the Dworkinian criterion for distinction, which attributes to rules (as opposed to principles) an all-or-nothing character and maintains that exceptions can generally be exhaustively listed.[10] Alexy asserts that *both* rules and principles have exceptions which cannot be exhaustively listed. According to him, rules only have an all-or-nothing character when one assumes a proviso limiting application of the rules to cases 'when no principle legally requires something else' or 'when no legally essential reasons demand something else.' But the problem is that, in this sense, even principles have an all-or-nothing character; thus, this distinguishing criterion can be dismissed.

Instead, Alexy suggests applying 'optimisation' as the differentiating criterion.[11] In this sense, principles are optimisation imperatives, that is, imperatives that can be fulfilled to varying degrees (optimisation postulate). In contrast, rules are norms that always can only be either fulfilled or not fulfilled.[12] They are, thus, definitive imperatives.[13] With this formulation, Alexy basically reformulates the Dworkinian criterion, so

[9] Neil MacCormick, *Legal Reasoning and Legal Theory*, Oxford, Clarendon Press 1978, 244–246; HLA Hart, *The Concept of Law*, Oxford, Clarendon Press ²1994, 263–268.

[10] Alexy, *Zum Begriff* (n. 2) 68–71. For a similar criticism against Dworkin, see Frederick Schauer, *Playing by the Rules: A Philosophical Examination of Rule-Based Decision-Making in Law and in Life*, Oxford, Clarendon Press 1991, 12–15.

[11] Alexy still speaks of 'ideal' and 'real' Ought (*Sollen*). See Alexy, *Zum Begriff* (n. 2) 79–82. In this sense, an ideal Ought is any Ought that does not require that its content actually and legally be possible in its entirety, but requires that fulfilment be as extensive or approximating as possible. *Id.* at 81. The other differences (degree of universality or how they handle cases of conflict; these will be addressed below) can be explained on the basis of this difference. However, in his more recent summary, he no longer mentions the concept, instead discussing optimisation as criterion for distinction. See Alexy, *Zur Struktur* (n. 2) 31–52. Thus, we will not deal with the complicated and vague criterion of 'ideal obligation' here; rather, we will focus only on Alexy's most recent formulation of the distinguishing criterion.

[12] Alexy, *Zur Struktur* (n. 2) 32.

[13] It is not entirely clear, how Alexy would find out whether a general norm we are dealing with is actually just a general rule (with 'rule-structure') or whether it is a principle with its 'principle-structure'. After the legal reasoning has taken place (*a posteriori*), the explanation in Alexian terms is possible, but before that (*a priori*) it is not entirely clear which type we are dealing with.

that it is no longer vulnerable to the above-mentioned objection regarding provisos.

The other difference between rules and principles, asserts Alexy, becomes clear in cases of conflict. In the conflict of rules, the collision is either resolved by rules of conflict (for example, *lex posterior*), or one of the rules is declared invalid. Conflicts of principles, however, are settled within a contingent relation of precedence between the two relevant principles, considering the circumstances of the case.[14] Precedence means that the legal consequence attached to the given supreme principle obtains, as opposed to the consequence of the conflicting principle. Typical conflicts of principles include conflicts between two fundamental rights.

And the final difference between rules and principles according to Alexy is that principles involve a 'the more X, the more Y' formula. The reasoning proceeds thus: if one violates a principle in the name of another principle, then the more the intrusion in the former, the more the need for justification by the latter.[15] Thus, the judge need not 'apply' a norm *(subsumptio)* in such cases – as opposed to cases involving rules – rather, she or he must balance competing principles. It follows from this weighing and balancing that the theory of principles implies the principle of proportionality, and the other way around.[16]

### 13.1.2 *The objection: superfluous concept*

There is, however, a serious problem with the above theory: the concept of 'principles logically distinct from rules' is simply superfluous.[17]

In order to understand fully this objection, we must digress briefly through the nature of *Verfassungsdogmatik* (for more details see above Chapter 4). *Verfassungsdogmatik* consists of different types of concepts. Some of them are not to be found as such in written constitutions (and they are not even defined by courts), but legal scholars develop them in

[14] *Id.* at 34. [15] *Id.* at 36.

[16] *Id.* at 35. The present author disagrees with the idea of mutual implication of 'proportionality' and 'principles theory'; see similarly Kai Möller, Constructing the Proportionality Test: An Emerging Global Conversation, in: Liora Lazarus – Christopher McCrudden – Nigel Bowles (eds.), *Reasoning Rights: Comparative Judicial Engagement*, Oxford, Hart 2014, 31–40, esp. 32. The present critique is not directed against proportionality, but only against the terminology of Alexyan principles.

[17] András Jakab, *A magyar jogrendszer szerkezete*, Budapest, Pécs, Dialóg Campus 2007, 52–64.

order to explain the mechanisms and structures of a legal order.[18] Such concept's definition is not 'true' or 'false'; rather, it is more or less expedient. One can speak of the truth or falsehood of the definition of a concept of positive law. For example, Art. 116(1) *Grundgesetz* (German Constitution; hereinafter 'GG') defines 'German' as follows: 'Unless otherwise provided by a law, a German within the meaning of this Basic Law is a person who possesses German citizenship or who has been admitted to the territory of the German Reich within the boundaries of 31 December 1937 as a refugee or expellee of German ethnic origin or as the spouse or descendant of such person.' Anyone who uses a conflicting definition in the context of the German Basic Law, then, might be blamed for using a *false* definition. Concepts developed by scholars, however, are significantly more complicated in this respect. Specifically, they do not employ any direct standard.[19] All that matters is the expediency, which is to say, its explanatory force, its ability to explain. A given conceptual system that was developed by a legal scholar, therefore, is better, if within its framework, (1) the greater number of legal phenomena can be explained (2) coherently and (3) with the highest possible degree of simplicity ((4) political and ideological factors can sometimes also play a role[20]).

This yields another important difference between the conceptual approach of positive law and that of legal scholars. We may not simply 'forget' concepts in positive law. We can debate various definitions (or exclude certain specific definitions as we did with the traditional implied definition of *Staat*, see above Chapter 11); but one thing we may not do is

[18] Friedrich Koja – Walter Antoniolli, *Allgemeines Verwaltungsrecht*, Wien, Manz $^{3}$1996, 2. For a similar analysis using different terminology, see Gustav Radbruch, *Rechtsphilosophie*, Stuttgart, Koehler $^{8}$1973, 215 (distinguishing *Rechtsbegriffe* ('concepts of law') and *rechtswissenschaftliche Begriffe* ('concepts of legal science')).

[19] Unless we were to use definitions such as '"the concept of principles", for Alexy, means . . . or "under principles, such and such is usually understood."' In these cases, one can of course say that the definition is true or false. But these would only be secondary statements of legal theory, dealing with what others have thought about the law. This is, however, not the case with primary definitions, which aim at a direct explication of certain legal phenomena.

[20] Generally, see Roger Cotterrell, *The Politics of Jurisprudence*, London, LexisNexis $^{2}$2003, 11–19. As to the ideological background of the division of the legal order into public and private law, see the speech of Robert Walter (in Strobl am Wolfgangsee, Austria, on June 6–7, 1969), in: *Zur Erneuerung der Struktur der Rechtsordnung. Gespräch über Wege zur Vermeidung der Zersplitterung des Privatrechts und zur Überwindung des Dualismus von öffentlichem Recht und Privatrecht*, Wien, Manz [1970], 49–62, especially 50–53. As to the ideological background of the *Stufenbaulehre* (doctrine of hierarchical, or 'step-structured,' legal order), see above Chapter 12.

to dismiss a relevant concept as superfluous. This we may only do with concepts that were developed by legal scholars, more specifically, when they have less explanatory force than the definitions of concepts of another (competing) scholarly conceptual system. If we can better deliver an explanation of the given legal order with a new concept (or conceptualisation), then we can discard the old one.

Our thesis postulates as follows: the concept that describes a principle as having a logical structure distinct from that of rules is simply superfluous. The phenomena explained by the concept can also be otherwise explained. Its introduction, thus, only superfluously, unnecessarily complicates the explanation, since the presence of multiple concepts of legal theory explains in a more complicated way.

And what exactly does this concept – that is, principles logically distinct from rules – explain? It explains legal reasoning and the application of law. The query is whether there might be a simpler (conceptually more economical)[21] explanation without this concept. We believe that there is. Which is to say, 'principles logically distinct from rules' can also be understood as indefinite, abstract rules that are to be concretised through adjudication.

Here, we will consider the German Federal Constitutional Court's decision in *Lebach* – which Alexy also analysed – as our case study.[22] This judgment is intentionally selected, so that Alexy's 'good example' can be repudiated.

The case involved the television station ZDF, which wanted to air a programme about a murder in the town of Lebach. The programme included the naming of an accomplice. After a court rejected the accomplice's motion for a preliminary injunction preventing the broadcast, he filed a constitutional complaint with the Federal Constitutional Court.

The legal issue of the case, *explained by way of principles* (which is how Alexy describes it), is as follows.[23] The principle of the protection of personality (Art. 2(1) in connection with Art. 1(1) GG) and the principle of the freedom of reporting by means of broadcast (second sentence of Art. 5(1) GG), here, stand in conflict with each other. The determination of which principle takes precedence depends on a weighing and balancing of the *concrete circumstances*. Based on this balancing of competing

[21] For the concept of *Denkökonomie*, see Leonidas Pitamic, Denkökonomische Voraussetzungen der Rechtswissenschaft, *Zeitschrift für öffentliches Recht* 3 (1916–1918) 339–367, 347.

[22] BVerfGE 35, 202.

[23] Alexy, *Theorie* (n. 2) 79–87.

factors, the Federal Constitutional Court ultimately gave precedence in this concrete case to the protection of personality.

But we can explain this case using (Alexian) *rules*, as well. Both rules (Art. 1(1) GG in connection with Art. 2(1) GG on the one hand, and Art. 5(1) GG on the other) are very general (i.e., indeterminate in content) rules which must be concretely interpreted in a concrete case. The Federal Constitutional Court held the freedom of reporting, here, inapplicable (that is, it interpreted this constitutional provision such that it did not cover this concrete case). In contrast, the Court found Art. 2(1) GG in connection with Art. 1(1) GG applicable to the case. This was, *not* because 'balancing prefers the one principle or the other,' but because 'the relevant rules were interpreted such that the case only falls within the scope of the one'. Once we have drawn the borderline between the two principles, there remains no doubt or discretion whether our case is under the scope of one or the other. It is either under it or not, *tertium non datur*. If there is a different case, we might define the borderline more precisely, which should now also deal with the special new problem that has occurred, but if the material facts of the two cases are the same, then there is no need to deal with making the borderline any more defined or precise. A balancing only takes place insofar as it is always the case with teleological (or purposive) interpretation and only before drawing the borderline.

The approach of rules is also better as regards legal certainty: the Alexian principles imply namely that the next time with the same material facts a different decision could be made (it is just a question of different balancing . . .). Therefore it is argued here that we should assume that the so-called principles have the same type of normativity (i.e., they are either applicable or not; and if they are, then they mean conclusively concrete legal consequences) as the rules – and it is merely their scope which is uncertain because of the vague and general expressions contained in their linguistic form.[24]

So we can deduce from all this that the concept, 'principles logically distinct from rules', is simply *superfluous* since the problems of applying the law it explains can be explained without it.

[24] And more generally: the fewer processes of thought in judicial justifications we accept (or: the fewer models of thought we accept for the reconstruction of judicial thinking), the better the chance to fight arbitrary decisions, because new structural types of judicial thinking make the decisions less foreseeable. So, the burden of proof is on the introduction of the new model of thought.

### *13.1.3 Possible (counter-)objections against this purely rule-based paradigm*

(1) The objection might be brought against my reasoning above that some norms evaluate facts *prima facie* as a breach of law, but later (after considering the relevant circumstances) we might consider these facts rather as *not* a breach of law. It is typically the situation with fundamental rights, where, for instance, we see a problem concerning (breach of) the freedom of expression, but eventually (typically in order to protect another fundamental right) we do not perceive it as a breach of the freedom of expression. Other norms, however, like the time limits in civil procedure, do not comprehend this two-step application, where the *prima facie* breach and the actual (eventual) breach differ. And according to the objection against my reasoning, this latter type of norms could be identified with Alexian rules, the former type with Alexian principles.

This objection is, however, mistaken. It does nothing but confuse the limitation (*Eingriff*) of a fundamental right with its breach (*Verletzung*). The constitutional provisions protecting fundamental rights (to stay with our example: the freedom of speech) do not prohibit a limitation (e.g., any libel suit) of the freedom of expression, only its breach. The contents of the freedom of speech is therefore not 'it is prohibited to limit the freedom of speech' but rather 'it is prohibited to breach the freedom of speech', where breach means a limitation without (appropriate) justification (*Rechtfertigung*). Thus, it is *not* the case that norms of fundamental rights would *prima facie* prohibit any limitation, but that later in the case of good (justifying) reasons it could not counter to the justified limitation. Actually, there is no *prima facie* prohibition of limitations. There is only one type of prohibition: the one of breaching the fundamental right. We came to this result at the end of a doctrinal test, but the final result of the test (breach or no breach) should strictly be differentiated from the intermediate steps (like limitation or no limitation). To stay with our example: the meaning of the freedom of speech is not that 'it is prohibited to limit the freedom of speech' but rather that 'it is prohibited to limit the freedom of speech *without* (appropriate) *justification*'. This prohibitory norm either prohibits an act or not: it is either under its scope or not. *Tertium non datur*. There are no 'less prohibited' and 'more prohibited' acts; there are only prohibited and non-prohibited acts ('either-or').

(2) Another objection might state that in the purely rule-based paradigm we cannot explain how two principles are weighed against each

other, and especially we cannot explain *why* one principle was given precedence over the other.

It is indeed true that my theory does not explain the reasons in weighing (*Abwägung*), because it belongs to a different problematic of legal theory. If we have two principles to be 'weighed' against each other, then in fact we just interpret the first principle in the light of the other and *vice versa* (i.e., we determine the scope of that principle with the help of the other one). How we do it exactly (and why precisely a certain interpretation is chosen) belongs to the general problematic of legal interpretation not to be confused with the logical structure of norms.

(3) A third objection emphasises the problematic of optimisation (*Optimierung*). According to this, the simpler rule-paradigm cannot explain the optimising nature of principles.

In order to answer this objection, we have to make a difference between the repetition of a legal reasoning on the one hand and its reconstruction by re-conceptualisation on the other. Judges might indeed talk about optimisation in their justification (or without mentioning the word, they might refer to the concept). It does not mean, however, that we have to follow them by doing so, when we analyse their decisions. If we can explain what they actually did by using a different conceptual framework, then we can do so. The concept of 'optimisation' might be a useful concept in the principle-paradigm, but it is as superfluous in the purely rule-paradigm as it is the Alexian concept of principle. We explained the problematic without it (see above in the discussion of *Lebach*).

(4) A final objection asks how the fundamental rights limitation tests can be explained in my theory and whether the individual steps of the test are separate rules.

This objection is similar to objection (1) mentioned above and presupposes that fundamental rights provisions are about the prohibition of fundamental rights *limitations*. This is, however, as shown above, a false assumption. Fundamental rights limitations are *per se* not prohibited in liberal constitutions. Fundamental rights provisions are actually about the prohibition of *breach* (i.e., limitation without appropriate justification). It means that this problem has been transformed into a problem of interpretation (i.e., determination of the scope of the 'prohibition of breach') again. The weighing of two principles is nothing other than *interpreting restrictively* one rule (principle) in the light of the other.

The *classical three step proportionality test* (1. suitability, 2. necessity, 3. proportionality in a narrow sense) can be translated into the rule paradigm as the following questions:[25] 1. Can we interpret rule *A* restrictively in the light of rule *B*? Is rule *B* a possible reason to interpret rule *A* restrictively? (suitability) 2. Do we have to do so, in order to gain in *B*? Is the restrictive interpretation of rule *A* necessary in the concrete situation in order to keep the non-restrictive interpretation of rule *B*? (necessity) 3. Is the restrictive interpretation of rule *A* not too radical as to the gain in *B*? Or would the restriction in interpretation be less severe if we were to interpret that other rule (i.e., *B*) restrictively in the light of the first (i.e., *A*)? Or should we rather interpret both slightly restrictively in the light of the other? (proportionality in a narrow sense)[26] We can thus conceptualise the proportionality test without using the terminology of Alexyan principles.

### 13.1.4 *So what* are *principles?*

Thus, principles are not logically different from rules in structure. Principles are *very important* (or fundamental, or basic) general (i.e., indeterminate in content) rules (or in other words: structural decisions, *Strukturentscheidungen*). The designation as a 'principle' expresses this importance.[27] So whether or not we designate a general rule as a principle functions as a *rhetorical* handle. Such a terminological promotion, however, is only to be used in cases of very general rules.[28] Normally, it would be implausible to speak of the fundamental *importance* of a minutely concrete rule.[29]

This rhetorical nature of principles should not be (mis)understood as pejorative. It simply indicates that the difference between principles and other general rules does not pertain to its legal-logical nature. To put it another (better) way: the designation as a principle can only have

25 The proportionality test itself is an abstract, often unwritten and very important rule (consisting of three sub-rules) of many legal systems.

26 For a similar objection, tracing back general problems of the principles theory to concrete fundamental rights limitation tests, see Ralf Poscher, Principles: How Many Theories? What Merit?, in: Matthias Klatt (ed.), *Institutionalized Reason. The Jurisprudence of Robert Alexy*, Oxford, Oxford University Press 2012, 218–247, especially 245–246.

27 It does not mean that *every* important rule will be designated as a principle. It means simply: only important rules have a chance to be promoted to 'principles'. The criteria of promotion (and their weigh) are far from clear, and will be dealt with later.

28 Cf. Jean-Louis Bergel, *Théorie générale du droit*, Paris, Dalloz [4]2003, 100 ('c'est la généralité').

29 Even more rhetorically emphasised is the expression 'general principle' (*principe général, allgemeiner Rechtsgrundsatz*). If principles are to be understood as 'very important' rules, then the expression 'general principle' can be decoded as 'very, very important rule'.

normative relevance, when construed as evidence of the legislature's decision about the rule's importance. Thereby, in turn (by historical or subjectively teleological interpretation), precedence is to be given to whichever of two possible interpretations conforms with so-called principles.

And why do we promote some rules to 'principles'? Of course, there is no simple, single answer.[30] Some would emphasise the explicit nature of their evaluative content;[31] their referentiality to the idea of law[32] or to a supreme legal rule;[33] their significance to the legal order;[34] their nature ensuring rights;[35] the certainty of their insight; or their universality. Others would speak of principles' specific meta-normative functions. These will be discussed below (*13.3.3 Meta-normative functions*).

It seems appropriate at this point to mention some relevant differences of opinion between Esser and Dworkin. First, for Esser, a principle implies greater discretion for the judge, since she or he must shape such principles. For Dworkin, in contrast, a principle serves to restrict judicial discretion.[36] Esser sees principles as the justification for decision; Dworkin sees them as instructive (legallybinding guidelines).[37] Secondly, Esser characteristically excludes ethics from the analysis,[38] but Dworkin considers principles to be ethical principles, whose very presence in the legal order is evidence of the untenability of the positivistic division

[30] The following overview is based on Alexy, *Zum Begriff* (n. 2) 65–66.

[31] Claus-Wilhelm Canaris, *Systemdenken und Systembegriff in der Jurisprudenz*, Berlin, Duncker & Humblot 1969, 50.

[32] Karl Larenz, *Methodenlehre der Rechtswissenschaft*, Berlin, Springer [6]1991, 226–227, 421.

[33] Hans Julius Wolff, Rechtsgrundsätze und verfassungsgestaltende Grundentscheidungen als Rechtsquellen, in: Otto Bachoff (ed.), *Forschungen und Berichte aus dem öffentlichen Recht. Festschrift für Walter Jellinek*, München, Isar Verlag 1955, 33–52, 37–39.

[34] Larenz (n. 32) 480; Aleksander Peczenik, Principles of Law: The Search for Legal Theory, *Rechtstheorie* 1971, 17–36, 30.

[35] On the fact that Dworkin identifies arguments of principle with arguments about rights, see Donald H Regan, Glosses on Dworkin: Rights, Principles, and Policies, in: Marshall Cohen (ed.), *Ronald Dworkin and Contemporary Jurisprudence*, Totowa, NJ, Rowman & Allanheld 1983, 119–160, 132.

[36] See José Antonio Pascua, Die Grundlage rechtlicher Geltung von Prinzipien: eine Gegenüberstellung von Dworkin und Esser, in: Giuseppe Orsi (ed.), *Prinzipien des Rechts*, Frankfurt aM, Lang 1996, 7–33, 24.

[37] Cf. Esser (n. 2) 51–52.

[38] See Pascua (n. 36) 22 n. 31. This is why Esser can be counted amongst the positivists. See Ewald Wiederin, Regel – Prinzip – Norm: Zu einer Kontroverse zwischen Hans Kelsen und Josef Esser, in: Stanley L Paulson – Robert Walter (eds.), *Untersuchungen zur Reinen Rechtslehre: Ergebnisse eines Wiener Rechtstheoretischen Seminars 1985–86*, Wien, Manz 1986, 137–166, 155. On similarities between Hart and Esser, see Pascua (n. 36) 18.

between law and morality. And, thirdly, legal principles for Esser are only created by way of their use in judicial decision-making.[39] For Dworkin, legal principles are valid *because they are just* (assuming they are coherent with the respective legal order).[40] Which author correctly answers these questions will be discussed now in turn.

First, the question, whether the presence of principles in a legal order contradicts the positivistic division between law and morality, can be answered with an unequivocal 'no'. Even if we were to recognise structurally distinct principles, this would not necessarily imply the end of the positivist division between law and morality.[41] At any rate, we have just refuted the logical difference. Secondly, the two authors disputed the nature of principles' validity. But nothing compels the acceptance of a (non-positivistic) nature of validity that is distinct from that of (other) rules.[42] Thirdly, Esser and Dworkin dispute whether a principle gives a judge greater or less discretion; the answer depends on the moment of analysis and whether the principle is 'positivised'. (a) When dealing with a positive (or 'positivised') principle, that is, when the principle can be found in a normative text (like a statute), then the moment of analysis makes no difference. The interpretive discretion, here, is certainly greater than with rules because the principle's higher generality permits more room for interpretation.[43] Discretion is, of course, less than with a rule that itself confers discretion. (b) A principle developed by judicial practice, however, restricts previous discretion, but only from the moment at which the principle actually becomes binding. Thus, this does not apply to the initial point in time, for example, when the principle is first formulated in an opinion. This restrictive effect, then, only becomes observable in later judgments.[44]

[39] See Pascua (n. 36) 19–20. [40] *Id.* at 28.

[41] Joseph Raz, Legal Principles and the Limits of Law, *Yale Law Journal* 81 (1972) 823–854, 851–854.

[42] See *id.* at 852 (coming to the same conclusion). [43] Cf. *id.* at 846.

[44] In this sense, too, we can understand the effect that codification (or 'positivisation') of principles has on the separation of powers. (1) The judiciary exercises greatest discretion when the legislature has prescribed neither concrete rules nor principles. This case is of course normally irrelevant, as in such a case the judiciary has not been given jurisdiction to decide anyway (without at least a prescription of principles, the empowerment would at any rate only be based on arbitrary decision). (2) When the legislature does not pass any detailed rules (instead, only a *principle*), greater discretionary room is left open to the judiciary than with concrete rules. (3) But, when the legislature passes concrete rules and positivises an (underlying) principle, it thereby actually restricts the judiciary's room for discretion (as against the legislature), because principles further restrict judicial interpretation of concrete rules (which leave less room for discretion anyway).

## 13.2 How can principles be ascertained (recognised)?

The next question regarding principles asks how they can be ascertained, or recognised, in a concrete legal order. This inquiry may not be as decisive as if the difference between rules and principles were a logical, structural one, but it remains nonetheless unavoidable (because of the special functions of principles as described below).

(1) The first case is when a principle is expressly anchored in a legal text.[45] (1/A) Within this category, the text itself can call its rule a 'principle.' (1/B) In other instances, only the general rule is anchored, without being dubbed a 'principle' by the text itself. Such a designation usually occurs in the course of judicial application or amongst legal scholars. In these examples, it is more appropriate to speak of the *recognition* of principles.

(2) Another constellation has the principle ascertained (or manufactured) through analysis of positive law.[46] This analysis can take place by way of either abstraction[47] from concrete rules or from concrete rules by scrutiny of the political and moral context. The former is the traditional method; Dworkin makes use of the latter. According to Dworkin, the principles of a given society's political morality manifest themselves in the constitution, the laws and legal precedents.[48] Thus, the emergence of a principle out of positive law requires that political morality be kept in view. Only in this way can the legal system be justified, thereby also justifying the ascertainment of its most important norms as proceeding from political morality.[49]

(3) Principles can ultimately also be newly introduced simply through judicial practice or within legal scholarship.[50] This, however, seldom

[45] Ota Weinberger, *Revision des traditionellen Rechtssatzkonzeptes*, in: Schilcher (n. 2) 53–68, 60.

[46] *Id.*; see also Stefan Vogenauer, *Die Auslegung von Gesetzen in England und auf dem Kontinent*, Tübingen, Mohr Siebeck 2001, 1257–1260 and 1273–1274 (discussing British and French courts' role in this respect).

[47] For Pütter's attempt, see Sigrid Jacoby, *Allgemeine Rechtsgrundsätze. Begriffsentwicklung und Funktion in der europäischen Rechtsgeschichte*, Berlin, Duncker & Humblot 1997, 38–42. The introduction of a legal principle by the legislature is outside the scope of the present chapter, since a valid legal order is presupposed as the object of the present analysis.

[48] Dworkin (n. 2) 66, 126.

[49] Johann Friedrich Reitemeier (1755–1839) made a similar attempt, seeking to derive the general legal principles from the constitution, customs and religion of a given country. See Jacoby (n. 47) 45.

[50] Weinberger (n. 45) 60.

occurs, since such principles are vulnerable to accusations of arbitrariness. In such cases, the lack of a basis in positive law is offset by moral arguments (for example, natural law).[51]

(4) Finally, a combination of the above-named methods is of course possible too. If, for instance, a general rule is explicitly mentioned in a legal text *and* has been given shape through much detailed regulation, then it has a good chance of being promoted by legal academia or in judicial practice to the rhetorical rank of 'principle.'

## 13.3 What is the function of principles?

And what, then, is the function of these *very important* general rules? They can, naturally, have the usual function of norms: they can be rules of conduct.[52] Due to their usually very general nature, this means they would act mostly indirectly, though not directly, to control conduct (that is, by way of interpretation of concrete rules). At the same time, this does not rule out principles' direct control of conduct.[53] But we are interested here in the particular functions of principles, which is to say, those *not* also characteristic of other rules. Let us now take a look at this point further.

### *13.3.1 Heuristic function*

Legal principles, ascertained through analysis of positive law, often have a heuristic function. They assist in structuring and systematising legal material to make it manageable.[54] This use of principles was characteristic of, for example, the Germanists (lawyers dealing with traditional non-Roman law in nineteenth-century Germany), who confronted an unmanageable and contradictory mass of laws. Therefore, they attempted

[51] Giorgio Del Vecchio, *Les principes généraux du droit*, in: *Recueil d'études sur les sources du droit en l'honneur de François Gény*, Paris, Sirey 1934, 69–84, 73–76 (asserting that principles cannot be ascertained through induction from the rules).

[52] For an erroneous analysis, see Hyman Gross, Standards as law, *Annual Survey of American Law* 1968–69, 575–580, especially 578. For him, principles are only rules of argumentation (as opposed to rules, which are rules of conduct). This, indeed, is one of their functions, but not the only. For an equally misguided opinion, see Torstein Eckhoff, Guiding Standards in Legal Reasoning, *Current Legal Problems* 1976, 205–219, especially 207.

[53] Raz (n. 41) 841 ('Principles as the sole ground for action in particular cases').

[54] Compare Betti's viewpoint on principles as general educational figures, in: Pascua (n. 36) 8.

to trace local and customary laws back to so-called leading principles in order to effect a manageable, comprehensible structuring of the law.[55] A similar function, amongst others, is ascribed to the respective principles of democracy, the rule of law, and federalism in Konrad Hesse's standard textbook on German constitutional law.[56]

Structure and manageability of the law are also necessary for legal certainty,[57] which is in turn indispensable to the efficient operation of any society. It should also be noted here that a structure that serves purely epistemological purposes can also have normative effect. Namely, when we describe the law, and this is broadly accepted, we thereby also alter the law.[58]

### *13.3.2 Practical legal functions in applying the law*

In application of the law, principles also have practical legal functions. (1) They play an important role in legal argumentation; in this sense, they regulate legal reasoning.[59]

(1/1) The most apparent function is the interpretive function.[60] Specialised regulations must be interpreted in conformity with general regulation.[61] Thus, where two interpretations of a law are possible, preference is given to whichever is (more) compatible with legal principles (i.e., general regulation).[62] This method, however, is inapplicable when dealing with clear wording; from which, again, exceptions are possible depending on the specific legal order.[63] Legal provisions which limit principles must themselves be interpreted restrictively.[64]

[55] Jacoby (n. 47) 139–150.

[56] See Konrad Hesse, *Grundzüge des Verfassungsrechts der Bundesrepublik Deutschland*, Heidelberg, CF Müller [20]1999, 55–121. For the Hungarian counterpart in constitutional scholarship with a similar structure as given by the constitutional principles, see József Petrétei, *Magyar alkotmányjog*, vol. I, Budapest, Dialóg Campus 2002, 83–113.

[57] Cf. Armin von Bogdandy, Europäische Prinzipienlehre, in: *id.* (ed.), *Europäisches Verfassungsrecht*, Berlin, Springer 2003, 149–203, 152–153.

[58] András Sajó, *Kritikai értekezés a jogtudományról*, Budapest, Akadémiai 1983, 25–26, 108–109; Georg Jellinek, *Allgemeine Staatslehre*, Berlin, Häring [3]1914, 50; Neil MacCormick, *Questioning Sovereignty: Law, State, and Nation in the European Commonwealth*, Oxford, Oxford University Press 1999, 113.

[59] Eckhoff (n. 52) 205–19, especially 207; Gross (n. 52) 575–80, especially 578.

[60] John A Usher, *General principles of EC law*, London, Longman 1998, 122–123.

[61] Raz (n. 41) 839 ('Principles as grounds for interpreting laws').

[62] Vogenauer (n. 46) 1274. [63] *Id.* [64] *Id.* at 1275.

(1/2) Principles can also act as a corrective and as an argumentative support for a desired outcome, to which the concrete rules would not lead (or would not *unequivocally* lead).[65] Principles carry out this function particularly in the application of law wherever the method of applying an inherent system of law – that is, where only valid *positive law, currently in force*, can be cited. An example is the Romanists of the historical school in nineteenth-century Germany.[66] The Romanists used legal principles as a corrective and as an argumentative support when positive law failed to yield (unequivocally) the desired result.

Furthermore, the US case-law which Dworkin made famous can also be, in my view, classified here.[67] In the first case, *Riggs v. Palmer*,[68] the concrete rules foresaw inheritance by a grandson, but these rules failed to answer the case because he had killed his grandfather. Invoking the principle, 'no one shall be permitted to take advantage of his own wrong', the court identified an exception to the concrete provisions. In the second case, *Henningsen v. Bloomfield Motors, Inc.*,[69] the court held, contrary to the concrete contractual provisions, in favour of an ordinary consumer in the name of a general principle.

(1/3) Reaffirmation of the holding. In Austria, § 7 of the General Austrian Civil Code (ABGB) was often applied, though only as additional authority for the reasoning and the holding, which had already been derived from concrete positive law.[70]

(2) A principle's abstractness (i.e., generality or indeterminacy) also permits for the possibility of applying rules *formally not in force* within the legal order of law that *is* in force.

(2/1) As a gateway for legal rules formally *no longer* in force. In this way, for instance, after the passing of the *Code civil* in France, Roman law could continue to have effect in the *principes généraux*, although the legislator had actually derogated Roman law.[71] The 'general principles' (*allgemeine Rechtsgrundsätze*) of § 7 of the Austrian Civil Code (1811 in

[65] Raz (n. 41) 840 ('Principles as grounds for particular exceptions to laws').
[66] Jacoby (n. 47) 115–138. [67] Dworkin (n. 2) 23–24.
[68] 115 N.Y. 506, 22 N.E. 188 (1889). [69] 32 N.J. 358, 161 A.2d 69 (1960).
[70] Jacoby (n. 47) 89–100 on § 7 ABGB: 'If a case cannot be decided with reference to the words of the law, regard shall be had to analogous cases explicitly dealt with in the Code and to the policies underlying other kindred laws. If the case still remains in doubt, it shall with careful consideration of the surrounding circumstances, be decided according to the principles of natural law.'
[71] *Id.* at 75–81.

Austria) had a similar function.[72] They meant, in reality, 'principles of Roman law'. Similar interpretations were used for the equivalent provisions of the *Codex Maximilianeus Bavaricus Civilis* (1756 in Bavaria), the Prussian *Allgemeines Landrecht* (1794 in Prussia) and the *Badisches Landrecht* (1810 in Baden).[73]

Whether and how these provisions were applied in *practice*, however, is a separate matter. The two poles are Prussia and France. In the former, application of law based on introductory Art. 49 of the *Allgemeines Landrecht* virtually never took place.[74] But in France the *principes généraux* were truly the normative bases for numerous decisions, namely, the basis for application of the rules of the (formally no longer in force) Roman law.[75]

(2/2)As a gateway for rules of *other* legal orders, or a bridging function between different legal orders. Principles permit the discovery of common ground amongst multiple legal cultures. This function has a heightened importance where representatives of multiple legal cultures simultaneously participate in the determination of law (as with EU law or international law)[76] without any detailed regulation about the legal basis of decisions. In such cases, the legal solutions of state legal orders are analogously applied.

(2/3) As a gateway for ideas of (social and political) morality. Interestingly, both positivists (Kelsen, Merkl) and the natural law scholar Giorgio del Vecchio emphasised this function of principles. The positivists always saw within the very general rules a possibility for discretion.[77] And 'discretion is the doorway in the legal building through which extralegal motivations can break in'.[78] For these two authors, extralegal motivations would include, for example, notions of morality. The Italian natural law scholar Giorgio del Vecchio proceeds from an entirely other origin to a similar endpoint. He considers the presence of principles in various legal codes to be an indication that even the legislator agreed: without these moral rules, no legal code can operate.[79] Thus, Vecchio not only contemplates principles as an open door for any and all notions of

[72] *Id.* at 63–70. [73] *Id.* at 57–62, 81–87. [74] *Id.* at 100–104.

[75] *Id.* at 104–109. Austria's middle position has already been mentioned above (as 'reaffirmation of the holding').

[76] See *id.*, 184–189 (citing examples from international law); see also *id.*, at 210–238 (citing examples from Community law based on the then-valid Art. 215(2) of the EEC Treaty).

[77] Kelsen, however, is sceptical of law development by the judiciary. See Wiederin (n. 38) 146; Hans Kelsen, *Allgemeine Theorie der Normen*, Wien, Manz 1979, 97.

[78] Adolf Merkl, *Allgemeines Verwaltungsrecht*, Berlin, Springer 1927, 152.

[79] Vecchio (n. 51) 78–79.

morality (as do Kelsen or Merkl); rather, principles themselves are natural law merely codified into positive law.[80]

(3) And one last function follows from the previously discussed practical legal functions, namely, developing the law.[81] A decisive novelty of Esser's theory – as opposed to the earlier methodological theory which described judges as 'discovering' principles – is precisely its emphasis on principles' function to develop (change) the law.[82] This function is characteristic in legal practice, in particular where the legal order in certain aspects is underdeveloped and, thus, more dependent on the borrowing of other legal orders' solutions (again, as in international law or EU law).[83]

Some argue that the legal force of legal acts is sometimes made dependent on their correspondence with legal principles (function as criterion of validity).[84] But one must keep in mind that this point of view can mislead. Granted, important rules are indeed often packed into higher-ranking legal acts (for instance, into constitutions) as 'principles', subsequently serving as a standard, against which the validity of lower rules is tested. And a given constitutional court (or the European Court of Justice) sometimes develops principles, treating them as constitutional law, though without an explicit constitutional reference (invisible constitution).[85] However, it is essential to bear in mind that these principles act as a standard, not because they *are* principles, but because the have a higher rank (or, perhaps, because they are treated thus: invisible constitution). Naturally, principles have a greater chance of being incorporated into the constitution or being treated as constitutional law by the given constitutional court. But, while the correlation is certainly probable, it is also not inevitable. Some principles (such as the principles of civil law) are not incorporated into the constitution. This function of a criterion of validity, thus, is not specifically related to the nature of *principles* but instead relates to *hierarchy*.

80 Vecchio (n. 51) 82. 81 Raz (n. 41) 841 ('Principles as grounds for making new rules').

82 Wiederin (n. 38) 139; Esser (n. 2) 83. Gény also emphasised this instructive function. See François Gény, *Méthode d'interprétation et sources en droit privé positif*, vol. 1, Paris, Librairie Générale de Droit et de Jurisprudence [2]1919, 41–53; Bergel (n. 28) 98.

83 Jacoby (n. 47) 170–208, 209–281. 84 Usher (n. 60) 123–124.

85 The Hungarian Constitutional Court serves as an example. See, e.g., 23/1990. (X.31.) AB, ABH 1990, 88, translated in László Sólyom – Georg Brunner, *Constitutional Judiciary in a New Democracy: The Hungarian Constitutional Court*, Michigan, Ann Arbor, University of Michigan Press 2000, 126.

### 13.3.3 *Meta-normative functions*

Principles can also fulfil meta-normative functions. Namely, (1) *ex ante* (e.g., programming the legislation)[86] and (2) *ex post* (the justification for rules).[87]

The literature especially emphasises this justifying function, which can be based either on the legal order as a whole (the ideological-legitimising function)[88] or, more often, only on a concrete rule or group of rules and institutions. It is another question, whether these justifying principles themselves can be used in application of the law.[89]

I assume that principles themselves can apply, assuming they have been 'positivised'; that is, they exist either in a legal norm or within judicial practice. But the mere fact that they justify and underlie other norms, of course, does not alone make them directly applicable.

### 13.3.4 *Social functions*

Noteworthy social functions of a principle include (1) the reconciliatory integrating function and (2) the value-integrating function.

The former signifies that the generality of principles also covers (regulates) those social conflicts not covered by concrete rules. Thus, such conflicts can be resolved in a legal framework, so there remain no legally unresolved conflicts leading to disintegration. This function, however, characterises any very general regulation.

The latter signifies that the designation as 'principle' underscores importance. This permits emphasis and explication of a society's common, important values, which in turn tends to promote integration.[90] After all, that which is highlighted as 'important' – those general rules worthy of the noble title of 'principle' – is a question of value judgement.

[86] See Pascua (n. 36) 10 (explaining the programming or orientating function); Raz (n. 41) 840 ('Principles as grounds for changing the laws').

[87] See Raz (n. 41) 839 (analysing principles as values in law); Neil MacCormick, 'Principles' of Law, *Juridical Review* 19 (1974) 217–226, 224 ('underlying reasons and values').

[88] Dworkin (n. 2) 105.

[89] Cf. Larenz (n. 32) 226–227, 421 (answering negatively), Franz Bydlinski, *Juristische Methodenlehre und Rechtsbegriff*, Wien, New York, Springer $^{2}$1991, 132–139 (answering negatively), Bergel (n. 28) 106 (answering affirmatively).

[90] See von Bogdandy (n. 57) 154 (detailing the task of a European doctrine of principles to promote identity).

# 14

## Public law–private law divide?

> Eine Einteilung des Rechts in ein spezielles Rechtsgebiet für den Zwang und eines für die Freiheit macht unter demokratischen und rechtsstaatlichen Verhältnissen keinen Sinn mehr. . . . [Die heutigen] theoretischen Debatten um die Abgrenzung von öffentlichem Recht und Privatrecht [sind] eine Art Sternenlicht, das auch dann noch unterwegs ist, wenn seine Quelle schon erloschen ist.[1]

Analyses about the distinction between public and private law traditionally begin with a quotation from Ulpian (*publicum ius est quod ad statum rei Romanae spectat, privatum quod ad singulorum utilitatem*, D 1.1.1.2.), then continue by stating that this fundamental categorisation (*summa divisio*) was already known to the Romans, and that (since then continuously) it holds even today.[2]

We are going to follow here a more sceptical path, and we are rather showing that the distinction both lacks descriptive force and has practical consequences which are difficult to reconcile with either the rule of law or democracy.[3] Consequently, we are going to conclude that the usage of the terms 'public law' and 'private law' only reflect a series of legal problems shaped by tradition, which we inherited from past centuries. There are public lawyers (as a sociological group), and therefore one can still speak of public law scholarship, but there is no such thing as public law (at least

[1] Michael Stolleis, Öffentliches Recht und Privatrecht im Prozeß der Entstehung des modernen Staates, in: Wolfgang Hoffmann-Riem – Eberhard Schmidt-Aßmann (eds.), *Öffentliches Recht und Privatrecht als wechselseitige Auffangordnungen*, Baden-Baden, Nomos 1996, 41–61, 59. ('The division of the law into a special legal branch of constraint and another one of freedom no longer makes sense under the circumstances of democracy and the rule of law. . . [Today's] theoretical debates on the differentiation between public law and private law [are] a kind of starlight which is still travelling even after its source becomes extinct.')

[2] E.g., Arno Scherzberg, *Wozu und wie überhaupt noch öffentliches Recht?*, Berlin, de Gruyter 2003, 8.

[3] For useful remarks and valuable criticism I am grateful to Antal Ádám, Péter Cserne, Matthias Goldmann, Gábor Hamza and Stephan Hinghofer-Szalkay.

not in a sense that would be theoretically consistent and relevant for European constitutional theory). We will, therefore, suggest avoiding using these concepts as constitutional terms.

## 14.1 Historical roots

There are several problems with the Ulpian-continuity thesis. First, the Romans did not regard that division as a theoretical dichotomy of the legal system, but as a merely didactic distinction.[4] Thus, they did not understand it as a strict disjunction, but just as shorthand for a bunch of more or less separable characteristics.[5] For most of the Middle Ages, the concepts were not in use even as such 'soft' categories.[6]

When the concept of *ius publicum* appeared again in the early modern (sixteenth-and seventeenth-century) Holy Roman Empire, it was regarded as a field of research discussed in books and taught at universities.[7] For most of the Middle Ages, law was divided into two parts: *ius civile* and *ius canonicum*, and the 'public law'–'private law' divide was only rarely used.[8] Even if it was used (with reference to Ulpian's formula), it was taken to refer merely to two domains of the legal order (as two intersecting circles, still without the notion of a strict *tertium non datur*).

From the mid-eighteenth century, as a consequence of the systematising categorisation of the *Vernunftrecht* school(s), Ulpian's formula began to be understood as a distinction between categories.[9] Here, public law was regarded as a domain of law 'without judicial control'. That

[4] Georges Chevrier, Remarques sur la distinction et les vicissitudes de la distinction du 'jus privatum' et du 'jus publicum' dans les oeuvres des anciens juristes français, *Archives de philosophie du droit* 1 (1952) 5–77, especially 77; Martin Bullinger, *Öffentliches Recht und Privatrecht. Studien über Sinn und Funktion der Unterscheidung*, Stuttgart, W. Kohlhammer 1968, 13–16.

[5] Such a systematic distinction would not have been compatible with the case method of Roman lawyers; see Max Kaser, Jus Publicum – Jus Privatum, *Studia et Documenta Historiae et Juris* 1951, 267–279, 267–270.

[6] Stolleis (n. 1) 46; Gábor Hamza, The Classification (divisio) into 'Branches' of Modern Legal Systems and Roman Law Traditions, *European Journal of Law Reform* 2006, 361–382, especially 362; Heinz Mohnhaupt, Römisch-rechtliche Einflüsse im 'ius publicum'/'Öffentliches Recht' des 18. und 19. Jahrhunderts in Deutschland, in: *id.*, *Historische Vergleichung im Bereich von Staat und Recht*, Frankfurt aM, Klostermann 2000, 123–150, 126.

[7] Bullinger (n. 4) 17–18; Michael Stolleis, *Geschichte des öffentlichen Rechts in Deutschland*. vol. 1, München, Beck 1988, 126–224.

[8] Stolleis (n. 7) 65.

[9] Criminal law and feudal law (*Lehnsrecht*) were, however, classified as private law, see Bullinger (n. 4) 31.

understanding served the interests of both the monarch[10] and the upcoming bourgeoisie. The former is rather obvious, while for the latter the explanation is that it eliminated the judicial enforceability of feudal industrial privileges, which belonged to public law.[11] What the concept was meant to do in practice, then, was to secure the rule of law needed by the bourgeoisie (with the resort to the judicial way in private law), without introducing the judicial enforceability of public-law positions (the prerogatives of the absolute monarch and the feudal privileges). In a somewhat different manner, in the nineteenth century the division was regarded as the consequence of the separation of 'state and society'.[12] Another nineteenth-century development was the strict conceptual design of the German Pandectists, which likewise contributed to the emergence of a strict dichotomy.[13] However, it can be stated that the division was never a complete and consistent one,[14] as there have always been important exceptions.[15] Nor was it applicable to each legal system.[16]

[10] See Hans Kelsen, Zur Lehre vom öffentlichen Rechtsgeschäft, *Archiv des öffentlichen Rechts* 31 (1913) 190–249, 218: 'the separation of public and private law is irreconciliable with the rule of law'. In the same way Stolleis (n. 1) 53.

[11] Bullinger (n. 4) 51–53; Dieter Grimm, *Das Öffentliche Recht vor der Frage nach seiner Identität, mit Kommentaren von Otto Depenheuer und Ewald Wiederin*, Tübingen, Mohr Siebeck 2012, 11–12; Carl von Rotteck, *Lehrbuch des Vernunftrechts und der Staatswissenschaften*, Stuttgart, Franck 1829–1830, vol. 1, 106, vol. 2, 146–147.

[12] Bullinger (n. 4) 69–72; Stolleis (n. 1) 55. Cf. above 11.2.6. [13] Stolleis (n. 1) 57.

[14] Illustrated with the problem of the classification of criminal law by Isabelle Rorive, Les structures du système juridique belge, in: Olivier Morétau – Jacques Venderlinden (eds.), *La structure des systèmes juridiques*, Bruxelles, Bruylant 2003, 177–194, 188 and 191. The same with the problem (debate on the classification) of private procedural law, see Hamza (n. 6) 376

[15] Martin Bullinger, Die Funktionelle Unterscheidung von öffentlichem Recht und Privatrecht als Beitrag zur Beweglichkeit von Verwaltung und Wirtschaft in Europa, in: Hoffmann-Riem – Schmidt-Aßmann (n. 1) 239–260, 244 with examples from legal history.

[16] Thus, the famous claim of Radbruch mistaken, see Gustav Radbruch, *Rechtsphilosophie*, Stuttgart, Koehler [8]1973, 221: '*The concepts of "private law" and "public law" are not positive-law concepts, which may as well be absent from a system of positive law; rather, these pre-exist to, and are ab ovo valid for, any kind of legal experience. These are a priori legal concepts.*' A position similar to mine is taken by Dieter Grimm, Öffentliches Recht, in: Görres-Gesellschaft (ed.), *Staatslexikon*, vol. 4, Freiburg, Herder [7]1988, 119–124, 120, and G Chevrier, Droit public – droit privé, in: Åke Malmström – Stig Strömholm (eds.), *Rapports généraux au VII^e^ Congrès international de droit comparé*, Stockholm, Almquist & Wiksell 1968, 37–41. On the lack of such a distinction in canon law, see A Bernárdez Canton, Droit public – droit privé en droit canonique, in: *ibid.* 42. Until the 1980s (*O'Reilly v. Mackmann* [1982] All ER 1124, House of Lords), the distinction played no role in English law either; see Ian McLeod, *Legal Method*, Basingstoke, New York, Palgrave [7]2009, 35–36.

## 14.2 The distinction today

The distinction between public and private law may be one of legal theory or one of positive law (on the different types of concepts, see above Chapter 4). In the first case, the legal system is divided only to enable explanations. In the second case, in turn, the legislator or the judge presupposes the distinction, using the respective concepts, and thus it has legal consequences.

### *14.2.1 Public law and private law as concepts of legal theory*

#### 14.2.1.1 Interest theory

According to this, public law serves the public interest, while private law serves private interests.[17] There are several possible objections to this theory. In particular: (1) private associations are often created for a purpose related to the public interest; (2) state actions regulated by the Civil Code of the given legal system belong to public law; (3) fundamental rights are often not exerted in the public interest, even though they are considered as being part of public law;[18] (4) a claim for a building permit apparently serves a private interest, but is regarded as one of public (more precisely: administrative) law.[19] (5) And finally, all rights (even the rights enshrined in civil codes) are supposed to serve the public interest to some extent.[20] The objections seem convincing enough to refute the interest theory (*Interessentheorie*).

#### 14.2.1.2 Subordination theory

According to this theory, public law is characterised by subordination,[21] while private law by the equality of the parties (and by private

[17] See the sentence of Ulpian quoted at the beginning of the chapter. For a modern European application (but with an additional category of 'social law'), see Loïc Azoulai, Sur un sens de la distinction public/privé dans le droit de l'Union européenne, *Revue trimestrielle du droit européen* 2010/oct.-déc., 842–860, especially 844 and 858–860.

[18] Ludwig Schöne, *Privatrecht und öffentliches Recht. Geschichte, Inhalts- und Bedeutungswandel eines juristischen Grundbegriffes*, Diss. jur. Freiburg 1955, 47.

[19] Detlef Schmidt, *Die Unterscheidung von privatem und öffentlichem Recht*, Baden-Baden, Nomos 1985, 92.

[20] See Erich Molitor, *Über öffentliches Recht und Privatrecht. Eine rechtssystematische Studie*, Karlsruhe, Müller 1949, 30; and Klaus F Röhl – Hans Christian Röhl, *Allgemeine Rechtslehre*, München, Carl Heymanns $^{3}$2008, 421–422.

[21] Martin Loughlin, *The Idea of Public Law*, Oxford, Oxford University Press 2004, 153: public law as the expression of the difference between 'members' and 'officers'.

autonomy).[22] The problems here are the following: (1) administrative law contracts exist in most European legal orders, and by definition they mean equality, whereas they are still categorised as public law;[23] (2) in the organisation of public administration, equality occurs quite often (e.g., the relationship between two municipalities that can make contracts with each other); (3) in family law or in employment law one finds subordination, yet these are not regarded as being part of public law; (4) the citizen is not 'subordinate' to the state (fundamental rights, right to vote).[24] This latter also highlights the anti-democratic premises of this theory,[25] which can hardly be reconciled with popular sovereignty.[26]

Thus, the subordination theory (*Subjektionstheorie, Subordinationstheorie*)[27] has to be rejected, as well.

[22] Georg Jellinek, *Allgemeine Staatslehre*, Berlin, Häring $^{3}$1914, 384; similarly Savigny; see Günter Stratenwerth, Zum Verhältnis von Privatrecht, öffentlichem Recht und Strafrecht. Eine Auseinandersetzung mit Walter Burckhardt, in: Juristische Fakultät der Universität Basel (ed.), *Privatrecht – Öffentliches Recht – Strafrecht. Grenzen und Grenzüberschreitungen*, Basel, Helbing & Lichtenhahn 1985, 415–429, 421, with detailed references. On similar positions in English doctrine, see Jack Beatson, 'Public' and 'Private' in English Administrative Law, *Law Quarterly Review* 103 (1987) 34–65, 52–54. A special form of the subordination theory is the legal form theory (*Rechtsformentheorie*), cf. Charles Szladits, The Civil Law System, in: René David (ed. in chief), *International Encylopedia of Comparative Law. II/2. Structure and Divisions of the Law*, Tübingen, Mohr 1974, 22. According to that, public law is the domain of state rule over the individual, characterised by command and constraint; private law, in turn, is the realm of relationships between equals, characterised by claim and litigation. See Fritz Fleiner, *Institutionen des deutschen Verwaltungsrechts*, Tübingen, Mohr $^{8}$1928, 50–51.

[23] Willibalt Apelt, *Der verwaltungsrechtliche Vertrag. Ein Beitrag zur Lehre von der rechtswirksamen Handlung im öffentlichen Rechte*, Leipzig, Meiner 1920, 125–127.

[24] Manfred Zuleeg, Die Anwendungsbereiche des öffentlichen Rechts und des Privatrechts, *Verwaltungsarchiv* 1982, 384–404, especially 391, with further references.

[25] Cf. Albert Venn Dicey, *Introduction to the Study of the Law of the Constitution*, London, Macmillan $^{10}$1959, 384–385, who argues that the continental distinction between public and private law is not accepted in England as there the citizens as well as the officers are subject to the same ordinary law. The citizen is not subordinate to the officer, but both are subject to the law (*rule of law*).

[26] Jörn Ipsen – Thorsten Koch, Öffentliches und privates Recht – Abgrenzungsprobleme bei der Benutzung öffentlicher Einrichtungen, *Juristische Schulung* 1992, 809–816, 811.

[27] Or, with Kelsen's term, *Mehrwerttheorie*, see Kelsen (n. 10) 192, and Hans Kelsen, *Allgemeine Staatslehre*, Berlin, Springer 1925, 82. Why Kelsen rejected the traditional division (or its overemphasis) is discussed by Dieter Wyduckel, Über die Unterscheidung von öffentlichem Recht und Privatrecht in der Reinen Rechtslehre, in: Werner Krawietz – Helmut Schelsky (eds.), *Rechtssystem und gesellschaftliche Basis bei Hans Kelsen* [Rechtstheorie Beiheft 5], Berlin, Duncker & Humblot 1984, 113–128.

#### 14.2.1.3 Subject theory

According to this theory, the regulation of the legal status of the state belongs to public law, while that of private persons to private law.[28] The problem here is that civil codes apply to the state as well. A solution may be to differentiate between 'the state in its private capacity' and 'the state in its public capacity (i.e., *qua* the state)', and to say that only the latter is regulated by public law. This may at first sight seem a satisfactory criterion of distinction.

This way, however, we obtain a definition that is circular.[29] For if we ask when exactly the state acts in its 'public capacity (*qua* the state)', then the answer is 'when its actions are regulated by public law'. But our original question was what 'public law' actually is.[30]

Moreover, this theory fails to provide an explanation as to why the horizontal effect of fundamental rights (*Drittwirkung*) is a problem of public law, as it refers to relationships between private parties.[31] A further problem of the theory is the definition of the 'state' which is far from clear (see above 11.2.3).

Thus, the subject theory (*Subjektstheorie*) has to be rejected too.

#### 14.2.1.4 Trusteeship theory

According to this theory, rules which regulate situations in which one of the parties is obliged to act as the trustee (*Sachwalter*) of the public interest (the common good) belong to public law.[32] The problem with this theory is that if this were the case, then the relationship between two private associations created for public purposes would belong to

[28] Jean Carbonnier, *Introduction au droit civil*, Paris, Presses Universitaires de France [23]1995, 95; Otto Mayer, *Lehrbuch des deutschen Verwaltungsrechts*, vol. 1, Leipzig, Duncker & Humblot [2]1914, 16; Beatson (n. 22) 48–51; Dawn Oliver, Common Values in Public and Private Law and the Public/Private Divide, *Public Law* 1997, 630–646, 645–646; Michel Rosenfeld, Rethinking the Boundaries between Public Law and Private Law for the Twenty-First Century, *International Journal of Constitutional Law* 11 (2013) 125–128 (doubting himself the usefulness of the distinction).

[29] Christoph Möllers, *Staat als Argument*, Tübingen, Mohr [2]2011, 301. On the circular nature of definitions of 'public law' see Wiederin, in: Grimm (n. 116) 92.

[30] Schmidt (n. 19) 118–119.

[31] A special form of the subject theory is the 'special law theory' (*Sonderrechtslehre*), according to which private law is valid for all subjects (i.e., also public-law subjects can make private-law contracts), while public law only for a specific, narrow circle. See Hans J Wolff, Der Unterschied zwischen öffentlichem und privatem Recht, *Archiv des öffentlichen Rechts* 76 (1950–1951) 205–217. This theory cannot account for the *Drittwirkung* either.

[32] Norbert Achterberg, *Allgemeines Verwaltungsrecht*, Heidelberg, Müller 1982, 11.

public law. Thus, the trusteeship theory (*Sachwaltertheorie*) also has to be rejected.[33]

#### 14.2.1.5 Disposition theory

In this theory, public law rules are strictly binding *(cogens),* while private law are rather just subsidiary (they apply if the parties do not wish otherwise).[34] That is to say, in private law the parties may dispose of their rights autonomously.[35] The problem with this theory is that in most European legal orders there is such a thing as non-strictly binding public law (constitutional organs have rights, the use of which is at their discretion), and there is strictly binding private law (e.g., the requirement of personal presence for marriage).[36] Thus, the disposition theory (*Verfügungstheorie*) also has to be rejected.

#### 14.2.1.6 Combined theories

We may also experiment with a combination of the above theories,[37] but it has to be borne in mind that the distinctions of those theories are not completely the same. Thus, if we state that public law is the law of 'subordination, public interest, strictly binding rules, applicable to the state', and private law the law of 'equality, private interests, non-strictly-binding rules, applicable to private individuals', then

(1) If we were to use the criteria conjunctively, then a number of fields or relationships will not be covered (e.g., non-strictly binding rules concerning the state), or
(2) If we were to regard them as alternatives, then we shall have overlapping categories (and consequently, the conceptual framework would not allow for a clear and logical description of the structure of the legal order).

[33] Schmidt (n. 19) 110–111.

[34] Walter Burckhardt, *Die Organisation der Rechtsgemeinschaft*, Zürich, Polygraphischer Verlag $^{2}$1944.

[35] Cf. Hamza (n. 6) 362 for a presentation and a convincing refutation of the quotation from Papinian (*'Ius publicum privatorum pactis mutari non potest'* [D. 2.14.28.]).

[36] Hans Nawiasky, *Allgemeine Staatslehre*. vol. 3, Einsiedeln, Benziger 1956, 163; Stratenwerth (n. 22) 417.

[37] Jean-Bernard Auby, Le rôle de la distinction du droit public et du droit privé dans le droit français, in: Mark Freedland – Jean-Bernard Auby (eds.), *The Public Law/Private Law Divide*, Oxford, Hart 2006, 11–19, especially 12–15; Péter Szigeti, *Jogtani és államtani alapvonalak*, Budapest, Rejtjel 2002, 130–131.

We may also try to get away by saying that these are not criteria but only characteristics. This, however, would presuppose the distinction, without answering the question about the basis of that distinction.

### *14.2.2 Private law and public law as positive-law concepts*

We have seen that 'public law' and 'private law' are not useful concepts as concepts of legal theory. But there are legal systems in Europe, where the term 'public law' occurs too in positive law (statutes or case-law), for instance, in Germany, in the jurisdictional rules of the administrative courts).[38] In these countries we are compelled to find a definition, as otherwise the rules containing these concepts cannot be applied.

In some European legal systems, the distinction has no such importance (e.g., in Hungary),[39] and the distinction plays no role in EU law[40] or in the European Convention of Human Rights, either.[41] But for the sake

[38] Schmidt (n. 19) 45–79 and Bullinger (n. 4) 106–110, with further references. Today (since 1982, see n. 16 above), the situation is similar in English law, too; see Beatson (n. 22) 34–65. On the relevance of the distinction in French, Italian, Swiss and Austrian positive law, see Szladits (n. 22) 24–41.

[39] The distinction was used once by the Constitutional Court, in the reasoning to the decision No. 30/1998. (VI. 25.) AB (ABH 1998. 220). The singular and theoretically unfounded (not sufficiently argued) argument was pertinently criticised by Imre Vörös, The Legal Doctrine and Legal Policy Aspects of EU-Accession, *Acta Juridica Hungarica* 2003, 141–163, 149–152. Where the terms are used, they only serve to emphasise the irrelevance of the distinction (in phrases like 'public law as well as private law'); see, e.g., Act No. 16 of 1998 on the publication of the Framework Treaty between the Republic of Hungary and the European Investment Bank (EIB) concerning the activity of the EIB in Hungary, signed in Hong Kong, on 22 September, 1997, Art. 1. For a comparative overview, see Matthias Ruffert (ed.), *The Public-Private Law Divide: Potential for Transformation?*, London, BIICL 2009.

[40] Wassilios Skouris, *Der Einfluß des europäischen Gemeinschaftsrechts auf die Unterscheidung zwischen Privatrecht und öffentlichem Recht. Dargestellt für das öffentliche Auftragswesen und die Privatisierung*, Bonn, Zentrum für Europäisches Wirtschaftsrecht 1996. For the argument that a national concept of 'public law' is irrelevant for the EC-law concept of 'public service', i.e., for the limitation of the freedom of work, see 149/79, Commission v. Belgium (1980), ECR 3881. The irrelevance of the distinction is made explicit elsewhere by the Treaty on the Functioning of the European Union (Arts 54 and 272: 'public or private law'). In other passages, the prohibition of privileges against private-law subjects is mentioned [TFEU Art. 123 para (1), Art. 124, Art. 125 para (1).].

[41] The case-law of ECtHR works with concepts of 'public' and 'private' very much different from those of the traditional 'public law' and 'private law'. This is criticised in the name of legal certainty by Paul Tavernier, La Convention européenne des droits de l'homme et distinction droit public – droit privé, in: Gérard Cohen Jonathan – Jean-François Flauss –Pierre Lambert (eds.), *Liber amicorum Marc-André Eissen*, Bruxelles,

of those countries where it does, we should have a strategy about how to approach the problem.

Thus, if the term 'public law' occurs in a rule regulating judicial authorities (or in a statute on administrative procedure), giving a definition cannot be avoided. In my view, however (as we have seen), neither of the above theories can serve as the basis of the traditional distinction.

It seems therefore easier to admit that as a first approach the *traditional* interpretation prevails. One may argue that 'these affairs are *usually* considered to belong to public law'. This is a rather safe and plausible way in the European legal systems, but it cannot give an answer to newly arising questions (i.e., new rules for which it is unclear whether they belong to public law or private law). For new problems have the characteristic that there is no traditional interpretation we could rely on. The definition we are looking for should comply with traditional interpretation (for the sake of legal certainty), but it should also be able to categorise unprecedented cases. Therefore, in these countries one has to focus on the key concepts (especially the rule of law, including protection of rights) when defining the term 'public law' as contained in positive law.

Thus, the proposed definition would be the following: (1) public law comprises the affairs/rules that are traditionally regarded as belonging to public law; (2) in (new) cases of doubt, that is, where the former traditional interpretation does not help, the decisive factor should be that no individual should lack the access to the protection of rights (redress).[42] When defining public law in positive law, this pragmatic approach also helps to avoid those concepts that are similarly difficult to define or are defined in too many (debatable) ways (as, e.g., public power, public authority,[43] public law, subordination, or public interest).[44]

Bruylant 1995, 399–413. See also, for the details, Dawn Oliver, The Human Rights Act and Public Law/Private Law Divides, *European Human Rights Law Review* 2000, 343–355.

42 This refers to an 'efficient' and, as a last resort, judicial protection through a fair process according to GG Art. 19 para. (4). For a thorough doctrinal analysis of the concept, see, e.g., Michael Sachs (ed.), *Grundgesetz. Kommentar*, München, Beck $^{5}$2009, 769–772.

43 Public authority is defined as the 'legal capacity to determine others and to reduce their freedom, i.e., to unilaterally shape their legal or factual situation' by Armin von Bogdandy – Philipp Dann – Matthias Goldmann, Developing the Publicness of Public International Law: Towards a Legal Framework for Global Governance Activities, *German Law Journal* 9 (2008) 1375–1400, 1381–1382; and 'public law' is defined by 'public authority' (*ibid.* 1380). This definition is vulnerable to objections we have already mentioned (e.g., family law and employment law would also be comprised in this concept).

44 A similar logic is followed by Beatson (n. 22) 59–64, on the basis of the case *Wandsworth L.B.C. v. Winder* [1985] A.C. 461.

### 14.3 What could be the constitutional purpose behind the distinction?

Even though the distinction does not serve as an explanation on the nature of the legal order, and in most European countries it is not a positive-law concept, we could still argue that we should retain it, if we were to find some general purpose (or constitutional principle) behind it.

As a matter of fact, it has been argued that the distinction between public law and private law reflects the separation of state and society,[45] and therefore it follows from the principles of the rule of law and freedom.[46] Private law – so the argument goes – would then be the domain untouched by the state (thus the 'sphere of liberty').[47]

The idea of the separation of state and society is, however, open to several objections which we have already dealt with above (12.2.6). Moreover, the distinction between public and private law *does not follow* from the separation of state and society. Private law, as well as public law, is a state-imposed order: the distinction between public and private law is one within the domain of the state.[48] Another problem is that this line of thought suggests (or at least implies) that 'public law' does not protect private autonomy or freedom (or protects it less), and this would contradict our ideas of democracy and the rule of law.

As the conceptual scopes are very similar, (1) any constitutional justification of the concept of 'public law' could either (partly) repeat the content of key concepts analysed in Part II of this book (especially democracy and the rule of law), and then it would be superfluous (and loaded with the unnecessary historical baggage of pre-democratic

[45] Eberhard Schmidt-Aßmann, Öffentliches Recht und Privatrecht als wechselseitige Auffangordnungen – Einleitende Problemskizze, in: Hoffmann-Riem – Schmidt-Aßmann (n. 11) 7–40, especially 19; Reinhard Damm, Risikosteuerung im Zivilrecht, in: Hoffmann-Riem – Schmidt-Aßmann (n. 11) 85–142, 139.

[46] Radbruch (n. 16) 157; Helmut Coing, *Grundzüge der Rechtsphilosophie*, Berlin, de Gruyter [3]1976, 189–191.

[47] René Savatier, Droit privé et droit public, *Recueil Dalloz* 1946 (chronique) 25–28, especially 25. 'Private' as protected against intervention: Beate Rössler, *Der Wert des Privaten*, Frankfurt, Suhrkamp 2001, 23.

[48] Möllers (n. 29) 303; cf. also Murray Hunt, The Horizontal Effect of Human Rights Act: Moving beyond the Public-Private Distinction, in: Jeffrey Jowell – Jonathan Cooper (eds.), *Understanding Human Rights Principles*, Oxford, Hart 2001, 161–178, especially 173, arguing that 'there is no such firm distinction [between public law and private law], because the very presence of the law introduces a public element: private relations are in part constituted by both statute and common law, and the State lurks behind both.'

connotations); or (2) it could even derogate from the content of these key concepts.[49]

Thus, we see that there is no longer any acceptable constitutional justification for the distinction.[50]

## 14.4 Further possible meanings of public law and private law

Quite often, we find statements that the border between public and private law becomes relativised,[51] or that private law yields to public law.[52] One wonders, however, what all these statements could mean, seeing, as we have, that there never was a clear and consistent border between the two domains.

Actually, 'public law' and 'private law' refer in these statements to *typical methods* of regulation[53] (and the related protection of rights or rules of responsibility).[54] More specifically, public law is taken to mean typical methods of administrative law, and private law those of private law. To be more precise, we should rather speak of 'contracts' or 'unilateral acts', avoiding the expressions 'public law' and 'private law'.[55]

49 See the proudly anti-constitutionalist approach in Loughlin (n. 21).

50 The historical motivation mentioned above (the interest of the bourgeoisie) does not exist anymore. See Stolleis (n. 1) 59.

51 '. . . the mixing of pubic-law elements into private law', see Justus Wilhelm Hedemann, *Einführung in die Rechtswissenschaft*, Berlin, de Gruyter [2]1927, 134. For similar voices in the French literature, see René Savatier, *Du droit civil au droit public*, Paris, Pichon & Durand-Auzias 1945.

52 'Everything becomes public law'; 'the publicisation of the legal', see Georges Ripert, *Le déclin du droit*, Paris, Librairie générale de droit et de jurisprudence 1949, 37–38; 'public law took over'; see Franz Wieacker, *Industriegesellschaft und Privatrechtsordnung*, Frankfurt aM: Athenaeum-Fischer-Taschenbuch Verlag 1974, 36; similarly: Tamás Lábady, *A magyar magánjog (polgári jog) általános része*, Budapest-Pécs, Dialóg Campus 1997, 22–27.

53 Public law as unilateral state intervention, private law as market(-like) solutions: Christian Kirchner, Regulierung durch öffentliches Recht und/oder Privatrecht aus der Sicht der ökonomischen Theorie des Rechts, in: Hoffmann-Riem – Schmidt-Aßmann (n. 11) 63–84, 70; Wolfgang Hoffmann-Riem, Öffentliches Recht und Privatrecht als wechselseitige Auffangordnungen – Systematisierung und Entwicklungspersektiven, in: Hoffmann-Riem – Schmidt-Aßmann (n. 11) 261–336, 300–304; Gustav Boehmer, *Grundlagen der bürgerlichen Rechtsordnung. Erstes Buch*, Tübingen, Mohr 1950, 166–167; Allan Kanner, Public and Private Law, *Tulane Environmental Law Journal* 1997, 235–277; Jacques Caillosse, Droit public-droit privé: sens et portée d'un partage académique, *L'Actualité juridique – Droit administratif* 20.12.1996, 955–964.

54 Schmidt-Aßmann (n. 45) 8–40, especially 15, 16 and 29; the 'flight into private law' of state activity (from public-law control) as a problem, see Fleiner (n. 22) 326.

55 Bullinger (n. 4) 116.

## 14.5 Should we use the concepts 'public law' and 'private law' in European constitutional discourse?

From the above, it would follow that the expressions 'public law' and 'private law' make no sense. This, however, is not entirely the case. We all have some ideas about what rules belong to the one or to the other.[56] But this is not because there is a consistent theory that provides for firm criteria or reasons for the distinction. This distinction is just a traditional one, not without flaws and indeed with a good deal of fuzziness.[57] Our knowledge of which legal rules belong to public law and which to private law is the result of some kind of a 'lawyerly folklore'. It was passed on to us by the previous generation mainly through legal education, in the same way as they received it from their predecessors.

Thus, it is not worthwhile to face the hopeless task of looking for a theoretical criterion of distinction, as the distinction is conceptually unclear (or circular or both),[58] and the categorisation is due to (legal) historical contingencies. The political interests underlying the distinction between public and private law have now disappeared. The distinction does not follow from the separation of 'state' and 'society' (which in itself is questionable). In those countries where these concepts appear in positive law, they have to be defined partly following the traditional interpretation, and partly (in unprecedented cases) focusing on the protection of fundamental rights.

[56] See, e.g., Patrick Birkinshaw, *European Public Law*, London, LexisNexis 2003, which does not contain a definition of 'public law' despite of its title containing the term.

[57] Dieter Medicus, *Allgemeiner Teil des BGB*, Heidelberg, Müller 1982, 6. Called tradition theory (*Traditionstheorie*) by Günter Püttner, *Allgemeines Verwaltungsrecht*, Düsseldorf, Werner [5]1979, 78. This doctrine is in fact the acceptance that there is no theoretically sound criterion of division, just the uncertain boundaries that stem from (legal) historical eventualities. For a somewhat similar opinion, see Grimm (n. 11) 72.

[58] For a circular definition, see, e.g., 'To the non lawyers a few words of explanation must be offered. Public law denotes that system of law that deals with our public affairs. It denotes the public sphere, defines its extent, the relationship between different tiers in the public sphere and between those tiers and individuals, corporate or personal, citizen or alien. Public law is primarily concerned with the exercise or non exercise of public power, sometimes by private actors, and its fairness, rationality, legality and proportionality.' Patrick Birkinshaw, Does European Public Law Exist?, *Queen's Papers on Europeanisation* 9/2001, 1. So he defines *public* law by reference to *public* sphere and *public* power. What actually 'public' means remains, however, undefined; only some examples are given. For similar conceptual problems, see Peter Cane, Public Law and Private Law: A Study of the Analysis and Use of a Legal Concept, in: John Eekelaar – John Bell (eds.), *Oxford Essays in Jurisprudence*. Third Series, Oxford, Clarendon Press 1987, 57–78.

In statements concerning the weakening of the boundaries between public and private law, the expressions 'public law' and 'private law' refer to *typical methods* of regulation (and the related protection of rights or rules of responsibility). To be more precise, we should rather speak of 'contracts' or 'unilateral state acts', avoiding the expressions 'public law' and 'private law'.

The terms 'public law' and 'private law' reflect nothing other than a series of legal problems shaped by tradition, which we inherited from past centuries.[59] To put it somewhat bluntly, one might say that there are public lawyers (as a sociological group), and therefore one can still speak of public law scholarship,[60] but there is no such thing as public law (at least not in a sense that would be theoretically consistent and relevant for European constitutional theory). Therefore, if possible, we should avoid using these concepts as constitutional terms.

[59] This is probably the only element that binds loosely together the otherwise excellent contributions in Cormac Mac Amhlaigh - Claudio Michelon - Neil Walker (eds.), *After Public Law*, Oxford, Oxford University Press 2013.

[60] See the impressive volumes of Michael Stolleis, *Geschichte des öffentlichen Rechts in Deutschland,* vols. I–IV, München, Beck 1988, 1992, 1999, 2012. For a similar approach, see Charles Eisenmann, Droit public et droit privé (en marge d'un livre sur l'évolution du droit civil français du XIXè au XXè siècle), *Revue du droit public et de la science politique* 1952, 904–979, especially 959–960. A different approach, which presupposes the legal (and not just scholarly) nature of the concept 'public law', is taken by the Societas Iuris Publici Europaei (SIPE) and the Ius Publicum Europaeum (IPE) project; see Armin von Bogdandy - Stephan Hinghofer-Szalkay, Das etwas unheimliche Ius Publicum Europaeum, *Zeitschrift für ausländisches öffentliches Recht und Völkerrecht* 2013, 209–248, 216–220 with further references.

# PART IV

## Concluding remarks

The present work analyses the language of constitutionalism, with a special emphasis on Europe. Most social issues can be expressed in this language; one just has to follow its grammar and learn its vocabulary. Constitutional lawyers speak this language by profession; their job is to translate social issues into constitutional ones and *vice versa*. Constitutional theorists (as the present author himself understands) see their role as describing this language and even in influencing its use through advising constitutional lawyers about its correct use. My general advice in this book is to have a look at the social challenges to which the different elements of this language were a response in the time in which they were invented, and to find their current meaning in the light of today's challenges.

The grammar of this constitutional language; that is, the rules of constitutional reasoning, are slightly different in every country, but generally, I have argued for a more frequent use of 'objective teleological' arguments (i.e., reference to the 'objective purpose' of the norm when explaining the content of constitutional norms) whenever and wherever it is possible. This term does *not* mean that the objective purpose can be established in an entirely objective way, the word 'objective' simply refers to the origin of the purpose: we establish it on the basis of an object, that is, the norm (and not on the basis of a subject, i.e., the law-maker), supposing that the norm serves a socially reasonable purpose. What actually this purpose (in Greek: *telos*) is, is very much open to the partly subjective interpretations of scholars and judges.

In the main part of the book, I have shown how this objective teleological interpretation can be applied in practice to key concepts of the constitutional language. I have suggested the use of a core vocubulary which includes 'sovereignty' (in a strongly redefined form, only as a 'claim of supreme exclusive power', which consequently does not impede European integration); the 'rule of law' and 'fundamental rights' (in an unchanged form, in spite of today's terrorist challenge); 'constitution' (also including the founding treaties of the European Union); 'democracy' (ensuring both the loyalty of citizens and the self-correction mechanism, which in the case of the European Union requires a practically exclusive role of the European Parliament in electing the European Commission); and 'nation' (meaning by it also all European citizens as a European nation).

In a short final part, I have highlighted a few conceptual dead-ends, referring to them as 'redundant vocabulary'. These were rejected partly because they are conceptually incoherent, and partly because they imply pre-democratic and pre-constitutional ideas on how a legal order functions. The redundant vocabulary includes the conceptual framework of *Staatslehre* (i.e., using the concept of a pre-legal state administration in constitutional reasoning); *Stufenbaulehre* (the Kelsenian terminology explaining the validity of norms); principles as norms logically distinct from rules (as exemplified by the theory of Robert Alexy); and the traditional public law–private law divide (which is both conceptually flawed and which also implies pre-democratic ideas of hierarchy between the state and its citizens).

This book describes a European constitutional language which is already widely used but very often in an unconscious and, in some cases, in a substantively different way. The suggested grammar (i.e., the pre-eminence of objective teleological arguments) could be used anywhere in the world. There is currently no specifically European grammar, but the suggested vocabulary with its partly redefined content is distinctively European. The definitions and and social challenges which motivate those definitions are all to be understood in the context of European integration. This volume is thus not just a methodological exercise in constitutional theory, but also a conscious effort to choose, clean and clarify the core constitutional vocabulary of the European constitutional discourse.

# BIBLIOGRAPHY


Aarnio, Aulis, *Denkweisen der Rechtswissenschaft*, Wien, Springer 1979.

Aarnio, Aulis, *Essays on the Doctrinal Study of Law*, Dordrecht, Springer 2011.

Aarnio, Aulis, e.a. (eds.) *Rechtsnorm und Rechtswirklichkeit. Festschrift für Werner Krawietz zum 60. Geburtstag*, Berlin, Duncker & Humblot 1993.

Abizadeh, Arash, Does Democracy Presuppose a Cultural Nation?, *American Political Science Review* 96 (2002) 495–509.

Acemoglu, Daron – James Robinson, *Why Nations Fail: The Origins of Power, Prosperity and Poverty*, New York, Random House 2012.

Achterberg, Norbert, Kriterien des Gesetzesbegriffs unter dem Grundgesetz, *Die öffentliche Verwaltung* 1973, 289–298.

Achterberg, Norbert, Hans Kelsens Bedeutung in der gegenwärtigen deutschen Staatslehre, *Die öffentliche Verwaltung* 1974, 445–454.

Achterberg, Norbert, *Allgemeines Verwaltungsrecht*, Heidelberg, Müller 1982.

Ackerman, Bruce, *We the People. 1:* Foundations, Cambridge, Mass., Belknap Press of Harvard University Press 1991.

Ackerman, Bruce, The Rise of World Constitutionalism, *Virginia Law Review* 83 (1997) 771–794.

Ackerman, Bruce, The Emergency Constitution, *Yale Law Journal* 113 (2003–2004) 1029–1091.

Ackerman, Bruce, This Is Not a War, *Yale Law Journal* 113 (2003–2004) 1871–1907.

Ackerman, Bruce, *Before the Next Attack. Preserving Civil Liberties in an Age of Terrorism*, New Haven, London, Yale University Press 2006.

Adamovich, Ludwig – Bernd-Christian Funk – Gerhart Holzinger, *Österreichisches Staatsrecht*, vol. 1, Wien, Springer 1997.

Aguirre, Mariano – José Antonio Sanahuja, Haiti: Demokratie durch Einmischung?, in: Tobias Debiel – Franz Nuscheler (eds.), *Der neue Interventionismus*, Bonn, Dietz 1996, 155–184.

Albi, Anneli, Postmodern versus Retrospective Sovereignty: Two Different Discourses in the EU and the Candidate Countries, in: Neil Walker (ed.), *Sovereignty in Transition*, Oxford, Hart 2003, 401–422.

Albi, Anneli, *EU Enlargement and the Constitutions of Central and Eastern Europe*, Cambridge, Cambridge University Press 2005.

Albi, Anneli, Introduction: The European Constitution and National Constitutions in the Context of 'Post-national Constitutionalism', in: Anneli Albi – Jacques Ziller (eds.), *The European Constitution and National Constitutions. Ratification and Beyond*, Alphen aan den Rijn, Kluwer Law International 2007, 1–14.

Albi, Anneli – Jacques Ziller (eds.), *The European Constitution and National Constitutions: Ratification and Beyond*, Alphen aan den Rijn, Kluwer Law International 2007.

Alder, John, *Constitutional and Administrative Law*, New York, Palgrave Macmillan $^{5}$2005.

Alexander, Larry, Striking Back at the Empire: A Brief Survey of Problems in Dworkin's Theory of Law, *Law and Philosophy* 6 (1987) 419–438.

Alexander, Larry – Ken Kress, Against Legal Principles, in: Andrei Marmor (ed.), *Law and Interpretation*, Oxford, Clarendon Press 1995, 279–327.

Alexander, Larry – Frederick Schauer, On Extrajudicial Constitutional Interpretation, *Harvard Law Review* 110 (1997) 1359–1387.

Alexy, Robert, Zum Begriff des Rechtsprinzips, in: Werner Krawietz e.a. (eds.), *Argumentation und Hermeneutik in der Jurisprudenz*, Rechtstheorie, Beiheft 1, Berlin, Duncker & Humblot 1979, 59–87.

Alexy, Robert, Zur Struktur der Rechtsprinzipien, in: Bernd Schilcher e.a. (eds.), *Regeln, Prinzipien und Elemente im System des Rechts*, Wien, Verlag Österreich 2000, 31–52.

Alexy, Robert, *Theorie der Grundrechte*, Frankfurt aM, Suhrkamp 2001.

Alexy, Robert – Aleksander Peczenik, The Concept of Coherence and Its Significance for Discursive Rationality, *Ratio Juris* 3 (1990) 130–147.

Allan, TRS, *The Sovereignty of Law: Freedom, Constitution, and Common Law*, Oxford, Oxford University Press 2013.

Alter, Peter, *Nationalismus*, Frankfurt aM, Suhrkamp 1985.

Álvarez, Leonardo, Die spanische Dogmatik der Verfassungstreue. Geschichte einer fehlgeschlagenen Rezeption des deutschen Verfassungsdenkens, *Zeitschrift für ausländisches öffentliches Recht und Völkerrecht* 2010, 433–458.

Álvarez Junco, José, El nacionalismo español: las insuficiencias en la acción estatal, *Historia social* 40 (2001) 29–51.

Alzaga Villaamil, Oscar, La Nación como Poder Constituyente en los preambulos de las *leges superiores*. El Estatut de 2006 y la STC 31/2010, *Teoría y Realidad Constitucional* no. 27 (2011/1) 131–176.

Amtenbrink, Fabian – Peter AJ van den Berg (eds.), *The Constitutional Intergrity of the European Union*, The Hague, TMC Asser 2010.

Anderle, Othmar, *Das universalhistorische System Arnold Joseph Toynbees*, Frankfurt aM, Humboldt 1955.

Anderson, Benedict, I like Nationalism's Utopian Elements, interview with Lorenz Khazaleh, 2005 www.culcom.uio.no/english/news/2005/.

Anderson, Benedict, *Imagined Communities*, London, New York, Verso $^{2}$2006.

Andreski, Stanislav, *Military Organization and Society*, Berkeley, University of California Press 1968.

Annus, Taavi, Comparative Constitutional Reasoning: The Law and Strategy of Selecting the Right Argument, *Duke Journal of Comparative & International Law* 14 (2004) 301–350.

Anschütz, Gerhard – Richard Thoma (eds.), *Handbuch des deutschen Staatsrechts*, vol. 2, Tübingen, Mohr 1932.

Antieau, Chester James, *Constitutional Construction*, London, Oceana 1982.

Antoniolli, Walter, e.a., *Hans Kelsen zum Gedenken*, Wien, Europaverlag 1974.

Apelt, Willibalt, *Der verwaltungsrechtliche Vertrag. Ein Beitrag zur Lehre von der rechtswirksamen Handlung im öffentlichen Rechte*, Leipzig, Meiner 1920.

Arbós Marín, Xavier – Fernando Domínguez García, Cataluña como nación y los símbolos nacionales, *Revista catalana de dret públic* [Especial Sentencia 31/2010] 2010, 101–114.

Armstrong, John A, *Nations before Nationalism*, Chapel Hill, University of North Carolina Press 1982.

Armstrong, Kenneth A, United Kingdom – Divided on Sovereignty, in: Neil Walker (ed.), *Sovereignty in Transition*, Oxford, Hart 2003, 327–350.

Arndt, Adolf, Der Rechtsstaat und sein polizeilicher Verfassungsschutz, *Neue Juristische Wochenschrift* 1961, 897–902.

Arndt, Adolf, Demokratie. Wertsystem des Rechts, in: Adolf Arndt – Michael Freund (eds.), *Notstandsgesetz – aber wie?*, Köln, Verlag Wissenschaft und Politik 1962, 7–66.

Arndt, Adolf – Michael Freund (eds.), *Notstandsgesetz – aber wie?*, Köln, Verlag Wissenschaft und Politik 1962.

Arnold, Rainer, Réflexions sur l'argumentation juridique en droit constitutionnel allemande, in: Otto Pfersmann – Gérard Timsit (eds.), *Raisonnement juridique et interprétation*, Paris, Sorbonne 2001, 49–63.

Aron, Raymond, *Peace and War*, Malabar, Krieger 1962.

Atienza, Manuel, *Las razones del Derecho. Teorías de la argumentación jurídica*, Madrid, Centro de Estudios Constitucionales 1991.

Atiyah, Patrick S – Robert S Summers, *Form and Substance in Anglo-American Law. A Comparative Study of Legal Reasoning, Legal Theory and Legal Institutions*, Oxford, Clarendon Press 1987.

Auby, Jean-Bernard, Le rôle de la distinction du droit public et du droit privé dans le droit français, in: Mark Freedland – Jean-Bernard Auby (eds.), *The Public Law / Private Law Divide*, Oxford, Hart 2006, 11–19.

Auerbach, Erich, *Mimesis: The Representation of Reality in Western Literature*, Princeton, Princeton University Press 1957.

Austin, John, *The Province of Jurisprudence Determined*, London, John Murray 1832.

Austin, John, *The Province of Jurisprudence Determined and The Uses of the Study of Jurisprudence*, London, Weidenfeld and Nicolson 1971.

Avbelj, Matej – Jan Komárek (eds.), Four Visions of Constitutional Pluralism, *EUI Working Papers Law* 2008/21.

Avbelj, Matej e.a. (eds.), *Constitutional Pluralism in the European Union and Beyond*, Oxford, Hart 2012.

Azoulai, Loïc, Sur un sens de la distinction public/privé dans le droit de l'Union européenne, *Revue trimestrielle du droit européen* 2010/oct.-déc., 842–860.

Baár, Monika, *Historians and Nationalism*, Oxford, Oxford University Press 2010.

Bachoff, Otto (ed.), *Forschungen und Berichte aus dem Öffentlichen Recht. Festschrift für Walter Jellinek*, München, Isar Verlag 1955.

Bacot, Guillaume, *Carré de Malberg et l'origine de la distinction entre souveraineté du peuple et souveraineté nationale*, Paris, Édition du CNRS 1985.

Bacqué, Jorge A, Stufenbau der Rechtsordnung oder Einebnung der Nor-men-pyra-mide, in: Eugenio Bulygin – Ernesto Garzón Valdés (eds.) *Argentinische Rechtstheorie und Rechtsphilosophie heute*, Berlin, Duncker & Humblot 1987, 111–116.

Badura, Peter, Bewahrung und Veränderung demokratischer und rechtsstaatlicher Verfassungsstruktur in den internationalen Gemeinschaften, *Veröffentlichungen der Vereinigung der Deutschen Staatsrechtslehrer* 1966, 34–104.

Badura, Peter, Verfassung und Verfassungsgesetz, in: Horst Ehmke (ed.), *Festschrift für Ulrich Scheuner zum 70. Geburtstag*, Berlin, Duncker & Humblot 1973, 19–39.

Badura, Peter, *Methoden der neueren Allgemeinen Staatslehre*, Goldbach, Keip $^{2}$1998.

Badura, Peter, *Staatsrecht*, München, CH Beck $^{5}$2012.

Badura, Peter – Horst Dreier (eds.), *Festschrift 50 Jahre Bundesverfassungsgericht*, vol. I, Tübingen, Mohr Siebeck 2001.

Bagehot, Walter, *Physics and Politics*, London, King 1887.

Bakke, Elisabeth, Towards a European Identity?, *ARENA Working Paper* 10/95, Oslo.

Bakke, Elisabeth, The Principle of National Self-Determination in Czechoslovak Constitutions 1920–1992, *Central European Political Science Review* 3 (2002) no. 10, 173–198.

Balaguer Callejón, María Luisa, *Interpretación de la Constitución y ordenamiento jurídico*, Madrid, Tecnos 1997.

Balakrishnan, Gopal (ed.), *Mapping the Nation*, London, Verso 1996.

Balcells, Albert, *Catalan Nationalism: Past and Present*, London, Macmillan 1995.

Balkin, Jack M – Sanford Levinson, Constitutional Grammar, *Texas Law Review* 72 (1994) 1771–1803.

Balkin, Jack M, Framework Originalism and the Living Constitution, *Northwestern University Law Review* 103 (2009) 549–614.

Ballreich, Hans e.a. (eds.), *Das Staatsnotrecht in Belgien, Frankreich, Großbritannien, Italien, den Niederlanden, der Schweiz und den Vereinigten Staaten von Amerika*, Köln, Heymann 1955.

Banaszak, Bogusław – Tomasz Milej, *Polnisches Staatsrecht*, Warszawa, Beck 2009.

Baquero Cruz, Julio, Alternativas a las condiciones de revisión y entrada en vigor, in: Iñigo Méndez de Vigo (ed.), *¿Qué fue de la Constitución Europea?*, Barcelona, Planeta 2007, 293–306.

Barak, Aharon, *Purposive Interpretation in Law*, Princeton, Princeton University Press 2005.

Barak, Aharon, Human Rights in Times of Terror – A Judicial Point of View, *Legal Studies* 2008, 493–504.

Barber, Nicholas William, *The Constitutional State*, Oxford, Oxford University Press 2010.

Barion, Hans – Ernst Forsthoff – Werner Weber (eds.), *Festschrift für Carl Schmitt zum 70. Geburtstag*, Berlin, Duncker & Humblot 1959.

Barnard, Frederick M, National Culture and Political Legitimacy: Herder and Rousseau, *Journal of the History of Political Ideas* 1983, 231–253.

Barnard, Frederick M, Patriotism and Citizenship in Rousseau, *Review of Politics* 46 (1984) 244–265.

Barnett, Hilaire, *Constitutional & Administrative Law*, London, New York, Routledge [9]2011.

Barry, Brian, Nationalism, in: David Miller (ed.), *The Blackwell Encyclopaedia of Political Thought*, Oxford, Blackwell 1987, 352–354.

Barth, Fredrik, *Ethnic Groups and Boundaries*, Boston, Little, Brown and Co. 1969.

Bast, Jürgen, Handlungsformen, in: Armin von Bogdandy (ed.), *Europäisches Verfassungsrecht*, Berlin, Springer 2003, 497–537.

Bates, David, Political Unity and the Spirit of the Law: Juridical Concepts of the State in the Late Third Republic, *French Historical Studies* 28 (2005) 69–101.

Batory, Agnes, Kin-State Identity in the European Context: Citizenship, Nationalism and Constitutionalism in Hungary, *Nations and Nationalism* 2010, 31–48.

Battis, Ulrich – Christoph Gusy, *Einführung in das Staatsrecht*, Berlin, de Gruyter 2011.

Bauböck, Rainer (ed.), *Migration and Citizenship*, Amsterdam, Amsterdam University Press 2006.

Bauböck, Rainer – Eva Ersbøll – Kees Groenendijk – Harald Waldrauch (eds.), *Acquisition and Loss of Nationality*, vols. I–II, Amsterdam, Amsterdam University Press 2006.

Bauer, Otto, The Nation [1924], in: Gopal Balakrishnan (ed.), *Mapping the Nation*, London, Verso 1996, 39–77.

Baycroft, Timothy, Ethnicity and Revolutionary Tradition in France, in: Timothy Baycroft – Mark Hewitson (eds.), *What Is a Nation? Europe 1789–1914*, Oxford, Oxford University Press 2006, 28–41.

Baycroft, Timothy – Mark Hewitson (eds.), *What Is a Nation? Europe 1789–1914*, Oxford, Oxford University Press 2006.

Bayefsky, Anne F (ed.), *Self-Determination in International Law: Quebec and Lessons Learned*, The Hague, Kluwer 2000.

Bazard, Saint-Amand – Barthélémy Prosper Enfantin, *Doctrine de Saint-Simon, Exposition première année (1828–1829)*, Paris, Bureau de l'organisateur $^{3}$1831.

Beatson, Jack, 'Public' and 'Private' in English Administrative Law, *Law Quarterly Review* 103 (1987) 34–65.

Beatty, David M, The Forms and Limits of Constitutional Interpretation, *American Journal of Comparative Law* 49 (2001) 79–120.

Beaud, Olivier, *La puissance de l'État*, Paris, Presses Universitaires de France 1994.

Beaud, Olivier – Erk Volkmar Heyen (eds.), *Eine deutsch-französische Rechtswissenschaft?*, Baden-Baden, Nomos 1999.

Beaulac, Stéphane, *The Power of Language in the Making of International Law*, Leiden, Nijhoff 2004.

Beck, Gunnar, *The Legal Reasoning of the Court of Justice of the EU*, Oxford, Hart 2012.

Becker, Florian, Staat und Krone im Vereinigten Königreich, in: Peter Axer e.a. (eds.), *Staat um Wort. Festschrift für Josef Isensee*, Heidelberg, CF Müller 2007, 471–488.

Beer, Samuel H, *To Make a Nation: The Rediscovery of American Federalism*, Cambridge, Mass., Harvard University Press 1994.

Beestermöller, Gerhard, Folter – Daumenschrauben an der Würde des Menschen. Zur Ausnahmelosigkeit eines Absoluten Verbotes, in: Gerhard Beestermöller – Hauke Brunkhorst (eds.), *Rückkehr der Folter. Rechtsstaat im Zwielicht?*, München, Beck 2006, 115–129.

Beestermöller, Gerhard – Hauke Brunkhorst (eds.), *Rückkehr der Folter. Rechtsstaat im Zwielicht?*, München, Beck 2006.

Beetham, David, *Max Weber and the Theory of Modern Politics*, Cambridge, Polity Press 1985.

Behrend, Jürgen, *Untersuchungen zur Stufenbaulehre Adolf Merkls und Hans Kelsens*, Berlin, Duncker & Humblot 1977.

Behrendt, Christian – Frédéric Bouhon, *Introduction à la théorie générale de l'État*, Bruxelles, Larcier $^{2}$2011.

Beiner, Ronald, Introduction: Nationalism's Challenge to Political Philosophy, in: id. (ed.), *Theorizing Nationalism*, New York, State University of New York Press 1999, 1–25.

Beiner, Ronald (ed.), *Theorizing Nationalism*, New York, State University of New York Press 1999.

Beiner, Ronald – Wayne Norman (eds.), *Canadian Political Philosophy: Contemporary Reflections*, Oxford, Oxford University Press 2001.

Bell, Jeannine, 'Behind this Mortal Bone': The (In)Effectiveness of Torture, *Indiana Law Journal* 83 (2008) 339–361.

Bell, John, *Policy Arguments in Judicial Decisions*, Oxford, Oxford University Press 1983.

Bell, John, *French Constitutional Law*, Oxford, Clarendon Press 1992.

Bellah, Robert N, Civil Religion in America, *Daedalus* 1967, 1–21.

Bellah, Robert N, *The Broken Covenant*, New York, Seabury 1975.

Bellamy, Richard, Sovereignty, Post-Sovereignty and Pre-Sovereignty, in: Neil Walker (ed.), *Sovereignty in Transition*, Oxford, Hart 2003, 167–190.

Bellamy, Richard, *Political Constitutionalism*, Cambridge, Cambridge University Press 2007.

Bengoetxea, Joxerammon, *The Legal Reasoning of the European Court of Justice: Towards a European Jurisprudence*, Oxford, Clarendon Press 1993.

Bengoetxea, Joxerramon, Multilingual and Multicultural Legal Reasoning: The European Court of Justice, in: Anne Lise Kjær – Silvia Adamo (eds.), *Linguistic Diversity and European Democracy*, Farnham, Ashgate 2011, 97–122.

Benner, Erica, Is There a Core National Doctrine?, *Nations and Nationalism* 2001, 155–174.

Berding, Helmut e.a. (eds.), *Vom Staat des Ancien régime zum modernen Parteienstaat. Festschrift für Theodor Schieder*, München, Oldenbourg 1978.

Berent, Moshe, The ethnic democracy debate, *Nations and Nationalism* 2010, 657–674.

Bergel, Jean-Louis, *Méthodologie juridique*, Paris, Presses Universitaires de France 2001.

Bergel, Jean-Louis, *Théorie générale du droit*, Paris, Dalloz [4]2003.

Berger, Stefan, Ethnic Nationalism Par Excellence? Germany 1789–1914, in: Timothy Baycroft – Mark Hewitson (eds.), *What Is a Nation? Europe 1789–1914*, Oxford, Oxford University Press 2006, 42–62.

Berggen, Niclas – Nils Karlson – Joakim Nergelius (eds.), *Why Constitutions Matter*, Stockholm, City University Press 2000.

Berka, Walter, *Die Grundrechte*, Wien, Springer 1999.

Berlin, Isaiah, *Vico and Herder*, London, Hogarth 1976.

Berman, Harold J, The Origins of Western Legal Science, in: JC Smith – David N Weisstub (eds.), *The Western Idea of Law*, London, Butterworths 1983, 399–413.

Bernárdez Canton, A, Droit public – droit privé an droit canonique, in: Åke Malmström – Stig Strömholm (eds.), *Rapports généraux au VII$^{e}$ Congrès international de droit comparé*, Stockholm, Almquist & Wiksell 1968, 42.

Bernstorff, Jochen von, *Der Glaube an das universale Recht. Zur Völkerrechtstheorie Hans Kelsens und seiner Schüler*, Baden-Baden, Nomos 2001.

Besselink, Leonard, The Notion and Nature of the European Constitution after the Lisbon Treaty, in: Jan Wouters – Luc Verhey – Philipp Kiiver (eds.), *European Constitutionalism beyond Lisbon*, Antwerp, Intersentia 2009, 261–281.

Besson, Samantha, Sovereignty in Conflict, *European Integration online Papers (EIoP)* vol. 8 (2004) N 15, 1–50.

BGG, Cuatro años de encarnizada batallas política, *El País* 16.04.2010.

Bielefeldt, Heiner, Die Absolutheit des Folterverbots. Über die Unabwägbarkeit der Menschenwürde, in: Gerhard Beestermöller – Hauke Brunkhorst (eds.), *Rückkehr der Folter. Rechtsstaat im Zwielicht?*, München, Beck 2006, 109–114.

Bierling, Ernst Rudolf, *Juristische Prinzipienlehre*, vol. II, Freiburg, Mohr 1898.

Bignami, Francesca E, The Democratic Deficit in European Community Rulemaking: A Call for Notice and Comment in Comitology, *Harvard International Law Journal* 40 (1999) 415–515.

Billier, Jean-Cassien – Aglaé Maryioli, *Histoire de la philosophie du droit*, Paris, Armand Collin 2001.

Billig, Michael, *Banal Nationalism*, London, Sage 1995.

Bindreiter, Uta, *Why Grundnorm? A Treatise on the Implications of Kelsen's Doctrine*, The Hague, Kluwer Law International 2002.

Bingham, Lord of Cornhill, The Rule of Law and the Sovereignty of Parliament, *King's Law Journal* 19 (2008) 223–234.

Bingham, Tom, *The Rule of Law*, London, Allen Lane 2010.

Birkinshaw, Patrick, Does European Public Law Exist?, *Queen's Papers on Europeanisation* 9/2001.

Birkinshaw, Patrick, *European Public Law*, London, LexisNexis 2003.

Birtles, William, e.a. (eds.), *Die Zulässigkeit des Einsatzes staatlicher Gewalt in Ausnahmesituationen*, Karlsruhe, Müller 1976.

Bjørn, Claus, e.a. (eds.), *Nations, Nationalism and Patriotism in the European Past*, Copenhagen, Academic Press Copenhagen 1994.

Blackstone, William, *Commentaries on the Laws of England*, Oxford, Clarendon Press [8]1765.

Blackstone, William, *An Analysis of the Laws of England*, Oxford, Clarendon Press [6]1771.

Blas Guerrero, Andrés de (ed.), *Teoria del Estado*, Madrid, UNED 2010.

Bleckmann, Albert, Monismus mit Primat des Völkerrechts. Zur Kelsenschen Konstruktion des Verhältnisses von Völkerrecht und Landesrecht, in: Werner Krawietz – Helmut Schelsky (eds.), *Rechtssystem und gesellschaftliche Basis bei Hans Kelsen*, Rechtstheorie, Beiheft 5, Berlin, Duncker & Humblot 1984, 337–347.

Blount, Justin, Participation in constitutional design, in: Tom Ginsburg – Rosalind Dixon, *Comparative Constitutional Law*, Cheltenham, Edward Elgar 2011, 38–56.

Bluntschli, Johann Caspar, Die nationale Staatenbildung und der moderne deutsche Staat, in: id., *Gesammelte kleine Schriften*, vol. 2, Nördlingen, Beck 1881, 70–113.

Bluntschli, Johann Caspar, *Gesammelte kleine Schriften*, vol. 2, Nördlingen, Beck 1881.

Bluntschli, Johann Caspar, *Die schweizerische Nationalität*, Zürich, Rascher und Cie. 1915 [1875].

Bobbio, Norberto, *Teoria generale del diritto*, Torino, Giappichelli 1993.

Bobbitt, Philip, *The Shield of Achilles: War, Peace, and the Course of History*, New York, Anchor 2002.

Böckenförde, Ernst-Wolfgang, *Die verfassungstheoretische Unterscheidung von Staat und Gesellschaft als Bedingung der individuellen Freiheit*, Opladen, Westdeutscher Verlag 1973.

Böckenförde, Ernst-Wolfgang, Die Methoden der Verfassungsinterpretation, *Neue Juristische Wochenschrift* 1976, 2089–2099.

Böckenförde, Ernst-Wolfgang (ed.), *Staat und Gesellschaft*, Darmstadt, Wissenschaftliche Buchgesellschaft 1976.

Böckenförde, Ernst-Wolfgang, Der verdrängte Ausnahmezustand, *Neue Juristische Wochenschrift* 1978, 1881–1890.

Böckenförde, Ernst-Wolfgang, Ausnahmerecht und demokratischer Rechtsstaat, in: Hans-Jochen Vogel (ed.), *Die Freiheit des Anderen. Festschrift für Martin Hirsch*, Baden-Baden, Nomos 1981, 259–272.

Böckenförde, Ernst-Wolfgang, Mittelbare/repräsentative Demokratie als eigentliche Form der Demokratie. Bemerkungen zu Begriff und Verwirklichungsproblemen der Demokratie als Staats- und Regierungsfrom, in: Georg Müller e.a. (eds.), *Staatsorganisation und Staatsfunktion im Wandel. Festschrift für Kurt Eichenberger, Basel*, Frankfurt aM, Helbing & Lichtenhahn 1982, 301–328.

Böckenförde, Ernst-Wolfgang, Zur Kritik der Wertbegründung des Rechts, in: Ralf Dreier (ed.), *Rechtspositivismus und Wertbezug des Rechts*, Stuttgart, Steiner 1990, 33–46.

Böckenförde, Ernst-Wolfgang, Demokratie als Verfassungsprinzip, in: id., *Staat, Verfassung, Demokratie*, Frankfurt aM, Suhrkamp 1991, 291–378.

Böckenförde, Ernst-Wolfgang, Die Eigenart des Staatsrechts und der Staatsrechtswissenschaft, in: id., *Staat, Verfassung, Demokratie*, Frankfurt aM, Suhrkamp 1991, 11–28.

Böckenförde, Ernst-Wolfgang, Geschichtliche Entwicklung und Bedeutungswandel der Verfassung, in: id., *Staat, Verfassung, Demokratie*, Frankfurt aM, Suhrkamp 1991, 29–52.

Böckenförde, Ernst-Wolfgang, *Staat, Verfassung, Demokratie*, Frankfurt aM, Suhrkamp 1991.

Böckenförde, Ernst-Wolfgang, Rechtsstaat, in: Joachim Ritter – Karlfried Gründer (eds.), *Historisches Wörterbuch der Philosophie*, vol. 8, Darmstadt, Wissenschaftliche Buchgesellschaft 1992, 332–342.

Böckenförde, Ernst-Wolfgang, *Welchen Weg geht Europa?*, München, Carl-Friedrich-von-Siemens-Stiftung 1997.

Böckenförde, Ernst-Wolfgang, Begriff und Probleme des Verfassungsstaates, in: id., *Staat, Nation, Europa*, Frankfurt aM, Suhrkamp 1999, 127–140.

Böckenförde, Ernst-Wolfgang, *Staat, Nation, Europa*, Frankfurt aM, Suhrkamp 1999.

Böckenförde, Ernst Wolfgang, Die Würde des Menschen war unantastbar, *Frankfurter Allgemeine Zeitung*, 3 September 2003, 33.

Boehmer, Gustav, *Grundlagen der bürgerlichen Rechtsordnung. Erstes Buch*, Tübingen, Mohr 1950.

Boehmer, Gustav, *Grundlagen der bürgerlichen Rechtsordnung. 2.1. Dogmengeschichtliche Grundlagen des bürgerlichen Rechtes*, Tübingen, Mohr 1951.

Bogdandy, Armin von, *Supranationaler Föderalismus als Wirklichkeit und Idee einer neuen Herrschaftsform*, Baden-Baden, Nomos 1999.

Bogdandy, Armin von (ed.), *Europäisches Verfassungsrecht*, Berlin, Springer 2003.

Bogdandy, Armin von, Europäische Prinzipienlehre, in: id. (ed.), *Europäisches Verfassungsrecht*, Berlin, Springer 2003, 149–203.

Bogdandy, Armin von, Europäische und nationale Identität: Integration durch Verfassungsrecht?, *Veröffentlichungen der Vereinigung der Deutschen Staatsrechtslehrer* 62 (2003) 156–193.

Bogdandy, Armin von – Philipp Dann – Matthias Goldmann, Developing the Publicness of Public International Law: Towards a Legal Framework for Global Governance Activities, *German Law Journal* 9 (2008) 1375–1400.

Bogdandy, Armin von – Jürgen Bast, The Constitutional Approach to EU Law – From Taming Intergovernmental Relationships to Framing Political Processes, in: Armin von Bogdandy – Jürgen Bast (eds.), *Principles of European Constitutional Law*, Oxford, Hart [2]2010, 1–7.

Bogdandy, Armin von – Jürgen Bast (eds.), *Principles of European Constitutional Law*, Oxford, Hart [2]2010.

Bogdandy, Armin von – Stephan Hinghofer-Szalkay, Das etwas unheimliche Ius Publicum Europaeum, *Zeitschrift für ausländisches öffentliches Recht und Völkerrecht* 2013, 209–248.

Bogdandy, Armin von – Peter M Huber (eds.), *Ius Publicum Europaeum*, vols. I–VII, Heidelberg, CF Müller, 2007–2015.

Bogdandy, Armin von – Matthias Kottmann – Carlino Antpöhler – Johanna Dickschen – Simon Hentrei – Maja Smrkolj, Reverse Solange – Protecting the Essence of Fundamental Rights against EU Member States, *Common Market Law Review* 2012/2, 489–519.

Bogs, Harald, *Die verfassungskonforme Auslegung von Gesetzen*, Stuttgart, Kohlhammer 1966.

Boldt, Hans, *Deutsche Staatslehre im Vormärz*, Düsseldorf, Droste 1975.

Boldt, Hans – Werner Conze – Görg Haverkate – Diethelm Klippel – Reinhart Koselleck, Staat und Souveränität, in: Otto Brunner e.a. (eds.), *Geschichtliche Grundbegriffe*, vol. 6, Stuttgart, Klett-Cotta 2004, 1–154.

Bomhoff, Jacco, *Balancing Constitutional Rights: The Origins and Meanings of Postwar Legal Discourse*, Cambridge, Cambridge University Press 2013.

Bork, Robert, Neutral Principles and Some First Amendment Problems, *Indiana Law Journal* 47 (1971) 1–35.

Borowski, Martin, *Grundrechte als Prinzipien*, Baden-Baden, Nomos 2007.

Bourdieu, Pierre, La force du droit. Éléments pour une sociologie du champs juridique, *Actes de la recherche en sciences sociales* no. 64/9 (1986) 3–19.

Bowen, John R, *Why the French Don't Like Headscarves: Islam, the State, and Public Space*, Princeton, Princeton University Press 2006.

Bradley, Curtis A, The Charming Betsy Canon and the Separation of Powers. Rethinking the Interpretive Role of International Law, *Georgetown Law Journal* 86 (1998) 479–537.

Bradley, Kieran St C, La transparence de l'Union Européenne, *Cahiers de droit européen*, N° 3–4 (1999) 285–362.

Brass, Paul R, *Ethnicity and Nationalism: Theory and Comparison*, New Delhi, Sage 1991.

Bredimas, Anna, *Methods of Interpretation and Community Law*, Amsterdam, North Holland Publishing 1978.

Brennan, Geoffrey – Alan Hamlin, Constitutions as Expressive Documents, in: Barry R Weingast – Donald A Wittman (eds.), *The Oxford Handbook of Political Economy*, Oxford, Oxford University Press 2006, 329–341.

Brenneisen, Hartmut, Grenzlinie Folter, in: Heribert Ostendorf (ed.), *Folter. Praxis, Verbot, Verantwortlichkeit*, Münster, LIT Verlag 2005, 53–80.

Breslin, Beau, *The Communitarian Constitution*, Baltimore, Johns Hopkins University Press 2004.

Breuilly, John, *Nationalism and the State*, Manchester, Manchester University Press ²1993.

Breuilly, John, Approaches to Nationalism, in: Gopal Balakrishnan (ed.), *Mapping the Nation*, London, Verso 1996, 146–174.

Breuilly, John, Dating the Nation: How Old Is an Old Nation?, in: Atsuko Ichijo – Gordana Uzelac (eds.), *When Is the Nation?*, London, Routledge 2005, 15–39.

Breyer, Stephen, *Active Liberty: Interpreting Our Democratic Constitution*, New York, Alfred Knopf 2005.

Brison, Susan J – Walter Sinnott-Armstrong (eds.), *Contemporary Perspectives on Constitutional Interpretation*, Boulder, Westview 1993.

Brison, Susan J – Walter Sinnott-Armstrong, A Philosophical Introduction to Constitutional Interpretation, in: Susan J Brison – Walter Sinnott-Armstrong (eds.), *Contemporary Perspectives on Constitutional Interpretation*, Boulder, Westview 1993, 1–25.

Brodocz, André, *Die symbolische Dimension der Verfassung*, Wiesbaden, Westdeutscher Verlag 2003.

Bronaugh, Richard, Persuasive Precedent, in: Laurence Goldstein (ed.), *Precedent in Law*, Oxford, Clarendon Press 1987, 217–247.

Brubaker, Rogers, *Citizenship and Nationhood in France and Germany*, Cambridge, Mass., Harvard University Press 1992.

Brubaker, Rogers, *Nationalism Reframed: Nationhood and the National Question in the New Europe*, Cambridge, Cambridge University Press 1996.

Brubaker, Rogers, Religion and Nationalism, *Nations and Nationalism* 2012, 2–20.

Brugger, Winfried, Darf der Staat ausnahmweise foltern?, *Der Staat* 35 (1996) 67–97.

Brugger, Winfried, May Government Ever Use Torture? Two Responses from German Law, *American Journal of Comparative Law* 48 (2000) 661–678.

Brugger, Winfried, Vom unbedingten Verbot der Folter zum bedingten Recht auf Folter?, *JuristenZeitung* 2000, 165–173.

Brugger, Winfried, Darf der Staat foltern?, *Podiumsdiskussion Humboldt Universität Berlin am 28.6.2001*, available at http://www.humboldt-forum-recht.de/english /4–2002/index.html.

Brugger, Winfried, *Freiheit und Sicherheit*, Baden-Baden, Nomos 2004.

Brunkhorst, Hauke, Folter, Würde und repressive Liberalismus, in: Gerhard Beestermöller – Hauke Brunkhorst (eds.), *Rückkehr der Folter. Rechtsstaat im Zwielicht?*, München, Beck 2006, 88–100.

Brünneck, Alexander von, Die öffentliche Meinung in der EG als Verfassungsproblem, *Europarecht* 1989, 249–261.

Brunner Otto – Werner Conze – Reinhart Koselleck (eds.), *Geschichtliche Grundbegriffe*, vols. 1–8, Stuttgart, Klett-Cotta 2004.

Bryde, Brun-Otto, Konstitutionalisierung des Völkerrechts und Internationalisierung des Verfassungsrechts, *Der Staat* 42 (2003) 61–75.

Buchanan, Allen, *Secession: The Morality of Political Divorce from Sumter to Lithuania and Quebec*, Boulder, Colo, Westview 1991.

Buchanan, James M, The Domain of Constitutional Economics, *Constitutional Political Economy* 1990, 1–18.

Buchanan, James M, Why Do Constitutions Matter?, in: Niclas Berggen e.a. (eds.), *Why Constitutions Matter*, Stockholm, City University Press 2000, 1–16.

Bucher, Eugen, Was ist 'Begriffsjurisprudenz'?, in: Werner Krawietz (ed.), *Theorie und Technik der Begriffsjurisprudenz*, Darmstadt, Wissenschaftliche Buchgesellschaft 1976, 358–389.

Bullinger, Martin, *Öffentliches Recht und Privatrecht. Studien über Sinn und Funktion der Unterscheidung*, Stuttgart, W. Kohlhammer 1968.

Bullinger, Martin, Die Funktionelle Unterscheidung von öffentlichem Recht und Privatrecht als Beitrag zur Beweglichkeit von Verwaltung und Wirtschaft in Europa, in: Wolfgang Hoffmann-Riem – Eberhard Schmidt-Aßmann (eds.),

*Öffentliches Recht und Privatrecht als wechselseitige Auffangordnungen*, Baden-Baden, Nomos 1996, 239–260.

Bulygin, Eugenio – Ernesto Garzón Valdés (eds.) *Argentinische Rechtstheorie und Rechtsphilosophie heute*, Berlin, Duncker & Humblot 1987.

Bulygin, Eugenio, Normative Positivism vs. the Theory of Legal Argumentation, in: Tomasz Gizbert-Studnicki – Jerzy Stelmach (eds.), *Law and Legal Cultures in the 21st Century: Diversity and Unity*, Warszawa, Oficyna 2007, 221–228.

[s.n.], *Das Bundesverfassungsgericht*, Karlsruhe, Müller 1963.

Burckhardt, Walter, *Die Organisation der Rechtsgemeinschaft*, Zürich, Polygraphischer Verlag $^{2}$1944.

Burdeau, Georges, *La démocratie*, Paris, Le Seuil 1956.

Burke, Edmund, Speech on the Representation of the Commons in Parliaments (1782), in: PJ Stanlis (ed.), *Selected Writings and Speeches of Edmund Burke*, Garden City, NY, Doubleday 1963, 330–331.

Burmeister, Joachim, *Die Verfassungsorientierung der Gesetzesauslegung*, Berlin, Frankfurt aM, Franz Vahlen 1966.

Burmeister, Joachim, e.a. (eds.), *Verfassungsstaatlichkeit. Festschrift Klaus Stern*, München, Beck 1997.

Burton, Steven J, *An Introduction to Law and Legal Reasoning*, Boston, Toronto, Little, Brown and Company 1985.

Bydlinski, Franz, *Juristische Methodenlehre und Rechtsbegriff*, Wien, New York, Springer $^{2}$1991.

Caillosse, Jacques, Droit public-droit privé: sens et portée d'un partage académique, *L'Actualité juridique – Droit administratif*, 20 December 1996, 955–964.

Calhoun, Craig, Nationalism and Ethnicity, *Annual Review of Sociology* 19 (1993) 211–239.

Calhoun, Craig, *Nationalism*, Buckingham, Open University Press 1997.

Calhoun, Craig, *Nations Matter: Culture, History, and the Cosmopolitan Dream*, London, New York, Routledge 2007.

Callies, Christian, Sicherheit im freiheitlichen Rechtsstaat. Eine verfassungsrechtliche Gratwanderung mit staatstheoretischem Kompass, *Zeitschrift für Rechtspolitik* 2002, 1–7.

Callies, Christian, Gewährleistung von Freiheit und Sicherheit im Lichte unterschiedlicher Staats- und Verfassungsverständnisse, *Deutsches Verwaltungsblatt* 118 (2003) 1096–1105.

Caemmerer, Ernst von –Soia Mentschikoff – Max Rheinstein – Konrad Zweigert (eds.), *Ius privatum gentium. Festschrift für Max Rheinstein*. vol. I, Tübingen, Mohr Siebeck 1969.

Canaris, Claus Wilhelm, *Systemdenken und Systembegriff in der Jurisprudenz*, Berlin, Duncker & Humblot 1969.

Cane, Peter, Public Law and Private Law: A Study of the Analysis and Use of a Legal Concept, in: John Eekelaar – John Bell (eds.), *Oxford Essays in Jurisprudence. Third Series*, Oxford, Clarendon Press 1987, 57–78.

Canovan, Margaret, *Nationhood and Political Theory*, Cheltenham, Edward Elgar 1996.

Cappelletti, Mauro, *Judicial Review in the Contemporary World*, New York, Bobbs-Merrill Inc. 1971.

Carbonnier, Jean, *Introduction au droit civil*, Paris, Presses Universitaires de France [23]1995.

Cardozo, Benjamin L, *The Nature of the Judicial Process*, New Haven, Yale University Press 1921.

Carens, Joseph H, Nationalism and the Exclusion of Immigrants: Lessons from Australian Immigration Policy, in: Mark Gibney (ed.), *Open Borders? Closed Societies*, Westport, Conn., Greenwood 1988, 41–60.

Carré de Malberg, Raymond, *Contribution à la Théorie Générale de l'État*, vols. 1–2, Paris, Sirey 1920–1922.

Cassese, Antonio, *International Law*, Oxford, Oxford University Press [2]2005.

Castellani, Arrigo, Quanti erano gl'italofoni nel 1861?, *Studi linguistici italiani* 1982, 3–26.

Chaltiel, Florence, *La souveraineté de l'État et l'Union européenne, l'exemple français*, Paris, LGDJ 2000.

Checkel, Jeffrey, International Institutions and Socialization in Europe, *International Organization* 2005, 801–826.

Chemerinsky, Erwin, *Interpreting the Constitution*, New York, Praeger 1987.

Chevrier, Georges, Remarques sur la distinction et les vicissitudes de la distinction du 'jus privatum' et du 'jus publicum' dans les oeuvres des anciens juristes français, *Archives de philosophie du droit* 1 (1952) 5–77.

Chevrier, G[eorges], Droit public – droit privé, in: Åke Malmström – Stig Strömholm (eds.), *Rapports généraux au VII[e] Congrès international de droit comparé*, Stockholm, Almquist & Wiksell 1968, 37–41.

Choudhry, Sujit, Globalization in Search of Justification: Toward a Theory of Comparative Constitutional Interpretation, *Indiana Law Journal* 74 (1998–1999) 819–892.

Choudhry, Sujit, Does the World Need More Canada?, in: Sujit Choudhry (ed.), *Constitutional Design for Divided Societies: Integration or Accommodation?*, Oxford, Oxford University Press 2008, 141–172.

Choudhry, Sujit, Bridging Comparative Politics and Comparative Constitutional Law, in: Sujit Choudhry (ed.), *Constitutional Design for Divided Societies: Integration or Accommodation?*, Oxford, Oxford University Press 2008, 3–40.

Choudhry, Sujit (ed.), *Constitutional Design for Divided Societies: Integration or Accommodation?*, Oxford, Oxford University Press 2008.

Cicero, *Pro Milone* (transl. by NH Watts), Cambridge, Cambridge University Press $^{5}$1972.

Classen, Claus Dieter, Europäische Integration und demokratische Legitimation, *Archiv des öffentlichen Rechts* 119 (1994) 238–260.

Closa, Carlos, Some Foundations for the Normative Discussion on Supranational Citizenship and Democracy, in: Ulrich K Preuß – Ferrán Requejo (eds.), *European Citizenship, Multiculturalism and the State*, Baden-Baden, Nomos 1998, 105–124.

Cohen-Eliya, Moshe – Iddo Porat, *Proportionality and Constitutional Culture*, Cambridge, Cambridge University Press 2013.

Cohen-Jonathan, Gérard, e.a. (eds.), *Liber Amicorum Marc-André Eissen*, Bruxelles, Bruylant 1995.

Coing, Helmut, *Grundzüge der Rechtsphilosophie*, Berlin, de Gruyter $^{3}$1976.

Coke, Edward, Speech on 17.05.1628, in: TC Hansard (ed.), *The Parliamentary History of England, from the Earliest Period to the Year 1803*, vol. 2, London, Hansard 1807, 356–358.

Cole, David, The Priority of Morality: The Emergency Constitution's Blind Spot, *Yale Law Journal* 113 (2003–2004) 1753–1800.

Cole, David – James X Dempsey, *Terrorism and the Constitution*, New York, London, New Press $^{3}$2006.

Colón-Ríos, Joel, Five Conceptions of Constituent Power, *Law Quarterly Review* 130 (2014) 306–336.

Comaroff, John L – Paul C Stern (eds.), *Perspectives on Nationalism and War*, Amsterdam, Gordon and Breach 1995.

Conacher, James B, *The Emergence of British Parliamentary Democracy in the Nineteenth Century*, New York, Wiley 1971.

Connor, Walker, *The National Question in Marxist-Leninist Theory and Strategy*, Princeton, Princeton University Press 1984.

Connor, Walker, The Timelessness of Nations, in: Montserrat Guibernau – John Hutchinson (eds.), *History and National Destiny: Ethnosymbolism and Its Critics*, Oxford, Blackwell 2004, 35–47.

Constant, Benjamin, De la liberté des Anciens comparée à celle des Modernes [1819], in: id., *Écrits politiques*, Paris, Gallimard/Folio, 1997, 591–619.

Constant, Benjamin, *Écrits politiques*, Paris, Gallimard/Folio, 1997.

Constantinou, Costas, Aporias of Identity: Bicommunalism, Hybridity and the 'Cyprus Problem', *Cooperation and Conflict* 2007, 247–270.

Contiades, Xenophon (ed.), *Engineering Constitutional Change*, London, Routledge 2013.

Conway, Gerard, *The Limits of Legal Reasoning of the European Court of Justice*, Cambridge, Cambridge University Press 2012.

Conze, Werner, Sicherheit, Schutz, in: Otto Brunner e.a. (eds.), *Geschichtliche Grundbegriffe*, vol. 5, Stuttgart, Klett-Cotta 2004, 831–862.

Cooter, Robert C, *The Strategic Constitution*, Princeton, NJ, Princeton University Press 2000.

Corbett, Richard – Francis Jacobs – Michael Shackleton, *The European Parliament*, London, Catermill [3]1995.

Corwin, Edward S, The Constitution as Instrument and as Symbol, *American Political Science Review* 30 (1936) 1071–1085.

Côté, Pierre-André, *Interprétation des lois*, Montréal, Yvon Blanc [2]1990.

Cotterrell, Roger, *The Politics of Jurisprudence*, London, LexisNexis [2]2003.

Courchene, Thomas J – Donald J Savoie (eds.), *The Art of the State*, Montréal, IRPP 2003.

Couzigou, Irène, *L'évolution du statut international de l'Allemagne depuis 1945*, Bruxelles, Bruylant 2011.

Craig, Paul, Britain in the EU, in: Jeffrey Jowell – Dawn Oliver (eds.), *The Changing Constitution*, Oxford, Oxford University Press [4]2000, 61–88.

Craig, Paul, Constitutions, Constitutionalism, and the European Union, *European Law Journal* 7 (2001) 125–150.

Craig, Paul – Graínne de Búrca, *EU Law*, Oxford, Oxford University Press [3]2003.

Craig, Paul, The European Union Act 2011: Locks, Limits and Legality, *Common Market Law Review* 2011, 1915–1944.

Cram, Laura, Identity and European Integration, *Nations and Nationalism* 2009, 109–128.

Crawford, James R, State Practice and International Law in Relation to Unilateral Secession, in: Anne F Bayefsky (ed.), *Self-Determination in International Law: Quebec and Lessons Learned*, The Hague, Kluwer 2000, 31–61.

Crawford, James R, State, in: Rüdiger Wolfrum (ed.): *Max Planck Encyclopedia of Public International Law*, Oxford, Oxford University Press 2011, available at http://www.mpepil.com/.

Cremer, Hans-Joachim, Regeln der Konventionsinterpretation, in: Rainer Grote – Thilo Marauhn (eds.), *EMRK/GG. Konkordanzkommentar zum europäischen und deutschen Grundrechtsschutz*, Tübingen, Mohr Siebeck 2006, 155–230.

Creveld, Martin von, *Aufstieg und Untergang des Staates*, München, Gerling 1999.

Csehi, Zoltán, e.a. (eds.), *Viva Vox Iuris Civilis. Tanulmányok Sólyom László tiszteletére*, Budapest, Szent István Társulat 2012.

Csekey, Stephan, *Die Verfassung Ungarns*, Budapest, Danubia 1944.

Cserne, Péter – Miklós Könczöl (eds.), *Legal and Political Theory in the Post-National Age*, Frankfurt aM, Peter Lang 2011.

Csink, Lóránt – Balázs Schanda – András Zs Varga (eds.), *The Basic Law of Hungary*, Dublin, Budapest, Clarus, NIPA 2012.

Curtin, Deirdre M, *Postnational Democracy: The European Union in Search of a Political Philosophy*, The Hague, Kluwer Law International 1997.

Cusimano, Maryann K (ed.), *Beyond Sovereignty: Issues for a Global Agenda*, Boston, Bedford/St. Martin's 2000.

Cvijic, Srdjan – Lorenzo Zucca, Does the European Constitution Need Christian Values?, *Oxford Journal of Legal Studies* 24 (2004) 739–748.

Dahl, Robert A, *Democracy and Its Critics*, New Haven, Yale Universiy Press 1989.

Dahl, Robert A – Edward R Tufte, *Size and Democracy*, Stanford, Stanford University Press 1973.

Dahlmann, Christian, The Trinity in Kelsen's Basic Norm Unravelled, *Archiv für Rechts- und Sozialphilosophie* (2004) 147–162.

Damm, Reinhard, Risikosteuerung im Zivilrecht, in: Wolfgang Hoffmann-Riem – Eberhard Schmidt-Aßmann (eds.), *Öffentliches Recht und Privatrecht als wechselseitige Auffangordnungen*, Baden-Baden, Nomos 1996, 85–142.

Dani, Marco, Economic and Social Conflicts, Integration and Constitutionalism in Contemporary Europe, *LSE 'Europe in Question' Discussion Paper Series* 13/2009, available at http://www2.lse.ac.uk/europeanInstitute/LEQS/LEQSPaper13b.pdf.

Dann, Otto, Nationalismus und Sozialer Wandel in Deutschland 1806–1850, in: id. (ed.), *Nationalismus und sozialer Wandel*, Hamburg, Hoffmann und Campe 1978, 77–128.

Dann, Otto (ed.), *Nationalismus und sozialer Wandel*, Hamburg, Hoffmann und Campe 1978.

Dann, Otto – John Dinwiddy (eds.), *Nationalism in the Age of the French Revolution*, London, Hambledon 1988.

Dann, Philipp, *Parlamente im Exekutivföderalismus*, Berlin, Springer 2004.

Dardanelli, Paolo – Nenad Stojanovic, The Acid Test: Competing Theses on Nationality-Democracy Nexus and the Case of Switzerland, *Nations and Nationalism* 2011, 357–376.

David, René (ed. in chief), *International Encylopedia of Comparative Law. II/2. Structure and Divisions of the Law*, Tübingen, Mohr 1974.

Davis, DM, Constitutional Borrowing: The Influence of Legal Culture and Local History in the Reconstruction of Comparative Influence: The South African Experience, *International Journal of Constitutional Law* 1 (2003) 181–195.

Debiel, Tobias – Franz Nuscheler (eds.), *Der neue Interventionismus*, Bonn, Dietz 1996.

de Búrca, Gráinne, The Language of Rights and European Integration, in: Jo Shaw – Gillian More (eds.), *New Legal Dynamics of European Union*, Oxford, Clarendon 1995, 29–54.

de Búrca, Gráinne, Sovereignty and the Supremacy Doctrine of the European Court of Justice, in: Neil Walker (ed.), *Sovereignty in Transition*, Oxford, Hart 2003, 449–460.

Deflem, Mathieu – Fred C Pampel, The Myth of Postnational Identity: Popular Support for European Unification, *Social Forces* 75 (1996) 119–143.

Delanty, Gerard – Krishan Kumar (eds.), *The SAGE Handbook of Nations and Nationalism*, London, Sage 2006.

Delpérée, Francis, La Constitution et son interprétation, in: Michel van de Kerchove (ed.), *L'interprétation en droit. Approche pluridisciplinaire*, Bruxelles, Facultés universitaires Saint Louis 1978, 187–210.

Del Vecchio, Giorgio, *Les principes généraux du droit, in: Recueil d'études sur les sources du droit en l'honneur de François Gény*, Paris, Sirey 1934, 69–84.

De Mauro, Tullio, *Storia linguistica dell'Italia unita*, Bari, Laterza 1970.

Depenheuer, Otto, *Selbstbehauptung des Rechtsstaates*, Paderborn, Schöningh 2007.

Depenheuer, Otto – Christoph Grabenwarter (eds.), *Verfassungstheorie*, Tübingen, Mohr Siebeck 2010.

Depenheuer, Otto – Markus Heintzen – Matthias Jestaedt – Peter Axer (eds.), *Staat um Wort. Festschrift für Josef Isensee*, Heidelberg, CF Müller 2007.

Derlén, Mattias, *Multilingual Interpretation of European Union Law*, Alphen aan den Rijn, Kluwer Law International 2009.

Dershowitz, Alan M, *Why Terrorism Works – Understanding the Threat, Responding to the Challenge*, New Haven, Yale University Press 2002.

Dershowitz, Alan M, Tortured Reasoning, in: Sanford Levinson (ed.), *Torture: A Collection*, Oxford, Oxford University Press 2004, 281–290.

Deutsch, Karl W, *Nationalism and Social Communication: An Inquiry into the Foundations of Nationalism*, Cambridge, Mass., Technology Press 1953.

Deutsch, Karl W, e.a., *Political Community and the North Atlantic Arena*, New York, Greenwood 1957.

Detjen, Joachim, *Die Werteordnung des Grundgesetzes*, Wiesbaden, VS 2009.

de Witte, Bruno, Sovereignty and European Integration: The Weight of a Legal Tradition, in: Neil Walker (ed.), *Relocating Sovereignty*, Aldershot, Ashgate 2006, 491–520.

de Witte, Bruno, The Rules of Change in the European Union: The Lost Balance between Rigidity and Flexibility, in: Catherine Moury – Luís de Sousa (eds.), *Institutional Challenges in Post-Constitutional Europe*, London, New York, Routledge 2009, 33–42.

Díaz-Andreu, Margarita – Timothy C Champion, *Nationalism and Archaeology in Europe*, London, UCL Press 1996.

Dicey, Albert Venn, *Lectures Introductory to the Study of the Law of the Constitution*, London, Macmillan $^{2}$1886.

Dicey, Albert Venn, *Introduction to the Study of the Law of the Constitution*, London & New York, Macmillan $^{10}$1959.

Dickinson, HT – Michael Lynch, Introduction, in: HT Dickinson – Michael Lynch (eds.), *The Challenge to Westminster: Sovereignty, Devolution and Independence*, East Linton, Tuckwell 2000, 1–11.

Dickinson, HT – Michael Lynch (eds.), *The Challenge to Westminster: Sovereignty, Devolution and Independence*, East Linton, Tuckwell 2000.

Diderot, Denis – Jean d'Alembert (eds.), *Encyclopédie ou Dictionnaire raisonné des sciences, des arts et des métiers*, vol. 15, Neufchatel, Samuel Faulche 1765.

Dieckhoff, Alain (ed.), *The Politics of Belonging*, Lanham, Md., Lexington Press 2004.

Di Fabio, Udo, Der neue Art. 23 des Grundgesetzes, *Der Staat* 32 (1993) 191–217.

Di Fabio, Udo, *Die Staatsrechtslehre und der Staat*, Paderborn, Ferdinand Schöningh 2003.

Dobner, Petra – Martin Loughlin (eds.), *The Twilight of Constitutionalism?*, Oxford, Oxford University Press 2010.

Doehring, Karl, Das Staatsnotrecht in den Vereinigten Staaten von Amerika, in: Hans Ballreich e.a. (eds.), *Das Staatsnotrecht in Belgien, Frankreich, Großbritannien, Italien, den Niederlanden, der Schweiz und den Vereinigten Staaten von Amerika*, Köln, Heymann 1955, 209–247.

Doehring, Karl, *Das Staatsrecht der Bundesrepublik Deutschland*, Frankfurt aM, Metzner [3]1984.

Doehring, Karl, Staat und Verfassung in einem zusammenwachsenden Europa, *Zeitschrift für Rechtspolitik* 1993/3, 98–103.

Doehring, Karl, Allgemeine Staatslehre aus der Sicht des Völkerrechts, in: Herbert Haller e.a. (eds.), *Festschrift für Günther Winkler. Staat und Recht*, Wien, Springer 1997, 179–192.

Doehring, Karl, *Allgemeine Staatslehre*, Heidelberg, CF Müller [3]2004.

Dreier, Horst, *Rechtslehre, Staatssoziologie und Demokratietheorie bei Hans Kelsen*, Baden-Baden, Nomos 1986.

Dreier, Horst, Souveränität, in: Görres-Gesellschaft (ed.), *Staatslexikon*, vol. 4., Freiburg, Herder [4]1988, 1203–1209.

Dreier, Horst, e.a., *Rezeption und Rolle der Reinen Rechtslehre*, Wien, Manz 2001.

Dreier, Ralf, *Recht – Moral – Ideologie. Studien zur Rechtstheorie*, Frankfurt aM, Suhrkamp 1981.

Dreier, Ralf, Zur Problematik und Situation der Verfassungsinterpretation, in: id., *Recht – Moral – Ideologie. Studien zur Rechtstheorie*, Frankfurt aM, Suhrkamp 1981, 106–145.

Dreier, Ralf, Bemerkungen zur Theorie der Grundnorm, in: Hans-Kelsen-Institut (ed.), *Die Reine Rechtslehre in wissenschaftlicher Diskussion*, Wien, Manz 1982, 38–46.

Dreier, Ralf (ed.), *Rechtspositivismus und Wertbezug des Rechts*, Stuttgart, Steiner 1990.

Drobnig, Ulrich, The Use of Comparative Law by Courts, in: Ulrich Drobnig – Sjef van Erp (eds.), *The Use of Comparative Law by Courts*, The Hague, Kluwer Law International 1999, 3–21.

Drobnig, Ulrich – Sjef van Erp (eds.), *The Use of Comparative Law by Courts*, The Hague, Kluwer Law International 1999.

Due, Ole – Marcus Lutte – Jürgen Schwarze (eds.), *Festschrift für Ulrich Everling*, vol. I, Baden-Baden, Nomos 1995.

Duke, Vic – Liz Crolley, *Football, Nationality and the State*, Harlow, Longman 1996.

Dumont, Louis, *Essais sur l'individualisme*, Paris, Seuil 1983.

Dunn, John, *Setting the People Free: The Story of Democracy*, London, Atlantic Books 2005.

Dunn, John (ed.), *Democracy: The Unfinished Journey 508 BC to AD 1993*, Oxford, Oxford University Press 1994.

du Plessis, Lourens, Interpretation, in: Stuart Woolman e.a. (eds.), *Constitutional Law of South Africa*, Cape Town, Juta $^{2}$2008, Chapter 32, 1–193.

Dupré, Catherine, *Importing the Law in Post-Communist Transitions: The Hungarian Constitutional Court and the Right to Human Dignity*, Oxford, Hart 2003.

Durandin, Catherine, *Histoire des Roumains*, Paris, Fayard 1995.

Dürig, Günter, Artikel 87a, in: Theodor Maunz – Günter Dürig (eds.), *Das Grundgesetz*, München, Beck (looseleaf edition, update of 1971).

Dworkin, Ronald, *Taking Rights Seriously*, London, Duckworth 1977.

Dworkin, Ronald, *Law's Empire*, London, Fontana 1986.

Dworkin, Ronald, Terror and the Attack on Civil Liberties, *New York Review of Books* 6 November 2003, 37–41.

Dworkin, Ronald, What the Court really said, *New York Review of Books*, 12 August 2004, 26–29.

Dyevre, Arthur, Technocracy and Distrust: Revisiting the Rationale for Constutional Review, *International Journal of Constitutional Law* 13 (2015) 30–60.

Dyson, Kenneth HF, Die Ideen des Staates und der Demokratie. Ein Vergleich 'staatlich verfaßter' und 'nicht staatlich verfaßter' Gesellschaften, *Der Staat* 19 (1980) 485–515.

Dyzenhaus, David, Introduction: Why Carl Schmitt?, in: id. (ed.), *Law as Politics: Carl Schmitt's Critique of Liberalism*, Durham, Duke University Press 1998, 1–20.

Dyzenhaus, David (ed.), *Law as Politics: Carl Schmitt's Critique of Liberalism*, Durham, Duke University Press 1998.

Eckhoff, Torstein, Guiding Standards in Legal Reasoning, *Current Legal Problems* 1976, 205–219.

Eckstein, Harry, On the 'Science' of State, *Daedalus* 1979/4, 1–20.

Eekelaar, John – John Bell (eds.), *Oxford Essays in Jurisprudence. Third Series*, Oxford, Clarendon Press 1987.

Ehmke, Horst, Staat und Gesellschaft als verfassungstheoretisches Problem, in: Konrad Hesse e.a. (eds.), *Festgabe für Rudolf Smend*, Tübingen, Mohr 1962, 23–49.

Ehmke, Horst (ed.), *Festschrift für Ulrich Scheuner zum 70. Geburtstag*, Berlin, Duncker & Humblot 1973.

Eisenberg, Avigail – Jeff Spinner-Halev (eds.), *Minorities within Minorities*, Cambridge, Cambridge University Press 2005.

Eisenberg, Melvin Aron, *The Nature of the Common Law*, Cambridge, Mass., Harvard University Press 1988.

Eisenmann, Charles, Droit public et droit privé (en marge d'un livre sur l'évolution du droit civil français du XIXè au XXè siècle), *Revue du droit public et de la science politique* 1952, 904–979.

Elkins, Zachary – Tom Ginsburg – James Melton, *The Endurance of National Constitutions*, Cambridge, Cambridge University Press 2009.

Elster, Jon, *Ulysses and the Sirens: Studies in Rationality and Irrationality*, Cambridge, Melbourne, Cambridge University Press, Paris, Maison des Sciences de l'Homme 1984.

Ely, John Hart, *Democracy and Distrust*, Cambridge, Mass., Harvard University Press 1981.

Engel, Salo (ed.), *Law, State, and International Legal Order. Essays in Honor of Hans Kelsen*, Knoxville, University of Tennessee Press 1964.

Eötvös, József, *A XIX. század uralkodó eszméinek befolyása az államra I.*, Budapest, Magyar Helikon 1981.

Erb, Volker, Folterverbot und Notwehrrecht, in: Peter Nitschke (ed.), *Rettungsfolter im modernen Rechtsstaat*, Bochum, Kamp 2005, 149–167.

Eriksen, Thomas Hylland, *Ethnicity and Nationalism*, London, Pluto [3]2010.

Ermacora, Felix, Die Grundrechte in der Verfassungsfrage 1919/1920, in: Rudolf Neck – Adam Wandruszka (eds.), *Die österreichische Verfassung von 1918 bis 1938*, München, Oldenburg 1980, 53–61.

Ermacora, Felix, *Österreichische Verfassungslehre*, Wien, Verlag Österreich 1998.

Ermacora, Felix (ed.), *Die österreichische Bundesverfassung und Hans Kelsen*, Wien, Braumueller 1982.

Eskridge, William N, Politics without Romance: Implications of Public Choice Theory for Statutory Interpretation, *Virginia Law Review* 74 (1988) 275–338.

Esser, Josef, *Grundsatz und Norm in der richterlichen Fortbildung des Privatrechts*, Tübingen, Mohr 1956.

Esterházy, Péter, *A szavak csodálatos életéből*, Budapest, Magvető 2003.

Evans, Peter B – Dietrich Rueschemeyer – Theda Skocpol (eds.), *Bringing the State Back In*, Cambridge, Cambridge University Press 1985.

Everson, Michelle, 'Subjects' or 'Citizens of Erewhon'? Law and Non-Law in the Development of 'British Citizenship', *Citizenship Studies* 2003/1, 57–85.

Fabbrini, Federico, Kelsen in Paris: France's Constitutional Reform and the Introduction of a Posteriori Constitutional Review of Legislation, *German Law Journal* 9 (2008) 1297–1312.

Fallon, Richard H, A Constructivist Coherence Theory of Constitutional Interpretation, *Harvard Law Review* 100 (1987) 1189–1286.

Fassbender, Bardo, Sovereignty and Constitutionalism in International Law, in: Neil Walker (ed.), *Sovereignty in Transition*, Oxford, Hart 2003, 115–143.

Favoreu, Louis – Patrick Gaïa – Richard Ghevontian – Jean-Louis Mestre – Otto Pfersmann – André Roux – Guy Scoffoni, *Droit constitutionnel*, Paris, Dalloz [14]2011.

Featherstone, Kevin, Jean Monnet and the Democratic Deficit in the European Union, *Journal of Common Market Studies* 1994, 149–170.

Federmann, Falco, *Die Konstitutionalisierung der Europäischen Union*, Lohmar, Josef Eul 2007.

Ferry, Jean-Marc, *La question de l'État européen*, Paris, Gallimard 2000.

Finn, Peter, Police Torture Threat Sparks Painful Debate in Germany, *Washington Post*, 8 March 2003, A19.

Firth, Raymond, *Symbols, Public and Private*, London, Allen & Unwin 1973.

Fish, Stanley, *Doing What Comes Naturally: Change, Rhetoric and the Practice of Theory in Literary and Legal Studies*, Durham, Duke University Press & Clarendon Press 1989.

Fladmark, J Magnus (ed.), *Heritage and Museums: Shaping National Identity*, Shaftesbury, Donhead 2000.

Fleiner, Fritz, *Institutionen des deutschen Verwaltungsrechts*, Tübingen, Mohr $^{8}$1928.

Fleiner, Thomas – Lidija R Basta Fleiner, *Allgemeine Staatslehre*, Berlin, Springer $^{3}$2004.

Fletcher, George P, Comparative Law as a Subversive Discipline, *American Journal of Comparative Law* 46 (1998) 683–700.

Fletcher, Laurel L – Eric Stover, *Guantánamo and its Aftermath: U.S. Detention and Interrogation Practices and Their Impact on Former Detainees*, Berkeley, University of California Press 2008.

Flor, Georg, Staatsnotstand und rechtliche Bindung, *Deutsches Verwaltungsblatt* 73 (1958) 149–152.

Foley, Michael, *The Silence of Constitutions: Gaps, Abeyances and Political Temperament in the Maintenance of Government*, London, Routledge 1989.

Fontanelli, Filippo – Giuseppe Martinico – Paolo Carrozza (eds.), *Shaping Rule of Law through Dialogue: International and Supranational Experiences*, Groningen, Europa Law Publishing 2010.

Forsthoff, Ernst, Die Umbildung des Verfassungsgesetzes, in: Hans Barion – Ernst Forsthoff – Werner Weber (eds.), *Festschrift für Carl Schmitt zum 70. Geburtstag*, Berlin, Duncker & Humblot 1959, 35–62.

Forsthoff, Ernst, *Zur Problematik der Verfassungsauslegung*, Stuttgart, Kohlhammer 1961.

Fossum, John Erik – Agustín José Menéndez, *The Constitution's Gift: A Constitutional Theory for a Democratic European Union*, Lanham, Md., Rowman & Littlefield 2011.

Foucault, Michel, *The Archaeology of Knowledge*, London, New York, Routledge 2002.

Foucault, Michel, *'Society Must Be Defended': Lectures at the Collège de France 1975–1976*, New York, Picador 2003.

Fowler, Brigid, Fuzzing Citizenship, Nationalising Political Space, *ESRC 'One Europe or Several' Programme Working Paper* 2002, 40/02.

Francis, Emerich K, *Ethnos und Demos*, Berlin, Duncker & Humblot 1965.

Francis, Emerich K, *Interethnic Relations. An Essay in Sociological Theory*, New York, Elsevier 1976.

Franck, Thomas, *Fairness in International Law and Institutions*, Oxford, Clarendon Press 1995.

Franck, Thomas M, *The Empowered Self: Law and Society in the Age of Individualism*, Oxford, Oxford University Press 1999.

Frankenberg, Günter, Critical Comparisons: Re-Thinking Comparative Law, *Harvard International Law Journal* 26 (1985) 411–455.

Frankenberg, Günter, Folter, Feindstrafrecht und Sonderpolizeirecht. Anmerkungen zu Phänomenen des Bekämpfungsrechts, in: Gerhard Beestermöller – Hauke Brunkhorst (eds.), *Rückkehr der Folter. Rechtsstaat im Zwielicht?*, München, Beck 2006, 56–68.

Franklin, Mark N, How Structural Factors Cause Turnout Variations at European Parliament Elections, *European Union Politics* 2001, 309–328.

Freedland, Mark – Jean-Bernard Auby (eds.), *The Public Law / Private Law Divide*, Oxford, Hart 2006.

Frick, Marie-Luisa, *Das Folterverbot im Rechtsstaat. Ethische Grundlagen und aktuelle Diskussion*, Saarbrücken, VDM 2007.

Frickey, Philip P, The Status and Rights of Indigenous Peoples in the United States, *Heidelberg Journal of International Law* 1999, 383–404.

Frowein, Jochen Abr, Die Verfassung der Europäischen Union aus der Sicht der Mitgliedstaaten, *Europarecht* 1995, 315–333.

Frowein, Jochen Abr – Thilo Marauhn (eds.), *Grundfragen der Verfassungsgerichtsbarkeit in Mittel- und Osteuropa*, Berlin, Springer 1998.

Frydman, Benoît, *Le sens des lois. Histoire de l'interprétation et de la raison juridique*, Paris, Bruxelles, Librairie Générale de Droit et de Jurisprudence – Bruylant 2005.

Fukuyama, Francis, *The End of History and the Last Man*, New York, Free Press 1992.

Funk, Bernd-Christian (ed.), *Staatsrecht und Staatswissenschaft in Zeiten des Wandels. Festschrift für Ludwig Adamovich*, Wien, Springer 1992.

Fusaro, Carlo, Italy, in: Dawn Oliver – Carlo Fusaro (eds.), *How Constitutions Change*, Oxford, Hart 2011, 211–234.

Gagnon, Alain – James Tully (eds.), *Multinational Democracies*, Cambridge, Cambridge University Press 2001.

Gall, Lothar, Liberalismus und Nationalstaat. Der deutsche Liberalismus und die Reichsgründung, in: Helmut Berding – Kurt Düwell – Lothar Gall – Wolfgang J Mommsen – Hans-Ulrich Wehler (eds.), *Vom Staat des Ancien régime zum modernen Parteienstaat. Festschrift für Theodor Schieder*, München, Oldenbourg 1978, 287–300.

Gallie, WB, Essentially Contested Concepts, *Proceedings of the Aristotelian Society* 56 (1956) 167–198.

Gamper, Anna, *Regeln der Verfassungsinterpretation*, Wien, Springer 2012.

Gamper, Anna, *Staat und Verfassung*, Wien, Facultas $^{3}$2014.

García de Enterría, Eduardo, *Le lengua de los derechos. La formación del Derecho Público europeo tras la Revolución Francesa*, Madrid, Real Academia Española 1994.

García-Pelayo, Manuel, *Derecho constitucional comparado*, Madrid, Revista Occidente 1950.

García-Pelayo, Manuel, *Obras completas*, Madrid, Centro de Estudios Políticos y Constitucionales [2]2009.

Gardbaum, Stephen, *The New Commonwealth Model of Constitutionalism*, Cambridge, Cambridge University Press 2013.

Garlicki, Leszek, *Polskie prawo konstytucyjne. Zarys wykładu*, Warszawa, Liber 1999.

Gavison, Ruth, What Belongs in a Constitution?, in: Stefan Voigt (ed.), *Constitutions, Markets and Law: Recent Experiences in Transition Economies*, Cheltenham, Edward Elgar 2002, 1–25.

Geary, Patrick J, *The Myth of Nations: The Medieval Origins of Europe*, Princeton, Princeton University Press 2002.

Gebhardt, Jürgen, Die Idee der Verfassung. Symbol und Instrument, in: Adolf Kimmel (ed.), *Verfassungen als Fundament und Instrument der Politik*, Baden-Baden, Nomos 1995, 9–23.

Gellner, Ernest, *Thought and Change*, London, Weidenfeld and Nicolson 1964.

Gellner, Ernest, *Nations and Nationalism*, Oxford, Blackwell [2]2006.

Gény, François, *Méthode d'interprétation et sources en droit privé positif*, vol. 1, Paris, Librairie Générale de Droit et de Jurisprudence [2]1919.

Gerber, Carl Friedrich von, *Über öffentliche Rechte*, Tübingen, Laupp 1852.

Gerber, Carl Friedrich von, *Grundzüge eines Systems des deutschen Staatsrechts*, Leipzig, Tauschnitz 1865.

Gerber, Carl Friedrich von, *Grundzüge des deutschen Staatsrechts*, Leipzig, Tauschnitz [3]1880.

Gergely, András – Gábor Máthé (eds.), *The Hungarian State: Thousand Years in Europe*, Budapest, Korona 2000.

Gibney, Mark (ed.), *Open Borders? Closed Societies*, Westport, Conn., Greenwood 1988.

Gibson, Ralph, The Intensification of Nationalist Consciousness in Modern Europe, in: Claus Bjørn e.a. (eds.), *Nations, Nationalism and Patriotism in the European Past*, Copenhagen, Academic Press Copenhagen 1994, 177–197.

Gicquel, Jean, *Droit constitutionnel et institutions politiques*, Paris, Montchrestien [22]2008.

Gillespie, Alisdair A, *The English Legal System*, Oxford, Oxford University Press 2007.

Gilmore, Piper, *Arguments from Roman Law in Political Thought, 1220–1600*, Cambridge, Mass., Harvard University Press 1941.

Ginsburg, Tom (ed.), *Comparative Constitutional Design*, Cambridge, Cambridge University Press 2012.

Ginsburg, Tom – Justin Blount – Zachary Elkins, Does the Process of Constitution-Making Matter?, in: Tom Ginsburg (ed.), *Comparative Constitutional Design*, Cambridge, Cambridge University Press 2012, 31–65.

Ginsburg, Tom – Rosalind Dixon, *Comparative Constitutional Law*, Cheltenham, Edward Elgar 2011.

Gizbert-Studnicki, Tomasz – Jerzy Stelmach (eds.), *Law and Legal Cultures in the 21st Century: Diversity and Unity*, Warszawa, Oficyna 2007.

Glaeßner, Gert-Joachim, *Sicherheit in Freiheit*, Opladen, Leske & Budrich 2003.

Glenn, H Patrick, Persuasive Authority, *McGill Law Journal* 32 (1987) 261–299.

Glenn, H Patrick, *The Cosmopolitan State*, Oxford, Oxford University Press 2013.

Godechot, Jacques, The New Concept of the Nation, in: Otto Dann – John Dinwiddy (eds.), *Nationalism in the Age of the French Revolution*, London, Hambledon 1988, 13–26.

Golding, Martin P, *Legal Reasoning*, New York, Knopf 1984.

Goldstein, Laurence (ed.), *Precedent in Law*, Oxford, Clarendon Press 1987.

Goldsworthy, Jeffrey, Originalism in Constitutional Interpretation, *Federal Law Review* 25 (1997) 1–50.

Goldsworthy, Jeffrey, *The Sovereignty of Parliament*, Oxford, Clarendon Press 1999.

Goldsworthy, Jeffrey, The Development of Parliamentary Sovereignty, in: HT Dickinson – Michael Lynch (eds.), *The Challenge to Westminster: Sovereignty, Devolution and Independence*, East Linton, Tuckwell 2000, 12–21.

Goldsworthy, Jeffrey, The Debate About Sovereignty in the United States, in: Neil Walker (ed.), *Sovereignty in Transition*, Oxford, Hart 2003, 423–446.

Goldsworthy, Jeffrey, Introduction, in: Jeffrey Goldsworthy (ed.), *Interpreting Constitutions: A Comparative Study*, Oxford, Oxford University Press 2006, 1–6.

Goldsworthy, Jeffrey, *Parliamentary Sovereignty*, Cambridge, Cambridge University Press 2010.

Goldsworthy, Jeffrey (ed.), *Interpreting Constitutions: A Comparative Study*, Oxford, Oxford University Press 2006.

Goodhart, Arthur L, Determining the *Ratio Decidendi* of a Case, *Yale Law Journal* 40 (1930) 161–183.

Goodhart, Arthur L, The *Ratio Decidendi* of a Case, *Modern Law Review* 22 (1959) 117–124.

Goodman, Sara Wallace, Naturalisation Policies in Europe, *Eudo* 2010, available at http://eudo-citizenship.eu/docs/7-Naturalisation%20Policies%20in%20Europe.pdf.

Goodrich, Peter, *Reading the Law: A Critical Introduction to Legal Method and Techniques*, New York, London, Basil Blackwell 1986.

Gordon, David (ed.), *Secession, State and Liberty*, New Brunswick, Transaction Publishers 1998.

Görlich, Helmut – Wolfgang Huber – Karl Lehrmann, *Verfassung ohne Gottesbezug?*, Leipzig, Evangelische Verlagsanstalt 2004.

Görres-Gesellschaft (ed.), *Staatslexikon*, vols. 1–7, Freiburg, Herder [4]1988.

Goutal, Jean Louis, Characteristics of Judicial Style in France, Britain, and the USA, *American Journal of Comparative Law* 24 (1976) 43–72.

Grabenwarter, Christoph, Die Verfassung in der Hierarchie der Rechtsordnung, in: Otto Depenheuer – Christoph Grabenwarter (eds.), *Verfassungstheorie*, Tübingen, Mohr Siebeck 2010, 391–413.

Graham, Cosmo, A Very British Affair – Jackson v. Attorney General, *European Public Law* 12 (2006) 501–513.

Graumann, Carl F, Soziale Identitäten, in: Reinhold Viehoff – Rien T Segers (eds.), *Kultur, Identität, Europa*, Frankfurt am Main, Suhrkamp 1999, 59–74.

Greenberg, Karen J (ed.), *The Torture Debate in America*, Cambridge, Cambridge University Press 2006.

Grewe, Constance – Christoph Gusy (eds.), *Französisches Staatsdenken*, Baden-Baden, Nomos 2002.

Grewe, Constance – Michael Riegner, Internationalised Constitutionalism in Ethnically Divided Societies, *Max Planck Yearbook of UN Law* 2011, 1–64.

Grewe, Wilhelm G, *The Epochs of International Law*, Berlin, New York, de Gruyter 2000.

Griffith, JAG, The Political Constitution, *Modern Law Review* 42 (1979) 1–21.

Grimm, Dieter, Der Staat in der kontinentaleuropäischen Tradition, in: id., *Recht und Staat der bürgerlichen Gesellschaft*, Frankfurt aM, Suhrkamp 1987, 54–81.

Grimm, Dieter, *Recht und Staat der bürgerlichen Gesellschaft*, Frankfurt aM, Suhrkamp 1987.

Grimm, Dieter, Öffentliches Recht, in: Görres-Gesellschaft (ed.), *Staatslexikon*, vol. 4, Freiburg, Herder [7]1988, 119–124.

Grimm, Dieter, *Braucht Europa eine Verfassung?*, München, Carl Friedrich von Siemens Stiftung 1995.

Grimm, Dieter, Does Europe Need a Constitution?, *European Law Journal* 1 (1995) 282–302.

Grimm, Dieter, Verfassung II, in: Otto Brunner – Werner Conze – Reinhart Koselleck (eds.), *Geschichtliche Grundbegriffe*, vol. 6, Stuttgart, Klett-Cotta [1990] 2004, 863–899.

Grimm, Dieter, *Das Öffentliche Recht vor der Frage nach seiner Identität, mit Kommentaren von Otto Depenheuer und Ewald Wiederin*, Tübingen, Mohr Siebeck 2012.

Groppi, Tania – Marie-Claire Ponthoreau, Conclusion. The Use of Foreign Precedents by Constitutional Judges: A Limited Practice, An Uncertain Future, in: id. (eds.), *The Use of Foreign Precedents by Constitutional Judges*, Oxford, Hart 2013, 411–431.

Groppi, Tania - Marie-Claire Ponthoreau (eds.), *The Use of Foreign Precedents by Constitutional Judges*, Oxford, Hart 2013.

Gross, Emanuel, Democracy in the War Against Terrorism - The Israeli Experience, *Loyola of Los Angeles Law Review* 35 (2002) 1161–1216.

Gross, Hyman, Standards as Law, *Annual Survey of American Law* 1968–69, 575–580.

Gross, Oren, Chaos and rules: Should Responses to Violent Crises Always Be Constitutional?, *Yale Law Journal* 112 (2003) 1011–1034.

Gross, Oren, The Prohibition on Torture and the Limits of Law, in: Sanford Levinson (ed.), *Torture: A Collection*, Oxford, Oxford University Press 2004, 229–253.

Groß, Thomas, Terrorbekämpfung und Grundrechte - Zur Operationalisierung des Verhältnismäßigkeitsgrundsatzes, *Kritische Justiz* 35 (2002) 1–17.

Grote, Rainer, Rule of Law, Rechtsstaat and État de droit, in: Christian Starck (ed.), *Constitutionalism, Universalism and Democracy - A Comparative Analysis*, Baden-Baden, Nomos 1999, 269–306.

Grote, Rainer - Thilo Marauhn (eds.), *EMRK/GG. Konkordanzkommentar zum europäischen und deutschen Grundrechtsschutz*, Tübingen, Mohr Siebeck 2006.

Grussmann, Wolf-Dietrich, *Adolf Julius Merkl. Leben und Werk*, Wien, Manz 1989.

Gschnitzer, Fritz - Reinhart Koselleck - Bernd Schönemann - Karl Ferdinand Werner, Volk, Nation, Nationalismus, Masse, in: Otto Brunner - Werner Conze - Reinhart Koselleck (eds.), *Geschichtliche Grundbegriffe*, vol. 7, Stuttgart, Klett-Cotta 2004, 141–431.

Guastini, Riccardo, *L'interpretazione dei documenti normativi*, Milano, Guiffrè 2004.

Guéhenno, Jean-Marie, *La fin de la démocratie*, Paris, Flammarion 1993.

Guibernau, Montserrat, *Nationalisms: The Nation-State and Nationalism in the Twentieth Century*, London, Polity 1996.

Guibernau, Montserrat - John Hutchinson (eds.), *History and National Destiny: Ethnosymbolism and Its Critics*, Oxford, Blackwell 2004.

Günther, Klaus, Darf der Staat foltern, um Menschenleben zu retten?, in: Gerhard Beestermöller - Hauke Brunkhorst (eds.), *Rückkehr der Folter. Rechtsstaat im Zwielicht?*, München, Beck 2006, 101–108.

Gusy, Christoph, Demokratiedefizite postnationaler Gemeinschaften unter Berücksichtigung der EU, *Zeitschrift für Politik* 1998, 267–281.

Gusy, Christoph, Gewährleistung von Freiheit und Sicherheit im Lichte unterschiedlicher Staats- und Verfassungsverständnisse, *Veröffentlichungen der Vereinigung der Deutschen Staatsrechtslehrer* 2004, 151–190.

Gusy, Christoph, Brauchen wir eine juristische Staatslehre? *Jahrbuch des öffentlichen Rechts der Gegenwart* 55 (2007) 41–71.

Gutmann, Amy (ed.), *A Matter of Interpretation*, Princeton, Princeton University Press 1997.

Haack, Stefan, *Verlust der Staatlichkeit*, Tübingen, Mohr Siebeck 2007.

Haas, Ernst, *The Uniting of Europe*, Stanford, Stanford University Press 1958.

Häberle, Peter, Staatslehre als Verfassungsgeschichte, *Archiv des öffentlichen Rechts* 102 (1977) 284–297.

Häberle, Peter, *Verfassung als öffentlicher Prozeß*, Berlin, Duncker & Humblot 1978.

Häberle, Peter, Grundrechtsgeltung und Grundrechtsinterpretation im Verfassungsstaat - Zugleich zur Rechtsvergleichung als 'fünfter' Auslegungsmethode, *Juristen-Zeitung* 1989, 913–919.

Häberle, Peter, Die Hauptstadtfrage als Verfassungsproblem, *Die öffentliche Verwaltung* 1990, 989–999.

Häberle, Peter, *Verfassung als öffentlicher Prozess*, Berlin, Duncker & Humblot ²1996.

Häberle, Peter, Ein 'Zwischenruf' zum Diskussionsstand in der deutschen Staatsrechtslehre, in: Theo Stammen e.a. (ed.), *Politik - Bildung - Religion. Festschrift Hans Maier*, Padeborn, Schöningh 1996, 327–339.

Häberle, Peter, *Verfassungslehre als Kulturwissenschaft*, Berlin, Duncker & Humblot ²1998.

Häberle, Peter, *Nationalhymnen als kulturelle Identitätselemente des Verfassungsstaates*, Berlin, Duncker & Humblot 2007.

Häberle, Peter, *Nationalflaggen. Bürgerdemokratische Identitätselemente und internationale Erkennungssymbole*, Berlin, Duncker & Humblot 2008.

Häberle, Peter, *Europäische Verfassungslehre*, Baden-Baden, Nomos ⁷2011.

Habermas, Jürgen, Citizenship and National Identity: Some Reflections on the Future of Europe, in: Ronald Beiner (ed.), *Theorizing Citizenship*, New York State University of New York Press 1995, 255–282.

Habermas, Jürgen, Remarks on Dieter Grimm's 'Does Europe need a Constitution?' *European Law Journal*, 1995, 303–307.

Habermas, Jürgen, *Between Facts and Norms*, Cambridge, Mass., MIT 1996.

Habermas, Jürgen, *Zur Verfassung Europas*, Berlin, Suhrkamp 2011.

Häcki, Rafael, Im Westen nichts Neues, *JuWiss* 21. February 2013 http://www.juwiss.de/im-westen-nichts-neues/.

Haferkamp, Hans-Peter, *Georg Friedrich Puchta und die 'Begriffsjurisprudenz'*, Frankfurt aM, Klostermann 2004.

Haft, Fritjof, Recht und Sprache, in: Arthur Kaufmann - Winfried Hassemer (eds.), *Einführung in die Rechtsphilosophie und Rechtstheorie der Gegenwart*, Heidelberg, Müller ⁶2006, 269–291.

Halász, Iván, A nemzetfogalom nyelvi-kulturális elemei a modern kelet- és középeurópai demokratikus alkotmányokban, in: Iván Halász - Balázs Majtényi - László Szarka (eds.), *Ami összeköt?*, Budapest, Gondolat 2004, 27–41.

Halász, Iván - Balázs Majtényi - László Szarka (eds.), *Ami összeköt?*, Budapest, Gondolat 2004.

Hall, John - Ian Jarvie (eds.), The Social Philosophy of Ernest Gellner, *Amsterdam and Atlanta, Rodopi* 1996.

Hall, John (ed.), *The State of the Nation: Ernest Gellner and the Theory of Nationalism*, Cambridge, Cambridge University Press 1998.

Hall, Stuart, Introduction: Who Needs 'Identity'?, in: Stuart Hall - Paul du Gay (eds.), *Questions of Cultural Identity*, London, Sage, 1996, 1–17.

Hall, Stuart - Paul du Gay (eds.), *Questions of Cultural Identity*, London, Sage, 1996.

Haller, Herbert, e.a. (eds.), *Festschrift für Günther Winkler. Staat und Recht*, Wien, Springer 1997.

Hallstein, Walter, *Europe in the Making*, London, Allen & Unwin 1972.

Halmai, Gábor, The Use of Foreign Law in Constitutional Interpretation, in: Michel Rosenfeld - András Sajó (eds.), *The Oxford Handbook of Comparative Constitutional Law*, Oxford, Oxford University Press 2012, 1328–1348.

Haltern, Ulrich R, *Verfassungsgerichtsbarkeit, Demokratie und Mißtrauen*, Berlin, Duncker & Humblot 1998.

Hammer, Stefan, Kelsens Grundnormkonzeption als neukantische Erkenntnistheorie des Rechts?, in: Stanley L Paulson - Robert Walter (eds.), *Untersuchungen zur Reinen Rechtslehre. Ergebnisse eines Wiener Rechtstheoretischen Seminars 1985/86*, Wien, Manz 1986, 210–231.

Hammon, Francis - Michel Troper, *Droit constitutionnel*, Paris, LGDJ [29]2005.

Hamza, Gábor, The Classification (Divisio) into 'Branches' of Modern Legal Systems and Roman Law Traditions, *European Journal of Law Reform* 2006, 361–382.

Hans-Kelsen-Institut (ed.), *Die Reine Rechtslehre in wissenschaftlicher Diskussion*, Wien, Manz 1982.

Hansard, TC (ed.), *The Parliamentary History of England, from the Earliest Period to the Year 1803*, vol. 2, London, Hansard 1807.

Hanschmann, Felix, Kalkulation des Unverfügbaren. Das Folterverbot in der Neu-Kommentierung von Art. 1 Abs. 1 GG im Maunz-Dürig, in: Gerhard Beestermöller - Hauke Brunkhorst (eds.), *Rückkehr der Folter. Rechtsstaat im Zwielicht?*, München, Beck 2006, 130–141.

Hansen, Mogens H, *The Athenian Democracy in the Age of Demosthenes*, Oxford, Blackwell 1991.

Haquet, Arnaud, *Le concept de souveraineté en droit constitutionnel français*, Paris, Presses Universitaires de France 2004.

Hardin, Russell, *One for All: The Logic of Group Conflict*, Princeton, Princeton University Press 1995.

Harding, Christopher - CL Lim, The Significance of Westphalia: An Archaeology of the International Legal Order, in: Christopher Harding (ed.), *Renegotiating Westphalia*, The Hague, Kluwer Law International 1999, 1–23.

Harding, Christopher (ed.), *Renegotiating Westphalia*, The Hague, Kluwer Law International 1999.

Harris, José, Society and the state in twentieth-century Britain, in: FML Thompson (ed.), *The Cambridge Social History of Britain 1750–1950*, vol. III, Cambridge, Cambridge University Press 1990, 63–118.

Harris, JW, When and Why Does the Grundnorm Change?, *Cambridge Law Journal* 29 (1971) 103–133.

Harris, JW, *Law and Legal Science: An Inquiry into the Concepts Legal Rule and Legal System*, Oxford, Clarendon Press 1979.

Hart, HLA, Definition and Theory in Jurisprudence, *Law Quarterly Review* 70 (1954) 37–60.

Hart, HLA, Introduction, in: John Austin, *The Province of Jurisprudence Determined and The Uses of the Study of Jurisprudence*, London, Weidenfeld and Nicolson 1971, vii–xviii.

Hart, HLA, *The Concept of Law*, Oxford, Clarendon Press [2]1994.

Haseler, Stephen, *The English Tribe*, London, New York, Macmillan 1996.

Hastings, Adrian, *The Construction of Nationhood*, Cambridge, Cambridge University Press 1997.

Haverkate, Görg, *Verfassungslehre*, München, Beck 1992.

Hayden, Robert M, Constitutional Nationalism in the Former Yugoslav Republics, *Slavic Review* 51 (1992) 654–673.

Hayek, Friedrich August von, *Die Verfassung der Freiheit*, Tübingen, Mohr 1971 (1960).

Hayes, Carlton JH, *Essays on Nationalism*, New York, Macmillan 1926.

Hayes, Carlton JH, *Nationalism: A Religion*, New York, Macmillan 1960.

Hayes-Renshaw, Fiona – Helen Wallace, Executive Power in the European Union: The Functions and Limits of the Council of Ministers, *Journal of European Public Policy* 2 (1995) 559–582.

Hazard, John M, Socialism and Federation, *Michigan Law Review* 1984, 1182–1194.

Heard, Andrew, *Canadian Constitutional Conventions: The Marriage of Law and Politics*, Toronto, Oxford University Press 1991.

Hechter, Michael, *Containing Nationalism*, Oxford, New York, Oxford University Press 2000.

Heck, Philipp, Was ist die Begriffsjurisprudenz, die wir bekämpfen?, *Deutsche Juristenzeitung* 1909, 1457–1461.

Hedemann, Justus Wilhelm, *Einführung in die Rechtswissenschaft*, Berlin, de Gruyter [2]1927.

Held, David, *Democracy and Global Order*, Stanford, California, Stanford University Press 1995.

Heller, Hermann, *Die Souveränität*, Berlin – Leipzig, de Gruyter 1927.

Heller, Hermann, *Staatslehre*, Leiden, Sijthoff 1934.

Hemke, Katja, *Methodik der Analogiebildung im öffentlichen Recht*, Berlin, Duncker & Humblot 2006.

Henke, Horst-Eberhard, Wie tot ist die Begriffsjurisprudenz?, in: Werner Krawietz (ed.), *Theorie und Technik der Begriffsjurisprudenz*, Darmstadt, Wissenschaftliche Buchgesellschaft 1976, 390–415.

Herdegen, Matthias, Art. 1 Abs. 1, in: Theodor Maunz – Günter Dürig (eds.), *Grundgesetz. Kommentar* (München, Beck, looseleaf edition since 1958, state of August 2005).

Herodotus, *History*, transl. by AD Godley, Cambridge, Mass., Harvard University Press 1922.

Herzog, Roman, *Allgemeine Staatslehre*, Frankfurt aM, Athenaeum 1971.

Hespanha, António Manuel, *Cultura jurídica europea. Síntesis de un milenio*, Madrid, Tecnos 2002.

Hesse, Konrad, Ausnahmezustand und Grundgesetz, *Die öffentliche Verwaltung* (1955) 741–746.

Hesse, Konrad, *Die normative Kraft der Verfassung*, Tübingen, Mohr 1959.

Hesse, Konrad, *Grundzüge des Verfassungsrechts der Bundesrepublik Deutschland*, Heidelberg, Müller [20]1999.

Hesse, Konrad – Siegfried Reicke – Ulrich Scheuner (eds.), *Festgabe für Rudolf Smend*, Tübingen, Mohr 1962.

Hestermeyer, Holger, *Staatsvolk and Homogeneity* [manuscript on file with the author].

Heun, Werner – Martin Honecker – Martin Morlok – Joachim Wieland (eds.), *Evangelisches Staatslexikon*, Stuttgart, Kohlhammer [2]2006.

Heuschling, Luc, Die Struktur der demokratischen Legitimität im französischen Recht: zwischen Monismus und Pluralismus, zwischen Subjekt-Symbolik und Gewaltenmechanik, *Europäische Grundrechte-Zeitschrift* 33 (2006) 338–353.

Heuschling, Luc, Verfassungsinterpretation in Frankreich, in: Georg Lienbacher (ed.), *Verfassungsinterpretation in Europa*, Wien, Jan Sramek 2011, 37–68.

Hilf, Meinhard, Die sprachliche Struktur der Verfassung, in: Josef Isensee – Paul Kirchhof (eds.), *Handbuch des Staatsrechts der Bundesrepublik Deutschland VII.: Normativität und Schutz der Verfassung – internationale Beziehungen*, Heidelberg, CF Müller 1992, 79–102.

Hilpold, Peter – Christoph Perathoner, *Die Schutzfunktion des Mutterstaates im Minderheitenrecht (the 'kin-state'). Eine völkerrechtliche und europarechtliche Untersuchung unter besonderer Berücksichtigung der Schutzfunktion Österreichs gegenüber der deutsch- und ladinischsprachigen Volksgruppe in Südtirol sowie der Diskussion um das ungarische Statusgesetz*, Wien, Neuer Wissenschaftlicher Verlag 2006.

Hilty, Carl, *Die schweizerische Nationalität*, Bern, Max Fiala 1875.

Hintze, Otto, Das monarchische Prinzip und die konstitutionelle Verfassung (1911), in: id., *Staat und Verfassung. Gesammelte Abhandlungen*, vol. 1, Göttingen, Vandenhoeck & Ruprecht [2]1962, 359–389.

Hintze, Otto, *Staat und Verfassung. Gesammelte Abhandlungen*, vol. 1, Göttingen, Vandenhoeck & Ruprecht [2]1962.

Hippel, Ernst von, *Allgemeine Staatslehre*, Berlin, Vahlen 1963.

Hirschl, Ran, *Towards Juristocracy*, Cambridge, Mass., Harvard University Press 2004.

Hirschman, Albert O, *Exit, Voice, and Loyalty. Responses to Decline in Firms, Organizations, and States*, Cambridge, Mass., Harvard University Press 1970.

Hix, Simon, Legislative Behaviour and Party Competition in the European Parliament, *Journal of Common Market Studies* 2001, 663–688.

Hix, Simon, *The Political System of the European Union*, New York, Palgrave Macmillan [2]2005.

Hix, Simon – Bjørn Høyland, *The Political System of the European Union*, London, Palgrave Macmillan [3]2011.

Hobe, Stephan, *Der offene Verfassungsstaat zwischen Souveränität und Interdependenz*, Berlin, Duncker & Humblot 1998.

Hobsbawm, Eric, Introduction, in: Eric Hobsbawm – Terence Ranger (eds.), *The Invention of Tradition*, Cambridge, Cambridge University Press 1983, 1–14.

Hobsbawm, Eric, Mass-Producing Traditions: Europe, 1870–1914, in: Eric Hobsbawm – Terence Ranger (eds.), *The Invention of Tradition*, Cambridge, Cambridge University Press 1983, 263–307.

Hobsbawm, Eric, *Nations and Nationalism since 1780: Programme, Myth, Reality*, Cambridge, Cambridge University Press 1990.

Hobsbawm, Eric, *Nations and Nationalism since 1780*, Cambridge, Cambridge University Press [2]1992.

Hobsbawm, Eric, Ethnicity and Nationalism in Europe Today, in: Gopal Balakrishnan (ed.), *Mapping the Nation*, London, Verso 1996, 255–266.

Hobsbawm, Eric – Terence Ranger (eds.), *The Invention of Tradition*, Cambridge, Cambridge University Press 1983.

Hoerster, Norbert, Kritischer Vergleich der Theorien der Rechtsgeltung von Hans Kelsen und H. L. A. Hart, in: Stanley L Paulson – Robert Walter (eds.), *Untersuchungen zur Reinen Rechtslehre. Ergebnisse eines Wiener Rechtstheoretischen Seminars 1985/86*, Wien, Manz 1986, 1–19.

Hoffmann-Riem, Wolfgang, Öffentliches Recht und Privatrecht als wechselseitige Auffangordnungen – Systematisierung und Entwicklungspersektiven, in: Wolfgang Hoffmann-Riem – Eberhard Schmidt-Aßmann (eds.), *Öffentliches Recht und Privatrecht als wechselseitige Auffangordnungen*, Baden-Baden, Nomos 1996, 261–336.

Hoffmann-Riem, Wolfgang – Eberhard Schmidt-Aßmann (eds.), *Öffentliches Recht und Privatrecht als wechselseitige Auffangordnungen*, Baden-Baden, Nomos 1996.

Hoffschulte, Heinrich, *Christliches Menschenbild und Gottesbezug in der Verfassung der Europäischen Union*, Münster, Akademie Franz Hitze Haus 2004.

Hofmann, Hasso, Von der Staatssoziologie zur Soziologie der Verfassung, *JuristenZeitung* 1999, 1065–1074.

Hogg, Peter W, Canada: From Privy Council to Supreme Court, in: Jeffrey Goldsworthy (ed.), *Interpreting Constitutions: A Comparative Study*, Oxford, Oxford University Press 2006, 85–87.

Holland, James - Julian Webb, *Learning Legal Rules*, Oxford, Oxford University Press [6]2006.

Holländer, Pavel, *Verfassungsrechtliche Argumentation - zwischen dem Optimismus und der Skepsis*, Berlin, Duncker & Humblot 2007.

Hollis, Christopher, *Parliament and Its Sovereignty*, London, Hollis & Carter 1973.

Holmes, Stephen, *Passions and Constraint: On the Theory of Liberal Democracy*, Chicago, University of Chicago Press 1995.

Holzhey, Helmut, Kelsens Rechts- und Staatslehre in ihrem Verhältnis zum Neukantianismus, in: Stanley L Paulson - Robert Walter (eds.), *Untersuchungen zur Reinen Rechtslehre. Ergebnisse eines Wiener Rechtstheoretischen Seminars 1985/86*, Wien, Manz 1986, 167–192.

Homer, *The Odyssey* [tr. Martin Hammond], London, Duckworth 2000.

Hong, Mathias, Das grundgesetzliche Folterverbot und der Menschenwürdegehalt der Grundrechte - eine verfassungsjuristische Betrachtung, in: Gerhard Beestermöller - Hauke Brunkhorst (eds.), *Rückkehr der Folter. Rechtsstaat im Zwielicht?*, München, Beck 2006, 24–35.

Honoré, AM, Legal Reasoning in Rome and Today, *South African Law Journal* 1974, 84–94.

Hooper, John, Germans Wrestle with Rights and Wrongs of Torture, *The Guardian*, 27 February 2003, 18.

Horak, Franz, Zur rechtstheoretischen Problematik der Begründung, in: Rainer Sprung (ed.), *Die Entscheidungsbegründung in europäischen Verfahrensrechten und im Verfahren vor internationalen Gerichten*, Wien, Springer 1974, 1–26.

Höreth, Marcus, *Die Europäische Union im Legitimationstrilemma*, Baden-Baden, Nomos 1999.

Horkay Hörcher, Ferenc, The National Avowal, in: Lóránt Csink - Balázs Schanda - András Zs Varga (eds.), *The Basic Law of Hungary*, Dublin, Clarus, NIPA 2012, 25–45.

Hornblower, Simon, Democratic Institutions in Ancient Greece, in: John Dunn (ed.), *Democracy: The Unfinished Journey 508 BC to AD 1993*, Oxford, Oxford University Press 1994, 1–16.

Hornburg, Helge, The Concept of Nation in the Hungarian Legal Order, in: András Jakab - Péter Takács - Allan F Tatham (eds.), *The Transformation of the Hungarian Legal Order 1985-2005*, The Hague, Kluwer Law International 2007, 507–520.

Horowitz, Donald L, Self-Determination: Politics, Philosophy, and Law, in: Margaret Moore (ed.), *National Self-Determination and Secession*, Oxford, Oxford University Press 1998, 181–214.

Hosking, Geoffrey - George Schöpflin (eds.), *Myth and Nationhood*, London, Christopher Hurst 1997.

Hroch, Miroslav, *Die Vorkämpfer der nationalen Bewegung bei den kleinen Völkern Europas*, Prague, Univerzita Karlova 1968.

Hroch, Miroslav, From National Movement to the Fully-Formed Nation: The Nation-Building Process in Europe, *New Left Review* 198 (1993) 3–20.

Hroch, Miroslav, Real and Constructed: The Nature of the Nation, in: John Hall (ed.), *The State of the Nation: Ernest Gellner and the Theory of Nationalism*, Cambridge, Cambridge University Press 1998, 91–106.

Huber, Ernst Rudolf, *Deutsche Verfassungsgeschichte*, vol. 1, Stuttgart, Kohlhammer 1960.

Hufeld, Ulrich, *Die Verfassungsdurchbrechung*, Berlin, Duncker & Humblot 1997.

Huizinga, Johan, *Men and Ideas*, Cambridge, Cambridge University Press 1984 (orig. 1940).

Hunt, Murray, The Horizontal Effect of Human Rights Act: Moving beyond the Public-Private Distinction, in: Jeffrey Jowell – Jonathan Cooper (eds.), *Understanding Human Rights Principles*, Oxford, Hart 2001, 161–178.

Hurd, John C, *The Theory of Our National Existence*, Boston, Little, Brown and Company 1881.

Husserl, Edmund, *Logische Untersuchungen. 1. Prolegomena zur reinen Logik*, Halle aS, Niemeyer 1900.

Huster, Stefan – Karsten Rudolph, Vom Rechtsstaat zum Präventionsstaat?, in: Stefan Huster – Karsten Rudolph (eds.), *Vom Rechtsstaat zum Präventionsstaat*, Frankfurt aM, Suhrkamp 2008, 9–22.

Huster, Stefan – Karsten Rudolph (eds.), *Vom Rechtsstaat zum Präventionsstaat*, Frankfurt aM, Suhrkamp 2008.

Hutchinson, John, *Nations as Zones of Conflict*, London, Sage 2005.

Hyman, Paula, *The Jews of Modern France*, Berkeley, University of California Press 1998.

Ichijo, Atsuko – Gordana Uzelac (eds.), *When Is the Nation?*, London, Routledge 2005.

Ignatieff, Michael, Nationalism and Narcissism of Minor Differences, in: Ronald Beiner (ed.), *Theorizing Nationalism*, New York, State University of New York Press 1999, 91–102.

Ignatieff, Michael, *The Lesser Evil: Political Ethics in an Age of Terror*, Edinburgh, Edinburgh University Press 2004.

Imboden, Max, e.a. (eds.), *Festschrift für Adolf J Merkl zum 80. Geburtstag*, München, Funk 1970.

Institute of Comparative Law Waseda University (ed.), *Law in East and West. Recht in Ost und West*, Tokyo, Waseda University Press 1988.

Ipperciel, Donald, Constitutional democracy and civic nationalism, *Nations and Nationalism* 2007, 395–416.

Ipsen, Hans Peter, *Fusionsverfassung Europäische Gemeinschaften*, Bad Homburg, Gehlen 1969.

Ipsen, Hans Peter, *Europäisches Gemeinschaftsrecht*, Tübingen, Mohr 1972.

Ipsen, Hans Peter, Die deutsche Staatsrechtswissenschaft im Spiegel der Lehrbücher, *Archiv des öffentlichen Rechts* 106 (1981) 161–204.

Ipsen, Jörn – Thorsten Koch, Öffentliches und privates Recht – Abgrenzungsprobleme bei der Benutzung öffentlicher Einrichtungen, *Juristische Schulung* 1992, 809–816.

Isensee, Josef, *Das Grundrecht auf Sicherheit*, Berlin, de Gruyter 1983.

Isensee, Josef, Vorrang des Europarechts und deutsche Verfassungsvorbehalte – offener Dissens, in: Joachim Burmeister e.a. (eds.), *Verfassungsstaatlichkeit. Festschrift Klaus Stern*, München, Beck 1997, 1239–1268.

Isensee, Josef, Der Verfassungsstaat als Friedensgarant, *Die politische Meinung* 2004, 66–72.

Isensee, Josef, Staat und Verfassung, in: Josef Isensee – Paul Kirchhof (eds.), *Handbuch des Staatsrechts der Bundesrepublik Deutschland, vol.* II.: *Verfassungsstaat*, Heidelberg, Müller [3]2004, 3–106.

Isensee, Josef, Die Staatlichkeit der Verfassung, in: Otto Depenheuer – Christoph Grabenwarter (eds.), *Verfassungstheorie*, Tübingen, Mohr Siebeck 2010, 199–270.

Isensee, Josef – Paul Kirchhof (eds.), *Handbuch des Staatsrechts der Bundesrepublik Deutschland*. vols. I–X, Heidelberg, CF Müller 1987–2001.

Isensee, Josef – Paul Mikat – Martin Honecker – Ernst Chr Suttner, Staat, in: Görres-Gesellschaft (ed.), *Staatslexikon*, vol. 5, Freiburg, Herder [7]1989, 133–170.

Itzcovich, Giulio, The Interpretation of Community Law by the European Court of Justice, *German Law Journal* 10 (2009) 537–559.

Ivie, Robert L – Timothy W Waters, Discursive Democracy and the Challenge of State Building in Divided Societies: Reckoning with Symbolic Capital in Bosnia and Herzegovina, *Nationalities Papers* 2010/4, 449–468.

Jacas, Joaquim Ferret, Nació, símbols i drets històrics, *Revista d'Estudis Autonòmics i Federals* 12 (2011) 44–60.

Jachtenfuchs, Markus – Beate Kohler-Koch (eds.), *Europäische Integration*, Opladen, Leske & Budrich 1996.

Jackson, Robert H, International Community beyond the Cold War, in: Gene M Lyons – Michael Mastanduno (eds.), *Beyond Westphalia?*, Baltimore, Johns Hopkins University Press 1995, 59–83.

Jackson, Vicki C, Holistic Interpretation: Fitzpatrick v. Bitzer and Our Bifurcated Constitution, *Stanford Law Review* 53 (2001) 1259–1310.

Jackson, Vicki C, *Constitutional Engagement in a Transnational Era*, Oxford, Oxford University Press 2010.

Jackson, Vicki C – Mark Tushnet (eds.), *Defining the Field of Comparative Constitutional Law*, Westport, Conn., Fraeger 2002.

Jacob, Marc, *Precedents and Case-Based Reasoning in the European Court of Justice*, Cambridge, Cambridge University Press 2014.

Jacobson, Stephen, Spain, in: Timothy Baycroft – Mark Hewitson (eds.), *What Is a Nation? Europe 1789–1914*, Oxford, Oxford University Press 2006, 210–227.

Jacoby, Sigrid, *Allgemeine Rechtsgrundsätze. Begriffsentwicklung und Funktion in der Europäischen Rechtsgeschichte*, Berlin, Duncker & Humblot 1997.

Jaconelli, Joseph, Do Constitutional Conventions Bind?, *Cambridge Law Journal* 64 (2005) 149–176.

Jahrreiss, Hermann, e.a. (eds.), *Um Recht und Gerechtigkeit. Festgabe für Erich Kaufmann*, Stuttgart, Kohlhammer 1950.

Jakab, András, Az osztrák EU-csatlakozás alkotmányjogi szempontból [The Austrian EU-Access from the Perspective of Constitutional Law], *Jogelméleti Szemle* (http://jesz.ajk.elte.hu/) (2002/1) II./1.3.2.

Jakab, András, *A jogszabálytan főbb kérdéseiről* [On the Main Questions of a Theory of Legal Rules], Budapest, Unió 2003.

Jakab, András, Die Verfassungscharta von Serbien und Montenegro, *Heidelberg Journal of International Law* 2003/3, 101–115.

Jakab, András, Kelsen's Doctrine of International Law between Epistemology and Politics, *Austrian Review of International and European Law* (ARIEL) 2004, 49–62.

Jakab, András, Kelsens Völkerrechtslehre zwischen Erkenntnistheorie und Politik, *Zeitschrift für ausländisches öffentliches Recht und Völkerrecht* 2004, 1045–1057.

Jakab, András, German Constitutional Law and Doctrine on State of Emergency – Paradigms and Dilemmas of a Traditional (Continental) Discourse, *German Law Journal* 5 (2006) 453–477.

Jakab, András, Neutralizing the Sovereignty Question: Compromise Strategies in Constitutional Argumentations about the Concept of Sovereignty before European Integration and Since, *European Constitutional Law Review* 2 (2006) 375–397.

Jakab, András, *A magyar jogrendszer szerkezete*, Budapest, Pécs, Dialóg Campus 2007.

Jakab, András, Közjog, magánjog, polgári jog – A dogmatikatörténet Próteuszai és az új Ptk. tervezete, *Állam- és Jogtudomány* 2007/1, 3–27.

Jakab, András, Problems of the Stufenbaulehre: Kelsen's Failure to Derive the Validity of a Norm from Another Norm, *Canadian Journal of Law and Jurisprudence* 2007, 35–68.

Jakab, András, Surviving Socialist Legal Concepts and Methods, in: András Jakab – Péter Takács – Allan F Tatham (eds.), *The Transformation of the Hungarian Legal Order 1985–2005*, The Hague, Kluwer Law International 2007, 606–619.

Jakab, András, What Makes a Good Lawyer?, *Zeitschrift für öffentliches Recht* 62 (2007) 275–287.

Jakab, András, Wissenschaft und Lehre des Verfassungsrechts in Ungarn, in: Armin von Bogdandy – Pedro Cruz Villalón – Peter M Huber (eds.), *Ius Publicum Europaeum*, vol. II, Heidelberg, CF Müller 2007, 773–801.

Jakab, András, Problems of the Stufenbaulehre: Kelsen's Failure to Derive the Validity of a Norm from Another Norm, *Canadian Journal of Law and Jurisprudence* 20 (2007) 35–68.

Jakab, András, Az Alkotmány kommentárjának feladata, in: András Jakab (ed.), *Az Alkotmány kommentárja*, Budapest, Századvég ²2009, 5–80.

Jakab, András, Two Opposing Paradigms of Continental European Constitutional Thinking: Austria and Germany, *International and Comparative Law Quarterly* 58 (2009) 933–955.

Jakab, András, Az alkotmányozás előkérdéseiről, *Iustum Aequum Salutare* 2010/4, 11–17.

Jakab, András, *Az új Alaptörvény keletkezése és gyakorlati következményei*, Budapest, HVG Orac 2011.

Jakab, András, Breaching Constitutional Law on Moral Grounds in the Fight against Terrorism: Implied Presuppositions and Proposed Solutions in the Discourse on 'the Rule of Law vs. Terrorism', *International Journal of Constitutional Law* 9 (2011) 58–78.

Jakab, András, Seven Role Models of Legal Scholars, *German Law Journal* 12 (2011) 757–784.

Jakab, András, Trianon Peace Treaty (1920), in: Rüdiger Wolfrum (ed.), *Max Planck Encyclopedia of Public International Law*, Oxford, Oxford University Press 2011, available at http://www.mpepil.com/.

Jakab, András, Wissenschaft vom Verwaltungsrecht: Ungarn, in: Armin von Bogdandy – Sabino Cassese – Peter M Huber (eds.), *Ius Publicum Europaeum IV., Heidelberg, CF Müller* 2011, 365–396.

Jakab, András, Full Parliamentarisation of the EU without Changing the Treaties: Why We Should Aim for It and How Easily It Can Be Achieved, *Jean Monnet Working Papers* 2012/3.

Jakab, András, On the Legitimacy of a New Constitution: Remarks on the Occasion of the New Hungarian Basic Law of 2011, in: Miodrag Jovanović – Đorđe Pavićević (eds.), *Crisis and Quality of Democracy in Eastern Europe, The Hague, Eleven* 2012, 61–76.

Jakab, András, Judicial Reasoning in Constitutional Courts: A European Perspective, *German Law Journal* 14 (2013) 1215–1278.

Jakab, András, Why the Debate between Kumm and Armstrong Is about the Wrong Question, *verfassungsblog.de* 20. June 2014, available at http://www.verfassungsblog.de/debate-kumm-armstrong-wrong-question/#.U6RIbfl_uqg.

Jakab, András, *Sustainability in European Constitutional Law* (April 11, 2015), available at SSRN: http://ssrn.com/abstract=2593371.

Jakab, András (ed.), *Az Alkotmány kommentárja*, Budapest, Századvég ²2009.

Jakab, András – Pál Sonnevend, Kontinuität mit Mängeln. Das neue ungarische Grundgesetz, *Zeitschrift für ausländisches öffentliches Recht und Völkerrecht* 2012, 79–102.

Jakab, András – Péter Takács – Allan F Tatham (eds.), *The Transformation of the Hungarian Legal Order 1985–2005*, The Hague, Kluwer Law International 2007.
Jakab, András – Arthur Dyevre – Giulio Itzcovich (eds.), Comparative Constitutional Reasoning, Cambridge: Cambridge University Press, forthcoming.
Jakobs, Günther, Bürgerstrafrecht und Feindstrafrecht, *HRRS-Online Zeitschrift für Höchstrichterliche Rechtsprechung zum Strafrecht* 3 (2004) 88–95.
Jefferson, Thomas, *Notes on the State of Virginia*, New York, Harper 1964.
Jefferson, Thomas, Letter to Samuel Kercheval (12 July 1816), in: Merrill D Peterson (ed.), *The Portable Jefferson*, New York, Penguin 1975, 558–559.
Jellinek, Georg, *Die rechtliche Natur der Staatenverträge*, Wien, Hoelder 1880.
Jellinek, Georg, *Die Lehre von den Staatenverbindungen*, Wien, Hoelder 1882.
Jellinek, Georg, *Verfassungsänderung und Verfassungswandlung*, Berlin, Häring 1906.
Jellinek, Georg, *Allgemeine Staatslehre*, Berlin, Häring [3]1914.
Jenkins, John R, *Jura Separatism in Switzerland*, Oxford, Clarendon Press 1986.
Jennings, Ivor, *The Approach of Self-Government*, Cambridge, Cambridge University Press 1956.
Jennings, Ivor, *The Law and the Constitution*, London, University of London Press [5]1959.
Jestaedt, Matthias, Phänomen Bundesverfassungsgericht, in: Christoph Schönberger e.a., *Das entgrenzte Gericht*, Berlin, Suhrkamp 2011, 77–158.
Jestaedt, Matthias (ed.), *Hans Kelsen und die deutsche Staatsrechtslehre*, Tübingen, Mohr Siebeck 2013.
Jestaedt, Matthias – Oliver Lepsius – Christoph Möllers, Christoph Schönberger, *Das entgrenzte Gericht*, Berlin, Suhrkamp 2011.
Jhering, Rudolph von, *Scherz und Ernst in der Jurisprudenz*, Leipzig, Breitkopf & Härtel 1884.
Jhering, Rudolf von, *Der Zweck im Recht*, Leipzig, Breitkopf & Haertel [8]1923.
Johnson, Nevil, Law as the Articulation of the State in Western Germany: A German Tradition from a British Perspective, *West European Politics* 1 (1978) 177–192.
Jones, HS, *The French State in Question: Public Law and Political Argument in the Third Republic*, Cambridge, Cambridge University Press 1993.
Jones, Timothy M – Penelope Sheets, Torture in the Eye of the Beholder: Social Identity, News Coverage, and Abu Ghraib, *Political Communication* 2009, 278–295.
Jouanjan, Olivier, Synthese, in: Constance Grewe – Christoph Gusy (eds.), *Französisches Staatsdenken*, Baden-Baden, Nomos 2002, 242–252.
Jouanjan, Olivier, Braucht das Verfassungsrecht eine Staatslehre? Eine französische Perspektive, *Europäische Grundrechte-Zeitschrift* 31 (2004) 362–370.
Jouvenel, Bertrand de, *Souveraineté. Á la recherche du bien politique*, Paris, Génin 1955.
Jovanović, Miodrag, *Constitutionalizing Secession in Federalized States: A Procedural Approach*, Utrecht, Eleven 2007.

Jovanović, Miodrag, *Collective Rights: A Legal Theory*, Cambridge, Cambridge University Press 2011.

Jovanović, Miodrag – Đorđe Pavićević (eds.), *Crisis and Quality of Democracy in Eastern Europe*, The Hague, Eleven 2012.

Jowell, Jeffrey – Jonathan Cooper (eds.), *Understanding Human Rights Principles*, Oxford, Hart 2001.

Jowell, Jeffrey – Dawn Oliver (eds.), *The Changing Constitution*, Oxford, Oxford University Press [4]2000.

Juristische Fakultät der Universität Basel (ed.), *Privatrecht – Öffentliches Recht – Strafrecht. Grenzen und Grenzüberschreitungen*, Basel, Helbing & Lichtenhahn 1985.

Kadish, Sanford H, Torture, the State, and the Individual, *Israel Law Review* 23 (1989) 345–356.

Kägi, Werner, *Die Verfassung als rechtliche Grundordnung des Staates*, Zürich, Polygraph 1945.

Kalmo, Hent – Quentin Skinner (eds.), *Sovereignty in Fragments*, Cambridge, Cambridge University Press 2010.

Kanner, Allan, Public and Private Law, *Tulane Environmental Law Journal* 1997, 235–277.

Kant, Immanuel, *Kritik der reinen Vernunft*, Hamburg, Meiner 1956.

Kapferer, Bruce, Nationalist Ideology and Comparative Anthropology, *Ethnos* 54 (1989) 161–199.

Karpen, Ulrich, *Auslegung und Anwendung des Grundgesetzes*, Berlin, Duncker & Humblot 1987.

Kaser, Max, Jus Publicum – Jus Privatum, *Studia et Documenta Historiae et Juris* 1951, 267–279.

Kaufmann, Arthur – Winfried Hassemer (eds.), *Einführung in die Rechtsphilosophie und Rechtstheorie der Gegenwart*, Heidelberg, Müller [6]2006.

Kaufmann, Erich, *Zur Problematik des Volkswillens*, Berlin, de Gruyter 1931.

Kaufmann, Marcel, *Europäische Integration und Demokratieprinzip*, Baden-Baden, Nomos 1997.

Kaufmann, Marcel, The Legitimation of the European Union – Democracy versus Integration, in: Hermann Pünder – Christian Waldhoff (eds.), *Debates in German Public Law*, Oxford, Hart 2014, 263–281.

Keane, John, *The Life and Death of Democracy*, London, Simon & Schuster 2009.

Keating, Michael, *Plurinational Democracy, Stateless Nations in a Post-Sovereignty Era*, Oxford, Oxford University Press 2001.

Keating, Michael, *Nations against the State: The New Politics of Nationalism in Quebec, Catalonia and Scotland*, London, Palgrave Macmillan [2]2001.

Keating, Michael, Sovereignty and Plurinational Democracy, in: Neil Walker (ed.), *Sovereignty in Transition*, Oxford, Hart 2003, 191–208.

Keating, Michael - John McGarry (eds.), *Minority Nationalism and the Changing International Order*, Oxford, Oxford University Press 2001.

Kecskés, László, Indító tézisek a Magyar Köztársaság Alkotmánya EU-vonatkozású szabályainak továbbfejlesztéséhez, *Európai Jog* 2004, 3–11.

Kedourie, Elie, *Nationalism*, Oxford, Blackwell [4]1993.

Kegley, Charles W - Gregory A Raymond, *Exorcising the Ghost of Westphalia - Building World Order in the New Millennium*, Upper Saddle River, NJ, Prentice Hall 2002, 154–175.

Kelemen, Katalin, The Road from Common Law to East-Central Europe, in: Péter Cserne - Miklós Könczöl (eds.), *Legal and Political Theory in the Post-National Age*, Frankfurt aM, Peter Lang 2011, 118–134.

Kellas, James G, *The Politics of Nationalism and Ethnicity*, London, Macmillan 1991.

Kelsen, Hans, *Hauptprobleme der Staatsrechtslehre entwickelt aus der Lehre vom Rechtssatze*, Tübingen, Mohr 1911.

Kelsen, Hans, Zur Lehre vom öffentlichen Rechtsgeschäft, *Archiv des öffentlichen Rechts* 31 (1913) 190–249.

Kelsen, Hans, Reichsgesetz und Landesgesetz nach österreichischer Verfassung, *Archiv des öffentlichen Rechts* 32 (1914) 202–245.

Kelsen, Hans, *Das Problem der Souveränität und die Theorie des Völkerrechts. Beitrag zu einer reinen Rechtslehre*, Tübingen, Mohr 1920.

Kelsen, Hans, *Hauptprobleme der Staatsrechtslehre entwickelt aus der Lehre vom Rechtssatze*, Tübingen, Mohr [2]1923.

Kelsen, Hans, *Allgemeine Staatslehre*, Berlin, Springer 1925.

Kelsen, Hans, Les rapports de système entre le droit interne et le droit international public, *Recueil des Cours* 1926, 231–329.

Kelsen, Hans, Wesen und Entwicklung der Staatsgerichtsbarkeit, *Veröffentlichungen der Vereinigung der Deutschen Staatsrechtslehrer* 1929, 30–88.

Kelsen, Hans, *Vom Wesen und Wert der Demokratie*, Tübingen, Mohr [2]1929.

Kelsen, Hans, Der Wandel des Souveränitätsbegriffes, *Studi filosofico-giuridici dedicati a Giorgio del Vecchio*, vol. II, Modena, Società Tipografico Modenese 1931, 1–11.

Kelsen, Hans, *Reine Rechtslehre*, Leipzig, Franz Deuticke 1934.

Kelsen, Hans, *Law and Peace in International Relations*, Cambridge, Mass., Harvard University Press 1942.

Kelsen, Hans, The Principle of Sovereign Equality of States as a Basis for International Organization, *Yale Law Journal* 53 (1944) 207–220.

Kelsen, Hans, *General Theory of Law and State*, Cambridge, Mass., Harvard University Press 1949.

Kelsen, Hans, *Principles of International Law*, New York, Rinehart 1952.

Kelsen, Hans, Adolf Merkl zu seinem 70. Geburtstag, *Zeitschrift für öffentliches Recht* 10 (1959–1960) 313–323.

Kelsen, Hans, Die Funktion der Verfassung, *Forum* 11 (1964) 583–586.

Kelsen, Hans, Recht, Rechtswissenschaft und Logik, *Archiv für Rechts- und Sozialphilosophie* 52 (1966) 545–552.

Kelsen, Hans, Der Begriff der Rechtsordnung [1958], in: Hans Klecatsky – René Marcic – Herbert Schambeck (eds.), *Hans Kelsen – Adolf Merkl – Alfred Verdross. Die Wiener Rechtstheoretische Schule*, Wien, Europa-Verlag 1968, 1395–1416.

Kelsen, Hans, Naturrechtslehre und Rechtspositivismus [1961], in: Hans Klecatsky e.a. (eds.), *Hans Kelsen – Adolf Merkl – Alfred Verdross: Die Wiener Rechtstheoretische Schule*, Wien, Europa-Verlag 1968, 817–832.

Kelsen, Hans, Die philosophischen Grundlagen der Naturrechtslehre und des Rechtspositivismus [1928], in: Hans Klecatsky e.a. (eds.), *Hans Kelsen – Adolf Merkl – Alfred Verdross: Die Wiener Rechtstheoretische Schule*, Wien, Europa-Verlag 1968, 281–350.

Kelsen, Hans, *The Pure Theory of Law* (transl. by Max Knight), Clark, New Jersey, Lawbook Exchange 1970.

Kelsen, Hans, *Allgemeine Theorie der Normen*, Wien, Manz 1979.

Kelsen, Hans, *General Theory of Norms* (transl. by Michael Hartney), Oxford, Clarendon Press 1991.

Kelsen, Hans, *Introduction to the Problems of Legal Theory* (transl. by Bonnie Litschewski Paulson and Stanley L Paulson), Oxford, Clarendon Press 1992.

Kemiläinen, Aira, *Nationalism*, Jyväskylä, Kustantajat 1964.

Kersten, Jens, *Georg Jellinek und die klassische Staatslehre*, Tübingen, Mohr 2000.

Keynes, John Maynard, *The General Theory of Employment, Interest and Money*, London, Palgrave Macmillan 1936.

Kielmansegg, Peter Graf, Integration und Demokratie, in: Markus Jachtenfuchs – Beate Kohler-Koch (eds.), *Europäische Integration*, Opladen, Leske & Budrich 1996, 49–84.

Kilényi, Géza, A képviseleti és a közvetlen demokrácia viszonya a magyar államszervezetben, *Magyar Közigazgatás* 1999, 673–681.

Kimmel, Adolf (ed.), *Verfassungen als Fundament und Instrument der Politik*, Baden-Baden, Nomos 1995.

Kirchhof, Paul, Die Zulässigkeit des Einsatzes staatlicher Gewalt in Ausnahmesituationen, in: William Birtles e.a. (eds.), *Die Zulässigkeit des Einsatzes staatlicher Gewalt in Ausnahmesituationen*, Karlsruhe, Müller 1976, 83–118.

Kirchhof, Paul, Der deutsche Staat im Prozeß der europäischen Integration, in: Josef Isensee – Paul Kirchhof (eds.), *Handbuch des Staatsrechts der Bundesrepublik Deutschland, Vol. VII: Normativität und Schutz der Verfassung – Internationale Beziehungen*, Heidelberg, CF Müller 1992, 855–887.

Kirchhof, Paul, Die Identität der Verfassung, in: Josef Isensee – Paul Kirchhof (eds.), *Handbuch des Staatsrechts der Bundesrepublik Deutschland, Vol. II: Verfassungsstaat*, Heidelberg CF Müller [3]2004, 261–316.

Kirchner, Christian, Regulierung durch öffentliches Recht und/oder Privatrecht aus der Sicht der ökonomischen Theorie des Rechts, in: Wolfgang

Hoffmann-Riem – Eberhard Schmidt-Aßmann (eds.), *Öffentliches Recht und Privatrecht als wechselseitige Auffangordnungen*, Baden-Baden, Nomos 1996, 63–84.

Kis, János, From Costs and Benefits to Fairness: Comments on Richard Posner, *East European Constitutional Review* 1995/Summer, 84–87.

Kis, János, *Alkotmányos demokrácia*, Budapest, Indok 2000.

Kiss, Géza, *A jogalkalmazás módszeréről*, Budapest, Athaeneum 1909.

Kischel, Uwe, *Die Begründung*, Tübingen, Mohr Siebeck 2003.

Kissane, Bill – Nick Sitter, National Identity and Constitutionalism in Europe, *Nations and Nationalism* 2010, 1–5.

Kjær, Anne Lise – Silvia Adamo (eds.), *Linguistic Diversity and European Democracy*, Farnham, Ashgate 2011.

Klatt, Matthias (ed.), *Institutionalized Reason: The Jurisprudence of Robert Alexy*, Oxford, Oxford University Press 2012.

Klausen, Jytte, *The Cartoons that Shook the World*, New Haven, Yale University Press 2009.

Klecatsky, Hans, e.a. (eds.), *Hans Kelsen – Adolf Merkl – Alfred Verdross: Die Wiener Rechtstheoretische Schule*, Wien, Europa-Verlag 1968.

Kleijkamp, Gerda, Comparing the Application and Interpretation of the United States Constitution and The European Convention on Human Rights, *Transnational Law and Contemporary Problems* 12 (2002) 307–334.

Klein, Claude, *Théorie et pratique du pouvoir constituant*, Paris, Presses Universitaires de France 1996.

Klein, Claude – András Sajó, Constitution-Making: Process and Substance, in: Michel Rosenfeld – András Sajó (eds.), *The Oxford Handbook of Comparative Constitutional Law*, Oxford, Oxford University Press 2012, 419–441.

Klein, Eckart, Der innere Notstand, in: Josef Isensee – Paul Kirchhof (eds.), *Handbuch des Staatsrechts der Bundesrepublik Deutschland, vol. 7: Normativität und Schutz der Verfassung – internationale Beziehungen*, Heidelberg, CF Müller 1992, 387–414.

Klein, Hans H, *Bundesverfassungsgericht und Staatsraison*, Frankfurt aM, Metzner 1968.

Kleinlein, Thomas, *Konstitutionalisierung im Völkerrecht*, Heidelberg, Springer 2012.

Klenner, Hermann, *Rechtsleere. Die Verurteilung der Reinen Rechtslehre*, Berlin, Verlag Marxistische Blätter 1972.

Klug, Ulrich, Die Reine Rechtslehre von Hans Kelsen und die formallogische Rechtfertigung der Kritik an dem Pseudoschluss vom Sein auf Sollen, in: Salo Engel (ed.), *Law, State, and International Legal Order: Essays in Honor of Hans Kelsen*, Knoxville, University of Tennessee Press 1964, 153–169.

Kluth, Winfried, *Die demokratische Legitimation der Europäischen Union*, Berlin, Duncker & Humblot 1995.

Kochenov, Dimitry, The Essence of EU Citizenship Emerging from the Last Ten Years of Academic Debate: Beyond the Cherry Blossoms and the Moon, *International and Comparative Law Quarterly* 62 (2013) 97–136.

Kohl, Philip L – Clare P Fawcett (eds.), *Nationalism, Politics and the Practice of Archaeology?*, Cambridge, Cambridge University Press 1995.

Koja, Friedrich, *Der Staatsnotstand als Rechtsbegriff*, Salzburg, Pustet 1979.

Koja, Friedrich, Die Verfassung, in: Heinz Mayer –Clemens Jabloner – Kucsko-Stadlmayer, – Rene Laurer –Kurt Ringhofer – Rudolf Thienel (eds.), *Staatsrecht in Theorie und Praxis: Festschrift für Robert Walter*, Wien, Manz 1991, 349–361.

Koja, Friedrich, Der Begriff der Allgemeinen Staatslehre, in: Bernd-Christian Funk (ed.), *Staatsrecht und Staatswissenschaft in Zeiten des Wandels. Festschrift für Ludwig Adamovich*, Wien, Springer 1992, 244–252.

Koja, Friedrich, *Allgemeine Staatslehre*, Wien, Manz 1993.

Koja, Friedrich – Walter Antoniolli, *Allgemeines Verwaltungsrecht*, Wien, Manz $^{3}$1996.

Komárek, Jan, Playing with Matches: The Czech Constitutional Court Declares a Judgment of the Court of Justice of the EU Ultra Vires, *European Constitutional Law Review* 8 (2012) 323–337.

Kommers, Donald P, Comparative Constitutional Law: Its Increasing Relevance, in: Vicki C Jackson – Mark Tushnet (eds.), *Defining the Field of Comparative Constitutional Law*, Westport, Fraeger 2002, 61–70.

Kommers, Donald P, Germany: Balancing Rights and Duties, in: Jeffrey Goldsworthy (ed.), *Interpreting Constitutions: A Comparative Study*, Oxford, Oxford University Press 2006, 161–214.

Koopmans, T, Comparative Law and the Courts, *International and Comparative Law Quarterly* 45 (1996) 545–556.

Korinek, Karl, Zur Interpretation von Verfassungsrecht, in: Heinz Mayer (ed.), *Staatsrecht in Theorie und Praxis. Festschrift für Robert Walter*, Wien, Manz 1991, 363–385.

Kortmann, Constantijn AJM – Joseph Fleuren – Wim Voermans (eds.), *Constitutional Law of 10 EU Member States*, Deventer, Kluwer 2006.

Koskenniemi, Martti, *From Apology to Utopia: The Structure of International Legal Argument*, Cambridge, Cambridge University Press 2005.

Kostakopoulou, Dora, European Union Citizenship: Writing the Future, *European Law Journal* 13 (2007) 623–646.

Kötz, Hein, Über den Stil höchstrichterlicher Entscheidungen, *Rabels Zeitschrift für ausländisches und internationales Privatrecht* 1973, 245–263.

Kovács, Péter, *International Law and Minority Protection*, Budapest, Akadémiai 2000.

Krabbe, Hugo, *Lehre der Rechtssouveränität*, Groningen, Wolters 1906.

Kraler, Albert, The Legal Status of Immigrants and Their Access to Nationality, in: Rainer Bauböck (ed.), *Migration and Citizenship*, Amsterdam, Amsterdam University Press 2006, 33–65.

Krauthammer, Charles, The Truth about Torture, in: Sanford Levinson (ed.), *Torture: A Collection*, Oxford, Oxford University Press 2004, 307–316.

Krawietz, Werner, Grundnorm, in: Joachim Ritter (ed.), *Historisches Wörterbuch der Philosophie*, vol. 3, Darmstadt, Wissenschaftliche Buchhandlung 1974, 918–922.

Krawietz, Werner, Begriffsjurisprudenz, in: Werner Krawietz (ed.), *Theorie und Technik der Begriffsjurisprudenz*, Darmstadt, Wissenschaftliche Buchgesellschaft 1976, 432–437.

Krawietz, Werner, Reinheit der Rechtslehre als Ideologie?, in: Werner Krawietz – Ernst Topitsch – Peter Koller (eds.), *Ideologiekritik und Demokratietheorie bei Hans Kelsen, Rechstheorie*, Beiheft 4, Berlin, Duncker & Humblot 1982, 345–421, 413.

Krawietz, Werner, Die Lehre vom Stufenbau des Rechts – eine säkularisierte politische Theologie?, in: Werner Krawietz – Helmut Schelsky (eds.), *Rechtssystem und gesellschaftliche Basis bei Hans Kelsen*, Rechtstheorie, Beiheft 5, Berlin, Duncker & Humblot 1984, 255–271.

Krawietz, Werner (ed.), *Theorie und Technik der Begriffsjurisprudenz*, Darmstadt, Wissenschaftliche Buchgesellschaft 1976.

Krawietz, Werner – Kazimierz Opalek – Aleksander Peczenik – Alfred Schramm (eds.), *Argumentation und Hermeneutik in der Jurisprudenz*, Rechtstheorie, Beiheft 1, Berlin, Duncker & Humblot 1979.

Krawietz, Werner e.a. (eds.), *Ideologiekritik und Demokratietheorie bei Hans Kelsen*, Rechstheorie, Beiheft 4, Berlin, Duncker & Humblot 1982.

Krawietz, Werner – Helmut Schelsky (eds.), *Rechtssystem und gesellschaftliche Basis bei Hans Kelsen*, Rechtstheorie, Beiheft 5, Berlin, Duncker & Humblot 1984.

Krenzler, Michael, *An den Grenzen der Notstandsverfassung. Ausnahmezustand und Staatsnotrecht im Verfassungssystem des Grundgesetzes*, Berlin, Duncker & Humblot 1974.

Kriele, Martin, *Theorie der Rechtsgewinnung entwickelt am Problem der Verfassungsinterpretation*, Berlin, Duncker & Humblot $^{2}$1976.

Kriele, Martin, *Einführung in die Staatslehre*, Stuttgart, Kohlhammer $^{6}$2003.

Krisch, Nico, *Beyond Constitutionalism: The Pluralist Structure of Postnational Law*, Oxford, Oxford University Press 2010.

Krockow, Christian Graf von, Staat, Gesellschaft, Freiheitsbewahrung, in: Ernst-Wolfgang Böckenförde (ed.), *Staat und Gesellschaft*, Darmstadt, Wissenschaftliche Buchgesellschaft 1976, 432–483.

Krüger, Herbert, *Allgemeine Staatslehre*, Stuttgart, Kohlhammer $^{2}$1966.

Krüger, Herbert, Verfassungsvoraussetzungen und Verfassungserwartungen, in: Horst Ehmke (ed.), *Festschrift für Ulrich Scheuner zum 70. Geburtstag*, Berlin, Duncker & Humblot 1973, 285–306.

Krygier, Martin, The Rule of Law: Legality, Teleology, Sociology, in: Gianluigi Palombella – Neil Walker (eds.), *Relocating the Rule of Law*, Oxford, Hart 2009, 45–69.

Krynen, Jacques – Albert Rigaudière (eds.), *Droits savants et pratiques françaises du pouvoir, 11e–15e siècles*, Bordeaux, Presses Universitaires de Bordeaux 1992.

Kucsko-Stadlmayer, Gabriele, Der Beitrag Adolf Merkls zur Reinen Rechtslehre, in: Robert Walter (ed.), *Schwerpunkte der Reinen Rechtslehre*, Wien, Manz 1992, 107–121.

Kumm, Mattias, Why Europeans Will Not Embrace Constitutional Patriotism, *International Journal of Constitutional Law* 6 (2008) 117–136.

Kunz, Josef L, *Völkerrechtswissenschaft und reine Rechtslehre*, Leipzig, Deuticke 1923.

Kurz, Hanns, *Volkssouveränität und Volksrepräsentation*, Köln, Heymanns 1965.

Kymlicka, Will, *Multicultural Citizenship*, Oxford, Oxford University Press 1995.

Kymlicka, Will, Citizenship in the Era of Globalization, in: Ian Shapiro – Casiano Hacker-Cordón (eds.), *Democracy's Edge*, London, Cambridge University Press 1999, 112–126.

Kymlicka, Will [interview with Ruth Rubio-Marín], Liberalism and Minority Rights, *Ratio Juris* 12 (1999) 133–152.

Kymlicka, Will, Misunderstanding Nationalism, in: Ronald Beiner (ed.), *Theorizing Nationalism*, New York, State University of New York Press 1999, 131–140.

Kymlicka, Will, *Politics in the Vernacular*, Oxford, Oxford University Press 2001.

Kymlicka, Will, The New Debate on Minority Rights, in: Ronald Beiner – Wayne Norman (eds.), *Canadian Political Philosophy: Contemporary Reflections*, Oxford, Oxford University Press 2001, 159–176.

Kymlicka, Will, The New Debate over Minority Rights, in: Ferran Requejo (ed.), *Democracy and National Pluralism*, London, Routledge 2001, 15–39.

Kymlicka, Will, New Forms of Citizenship, in: Thomas J Courchene – Donald J Savioe (eds.), *The Art of the State*, Montréal, IRPP 2003, 265–309.

Kymlicka, Will, The Internationalization of Minority Rights, in: Sujit Choudhry (ed.), *Constitutional Design for Divided Societies: Integration or Accommodation?*, Oxford, Oxford University Press 2008, 111–140.

Lábady, Tamás, *A magyar magánjog (polgári jog) általános része*, Budapest, Pécs, Dialóg Campus 1997.

Laband, Paul, Das Budgetrecht nach den Bestimmungen der Preußischen Verfassungsurkunde unter Berücksichtigung der Verfassung des Norddeutschen Bundes, *Zeitschrift für Gesetzgebung und Rechtspflege in Preußen* 4 (1870) 619–707.

Laband, Paul, *Die Wandlungen der deutschen Reichsverfassung*, Dresden, Zahn & Jaensch 1895.

Laband, Paul, *Das Staatsrecht des Deutschen Reiches*, vol. II, Tübingen, Mohr [5]1911.

Laband, Paul, *Staatsrechtliche Vorlesungen* [ed. Bernd Schlüter], Berlin, Duncker & Humblot 2004.

Lacroix, Justine, For a European Constitutional Patriotism, *Political Studies* 2002, 944–958.

Laitin, David D, *Nations, States and Violence*, Oxford, Oxford University Press 2007.

Lakin, Stuart, Debunking the Idea of Parliamentary Sovereignty: The Controlling Factor of Legality in the British Constitution, *Oxford Journal of Legal Studies* 28 (2008) 709–734.

Lambert, Édouard, *Le gouvernement des juges et la lutte contre la législation sociale aux États-Unis. L'expérience américaine du contrôle judiciaire de la constitutionnalité des lois*, Paris, M Giard & Cie 1921.

Lamont, Grant, *Precedent and Analogy in Legal Reasoning*, in: Edward N Zalta (ed.), *Stanford Encyclopedia of Philosophy* 2006, available at plato.stanford.edu/.

Lamprecht, Florian, *Darf der Staat foltern um Leben zu retten?*, Paderborn, Mentis-Verlag 2009.

Landau, David, Abusive Constitutionalism, 47 *UC Davis Law Review* 2013, 189–260.

Landesvereinigung der Arbeitsverbände Nordrhein-Westfalen e.V. und Verband der Metall- und Elektro-Industrie Nordrhein-Westfalen (eds.), *Festschrift für Jochen F. Kirchhoff zum 75. Geburtstag*, Köln, Schmidt 2002.

Lane, Jan-Erik, *Constitutions and Political Theory*, Manchester, Manchester University Press [2]2011.

Langbein, John H, The Legal History of Torture, in: Sanford Levinson (ed.), *Torture: A Collection*, Oxford, Oxford University Press 2004, 93–103.

Langheid, Theo, *Souveränität und Verfassungsstaat. The Sovereignty of Parliament*, Köln, Köln Diss. 1984.

Lansing, Robert, *The Peace Negotiations: A Personal Narrative*, Orlando, Houghton Mifflin 1921.

Larenz, Karl, *Methodenlehre der Rechtswissenschaft*, Berlin, Springer [6]1991.

Lassalle, Ferdinand, *Gesammelte Reden*, vol. 2, Berlin, Paul Cassirer 1919.

Lassalle, Ferdinand, Über Verfassungswesen [1862], in: id., *Gesammelte Reden*, vol. 2, Berlin, Paul Cassirer 1919, 24–61.

Laski, Harold J, *Studies in the Problem of Sovereignty*, New Haven, Yale University Press 1917.

Lasser, Mitchel de S-O-l'E, *Judicial Deliberations: A Comparative Analysis of Judicial Transparency and Legitimacy*, Oxford, Oxford University Press 2004.

Laun, Rudolf von, Der Staatsrechtslehrer und die Politik, *Archiv des öffentlichen Rechts NF* 2 (1922) 145–199.

Laurer, Hans René, Europarecht und österreichische Rechtsordnung. Rechtsnormen in einem einheitlichen Stufenbau?, *Österreichische Juristen-Zeitung* 52 (1997) 801–810.

Laven, David, Italy, in: Timothy Baycroft – Mark Hewitson (eds.), *What Is a Nation? Europe 1789–1914*, Oxford, Oxford University Press 2006, 255–271.

Law, David S – Mila Versteeg, The Declining Influence of the United States Constitution, *New York University Law Review* 87 (2012) 762–858.

Lawson, FH, Doctrinal Writing: A Foreign Element in English Law, in: Ernst von Caemmerer e.a. (eds.), *Ius privatum gentium. Festschrift für Max Rheinstein.* vol. I, Tübingen, Mohr Siebeck 1969, 191–210.

Lazarus, Liora – Christopher McCrudden – Nigel Bowles (eds.), *Reasoning Rights: Comparative Judicial Engagement*, Oxford, Hart 2014.

Lecours, André, Ethnic and Civic Nationalism: Towards a New Dimension, *Space & Polity* 4 (2000) 153–165.

Legrand, Pierre, *Le droit comparé*, Paris, Presses Universitaires de France 1999.

Lemberg, Eugen, *Nationalismus*, vol. II, Reinbek bei Hamburg, Rowohlt 1964.

Lenaerts, Koen, Civis Europaeus Sum: From the Cross-border Link to the Status of Citizen of the Union, *Online Journal on Free Movement of Workers within the European Union* 3 (2011) 6–18.

Leone, Richard C – Greg Anrig Jr. (eds.), *The War on Our Freedoms*, New York, Public Affairs 2003.

Leonhard, Jörn, Nation-States and Warfare, in: Timothy Baycroft – Mark Hewitson (eds.), *What Is a Nation? Europe 1789–1914*, Oxford, Oxford University Press 2006, 231–254.

Leoussi, Athena S (ed.), *Encyclopaedia of Nationalism*, New Brunswick, London, Transaction 2001.

Lepsius, Oliver, Freiheit, Sicherheit und Terror. Die Rechtslage in Deutschland, *Leviathan* 2004, 64–88.

Lepsius, Oliver, Braucht das Verfassungsrecht eine Theorie des Staates? *Europäische Grundrechte-Zeitschrift* 31 (2004) 370–381.

Lepsius, Oliver, L'influence du droit public français sur la doctrine juridique allemande de la République Fédérale, *Revue d'histoire des facultés de droit et de la science juridique* 24 (2004) 205–227.

Lepsius, Oliver, Die maßstabsetzende Gewalt, in: Christoph Schönberger e.a., *Das entgrenzte Gericht*, Berlin, Suhrkamp 2011, 159–279.

Lepsius, Oliver, Funktion und Wandel von Staatsverständnissen, in: Andreas Voßkuhle – Christian Bumke – Florian Meinel (eds.), *Verabschiedung und Wiederentdeckung des Staates im Spannungsfeld der Disziplinen*, Berlin, Duncker & Humblot 2013, 37–58.

Lepsius, Oliver, Rechtswissenschaft in der Demokratie, *Der Staat* 2013, 157–186.

Lerche, Peter, Stil und Methode verfassungsgerichtlicher Entscheidungspraxis, in: Peter Badura – Horst Dreier (eds.), *Festschrift 50 Jahre Bundesverfassungsgericht*, vol. I, Tübingen, Mohr Siebeck 2001, 333–361.

Lerner, Max, Constitution and Court as Symbols, *Yale Law Journal* 46 (1937) 1290–1319.

Lesaffer, Randall, *European Legal History*, Cambridge, Cambridge University Press 2009.

Le Sueur, Andrew – Maurice Sunkin, *Public Law*, London, New York, Longman 1997.

Letsas, George, *A Theory of Interpretation of the European Court of Human Rights*, Oxford, Oxford University Press 2007.

Levi, Edward H, *An Introduction to Legal Reasoning*, Chicago, London, University of Chicago Press 1949.

Levin, Michael, The Case for Torture, *Newsweek* 7 June 1982.

Levinson, Sanford, Is Liberal Nationalism an Oxymoron? An Essay for Judith Shklar, *Ethics* 1995/3, 626–645.

Levinson, Sanford, Do Constitutions Have a Point? Reflections on 'Parchment Barriers' and Preambles, in: Ellen Frankel Paul – Fred D Miller, Jr – Jeffrey Paul (eds.), *What Should Constitutions Do?*, Cambridge, Cambridge University Press 2011, 150–178.

Levinson, Sanford (ed.), *Torture: A Collection*, Oxford, Oxford University Press 2004.

Levitsky, Jonathan E, The Europeanization of the British Legal Style, *American Journal of Comparative Law* 42 (1994) 347–380.

Levy, Jacob T, *The Multiculturalism of Fear*, Oxford, Oxford University Press 2000.

Levy, Jacob T, National Minorities without Nationalism, in: Alain Dieckhoff (ed.), *The Politics of Belonging*, Lanham, Lexington Press 2004, 155–174.

Levy, Jacob T, Federalism, Liberalism, and the Separation of Loyalties, *American Political Science Review* 101 (2007) 459–477.

Lienbacher, Georg (ed.), *Verfassungsinterpretation in Europa*, Wien, Jan Sramek 2011.

Lijphart, Arend, *Democracy in Plural Societies*, New Haven, Yale University Press 1977.

Lijphart, Arend, *Democracies*, New Haven, London, Yale University Press 1984.

Lijphart, Arend, Constitutional Design for Divided Societies, *Journal of Democracy* 2004/2, 96–109.

Lindahl, Hans, Sovereignty and Representation in the European Union, in: Neil Walker (ed.), *Sovereignty in Transition*, Oxford, Hart 2003, 87–114.

Linz, Juan J, Early State Building and Late Peripheral nationalism against the State: The Case of Spain, in: Stein Rokkan (ed.), *Building States and Nations*, vol. 2, Beverly Hills, Calif., Sage 1973, 32–116.

Lippold, Rainer, *Recht und Ordnung. Statik und Dynamik der Rechtsordnung*, Wien, Manz 2000.

Livingston, Donald W, The Secession Tradition in America, in: David Gordon (ed.), *Secession, State and Liberty*, New Brunswick, Transaction Publishers 1998, 1–33.

Llobera, Josep R, *The God of Modernity: The Development of Nationalism in Western Europe*, Oxford, Berg 1994.

López Basaguren, Alberto, Nación y lengua en el Estatuto de Autonomía de Cataluña. Consideraciones sobre la STC 31/2010, *Revista General de Derecho Constitucional* 13 (2011) 1–26.

Loughlin, Martin, The State, the Crown and the Law, in: Maurice Sunkin – Sebastian Payne (eds.), *The Nature of the Crown*, Oxford, Oxford University Press 1999, 33–76.

Loughlin, Martin, *The Idea of Public Law*, Oxford, Oxford University Press 2004.

Loughlin, Martin, In Defence of Staatslehre, *Der Staat* 48 (2009) 1–28.

Loughlin, Martin, *Foundations of Public Law*, Oxford, Oxford University Press 2010.

Loughlin, Martin, What Is Constitutionalisation?, in: Petra Dobner – Martin Loughlin (eds.), *The Twilight of Constitutionalism?*, Oxford, Oxford University Press 2010, 47–70.

Löwenstein, Karl, *Verfassungslehre*, Tübingen, Mohr $^{4}$2000.

Luban, David, Liberalism, Torture and the Ticking Bomb, in: Karen J Greenberg (ed.), *The Torture Debate in America*, Cambridge, Cambridge University Press 2006, 35–83.

Luchaire, François – Gérard Conac – Xavier Prétot (eds.), *La Constitution de la République française*, Paris, Economica $^{3}$2009.

Lugo, Luis E (ed.), *Sovereignty at the Crossroads? Morality and International Politics in the Post-Cold War Era*, Lanham, Md., Rowman Littlefield 1996.

Luhmann, Niklas, *Gibt es in unserer Gesellschaft noch unverzichtbare Normen?*, Heidelberg, Müller 1993.

Lukács, Georg, *Die Zerstörung der Vernunft*, Berlin, Aufbau Verlag 1955.

Lungu, Ioana, Romanian Constitutional Nationalism, *Polish Sociological Review* 2002 (140) 397–412.

Lyons, Gene M – Michael Mastanduno (eds.), *Beyond Westphalia?*, Baltimore, Johns Hopkins University Press 1995.

Mac Amhlaigh, Cormac – Claudio Michelon – Neil Walker (eds.), *After Public Law*, Oxford, Oxford University Press 2013.

MacCormick, Neil, 'Principles' of Law, *Juridical Review* 19 (1974) 217–226.

MacCormick, Neil, *Legal Reasoning and Legal Theory*, Oxford, Clarendon Press 1978.

MacCormick, Neil, Coherence in Legal Justification, in: Aleksander Peczenik, e.a. (eds.), *Theory of Legal Science*, Dordrecht, Reidel Publishing 1984, 235–251.

MacCormick, Neil, Nations and Nationalism, in: Ronald Beiner (ed.), *Theorizing Nationalism*, New York, State University of New York Press 1999, 189–204.

MacCormick, Neil, *Questioning Sovereignty*, Oxford, Oxford University Press 1999.

MacCormick, Neil, Is There a Constitutional Path to Scottish Independence?, *Parliamentary Affairs* 53 (2000) 721–736.

MacCormick, Neil – Robert S Summers (eds.), *Interpreting Statutes*, Aldershot, Dartmouth 1991.

MacCormick, Neil – Robert S Summers (eds.), *Interpreting Precedents: A Comparative Study*, Aldershot: Ashgate 1997.

Maddox, Graham, A Note on the Meaning of 'Constitution', *American Political Science Review* 56 (1982) 805–809.

Madison, James, e.a., *The Federalist Papers*, ed. Isaac Kramnick, Harmondsworth, Penguin 1988.

Maduro, Miguel Poiares, Contrapunctual Law: Europe's Constitutional Pluralism in Action, in: Neil Walker (ed.), *Sovereignty in Transition*, Oxford, Hart 2003, 501–537.

Maduro, Miguel Poiares, The Importance of Being Called a Constitution, *International Journal of Constitutional Law* 3 (2005) 332–356.

Magiera, Siegfried, Das Europäische Parlament als Garant der demokratischen Legitimation in der Europäischen Union, in: Ole Due – Marcus Lutte – Jürgen Schwarze (eds.), *Festschrift für Ulrich Everling*, vol. I, Baden-Baden, Nomos 1995, 789–801.

Mair, Peter, Political Opposition and the European Union, *Government and Opposition* 2007, 1–17.

Maitland, Frederick William, *The Constitutional History of England*, Cambridge, Cambridge University Press 1908.

Majone, Giandomenico, *Regulating Europe*, London, Routledge 1996.

Majone, Giandomenico, Europe's 'Democratic Deficit': The Question of Standards, *European Law Journal* 4 (1998) 5–28.

Majtényi, Balázs, *A nemzetállam új ruhája*, Budapest, Gondolat 2007.

Malesevic, Sinisa, *Identity as Ideology*, Basingstoke, Palgrave Macmillan 2006.

Malmström, Åke – Stig Strömholm (eds.), *Rapports généraux au VII<sup>e</sup> Congrès international de droit comparé*, Stockholm, Almquist & Wiksell 1968.

Mancini, Susanna, Rethinking the Boundaries of Democratic Secession: Liberalism, Nationalism, and the Right of Minorities to Self-Determination, *International Journal of Constitutional Law* 6 (2008) 553–584.

Mangoldt, Hermann von – Friedrich Klein – Christian Starck (eds.), *Kommentar zum Grundgesetz*, München, Vahlen [6]2010.

Mann, Michael, A Political Theory of Nationalism and Its Excesses, in: Sukumar Periwal (ed.), *Notions of Nationalism*, Budapest, Central University Press 1995, 42–64.

Mann, Michael, The Emergence of Modern European Nationalism, in: John Hall – Ian Jarvie (eds.), *The Social Philosophy of Ernest Gellner*, Amsterdam, Rodopi 1996, 147–170.

Manning, John F, Textualism as a Nondelegation Doctrine, *Columbia Law Review* 97 (1997) 673–739.

Manow, Philip – Holger Döring, Electoral and Mechanical Causes of Divided Government in the European Union, *Comparative Political Studies* 2008, 1349–1370.

Marcic, René, Das Naturrecht als Grundnorm der Verfassung, in: Franz-Martin Schmölz (ed.), *Das Naturrecht in der politischen Theorie*, Wien, Springer 1963, 69–90.

Marcou, Gérard, Le principe d'indivisibilité de la République, *Pouvoirs* 100 (2002) 45–65.

Maritain, Jacques, *Man and the State*, Chicago, Chicago University Press 1951.

Markesinis, Basil, Conceptualism, Pragmatism and Courage, *American Journal of Comparative Law* 34 (1986) 349–367.

Markesinis, Basil, A Matter of Style, *Law Quarterly Review* 110 (1994) 607–628.

Markides, Alecos, The Republic of Cyprus, in: Constantijn Kortmann e.a. (eds.), *Constitutional Law of 10 EU Member States*, Deventer, Kluwer 2006, I.3–I.76.

Markoff, John, *Waves of Democracy: Social Movements and Political Change*, London, Pine Forge 1996.

Marmor, Andrei (ed.), *Law and Interpretation*, Oxford, Clarendon Press 1995.

Marquand, David, *Parliament for Europe*, London, Jonathan Cape Ltd 1979.

Marshall, Geoffrey, *Constitutional Theory*, Oxford, Clarendon Press 1971.

Marshall, Geoffrey, *Constitutional Conventions*, Oxford, Oxford University Press 1984.

Martinek, Oswin, e.a (eds.), *Arbeitsrecht und soziale Grundrechte. Festschrift für Hans Floretta*, Wien, Manzsche 1983.

Martínez-Herrera, Enric – Djaouida Moualhi, Predispositions to Discriminatory Immigration Policies in Western Europe: An Exploration of Political Causes, *Portuguese Journal of Social Sciences* 2007/3, 215–233.

Martínez-Herrera, Enric – Thomas Jeffrey Miley, The Constitution and the Politics of National Identity in Spain, *Nations and Nationalism* 2010, 6–30.

Martinico, Giuseppe, *The Tangled Complexity of the EU Constitutional Process: The Frustrating Knot of Europe*, London, Routledge 2012.

Marx, Anthony W, *Faith in Nation: Exclusionary Origins of Nationalism*, Oxford, Oxford University Press 2003.

Mastronardi, Philippe A, *Juristisches Denken*, Bern, Haupt 2001.

Mattera, Alfonso, L'européanité est-elle chrétienne?, *Revue du droit de l'Union européenne* 2003, 352–342.

Mattila, Mikko, Why Bother? Determinants of Turnout in the European Elections, *Electoral Studies* 2003, 449–468.

Maunz, Theodor – Reinhold Zippelius, *Deutsches Staatsrecht*, München, CH Beck $^{30}$1998.

Maunz, Theodor - Günter Dürig (eds.), *Grundgesetz. Kommentar* (München, Beck, looseleaf edition since 1958, state of August 2005).

Maurer, Andreas - Wolfgang Wessels, *Das Europäische Parlament nach Amsterdam und Nizza: Akteur, Arena oder Alibi?*, Baden-Baden, Nomos 2003.

Maurer, Hartmut, *Staatsrecht I.*, München, CH Beck $^{6}$2010.

Mayer, Franz C, *Kompetenzüberschreitung und Letztentscheidung*, München, Beck 2000.

Mayer, Heinz, Die Theorie des rechtlichen Stufenbaues, in: Robert Walter (ed.), *Schwerpunkte der Reinen Rechtslehre*, Wien, Manz 1992, 37–46.

Mayer, Heinz e.a. (eds.), *Staatsrecht in Theorie und Praxis: Festschrift für Robert Walter*, Wien, Manz 1991.

Mayer, Otto, *Lehrbuch des deutschen Verwaltungsrechts*, vol. I, Leipzig, Duncker & Humblot $^{2}$1914.

Mayer, Tilman, *Prinzip Nation*, Opladen, Leske & Budrich 1986.

McCain, John, Torture's Terrible Toll, *Newsweek* 21 November 2005.

McCrone, David, *The Sociology of Nationalism*, London, Routledge 1998.

McCrudden, Christopher, A Common Law of Human Rights? Transnational Judicial Conversation on Constitutional Rights, *Oxford Journal of Legal Studies* 20 (2000) 499–532.

McGarry, John - Michael Keating (eds.), *European Integration and the Nationalities Question*, New York, Routledge 2006.

McGarry, John - Michael Keating - Margaret Moore, Introduction: European Integration and the Nationalities Question, in: John McGarry - Michael Keating (eds.), *European Integration and the Nationalities Question*, New York, Routledge 2006, 1–20.

McGarry, John - Brendan O'Leary - Richard Simeon, Integration or Accommodation?, in: Sujit Choudhry (ed.), *Constitutional Design for Divided Societies: Integration or Accommodation?*, Oxford, Oxford University Press 2008, 41–88.

McInnes, Colin - Nicholas J Wheeler (eds.), *Dimensions of Western Military Intervention*, London, Frank Cass 2002.

McIntire, CT - Marvin Perry, Toynbee's Achievement, in: CT McIntire - Marvin Perry (eds.), *Toynbee. Reappraisals*, Toronto, University of Toronto Press 1989, 3–31.

McIntire, CT - Marvin Perry (eds.), Toynbee: Reappraisals, Toronto, University of Toronto Press 1989.

McLean, Janet, *Searching for the State in British Legal Thought*, Cambridge, Cambridge University Press 2012.

McLeod, Ian, *Legal Method*, Basingstoke, Palgrave $^{7}$2009.

McNeill, William H, *Polyethnicity and National Unity in World History*, Toronto, Toronto University Press 1986.

McRoberts, Kenneth, *Catalonia: Nation Building without a State*, Toronto, University of Toronto Press 2001.

Medicus, Dieter, *Allgemeiner Teil des BGB*, Heidelberg, Müller 1982.

Meinecke, Friedrich, *Weltbürgertum und Nationalstaat*, München, Oldenbourg $^{2}$1969 [1907].

Melucci, Alberto, *Nomads of the Present: Social Movements and Individual Needs in Contemporary Society*, London, Hutchinson, 1989.

Mencken, Henry Louis, The Divine Afflatus, in: *A Mencken Chrestomathy: His Own Selection of His Choicest Writings*, New York, AA Knopf 1949, 443.

Mencken, Henry Louis, *A Mencken Chrestomathy: His Own Selection of His Choicest Writings*, New York, AA Knopf 1949.

Mendes, Conrado Hübner, *Constitutional Courts and Deliberative Democracy*, Oxford, Oxford University Press 2013.

Méndez de Vigo, Iñigo (ed.), *¿Qué fue de la Constitución Europea?*, Barcelona, Planeta 2007.

Menéndez, Agustín José, A Christian or a Laic Europe? Christian Values and European Identity, *Ratio Juris* 18 (2005) 179–205.

Menéndez, Agustín José, A Pious Europe? Why Europe Should Not Define Itself as Christian, *European Law Review* 30 (2005) 133–148.

Menzel, Jörg (ed.), *Verfassungsrechtssprechung*, Tübingen, Mohr Siebeck 2000.

Merkl, Adolf, *Die Lehre von der Rechtskraft entwickelt aus dem Rechtsbegriff*, Leipzig, Deuticke 1923.

Merkl, Adolf, *Allgemeines Verwaltungsrecht*, Berlin, Springer 1927.

Merkl, Adolf, Prolegomena einer Theorie des rechtlichen Stufenbaues [1931], in: Hans Klecatsky e.a. (eds.), *Hans Kelsen - Adolf Merkl - Alfred Verdross: Die Wiener Rechtstheoretische Schule*, Wien, Europa-Verlag 1968, 1311–1361.

Merkl, Adolf, Das doppelte Rechtsantlitz [1918], in: Hans Klecatsky e.a. (eds.), *Hans Kelsen - Adolf Merkl - Alfred Verdross. Die Wiener Rechtstheoretische Schule*, Wien, Europa-Verlag 1968, 1091–1113.

Merkl, Adolf, Gesetzesrecht und Richterrecht [1922], in: Hans Klecatsky e.a. (eds.), *Hans Kelsen - Adolf Merkl - Alfred Verdross: Die Wiener Rechtstheoretische Schule*, Wien, Europa-Verlag 1968, 1615–1624.

Merkl, Adolf, Die Unveränderlichkeit von Gesetzen - ein normlogisches Prinzip [1917], in: Hans Klecatsky e.a. (eds.), *Hans Kelsen - Adolf Merkl - Alfred Verdross: Die Wiener Rechtstheoretische Schule*, Wien, Europa-Verlag 1968, 1079–1090.

Métall, Rudolf Aladár, *Hans Kelsen. Leben und Werk*, Wien, Deuticke 1969.

Meyer, Georg - Gerhard Anschütz, *Lehrbuch des deutschen Staatsrechts*, München, Duncker & Humblot $^{7}$1919.

Miersch, Matthias, *Der sogenannte référé legislatif*, Baden-Baden, Nomos 2000.

Mik, Cezary, Sovereignty and European Integration in Poland, in: Neil Walker (ed.), *Sovereignty in Transition*, Oxford, Hart 2003, 367–400.

Mill, John Stuart, *Utilitarianism, Liberty and Representative Government*, Everyman, London 1910.

Millard, Gregory, The Secession Reference and National Reconciliation: A Critical View, *Canadian Journal of Law and Society* 14 (1999) 1–19.

Miller, David, In Defence of Nationality, in: Paul Gilbert – Paul Gregory (eds.), *Nations, Cultures, and Markets*, Abingdon, Avebury 1994, 15–32.

Miller, David, *On Nationality*, Oxford, Clarendon Press 1995.

Miller, David (ed.), *The Blackwell Encyclopaedia of Political Thought*, Oxford, Blackwell 1987.

Mimin, Pierre, *Le style des jugements. Vocabulaire – Construction – Dialectique – Formes juridiques*, Paris, Librairies techniques 1978.

Mittelstraß, Jürgen, *Enzyklopädie Philosophie und Wissenschaftstheorie*, vol. 2, Mannheim, Bibliographisches Institut 1984.

Moeckli, Daniel, *Human Rights and Non-Discrimination in the 'War on Terror'*, Oxford, Oxford University Press 2008.

Mohl, Robert von, *Geschichte und Literatur der Staatswissenschaften*, vol. 1, Erlangen, Enke 1855.

Mohnhaupt, Heinz, *Historische Vergleichung im Bereich von Staat und Recht*, Frankfurt aM, Klostermann 2000.

Mohnhaupt, Heinz, Römisch-rechtliche Einflüsse im 'ius publicum'/'Öffentliches Recht' des 18. und 19. Jahrhunderts in Deutschland, in: id., *Historische Vergleichung im Bereich von Staat und Recht*, Frankfurt aM, Klostermann 2000, 123–150.

Molitor, Erich, *Über öffentliches Recht und Privatrecht. Eine rechtssystematische Studie*, Karlsruhe, Müller 1949.

Möller, Kai, Constructing the Proportionality Test: An Emerging Global Conversation, in: Liora Lazarus e.a. (eds.), *Reasoning Rights: Comparative Judicial Engagement*, Oxford, Hart 2014, 31–40.

Möllers, Christoph, *Staat als Argument*, München, CH Beck 2000.

Möllers, Christoph, Staat, in: Werner Heun e.a. (eds.), *Evangelisches Staatslexikon*, Stuttgart, Kohlhammer $^{2}$2006, 2272–2283.

Möllers, Christoph, *Demokratie. Zumutungen und Versprechen*, Berlin, Klaus Wagenbach 2008.

Möllers, Christoph, *Die drei Gewalten*, Göttingen, Velbrück 2008.

Möllers, Christoph, *Der vermisste Leviathan*, Frankfurt aM, Suhrkamp 2008.

Möllers, Christoph, Pouvoir Constituant – Constitution – Constitutionalism, in: Armin von Bogdandy – Jürgen Bast (eds.), *Principles of European Constitutional Law*, Oxford, Hart $^{2}$2010, 169–205.

Möllers, Christoph, *Staat als Argument*, Tübingen, Mohr Siebeck $^{2}$2011.

Montagu, MF Ashley (ed.), *Toynbee and History: Critical Essays and Reviews*, Boston, Porter Sargent 1956.

Moore, Barrington, Jr., *Social Origins of Dictatorship and Democracy*, Boston, Beacon Press 1966.

Moore, Margaret, *The Ethics of Nationalism*, Oxford, Oxford University Press 2001.

Moore, Margaret, Globalization, Cosmopolitanism, and Minority Nationalism, in: Michael Keating – John McGarry (eds.), *Minority Nationalism and the Changing International Order*, Oxford, Oxford University Press 2001, 44–60.

Moore, Margaret (ed.), *National Self-Determination and Secession*, Oxford, Oxford University Press 1998.

Moravcsik, Andrew, The Myth of Europe's 'Democratic Deficit', *Intereconomics: Journal of European Economic Policy* November-December 2008, 331–340.

Morawski, Lech – Marek Zirk-Sadowski, Precedent in Poland, in: Neil MacCormick – Robert S Summers (eds.), *Interpreting Precedents: A Comparative Study*, Aldershot, Ashgate 1997, 219–258.

Moreno, Luis, e.a., Multiple Identities in Decentralized Spain, *Regional and Federal Studies* 8 (1998) 65–88.

Moreso, José Juan, *Legal Indeterminacy and Constitutional Interpretation*, Dordrecht, Kluwer 1998.

Morétau, Olivier – Jacques Venderlinden (eds.), *La structure des systèmes juridiques*, Bruxelles, Bruylant 2003.

Morlok, Martin, *Was heißt und zu welchem Ende studiert man Verfassungstheorie?*, Berlin, Duncker & Humblot 1988.

Möstl, Markus, *Die staatliche Garantie für die öffentliche Sicherheit und Ordnung*, Tübingen, Mohr Siebeck 2002.

Möstl, Markus, Regelungsfelder der Verfassung, in: Otto Depenheuer – Christoph Grabenwarter (eds.), *Verfassungstheorie*, Tübingen, Mohr Siebeck 2010, 569–597.

Moury, Catherine – Luís de Sousa (eds.), *Institutional Challenges in Post-Constitutional Europe*, London, Routledge 2009.

Moyrand, Alain – Tony Angelo, International Law Perspectives on the Evolution in Status of the French Overseas Territories, *La Revue Juridique Polynésienne* 5 (1999) 49–69, available at http://www.upf.pf/Revue-no-5-1999.html?lang=fr.

Mullen, Tom, Reflections on Jackson v. Attorney General: Questioning Sovereignty, *Legal Studies* 27 (2007) 1–25.

Müller, Georg e.a. (eds.), *Staatsorganisation und Staatsfunktion im Wandel. Festschrift für Kurt Eichenberger*, Basel, Frankfurt aM, Helbing & Lichtenhahn 1982.

Müller, György, Kormányzati viszonyainkról az új alkotmánykommentár 'A Kormány' című fejezete kapcsán, *Jogelméleti Szemle* 2010/1, http://jesz.ajk.elte.hu/muller41.html.

Müller, Jan-Werner, A European Constitutional Patriotism? The Case Restated, *European Law Journal* 14 (2008) 542–557.

Müller, Jan-Werner, *Verfassungspatriotismus*, Berlin, Suhrkamp 2010.

Müller-Freienfels, Wolfram, Zur Rangstufung rechtlicher Normen, in: Institute of Comparative Law Waseda University (ed.), *Law in East and West. Recht in Ost und West*, Tokyo, Waseda University Press 1988, 3–39.

Munro, Colin R, *Studies in Constitutional Law*, London, Butterworths [2]1999.

Murkens, Jo Eric Khushal, The Future of Staatsrecht: Dominance, Demise or Demystification?, *Modern Law Review* 2007, 731–758.

Murkens, Jo Eric Khushal, *From Empire to Union: Conceptions of German Constitutional Law since 1871*, Oxford, Oxford University Press 2013.

Murphy, Walter F – James E Fleming – Sotirios A Barber – Stephen Macedo *American Constitutional Interpretation, American Constitutional Interpretation*, New York, Foundation Press [3]2003.

Murschetz, Verena, *Verwertungsverbote bei Zwangsmaßnahmen gegen den Beschuldigten im amerikanischen und österreichischen Strafprozess*, Innsbruck, Verlag Österreich 1999.

Namier, Lewis, *1848: The Revolution of Intellectuals*, Oxford, Oxford University Press 1992.

Navot, Suzie, Israel, in: Dawn Oliver – Carlo Fusaro (eds.), *How Constitutions Change*, Oxford, Portland, Hart 2011, 191–209.

Nawiasky, Hans, Kritische Bemerkungen zur Lehre vom Stufenbau des Rechtes, *Zeitschrift für öffentliches Recht* 6 (1926/27) 488–496.

Nawiasky, Hans, *Allgemeine Staatslehre*, vol. 2/2, Einsiedeln, Benziger 1955.

Nawiasky, Hans, *Allgemeine Staatslehre*. vol. 3, Einsiedeln, Benziger 1956.

Neck, Rudolf – Adam Wandruszka (eds.), *Die österreichische Verfassung von 1918 bis 1938*, München, Oldenburg 1980.

Neframi, Eleftheria, Mixed Agreements as a Source of European Union Law, in: Enzo Cannizzaro – Paolo Palchetti – Ramses A Wessel (eds.), *International Law as Law of the European Union*, Leiden, Martinus Nijhoff 2012, 325–349.

Neumann, Ulfrid – Joachim Rahlf – Eike von Savigny *Juristische Dogmatik und Wissenschaftstheorie*, München, CH Beck 1976.

Neumann, Ulfrid, Wissenschaftstheorie der Rechtswissenschaft, in: Arthur Kaufmann – Winfried Hassemer – Ulfrid Neumann (eds.), *Einführung in die Rechtsphilosophie der Gegenwart*, Heidelberg, Müller [8]2011, 385–400.

Newman, Gerald L, The Uses of International Law in Constitutional Interpretation, *American Journal of International Law* 98 (2004) 82–90.

Newman, Michael, *Democracy, Sovereignty and the European Union*, London, C Hurst and Co. Publishing 1996.

Ni Aoláin, Fionnuala, Truth Telling, Accountability and the Right to Life, *European Human Rights Law Review* 5 (2002) 572–590.

Nielsen, Kain, Cultural Nationalism, Neither Ethnic nor Civic, in: Ronald Beiner (ed.), *Theorizing Nationalism*, New York, State University of New York Press 1999, 119–130.

Nimni, Ephraim J, Introduction for the English-Reading Audience, in: Otto Bauer, *The Questions of Nationalities and Social Democracy*, Minneapolis, University of Minnesota Press [1924] 2000, xvii–xviii.

Nitschke, Peter (ed.), *Rettungsfolter im modernen Rechtsstaat*, Bochum, Kamp 2005.

Nolte, Georg (ed.), *European and US Constitutionalism*, Strasbourg, Council of Europe Publishing 2005.

Nootens, Geneviève, Liberal Nationalism and the Sovereign Territorial Ideal, *Nations and Nationalism* 2006, 35–50.

Norman, Wayne, Secession and (Constitutional) Democracy, in: Ferran Requejo (ed.), *Democracy and National Pluralism*, London, Routledge 2001, 84–102.

Norman, Wayne, *Negotiating Nationalism: Nation-Building, Federalism, and Secession in the Multinational State*, Oxford, Oxford University Press 2006.

Oberreuter, Heinrich, *Notstand und Demokratie*, München, Vögel 1978.

Oebbecke, Janbernd (ed.), *Nicht-normative Steuerung in dezentralen Systemen*, Stuttgart, Franz Steiner 2005.

Oehmichen, Anna, *Terrorism and Anti-Terror Legislation: The Terrorised Legislator? A Comparison of Counter-Terrorism Legislation and Its Implications on Human Rights in the Legal Systems of the United Kingdom, Spain, Germany and France*, Antwerp, Intersentia 2009.

Oeter, Stefan, Souveränität und Demokratie in der 'Verfassungsentwicklung' der Europäischen Union, *Zeitschrift für ausländisches öffentliches Recht und Völkerrecht* 1995, 659–712.

Offe, Claus, Homogeneity and Constitutional Democracy: Coping with Identity Conflicts through Group Rights, *Journal of Political Philosophy* 6 (1998) 113–141.

Öhlinger, Theo, *Der Stufenbau der Rechtsordnung. Rechtstheoretische und ideologische Aspekte*, Wien, Manz 1975.

Öhlinger, Theo, Unity of the Legal System or Legal Pluralism: The Stufenbau Doctrine in Present-Day Europe, in: Antero Jyränki (ed.), *National Constitutions in the Era of Integration*, The Hague, Kluwer Law International 1999, 163–173.

Öhlinger, Theo – Harald Eberhard, *Verfassungsrecht*, Wien, Facultas [9]2012.

Oklopcic, Zoran, Populus Interruptus, *Leiden Journal of International Law* 22 (2009) 677–702.

Oklopcic, Zoran, The Territorial Challenge: From Constitutional Patriotism to Unencumbered Agonism in Bosnia and Herzegovina, *German Law Journal* 13 (2012) 23–50.

O'Leary, Brendan, Instrumentalist Theories of Nationalism, in: Athena S Leoussi (ed.), *Encyclopaedia of Nationalism*, New Brunswick, London, Transaction 2001, 148–153.

O'Leary, Brendan, An Iron Law of Nationalism And Federation? A (Neo-Diceyan) Theory of the Necessity of a Federal Staatsvolk, and of Consociational Rescue, *Nations and Nationalism* 2001, 273–296.

Oliver, Dawn, Common Values in Public and Private Law and the Public/Private Divide, *Public Law* 1997, 630–646.

Oliver, Dawn, The Human Rights Act and Public Law/Private Law Divides, *European Human Rights Law Review* 2000, 343–355.

Oliver, Dawn – Carlo Fusaro (eds.), *How Constitutions Change*, Oxford, Portland, Hart 2011.

Ooyen, Robert Chr van, *Der Begriff des Politischen des Bundesverfassungsgerichts*, Berlin, Duncker & Humblot 2005.

Ooyen, Robert Chr van, *Die Staatstheorie des Bundesverfassungsgerichts und Europa*, Baden-Baden, Nomos [4]2011.

Orfield, Lester Bernhard, *The Amending of the Federal Constitution*, Ann Arbor, University of Michigan Press 1942.

Orgad, Liav, The Preamble in Constitutional Interpretation, *International Journal of Constitutional Law* 8 (2010) 714–738.

Osiatynski, Wiktor, Paradoxes of Constitutional Borrowing, *International Journal of Constitutional Law* 1 (2003) 244–268.

Ossenbühl, Fritz, Maastricht und das Grundgesetz, *Deutsches Verwaltungsblatt* 108 (1993) 629–637.

Ost, François, L'interprétation logique et systématique et le postulat de rationalité du législateur, in: Michel van de Kerchove (ed.), *L'interprétation en droit. Approche pluridisciplinaire*, Bruxelles, Facultés universitaires Saint Louis 1978, 97–184.

Ost, François – Michel van de Kerchove, Les directives d'interprétation en théorie du droit et en droit positif belge. La lettre et l'esprit, in: Jean-François Perrin (ed.), *Les règles d'interprétation*, Fribourg, Éditions Universitaires Fribourg Suisse 1989, 7–39.

Ost, François – Michel van de Kerchove, *Entre la lettre et l'esprit. Les directives d'interprétation en droit*, Bruxelles, Bruylant 1989.

Ostendorf, Heribert (ed.), *Folter. Praxis, Verbot, Verantwortlichkeit*, Münster, LIT Verlag 2005.

Osterkamp, Jana, *Verfassungsgerichtsbarkeit in der Tschechoslowakei (1920–1939)*, Frankfurt aM, Vittorio Klostermann 2009.

Özkirimli, Umut, *Theories of Nationalism*, Basingstoke, Palgrave Macmillan [2]2010.

Paine, Thomas, The Rights of Man (1791), in: Moncure Daniel Conway (ed.), *Writings of Thomas Paine*, vol. 2, New York, AMS Press 1967, 265–523.

Palmer, Robert R, *The Age of Democratic Revolution: A Political History of Europe and America, 1760–1800*, vol. 1, Princeton, NJ, Princeton University Press 1959.

Palombella, Gianluigi, The Rule of Law and its Core, in: Gianluigi Palombella – Neil Walker (eds.), *Relocating the Rule of Law*, Oxford, Hart 2009, 17–42.

Palombella, Gianluigi – Neil Walker (eds.), *Relocating the Rule of Law*, Oxford, Hart 2009.

Palumbo, Michael - William Oswald Shanahan (eds.), *Nationalism: Essays in Honour of Louis L Snyder*, Westport, Conn., Greenwood 1981.

Papaioannou, Elias - Gregorios Siourounis, Democratization and Growth, *CEDI Working Papers* 2007-13, available at http://ideas.repec.org/p/edb/cedidp/07-13.html.

Parche, Hans M, *Der Einsatz von Streitkräften im inneren Notstand. Zugleich ein Beitrag zur Lehre vom rechtsstaatlichen Handeln der Exekutive und seiner Kontrolle*, Münster, univ. diss. 1974.

Pascua, José Antonio, Die Grundlage rechtlicher Geltung von Prinzipien. Eine Gegenüberstellung von Dworkin und Esser, in: Giuseppe Orsi (ed.), *Prinzipien des Rechts*, Frankfurt aM, Lang 1996, 7-33.

Pasquino, Pasquale, *Sieyès et l'invention de la Constitution en France*, Paris, Odile Jacob 1998.

Patyi, András, *Közigazgatási bíráskodásunk modelljei*, Budapest, Logod 2012.

Paul, Ellen Frankel, e.a. (eds.), *What Should Constitutions Do?*, Cambridge, Cambridge University Press 2011.

Paulson, Stanley L, Zur Stufenbaulehre Merkls in ihrer Bedeutung für die Allgemeine Rechtslehre, in: Robert Walter (ed.), *Adolf J Merkl. Werk und Wirksamkeit*, Wien, Manz 1990, 93-105.

Paulson, Stanley L - Robert Walter (eds.), *Untersuchungen zur Reinen Rechtslehre. Ergebnisse eines Wiener Rechtstheoretischen Seminars 1985/86*, Wien, Manz 1986.

Pauly, Walter, *Methodenwandel im deutschen Spätkonstitutionalismus*, Tübingen, Mohr 1993.

Paye, Jean-Claude, *La fin de l'État de droit. Lutte antiterrorist - de l'état d'exception à la dictature*, Paris, La Dispute 2004.

Pecora, Vincent P (ed.), *Nations and Identities: Classic Readings*, Oxford, Blackwell 2001.

Peczenik, Aleksander, Principles of Law: The Search for Legal Theory, *Rechtstheorie* 1971, 17-36.

Peczenik, Aleksander, Two Sides of Grundnorm, in: Hans-Kelsen-Institut (ed.), *Die Reine Rechtslehre in wissenschaftlicher Diskussion*, Wien, Manz 1982, 58-62.

Peczenik, Aleksander, *On Law and Reason*, Dordrecht, Kluwer 1989.

Peczenik, Aleksander - Lars Lindahl - Bert van Roermund (eds.), *Theory of Legal Science*, Dordrecht, Reidel Publishing 1984.

Perelman, Chaïm, *Logique juridique - nouvelle rhétorique*, Paris, Dalloz 1976.

Periwal, Sukumar (ed.), *Notions of Nationalism*, Budapest, Central University Press 1995.

Pernice, Ingolf, Maastricht, Staat und Demokratie, *Die Verwaltung* 1993, 449-488.

Pernice, Ingolf, Europäisches und nationales Verfassungsrecht, *Veröffentlichungen der Vereinigung der Deutschen Staatsrechtslehrer* 2001, 149-193.

Pernice, Ingolf, Die Europäische Verfassung, *Walter Hallstein-Institut Papers* 12/01, 1-22.

Pernice, Ingolf, Multilevel Constitutionalism in the European Union, *European Law Review* 2002, 511-529.

Pernice, Ingolf, Europawissenschaft oder Staatsrechtslehre?, in: Helmuth Schulze-Fielitz (ed.), *Staatslehre als Wissenschaft*, Berlin, Duncker & Humblot 2007, 225–251.

Pernice, Ingolf – Jiri Zemanek (eds.), *A Constitution for Europe: The IGC, the Ratification Process and Beyond*, Baden-Baden, Nomos 2005.

Pernthaler, Peter, *Der Verfassungskern*, Wien, Manz 1998.

Pernthaler, Peter – Peter Pallwein-Prettner, Die Entscheidungsbegründung des österreichischen Verfassungsgerichtshofs, in: Rainer Sprung (ed.), *Die Entscheidungsbegründung in europäischen Verfahrensrechten und im Verfahren vor internationalen Gerichten*, Wien, Springer 1974, 199–227.

Perry, Marvin, *Arnold Toynbee and the Western Tradition*, New York, Peter Lang 1996.

Pescatore, Pierre, *Introduction à la science du droit*, Luxembourg, Centre Universitaire de l'État 1960.

Pescatore, Pierre, Les exigences de la démocratie et la legitimité de la Communauté européenne, *Cahiers de droit européen* 1974, 499–514.

Peters, Anne, *Elemente einer Theorie der Verfassung Europas*, Berlin, Duncker & Humblot 2001.

Petersen, Niels, Avoiding the Common-Wisdom Fallacy: The Role of Social Sciences in Constitutional Adjudication, *International Journal of Constitutional Law* 2013, 294–318.

Petersmann, Hans G, *Die Souveränität des Britischen Parlaments in den Europäischen Gemeinschaften*, Baden-Baden, Nomos 1972.

Peterson, Merrill D (ed.), *The Portable Jefferson*, New York, Penguin 1975.

Petrétei, József, *Magyar alkotmányjog*, vol. I, Budapest, Dialóg Campus 2002.

Pfersmann, Otto, Ontologie des normes juridiques et argumentation, in: Otto Pfersmann – Gérard Timsit (eds.), *Raisonnement juridique et interpretation*, Paris, Sorbonne 2001, 11–34.

Pfersmann, Otto, Le sophisme onomastique: changer au lieu de connaître. L'interprétation da la Constitution, in: Ferdinand Mélin-Soucramanien (ed.), *L'interprétation constitutionnelle*, Paris, Dalloz 2005, 33–60.

Pfersmann, Otto – Gérard Timsit (eds.), *Raisonnement juridique et interprétation*, Paris, Sorbonne 2001.

Pierré-Caps, Stéphane, Karl Renner et l'État multinational, *Droit et Société* 27 (1994) 421–441.

Pierré-Caps, Stéphane, Le constitutionnalisme et la nation, in: Jean-Claude Colliard – Yves Jegouzo (eds.), *Le nouveau constitutionnalisme. Mélanges en l'honneur de Gérard Conac*, Paris, Economica 2001, 67–86.

Pitamic, Leonidas, Denkökonomische Voraussetzungen der Rechtswissenschaft, *Zeitschrift für öffentliches Recht* 3 (1916–1918) 339–367.

Plog, Karsten, *Die Krise der Allgemeinen Staatslehre in der Wissenschaftsgeschichte der Politik*, München, Schön 1969.

Plucknett, Theodore FT, Bonham's Case and Judicial Review, *Harvard Law Review* 40 (1926–1927) 30–70.

Pogge, Thomas W, How to Create Supra-National Institutions Democratically, in: Andreas Føllesdahl – Peter Koslowski (eds.), *Democracy and the European Union*, Berlin, Springer 1998, 160–185.

Pogonyi, Szabolcs – Mária M Kovács – Zsolt Körtvélyesi, The Politics of External Kin-State Citizenship in East Central Europe, *Eudo* 2010, available at http://eudo-citizenship.eu/docs/ECEcompreport.pdf.

Popper, Karl Raimund, *The Open Society and Its Enemies*, London, Routledge 2006.

Poscher, Ralf, Menschenwürde als Tabu. Die verdeckte Rationalität eines absoluten Rechtsverbots der Folter, in: Gerhard Beestermöller – Hauke Brunkhorst (eds.), *Rückkehr der Folter. Rechtsstaat im Zwielicht?*, München, Beck 2006, 75–87.

Poscher, Ralf, Principles: How Many Theories? What Merit?, in: Matthias Klatt (ed.), *Institutionalized Reason: The Jurisprudence of Robert Alexy*, Oxford, Oxford University Press 2012, 218–247.

Posen, Barry R, Nationalism, Mass Army, and Military Power, *International Security* 18 (1993) 80–124.

Posner, Eric – Adrian Vermeule, *Terror in the Balance: Security, Liberty, and the Courts*, Oxford, Oxford University Press 2007.

Posner, Richard A, Interpretation Revisited, in: Susan J Brison – Walter Sinnott-Armstrong (eds.), *Contemporary Perspectives on Constitutional Interpretation*, Boulder, Westview 1993, 102–117.

Posner, Richard A, The Costs of Enforcing Legal Rights, *East European Constitutional Review* 1995/Summer 71–83.

Posner, Richard A, The Problematics of Moral and Legal Theory, *Harvard Law Review* 111 (1997–1998) 1637–1715.

Posner, Richard A, *The Problematics of Moral and Legal Theory*, Cambridge, Mass., Belknap Press of Harvard University Press London, 1999.

Posner, Richard A, No Thanks, We Already Have Our Own Laws, *Legal Affairs* Aug. 2004, 40–42.

Posner, Richard A, Torture, Terrorism, and Interrogation, in: Sanford Levinson (ed.), *Torture: A Collection*, Oxford, Oxford University Press 2004, 291–298.

Posner, Richard A, *Not a Suicide Pact: The Constitution in a Time of National Emergency*, Oxford, Oxford University Press 2006.

Post, Robert C, Constitutional Scholarship in the United States, *International Journal of Constitutional Law* 7 (2009) 416–423.

Prélot, Marcel – Jean Boulouis, *Institutions politiques et droit constitutionnel*, Paris, Dalloz 1990.

Preuß, Hugo, *Gemeinde, Staat und Reich*, Berlin, Springer 1889.

Preuß, Ulrich K, Disconnecting Constitutions from Statehood, in: Petra Dobner – Martin Loughlin (eds.), *The Twilight of Constitutionalism?*, Oxford, Oxford University Press 2010, 23–46.

Preuß, Ulrich K – Ferrán Requejo (eds.), *European Citizenship, Multiculturalism and the State*, Baden-Baden, Nomos 1998.

Priester, Jens-Michael, Die Grundnorm als Chimäre, in: Werner Krawietz – Helmut Schelsky (eds.), *Rechtssystem und gesellschaftliche Basis bei Hans Kelsen*, Rechtstheorie, Beiheft 5, Berlin, Duncker & Humblot 1984, 211–244.

Pünder, Hermann – Christian Waldhoff (eds.), *Debates in German Public Law*, Oxford, Hart 2014.

Püttner, Günter, *Allgemeines Verwaltungsrecht*, Düsseldorf, Werner $^{5}$1979.

Quaritsch, Helmut, *Staat und Souveränität*, Frankfurt aM, Athenaeum 1970.

Quine, Willard VO, On Empirically Equivalent Systems of the World, *Erkenntnis* 9 (1975) 313–328.

Quinton, Anthony, *The Politics of Imperfection*, London, Faber & Faber 1978.

Rabkin, Jeremy A, *The Case for Sovereignty*, Washington, AEI Press 2004.

Radbruch, Gustav, *Einführung in die Rechtswissenschaft*, Stuttgart, KF Köhler Verlag $^{12}$1969.

Radbruch, Gustav, *Rechtsphilosophie*, Stuttgart, Koehler $^{8}$1973.

Ragone, Sabrina, *El control judicial de la reforma constitucional. Aspectos teóricos y comparativos*, Porrúa, Instituto Mexicano de Derecho Procesal Constitucional 2012.

Räikkä, Juha, Is a Membership-Blind Model of Justice False by Definition?, in: id. (ed.), *Do We Need Minority Rights? Conceptual Issues*, The Hague, Nijhoff 1996, 3–19.

Raisch, Peter, *Juristische Methoden. Vom antiken Rom bis zur Gegenwart*, Heidelberg, CF Müller 1995.

Rakove, Jack N, *American Federalism: Was There an Original Understanding?*, in: Mark R Killenbeck (ed.), *The Tenth Amendment and State Sovereignty*, Lanham, Md, Rowman & Littlefield 2002, 107–129.

Ramos Romeu, Francisco, The Establishment of Constitutional Courts: A Study of 128 Democratic Constitutions, *Review of Law and Economics* 2 (2006) 103–135.

Randelzhofer, Albrecht, Souveränität und Rechtsstaat: Anforderungen an eine Europäische Verfassung, in: Heiner Noske (ed.), *Der Rechtsstaat am Ende?*, München, Olzog 1995, 123–134.

Ranke, Leopold von, *Sämtliche Werke*, vols. 49–50, Leipzig, Duncker & Humblot 1887.

Raschauer, Bernhard, Art. 69, in: Karl Korinek – Michael Holoubek (eds.), *Österreichisches Bundesverfassungsrecht*, Wien, Springer [loose-leaf edn., December 2003].

Rasmusen, Eric B, Judicial Legitimacy as a Repeated Game, *Journal of Law, Economics & Organization* 1994/1, 63–83.

Rawlings, Richard e.a. (eds.), *Sovereignty and the Law*, Oxford, Oxford University Press 2013.

Raz, Joseph, Legal Principles and the Limits of Law, *Yale Law Journal* 81 (1972) 823–854.

Raz, Joseph, Kelsen's Theory of the Basic Norm, *American Journal of Jurisprudence* 19 (1974) 99–111.

Raz, Joseph, The Rule of Law and Its Virtue, in: id., *The Authority of Law*, Oxford, Oxford University Press 1979, 210–229.

Raz, Joseph, *The Concept of a Legal System: An Introduction to the Theory of Legal System*, Oxford, Clarendon Press $^{2}$1980.

Raz, Joseph, *Ethics in the Public Domain*, Oxford, Clarendon Press 1994.

Raz, Joseph, *The Authority of Law*, Oxford, Oxford University Press $^{2}$2009.

[s.n.], *Recueil d'études sur les sources du droit en l'honneur de François Gény*, Paris, Sirey 1934.

Reemtsma, Jan Philipp, *Folter im Rechtsstaat?*, Hamburg, Hamburger Edition 2005.

Reestman, Jan Herman, *Conseil Constitutionnel* on the Status of (Secondary) Community Law in the French Internal Order. Decision of 10 June 2004, 2004–496 DC, *European Constitutional Law Review* 1 (2005) 302–317.

Regan, Donald H, Glosses on Dworkin: Rights, Principles, and Policies, in: Marshall Cohen (ed.), *Ronald Dworkin and Contemporary Jurisprudence*, Totowa, NJ, Rowman & Allanheld 1983, 119–160.

Rehnquist, William H, The Notion of a Living Constitution, *Texas Law Review* 1976, 693–706.

Reid, John Philip, *Rule of Law: The Jurisprudence of Liberty in the Seventeenth and Eighteenth Centuries*, DeKalb, Northern Illinois University Press 2004.

Reimann, Hans Leo, Überlieferung und Rezeption im Mittelalter [der Demokratie], in: Otto Brunner – Werner Conze – Reinhart Koselleck (eds.), *Geschichtliche Grundbegriffe*, vol. 1, Stuttgart, Klett-Cotta 2004, 835–839.

Reiners, Edgar, *Die Normenhierarchie in den Mitgliedstaaten der europäischen Gemeinschaften*, vol. I, Hamburg, Fundament-Verlag 1971.

Rejali, Darius, *Torture and Democracy*, Princeton, Oxford, Princeton University Press 2007.

Renan, Ernest, What Is a Nation? [1882], in: Homi K Bhabha (ed.), *Nation and Narration*, London, Routledge 1990, 8–22.

Renner, Karl, State and Nation, in: Ephraim Nimni (ed.), *National Cultural Autonomy and Its Contemporary Critics*, London, Routledge 2005 [1899], 15–47.

Requejo, Ferran, Introduction, in: id. (ed.), *Democracy and National Pluralism*, London, Routledge 2001, 1–11.

Requejo, Ferran, Political Liberalism in Multinational States, in: Alain-G Gagnon – James Tully (eds.), *Multinational Democracies*, Cambridge, Cambridge University Press 2001, 110–132.

Requejo, Ferran, *Multinational Federalism and Value Pluralism: The Spanish Case*, London, Routledge 2005.

Requejo, Ferran (ed.), *Democracy and National Pluralism*, London, Routledge 2001.

Rescigno, Giuseppe Ugo, *Le convenzioni costituzionali*, Padua, Cedam 1972.

Resina, Joan Ramon, Post-National Spain? Post-Spanish Spain? *Nations and Nationalism* 8 (2002) 377–396.

Ridley, FF, There Is No British Constitution: A Dangerous Case of the Emperor's Clothes, *Parliamentary Affairs* 41 (1988) 340–361.

Riedel, Norbert K, Gott in der Europäischen Verfassung?, *Europarecht* 2005. 676–683.

Rigaux, François, Hans Kelsen on International Law, *European Journal of International Law* 9 (1998) 325–343.

Ripert, Georges, *Le déclin du droit*, Paris, Librairie générale de droit et de jurisprudence 1949.

Rishworth, Paul, New Zealand, in: Dawn Oliver - Carlo Fusaro (eds.), *How Constitutions Change*, Oxford, Portland, Hart 2011, 235–260.

Ritter, Joachim - Karlfried Gründer (eds.), *Historisches Wörterbuch der Philosophie*, vol. 8, Darmstadt, Wissenschaftliche Buchgesellschaft 1992.

Robbers, Gerhard, *Sicherheit als Menschenrecht*, Baden-Baden, Nomos 1987.

Robertson, David, *The Judge as Political Theorist*, Princeton, Princeton University Press 2010.

Roche, Maurice, Nations, Mega-events and International Culture, in: Gerard Delanty - Krishan Kumar (eds.), *The SAGE Handbook of Nations and Nationalism*, London, Sage 2006, 260–272.

Rodríguez Iglesias, Gil Carlos, Zur 'Verfassung' der Europäischen Gemeinschaft, *Europäische Grundrechte-Zeitschrift* 1996, 125–131.

Rodríguez-Ruiz, Blanca - Ruth Rubio-Marín (eds.), *The Struggle for Female Suffrage in Europe: Voting to Become Citizens*, Leiden, Brill 2012.

Röhl, Klaus F - Hans Christian Röhl, *Allgemeine Rechtslehre*, München: Carl Heymanns $^{3}$2008.

Rokkan, Stein (ed.), *Building States and Nations*, vol. 2, Beverly Hills, Calif., Sage 1973.

Roosevelt, Theodore, *True Americanism [1894]*, in: Theodore Roosevelt, *Works of Theodore Roosevelt*, vol. I, New York, Collier 1897, 31–50.

Roosevelt, Theodore, *Works of Theodore Roosevelt*, vol. I, New York, Collier 1897.

Rorive, Isabelle, Les structures du système juridique belge, in: Olivier Morétau - Jacques Venderlinden (eds.), *La structure des systèmes juridiques*, Bruxelles, Bruylant 2003, 177–194.

Rosas, Allan - Lorna Armati, *EU Constitutional Law*, Oxford, Oregon, Hart 2012.

Rosenfeld, Michel, Constitutional Adjudication in Europe and the United States: Paradoxes and Contrasts, in: Georg Nolte (ed.), *European and US Constitutionalism*, Strasbourg, Council of Europe Publishing 2005, 165–199.

Rosenfeld, Michel, Rethinking the Boundaries between Public Law and Private Law for the Twenty-First Century, *International Journal of Constitutional Law* 11 (2013) 125–128.

Rosenfeld, Michel – András Sajó (eds.), *The Oxford Handbook of Comparative Constitutional Law*, Oxford, Oxford University Press 2012.

Rosenkrantz, Carlos F, Against Borrowings and Other Nonauthoritative Uses of Foreign Law, *International Journal of Constitutional Law* 1 (2003) 269–295.

Ross, Alf, *International Law: An Introduction*, Copenhagen, Nyt Nordisk Forlag 1984 (in Danish).

Rössler, Beate, *Der Wert des Privaten*, Frankfurt, Suhrkamp 2001.

Roth, SJ, The Effects of Ethno-Nationalism on Citizens' Rights in the Former Communist Countries, in: András Sajó (ed.), *Western Rights? Post-Communist Application*, Leiden, Kluwer 1996, 273–290.

Rothfels, Hans, Die Nationalidee in westlicher und östlicher Sicht, in: id. e.a. (eds.), *Osteuropa und der deutsche Osten*, Köln, Rudolf Müller 1956, 7–18.

Rothfels, Hans, Grundsätzliches zum Problem der Nationalität, in: id., *Zeitgeschichtliche Betrachtungen*, Göttingen, Vandenhoeck & Ruprecht $^{2}$1963, 89–111.

Rothfels, Hans, *Zeitgeschichtliche Betrachtungen*, Göttingen, Vandenhoeck & Ruprecht $^{2}$1963.

Rothfels, Hans e.a. (eds.), *Osteuropa und der deutsche Osten*, Köln, Rudolf Müller 1956.

Rotteck, Carl von, *Lehrbuch des Vernunftrechts und der Staatswissenschaften*, vol. 1–2, Stuttgart, Franck 1829–1830.

Röttinger, Moritz, Die Hoheitszeichen der Europäischen Union – ein paar vielleicht nicht nur theoretische Rechtsfragen, *Europarecht* 2003, 1095–1108.

Rouland, Norbert, La tradition juridique française et la diversité culturelle, *Droit et société* 1994, 381–419.

Rousseau, Jean-Jacques, *Du contrat social*, Amsterdam, Rey 1762.

Rub, Alfred, *Hans Kelsens Völkerrechtslehre. Versuch einer Würdigung*, Zürich, Schulthess 1995.

Rudden, Bernard, Courts and Codes in England, France and Soviet Russia, *Tulane Law Review* 48 (1974) 1010–1028.

Ruffert, Matthias (ed.), *The Public-Private Law Divide: Potential for Transformation?*, London, BIICL 2009.

Ruggeri, Antonio – Antonino Spadaro, *Lineamenti de giustizia constituzionale*, Torino, Giapichelli 2004.

Ruiz-Miguel, Alfonso – Francisco J Laporta, Precedent in Spain, in: Neil MacCormick – Robert S Summers (eds.), *Interpreting Precedents: A Comparative Study*, Aldershot, Ashgate 1997, 259–292.

Rupp, Hans Heinrich, *Grundfragen der heutigen Verwaltungsrechtslehre*, Tübingen, Mohr 1965.

Rupp, Hans Heinrich, Europäische 'Verfassung' und demokratische Legitimation, *Archiv des öffentlichen Rechts* 120 (1995) 269–275.

Sachs, Michael (ed.), *Grundgesetz. Kommentar*, München, Beck $^{5}$2009.

Sacksofsky, Ute, e.a., Erosion von Verfassungsvoraussetzungen, *Veröffentlichungen der Vereinigung der deutschen Staatsrechtslehrer* 68 (2008).

Sajó, András, *Kritikai értekezés a jogtudományról*, Budapest, Akadémiai 1983.

Sajó, András, *Limiting Government: An Introduction to Constitutionalism*, Budapest, New York, Central European University Press 1999.

Sajó, András, Learning Co-Operative Constitutionalism the Hard Way: the Hungarian Constitutional Court Shying Away from EU Supremacy, *Zeitschrift für Staats- und Europawissenschaften* 2004, 351–371.

Sajó, András, EU Networks under the New Constitution, Impact on Domestic Constitutional Structures, in: Ingolf Pernice – Jiri Zemanek (eds.), *A Constitution for Europe: The IGC, the Ratification Process and Beyond*, Baden-Baden, Nomos 2005, 183–197.

Sajó, András, *Constitutional Sentiments*, New Haven, Yale University Press 2010.

Sajó, András (ed.), *Western Rights? Post-Communist Application*, Leiden, Kluwer 1996.

Sandel, Michael, *Democracy's Discontent*, Cambridge, Mass., Belknap Press of Harvard University Press 1996.

Sarasola, Fernández – Joaquín Varela Suanzes-Carpegna (eds.), *Conceptos de Constitución en la historia*, Oviedo, Junta General del Principado de Asturias 2010.

Šarčević, Edin, *Der Rechtsstaat*, Leipzig, Leipziger Universitätsverlag 1996.

Sartorius, Rolf, Hart's Concept of Law, in: Robert S Summers (ed.), *More Essays in Legal Philosophy*, Oxford, Blackwell 1971, 131–161.

Saunders, Cheryl, The Use and Misuse of Comparative Constitutional Law, *Indiana Journal of Global Legal Studies* 13 (2006) 37–76.

Sauvel, Tony, Histoire du jugement motivé, *Revue du droit public et de la science politique* 1955, 5–53.

Savatier, René, *Du droit civil au droit public*, Paris, Pichon & Durand-Auzias 1945.

Savatier, René, Droit privé et droit public, *Recueil Dalloz* 1946 (chronique) 25–28.

Savigny, Eike von, Methodologie der Dogmatik. Wissenschaftstheoretische Fragen, in: Ulfrid Neumann e.a., *Juristische Dogmatik und Wissenschaftstheorie*, München, CH Beck 1976, 7–13.

Savigny, Eike von, Die Rolle der Dogmatik – wissenschaftstheoretisch gesehen, in: Ulfrid Neumann e.a., *Juristische Dogmatik und Wissenschaftstheorie*, München, CH Beck 1976, 100–109.

Scalia, Antonin, Common Law Courts in a Civil-Law System: The Role of United States Federal Courts in Interpreting the Constitution and Laws, in: Amy Gutmann (ed.), *A Matter of Interpretation*, Princeton, Princeton University Press 1997, 3–48.

Scalia, Antonin, Response, in: Amy Gutmann (ed.), *A Matter of Interpretation*, Princeton, Princeton University Press 1997, 129–150.

Scalia, Antonin, Judicial Adherence to the Text of Our Basic Law: A Theory of Constitution Interpretation, The Progressive Conservative 5/225 (2003), www.proconservative.net/PCVol5Is225ScaliaTheoryConstlInterpretation.shtml.

Scalia, Antonin, Foreign Legal Authority in the Federal Courts, *American Society of International Law Proceedings* 2004, 305–310.

Scalia, Antonin, *Reading Law: The Interpretation of Legal Texts*, St. Paul, Thomson/West 2012.

Scarry, Elaine, Five Errors in the Reasoning of Alan Dershowitz, in: Sanford Levinson (ed.), *Torture. A Collection*, Oxford, Oxford University Press 2004, 281–290.

Schäffer, Heinz, *Verfassungsinterpretation in Österreich*, Wien, Springer 1971.

Schäller, Steven, Präjudizien als selbstreferentielle Geltungsressource des Bundesverfassungsgerichts, in: Hans Vorländer (ed.), *Die Deutungsmacht der Verfassungsgerichtsbarkeit*, Wiesbaden, VS-Verlag 2006, 205–234.

Schanda, Balázs, Considerations on the Place of Religion in Constitutional Law, in: Zoltán Csehi – Balázs Schanda – Pál Sonnevend (eds.), *Viva Vox Iuris Civilis. Tanulmányok Sólyom László tiszteletére*, Budapest, Szent István Társulat 2012, 278–285.

Scharpf, Fritz W, *Demokratietheorie zwischen Utopie und Anpassung*, Konstanz, Konstanz University Press 1970.

Scharpf, Fritz W, Democratic Polity in Europe, *European Law Journal* 2 (1996) 136–155.

Scharpf, Fritz W, *Regieren in Europa*, Frankfurt aM, Campus Verlag 1999.

Schauer, Frederick, Precedent, *Stanford Law Review* 39 (1987) 571–605.

Schauer, Frederick, *Playing by the Rules: A Philosophical Examination of Rule-Based Decision-Making in Law and in Life*, Oxford, Clarendon Press 1991.

Schauer, Frederick, On the Migration of Constitutional Ideas, *Connecticut Law Review* 37 (2004–2005) 907–919.

Scherzberg, Arno, *Wozu und wie überhaupt noch öffentliches Recht?*, Berlin, de Gruyter 2003.

Scheuner, Ulrich, Der Verfassungsschutz im Bonner Grundgesetz, in: Hermann Jahrreiss e.a. (eds.), *Um Recht und Gerechtigkeit. Festgabe für Erich Kaufmann*, Stuttgart, Kohlhammer 1950, 313–330.

Scheuner, Ulrich, Nationalstaatsprinzip und Staatenordnung, in: Theodor Schieder (ed.), *Staatsgründungen und Nationalitätsprinzip*, Wien, München, Oldenbourg 1974, 285–306.

Schieder, Theodor, *Nationale und übernationale Gestaltungskräfte in der Geschichte des europäischen Ostens*, Krefeld, Scherpe 1954.

Schieder, Theodor (ed.), *Staatsgründungen und Nationalitätsprinzip*, Wien, München, Oldenbourg 1974.

Schilcher, Bernd – Peter Koller – Bernd-Christian Funk (eds.), *Regeln, Prinzipien und Elemente im System des Rechts*, Wien, Verlag Österreich 2000.

Schild, Wolfgang, *Die Reinen Rechtslehren. Gedanken zu Hans Kelsen und Robert Walter*, 1975.

Schild, Wolfgang, Folter einst und jetzt, in: Peter Nitschke (ed.), *Rettungsfolter im modernen Rechtsstaat*, Bochum, Kamp 2005, 69–93.

Schilling, Theodor, *Rang und Geltung von Normen in gestuften Rechtsordnungen*, Berlin, Spitz 1994.

Schilling, Theodor, The Autonomy of the Community Legal Order, *Harvard International Law Journal* 37 (1996) 389–409.

Schilling, Theodor, Zum Verhältnis von Gemeinschafts- und nationalem Recht, *Zeitschrift für Rechtsvergleichung, Internationales Privatrecht und Europarecht* 1998, 149–151.

Schilling, Theodor, Justizrevolutionen, *Der Staat* 51 (2012) 525–558.

Schlesinger, Arthur, Nationalism in the Modern World, in: Michael Palumbo – William Oswald Shanahan (eds.), *Nationalism: Essays in Honour of Louis L Snyder*, Westport, Conn., Greenwood 1981, ix–xx.

Schliesky, Utz, *Souveränität und Legitimität von Herrschaftsgewalt. Die Weiterentwicklung von Begriffen der Staatslehre und des Staatsrechts im europäischen Mehrebenensystem*, Tübingen, Mohr Siebeck 2004.

Schlüter, Bernd, *Reichswissenschaft, Staatsrechtslehre, Staatstheorie und Wissenschaftspolitik im Deutschen Kaiserreich am Beispiel der Reichsuniversität Straßburg*, Frankfurt aM, Klostermann 2004.

Schmalz, Dieter, *Staatsrecht*, Baden-Baden, Nomos $^{4}$2000.

Schmid, Carlo, *Erinnerungen*, Bern, Scherz 1979.

Schmidt, Detlef, *Die Unterscheidung von privatem und öffentlichem Recht*, Baden-Baden, Nomos 1985.

Schmidt-Aßmann, Eberhard, Öffentliches Recht und Privatrecht als wechselseitige Auffangordnungen – Einleitende Problemskizze, in: Wolfgang Hoffmann-Riem – Eberhard Schmidt-Aßmann (eds.), *Öffentliches Recht und Privatrecht als wechselseitige Auffangordnungen*, Baden-Baden, Nomos 1996, 7–40.

Schmitt, Carl, *Die Diktatur. Von den Anfängen des modernen Souveränitätsgedankens bis zum proletarischen Klassenkampf*, München, Duncker & Humblot 1921.

Schmitt, Carl, *Verfassungslehre*, München, Duncker & Humblot 1928.

Schmitt, Carl, *Politische Theologie*, München, Duncker & Humblot $^{2}$1934.

Schmitt, Carl, Legalität und Legitimität, in: id., *Verfassungsrechtliche Aufsätze aus den Jahren 1924–1954*, Berlin, Duncker & Humblot 1958, 303–350.

Schmitt, Carl, *Verfassungsrechtliche Aufsätze aus den Jahren 1924–1954*, Berlin, Duncker & Humblot 1958.

Schmitt, Carl, *Political Theology*, Cambridge, Mass., MIT Press 1985.

Schmölz, Franz-Martin (ed.), *Das Naturrecht in der politischen Theorie*, Wien, Springer 1963.

Schneider, Hans-Peter, Verfassungsinterpretation aus theoretischer Sicht, in: Hans-Peter Schneider – Rudolf Steinberg (eds.), *Verfassungsrecht zwischen*

*Wissenschaft und Richterkunst. Konrad Hesse zum 70. Geburtstag*, Heidelberg, CF Müller 1990, 39–52.

Schneider, Hans-Peter – Rudolf Steinberg (eds.), *Verfassungsrecht zwischen Wissenschaft und Richterkunst. Konrad Hesse zum 70. Geburtstag*, Heidelberg, CF Müller 1990.

Schoepke, Peter, *Die rechtliche Bedeutung der Präambel des Grundgesetzes für die Bundesrepublik Deutschland. Eine Grundlegung mit rechtshistorischer Einführung und Abhandlung der Präambeln zu den Verfassungen der Länder in der Bundesrepublik Deutschland [Diss. Tübingen]*, Bamberg, Bamberger Fotodruck 1965.

Schöbener, Burkhard, *Allgemeine Staatslehre*, München, Beck 2009.

Schönberger, Christoph, *Das Parlament im Anstaltsstaat. Zur Theorie der parlamentarischen Repräsentation in der Staatsrechtslehre des Kaiserreichs*, Frankfurt aM, Klostermann 1997.

Schönberger, Christoph, Der 'Staat' der Allgemeinen Staatslehre: Anmerkungen zu einer eigenwilligen deutschen Disziplin im Vergleich mit Frankreich, in: Olivier Beaud – Erk Volkmar Heyen (eds.), *Eine deutsch-französische Rechtswissenschaft?*, Baden-Baden, Nomos 1999, 111–137.

Schönberger, Christoph, *Unionsbürger. Europas föderales Bürgerrecht in vergleichender Sicht*, Tübingen, Mohr Siebeck 2005.

Schönberger, Christoph, Lisbon in Karlsruhe: Maastricht's Epigones at Sea, *German Law Journal* 10 (2009) 1201–1218.

Schöne, Ludwig, *Privatrecht und öffentliches Recht. Geschichte, Inhalts- und Bedeutungswandel eines juristischen Grundbegriffes*, Freiburg, univ. diss. 1955.

Schöpflin, George, The Functions of Myth and a Taxonomy of Myths, in: Geoffrey Hosking – George Schöpflin (eds.), *Myth and Nationhood*, London, Christopher Hurst 1997, 19–35.

Schramm, Alfred, Zweistufige Rechtsakte – oder: Über Richtlinien und Grundsatzgesetze, *Zeitschrift für öffentliches Recht* 56 (2001) 65–96.

Schramm, Gottfried, *Ein Damm bricht. Die römische Donaugrenze und die Invasion des 5.-7. Jahrhunderts im Lichte von Namen und Wörtern*, München, Oldenbourg 1997.

Schreiber, Hans-Ludwig, *Der Begriff der Rechtspflicht*, Berlin, de Gruyter 1966.

Schröder, Jan, Zur gesamteuropäischen Tradition der juristischen Methodenlehre, *Akademie-Journal* 2002/2, 37–41.

Schröder, Meinhard, Staatsrecht an den Grenzen des Rechtsstaates, *Archiv des öffentlichen Rechts* 103 (1978) 121–148.

Schulze-Fielitz, Helmuth, *Der informale Verfassungsstaat*, Berlin, Duncker & Humblot 1984.

Schulze-Fielitz, Helmuth, Grundsatzkontroversen in der deutschen Staatsrechtslehre, *Die Verwaltung* 1999, 241–282.

Schulze-Fielitz, Helmuth, Was macht die Qualität öffentlich-rechtlicher Forschung aus?, *Jahrbuch des öffentlichen Rechts der Gegenwart. Band 50*, Tübingen, Mohr Siebeck 2002, 1–68.

Schulze-Fielitz, Helmuth, Staatsrechtslehre als Wissenschaft, in: id. (ed.), *Staatsrechtslehre als Wissenschaft*, Berlin, Duncker & Humblot 2007, 11–48.

Schulze-Fielitz, Helmuth, Konjunkturen der Klassiker-Rezeption in der deutschen Staatsrechtslehre – Vermutungen auch im Blick auf Hans Kelsen, in: Matthias Jestaedt (ed.), *Hans Kelsen und die deutsche Staatsrechtslehre*, Tübingen, Mohr Siebeck 2013, 147–174.

Schulze-Fielitz, Helmuth (ed.), *Staatsrechtslehre als Wissenschaft*, Berlin, Duncker & Humblot 2007.

Schumpeter, Joseph A, *Capitalism, Socialism, and Democracy*, London, Allen & Unwin [3]1950.

Schuppert, Gunnar Folke, *Staatswissenschaft*, Baden-Baden, Nomos 2003.

Schurdel, Harry D, *Nationalhymnen der Welt. Entstehung und Gehalt*, Zürich, Atlantis Musikbuch-Verlag 2006.

Schütze, Robert, *European Constitutional Law*, Cambridge, Cambridge University Press 2012.

Schwartz, Alex, Patriotism or Integrity? Constitutional Community in Divided Societies, *Oxford Journal of Legal Studies* 2011, 503–526.

Schwartz, Bernard, *Constitutional Law*, New York, The Macmillan Company 1972.

Schweber, Howard, *The Language of Liberal Constitutionalism*, Cambridge, Cambridge University Press 2007.

Schwetzel, Wolfram, *Freiheit, Sicherheit, Terror*, München, Vahlen 2007.

Sedley, Sir Stephen, Human Rights: A Twenty-First Century Agenda, *Public Law* 1995, 386–401.

Sen, Amartya, *Development as Freedom*, New York, Knopf 1999.

Seton-Watson, Hugh, Intelligentsia und Nationalismus in Osteuropa 1948–1918, *Historische Zeitschrift* 1962, 331–345.

Seton-Watson, Hugh, *Nations and States*, London, Methuen 1977.

Shapiro, Ian – Casiano Hacker-Cordón (eds.), *Democracy's Edge*, London, New York, Cambridge University Press 1999.

Shaw, Jo, 'Postnational Constitutionalism' in the European Union, *European Public Policy* 6 (1999) 579–597.

Shaw, Jo – Gillian More (eds.), *New Legal Dynamics of European Union*, Oxford, Clarendon 1995.

Sieberson, Stephen C, The Treaty of Lisbon and Its Impact on the European Union's Democratic Deficit, *Columbia Journal of European Law* 2007–2008, 445–465.

Sieyès, Emmanuel-Joseph, *Political Writings*, ed. Michael Sonenscher, Indianapolis, Hackett 2003.

Sieyès, Emmanuel-Joseph, What Is the Third Estate? (1789), in: id., *Political Writings*, ed. Michael Sonenscher, Indianapolis, Hackett 2003, 92–162.

Simeon, Richard - Daniel-Patrick Conway, Federalism and Management of Conflict in Multinational Societies, in: Alain Gagnon - James Tully (eds.), *Multinational Democracies*, Cambridge, Cambridge University Press 2001, 338–365.

Simmonds, Nigel E, *Central Issues in Jurisprudence. Justice, Law and Rights*, London, Sweet & Maxwell [2]2002.

Simoncini, Marta, Risk Regulation Approach to EU Policy against Terrorism in the Light of ECJ/CFI Jurisprudence, *German Law Journal* 10 (2009) 1526–1549.

Skinner, Quentin, The Italian City-Republics, in: John Dunn (ed.), *Democracy: The Unfinished Journey 508 BC to AD 1993*, Oxford, Oxford University Press 1994, 57–69.

Skouris, Wassilios, *Der Einfluß des europäischen Gemeinschaftsrechts auf die Unterscheidung zwischen Privatrecht und öffentlichem Recht. Dargestellt für das öffentliche Auftragswesen und die Privatisierung*, Bonn, Zentrum für Europäisches Wirtschaftsrecht 1996.

Slaughter, Anne-Marie, A Typology of Transjudicial Communication, *University of Richmond Law Review* 29 (1994) 99–137.

Smend, Rudolf, *Verfassung und Verfassungsrecht*, München, Leipzig, Duncker & Humblot 1928.

Smend, Rudolf, Festvortrag zur Feier des zehnjährigen Bestehens des Bundesverfassungsgerichts am 26. Januar 1962, in: *Das Bundesverfassungsgericht*, Karlsruhe, Müller 1963, 23–37.

Smith, Anthony D, *The Ethnic Origins of Nations*, Oxford, Blackwell 1986.

Smith, Anthony D, The Nation: Invented, Imagined, Reconstructed?, *Millennium: Journal of International Studies* 20 (1991) 353–368.

Smith, Anthony D, *National Identity*, London, Penguin 1991.

Smith, Anthony D, *Nations and Nationalism in a Global Era*, Cambridge, Polity Press 1995.

Smith, Anthony D, Opening Statement: Nations and Their Past, *Nations and Nationalism* 1996, 358–365.

Smith, Anthony D, *Nationalism and Modernism: A Critical Survey of Recent Theories of Nations and Nationalism*, London, New York, Routledge 1998.

Smith, Anthony D, *Myths and Memories of the Nation*, Oxford, New York, Oxford University Press 1999.

Smith, Anthony D, *The Cultural Foundations of Nations*, Oxford, Blackwell 2008.

Smith, David A - Dorothy J Solinger - Steven C Topik (eds.), *States and Sovereignty in the Global Economy*, London, Routledge 1999.

Smith, Graham - Andrew Wilson - Annette Bohr - Edward Allworth, *Nation-Building in the Post-Soviet Borderlands*, Cambridge, Cambridge University Press 1998.

Smith, JC - David N Weisstub (eds.), *The Western Idea of Law*, London, Butterworths 1983.

Smooha, Sammy, The Model of Ethnic Democracy, *ECMI (European Center for Minority Issues, Flensburg) Working Papers* No. 13 (2001).

Smooha, Sammy, Type of Democracy and Modes of Conflict Management in Ethnically Divided Societies, *Nations and Nationalism* 2002, 423–431.

Solozábal Echavarría, JJ, Constitución, in: Manuel Aragón Reyes (ed.), *Temas básicos de derecho constitucional*, vol 1., Madrid, Civitas 2001.

Sólyom, László, Aufbau und dogmatische Fundierung der ungarischen Verfassungsgerichtsbarkeit, *Osteuropa-Recht* 2000, 230–241.

Sólyom, László - Georg Brunner, *Constitutional Judiciary in a New Democracy: The Hungarian Constitutional Court*, Michigan, Ann Arbor 2000.

Somek, Alexander, Constitutional Treaty: A Comment on the Legal Language of the European Union, *Annual of German & European Law* 1 (2003) 310–322.

Somló, Felix, *Juristische Grundlehre*, Leipzig, Meiner 1917.

Sommermann, Karl-Peter, Verfassungsperspektiven für die Demokratie in der erweiterten Europäischen Union. Gefahr der Entdemokratisierung oder Fortentwicklung im Rahmen europäischer Supranationalität?, *Die öffentliche Verwaltung* 2003, 1009–1017.

Sonenscher, Michael, Introduction, in: Emmanuel-Joseph Sieyès, *Political Writings*, ed. Michael Sonenscher, Indianapolis, Hackett 2003, vii–lxiv.

Spielbüchler, Karl, Grundrecht und Grundrechtsformel, in: Oswin Martinek e.a (eds.), *Arbeitsrecht und soziale Grundrechte. Festschrift für Hans Floretta*, Wien, Manzsche 1983, 289–307.

Spinant, Dana, How to Make Elections Sexy: Give Voters a Say in Europe's Top Jobs, *European Voice* 5–11.02.2004, 12.

Sprung, Rainer (ed.), *Die Entsheidungsbegründung in europäischen Verfahrensrechten und im Verfahren vor internationalen Gerichten*, Wien, New York, Springer 1974.

Stammen, Theo - Heinrich Oberreuter - Paul Mikat (eds.), *Politik - Bildung - Religion. Festschrift Hans Maier*, Padeborn, Schöningh 1996.

Stanlis, PJ (ed.), *Selected Writings and Speeches of Edmund Burke*, Garden City, N.Y., Doubleday 1963.

Starck, Christian, Zur Notwendigkeit der Wertbegründung des Rechts, in: Ralf Dreier (ed.), *Rechtspositivismus und Wertbezug des Rechts*, Stuttgart, Steiner 1990, 47–61.

Starck, Christian, Die Verfassungsauslegung, in: Josef Isensee - Paul Kirchhof (eds.), *Handbuch des Staatsrechts der Bundesrepublik Deutschland*, vol. VII: *Normativität und Schutz der Verfassung - internationale Beziehungen*, Heidelberg, CF Müller 1992, 189–229.

Starck, Christian, Verfassung und Gesetz, in: Christian Starck (ed.), *Rangordnung der Gesetze*, Göttingen, Vandenhoeck & Ruprecht 1995, 29–38.

Starck, Christian, Art. 1 Abs. 1, in: Hermann von Mangoldt – Friedrich Klein – Christian Starck (eds.), *Kommentar zum Grundgesetz*, München, Vahlen [6]2010, 61–62.

Starck, Christian (ed.), *Rangordnung der Gesetze*, Göttingen, Vandenhoeck & Ruprecht 1995.

Starck, Christian (ed.), *Constitutionalism, Universalism and Democracy – A Comparative Analysis*, Baden-Baden, Nomos 1999.

Stein, Ekkehart – Götz Frank, *Staatsrecht*, Tübingen, Mohr Siebeck [21]2010.

Stern, Klaus, *Das Staatsrecht der Bundesrepublik Deutschland, vol. 2: Staatsorgane, Staatsfunktionen, Finanz- und Haushaltsverfassungen, Notstandsverfassung*, Munich, Beck 1980.

Sternberger, Dolf, Aspekte des bürgerlichen Charakters [1946] in: id., *Ich wünschte ein Bürger zu sein*, Frankfurt aM, Suhrkamp 1995, 10–27.

Sternberger, Dolf, *Ich wünschte ein Bürger zu sein*, Frankfurt aM, Suhrkamp 1995.

Steyn, Johan, Guantanamo Bay: The Legal Black Hole, *International and Comparative Law Quarterly* 53 (2004) 1–15.

Stoitzner, Bettina, Die Lehre vom Stufenbau der Rechtsordnung, in: Stanley L Paulson – Robert Walter (eds.), *Untersuchungen zur Reinen Rechtslehre. Ergebnisse eines Wiener Rechtstheoretischen Seminars 1985/86*, Wien, Manz 1986, 51–90.

Stolleis, Michael, *Geschichte des öffentlichen Rechts in Deutschland*, vols. I–IV, München, Beck 1988, 1992, 1999, 2012.

Stolleis, Michael, *Staatsrechtslehre und Politik*, Heidelberg, CF Müller 1996.

Stolleis, Michael, Öffentliches Recht und Privatrecht im Prozeß der Entstehung des modernen Staates, in: Wolfgang Hoffmann-Riem – Eberhard Schmidt-Aßmann (eds.), *Öffentliches Recht und Privatrecht als wechselseitige Auffangordnungen*, Baden-Baden, Nomos 1996, 41–61.

Stolleis, Michael, *Rechtsgeschichte als Kunstprodukt. Zur Entbehrlichkeit von 'Begriff' und 'Tatsache'*, Baden-Baden, Nomos 1997.

Stolleis, Michael, *Public Law in Germany 1800–1914*, Oxford, Berghahn Books 2001.

Stolleis, Michael, *Rechtsgeschichte schreiben. Rekonstruktion, Erzählung, Fiktion?*, Basel, Schwabe 2008.

Stone Sweet, Alec, Why Europe Rejected American Judicial Review: And Why It May Not Matter, *Michigan Law Review* 101 (2003) 2744–2780.

Stone Sweet, Alec, The Juridical Coup d'Etat and the Problem of Authority, *German Law Journal* 8 (2007) 915–927.

Stone Sweet, Alec – Jud Mathews, Proportionality Balancing and Global Constitutionalism, *Columbia Journal of Transnational Law* 47 (2008–2009) 72–161.

Stratenwerth, Günter, Zum Verhältnis von Privatrecht, öffentlichem Recht und Strafrecht. Eine Auseinandersetzung mit Walter Burckhardt, in: Juristische Fakultät der Universität Basel (ed.), *Privatrecht – Öffentliches Recht –*

*Strafrecht. Grenzen und Grenzüberschreitungen*, Basel, Helbing & Lichtenhahn 1985, 415–429.

Strauss, David A, *The Living Constitution*, Oxford, Oxford University Press 2010.

Strobel, Karl, Die Frage der rumänischen Ethnogenese. Kontinuität–Diskontinuität im unteren Donauraum in Antike und Frühmittelalter, *Balkan-Archiv* 30/32 (2005–2007) 59–166.

Suanzes-Carpegna, Joaquín Varela, La doctrina de la Constitución histórica de España, in: Fernández Sarasola – Joaquín Varela Suanzes-Carpegna (eds.), *Conceptos de Constitución en la historia*, Oviedo, Junta General del Principado de Asturias 2010, 307–359.

Sullivan, Andrew, The Abolition of Torture, in: Sanford Levinson (ed.), *Torture: A Collection*, Oxford, Oxford University Press 2004, 317–327.

Sulyok, Márton – László Trócsányi, Preambulum, in: András Jakab (ed.), *Az Alkotmány kommentárja*, Budapest, Századvég [2]2009, 83–105.

Summers, Robert S (ed.), *More Essays in Legal Philosophy*, Oxford, Blackwell 1971.

Summers, Robert S – Michele Taruffo, Interpretation and Comparative Analysis, in: Neil MacCormick – Robert S Summers (eds.), *Interpreting Statutes*, Aldershot, Dartmouth 1991, 461–510.

Sunkin, Maurice – Sebastian Payne (eds.), *The Nature of the Crown*, Oxford, Oxford University Press 1999.

Sunstein, Cass R, Constitutionalism and Secession, *University of Chicago Law Review* 58 (1991) 633–670.

Sunstein, Cass R, *Legal Reasoning and Political Conflict*, Oxford, Oxford University Press 1996.

Sunstein, Cass R – Adrian Vermeule, Interpretation and Institutions, *Michigan Law Review* 101 (2003) 885–951.

Svoboda, David, Nations under Siege: Interview with Historian Miroslav Hroch, *New Presence* 2004/4, 24–27.

Szabó, Miklós, *Ars juris, A jogdogmatika alapjai*, Miskolc, Bíbor 2005.

Szászy-Schwarz, Gusztáv, *Parerga*, Budapest, Athenaeum 1912.

Szente, Zoltán, A historizáló alkotmányozás problémái – a történeti alkotmány és a Szent Korona az új Alaptörvényben, *Közjogi Szemle* 2011/3, 1–13.

Szente, Zoltán, *Érvelés és értelmezés az alkotmányjogban*, Budapest, Pécs, Dialóg Campus 2013.

Szigeti, Péter, *Jogtani és államtani alapvonalak*, Budapest, Rejtjel 2002.

Szladits, Charles, The Civil Law System, in: René David (ed. in chief), *International Encylopedia of Comparative Law. II/2: Structure and Divisions of the Law*, Tübingen, Mohr 1974, 15–76.

Szűcs, Jenő, *Nation und Geschichte*, Budapest, Corvina 1981.

Tajadura Tejada, Javier, El pronunciamiento del Tribunal Constitucional sobre el preámbulo del Estatuto de Autonomía de Cataluña. nación, realidad nacional y derechos históricos, *Teoría y Realidad Constitucional* no. 27 (2011/1) 423–447.

Takács, Péter, *Államtan*, Budapest, Corvinus 2011.

Tamanaha, Brian Z, A Concise Guide to the Rule of Law, in: Gianluigi Palombella – Neil Walker (eds.), *Relocating the Rule of Law*, Oxford, Hart 2009, 3–15.

Tamir, Yael, *Liberal Nationalism*, Princeton, Princeton University Press 1993.

Tammelo, Ilmar, Von der reinen zu einer reineren Rechtslehre, in: Werner Krawietz – Helmut Schelsky (eds.), *Rechtssystem und gesellschaftliche Basis bei Hans Kelsen*, Rechtstheorie, Beiheft 5, Berlin, Duncker & Humblot 1984, 245–252.

Tarello, Giovanni, *L'interpretazione della legge*, Milano, Giuffrè 1980.

Tavernier, Paul, La Convention européenne des droits de l'homme et distinction droit public – droit privé, in: Gérard Cohen-Jonathan – Jean-François Flauss – Pierre Lambert (eds.), *Liber amicorum Marc-André Eissen*, Bruxelles, Bruylant 1995, 399–413.

Teich, Mikulás – Roy Porter, Introduction, in: Mikulás Teich – Roy Porter (eds.), *The National Question in Europe in Historical Context*, Cambridge, Cambridge University Press 1993, xv–xxii.

Teich, Mikulás – Roy Porter (eds.), *The National Question in Europe in Historical Context*, Cambridge, Cambridge University Press 1993.

Teitel, Ruti, Comparative Constitutionalism in a Global Age, *Harvard Law Review* 117 (2004) 2570–2596.

Térey, Vilmos, Csodaváróknak, *Jogelméleti Szemle* 2010/2, http://jesz.ajk.elte.hu/terey42.html.

Tettinger, Peter J, Freiheit in Sicherheit, in: Landesvereinigung der Arbeitsverbände Nordrhein-Westfalen e.V. und Verband der Metall- und Elektro-Industrie Nordrhein-Westfalen (eds.), *Festschrift für Jochen F. Kirchhoff zum 75. Geburtstag*, Köln, Schmidt 2002, 281–296.

Thiesse, Anne-Marie, *La création des identités nationales*, Paris, Seuil 2001.

Thoma, Richard, Der Vorbehalt der Legislative und das Prinzip der Gesetzmäßigkeit von Verwaltung und Rechtsprechung, in: Gerhard Anschütz – Richard Thoma (eds.), *Handbuch des deutschen Staatsrechts*, vol. 2, Tübingen, Mohr 1932, 221–236.

Thompson, FML (ed.), *The Cambridge Social History of Britain 1750–1950*, vol. III, Cambridge, Cambridge University Press 1990.

Thornhill, Chris, *A Sociology of Constitutions: Constitutions and State Legitimacy in Historical-Sociological Perspective*, Cambridge, Cambridge University Press 2011.

Thürer, Daniel – Thomas Burri, Secession, in: Rüdiger Wolfrum (ed.), *Max Planck Encyclopedia of Public International Law*, Oxford, Oxford University Press 2011, available at http://www.mpepil.com/.

Thürer, Daniel – Thomas Burri, Self-Determination, in: Rüdiger Wolfrum (ed.), *Max Planck Encyclopedia of Public International Law*, Oxford, Oxford University Press 2011, available at http://www.mpepil.com/.

Tierney, Stephen, *Constitutional Law and National Pluralism*, Oxford, Oxford University Press 2004.

Tierney, Stephen, Beyond the Ontological Question: Liberal Nationalism and the Task of Constitution-Building, *European Law Journal* 14 (2008) 128–137.

Tilly, Charles, States and Nationalism in Europe 1492–1992, in: John L Comaroff – Paul C Stern (eds.), *Perspectives on Nationalism and War*, Amsterdam, Gordon and Breach 1995, 187–204.

Tilly, Charles, *Durable Inequality*, Berkeley, University of California Press 1998.

Tilly, Charles (ed.), *The Formation of National States in Western Europe*, Princeton, Princeton University Press 1975.

Tocqueville, Alexis de, *De la démocratie en Amérique*, vols. I–II, Paris, Gosselin 1835–40.

Tomkins, Adam, *Our Republican Constitution*, Oxford, Hart 2005.

Tomuschat, Christian, *Verfassungsgewohnheitsrecht*, Heidelberg, Winter 1972.

Tomuschat, Christian, Das Endziel der europäischen Integration, *Deutsches Verwaltungsblatt* 1996, 1073–1082.

Tønnesson, Stein, Globalising National States, *Nations and Nationalism* 2004, 179–194.

Toynbee, Arnold J, *A Study of History*, vol. I, London, Oxford University Press 1933.

Toynbee, Arnold J, *A Study of History*, vol. VI, London, Oxford University Press 1939.

Treanor, William Michael, Judicial Review Before Marbury, *Stanford Law Review* 58 (2005) 455–562.

Tribe, Lawrence H, *The Invisible Constitution*, Oxford, Oxford University Press 2008.

Tribe, Lawrence H – Patrick O Gudridge, The Anti-Emergency Constitution, *Yale Law Journal* 113 (2003–2004) 1801–1870.

Triepel, Heinrich, *Staatsrecht und Politik*, Berlin, de Gruyter 1927.

Troper, Michel, Sur la théorie juridique de l'État, in: id., *Pour une théorie juridique de l'État*, Presses Universitaires de France 1994, 5–22.

Troper, Michel, *La théorie du droit, le droit, l'État*, Paris, Presses Universitaires de France 2001.

Troper, Michel, The Survival of Sovereignty, in: Hent Kalmo – Quentin Skinner (eds.), *Sovereignty in Fragments*, Cambridge, Cambridge University Press 2010, 132–150.

Trotter, Markus, *Der Ausnahmezustand im historischen und europäischen Rechtsvergleich*, Heidelberg, univ. diss. 1997.

Trupp, Andreas, Zur Kritik der Stufenbautheorie und wissenschaftstheoretischen Konzeption der Reinen Rechtslehre, in: Werner Krawietz – Helmut Schelsky (eds.), *Rechtssystem und gesellschaftliche Basis bei Hans Kelsen*, Rechtstheorie, Beiheft 5, Berlin, Duncker & Humblot 1984, 299–317.

Tsagourias, Nicholas (ed.), *Transnational Constitutionalism: International and European Models*, Cambridge, Cambridge University Press 2007.

Tsatsos, Dimitris Th (ed.), *Die Unionsgrundordnung*, Berlin, BWV 2010.

Tünnesen-Harmes, Christian – Jörn Westhoff, Hymne kraft Briefwechsels?, *Neue Justiz* 1993, 60–62.

Türk, Pauline – Isabelle Thumerel – Gilles Toulemonde, *Exercices corrigés. Théorie générale du droit constitutionnel*, Paris, Gualino 2010.

Turpin, Colin, *British Government and the Constitution*, London Butterworths $^{5}$2002.

Tushnet, Mark, The Possibilities of Comparative Constitutional Law, *Yale Law Journal* 108 (1999) 1225–1309.

Tushnet, Mark, The United States: Eclecticism in the Service of Pragmatism, in: Jeffrey Goldsworthy (ed.), *Interpreting Constitutions: A Comparative Study*, Oxford, Oxford University Press 2006, 7–55.

Tushnet, Mark, *The Constitution of the United States*, Oxford, Hart 2009.

Twining, William, Torture and Philosophy, *Proceedings of the Aristotelian Society, Supplementary Volumes* (52) 1978, 143–195.

Twining, William – David Miers, *How to Do Things with Rules: A Primer of Interpretation*, London, Weidenfeld and Nicolson $^{2}$1982.

Uhle, Arnd, *Freiheitlicher Verfassungsstaat und kulturelle Identität*, Tübingen, Mohr Siebeck 2004.

Uitz, Renáta, *Constitutions, Courts and History: Historical Narratives in Constitutional Adjudication*, Budapest, CEU Press 2005.

Usher, John A, *General principles of EC law*, London, Longman 1998.

Vallès, Josep M, Catalonia 1979–2001: A Self-Government Experience in the Globalisation Age, *Scottish Affairs* 2001, Special Issue: Stateless Nations in the 21th Century: Scotland, Catalonia, Quebec, 156–161.

van de Kerchove, Michel (ed.), *L'interprétation en droit. Approche pluridisciplinaire*, Bruxelles, Facultés universitaires Saint Louis 1978.

van den Berghe, Pierre L, Sociobiological Theory of Nationalism, in: Athena S Leoussi (ed.), *Encyclopaedia of Nationalism*, New Brunswick, London, Transaction 2001, 274–278.

van den Berghe, Pierre L, Multicultural Democracy: Can It Work?, *Nations and Nationalism* 2002, 433–449.

van der Lugt, Cornelis Theunis, *State Sovereignty or Ecological Sovereignty?*, Baden-Baden, Nomos 2000.

Van Duin, Pieter, Is National Mobilization in Slovakia on the Decline?, *Slovak Foreign Policy Affairs* 2001/Spring 121–128.

van Eikema Hommes, Hendrik J, The Development of Hans Kelsen's Concept of Legal Norms, in: Werner Krawietz – Helmut Schelsky (eds.), *Rechtssystem und gesellschaftliche Basis bei Hans Kelsen*, Rechtstheorie, Beiheft 5, Berlin, Duncker & Humblot 1984, 159–178.

van Gerven, Werner, *The European Union: A Polity of States and Peoples*, Oxford, Portland, Hart 2005.

Van Parijs, P, Europe's Linguistic Challenge, *Archives Européennes de Sociologie* 2004 (XLV/1) 113–154.

van Reenen, Tobias, Tendances actuelles dans l'interprétation de la Constitution de l'Afrique du Sud, *Revue française de droit constitutionnel* 2002, 355–375.

Varouxakis, Georgios, *Mill on Nationality*, London, Routledge 2002.

Vattel, Emer de, *Le droit des gens*, Washington, Carnegie Institution of Washington 1916 [London, 1758].

Veil, Winfried, *Volkssouveränität und Völkersouveränität in der EU*, Baden-Baden, Nomos 2007.

Verdery, Katherine, Whither 'Nation' and 'Nationalism'?, *Daedalus* 122 (1993) 37–46.

Verdross, Alfred, Zum Problem der Rechtsunterworfenheit des Gesetzgebers, *Juristische Blätter* 45 (1916) 471–473.

Verdross, Alfred, Völkerrecht und einheitliches Rechtssystem. Kritische Studie zu den Völkerrechtstheorien von Max Wenzel, Hans Kelsen und Fritz Sander, *Zeitschrift für Völkerrecht* 1923, 405–438.

Verhoeven, Amaryllis, *The European Union in Search of a Democratic and Constitutional Theory*, The Hague, Kluwer Law International 2002.

Vertovec, Steven – Susanne Wessendorf (eds.), *The Multiculturalism Backlash. European Discourses, Policies and Practices*, London, New York, Routledge 2010.

Vick, Brian, Language and Nation, in: Timothy Baycroft – Mark Hewitson (eds.), *What Is a Nation? Europe 1789–1914*, Oxford, Oxford University Press 2006, 155–170.

Viehoff, Reinhold – Rien T Segers (eds.), *Kultur, Identität, Europa*, Frankfurt am Main, Suhrkamp 1999.

Viehweg, Theodor, *Topik und Jurisprudenz*, München, Beck 1953.

Villiers, Michel de – Thierry Renoux (eds.), *Code constitutionnel*, Paris, LexisNexis $^{4}$2011.

Vincze, Attila, Die unmittelbare Anwendbarkeit der ungarischen Verfassung, *Jahrbuch für Ostrecht* 2009, 83–94.

Vincze, Attila, Das tschechische Verfassungsgericht stoppt den EuGH – zum Urteil des tschechischen Verfassungsgerichts Pl. ÚS 5/12 vom 14.2.2012, *Europarecht* 2013/2, 194–204.

Vogel, Hans-Jochen (ed.), *Die Freiheit des Anderen. Festschrift für Martin Hirsch*, Baden-Baden, Nomos 1981.

Vogenauer, Stefan, *Die Auslegung von Gesetzen in England und auf dem Kontinent*, Tübingen, Mohr Siebeck 2001.

Vogt, Andreas, *Der Gottesbezug in der Präambel des Grundgesetzes*, Hamburg, Kovač 2007.

Vogt, Joseph, *Wege zum historischen Universum*, Stuttgart, Kohlhammer 1961.

Voigt, Alfred, Ungeschriebenes Verfassungsrecht, *Veröffentlichungen der Vereinigung der Deutschen Staatsrechtslehrer* 1952, 33–45.

Voigt, Stefan, *Explaining Constitutional Change*, Cheltenham, Edward Elgar 1999.

Voigt, Stefan (ed.), *Constitutions, Markets and Law: Recent Experiences in Transition Economies*, Cheltenham, Edward Elgar 2002.

Vorländer, Hans, Verfassungsverehrung in Amerika, *Amerikastudien* 34 (1989) 69–82.

Vorländer, Hans (ed.), *Die Deutungsmacht der Verfassungsgerichtsbarkeit*, Wiesbaden, VS-Verlag 2006.

Vörös, Imre, The Legal Doctrine and Legal Policy Aspects of EU-Accession, *Acta Juridica Hungarica* 2003, 141–163.

Voßkuhle, Andreas, Die Renaissance der 'Allgemeinen Staatslehre' im Zeitalter der Europäisierung und Internationalisierung, *Juristische Schulung* 2004, 1–7.

Voßkuhle, Andreas, Die politischen Dimensionen der Staatsrechtslehre, in: Helmuth Schulze-Fielitz (ed.), *Staatsrechtslehre als Wissenschaft*, Berlin, Duncker & Humblot 2007, 135–158.

Voßkuhle, Andreas, e.a. (eds.), *Verabschiedung und Wiederentdeckung des Staates im Spannungsfeld der Disziplinen*, Berlin, Duncker & Humblot 2013.

Wahl, Rainer, Erklären staatstheoretische Leitbegriffe die Europäische Union?, *JuristenZeitung* 2005, 916–925.

Waldron, Jeremy, *Law and Disagreement*, Oxford, Clarendon Press 1999.

Waldron, Jeremy, Torture and Positive Law: Jurisprudence for the White House, *Columbia Law Review* 105 (2005) 1681–1750.

Walker, Neil, Late Sovereignty in the European Union, in: Neil Walker (ed.), *Sovereignty in Transition*, Oxford, Hart 2003, 3–32.

Walker, Neil (ed.), *Sovereignty in Transition*, Oxford, Hart 2003.

Walker, Neil (ed.), *Relocating Sovereignty*, Aldershot, Ashgate 2006.

Walter, Christian – Silja Vöneky – Volker Röben – Frank Schorkopf (eds.), *Terrorism as a Challenge for National and International Law: Security versus Liberty?*, Berlin, Springer 2004.

Walter, Christian, Dezentrale Konstitutionalisierung durch nationale und internationale Gerichte: Überlegungen zur Rechtsvergleichung als Methode im öffentlichen Recht, in: Janbernd Oebbecke (ed.), *Nicht-normative Steuerung in dezentralen Systemen*, Stuttgart, Franz Steiner 2005, 205–230.

Walter, Robert, Wirksamkeit und Geltung, *Zeitschrift für öffentliches Recht* 11 (1961) 532–541.

Walter, Robert, Die Gewohnheit als rechtserzeugender Tatbestand, *Österreichische Juristen-Zeitung* 18 (1963) 225–232.

Walter, Robert, *Der Aufbau der Rechtsordnung*, Graz, Leykam 1964.

Walter, Robert, Der gegenwärtige Stand der Reinen Rechtslehre, *Rechtstheorie* 1970, 69–95.

Walter, Robert e.a., *Zur Erneuerung der Struktur der Rechtsordnung. Gespräch über Wege zur Vermeidung der Zersplitterung des Privatrechts und zur Überwindung des Dualismus von öffentlichem Recht und Privatrecht*, Wien, Manz [1970], 49–62.

Walter, Robert, Die Lehre vom Stufenbau der Rechtsordnung, *Archivum Iuridicum Cracoviense* 13 (1980) 5–16.

Walter, Robert, Entstehung und Entwicklung des Gedankens der Grundnorm, in: Walter, Robert (ed.), *Schwerpunkte der Reinen Rechtslehre*, Wien, Manz 1992, 47–59.

Walter, Robert, Die Grundnorm im System der Reinen Rechtslehre, in: Aulis Aarnio e.a. (eds.) *Rechtsnorm und Rechtswirklichkeit. Festschrift für Werner Krawietz zum 60. Geburtstag*, Berlin, Duncker & Humblot 1993, 85–99.

Walter, Robert, Die Reine Rechtslehre – eine Theorie in steter Entwicklung. Einige Klarstellungen, *Juristische Blätter* 116 (1994) 493–495.

Walter, Robert, *Hans Kelsens Rechtslehre*, Baden-Baden, Nomos 1999.

Walter, Robert, Bemerkungen zu Kelsen, Geltung und Wirksamkeit des Rechts, in: id. e.a. (eds.), *Hans Kelsens stete Aktualität. Zum 30. Todestag Kelsens*, Wien, Manz 2003, 31–41.

Walter, Robert (ed.), *Adolf J Merkl. Werk und Wirksamkeit*, Wien, Manz 1990.

Walter, Robert (ed.), *Schwerpunkte der Reinen Rechtslehre*, Wien, Manz 1992.

Walter, Robert – Heinz Mayer – Gabriele Kucsko-Stadlmayer, *Grundriss des österreichischen Bundesverfassungsrechts*, Wien, Manz $^{10}$2007.

Walter, Robert, e.a. (eds.), *Hans Kelsens stete Aktualität. Zum 30. Todestag Kelsens*, Wien, Manz 2003.

Waluchow, Wil, Constitutions as Living Trees: An Idiot Defends, *Canadian Journal of Law and Jurisprudence* 18 (2005) 207–247.

Wank, Rolf, *Die Auslegung von Gesetzen*, München, Vahlen $^{5}$2011.

Ward, Cynthia, The Limits of 'Liberal Republicanism': Why Group-Based Remedies and Republican Citizenship Don't Mix, *Columbia Law Review* 91 (1991) 581–607.

Wassermann, Rudolf, *Terrorismus contra Rechtsstaat*, Darmstadt, Luchterhand 1976.

Watson, Blake A, John Marshall and Indian Land Rights, *Seton Hall Law Review* 2006, 481–549.

Weber, Albrecht, *Europäische Verfassungsvergleichung*, München, Beck 2010, 17–18.

Weber, Eugen, *Peasants into Frenchmen*, Stanford, Stanford University Press 1976.

Wehrs, Frank-Bodo von, *Zur Anwendbarkeit des Notstandsrechts der Bundesrepublik Deutschland*, Mainz, univ. diss. 1971.

Weiler, Joseph HH, Problems of Legitimacy in Post-1992 Europe, *Außenwirtschaft* 1991, 411–437.

Weiler, Joseph HH, The Transformation of Europe, *Yale Law Journal* 100 (1991) 2403–2483.

Weiler, Joseph HH, Does Europe Need a Constitution?, *European Law Journal* 1 (1995) 219–258.

Weiler, Joseph HH, The State 'über alles': Demos, Telos and the German Maastricht Decision, *Jean Monnet Working Papers* 1995/6.

Weiler, Joseph HH, The Reformation of European Constitutionalism, *Journal of Common Market Studies* 1997, 97–131.

Weiler, Joseph HH, European Democracy and Its Critics: Polity and System, in: id., *The Constitution of Europe*, Cambridge, Cambridge University Press 1999, 264–285.

Weiler, Joseph HH, *The Constitution of Europe*, Cambridge, Cambridge University Press 1999.

Weiler, Joseph HH, To Be a European Citizen: Eros and Civilization, in: id., *The Constitution of Europe*, Cambridge, Cambridge University Press 1999, 324–357.

Weiler, Joseph HH, *Ein christliches Europa* [introd. Ernst-Wolfgang Böckenförde], Salzburg, München, Pustet 2004.

Weiler, Joseph HH – M Wind (eds.), *European Constitutionalism Beyond the State*, Cambridge, Cambridge University Press 2003.

Weinberger, Ota, Revision des traditionellen Rechtssatzkonzeptes, in: Bernd Schilcher e.a. (eds.), *Regeln, Prinzipien und Elemente im System des Rechts*, Wien, Verlag Österreich 2000, 53–68.

Weingast, Barry R – Donald A Wittman (eds.), *The Oxford Handbook of Political Economy*, Oxford, Oxford University Press 2006.

Weinrib, Lorraine E, Constitutional Conceptions and Constitutional Comparativism, in: Vicki C Jackson – Mark Tushnet (eds.), *Defining the Field of Comparative Constitutional Law*, Westport, Fraeger 2002, 3–34.

Wendel, Mattias, Judicial Restraint and the Return to Openness: The Decision of the German Federal Constitutional Court on the ESM and the Fiscal Treaty of 12 September 2012, *German Law Journal* 14 (2013) 21–52.

Werbőczy, Stephanus, *Opus Tripartitum juris consuetudinarii inclyti regni Hungariae*, Wien, 1517.

Wheare, Kenneth, *Modern Constitutions*, London, Oxford University Press 1951.

Wieacker, Franz, *Industriegesellschaft und Privatrechtsordnung*, Frankfurt aM, Athenaeum-Fischer-Taschenbuch Verlag 1974.

Wiederin, Ewald, Regel – Prinzip – Norm: Zu einer Kontroverse zwischen Hans Kelsen und Josef Esser, in: Stanley L Paulson – Robert Walter (eds.), *Untersuchungen zur Reinen Rechtslehre: Ergebnisse eines Wiener Rechtstheoretischen Seminars 1985–86*, Wien, Manz 1986, 137–166.

Wiederin, Ewald, *Bundesrecht und Landesrecht*, Wien, Springer 1995.

Wiederin, Ewald, Denken vom Recht her. Über den modus austriacus in der Staatsrechtslehre, in: Helmuth Schulze-Fielitz (ed.), *Staatsrechtslehre als Wissenschaft*, Berlin, Duncker & Humblot 2007, 293–318.

Wiederin, Ewald, Verfassungsinterpretation in Österreich, in: Georg Lienbacher (ed.), *Verfassungsinterpretation in Europa*, Wien, Jan Sramek 2011, 81–114.

Wieser, Bernd, Das Rechtsphänomen Bundeshymne, *Juristische Blätter* 111 (1989) 496–508.

Wieser, Bernd, *Vergleichendes Verfassungsrecht*, Wien, Springer 2005.

Wilburg, Walter, *Elemente des Schadensrechts*, Marburg an der Lahn, Elwert 1941.

Wilburg, Walter, *Entwicklung eines beweglichen Systems im bürgerlichen Recht*, Graz, Kienreich 1950.

Wilhelm, Walter, *Zur juristischen Methodenlehre im 19. Jahrhundert. Die Herkunft der Methode Paul Labands aus der Privatrechtswissenschaft*, Frankfurt aM, Klostermann 1958.

Williams, Glanville, Language and the Law, *Law Quarterly Review* 61 (1945) 71–86, 179–195, 293–303, 384–406; 62 (1946) 387–406.

Williams, Paul, Fighting for Freetown: British Military Intervention in Sierra Leone, in: Colin McInnes – Nicholas J Wheeler (eds.), *Dimensions of Western Military Intervention*, London, Frank Cass 2002, 140–168.

Wilson, James G, American Constitutional Conventions, *Buffalo Law Review* 40 (1992) 645–738.

Wimmer, Andreas, A Swiss Anomaly?, *Nations and Nationalism* 2011, 718–737.

Wincott, Daniel, Does the European Union Pervert democracy? Questions of Democracy in New Constitutionalist Thought on the Future of Europe, *European Law Journal* 4 (1998) 411–428.

Wind, Marlene, *Sovereignty and European Integration: Towards a Post-Hobbesian Order*, Basingstoke, Palgrave 2001.

Winkler, Heinrich August (ed.), *Nationalismus*, Königstein, Athenaeum 1978.

Winkler, Heinrich August, Einleitung. Der Nationalismus und seine Funktionen, in: id. (ed.), *Nationalismus*, Königstein, Athenaeum 1978, 5–46.

Winterhoff, Christian, *Verfassung – Verfassunggebung – Verfassungsänderung*, Tübingen, Mohr Siebeck 2007.

Wisdom, John, Gods, *Proceedings of the Aristotelian Society* 1944, 185–194.

Wittes, Benjamin, *Law and the Long War: The Future of Justice in the Age of Terror*, New York, Penguin Press 2008.

Wittgenstein, Ludwig, *Philosophical Investigations*, Oxford, Blackwell 1953.

Wittram, Reinhard, *Nationalismus und Säkularisation*, Lüneburg, Heliand Verlag 1949.

Wittreck, Fabian, Menschenwürde und Folterverbot, *Die öffentliche Verwaltung* 2003, 873–882.

Wolff, Hans J, Der Unterschied zwischen öffentlichem und privatem Recht, *Archiv des öffentlichen Rechts* 76 (1950–1951) 205–217.

Wolff, Hans Julius, Rechtsgrundsätze und verfassungsgestaltende Grundentscheidungen als Rechtsquellen, in: Otto Bachoff (ed.), *Forschungen und Berichte aus dem Öffentlichen Recht. Festschrift für Walter Jellinek*, München, Isar Verlag 1955, 33–52.

Wolfrum, Rüdiger (ed.), *Max Planck Encyclopedia of Public International Law*, Oxford, Oxford University Press 2011, available at http://www.mpepil.com/.

Wollstein, Günter, *Das Großdeutschland der Paulskirche*, Düsseldorf, Droste 1977.

Woolman, Stuart, e.a. (eds.), *Constitutional Law of South Africa*, Cape Town, Juta [2]2008.

Wootton, David, The Levellers, in: John Dunn (ed.), *Democracy: The Unfinished Journey 508 BC to AD 1993*, Oxford, Oxford University Press 1994, 71–90.

Worsley, Peter, *The Three Worlds: Culture and World Development*, London, Weidenfeld and Nicholson 1984.

Wouters, Jan – Luc Verhey – Philipp Kiiver (eds.), *European Constitutionalism beyond Lisbon*, Antwerp, Intersentia 2009.

Wróblewski, Jerzy, Legal Reasoning in Legal Interpretation, *Logique et Analyse* 1969, 3–31.

Wyduckel, Dieter, Über die Unterscheidung von öffentlichem Recht und Privatrecht in der Reinen Rechtslehre, in: Werner Krawietz – Helmut Schelsky (eds.), *Rechtssystem und gesellschaftliche Basis bei Hans Kelsen* [Rechtstheorie Beiheft 5], Berlin, Duncker & Humblot 1984, 113–128.

Yack, Bernard, The Myth of the Civic Nation, in: Ronald Beiner (ed.), *Theorizing Nationalism*, New York, State University of New York Press 1999, 103–118.

Yack, Bernard, Popular Sovereignty and Nationalism, *Political Theory* 25 (2001) 517–536.

Yoo, John, *The Powers of War and Peace*, Chicago, London, University of Chicago Press 2005.

Yoo, John, *War by Other Means*, New York, Atlantic Monthly Press 2006.

Young, Alison L, Parliamentary Sovereignty Re-defined, in: Richard Rawlings – Peter Leyland – Alison Young (eds.), *Sovereignty and the Law*, Oxford, Oxford University Press 2013, 68–88.

Zacharias, Diana, Terminologie und Begrifflichkeit, in: Armin von Bogdandy e.a. (eds.), *Ius Publicum Europaeum*, vol. II, Heidelberg, CF Müller 2008, 843–891.

Zagrebelsky, Gustavo, *Historia y constitución*, Madrid, Trotta [2]2011.

Zagrebelsky, Gustavo – Valeria Marcenò, *Giustizia constituzionale*, Bologna, il Mulino 2012.

Zakaria, Fareed, *The Future of Freedom: Illiberal Democracy at Home and Abroad*, New York, W. W. Norton & Company 2007.

Zalta, Edward N (ed.), *Stanford Encyclopedia of Philosophy*, 2006, available at www.plato.stanford.edu/.

Zeller, Ernst, *Auslegung von Gesetz und Vertrag*, Zürich, Schulthess 1989.

Zihlmann, Rudolf, *Legitimität und Legalität des Notrechts*, Bern, Stämpfli 1950.

Ziller, Jacques, Sovereignty in France: Getting Rid of the Mal de Bodin, in: Neil Walker (ed.), *Sovereignty in Transition*, Oxford, Hart 2003, 261–277.

Zippelius, Reinhold, *Geschichte der Staatsideen*, München, Beck [10]2003.

Zippelius, Reinhold, *Allgemeine Staatslehre*, München, Beck [15]2007.

Zippelius, Reinhold – Thomas Würtenberger, *Deutsches Staatsrecht*, München, Beck [31]2005.

Žižek, Slavoj, Der Körper des Feindes, *Die Zeit* 6 December 2001.

Zorn, Phillip Karl Ludwig, *Das Staatsrecht des Deutschen Reiches*, vol. 1, Berlin, Guttentag 1880.

Zubrycki, Geneviève, 'We, the Polish Nation': Ethnic and Civic Visions of Nationhood in Post-Communist Constitutional Debates, *Theory and Society* 2001, 629–688.

Zucca, Lorenzo, *Constitutional Dilemmas: Conflicts of Fundamental Legal Rights in Europe and the USA*, Oxford, Oxford University Press 2007.

Zuleeg, Manfred, Demokratie in der Europäischen Gemeinschaft, *Juristen-Zeitung* 1993, 1069–1074.

Zuleeg, Manfred, What Holds a Nation Together? Cohesion and Democracy in the United States of America and in the European Union, *American Journal of Comparative Law* 45 (1997) 505–526.

Zuleeg, Manfred, Die Anwendungsbereiche des öffentlichen Rechts und des Privatrechts, *Verwaltungsarchiv* 1982, 384–404.

Zweifel, Thomas D, *Democratic Deficit: Institutions and Regulation in the European Union, Switzerland and the United States*, Lanham, Md., Lexington 2002.

Zweig, Egon, *Die Lehre vom Pouvoir Constituant. Ein Beitrag zum Staatsrecht der französischen Revolution*, Tübingen, Mohr Siebeck 1909.

# INDEX

*Note*: Boldface numbers indicate table

For EU product safety concerns, contact us at Calle de José Abascal, 56–1°, 28003 Madrid, Spain or eugpsr@cambridge.org.

www.ingramcontent.com/pod-product-compliance
Lightning Source LLC
LaVergne TN
LVHW011532200926
848484LV00001B/247